CATALOGUE

OF THE

NEW YORK STATE LIBRARY,

1872.

SUBJECT-INDEX

OF THE

GENERAL LIBRARY.

ALBANY:
VAN BENTHUYSEN PRINTING HOUSE.
1872.

PREFACE.

The last complete Catalogue of the General Library was published in 1856. A Supplement containing the additions of five years was published in 1861, which was larger than the previous volume, on account of the addition by exchange and donation of large numbers of pamphlets. A Catalogue of all the printed contents of the Library to the present time, on the same plan of full titles, including those of the collection of two thousand volumes of pamphlets, would fill more than thirty-five hundred pages.

Although the Trustees, under the existing Statute, would be authorized to publish such a Catalogue, they have deemed it best to issue instead a condensed Subject-Index Catalogue. Some of the largest libraries have abandoned all purpose of publishing full Catalogues, both on account of the expense, and because that in a short time the annual additions to a growing Library will have impaired the value of the work as one for reference. While this course was suggested by its economy, it commended itself also for the reason, that the larger number of readers in a reference library avail themselves of the index of subjects rather than of the alphabetical catalogue of authors. The number who wish to know what may be found in a particular department or on a topic in which they are interested, is much larger than the number of those who desire to see a list of the works of a particular author, or the exact title of a book.

It being decided to publish a condensed Subject-index instead of a full Catalogue, it became necessary that the titles should be short and abbreviated, otherwise a catalogue by subjects would make as large a work as a catalogue by authors. In the abridgment of the titles it has been intended to retain the words of the author, if necessary for identification.

So far as executed in accordance with the plan, the Index gives with regard to each book at least four facts: The *subject*, the *name of the author*, when not anonymous, *a portion of the title*, and the *date* of publication, or the period embraced in the work, or both. Under some one of the Topics, each volume is entered once, and some of them are entered several times under different topics. Of the fifty thousand pamphlets in the Library, all are entered by a reference to the number of the volume in which each is bound with others on the same subject, while many of the more important are entered by their specific titles under the subject of which they treat.

If the experiment of issuing a Catalogue of this nature as a substitute for the usual Catalogue of authors should prove successful, by increasing the utility of the Library at a moderate expense, it would be an encouragement to publish after a few years a similar one, improved in its system and execution. Many of the present titles as originally formed were designed as references to the printed Catalogue of authors, and not to be sufficient in themselves. The size of the volumes and Christian names of authors might be added; the dates also might be more uniformly given; and especially the contents of collections, as of learned societies, and of authors writing on a variety of topics, might be referred to more frequently.

The number of volumes in the Library at the date of the issue of this volume, is 86,800, of which 23,400 are in the Law Library, which contains also all State, Legislative and Parliamentary documents.

TRUSTEES AND OFFICERS OF THE LIBRARY.

THE REGENTS OF THE UNIVERSITY OF THE STATE OF NEW YORK,

EX OFFICIO.

Library Committee, 1872.

Officers of the Library.

THE LAWS AND REGULATIONS

RELATIVE TO THE

NEW YORK STATE LIBRARY.

I. EXTRACTS FROM THE LAWS OF THE STATE, RELATIVE TO THE LIBRARY.

SECTION 1.* The Regents of the University of the State of New York are hereby constituted, and shall continue, the Trustees of the State Library.
Laws of 1844: Chap. 255, sec. 1.

§ 2. The trustees hereby appointed shall have power from time to time to appoint a librarian to superintend and take care of said library, and to prescribe such rules and regulations for the government of the library as they shall think proper, and to remove the librarian at any time when they shall deem it expedient; but for the purpose of removing or appointing a librarian, twelve of the said trustees shall be required to form a quorum. Same chapter, sec. 3.

§ 3. The assistant librarian and messenger shall be appointed by the trustees of the library. Laws of 1848: Chap. 262, sec. 2.

In the Laws of 1862, chap. 435, it was enacted that the Librarians be henceforth designated as the Librarian of the Law Library, and the Librarian of the General Library, and the Messenger as Janitor. For Second Assistant, *see* Laws of 1855, chap. 538, sec. 1; and chap. 539, sec. 1; and 1862, chap. 435.

§ 4. The State Library shall be kept open every day in the year, Sundays excepted, during such hours in each day as the trustees of the said library may direct. Laws of 1844: Chap. 255, sec. 5.

§ 5. The librarian shall be constant in his personal attendance upon the library during the hours it shall be directed to be kept open, and shall perform such other duties as may be imposed by law or by the rules and regulations which may be prescribed by the said trustees. Same chapter, sec. 6.

§ 6. The acting trustees will from time to time give directions to the librarian in relation to the proper and safe keeping of the books, maps, charts, and other property belonging to the said library; and may, by way of amercement for every violation or neglect of duty, suspend or deduct from his salary or emolument any part thereof, not exceeding half of it in any one year.
Laws of 1840: Chap. 381, sec. 3.

§ 7. The trustees of the State Library may, from time to time, sell or exchange duplicate or imperfect books belonging to the library, not necessary for the use thereof. Laws of 1845: Chap. 85, sec. 3.

*The sections are, for convenience, numbered without reference to their original numbers.

§ 8. It shall be the duty of the trustees of the State Library annually to report to the legislature the manner in which the moneys by them received during the year preceding have been expended; together with a true and perfect catalogue of all the books, maps and charts which have been added to the library since the date of the last preceding annual report; and whether any, and, if so, what books, maps and charts have been lost; and, also, at the end of every five years, to report in like manner a full and perfect catalogue of all the books, maps and charts then remaining in the library.

Laws of 1844: Chap. 255, sec. 7.

§ 9. It shall be the duty of the trustees to provide, in their regulations, that any member of the senate or assembly, during the session of the legislature, or during the sitting of the court for the correction of errors*, or of the senate only, shall be permitted, under proper restrictions, forfeitures and penalties, to take to his boarding-house or private room any book belonging to the library, except such books as the trustees shall determine are necessary always to be kept in the library as books of reference; but no member of the legislature shall be permitted to take or detain from the library more than two volumes at any one time. R. S. Part 1, chapter 8, title 8, sec. 8.

§ 10. Before the President of the senate, or the Speaker of the assembly, shall grant to any member a certificate of the time of his attendance, he shall be satisfied that such member has returned all books taken out of the library by him, and has settled all accounts for fines for injuring such books or otherwise.

Same title, sec. 7.

§ 11. It shall also be the duty of the trustees to provide in their regulations that no book, map, or other publication shall be at any time taken out of the library by any other person than a member of the legislature, for any purpose whatever. Same title, sec. 8.

§ 12. The heads of the several departments, and the trustees of the State Library, shall have the same right to take books from the library, as is now enjoyed by members of the legislature. Laws of 1845: Chap. 85, sec. 1.

§ 13. The judges of the court of appeals, and the justices of the supreme court, shall be allowed to take books from the library under the same regulations as the members of the legislature. Laws of 1848: Chap. 262, sec. 3.

Concurrent Resolution of the Senate and Assembly, April 9, 1856.
(Laws of 1856, p. 364.)

Resolved, That the Trustees of the State Library be authorized and required to close the said library for the period of fifteen days in each year, to wit, from the fifth to the twentieth day of August, for the purpose of cleaning and dusting the books of the said library, and for making such internal arrangements as the trustees may think proper.

II. RULES AND REGULATIONS FOR THE GOVERNMENT OF THE LIBRARY, PRESCRIBED BY THE TRUSTEES.

1. The Library shall be open to the public daily as required by law (Sundays and fifteen days from the fifth to the twentieth of August excepted), from the hour of nine in the morning till five in the afternoon; and during the sessions of the Legislature, till six in the afternoon, except on Saturdays, when it will be closed at five. While the Court of Appeals, or any general term of the Supreme Court is in session in the Capitol during the recess of the Legislature, the Law Library will also be open till six o'clock in the afternoon, except on Saturdays as aforesaid.

* This Court was abolished under the State Constitution of 1846.

2. It shall be the duty of the Librarian and the Assistant Librarian, carefully to preserve the books, maps, charts, engravings, manuscripts, medals, furniture, and other property belonging to the Library. They will be severally held accountable for the full value of every article missing from their respective departments, and for every injury except from ordinary use, unless it can be shown that some other person is responsible for such loss or injury; the amount of such loss or injury to be deducted from the salary of such officer, pursuant to section 3 of chapter 381 of the Laws of 1840.

3. Whenever the Library is open, the Librarian and Assistant Librarians shall be in attendance: they shall preserve order, and exclude, if necessary, any disorderly person: they shall prevent smoking, loud talking, and all noise inappropriate to the quietness of a place of study.

4. Any person who wishes to obtain any book for perusal in the General Library, will be furnished at the desk of the Librarian in attendance, with a card, on which he will inscribe from the Catalogue the title of the book desired, and his own name. The book thus received must not be taken from the library hall, but be returned to the Librarian's desk, otherwise the person will remain responsible for the book. The Librarians will exercise a proper discrimination as to the delivery of such books as they may judge liable to be injured. Manuscripts, rare and valuable books, and plates are excluded from this rule: they will be shown only on special application to the Librarian in charge, and under such regulations as the circumstances of each case may in his judgment require.

5. In compliance with the provisions of the statute above set forth, any member of the Senate or Assembly, during the session of the Legislature or of the Senate only, is permitted, under the restrictions, forfeitures and penalties hereinafter mentioned, to take to his boarding-house or private room any book belonging to the Library, except such as are herein determined to be necessary always to be kept in the library as books of reference. The Judges of the court of appeals, the Justices of the Supreme court, the Heads of the several departments, and the Trustees of the Library, have by statute the same right to take books from the Library, and under the same regulations as the members of the Legislature. No book, map, manuscript, or other article belonging to the Library, shall be at any time taken out of the Library by any other person, for any purpose whatever. The restrictions and terms above referred to are contained in the next three rules.

6. No book can be taken from the Library, until its title, and the name of the person taking it, have been registered by the Librarian A card must also be given for it, in the manner required by the fourth rule.

7. No person can take or detain from the Library more than two volumes at any one time, or for a longer period than two weeks.

8. If, on reasonable notice from the Librarian or either of the Assistant Librarians that the time for which any book or books taken or detained has expired, any person shall omit to return to the Library any such book or books for more than three days after such notice shall have been given; or if any book, map, chart, engraving, medal, or other article belonging to the Library be lost or destroyed, or so far injured as to be equivalent, in the judgment of the Librarian or Assistant Librarian in charge, to a total loss for the purposes of the Library; the person by whom such loss, destruction or injury has been occasioned, or who shall fail to make such return, shall be charged the full value of the book or article so lost, destroyed, injured or not returned; and in case of the loss of a book, or its not being returned, if it belong to a set of two or more volumes, he shall be charged the value of the whole set, or as much as it may cost to perfect it, at the election of the Library Committee. For any injury not amounting to destruction to any book, map, chart, engraving, medal or other article as aforesaid, the person causing the same shall pay a sum sufficient to compensate for such injury. This rule shall be of general application.

9. The Trustees hereby declare, agreeably to the provisions of the Revised Statutes, that the following books are always to be kept in the Library as books of reference, to wit: All the books in the Law Library; and, in the General Library, all dictionaries, encyclopædias, registers, directories, newspapers, maps and engravings, and books which are valuable for their rarity or antiquity.

10. Books of reference referred to in the preceding article, cannot be taken from the Library; except that during the sessions of the Legislature or of the Courts, any member thereof may take to any room in the Capitol any such book, on leaving a card for the same, as required by the fourth rule, after being duly registered. The book must be returned on the same day on which it is taken.

11. No books belonging to the Law Library can be taken to the General Library for perusal; nor are books, maps, engravings, or any other article belonging to the General Library, to be taken to the Law Library for perusal or examination.

12. For the better preservation from injury of the more costly collections of engravings, and the rare works and maps belonging to the Library, neither the Librarian nor the Assistant Librarians shall exhibit them to any person other than those authorized to take books from the Library, except on a written request from a member of the Joint Library Committee of the Senate and Assembly, the Speaker of the Assembly, or one of the Trustees or the Secretary of the Library.

13. Three days before the day fixed for the adjournment of any session of the Legislature, or of the Senate only, the Librarian shall address a note to each member of the Legislature, or of the Senate, as the case may be, having any book belonging to the Library, requesting the return thereof within twenty-four hours.

14. After the expiration of the said twenty-four hours, the Librarian shall immediately make out a list of the members of each house who have omitted to return any books belonging to the Library, specifying the volumes retained by each; and a list of those against whom any charges for any injury to or loss of books exist, stating the amount of them; which list shall be alphabetically arranged according to the names of the respective members, and shall be certified to be correct. To the President of the Senate, the Librarian shall forthwith deliver the list relating to that body; and the list containing the names of the members of the Assembly, he shall forthwith deliver to the Speaker; and upon each list shall be written a copy of the section of the Revised Statutes in regard to the matter above set forth.

15. Twenty days before the opening of any annual session of the Legislature, the Librarian shall report in writing to the Trustees the title of every book, map, chart, print, engraving, or other article missing from the Library since the catalogue of the previous year was made out, or, if no such catalogue has been made, then since the date of the said Librarian's last annual report to the trustees; together with the name or names of the persons who appear, from the entries of the Librarian, to have borrowed or detained the same, to the end that such list may be submitted to the Legislature by the Trustees.

16. All penalties imposed under any of these rules may be remitted by the Library Committee, either wholly, or on such terms as they may deem proper.

SYNOPSIS

OF THE

PRINCIPAL TOPICS OF THE SUBJECT-INDEX.

The Names of persons and places are omitted in this list.

I. HISTORY. BIOGRAPHY.
II. LITERATURE. POLYGRAPHY.
III. POLITICS. SOCIOLOGY.
IV. SCIENCES. ARTS.
V. THEOLOGY. PHILOSOPHY.

I. HISTORY. BIOGRAPHY.

II. Literature. Polygraphy.

III. Politics. Sociology.

IV. Sciences. Arts.

V. Theology. Philosophy.

EXPLANATORY.

The abbreviations most frequently occurring have the following significations :

P., Pam. Pamphlets.
Pamp'r. Pamphleteer.
Cat. Catalogue.
V., v., vol. Volume.
Imp. Imperfect series.
B. C. Bleecker Collection.
L. Lib. Law Library.

The very frequent abbreviations like "U. S." for United States, "Gr. Br." for Great Britain, "Conv." for Convention, etc., it is believed, will be usually understood from the connection in which they occur.——The figures at the end of titles are either the date of the edition or editions, or indicate the period embraced in the book. Sometimes both are given.——The figures after "P." refer to the number of the volume in the Library Collection of pamphlets, in which the publication may be found.——The arrangement of subjects is alphabetical, as in an encyclopædia or dictionary. Under many subjects cross-references are given to topics with other names, containing titles cognate to the one in which the reader is interested. Cross-references are also frequently made from topics under one name, to the name of the same general meaning adopted by the editor. H. A. H.

NEW YORK STATE LIBRARY.

SUBJECT-INDEX

OF THE GENERAL LIBRARY.

A.

Aarau, Switzerland. Aarganisch. Klöster, 1841.

Abbot, A. Rogistor of G. Abbot.

Abbot, A. Tolland Co. Conn. Assoc'n.

Abbot, C. *See* Colchester, Lord.

Abbot, G. Abbot, A., Genealogy of family.

Abbot, J. L. Everett, Address concerning, 1814.

Abbot, S. Woods, L., Death of, 1812.

Abbott, J. Remarks on "Corner Stone."

Abeel, D. Williamson, G. R., Life of, 1848.

Abelard, P. Opera. (*Letters*), 1616.
Berrington, Life of, and letters, 1787.

Abendroth, A. Wurm, In memoriam, 1852.

Abercrombie, J. Bruce, J., Sermon on, 1844.

Abercromby, Gen. Sir R. Memoir, 1861.

Aberdeen. Thoms, History of, 1811.

Abernethy, John. Macilwain, G., Life of, 1853.

Abernethy, R. Curtis, L., Funer. discourse on.

Abington, Ms. Hobart, A., Hist. sketch of, 1839.
Centenn. celeb., 1862.

Abney, Mary. Price, S., Sermon on, 1750.

Aborigines. Engel, L'Amérique, comment peuplée ? 1767.
Hornius, De Originibus Americanis, 1652.

Aborigines (continued).
Motte, S., Legislation for, 1840.
Rafinesque, American Nations, 1836.
Rio, Cabrera's Research, 1822.
Sanford, E., United States Hist., 1819.
See Indians; Antiquities.

Abraham. Molesworth, Sacrifice of Isaac.

Abrantes (*Duchesse d'.*), **Madame Junot.** Memoirs.

Absenteeism. Agric. distress, 1834.
Hints to all parties, 1834.
List of, Ireland, 1730.

Absolution. Luther, upon the Keys, 1846.

Abyssinia. Baker, S. W., Nile tributaries of, 1868.
Beke, Mission to, 1846.
Ditson, Para papers, 1858.
Geddes, Church history of.
Gobat, Journal of residence in, 1850.
Lobo, Voyage to Abyssinia, Pinkerton, vol. 15.
Ludolfus, Historie van Abissinia, 1687.
" History of Ethiopia.
Poncet, Journey to, Pinkerton, vol. 15.
Rassam, British Mission, 1869.
Roth, Schilderung der Natur in, 1851.
Russell, M., Abyssinia, Edin. Cab. Lib. vol. 12.
Salt, H., Voyage to, 1814.
See Egypt; Africa.

Academies. *See* Education; Scientific Soc.
Catalogues of, Pam. vol. 458, 1317, 1638–46.
Catalogues of Female, Pam. vol. 459, 460, 1644, 1645.

Adventures (continued).
Bishop, N., Life of, 1744.
Davenport, R. A., Perilous adventures, 1846.
Edwards, M., Life of.
Harriot, G., Struggles through life, Travels of, 1807.
Trenck (Baron), Life and Adventures, 1798.
See Shipwrecks.

Advertisements of Arts and Trades. Pamphlets, vol. 402, 658, 1035, 1222, 1223, 1236.

Adwert Monastery. Hoppius, F., Vitæ ac gesta.

Aeronautics. *See* Balloons.

Affghanistan. Burnes, A., Cabool, etc., 1843.
Colonial Society, Causes of the war.
Conolly, Journey through, 1838.
Eyre, Mil. operations at Cabul, 1842.
Griffith, W., Travels in, 1847.
Harlan, Memoir of India and, 1842.
Masson, Journeys in Beloochistan, etc., 1844.
Rose, Sir G. H., The Afghans, etc., 1852.
Sale, Lady, Journal of disasters in, 1841.
Vigne, Visit to Cabul and, 1840.

Africa, with Central Africa. American Colonization Soc. Reports.
" African Repository.
Baker, S. W., Albert Nyanza, 1866.
Beke, on the Geog. of Africa, 1850.
Boteler, Voyage of discovery to, and Arabia, 1835.
Bowen, T. J., Miss'y labors in, 1849–56.
Bruce, Trav. to source of the Nile, 1790.
Burchardt, Travels in Nubia, 1819.
Burton, Lake Regions, 1860.
Caillié, Travels, Central Africa, 1824.
Campbell, R., My mother land, 1861.
Damburger, Travels from Good Hope to Morocco, 1781–97.
Dapper, Beschreibung, 1671.
Daumas, Le Grand Désert, 1848.
Davis, W., Travels through, 1755.
Denham, Discoveries in, 1822–24.
English, G. B., Dongola and Sennaar, 1823.
Grégoire, Intell. faculties of negroes, 1801.
Hanoteau, La langue Tamachek.
Hawkins, J., Voyage to coast, 1797.

Africa, with Central Africa (continued)
Herbert, Travel in, 1677.
Horneman, Trav. from Cairo to Mourzouk, 1797.
Journal d'un voy. sur les côtes d', 1730.
Kunstmann, Afrika vor den Entdeck. der Portugiesen, 1853. *See* Bav. Acad. Mem. vol. 2.
Legion of Liberty, 1843.
Levaillant, Voy. par le cap de Bonne Espérance, 1780–85.
Lewis, R. B., Light and Truth, 1836.
Madinier, Projet d'une expédit, 1856.
Marcus, L., Hist. des Wandales, 1836.
Martin, R. M., Brit. Colon. Lib. V. 3.
Murray, H., Narr. of discovery in, Edin. Cab. Lib. vol. 35.
Noah, Trav. Barbary States, 1813–15.
Owen, Voyages to shores of, 1833.
Pamphlets, vol. 956.
Park, M., Travels in the interior of, 1795.
" Journal of a mission to, 1805.
Petherick, Soudan and, 1861.
Recueil de divers voyages, 1674.
Relation du voyage, 1670–71.
Taylor, B., Journey to Central, 1854.
Werne, African wanderings, 1852.
See Cape of Good Hope, Egypt, Nile.

Africa, East. Baldwin, African hunting, 1863.
Barbosa, Description of, 1510.
Barnard, Three years' cruise, Mozambique channel, 1848.
Bradley's shipwreck, 1818.
Bruce, J., Travels on the Nile, 1768–70.
Cauché, Voyage à Madagascar, 1651.
Krapf, J. L., Travels, eastern Africa, 18 years, 1860.
Livingstone, Exped. to the Zambesi.
Saldanha, Colonias de Portugal, 1839.
Valentia, Voy. and trav. to Red Sea, Abyssinia, 1802–6.
See Abyssinia; Egypt; Africa.

Africa, North. Algiers, Rapport sur les Tribus Arabes, 1851.
Ali Bey, Travels in Morocco, 1816.
Barth, Travels, north and central 1849–55.
Botticher, Geschichte der Carthager, 1827.
Browne, W. G., Travels in Africa and Egypt, 1792–98.
Bruce, C. L. C., On Bruce's travels, 1837.
Bruce, J., Trav. to source of the Nile.
Daumas, La Kabylie.

Africa, North (continued).
Davis, N., Carthage.
Hamilton, J., Wanderings in.
Hanoteau, Langue Tamachek.
Hodgson, W. B., Notes on Northern Africa, 1844.
Jowett, Christian Researches, 1815–20.
Keatinge, Trav. in Eur. and Morocco, 1816.
La Motraye, Travels, 1732.
Lempriere, Tour through Morocco, 1813.
Mauroy, Commerce de l'Afrique septentrionale, 1845.
Mouette, Trav. in Fez and Morocco. *See* Lawson, J.
Noah, M. M., Travels in the Barbary States, 1813–15.
Paddock, Shipwreck, South Barbary, 1818.
Russell, M., Barbary States, Edin. Cab. Lib. vol. 17.
St. John, B., Adven. in Lybian desert, 1849.
Shaw, T., Travels, 1738.
Sumner, C., White Slavery in, 1847.
Tornberg, Annales regum Mauritaniæ, 1843.
Urquhart, D., Pillars of Hercules, 1848.
See Algiers; Morocco; Tripoli; Tunis; Slavery.

Africa, South. Anderson, C. J., Lake Ngame, Discoveries in S. W. Afr., 1854–5.
" Okavango river, 1860.
Barrow, Sir J., Travels in the interior of, 1797.
Bunbury, Residence at Cape of Good Hope, 1848.
Campbell, J., Travels in, 1815.
Cumming, Five years of a hunter's life, 1850.
Latrobe, Visit to, 1815, '16.
Livingstone, D., Resear. in South Af., 1857.
Mason, G. H., Life with Zulus, 1855.
Moffatt, Missionary labors in, 1845.
Moodie, Ten years in South Africa, 1835.
Pringle, T., Narrative of a residence in, 1840.
Prospectus, Delagoa Bay.
Rhyne, Ten, Account of, Churchill, vol. 4.
Thunberg, Cape of Good Hope, Pinkerton, vol. 16.

Africa, South (continued).
Tuckey, Exped. to R. Zaire or Congo, 1816.
See Cape of Good Hope.

Africa, West. Adams, R., Narrative of wreck, 1810.
Adanson, Voy. to Sénégal, Pinkerton, vol. 16.
Alexander, A., Hist. of colon. of W. Africa, 1846.
Allen, W., Expedition to the Niger, 1841.
Angelo, Voyage to Congo, Pinkerton, vol. 16.
Benezet, Hist. acct. of Guinea, 1771.
Beecham, J., Ashantee coast, 1840.
Burton, R. F., Abekouta.
Bosman, Descr. of coast of Guinea, Pinkerton, vol. 16.
Bowdich, E. T., From Cape Coast Castle to Ashantee, 1819.
Christian traveler, 1841.
Clapperton, Second Expedition.
Coker's Journal, 1820.
Cruikshank, Achttien jaren aan.
Delany, Niger River.
Du Chaillu, Explorations, 1861.
Duncan, J., Travels in, 1845.
Durand, Voyage au Sénégal, 1802.
Foote, Africa and the American flag, 1854.
Ford, H., Fevers of western Af. 1856.
Forbes, F. E., Afr. blockade, 1849.
Gray, W., Travels in western Af., 1818–21.
Gr. Brit. Danish possessions.
Hawthorne, Journal of an African Cruiser, 1845.
Honey, W., Captivity in, 1844.
Johnson, W. A. B., Memoir, 1853.
Labat, Voyage en Guinée, 1725–27.
Lajaille, Voyage au Sénégal, 1784-85.
Leonard, P., Voy. to western coast, 1830–32.
Liberia, Const., gov't and laws, 1825.
Lopez, Account of Congo, Churchill, Supp. 2.
Mayo, Kaloolah, 1849.
Mayer, Capt. Canot, an African slaver, 1854.
Miller, A., Liberia described.
Montefiore, Of Sierra Leone, 1794.
Pamphlets, vol. 956.
Phillips, Capt., Voy. to Montserrado, 1693 (Churchill, vol. 6).
Putnam, L. H., On Liberia.
Rawle, R., Mission to, 1851.

Africa, West (continued).
Reade, Savage Africa, 1864.
Riley's Narrative, 1851.
Spilsbury, Voyage to, 1805.
Tams, G., Portuguese possessions in, 1845.
Thompson, T., Miss. voy. to Guiney, 1758.
Tracy, Society Western Africa, 1845.
Valdez, Six years in, 1861.
Voy. aux côtes de Guinée, 1719.
Wadstrom on Colonization, 1794.
West African Sketches, 1824.
See Liberia; Sierra Leone.

Africa; Trade. Netherlands, Deductie, 1664.

African Colonization. *See* Colonization; Negroes.

African Languages. *See* Bibliography; Language.

Africans. Armistead, Tribute for the Negro, 1848.
Edwards, B., Maroon Negroes.
Gustavus Vassa, Life of, 1837.
Lee Boo, History of, 1822.
Lewis, Bowles' life.
Lyceum of N. H. of N. Y., Report, 1848, P., 273.
Sancho, I., Letters of, 1782.
Wheeler, P., Life of.
See Negroes.

Agincourt. Hunter's Tracts.

Agricultural Addresses. Allen, L. F., N. Y. St. Agr. Soc., 1849.
Boutwell, G. S., Hillsborough, N. H. 1852.
Cass, L., Kalamazoo Co., Mich. 1850.
Cheever, S., N. Y. Agr. Soc., 1856.
Colman, H., Monroe Co. N. Y., 1838–41. *See* Massachusetts.
Davis, G. R., Rensselaer Co., N. Y., 1852.
De Chaumont, J. L., Jefferson Co. 1824.
Everett, E., N. Y. St. Agr. Soc. 1857.
Faxton, N. Y. Agr. Soc., 1857.
Featherstonhaugh, G. W., Schenectady, 1822.
Geddes, G., Onondaga Co., 1854.
Genet, E. C., Rensselaer Co.
Greene Co., B. P. Johnson, 1837.
Hallet, J. W., Ontario Agr. Soc.
Hallowell, B., Loudoun Co., Va., 1853.
Jessup, W., N. Y. Agr. Soc., 1856.

Agricultural Addresses (continued).
Kelly, W., N. Y. St. Agr. Soc. 1855.
Kirby, E., Jefferson Co., 1831.
Lathrop, J. H., Wisconsin Agr. Soc. 1851.
Mack, E., Tompkins Co., N. Y., 1844.
Norton, J. P., Albany and Buffalo, 1848.
Pamphlets, vol. 949.
Quincy, J., N. Y. St. Agr. Soc. 1845.
Sedgwick, T., Berkshire Co., 1830.
Sheldon, J., Evans, N. Y., 1856.
Spencer, J. C., Buffalo, 1848.
Thomas, D., Aurora, 1845, Pam. 187.
Titus, J. H., Franklin Co, N. Y., 1853.
Tyson, J. R., Montgomery Co., Pa., 1856.
Watson, W. C., Essex Co., N. Y., 1854.
Winthrop, R. C., Bristol Co., Mass., 1852, Pam. 88.

Agricultural Advertisements. Pam. V. 1105.

Agricultural Books. *See* Bibliography.

Agricultural Essays. Pam. vol. 950.

Agricultural Periodicals and Almanacs. Agric. Almanack, Phila., 1819–1826.
Agric. Guide, Alm., N. Y., 1851.
Amer. Agr. Alm., 1844–45.
American Agriculturist.
Amer. Cultivator Alm., 1849.
American Farmer, 1822–27.
American Farmer, Skinner, 1820–21.
American Farmers' Magazine, N. Y., 1858.
Am. Quar. Journal of Agricul. and Sc. Albany, 1845–48.
Annales de l'Institut Agronomique, 1852, 4°.
Annales des Haras et de l', 1845-47.
Bath and West of Eng. Agr. Soc. Papers, 1802.
Bavaria Agr. Soc. Central Bla., 1844.
Canada, Board of, Trans., 1856–58.
Country Gentleman, 1853–67.
Cultivators' Almanac, 1840–41.
Farmer (The) and Mechanic, 1847–1850, 4°.
Farmer's Almanac, 1851, Lond.
Farmer's Journal, Montreal, 1858.
Farmer's Library and Journal, 1846–1848.
Farmer's Magazine, 1802–3.
Farmer's Mech Man. and Sportsman's Mag., 1827.

Agricultural Periodicals and Almanacs (continued).
Fellenberg, Landwirthschaftliche Blätter, 1813.
Gardener's Almanac, London, 1852.
Gardener's Chron. and Agr. Gazette, 1846–'51.
Gardener's Magazine, 1828.
Genesee Farmer, 1847–52.
Illustrated, N. Y., 1852.
Illust. Ann. Reg., 1855.
Jour. du Cultivateur, Canada, 1855–56.
Journal of Agriculture, Edinburgh, 1843–58.
Landwirthschaftlich Verein, Zeitschrift, 1859–60.
Mass. Agric. Society Repository, 1793–1832.
Medical and Agricultural Register, Boston, 1807.
Milburn's Agr. Almanac, Lond., 1852.
Moore's Rural New Yorker, 1853–56.
New England Farmer, 1822–35, 39–43.
N. Y. State Agr. Almanac, 1821–26.
" Agr. Soc. Journal, 1855–1869.
Plough Boy, Albany, 18'9–23.
Rural Mag., Hartford, 1819.
Southern Silk Manual, 1839.
U. S. Agr. Soc. Journal, 1857.
Year book of, 1855–56 (Wells).

Agricultural Societies. Adams Co., Ill., Report, 1855.
Agr. Associations in G. Britain, 1819, Pam. 430.
Agricultural societies of Mass. Trans.
Agricultural Soc. of Eng. Journal.
Albany Co. Agr. Soc. 1856, Pam. 266.
American Agr. Assoc. Trans. 1846.
Bavaria, Hauslandwirthschafts Kalender, 1854–58, 61, 64–67.
California Agr. Soc. Trans., 1858.
Connecticut State Agr. Soc. Trans., 1854–59.
Essex Agr. Soc Trans. 1818–65.
Franklin Co., N. Y., 1857.
Hawaiian Agr. Soc. 1854.
Highland Agricul. Soc. Trans. 1855–1859.
Illinois State Agr. Soc. Trans. 1853-57.
Indiana State Board, Trans. 1851–53, 1856.
Iowa State Agr. Soc. 1858.
Kentucky State, Reports, 1856–59.
Lewis Co., N. Y., 1858.
Maine State Soc. Trans., 1850–68.
Massachusetts Soc. for Prom., 1803.

Agricultural Societies (continued).
Mass. Board of Agriculture Trans., 1837–59.
Michigan State Agr. Soc., 1857, 65, 69.
Monroe Co., N. Y., History, 1857, Pam. 461.
New Eng. Soc. for Poultry, Reports, 1849–52.
New Hampshire Trans., 1854–58.
New Haven Agr. Soc. Trans., 1841.
New Jersey, Report, 1860.
New York, Board of Agr. Memoirs, 1821–24.
N. Y. State Agr. Soc. Journal, 1850–1869.
" Transactions, 1841–68.
N. A. Pomological Convention, Proc. 1849.
Norfolk Agr. Soc., Mass., 1855, 56, 58.
Ohio, Board of, Reports, 1850–67.
Oneida Co., N. Y., 1853, Pam. 103.
Onondaga Co., N. Y., 1854, Pam. 461.
Overijsselsche Vereeniging, 1841–56.
Pamphlets, vol. 951.
Pennsylvania Agr. Soc. Memoirs, 1824.
Philadelphia Soc. for promoting Agr. Memoirs, 1815–18.
Provincial Agr. Ass , Canada, 1856, Pam. 230.
Queen's Co., N. Y., 1858, Pam. 461.
Rock Co., Wis., 1856.
St. Louis Agr. and Mech. Ass., 1857.
Soc. Centrale d'Agriculture, Paris, 1801–50.
Soc. d'Agriculture de .... Lille, 1851-1852.
Société de Lozére, 1861–62.
Soc. for advance. of Useful Arts, N. Y., 1807–16.
Soc. for promot. of Agr. N. Y. Trans. 1791–99.
Soc. lib. d'Agr. du Dep. de l'Eure, 1841–50.
Society of Virginia, Memoirs, 1818.
Tennessee Reports, 1855.
U. S. Agr. Soc. Exhibition, 1855, 56, 1859.
Virginia Agr. Soc. Trans., 1853.
Warren Co., N. Y., Report, 1860.
Wisconsin Agr. Soc., 1851–52.
Workington Agr. Soc. Proc., 1809.

Agriculture, Colleges of.
Belgium, Ecoles d'Agr., 1850–51.
" Inspec. des Ecoles d'Agr. 1850.
Cornell University, Ithaca, N. Y., Catalogues, Reports, 1867–70.

Agriculture, Colleges of (continued).
DeWitt, on an Agr. College, 1819.
Hall, H. C. van, Landhuishoudkundige school, 1844.
Handley, On a nat. agr. institution, 1838, Pam. 430.
Koen. Landw. Centralschule, 1863.
Massachusetts Agr. College, 1851–71.
N. Y. State Agricultural College, 1853, Pam. 461.
Porter, J. A., Agricultural School, 1856, Pam. 231.

Agriculture, European. Allgemeine Zeitung, 1853, 4°.
Baden, Landwirthsch. Blatt. 1859.
Bavaria, Agr. Soc., 1855–58, 4°.
Brunswick, Land-und Forstwirthe, 1858.
Colman, H., European Agriculture.
Deby, Agr. en Europe et en Amérique, 1825.
Diggelen, Voorlezing, 1842.
Enklaar, Verhandeling, 1842.
Fraas, Geschichte der Landwirthschaft.
Fries, F., Prak. Anleitung, 1853.
Henz, Anleitung, 1856.
Hessische Gewerbverein, 1842–68.
Hoffmann, Fortschritte der Agr. chemie, 1861.
Hollandsche Maatsch., 1856.
Kervyn, Agriculture Flamande, 1849.
Landwirthschaftlich Verein, 1857–59.
Landwirthschaftlichen Versuch-Stationen, 1860.
Mengen, Festgabe, Braunschweig, 1858.
Portugal, Exposicao, 1852.
Royer, De l'Agricul. Allemande, 1847.
Schultz-Fleeth, Rationelle Ackerbau.
Sonsbeeck, Op den landbouw, 1849.
Verein für Land-und Forstwirthschaft, 1857.

Agriculture, French. Agriculture Française, 1843–47.
Almanach du Cultivateur, 1855, Alm. vol. 52.
Annuaire de l'Hortic. Française, 1855, Alm. 52.
Basset, Annuaire de l'Agr., 1855.
Becquerel, Des engrais inorganiques, 1848.
Belgium, Dèfrichement de la Campine, 1848.
" Exposition des produits d'agr. 1847–48.
" Bulletin du conseil supèrieur, 1847–51.

Agriculture, French (continued).
Bentz, L., Elèments d'Agriculture, 1845.
Bibliothéque Rurale, Bruxelles, 1849.
Bobierre, Des Engrais, 1854, Pam. 233.
Boitet, Le pin maritime, 1857.
Candolle (Aug. de), Deux voy. agronomiques, 1813.
Congrès central d'agriculture, 1844–50.
Debeauvoy, Guide de l'apiculteur, 1851.
Delafond, Pleuro-Pneumonie des Bêtes bovines, 1840.
" Maladie de poitrine du gros bétail, 1844.
Dict. d'Hist. Nat. appl. à l'agriculture, 1816–19.
Dombasle, Ann. Agricoles de Roville, 1828–48.
Duhamel, Plantations des arbres, 1760, 4°.
Dumas, Sur le Drainage.
Ecoles d'Agriculture, Belgique, 1850, 8°.
Eenens, Fertilisation de la Campine, 1849.
France, Agric. Bulletin, 1843–51.
" Agr. Compte Rendu, 1850.
" Min. d'Agr. Animaux reproducteurs, 1853–56.
" Animaux de boucherie, 1845, 51, 54, 56.
" Colonies Agric. de l'Algérie, 1851.
Gasparin, Cours d'Agriculture, 1844–1846.
Géra, De la fabrication du fromage, 1842.
Giovanetti, Des eaux qui servent aux irrigations, 1844.
Gossin, De la réunion territoriale, 1844.
Gourcy, Notes agricoles.
" Voyage Agricole, 1855.
Jamet, Cours d'Agriculture, 1846.
Ladoucette, Influence de location sur le produit, 1844.
Le Clerc-Chouin, L'agr. de l'ouest de la France, 1843.
Le Couteux, Agr. du département de la Seine, 1840.
Le Docte, Mém. sur. l'agriculture, 1849.
" Agriculture Luxembourgeoise, 1849.
Lescallier, Culture des terres basses dans la Guyane, 1791.
Malaguti, Chimie agricole, 1855.

Agriculture, French (continued).
Malo, Eléments de comptabilité rurale, 1841.
Martinelli, Manuel d'agriculture, 1846.
Mauny, Irrigations dans l'Allemagne, 1844.
Morin, Castration des vaches.
Nadault de Buffon, Traité des irrigations, 1843–44.
Nicolet, Atlas de Phys. et de Météor, 1855.
Normandie (La) Agricole, Journal d' 1843–48.
Ossaye, Les veillèes Canadiennes, 1852.
Picard, L'Agriculture raisonnée, 1844.
Richard, Dict. d'Agriculture, 1855.
Royer, Notes économiques, 1843.
Sauzeau, Agr. du Poitou, 1844.
Schmidt, J. P., Des .... engrais., 1825.
Schlippf, Manuel populaire d', 1844.
Seringe, Le petit agriculteur, 1841.
Stoltz, J. L., Manuel Elémentaire, 1842.
Travanet, Agromanie empirique, 1845.
Ysabeau, Engrais. *See* Encyc. Populaire.
" Opérations agricoles.
" Leçons élém., 1854.

Agriculture, miscellaneous. Agricola, Experimental Husbandman, 1726, 4°.
Anderson, Agric. chemistry, 1860.
Allen, R. L., American Farm-book, 1849.
Amand-Malo, Comptabilité rurale, 1841.
American Husbandry, 1775.
Armstrong, J., Treatise on, 1845.
Bancroft's Agr. Alm., 1828.
Barclay, Capt., Agri. Tour in U. S., 1842.
Beaumont, Utilité du Phosphore, 1857.
Beck, On Pelargonium.
Bement, Amer. Poulterer's companion, 1845.
Bentz, Elements of (Skinner).
Blaikie, Farm manure, 1818, Pam. 430.
Booke, A., ... how to plant and graffe, etc., 1575.
Bordley, R., Rotation of crops, etc., 1797.
Boussingault, Rural economy, 1845.
" Agronomie, 1860–61.
British Husbandry, 1834.
Browne, D. J., American Muck-Book, 1850.
Buckland, J. M., Agr. Statistics, 1821.

Agriculture, miscellaneous (continued)
Buel, J., Farmer's Companion, 1847.
" Farmer's Instructor, 1847.
Cabell, Early History of, in Va., Pam. 461.
Canada, Reports on Agr., 1850.
Cato, M. P., De re rustica. *See* Scriptores.
Cleghorn, Depressed state of, 1822.
Columella, De re rustica. *See* Scriptores rei.
Communications to Board of Agr. 1804-1811.
Darlington, Agricultural Botany, 1847.
Davis, H., Farming essays, 1850, Pam. 430.
Davis, N. S., Text Book on Agr. 1848.
Davy, Agr. chem., works, vol. 7, 8.
" Agricultural Chemistry.
Day, W., Mechanical Science and prize syst. in Agr., 1857.
Dawson, J. W., Improvement of in Nova Scotia, 1856.
Deane, S., N. E. Farmer's Dict. 1790.
Douglas, R., Agr. of Roxburgh, 1798.
Einhof, Grundriss der Chemie für Landwirthe, 1808.
Emery Brothers, Albany, Instruments, 1856, Pam. 266.
Emmons, E., Sci. agriculture.
Essays on divided commons, 1778.
Forbes, The new husbandry, 1786.
Forsyth, W., Management of Fruit Trees, 1803.
Fullerton, On soils, 1801.
Gardner, D. P., Farmer's Dict., 1846.
Gardener's Alm., 1860, Weathersfield, Conn.
Gaudry, Machines agricoles.
Gaylord, American Husbandry, 1847.
Gleanings from Books on, 1802.
Good, W. W., Theorists confected, 1851.
Gourcy, Voyages agricoles, 1861–62.
" 4th Voy. en Angleterre, 1859.
Great Britain, Patents, 1617–1870.
Holdridge, W., Essay on the Weeds of.
Holland, H., View of agr. of Cheshire. 1808.
Home, F., Principles of, 1759.
Hough, F. B., Farm record, 1860.
Houghton, Husbandry and Trade improved, 1727.
Howard, S., Grasses, Pam. 272.
Jay, J., Statist. view of, 1859.
Johnson, W., Nugæ georgicæ, 1815.
Johnston, J. F. W., Experimental agriculture, 1849.

Agriculture, miscellaneous (continued)

Johnson, J. F. W., Use of lime in agr. 1849.

" Agr. chemistry and geology, 1856.

" Analysis of soils, 1855.

Jourdier, Voy. Agronomique en Russie, 1861.

Kirwan, Manures to the sorts of soils, 1796.

Kollar, Insects injurious to farmers, 1840.

Liebig, J., von., On mod. agriculture.

" Organic chemistry, 1841.

" Relations of chemistry to, 1855.

" Letters on, 1859.

Loudon, J. C., Encyc. of Agric. 1835.

Lowe, R., Agr. of Nottingham, 1813.

McKillop, Harvest in Md., 1855.

Mac Neven, W. J., Application of chemistry to, 1825.

Manny's reaper.

Mapes's Illus. catal., 1861.

Marshall, W., Minutes on a farm of 300 acres, 1778, 4°.

Maryland, Higgins's Reports, 1853–58, Pam. 273, 461.

Massachusetts, Colman's Reports, 1838-1841.

" Sec. of Board, Reports, 1856–57.

Mechi, On British agriculture, 1851, Pam. 430.

Mitchell, D. G., Wet days at Edgewood, 1865.

" My farm at Edgewood, 1863.

Mitchell, J., Man. of agr. analysis, 1845.

Morton, J. C., Cyclopædia of agriculture, 1851.

Naismith, Agr. of Clydesdale, 1806.

Nat. anti-corn law league, prize essays.

Nesbit, Agric. chemistry, 1856.

New York, Nat. Hist. E. Emmons, 1854.

Nicholson, J., Farmer's Assistant, 1820.

Niles, H., Agric. in the U. S., 1827.

Norton, J. P., Elem. of Sci. Agriculture, 1850.

Palladius, De re rustica.

Pamphlets relating to, vol. 187, 430, 461, 505, 614, 667, 765, 949, 951, 1034, 1217, 1218, 1484, 1649, 1650, 1759, 1853, 2514.

Parkes, Salt in agr., 1819.

Partridge, W., Practical agric., 1849.

Agriculture, miscellaneous (continued)

Perrine, Raising tropical plants in Florida, 1838.

Phillips, P. L., Tropical agr., 1845.

Pierre, Culture des céréales et plantes industrielles.

Poellnitz, Essay, N. Y., 1790.

Prince, L. B., Agric. Hist. of Queens county, L. I., 1860.

Reasons and plans, Lond., 1836.

Rocque, On Lucerne, 1761.

Ruffin, Essays on, 1855.

Russell, R., Agriculture and climate of North America.

Salisbury, J. H., Prize Essays, 1849.

" Analyses of vegetables, 1850.

Sheppard, Hand-book of statistics, 1860.

Sinclair, Sir J., Correspondence, 1831.

" Memoir, 1853.

" Code of Agriculture, 1818.

Sketches, rotation of crops, 1796.

Slingerland, Report on.

Smith, J. A., Productive farming, 1843.

Sorsby, Horizon. plowing.

South Carolina, Agr. survey, 1843, 44, 1848.

Spurrer, The practical farmer, 1793.

Stafford, J. R., Production of cereal grains, 1848.

Stefano, Agri. nuova, 1591.

Stephens, H., Book of the farm, 1846–1847.

Talpa, or Chronicles of a clay farm. *See* H. C. W.

Taylor, J., Arator, 1818.

Taylor. J. O., Farmer's school book.

Thaer (Alb.), Principles of, 1845.

" Grundsatze der Landwirthschaft, 1810–13.

Thomas, J. J., Amer. Fruit Culturist, 1849.

" Farm implements, 1854.

Thomson, R. D., Food of cattle, 1846.

Topham, Chem. for agriculturists, 1853.

Tull, Horse-hoeing husbandry, 1733.

Tusser, 500 points of husbandry, 1744.

U. S. Commissioners' Reports, 1862–69.

Varlo, New system of, 1785.

Varo, M. T., De re rustica.

Vermont Conv. of fruit growers, 1848, Pam. 52.

Washington, G., Letters on, 1844.

Watson, E., Progress of Agricultural Society, 1820.

Weston, Tracts on, 1773.

Albigenses (continued).
Faureil, Hist. de la Croisade contre, 1837. *See* France Docts. inéd.
Roger, P., Archives historiques des., 1850.
Sismondi, Crusades against, 1843.
See Waldenses.

Albuera Medal. Long, C. E., P. 393.

Alchemy. Albineus, Bibliotheca, 1653.
Crollius, Mysteries of Nature, 1657.
Hitchcock, E. A., On alchymists, 1855-1857.
" Swedenborg, a Hermetic philosopher.
Red book of Appin.
See Delusions.

Alcohol. Anstie, F. E., Stimulants and narcotics, 1864.
Dampierre, Eaux de vie, 1858.
Graham, T., Methylated spirits.
Payen, A., De la distillation, 1858.
Youmans, Alcohol and the const. of man.
See Temperance; Wine; Distillation.

Alden, J. Descendants of, by E. Alden.

Aldine Editions. *See* Bibliography.

Ale. Dissertation concerning Barley wine, 1750.
Taylor, J., Ale in prose and verse, by Barry Gray, 1866.

Aleppo. Russell, A., Natural History of, 1756.

Alexander the Great. Curtius, De rebus Alexandri, 1670.

Alexander VI., Pope. Gordon, Life of.

Alexander, A. Alexander, J. W., Life of, 1845.

Alexander, J. H. Pinkney, Memoir of, 1867, P. 1856.

Alexander, J. W. 40 years' letters.

Alexander, W., Earl of Stirling. Duer, W. A., Life of.
See N. J. Hist. Coll., vol. 2.

Alfieri. Autobiography, 1845.
Copping, Life of.

Alfred, King. Asser, Life of. (Six old Eng. chron.)
Pauli, Life of, 1852–1854.
Spelman, Vita.
" Life of.
Tupper, Poems translated.

Algebra. *See* Mathematics.

Algeria, Algiers. Almanac d'Algérie, 1849–1855.

Algeria, Algiers (continued).
" Etat actuel, 1862.
Barthélemy, Etudes sur l'Algérie, 1840.
Blome, State of, 1678.
Chasseurs d'Afrique, Pam., vol. 10.
Dictionnaire, Fran.–Berbère.
Dureau, Province de Constantin, 1837.
Fillias, Etat actuel, 1862.
Fournel, Richesse minerale de, 1849.
France; Tableau de l', 1839, 54–59.
" Exploration, Scientifique, 1847–1853.
Hunt, G. J., American Algerine war, 1819.
Knight, F., Seven years slavery in, 1631, Churchill, Supp. 2.
Manert, Géog états barbaresques, 1842.
Mauroy, Question d'Alger, 1844.
Moll, Colonization et Agriculture de l'Algérie, 1845.
Morell, History of, etc., 1854.
Napoleon III, Voyage de, 1860.
Pulszky, The Tricolor on the Atlas, 1855.
St. Marie, Algeria in 1845.
Schmitz, D'Abd el Kader, 1845.
Shaler, Sketches of, 1826.
Stevens, J. W., Hist. account of, 1797.
Valliant, Culture du coton, 1854.
" Rapport sur, 1853.
Ville, Recherches sur les roches, etc., de, 1852.
Wagner, M., On Algeria. *See* Pulszky, F.
See Africa, North.

Ali Pasha. Vandencourt, Life of.

Aliens. Lowell, J., Review of Hay on Expatriation, 1814, Pam. 9 B. C.
Reeves, John, Two tracts on Americans....not aliens, 1814, Pam. 129.
Review on expatriation, 1814, Pam. 9 B. C.
See Emigration; Naturalization; Sedition Act.

Allan, J. Memorial of, 1864.

Allegiance. *See* Oaths of Allegiance.

Allegory. Barclay, Euphormion.

Alleine, J. Newton, G., Sermon on.

Allen Family of Medfield. Geneal., 1869.

Allen, B. Allen, T. G., Memoir of, 1832.

Allen, E. D. Sprague, W. B., Sermon, death of, 1843.

America, Discovery in (continued).
Murphy, H. C., Hudson in Holland, 1859.
Navarette, Descubrimentos que hicieron los Espanoles, 1825-37.
Nicholls, J. F., Cabot's life, 1869.
Novus orbis, Rot., 1616.
Pam. vol., 1219.
Perry, W. S., Am. disc. and Church of England, 1863.
Philoponus, H., Nova navigatio, 1621.
Rafn, Discovery in Tenth Century, 1838.
Read, J. M., Henry Hudson, a hist. inquiry, 1866.
Santarem, On Vespucius.
Smith, Capt. John, Descr. of New England, 1614.
" True relation of Virginia, 1608.
" Travels in Virginia, N. E., 1630.
Smith, Joshua T., Discovery by the Northmen, 1842.
Soto, Narr. of Florida Exp.
Squier, Collection of documents, 1860.
Stevens, H., Notes on the earliest maps, 1453–1530.
Steward, J., Hist. of.
Syllacius, De insulis nuper inventis, (Lenox), 1859.
Ternaux, Voyages, etc., pour servir à l'hist., etc., 1838–41.
Tonti, Découvertes de La Salle, Eng. and French, 1697.
Trumbull, H., Hist. of disc. of Am., 1828.
Ulloa, Mémoires sur la découverte de, 1787.
Varnhagen, Vespuce, premier voyage, 1858.
Williams, Disc. by Madoc., 1170.
Winchester, E., Oration on, 1792.
Witsius, H., Exercitationes, 1695.
Wytvliet, C., Descr. Ptolem. augmentum, 1597.
See Voyages; Discoveries; Columbus; Vespucius, etc.

America, History of, Travels in, etc.
Acosta, De Natura Novi orbis, 1596.
" Hist. nat. y moral, 1590.
Alcedo, Dic. geog. hist. de las Indias occid., 1786–89.
Almanach Américain, 1783–87.
American Notes and Queries, 1857.
American Gazetteer, 1762.
Alexander, J. E., Transatlantic sketches, 1833.

America, History of, Travels in, etc. (continued).
Bercy, L'Europe et l'Am. comparées, 1818.
Blaew, Geographia, 1662, Atlas of America.
Blome, His Majesty's territories in 1684.
Boletto, El nuevo mundo, 1701.
British Empire in America, Oldmixon, 1741.
Burke, European settlements in, 1770.
Callender, Sketches of the history of, 1797.
Campbell, J., Span. Empire in Am. 1747.
Castellanos, Elegias, 1589.
Chambo, Commerce de, par Marseille, 1764.
Charlevoix, Hist. et Desc. de la nouv. France, 1744.
Chateaubriand, Recollections of, 1816.
Chumacero, Excessos contra las naturales, 1632.
Clune, Dutch Colonies in, 1769.
Codice Dipl. Colombo-Americano, 1823.
Coke, Journal, 1792.
Cortès, H., Expeditions, Kerr. v. 3.
Cramer, Natur-wunder in Nord-Amer., 1840.
Dapper, Die unbekannte Newe Welt, 1673.
Dassie, Desc. gén. des costes de l', 1677.
Delafield, Origin of antiq. of, 1839.
Description (Exact) of the West-Ind., 1655.
Drake, S. G., Address, 1858.
Ebeling, Erdbeschreibung und Geschichte von, 1793–1816.
Engel, Comment a-t-elle été peuplée ? 1767.
" Situation des pays septentrionales, 1765.
" Extraits des voy. Septen., 1779.
Everett, A. H., Gen. Surv. of Western powers, 1827.
Frost, J., Remark. events in hist. of, 1848.
Genty, L'influence de la découverte de, 1788.
Goodrich, Pict. Hist. of N. and S. Am., 1850.
Gordon, T. F., History of America, 1831.
Gottfriedt, J. H., Newe Welt, 1655.
Grasset, Encyclopédie des voyages, 1796.

America, History of, Travels in, etc. (continued).

Green, J., Remarks on new chart of, 1753.

Helps, Spanish Conquest in, 1855, 57.

Herrera, History of the Continent of America, 1725.

" Novus orbis, descriptio, 1622.

" Historia general de lo Hecho, etc., 1730.

Hist. Nat. y moral de las Indias, Span. Eng. and Fr.

Historical Magazine, 1857–71.

Horne, G., De Originibus Americanis, 1652.

Hughes, American Physician, 1672.

Humboldt, Hist. de la Géog. du Nouveau Continent, 1836–39.

" Voyages, 1799–1803.

Jeffreys, N., Hist. of Spanish and Fr. Dominion, 1760.

Josselyn, Two voy. to N. England, 1672.

Kip, Early Jesuit missions in, 1846.

Las Casas (B. de), Œuvres, 1822.

" Istoria della distruttione, etc., 1630.

" Destruycion de las Indias, 1552.

Laon d'Aigremont, Relation du voyage au cap de Nord, 1654.

La Roche-Tilhac, Almanach Américain, etc., 1783-87.

Léry, Hist. Nav. in Brasiliam, 1594.

Long, Amer. and W. Indies geographically descr., 1845.

Macgregor, Progress of, from its disc., 1848.

Marmier, Letters sur l'Amérique, 1851.

Munoz, Historia del Nuevo Mundo, Span. and Eng., 1793.

Nuix, Humanidad de los Espanoles, 1782.

Pereira, Compendio narrativo, 1760.

Pernety, Examen des recherches de Pauw, 1770.

Pradt, L'Europe et l'Amérique, 1821.

Pritts, J., Mirror of Olden Time, 1849.

Rafinesque, American Nations, 1836.

Rafn, Antiq. Américaines.

Robertson, W., in Eng. and Fr., 1778.

Robinson, W. D., Cursory view, 1815.

Russell, Wm., Hist. of America, 1778.

Saintard, Roman politique, 1756.

Schérer, Recherches Hist. et Geog. sur, 1777.

Schmidt-Phiseldek, Europe and Amer., 1820.

Simms, W. G., Views and Reviews, 1845.

Smith, J. J., American Hist. and Lit. curiosities, 1847.

Snowdon, R., Hist. of N. and S. Am., 1817.

Society of Northern Antiquaries, 1837–63.

Solorzano, Politica Indiana, 1703.

Speed, Epitome of Great Britain, 1676.

Staden, Véritable Histoire, 1557.

Stokes, A., Views of America, 1783.

State of Great Britain and, 1765.

Thévet, La France antartique, 1558.

Torquemada, De la Monarquia Indiana, 1723.

Touron, Hist. générale de, 1769.

Ulloa, Noticias Americanas, 1792.

Uricoechea, Mapoteca Colombiana, 1860.

Vries, D. P., Voy. to Amer., 1632–44.

Wakefield, England and America, 1834.

Walton, W., State of Span. Colonies, 1810.

Warburton, E., Hochelaga, 1846.

Ward, M., Simple cobbler of Aggawam, 1843.

Waterton, C., Wanderings in, 1812–24.

West Indische.....Reizen door Nieuw Nederland, 1705.

Williamson, H., Obs. on climate of, 1811.

Winthrop, J., Journal of N. E. colonies, 1630–44.

Wood, W. M., Sketches of South Am. and California, 1849.

See North America; Central America; South America; United States; Florida; West Indies; Voyages, etc.; Historical Societies; United States; Political Pam., etc.

American Antiquities. *See* Antiquities; Aborigines.

American Board of Missions. Reports, 1816–71.

Cong. churches of N. Y.

Review of the Report of, India, 1856, Pam. 525.

American Books, Catalogues, Authors, Libraries. *See* Bibliography.

American Colonies. *See* British, French and Spanish Colonies.

Anatomy (continued).
Bell, J., Anatomy of the human body.
Bottman, Cours d'Anat., 1788.
Catalogue of anat. preparations, 1769.
Cox, Synopsis of the body.
Cutter, Treatise on, 1850.
Douglass, Myographia, 1707.
Draper, J. W., Legalization of.
Hildreth, C. T., Case of Notencephale.
Heyfelder, Ueber Amputationen.
Importance of, 1825.
Keill, The Anat. of the human body.
Kidd, J., Lect , Compar. Anat., 1824.
King, T., Anat. as Sci of organization.
Kobelt, Appareil génital, 1851.
Lambert, Popular anatomy, 1852.
Maclise, J., Comp. osteology, 1847.
Mass., Legalizing study of, 1833, Pam. 271.
Mussey, Cat. of Cabinet, Pam. 516.
Owen, Anat. of vertebrates, 1867.
" Of the Invertebrate Animals, 1855.
Paré, Œuvres, 1585.
Pinnock, Catechism of, 1826. Pam. 605.
Ruysch, Werken, 1744.
Smith, J. V. C., Class book, 1836.
Soemmering, De l'organe de l'Ouie, 1825.
Spurzheim, Anat. of the Brain.
Warren, Anat. Museum, 1870.
Weber, Atlasses von, Pam. 523.
See Bibliography; Surgery; Medicine; Zoölogy, comparative.

Andersen, H. C. Story of life of, 1847, 71.

Andes Mountains. Orton, J., Andes and Amazon, 1870.
U. S Naval Expedition, 1849–52.

Andover, Mass. Abbot, A., History of, 1847.
Andover fuss, 1853, Pam. 96.
Dana, D., Remonstrance, 1853, P. 96.
Edwards, J., Address, 1826.
Fuller, S., Education in, 1856, Pam. 241.
Jackson, S. C., Sermon, 1827.
Theol. Sem., Centen. Celeb., Catalogues.

Andover, N. H. Moore, J. B., Hist. of.

Andre, Maj. J. The Cow Chace, with notes, 1780.
Andreana, Phila., 1865.
Barbé-Marbois, Complot d'Arnold, 1816.

Andre, Maj. J. (continued).
Biddle, Washington and, 1857.
Clinton, G., Correspondence, 1842.
Lyon, C. H., Oration, 1839.
Raymond, H. J., Oration, Tarrytown, 1853.
Sargent, W., Life of, 1860.
Smith, J. H., Narrative of causes of his death, 1808.
Vindication of the Captors (Benson), 1817.

Andreis, F. de. Rosati, Life of.

Andrew, Gov. J. A. Messages and addresses, 1860–66.
Conspiracy to defame, 1862.
Nason's discourse on.
Stowe's Men of the time, 1868.

Andros, Sir E. Andros' Tracts, 1866.
Brodhead, Address (Hist Mag. N. Y.)
Revolution in N. E. justified.

Anecdotes. American Anecdotes, 1823.
Anecdotes, 1771.
Galland, Maximes des Orientaux.
Lemon, Jest book.
Miller, J., Jests.
Original anecdotes.
Percy anecdotes.
Railway anecdote book.
Smith, D , Anecdotes for the young.
Wanley, Wonders of the little world.
Yonge, Book of golden deeds.

Angelo, M. Duppa, Life of, 1846.
Eastlake, Contribu'ns, Sistine Chapel, 1848.
Grimm, H., Life of.
Oxford, Cartoons.
Vasari, Lives of Painters, 1850–52.

Angels. Lloyd, J., Ministration of, 1786.
Victorellus, De angel. custodia.

Angling. *See* Fishing.

Anglo-Saxons. Akerman, Remains of Pagan Saxondom.
Anglo-Saxon Chron. (Chron. of G B.)
Kemble, Codex diplomaticus. (Eng. Hist. Soc.)
Lingard, Hist. Ang. Sax. Church.
Miller, T., Hist. of the Anglo-Saxons, 1848.
Palgrave's Hist. of England, vol. 3, 1864.
Strutt, Chronicle of England, 1778.
Thrupp, The Anglo-Saxon home, 1862.
Turner, S., Hist. of the Anglo-Saxons, 1828.
Wright, T., Biographia Britan. literaria, 1846.
See Language; Great Britain.

Antiquities (continued).
Univ. of Penn'a, Rosetta Stone, 1859.
Willis' Current Notes, 1851-62.
Worsley, Museum Worsleyanum.
See France; Bibliography; Pre-historic times.

Antiquities, American. American Antiquarian Soc. Trans., 1820-26.
Antiquités Mexicaines, 1834.
Atwater, C., Writings, Western Antiquities, 1829.
Bibaud, Hist. fab. du contin Amèr.
Bollaert, Researches in New Granada.
Bradford, A. W., Am. Antiquities, 1841.
Brackenridge, Disc. in New Mexico, 1857.
Brasseur de Bourbourg, Popol-vuh.
Cabrera, Huehuetlapallan, 1822.
Clinton, De W., Ant. of Western New York, 1818, Pam. 4.
Comité d'Archæol. Amer., 1865.
Davis, A., Antiq. of Cent. Amer., 1841, Pam. 79.
Delafield, Origin of Antiq. of America, 1839.
Dupaix, Antiquités Mexicaines.
Gale, Mound Builders of the Mississippi.
Haven, S. F., Archæology of the U. S., 1856.
Humboldt, Monumens des peuples indigènes de l'Amérique, 1810.
" Vue des Cordillères, 1810.
Kingsborough, Mexican Antiquities.
Kongelige Nordiske Oldskrift Selskab, Antiquitates Americanæ, 1837-45.
" Mémoires, 1836-60.
" Annaler, 1836-45.
Lenoir, Alex., Monumens Américains et Egyptiens, 1834.
Longpérier Antiquités Américaines au Louvre, 1852.
McCulloh, Researches on Aborig. hist. of America, 1829.
Mayer, Mexican Archæology, 1857.
Mitchill, S. L., Antiq. and Ethn. of Amer. Am. Antiq. Soc., vol. 1.
Moreau, Pierre de Taunton.
Pidgeon, Mound Builders of, 1858.
Priest, American Antiquities, 1833.
Rio, Huehuetlapallan, 1822.
Rivero, Antiq. Peruanas.
" Peruvian antiquities, 1853.
Society of Northern Antiquaries. *See* Kongelige.

Antiquities, American (continued).
Squier, Publications on Amer. Antiq., 1851-52.
Stephens, Anc. Mon. of Central America.
Warden, D. B., Recherches sur l'Amérique, 1834.
Whittlesey, C., Ancient works in Ohio. Smith'n. Contr., v. 3.
Willson, M., American History, 1847.

Antiquities, Great Britain. Archæological Magazine, 1843.
Barnes, W., Notes on, 1858.
Boyle, Museum Britan., 1791.
Brit. Archæol. Association, Journal, 1847–54.
Camden, W., Remaines concerning Britaine, 1637.
Eccleston, Introd. to Eng. antiquities, 1847.
Hearne, Coll. of Antiquarian discourses, 1775.
Higgins, Celtic druids.
Kinnersley, Sepulchral curiosities, Eng. and America, 1823.
Petrie, Round Towers of Ireland. Roy. Irish Acad., v. 20.
Smith, C. J., Lit. and Hist. curiosities, 1840.
Society of Antiquaries, London, 1779-1846.
Soc. of Antiq. of Scotland. Proceedings.
Tindal, Hist. of Evesham, 1794.
Wright, T., Archæological Album, 1845.
See Great Britain; England.

Antiquities, Greek and Roman. Adam, A., Roman Antiquities, 1814.
Antiquities of Attica, 1833.
Antonides, Olymp–Speelen, 1732.
Begerus, Lucernæ ex cavernis Romæ, 1702.
" Ulysses syrenes prætervectus, 1703.
" Pœnæ infern. Ixionis, 1703.
Berosus, De antiquitatibus.
Cappele, Comment de ant. Pergamenis.
Cochin, Herculaneum, 1754.
Disney, Museum, marble bronzes.
Dobree, Greek inscriptions.
Ellis, Townley gallery of sculpture.
Elgin Marbles, Pamphleteer, v. 8.
Eschenburg, Classical antiquities, 1837.
Fellows, Discoveries in Lycia, 1841.

Antiquities, Greek and Roman (continued).
Fleetwood, Inscriptionum antiq. Sylloge, 1691.
Fordyce, Mem. concerning Herculaneum, 1750.
Gell, Pompeiana, 1852.
" Topography of Rome, 1834.
Graevius, Thesaurus Antiq. Romanarum Græcarumque, 1732–37.
Gronovius, Thesaurus antiquitatum Graecarum, 1732–37.
Gruterus, Inscriptiones antiquæ.
Hamilton, W. J., Researches in Asia Minor, etc., 1842.
Herculaneum et Pompéi, Roux et Barré, 1840.
Hoffmann, C. F., Der Römer städte an dem Rheine.
Kennett, B., Antiquities of Rome, 1820.
Lowe, Rom. theat. of Verulam.
Lumisden, Antiquities of Rome, 1812.
Montfaucon, Antiquity explained, 1725–31.
Musée des Antiques du Louvre, 1830.
Naples, Musée Bourbon, 1840, P. 499.
Ouvaroff, Mysteries of Eleusis.
Pompeii, Lib. E. K.
Remarks on Llandaff's Horæ Pelasg.
Rossi, Roma Sotteranea, 1864, 67.
Sarayna, De Orig. Veronæ, 1540.
Sickler, Herculaneum Rolls, 1817, Pam. 1011.
Smith, W., Classical Dictionary.
" Dict. of Gr. and Rom. Ant., 1849.
Streber, Etrurischen Bronce-Reliefs, 1834.
Stuart, J., Ant. of Athens, 1858.
Ternite, Wandgemälde aus Pompeii.
Thiersch, München Antiquarium, 1825.
" Der Akropolis von Athen, 1853.
Venuti, Scoperti d'Ercolano, 1748.
Winckelmann, Découvertes d'Herculanum, 1764.
" Sendschreiben von Herculaneum, 1792.
Worsley, Museum Worsleyanum.
Zahn, Herculaneum et Pompei, 1829–1842.
See Classical; Herculaneum, etc.

Antiquities, Northern. Depping, Wayland Smith.
Kong. Nord. Oldskrift Selskab, Mémoires, 1836–60.
" Annaler, 1836–45.

Antiquities, Northern (continued).
Kong. Nord. Antiquarisk Tidsskrift, 1843-1863.
" Aarboger, 1866.
" Guide to Northern Archæology, (Ellesmere).
Mallet, Northern antiquities, 1847.
Nordiske Literatur-Samfund. Oldskrifter, 12 v. 1847–51.
Weber, Illust. of Northern Antiq., 1814.
Worsæ, Primitive Denmark.

Anti-rent. Harrington, H. F., Sermon on, 1846.
Helderbergia, or the Apotheosis, 1855.
Johnson, A. G., Judicial usurpation.
Makgill, Rent no robbery, 1851, P. 76.
Pepper, C., Manor of Rensselaerwyck, 1846.

Antwerp. Nys, les Archives d'Anvers, 1852.

Apalachicola Land Co. Blatchford, Report to, 1837.

Apes, William. The experience of, 1829.

Aphorisms. *See* Maxims.

Apocrypha. Apostolical fathers, (Lake).
Mansel, S. P., Sermon on.

Apoplexy. Alexander, E., Diss. de apoplexia.

Apostles. Cave, W., Lives of.
Greenwood, F. W. P., Lives of the 12 Apostles.
Whiston, Essay on Apost. constitutions, 1711.

Apostolical Canons. Jenkins, R. C., Lond., 1856.

Apostolical Succession. Benson, C., Writings.
Davenport, J. S., The Apostolic Office, 1853. Pam. 104.
Luther, Apostolic Succession, 1842. Pam. 307.
McIlvaine, C. P., The Argument for, 1843. Pam. 543.
Muskett, W., Apost. Succession, 1848.
Perceval, A. P., Apology for.
Sinclair, J., Vindication of, 1839.
Stebbing, H., Misc. Observ, 1718.
See Episcopacy; Church of England.

Apparitions. Brierre de Boismont, History of.
De Foe, History of, v. 13.
Hobson, Account of.
Thacher, J., Essay on, 1831.
Young's Morristown ghost, 1825.
See Delusions; Witchcraft.

Appleton, N. Winthrop, Memoir of, 1861.

Appleton, S. Jewett, I. A., Memorial of, 1850.

Appleton, W. Robbins, C., Memoir of.

Apthorp, East. Nichols, Lit. Anec. III, 753. Life of.

Aquaria. Bishop, J., Handbook.
Edwards, A. M., Aquarium in America, 1858.
Gosse, Aquarium, 1854.
Humphreys, H. N., Ocean Gardens, 1857.
Sowerby, Natural History of, 1857.

Aqueducts. *See* Bridges; Water; Engineering.

Aquinas, Thomas. Hampden, Life of.

Arabia. Ante-Mahometan Hist. of, 1853.
Baker, S. W., Hamram Arabs.
Boteler, Voy. of discovery to, 1821–26.
Burckhardt, Notes on the Bedouins.
Crichton, Hist. of Arabia, Edin. Cab. Lib.
Daumas, Manners of the desert.
Dumas, Travels, 1839.
Forster, C., Hist. Geog. of Arabia.
Herbelot, Bibliot. Orientale, 1697.
Landseer, J., Sabæan researches, 1823.
Lepsius, Letters from Egypt and Sinaia, 1853.
Marigny, History of the Arabians.
Niebuhr, Travels through Arabia, 1792.
Ockley, History of Saracens.
Owen, Voyages, 1833.
Palgrave, Travels in, 1862–63.
Sédillot, Hist. des Arabes, 1854.
Stanley, Mount Sinai, 1857.
Wellsted, Travels in, 1838.
See Syria; Egypt; Mohammed.

Arabic. *See* Bibliography; Grammars; Language; Oriental.

Arabic Authors, literature. Abulfeda, Ann. Muslemici, 1789–92.
" De vita Muhamedis.
Abou Chodja, Jurisprudence Musulmane.
Ali ben Ali Taleb., Carmina.
Asiat. Soc. of Bengal, Bibliot. Indica.
Church of England, Prayer.
Carlyle, Spec. of Arab Poetry, 1796.
Cherbonneau, Les Fourberies de Delilah, 1856.
" Hist. de Chems-eddine, 1852.
Djemal-eddin, Alfiyya, Grammaire, 1833.

Arabic Authors, literature (continued)
Dozy, Script. Loci de Abbadidis, 1846, 1852.
Hamasæ Carmina.
Hariri, Les Séances de, in Arabic (De Sacy.)
" Makamat, in Engl. (Preston).
Harris, James, Philological Inquiries, 1781.
Hoogvliet, Diver. Script. de Apthtasid. fam. et Ibn Abduno, 1839.
Instit. de France, Notices de manuscrits.
Khaldoun, Prolégomènes, 1858.
Khalil, Juris. Musul. Malékite, 1855.
Koran, in Arabic, and Sales and Lane's translations.
Lokman, Fables, 1847.
Marracci, L'Alcoran, 1697.
Pocock, Spec. hist. Arabum.
Reinaud, Relation des voyages fait par les Arabes, 1845.
Roorda, Abul Abbasi Amedis....vita, 1825.
Rutgers, Hist. Jemanæ sub Hasano Pascha, 1838.
Soyouti, De Interpretibus Korani, 1839.
" De Nom. Relativis, 1851.
Tarikhi Kiniset, (Church History.)
Wakidi, De Expug. Memphidis, 1825.
Weyers, Locos Ibn Khacenis de Ibn Zeidouno, 1831.
" Arabische letters, 1840. Pam. 1056.
Zamakhshari, Lexicon Geog., 1856.

Arago, F. J. Quételet, Notice sur., 1855, Pam. 608.

Aram, E. Life and trial, 1842.
Account of the trial, 1832.
Trial and defence, Pamphletear, v. 23.

Ararat, Mt. *See* Armenia.

Arblay, F. B. D'. Diary.

Arbuthnot. Narrative of voy. and exec. of Arbuthnot and Ambrister, 1819.
United States, Mess of Prest., 1818.

Archæology. *See* Antiquities.

Archbold, R. Trail, J., Sermon on.

Archery. Hansard, G. A., The Book of.

Architecture. Aldrich, Civil Arch., 1824.
Annual retrospect, 1861.
Architect. Societies, 1856.
Aviler, D', Cours d'Architecture, 1750.
Barnard H., School Archi., 1848.
Barr, Anglican Church Archit., 1846.

Architecture (continued).
Bayer, Cathed., Strasbourg.
Belidor, La Science des ingénieurs, 1813.
Boisserée, Denkmale...am Nieder-Rhein, 1844.
Burrowes, Penn'a School Archi., 1855.
Builder's Dictionary, 1734.
Builder, The, London, 1867-69.
Building News, 1868-69.
Bury, De Marbrerie.
Calliat, Parallèle des Maisons de Paris, 1830.
Cambridge Camden Soc., 1842-43, Pam. 401.
Ceruti, Portici a Magazzini, 1848.
Civil Eng. and Arch. Journal, 1838-1867.
Considerations on the principles, 1843.
Dallaway, Architecture in England, 1833.
Daly, Motifs d'Architecture, 1869.
Dardel, Palais du commerce à Lyon, 1868.
Davy, Artificial foundations, 1839.
Denison, On Church building, 1856.
Didron, Cathédrale de Chartres, 1861.
Doellinger, Die Baukunst, 1833.
Elmes, Life of Wren.
Fergusson, Hand Book of Architecture, 1855.
" Hist. of Modern Architecture, 1862.
" Assyr. and Pers. Architecture, 1851.
Field, M., City Architecture, 1853.
Garbett, Rud. treat. on principles of design in.
Garnaud, Arch. Chrétienne, 1857.
Gaucherel, Décoration appliqué à, 1857.
Glossary of Architecture, 1850.
Gwilt, Encyc. of Archit., 1867.
Halfpenny, Chinese and Gothic, 1752.
Hart, J., Construction of oblique arches, 1839.
" J. C., Parish Churches, 1857.
Hopper, Westminster palace.
Hunt, T. F., Architettura campestre, 1827.
" Examples of Tudor architecture, 1841.
Johnson, W. R., Building Stones, 1850, Pam. 518.
Krafft, Maisons de Paris, 1849.
Kugler, F., Geschichte der, 1859.
Leeds, W. H, Rudimentary architecture, 1848.

Architecture (continued).
Legh, Music of the Eye.
Le Noir, Architecture monastique.
Lindsay, Hist. of Christian Art.
Merlini, Dei tetti degli edifici, 1842.
Milizia, Lives of Architects, 1826.
Moller, Deutschen Baukunst.
Moseley, Mech. Principles of, 1856.
Murphy, J. C., Arabian Antiq. of Spain.
New York Ecclesiologist, 1848-53.
Nicholson, Encyclopedia of, 1861.
" Treatise on Projection, 1840.
Otis, Specific. for Arsenal, 1858, P. 193.
Otte, Kirkl. Kunst. Archäologie, 1855.
Owen, R. D., Hints on public architecture, 1849.
Paddington new Church.
Paley, On Peterborough Cathed.
Palladio, L'Architettura, 1642.
Pamphlets, vols. 1221, 1235, 1652.
Papworth, Museums, 1853.
Pasley, Obs. on limes, cements, 1838.
Peake, Rudiments of Naval Archit., 1849.
Plans for Churches, 1854.
Poole, Churches, structure, 1845.
Popp, Arch. Gothique, 1841.
Prony, Archit. hydraulique, 1790, 96.
Pugin, A., Gothic ornaments, 1844.
" Timber gables, 1839.
Pugin A. W., Examples of Gothic arch., 1850-56.
" Remarks on Eccl. arch., 1850.
" An apology for "Contrasts," 1837.
Puttrich, Baukunst des Mittelälters, 1844-50.
" Bauku. i. d. Obersachsischen Ländern, 1852.
Ralph, J., Public Buildings of London.
Ranlett, W. H., The Architect, 1847.
Rowe, S., on Gothic archit.
Round Church, Restoration, 1845, Pam. 401.
Rudiments of ancient, 1821.
Ruskin, Stones of Venice, 1851.
" Seven Lamps of, 1854.
" Notes on Sheepfolds, 1851, Pam. 222.
Scamozzi, Œuvres d'Architecture, 1764.
Scheult, Architect. en Italie, 1830.
Schinkel, Sammlung Archit. Entwürfe, 1845.
" Werke de hôheren Baukunst, 1840.

Architecture (continued).
Schlegel, F., Misc. works, On Gothic Architecture, 1849.
Schnaase, Gesch. d. Bildenenen Künste bei den alten, 1843-64.
Shaw, Civil Architecture, 1836.
Simms, F. W., Public Works of Great Britain, 1838.
Smeaton, Builder's Companion, 1850.
Smith, W., Origin and Progress of, 1831.
Society for promoting ... Eastover church.
Soravia, Le chiese di Venezia, 1822.
Stichaner, Romisch. Denkmaeler in Baiern, 1808.
Stuart, R., Dictionary of Archit.
Sturm, Arch. Goldmannianæ, 1714.
Theory....of bridges, Weale, 1853.
Tower, Illus. of Croton aqueduct, 1843.
Tredgold, Principles of carpentry, 1837.
Tuthill, Hist. of Architecture, 1848.
Verdier, Arch. au Moyen age, 1858.
Viollet le Duc, Arch. mil. du Moyen age, 1854.
Vitri, Le Vignole de poche, 1840.
" Dict. d'Architecture civile, 1840.
Vitruvius, L'Architettura, 1758.
Von Steinwehr, Specifications, 1858.
Ware, W. R., Arch. instruction, 1860.
Weale, Dictionary of civil and naval Archit., 1849, 50.
Westminister Palace.
Wightwick, The Palace of Architect., 1840.
" Hints to young architects, 1847.
Wills, Anc. Engl. Arch., 1850.
Ziegler, Etudes céramiques, 1850.
See Bibliography; Church.

Architecture, Domestic. Allen, L. F., Rural Architecture, 1852.
Cleaveland, Villages and farm cottages.
Downing, A. J., Designs for rural cottages, 1844.
Fowler, Home for All, 1848.
Goodwin, Rural architecture, 1835.
Hunt, Picturesque domestic architecture, 1841.
Johnson, S. W., Rural Economy; Pise building, 1806.
Maatschappij, etc., Burgerlijke Bouwkunde.
Normand, Décorations pour Maisons.
Robinson, P. F., Ornamental cottages, 1838.
Strickland, Cottage construction.

Architecture, Domestic (continued).
Vaux, C., Villas and Cottages, 1857, 1864.
Wheeler, G., Homes for the people, 1855.
See Building.

Arctic Travels. Erman, Travels in Siberia, 1848.
Hayes, Open Polar sea. .
Hearne, Journey to Northern Ocean, 1769–72.
Lamont, Seasons with the sea-horses, 1861.
Leslie, Discoveries in Polar seas, 1831.
Mackenzie's Journal.
Mémoires, (Engel), 1765, 1779.
Scoresby, Description of, 1820.
Simpson, S., Discov. on North coast of America, 1836–39.
Tytler, P. F., Progress of discovery.
See Voyages (Arctic); Russia; North America.

Ardeche, France. Annuaire, 1836.

Ardenne, France. Podesta, Bords de la Semoy.

Argensola, L. Pellicer, Ensayo, 1778.

Argentine Confederation. Constit., 1826.
Azara, Histoire naturelle.
King, J. A., Twenty-four years in, 1846.
Nunez, Account of the United Provinces, 1825.
Page, T. J., Exploration of, 1853–56.
Pazos, Letters on the United Provinces, 1819.
Rosas, De la dictatura, 1849.
" Correspondencia, 1851.
Sarmiento, Life in, 1868.
See La Plata; Paraguay; Buenos Ayres.

Argyle, Duke of. Conduct reviewed, 1740.

Arians. Blackmore, R., Arian Hypothesis, 1721. Pam. 340.
" Modern Arians, 1721. P. 340.
Fulgentius, Opera.
Maimbourg, History of.
Potter, J., Charge, 1719.
Remarks upon Dr. Clark's Expos., 1730, Pam. 349.
Scriptures and A. compared, 1722.
Two Letters, 1751, 1756.
Whiston's writings, 1708–29.
See Unitarians.

Aristocracy. *See* Dignities; Rank.

Aristotle. Andronicus, Paraph. ethic., Ox., 1819.
Beloe, v. 4, Commentators on.
Blakesley, Life of.
Eustratius, Commentaria., Ven., 1536.
Simplicius, In IV lib. de Cœlo. Traj., 1865.

Arithmetics. Adams, D., Scholar's, 1833.
Alexander's System, 1802.
Amer. Tutor's Assistant, 1813.
Arithm. fragment, London.
Ballard, Gauging unmasked.
Bennett, T., Pract. Arith., Phila., 1818.
Bertrand, Arit. commerciale.
Bézout, Theor. and Pract. Arithmetic, 1825, B. C.
Blassière, Calcul numérique, 1770.
Bonnycastle, Scholar's guide.
Botham, First Book of.
Bowen, T. H., Self-multiplier.
Boydell, Merchant freighter.
Brion, Arith. industrielle, 1836.
Bruce, J. C., Mental arith., 1835.
Bullock, Hist. and Rudiments of, 1853.
Byrne, Dual arithmetic, Lond., 1864.
Cobb, L., N. Y., 1834.
Cocker, E., Lond., 1758.
Colburn, Boston, 1841.
Concise arithmetician, 1829.
Constantin, Arith. décimale, 1830.
Cornell's Trader's Reckoner.
Correct arith. tables.
Cruttenden, D. H., The Systematic Ar., 1848.
Daboll's Schoolmaster's Assistant.
Dalton, Arith. examples.
Davies, C., School arith., 1861.
" Intell. arithmetic.
" Univer. arithmetic.
" Grammar of, 1850.
De Morgan, Elements of arith., 1846.
Dilworth, 1784, 1802.
Docharty, Pract. arith., 1854.
Dodd, J. B., High School arith., 1853.
Doyle, Ready reckoner for boards, wages.
Eaton, J. S., Treatise on, 1857.
Eleméns d' arithmétique, 1833.
Emerson, F., N. Amer. arith., 1844.
Evans, J., Tables of discount, 1823.
Fuller, J. E., Telegraphic computer, 1852.
Gelder, De Cijferkunst, 1837.
Gordon, W., Universal Accountant, 1796.

Arithmetics (continued).
Greenleaf, Mental arith.
Hadden, Rudimentary arith , 1851.
Hunter, J , Modern arith., Lond., 1866.
Hutton, C., Key to.
King, J., New system, 1808.
Kruijtbosch, Pract. Rekenboek, 1852, 1855.
Lardner, Treatise on Arith., Cyclop. v. 66.
Lee, C., Am. Accomptant.
M'Kenney, F., Key to Bennett's, 1811.
Mailly, Science du Calcul, 1848.
Meursius, Denarius Pythagoricus, 1631.
Muelder, Calcul mental.
Newton, Sir I., Univ. Arithmetic.
Olney, System of.
Parke, N., Lect. on Philosophy of, 1850.
Partridge, S., Scale of proportion.
Peacock, Mental arith., 1826.
Penn, S., Of weight of diff. lengths, 1830.
Perkins, G. R., Arithmetics, 1849-51.
" Lecciones, 1856.
Pike, N., 1793, 97.
Preston, J., Introd. to, Albany, 1834.
Rihouey, Nouveau traité, 1830.
Ritt, Nouv. Arithmétique, 1858.
Saigey, Problèmes de, 1757.
" Solutions Raisonnées, 1857.
Saul, J., Tutor's Asst., 1815.
Scheutz, Calcul. Machine, 1857.
Smith, B., Class book of, 1864.
Smith, R. C., Pract. and mental, 1834.
" Federal calculator, 1836.
" Key to, 1844.
Sonnet, Leçons d', 1857.
Stevens, B., System of, 1822.
Stoddard, J. F., Amer. intel. arith., 1850.
" The Amer. Philoso., 1853.
Stoddard, W., Federal Calculator, 1815.
Thompson, J. B., Practical Ar., 1853.
" Ment. arith., 1854, 63.
Vogdes, U. S. Arithmetic, 1847.
Walsh, M., Mercantile Arith., 1807.
Walton, Intellectual Arith., 1866.
Young, J. R., Simple Arith., 1855.
See Mathematics; Tables.

Arizona. Arizona Miner., 1866-70, imp.
Bailey, Report on Indians of, 1858.
Browne, J. R., Adventures in, 1869.
Cram, T. J., Memoir on, 1858.
Cremony, Life with the Apaches, 1868.
Mowry, Resources of, 1859.

Arts (continued).

Brandon Paints.

Browne, D. J., Etymological Encyclopedia, 1832. B. C.

Buchanan, R., Mill work, etc., 1823.

Burgoyne, Quarrying of Stone, 1849.

Bulletin des sci. technologiques, 1826-1831.

Byrne, Metal-worker's Asst., 1852.

Canada, Exposition, 1855.

Canada et l'Exposition, 1855.

Crosby, P., Sawing lumber.

Denison, Treatise on clock-making, 1850.

Dobson, E., Manuf. of bricks, 1850.

Dossie, Observations on potash, 1767.

Dunlap, W., Progress of Arts of Design in America, 1834.

Elliot, S., American Museum, 1822.

Emporium of Arts and Sciences, 1812-1814.

Epitome of the Arts, 1811.

Evans, Young Millwright's Guide, 1795.

Ewbank, Hydraulic and other machines, 1842.

Exhibition, Lond., 1862.

Exposition universelle, 1851.

Exposition de Paris, 1867.

France, Expos. of, 1855.

Franke, Technological Dictionary.

Franklin Institute Journal, 1826-70.

Gill's Technological Repository, 1827-1830.

Gilroy, Art of Weaving, 1847.

Gobright, N. Y. Sketch Book, 1858.

Gregory, G., Dictionary of Arts and Sciences, 1815-16.

Gregory, O., Treatise on Mechanics, 1826.

Grumman, Surveyor's chains.

Guillery, Technologie.

" Arts céramiques.

Hay, D. R., Nomenclature of colours, etc., 1845.

Hazen, Pop. Technology.

Historical Essay, 1749.

History of silk, cotton, wool, etc., 1845.

Holland, J., Manufactures in metal. (Lard. Cycl.)

Holtzapfel, C., Turning and Mechan. manipulation, 1846-51.

Howard's Dredging machine.

Invention, L', Journal, Paris, 1857-60.

Jamieson, A., Mech. for practical men.

Journal des Connaissances usuelles, 1833.

Arts (continued).

Journal of Design and Manufact., 1849-52.

Kingsley's Mechanic's Pocket Book, 1851.

Lardner, Treatise on Mechanics.

Leonard, The Mechanical Principia, 1848.

Littlefield, D. G., Improvements, base burning stove.

Mass Char. Mech. Assoc. Addresses, 1837-48.

Mechanics' Magazine, London, 1823-70.

Mining Magazine, 1853-60.

Monge, Treatise on Statics, 1851.

Morris, Tasker & Co., Pascal Iron Works, Catal. of.

Mosely, Illustrations of Mechanics, 1829.

" Treatise on Mechanics, 1839.

Moxon, Mechanic Exercises, 1677.

Nicholson, J., Operative Mechanic, 1834.

Overman, Iron Moulder's Guide.

Pamphlets on the Arts, vols. 402, 658, 1035, 1222, 1223, 1235, 1653, 1854, 2507.

Parrish, Skeletonizing leaves.

Payen, Chemie industrielle.

Pilkington, J., Artist's Guide, 1841.

Potter, A., Science applied to Arts and Manuf., 1841.

Recueil d'Ouvrages, etc., Bance.

Reimann, Manuf. of aniline.

Repertory of Arts, 1794-1806.

Repertory of patent inventions, period. 1830-62.

Richardson, Metallic Arts and Diseases, 1790.

Scientific American, period., 1846-70.

Simmons' Edge Tools, 1855, P. 298.

Soc. Cen. d'Agric. Moulins à bras, 1821.

Society for the Encouragement of, etc., 1760, 1836.

Soc. for promot. of useful arts, N. Y., 1807.

Society of Arts, Journal, London, 1854-70.

Spafford, Wheel carriages, 1815.

Stearns, S., American Oracle, 1791.

Stokes, Cabinetmaker and upholsterer, 1850.

Swindell, S. G., Well-digging and pumpwork, 1849.

Symons, J. C., Arts and Artisans, 1839.

Arts (continued).
Timb's Year Book, 1839-55.
Tolhausen, Technological Dict., 1854, 1855.
Tomlinson, Cyclopædia, 1851,54. Supplement, 1868.
Tomlinson, C, Rudimentary mechanics, 1851.
Totten, Hydraulic and comm. mortar, 1842.
" Lime-burning, 1842.
Treatise on dyeing and calico-printing, 1846.
Turner, R., Introduction to Arts and Sciences, 1783.
United States Mag. of Science, Art, etc., 1854, 55.
United States Pat. Off. reports to 1868.
Ure, Dict. of Arts, Man. and Mines, 1840, 45. Supplement, 1863.
Ward, G. G., Essay on the lever, 1829.
Weisbach, Mech. of Machinery, 1847, 1848.
Whittock, Decorative painter's guide, 1841.
Wright, W. H., Treatise on mortars, 1845.
Wyatt, 11th French Exposition, 1849.
Young, T., Lecture on Mech. Arts, 1807.
Young Ladies' Book.
Ziegler, Etudes céramiques, 1850.
See Inventions; Patents; Scientific; Engineering; Exhibitions; Mech. Institutes; Hydraulics; Machinery; Fine Arts; Cements.

Asbury, F. Coke, Ord. Sermon of, 1784.
Strickland, W. P., Life of, 1858.

Ashbridge, G. W. Russell, J. T., Sermon on, 1834.

Ashburnham, M. Cushing, J., Century Sermon.

Ashland Co., Ohio, Knapp, H. S., History of.

Ashmun, J. Bacon, L., Discourse on, 1828, P. 61.
Gurley, R. R., Life of, 1835.

Ashton, J. Memoirs of, 1838.

Ashworth, C. Palmer, S., Serm. on.

Asia. Baldelli, Relazioni...dell Asia.
Barros, L'Asia, 1562.
Bell, J., Tr. to various parts of, 1764.
Bergeron, Voy. en Asie, XII-XV siècles.
Bernier, Tr. in the Mogul Empire, 1826.

Asia (continued).
Buckingham, Tr. in Oriental World, 1830.
Cartwright, J., Travels in, (Churchill's Coll.)
Chardin, Voyages, 1711.
Dapper, Beschryving van Asie, 1680.
Drummond, Sir W., Origines, 1824.
Engel, Situation des pays septentrionaux, 1765.
Herbert, Travel in, 1677.
Keppel, Journey from India to Eng., 1827.
Klaproth, Tableaux historiques.
La Motraye Travels, 1732.
Olearius, Travels, 1639.
Ouseley, Travels in the East, 1819-23.
Palmer, A. H., Commerce with, 1847.
Polo, Marco, Il milione.
" Travels in the 13th century, 1818, 1854.
Remusat, Mélanges Asiatiques.
Soc. Asiatique, Journal, 1823–67.
Tavernier, Six Voyages, 1676–77.
Turkish evening entertainments, 1850.

Asia, Central. Atkinson, T. W., Explor. in Central, 1858.
Burnes, A., Travels to Bokhara, 1831–1833.
Carpini, Travels in.
Conolly, Journey to North of India, 1838.
Hervey, T. K., Adventures in Tartary.
Hist. of the Tartars.
Moorcroft, Himalayan Provinces, 1841.
Ranking, Wars of the Mongols.
Timour, Histoire de, 1722.
Vambéry, Travels in Central, 1865.
Wolff, J., Travels, 1831–34.
" Mission to Bokhara, 1843–45.
Wood, J., Sources of the River Oxus, 1836-38.
See Persia; Affghanistan; Tibet.

Asia, Southern. Baron, S., Descript. of Tonqueen.
Crawfurd, Embassy to Ava, 1830.
" Embassy to Siam and Cochin China, 1830.
Earl, Phys. Geog. of South Eastern, 1853, P. 402.
Ireland, Five years in, 1859.
Malcom, Travels in South Eastern Asia, 1839.
Roberts, E., Embassy to Cochin China, etc., 1832-34.
Shaw, S., Journals, 1847.
Texeira, Tr. from India to Italy.

Astronomy (continued).
Bowditch, Mécan. céleste of La Place, 1829–39.
Bradford, D., Wond. of the heavens, 1837.
Brnunow, Comète de Vico, 1849.
Bureau des Longitudes, Annuaire, 1826–57, 59.
Burritt, E. H., Astron. Atlas, 1835.
" Geog. of the heavens.
Cary, Names of constellations.
Cassini, J. D., Elémens de l', vérifiés, 1684.
" Lumière céleste dans le Zodiaque, 1685.
" Satellites de Jupiter, 1693.
Chabert, Voyage, 1751.
Chambers, G. F., Descript. Astron., 1867.
Chappé, Observations de Vénus, 1769.
Clarke, H., Refraction and parallax, 1800.
Conant, Year Book, 1836.
Copernicus, De Revol. Orbium, 1543.
De La Rue, W., Solar physics, 1865.
" Solar eclipse, July 1860.
Dick, Practical Astronomer, 1848.
Downes, Occultations in United States, 1851, 52, 53.
Drummond, Œdipus Judaicus.
Dudley Observatory, Annals, vol. i, 1866; ii, 1871.
Dunkin, The midnight sky, 1872.
Dunn, Univ. planispheres.
Dupuis, Origine des cultes.
Eclipse (The Annular) of 1854.
Edwards, S., Copernicus, a poem.
Exam. of doct. of moon's rotation, 1847. P. 23.
Ferguson, Introd. to Astronomy, 1812.
" Astronomy explained, 1799.
Firmicus, J., Astronomicon, 1551.
Fleurieu, Voy. pour éprouver les horloges marines, 1768, 69.
Gassendi, P., Institutio Astronomica, 1656.
Gauss, Theory of the Motion, etc., 1857.
Georgetown Coll. Annals of Observat., 1852.
Gilliss, Obs. at Observatory, Wash., 1846.
" U. S. N. Astr. Exped., 1849–1852.
Goodacre, Expl. of the terms of, 1824. P. 24. B. C.
" Eight Lectures on, 1825.

Astronomy (continued).
Gould, B. A., Hist. of Disc. of Neptune, 1850.
Grant, R., Hist. of Physical Astron., 1852.
Guillemin, The heavens, 1871.
Guy, Elements of, 1832.
Hahn, Descr. of Planetarium, 1781. P. 402.
Haskins, R. W., Astr. for Schools, 1841.
" Essays on Comets, 1842.
Herschel, Outlines of Astron., 1849.
" Treatise on Astronomy.
" Treatise on (Walker's ed.), 1836.
" Obs. at the Cape of Good Hope, 1834–38.
" Obs. of Nebulæ at Slough, 1825–33.
Hind, The Solar system, 1852.
Humboldt, Observations astronomiques, 1799-1803.
Hevelius, Annus climactericus, 1685.
Holmboe, Chaldærnes astrolab.
Hough, G. W., Cataloguing machine, 1863.
Kendall, Uranography, 1824.
Keith, Use of globes.
Kreil, Einfluss des Mondes, 1853.
Lawson, H., Obs. on Uranus.
Leadbetter, C., Astronomy, 1727.
Le Gentil, Voyage .... passage de Vénus.
LeVerrier, Mouvement de Mercure, 1845.
Loomis, E., Progress of, in U. S., 1850.
Loomis, W. J., Origin of gravitation, etc.
Lovekin, Mental calculator, 1821.
Lubbock, Researches in phys. astron., 1830, 37.
Ludlam, French tech. terms in.
Manilius, Astronomicon, 1679.
Marsh, J., The Astrarium, 1806.
Maupertuis, Œuvres, 1756.
Maurice, Observations on astro. and anc. hist., 1816.
Maury, Obs. at Astr. Ob. Washington, 1845, 46, 47.
Meech, Heat of the Sun.
Mitchel, O. M., Planetary and stellar worlds, 1848.
" Address, Hamilton Coll., 1856.
" Astron. of the Bible, 1863.
Morgan, Aurora Borealis, Cambridge, 1847.

Autobiography (continued).
Delany, Mrs. M., Granville, 1862.
De Quincey, Writings, vol. 13, 1851.
D' Ewes, Sir Simonds, 1845.
Digby, Sir K., 1827.
Douglas, T., of Florida, 1856.
Douglass, Frederick, 1845, 1855.
Dundonald, Earl T., 1860.
Durand, J. R., 1820.
Dutens, Rev. L., 1806.
Edgeworth, R. L., 1844.
Edmundson, Journal of, 1774.
Fennell, J., 1814.
Finley, J. B., Pioneer life.
Fitz James, Z., Autobiography, 1855. Pam. 496.
Forman, S., 1552–1602.
Frederica, Margravine of Bareuth, 1828.
Freytag, Gen. J. D., 1824.
Fry, Caroline, 1849.
Gardiner, H., 1813.
Gates, T. R., Life of, 1818.
Genlis, Madame de, 1825.
Gibbon, Miscellaneous works, vol. 10.
Glendinning, W., 1795.
Godoy, Manuel de, 1836.
Goethe, W. J., 1849.
Goldoni, C., 1828.
Gordon, P. L., Personal Memoirs, 1830.
Hamilton, A., Count Grammont, 1811.
Hanger, Col. George, 1801.
Herbert, Edward, Lord, 1792, 1824.
Heron, Sir R., Notes, 1852.
Hicks, Elias, 1832.
Hodgson, John, 1806.
Holberg, Louis, 1827.
Holcroft, T., 1852.
Huet, Bp. P. D., 1810.
Hunt, Leigh, 1850.
Huntingdon, W., Bank of Faith, 1843.
Hutchins, L., 1865.
Hutton, W., 1841.
Iturbide, Augustin, 1824.
Jarratt, D., 1806.
Jerdan, W., 1853.
Ker, John, of Kersland, 1727.
Kotzebue, A. von, 1830.
Lafarge, Madame, 1841.
Lamartine, Memoirs of my youth, 1849.
Lamb, R., 1811.
Lancaster, Joseph, 1833.
Le Courayer, Last sentiments, 1787.
Leslie, C. R., 1860.
Lighton, W. B., 1854.
Lilly's life and times, 1602–1681.
Louis XVIII., 1832.
Lutfullah, a Mohammedan, 1857.

Autobiography (continued).
Maceroni, Col., Memoirs, 1838.
Marsden, J., Grace displayed, 1814.
Miller, Hugh, 1854.
Mirabeau, Mémoires.
Morgan, Lady, 1859.
Neal, John, Recollections, 1869.
Neill, W., D. D., Phila., 1861.
Pennant, Thomas, 1793.
Pepys, S., 1841.
Pfeiffer, Ida, Last travels and life, 1861.
Phases of Interior Life, 1856.
Piozzi, Mrs. Thrale, 1861.
Priestley, Joseph, 1795.
Robinson, Mrs. M., 1802.
Russell, S., of Boston, 1857.
Sampson, W., Memoir, 1807.
Schleiermacher, F. E., 1860.
Scott, Gen. W., 1864.
Scott, Sir W. *See* Lockhart.
Shepard, T., Of Cambridge, N. E., 1832.
Smith, Elias, Of Portsmouth.
Steffens, H., My Career, 1863.
Stilling, H. Jung, 1844.
Thomson, G., 1847.
Thorburn, G., 40 years residence in America.
Trumbull, J., 1756–1841.
Waterton, C., 1851.
White, J. Blanco, Life, 1845.
Wikoff, H., 1855.
Wilkinson, Gen. J., 1816.
Willett, M., His military actions, 1831.
Woodman, J., 1794.
Zschokke, H., 1845.
See Diaries; Letters.

Autographs. Bangs, Merwin & Co., Cat. 1858.
Bell, Cat. of, for sale, 1853.
Brotherhead, Book of the signers, 1861.
Corwin's Cat., with prices, N. Y., 1856.
Crelle, Catalogue, Berlin, prices, 1856.
Crowingshield's Cat., priced, 1860.
Gibson's Sale Catalogue, 1859.
Morse, Priced Catalogue, 1857.
Netherclift, Autograph Miscellany.
" Autograph Souvenir.
Norton, Cat. of, on sale, 1857.
Renouard, Cat. de la Bibliot. de, 1854.
Signers of the declaration of Independence. Letters by, in MS.
Smith, C. J., Hist. & Lit. curiosities, Lond., 1840.
Smith, J. J., Amer. Hist. & Lit. curiosities, 1st series, 1847; 2d series, 1860.
Soleinne, Bibliot. Dramatique, V. 3, 1843–45.

Autographs (continued).
Sotheby, Handwriting of Melancthon, 1839.
" Autog. of M. Luther, 1839.
Tefft, Sale Catalogue, 1867, priced.
Weigel, Verzeichniss. P. 471.

Avarice. Dancer, D., Anecdotes of. P. 1016.

Avignon. Grosjean, Précis historique sur la ville d', 1842.

Avon Springs. Salisbury, S., 1835. P. 79.

Ayscough, F. Case of, 1731.
Oxford University Proceedings, 1730.

Azani, Turkey. Keppel, Tour to, 1831.

Azores Is. Boid, Description of, 1835.
Bullar, Winter in the, 1841.
Major, Life of Prince Henry.
Steele, R., Tour, 1810.
Webster, J. W., Description of, 1821.

Aztec children. Conolly, Ethnolog. exhibition.

B.

Babajee, Hindoo. Read, H., Life of.

Babcock. Family genealogy, 1844.

Babcock, C. Robbins, A. R., Sermon on.

Babylon. Maurice, Observ. on, 1818.
Rich, C. J., On ruins of, 1816.
" Journey to.

Bache, B. F. Truth will out, 1798.

Backus, I. Fish, J., Exam. Examined, 1771.
Hovey, Memoir of.

Bacon, David. Stearns, S., Sermon on, 1810.

Bacon, Delia. Beecher, C. E., A narrative, 1850.
Hawthorne, Our old home.

Bacon, Francis. Dixon, Hist. of, 1861.
Fischer, Philosophy of.
Grosart, On the Christian paradoxes.
Mallet, D., Life of, 1740.
Napier, M., Bacon and Sir W. Raleigh.
Spedding, Life and corres. of, 1870.

Bacon, Leonard. Calhoun, G. A., Letter to.

Bacon, N. Burk's Virginia.
Campbell's Virginia.
Hopkins, S., Youth of the old dominion, 1856.
Tucker's Hansford.
Ware, W., Life of. Sparks. v. 13.

Bacon, Sam. Ashmun, J., Memoir of, 1822.

Bacon, W. Clark, O., Letter to, 1818.

Bacon, W. H. Memorial of, 1863.

Baden. Baden, Statistik, 1855.
Bingner, Literatur ueber, 1750–54.
Dietz, Gewerbe in Baden.
Vier briefe eines Demokraten, 1850.

Baffin's Bay. Sutherland, Journal of a voyage, 1850–51.

Bagdad. Marigny, History of the Arabians.
See Mesopotamia.

Bage, R. Scott, W., Life of.

Bahama Is. Catesby, Nat. Hist. of, 1754.
Edwards, B., Hist of Brit. West Ind., 1806, 10.
McKinnen, D., Description of, 1806.
Martin, R. M., Brit. Col. Lib. v. 4.
Townsend, P. S., Topog. and diseases of, 1826.
See Florida.

Bailey, Jacob. Bartlett, W. S., Mem. of, 1853.

Bailey, Robert. Life of, 1821.
Letters, 1637–62.

Bainbridge, W. Harris, T., Life of, 1837.

Baines, E. Baines, E., Life of, 1851.
Parsons, J., Sermon on.

Baird, Sir D. Hook, T., Life of, 1832.

Baird, R. Life of.
Sprague, W. B., Discourse on.

Baker, E. D. Fitch, T., Address on.

Balboa, V. N. De. Quintana, Life of, 1832.

Baldwin, H. Memoirs of Distinguished Americans, 1853. P. 254.

Baldwin, T. Chessman, Memoir of.
Sommers, Life of, 1835.

Baldwin, W. Letters, 1843.

Baldwin University, Ohio. Catalogues, 1854–69.

Balkan Mts. Keppel, Journey over.

Ball, A. N. W. Morse, O. A., On "rock me to sleep."

Ball, C. Life and adven., 1857.

Ball, N. Hyde, A., Fun. Serm. on, 1797.

Ballads. Allingham, British ballads.
Aytoun, Lays of the Scot. cavaliers.
Ballads (1200), British collected, 4 v.
Book of Scottish Ballads, 1853. (Whitelaw's.)
Bürger, G. A., Leonora.
" Ballads. *See* Uhland.
Child, English and Scotch ballads, 8 v.

Baptism (continued).
Beckwith, G. C., On the mode of Baptism, 1831. P. 82.
Beecher, E., Import and modes, 1849.
Bernard, D., Essay on.
Bradbury, T., Duty and doctrine of baptism, 1810.
Brett, Bap. by Laymen.
Brown, J., Essay on.
Case of house baptism, 1709.
Chadwick, J., New light on, 1832.
Clark, P., Scripture Grounds of, 1735.
Clayton, B., Letters concer., 1756.
Craps, J., View of, 1838.
Daniell, M., What is Baptism, 1838. P. 314.
Dell, Doct. of Baptisms, 1759.
Dissertation on, form of, 1726.
Dore, Sermons on, 1829.
Eastwood, M., Essay on.
Freeman, C., Import of.
Fuller, A., Uses of, 1814. P. 466.
Greatrake, L., Essay on.
Hall, E., Expos. of law of.
Harris, W., Pract. View of, 1816.
Hascall, Definitions of Bapto, etc. P. 466.
Hunt, T. P., The Bible Baptist, 1843. Muns. P. 9.
Illustrations of Fonts, 1844.
Jones, J. A., Joseph corrected, 1834.
Judson, A., Sermon on Baptism, 1832.
Laird, R. M., Essay on.
Lawrence, Lay-Baptism.
Martin, J., Miscellanies.
Meade, Companion to the font.
Morris, H., Sermons on the mode of.
Munro, J., Inquiry, 1825.
Obs. on Matt. xxviii, 19, 20, 1849. P. 313.
Pamphlets on Baptism, vols. 668, 669, 869, 952, 1225, 1855.
Pengilly, R., Script. Guide to. P. 623.
Phipps, J., Dissert. on, 1781.
Pirie, Dissert. on, 1803.
Platt, D., Foundations Exam., 1838.
Proud, J., Water-baptism.
Rahusen, Hand-boek over, 1790.
Reed, J., Essay on.
Relig. exercise for families
Strong, C., Inquiry, 1793.
Truair, Plain Truth on Baptism, 1829. P. 65.
Turney, E., The Command, 1849. P. 466.
Walker, J., Essays, 1838.
Wayland, F., Principles of Baptists, 1857.
Word Baptizo, Essay on.

Baptism of Infants. Addington, Reasons, 1771.
Austin, S., Examination, 1805.
Bostwick, Vindication of, 1790.
Chapman, W., Sermon on.
Clinton, J., Household Baptism, 1838.
Close, J., Infant Baptism, 1803.
Cobbet, Vind. of covenant, 1642.
Edwards, P., Antipædobaptism, 1802. P. 466.
Goodwin, J., Kata-Baptism, 1655.
Hammond, Defence of, 1656.
Inglis, C., On infant b., 1768.
Lathrop, J., Sprinkling, 1789.
" On the mode and subjects of, 1803.
Ollyffe, Defence of, 1694.
Perrouet, Defence of, 1749.
Presb. Church, Rep. on Bapt. Child., 1812. P. 536.
Richards, W., Of Antichrist.
Sacrament of Responsibility (Newland), 1852. P. 231.
Steele, E , Infant baptism.
Thoughts upon, 1807.
Tyler, B., Christian Nurture, 1847. P. 231.
Wall, W., Conference on.
Whiston, W., Prim. Infant Baptism, 1712. P. 314.
Witherell, On Subjects and Mode, 1817. P. 466.

Baptismal regeneration. Benson, C., Writings, 1817.
Brigg, Spiritual regeneration.
Cockburn, W., Some remarks.
Craik, The Divine life.
Dodsworth, On Gorham *vs.* Exeter, 1850.
Goode. W., Letter to Bishop of Exeter, 1850. P. 329.
Harrison, B., Charge, 1850.
High-Church Theory, 1853.
Lindsay, Gorham *v.* Exeter, 1850. P. 330.
Molyneux, Bapt. Regen. opposed, 1842.
Pamphlets, vol. 1270.
Phillpotts, Letter to Archb. of Canter., 1850. P. 200.
Piers, O., Bapt. Regen., 1843.
Scott, J., Effect of Baptism, 1817.
Scriptural Rev. of Liturgy, 1851. P. 329.
Spurgin, Voice of Warning, 1843.
See Tractarianism.

Baptist Church Associations, Minutes of. Abington Bapt. A., Pa.
Bapt. Gen. Assoc., Va., 1849, 57.
Bapt. Gen. Conven., 1814, 16, 17, 32, 38.
Berkshire, Mass., 1857.

Baptist Church Associations, Minutes of (continued).
Berkshire, N. Y., 1826–28.
Black River, N. Y., 1820–1859.
Bridgewater, Pa., 1827.
Canada Bapt. Ass'n, 1822. P. 466.
Cattaraugus Ass'n, N. Y., 1847.
Cayuga Ass'n, N. Y., 1817, 20, 25.
Chemung Ass'n, 1824, 30.
Chenango Ass'n, N.Y., 1833, 37, 42, 43.
Dane Bapt. Ass'n, Wis., 1856.
Eastern New Brunswick, 1856.
Essex Bapt. Ass'n, N. Y., 1815.
Franklin, Del. Co., N. Y., 1815, 16, 26.
Holland Purchase Ass'n, N. Y., 1821.
Hudson River Bapt. Ass'n, 1820, 23, 32–67.
Illinois Pastoral Union, 1857.
Madison Bapt. Ass'n, N. Y., 1810, 12-1832.
New London Ass'n, 1820.
N. Y. Bapt. Ass'n, 1820.
Oneida Bapt. Ass'n, N. Y., 1821.
Onondaga Ass'n, 1825.
Ontario Bapt. Ass'n, 1815.
Otsego, N. Y., 1796.
Pamphlets, vols. 1656, 1657.
Philadelphia Bapt. Ass'n, 1707–1807.
Rensselaerville, N. Y., 1815, 21, 56–68.
St. Lawrence Bapt. Ass'n, N. Y., 1841.
Saratoga, N. Y., 1821.
Stephentown Ass'n, N. Y., 1846, 57.
Warren Bapt. Ass'n, R. I., 1847.
Windham Co., Vt., 1848.
Worcester, N. Y., 1834.

Baptist Churches, United States. Amer. Bapt. Almanac, 1860.
Amer. Bapt. Memorial, 1855, 56.
Amer. Bapt. Year-book, 1871.
Amer. Bapt. Miss. Union Jubilee.
Asplund, J., Reg. of Bapt. Churches, 1791.
Backus, I., History of New England to 1784.
" Hist. of, to 1804.
Baptist Almanac, 1846–59.
Baptist Churches, 1858.
Baptist Memorial, 1848, 51.
Belcher, G., The Baptist pulpit in the U. S., 1850.
Benedict, D., History of, in the U. S., 1813, 48.
" Fifty years among, 1860.
Campbell, J. H., Georgia Baptists.
Clough, S., Christian denomination, 1827. P. 65.
Cone, S. H., Life of, 1856.
Cox, F. A., The Baptists in America, 1836.

Baptist Churches, United States (continued).
Ford *vs.* Everts, Louisville, Ky.
Free Will Baptist Foreign Mission Soc. 1855.
Gammell, Hist. of Baptist For. Mis., 1849.
Gano's life, 1806.
Hague, W., Hist. discourse, 1839.
Haynes, D. C., Baptist Denomination, 1856.
Haynes, T. W., Dict. of Bapt. Biog., 1848.
Hiscox, Church Directory, 1859.
Hist. sketch, South Reading.
Massachusetts Bapt. Conven. Reports, 1848, 49.
Millet, Hist. of, in Maine.
Pamphlets relating to, vols. 232, 314, 465, 466.
Peak, J., Memoir of.
Purefoy, Hist. Sandy Creek Ass'n, N. C.
Rogers, W., Letter, 1785.
Semple, Hist. of, in Virginia.
Smith, S. F., Mem. of Grafton.
Sprague, Annals of Am. Pulpit.
Stanton St. Church, N. Y.
Taylor, J. B., Lives of Va. Bap. Min. 1838.
U. S. Bapt. Ann. Reg., 1832, '71.
Worcester, N., Progress of, 1794.
Wright, S., Hist. of the Shaftsbury Assoc., 1781–1853.

Baptist Communion. Cummings, A., Sermon, 1821.
Gould, Open commun. Norwich, Eng.
Hall, R., Terms of communion, 1816. P. 465.
Robinson, R., On Free Communion, 1781.
Smith, J. H., Close Communion, 1853. P. 466.
Wright, R., Open Communion, 1809.

Baptists, European. Bapt. Ann. Reg., 1792, 4, 5.
Batelier, De drie Getuygen, 1672. P. 634.
Boerhave, Weder-dooperen, 1661.
" Der Mennoniten, 1660.
Booth, A., Apology for, 1812.
" Sermons, etc.
Carey, Vindication of the Calcutta Miss., 1828. P. 314.
Cate, Doopsgezinden in Friesland.
Caveat against Anabaptists, 1714. P. 125.
Crowell, Members' Hand book, 1853.
Cox, Hist. of Bapt. Miss. Soc.
Cutting, Vind. of Bap. History, 1859.
Davis, J., Hist. of Welsh Baptists.

Baptists, European (continued).
Dyer, J., Letter on India Miss.
Greenfield, E., Publications, 1825–49.
Griffith, J., Two discourses, 1707.
Hanserd Knollys Society Publications, 9 vols.
Harris, D., Real Facts Stated, 1832.
Ivimey, History of Engl. Bapt.
Johns, W., Serm. on India Miss.
Perkins, N., Origin of, 1789.
Robinson, R., History of Baptism, 1790.
Rues, S. F., Staet der Mennoniten, 1745.
Ryland, J., Writings.
Tallack, W., Fox and Baptists, 1868.
Taylor, A., History of Engl. Bapt.

Barbadoes. Hillary, Diseases of, 1811.
Ligon, Histoire de l'isle, 1674.
" History of, 1657.
Short History of, 1768.
Sketches (Desultory) of, 1840.
See West Indies.

Barbaro, F. Epistolæ, 1425-53.

Barbary States. Philemon, Voyages to.
See Africa, North; Algiers; Morocco; Tunis; Tripoli.

Barbe Marbois. Société Montyon, 1839.
N. A. Review, 1829.

Barber, W. H. Stephen, Sir G., The Royal Pardon of, 1852.

Barcelona. Records of the inquisition.

Bard, S. M'Vickar, Life of, 1822.

Barker, A. E. Eggleston, Funeral disc., 1863.

Barker, G. P. Bryan, G., Life of, 1849.

Barker, J. Life of, 1855.
Cooke, W., A few facts.

Barlass, W. Newton, J., Letters to.

Barnard, D. D. Writings collected, 5 v.
Newspapers, v. 157.

Barnard, F. J. Sprague, W. B., Sermon, Death of, 1856.

Barnard, T. Prince, J., Serm., Death of, 1814. P. 214.

Barnard, W. F. Memorial, 1864.

Barnes, A. Trial of, 1834, 36.
Life at three score, 1859.
Examination of his reply.
Junkin, G., History of trial before Synod, 1836.
Presby. Church, An Address, 1836.
Smith, G., Correspondence with.

Barney, Joshua. Barney, M., Memoirs, 1832.

Barnstable, Ms. Barnstable Conference, History of, 1846.
Cape Cod Cent. Celebration, 1839.
Clark, J. S., Hist. discourse.
Freeman, Hist. of Cape Cod.
Palfrey, Hist. Disc., 1839.

Barnum, P. T. Autobiography, 1855.
Humbugs of the world, 1866.

Barometer. *See* Meteorology.

Barr, J. W. Swift, E. P., Mem. of, 1833.

Barre, Col. I. Britton, Memoir of.

Barre, Ms. Thompson, Hist. disc., 1854.

Barrier Treaty. Some remarks, 1712.

Barrington, Geo. Memoirs, 1790.

Barrington, Sir Jonas. Per. sketches, 1832.

Barrington, Viscount W. W. Life of, 1815.

Barron, J. Decatur, S., Correspondence with, 1820. P. 50.

Barrow, Sir John. Autobiog. memoir, 1847.

Barstow, S. Memorial of, 1854.

Bartels, J. H. Redslob, In Memoriam, 1853.

Bartlet, W. Dana, D., Disc. on, 1841.

Barton, B. Memoirs and Letters, 1850.

Barton, J. Kenney, A. H., Fun. Serm.

Barton, W. Williams, Mrs., Life of, 1839.

Bartram, J. Darlington, Memorial of, 1849.

Bascom, H. B. Henkle, Life of.

Bascom, T. Geneal. record, 1870.

Basire, J. Correspondence, 1650-85.

Baskerville's ed. Brunet, Manuel, v. 5.

Basle. Eclaircissements sur, 1833.

Bassompierre, De. Mémoires, 1765.

Bastille, The. Latude, Account of.
Memoirs, 1834.
Mémoires sur.
Pamphlets relating to, vol. 770.

Batavia. Boom, Nederl. Oost Indie, 1864.
Gibson, Prison of Weltevreden, 1855.
See Java.

Batavia, N. Y. Seaver, W., Hist. Sketch of, 1849.

Bates, E. Gordon, J. W., For the Presidency.

Bates, Josh. Memorial of, 1865.
Boston merchants' tribute, 1864.

Bedell, G. T. Tyng, S. H., Memoir of.

Bedford, Duke of. *See* Russell.

Bedford, New Hamp. Woodbury, P. P., Hist. of, 1851.

Bedfordshire, Eng. Beauties of England and Wales.
Fisher, T., Hist. Collections, 1812–36.

Beecher, G. Biog. remains, 1844.

Beecher, H. W. Bartlett, D. W., Modern agitators, 1855.
Dix's Sketches.
Stowe, H. B., Men of our times.

Beecher, Lyman. Autobiog. and cor.
Bartlett, Modern agitators, 1855.
Dix's Sketches.

Bees. Bevan, E., Nat. Hist., etc., of the honey bee, 1838.
Debeauvoy, Guide de l'apiculteur, 1851.
Haughton, Cells of.
Huber, Nat. Hist. of bees.
Martin's Bee-house, 1846.
Miner, American Bee-keeper's manual, 1849.
Phelps, Bee-keeper's chart.
Richardson, The hive, 1854.
Weeks, Management of, 1839.

Beeston Cast'e. Hecklin, History of, 1845.

Beethoven, L. von. Letters, 1790–1826.

Beggars. Exposure of the various, etc.
Society for the suppression, etc., 1857.
See Poor.

Behaim, M. Ghillany, Geschichte des Seefahrers, 1853.

Belchertown, Ms. Doolittle, Historical Sketch of Cong. Ch., 1852.

Belgium. Académie des sciences, Annuaire, 1846–67.
Annuaire de l'Industrie Belge, 1838.
Belgium, Documents, sur l'instruction publique.
" Official pub., misc., 1849–62.
Bréval, Remarks on travel, 1723.
Dobson, E., Railways of, 1834–42.
Gachard, Anciennes Assemblées de la Belgique, 1845.
Gibson, W., Belgian Surgeons, 1848. P. 271.
Heuschling, Publications on Belgian Statistics, 1844–51.
Jottrand, Des rapports de la Belgique et de la France, 1841.
Le Roy, Université de Liège, 1869.
Louis XVIII, Journey, 1791.
Pamphlets relating to the Belgian revolution (1830), vols. 939–941.
Papendrecht Hist. Eccl. Ultrajectinæ, 1725.

Belgium (continued).
Poplimont, La Belgique héraldique, 1867.
Respublica Namurcensis, 1634.
Revolution en, 1830.
Tennent, J. E., Belgium, 1841.
Trollope, Belgium since 1830.
Univ. de Louvain, 1863, 64.
See Rhine; Netherlands; Bibliography.

Belief. *See* Opinions; Creeds; Reason.

Belisarius. Mahon, Lord, Life of, 1848.
Marmontel, History of, 1770. B. C.

Bell, Andrew. Southey, R., Life of, 1844.

Bell, B. Trial of.

Bell, Sir C. Arnott, Oration on, 1843.

Bell, H. Morris, E., Life of, 1854.

Bell, John. Past history. P. 1229.

Bellamy, George, Anne. Memoirs.

Bellamy, J., D.D. Works, Memoir.

Belleisle. Impartial Narrative, 1761.

Bellows, B. Bellows. H. W., Sketch of, 1854.

Bells. Baker, B., of Westminster.

Belles-lettres. *See* Literature; Poetry; Drama; etc.

Benecke, C. D. Lehmann, in Memoriam, 1853. P. 1102.

Benedict XI, Pope. Scoti, A., Memorie del, 1737.

Benedict. Family pedigree.
Genealogy, By H. W. Benedict, 1870.

Benedict, E. C. Run through Europe.

Benedict, L. & S. Memorial of.
Canal claims, 1862. P. 1872.

Benedict, Gen. L. Memorial, 1866.
Albany Bar Proc. 1864. P. 1591.

Benevolence. Church, Philosophy of.
Lawrence, E. A., Mission of the church.

Benevolent Societies. Pamphlets regarding, vols. 90, 97, 232, 263, 472, 509, 1487.
See Humane Institutions; Charities.

Benezet, A. Vaux, R., Memoirs of, 1817.

Bengal Directory, 1824.
See India.

Benjamin, S. M. Murdock, D., Sermon on.

Bennet, Mr. Featley, D., Sermon on, 1708. P. 381.

Bennet. T. Atterbury, Sermon on, 1706.

Bennett, J. Chickering, Sermon on.

Bennett, J. E. Parish and the minister, 1851.

Bennett, W. E. J. Griffith, Letter to, 1853.

Bennington, Vt. Butler, J. D., Address on Battle of, 1848.
Jennings, Memorials of, 1869.

Bentinck, Lord G. D'Israeli, A political biography, 1852.

Bentinck, W. C. East India Comp., Proc. on resignation, 1835.

Bentley, R. Middleton, C., Proceedings against, 1719.

Bentley, W. Craner, Testimony, 1757.
Rogers, J., Serm., Death of, 1751. P. 381.

Bentham, Jeremy. Colls, Utilitarianism.

Benton, T. H. Bates, E., Against, 1828.

Benzeville, S. Moore, J., Discours sur la mort de.

Beranger, P. J. Memoirs.

Berbice. Marryatt, J., Ans. to Commissioners, 1817.

Bergen family. Genealogy, 1866.

Bergen, N. J. 200th anniversary, 1861.
Taylor, B. C., History of, 1857.

Berkeley, Bp. Correspondence.
Mandeville, Letter to, 1732.

Berks and Lebanon Cos., Penna. Rupp, Hist. of, 1844.

Berkshire, Eng. Beauties of Eng. and Wales.
Berry, County genealogy.

Berkshire Co., Mass. Allen, T., Hist. of, 1808. P. 502.
Allen, W., Wunnissoo, a poem.
History of the County of, 1829.
Holland, Hist. of Western Massachusetts, 1855.
Hopkins, M., Jubilee Sermon, 1845.
See Pittsfield.

Bermuda Islands. Martin, R. M., Brit. Col. Lib. V. 6.
Plaine Description, 1609.

Bernadotte, C. J. King of Sweden. *See* Charles XIV.

Bernard, Saint. Les lettres de, 1772.
Morison, Life of.
Ratisbonne, Life of.

Bernard, J. Retrospections, 1830.

Bernard, Sir T. Baker, J., Life of.

Berry, Miss M. Correspondence, 1783-1852.

Berry, H. G. Butler, N., Fun. discourse, 1863.

Berryer, P. A. Galerie des Contem., 1; Vie de, 1845.
Senior, Biog. of.

Bertrand, Gen. Galerie des Côntem., Notice sur. 1845.

Berwick-upon-Tweed. Fuller, History of, 1799.

Berzelius. Galerie des Con., Vie de, 1845.

Best, H. Pers. and Lit. Memoirs, 1829.

Bethlehem Female Seminary. Reichel, History of, 1785–1858.

Bethune, G. W. Van Nest, Memoir of.

Bethune, Mrs. J. Bethune, Memoirs of.

Beverly, Ms. Stone, E. M., Hist. of, 1630-1842.

Bevois, M. Dew, S., Sermon on.

Bewick, T. Memoir, 1862.
Bell, Cat. of Books relating to, 1850.

Bible: Miscellaneous. Beecher. C. E., Appeal to the People.
Benson, C , On Scriptural difficulties.
Biblical Emendations, 1830, P. 15. B. C.
Boucher, L'homme en face de.
Castalio, Dialog. Sac. libri iv. 1722.
Chalmers, T., Scriptural Read's., 1849.
Chillingworth, Works, 1820.
Concise Examinations, 1856.
Eastman, J. W., The Bible Excellent, 1823. P. 559.
Excellence of, Hughes, 1803.
Female Scripture characters, 1816.
Gastrell, Christian Institutes.
Halsey, Literary Attractions of, 1858.
Higginson, T. W., Scripture Idolatry, 1854. P. 558.
How, T. Y., Address, N. Y., 1817.
Hunter, Sacred biography.
Hutchinson, Music of.
James, Bellum Papale; Hieron. editionem, 1678.
Jenks, W., Bible Atlas, 1847.
Kittredge, Scripture lands described, 1850.
Letter to a Friend, 1700.
Lewis, T., Bible and Science, 1856.
Livermore, G., Circulation of the Scriptures, 1849.
Macmillan, Bib., Natural History.
Manual of Reflections, 1801.
Manrice, F. D., Claims of, 1863.
Melmoth, Sublime of Scripture.
Nelson, H. A., Bible for the People, 1857. P. 468.
Nott, J. C., Bib. and Phys. Hist. of Man, 1849.
Payson E., Oracles of God, 1824. P. 111.
Skinner, T. H., Religion of the Bible.

Bible: Miscellaneous (continued).

Spring, G., The Rule of Faith, 1844.

Taylor, I., Transmission of books, 1859.

Turner, S., Sacred Hist. of the World, 1831. B. C.

Wadsworth, B., Sermon on, 1815.

Wells, Geography of, 1721–34.

Yates, J., Letter to Vice Chancellor, 1834. P. 317.

See Cosmogony; Christ. evid.; Bibliography.

Bible: Commentaries on, Critical and Practical. Bundel van.... Oeffeningen, 1757-63.

Bush, G., Illustrations of, 1836. B. C.

Butler, C., Horæ Biblicæ, 1817.

Cocceius Opera, 1689.

Critical Notes, Mann, 1747.

Doddridge, Family Expositor, 1836.

Drummond, W., Œdipus Judaicus.

Eichhorn, On "Word" and "Spirit," 1834. P. 313.

Emdre, Bybels Huis Boek, 1786.

Green, Wm, H., Inaug. Disc., 1851.

Haas, Exerc. Philologica, 1798.

Hamelsveld, Exercitatio in Scrip. Sac. 1763. P. 1016.

Hare, F., The Difficulties, etc., 1769.

Harmer, Obs. on var. passages.

Hawks, Egypt a witness for the Bible, 1850.

Hieronymus, Opera omnia, 1823-24.

Hodge, C., Importance of Bib. Literature, 1822. P. 93.

Hulsius, Verkl. der....Liederen in. 1726.

Lee, S., Prolegomena in Bib. Sac.

Lightfoot, Opera, 1686.

Lowth, R., Letter to Warburton, 1766.

Marsh, H., Hist. of Bib. interpretation.

Miscellanea Sacra, Shute.

Meyboom, Commen. Theol., 1840.

Montanus, Communes Hebr. ling. idiotismi, 1572.

Origen, Hexaplorum quæ supersunt.

Ostervald, Pract. Obs. on O. and N. T.

Ouboter, Verklaaring, 1791.

Palm, Van der, Aantekeningen tot de vertaling des, 1834. B. C.

Pamphlets relating to biblical criticism and literature, vols. 313, 769, 1232, 1262, 1267-1270, 1489, 1760.

Patrick, Comm. on the Bible, 1844.

Picus Mirandula, Heptaplus, 1479.

Planche, Introd. to sacred philology.

Poole, M., Synopsis Criticorum, 1669–1676.

Priestley, Notes on all the books of S., 1803, 4. B. C.

Reineccius, Manuale Biblicum, 1734.

Bible: Commentaries on, Critical and Practical (continued).

Rendell, E. D., Treatise on the peculiarities of, 1853. P. 93.

Rynink, Exerc. in Scr. Sac., 1765.

Sawyer, Elem. of B., interpretation.

Schutte, Heilige Jaarboeken, 1779.

Spinoza, B., Critical inquiry.

Theodoretus, Opera, 1573.

Theophylactus Comm. Greek and Latin, Opera, 1754–63.

Vermeer, Over Verschede Plaatsen, 1757.

Walker, J., Essays, 1838.

Bible: Commentaries, etc. on the old Testament: Various Books.

Alexander, J. A., Commentary on Psalms.

" On Isaiah.

Bonnet, Solomon's Prediger, 1792.

Bonomi, Nineveh, 1857.

Broadley, Evid. of Relig. of Moses, 1805. P. 335.

Bryant, Plagues of Egypt.

Buchanan, G., Paraph. Ps. Dav. Poet, 1790. B. C.

Catcott, A. S. The Elohim.

Chandler, S., Vindication of Old Testament, 1741.

Colenso, Bp., Pentateuch and Joshua critically examined, 1862, 63.

Coleridge, J., Judges 17, 18. 1768.

Compendio dell ant. testamento.

Costard, On the book of Job.

Cotton, J., Comm. on Ecclesiastes, 1657.

Critical dissertation on Is. VII, 1767.

Cumming, J., Colenso wrong, 1862.

Cunningham, Dr., Kennicott's method, 1760.

Cyprianus, Opera, 1726.

Cyrillus, Hom. in Jeremiam.

" On Leviticus.

Dimock, Notes on Genesis, Exodus, Isaiah, Jer.

" Notes on Psalms, Proverbs, Minor Prophets.

Diss. on destruction of Canaan.

Dod, J., On the Proverbs, 1606.

Doederlein, In vetus Test. Auctarium, 1779. B. C.

D'Oyly, Letters to Drummond, 1812.

Ens, Aanmerkingen over Iesaias XI, XII, 1764.

Good, J. M., Job translated.

Green, W. H., Answer to Colenso.

Gregorius, Comm. in Hexæmeron, 1553.

Gregory I., Opera, 1744.

Grotius, Annot. in Vetus Test., 1727.

Harcourt, Doctrines of the Deluge, 1838.

Bible: Commentaries, etc. on the old Testament: Various Books (continued).

Horne, G., Comm. on the Book of Psalms, 1820. B. C.

Houte, Van, Ps. cxlvi, 1736.

Hunt, T., Dissertation, 1743.

Kennicott, On MSS. of Hebrew.

" On Gen. I-III.

" On 1 Sam., vi, 19.

Lach, Van Iesaias, Chap. vi, 1739.

Lawson, Lectures on Ruth, 1816. B. C.

Letters of certain Jews.

Lettres de Quelques Juifs, 1769.

Levi, Defence of O. T., 1798.

Maclear, Shilling book of Hist. of.

Mahan, Answer to Colenso.

Marsh, H., Authenticity of Pentateuch.

" Moses Vindicated.

" On Michaelis's comment.

Marsh, W., On the Pentateuch.

Maurice, F. D., Patriarchs and law-givers, sermons.

Mulder, Letteryruchten, 1844.

Muntinghe, De Psalmen, 1772.

Musculus, Commentarii, 1578-1623.

Newcome, W., On Ezekiel, 1836.

Newton, S., Dissert. on the Prophecies, 1832. B. C.

Outrein, Over Psalm cxix, 1701.

Palfrey, Lect. on the Jewish Scriptures, 1838–40. B. C.

Pemble, W., On Ecclesiastes, 1628.

" On Zechariah, 1629.

Pilkington, Errors in the Heb., 1759.

Pintus, In Pro. Jeremiæ, 1581.

Popham, Pentateuch compared.

Pseaulmes de David, Estienne, 1552.

Rafinesque, Genius of Heb. Bib., 1838.

Rawlinson, Evidences of truth of, 1860.

Reply to the Letter to Dr. Waterland, 1732.

Rivetus, Med. in Psal. cxix, 1638.

Rogers, J., Lowth's corrections.

Rose, H. J., On the Mosaic law.

S. (D. M. B.), Explication du Cantique des Cantiques, 1689.

Schultens, Proverbia Salomonis.

Sharpe, G., On Merrick's Annotations, 1769. P. 334.

Sherlock, T., Case of Abraham, etc., 1746.

Simon, Hist. crit. du Vieux Test., 1685.

Stanley, A. P., Hist. of Jewish church, 1863-6.

Stebbing, H., Hist. of Abraham, 1746.

Stuart, M., On Daniel, 1850.

Thompson, J. P., Man in Genesis, 1869.

Bible: Commentaries, etc. on the old Testament: Various Books (continued).

Warburton, Defence of Div. Legation, 1747. P. 352.

Wardlaw. R., On Ecclesiastes.

Webber, F., Jewish Dispensation, 1738.

Whiston, W., On the true text of, 1722.

See Solomon's Song; Job.

Bible: Commentaries, etc., on the New Testament. Abrégé de la morale des Evangiles, 1689.

Adams, H., Letters on Gospels, 1824.

Adler, J. G. C., Novi. Test. Syriacæ, 1789.

Alexander, J. A., On Matthew.

Amersfoordt, Annot. Nov-Fœd., 1810.

Augustinus, Sur le Nouveau testament, 1689.

Ballou, H., Notes on the Parables, 1831. B. C.

Bengel, Gnomon of, 1857.

Blomfield, Use of Jewish Tradition, 1817. P. 313.

Bosch, De Magis ab Oriente, 1695. P. 634.

Brink, Over den 1 Joannes, 1806.

Burgess, T., Writings, Lond., 1815-35.

Calvin, On Epist. to Romans, 1836.

Carpenter, D., Supp. to Harm. of Four Gospels, 1838. P. 313.

Chapman, Notes on passages, 1819.

Chrysostom, On Galatians, 1833.

Colenso, Bp., On Romans, 1863.

Collet, S., Paraph. of Romans, Galatians and Hebrews, 1774.

Conybeare, St. Paul's life.

Crandall, A. L., Expl. of Revelation, 1841. P. 631.

Curtenius, Brieven v. Paulus aan Corin, 1769.

Cyrillus, On John.

Dwight, T., Genuineness of the N. T.

Ellicott, On Galatians, 1860.

Elsnerus, Brief aan de Romeinen, 1763.

Erasmus, In Evan. Joannis, 1542.

" In Novum Testamen. annot. 1522.

Eyton, Sermon on the Mount, 1808. P. 238.

Fleetwood, On Rom. xiii, 1710.

Furness, Remarks on the four gospels, 1836. B. C.

Goffine, Auslegung aller Epistelen, 1849.

Grotius, Annot. in Novum Test., 1826-34. B. C.

Gyles, S. F., On Luke 22: 38.

Haas, Openbaaring van Johannes, 1804-117.

Haldane, R., On Rom. i–v, 1806.

Bible: Commentaries, etc., on the New Testament (continued).

Heinsius, Exerc. ad Nov. Test., 1639.

Heylin, J., Theol. Lectures, 1749, 1761.

Hodge, C., On 2 Corinthians.

Hollman, Ad. C. iii et xiii, Pauli ad 1 Cor., 1819. P. 295.

Janeway, Exposition of Romans.

Jewell, Bp. J., On Thessalonians, 1583.

Jona, Annot. in Acta Apost.

Keil, Opus. Acad. ad N. T. interpretationem, 1821.

Kenrick, Exp. of Hist. books of N. T., 1828. B. C.

Knatchbull, N., In lib. Nov. Testamenti, 1677.

Koning, Corinth. lsten zendbrief, 1702.

Leighton, Works, Peter's Epistles.

Lorgion, De dicentibus in N. T. suo ingenio interpretandis.

Luther, Præfatio in Ep. ad Roman.

Maclear, Shilling book of hist., 1867.

McLeod, A., Lectures on the Prophecies of the Revelation, 1814.

Martin, D., Upon 1st John v. 7, 1718.

Maurice, F. D., Lect. on St. Luke.

Melancthon, In Evang. Joann. et Matt., 1523.

Mills, W., On 1 Cor. 15: 29.

Nahuys, Over d. brief v. Paulus aan de Philippensen.

Newcome, Harmony of the 4 Evangelists, 1809. B. C.

Newton, Sir I., On 1st John v. 7, 1754.

Oecolampadius, In Epist. Joannis.

Olshausen, Comm. on New Testament.

Owen, H., Obs. on four Gospels, 1764.

" The modes of Quotation vindicated, 1789.

Paley, Horæ Paullnæ, works, v. 2, 1830.

Peirce, James, Dissertat'n on six texts, 1727.

" Paraphrase and Notes on the Epistles, 1733.

Piscator, J., Comm. in omnes libros, N. T., 1613.

Plevier, Paulus, aan de Galateren, 1738.

Porteus, Lect. of Gosp. of Matthew, 1805. B. C.

Randolph, T., Proph. in the N. T.

Schleiermacher, On Gospel of St. Luke, 1825. B. C.

Sharp, G., Greek Defin. Article, 1798.

Socinus, Explicatio Cap. 1. Johannis.

Stuart, M., On the Ep. to the Hebrews.

" On the Apocalypse.

Sykes, Ep. to Hebrews, 1755. P. 1004.

Tholuck, On Gospel of St. John, 1836.

Tregelles, Lang. of Matthew's Gospel, 1850. P. 313.

Bible: Commentaries, etc., on the New Testament (continued).

Trench, Synonymes of the N. T.

Turner, S. H., Notes on the Romans, 1824.

Whately, Difficulties in Ep. of St. Paul, 1830. B. C.

Whitby, Last thoughts of, 1822. P. 304.

White, J. B., Diatessaron, 1800.

Zigabonus, Comm. in Evang. 1547.

See Bible; Theology; Revelation of St. John.

Bible Concordances. Cruden, A., 1817.

Englishman's Greek Conc. of the N. T., 1848. B. C.

Hugues de St. Cher S. S. Bib. vulg. ed. Concord., 1649.

Trommius, Nederl. Concord., 1750.

Bible: Dictionaries. Am. S. S. Union, Dictionary.

Calmet, Dictionary of, 1832. B. C.

Eastwood, Old Bible Words, 1866.

Fleming, Scripture Gazetteer, 1837.

Kitto, Cyclopædia of Bib. Literature, 1846. B. C.

Smith, W., Dictionary of, 1863.

" Hackett & Abbot's ed., 1871.

Bible: English Translation. Anderson, C., Annals of Eng. Bible, 1855.

Burges, On new Translation of.

Conant, History of, 1856.

Day, H. T., Inaccuracies of Engl.

Geddes, of a new Translation, 1787.

Lenox, J., King James' Bible.

McClure, Authors of Version.

Newman, Emend. of O. T., 1839.

Revision of the authorized, Dub., 1837.

Walter, H., Independence of the version, 1823-28.

Ward, T., Errata of the Protestant Bible, 1688.

Webster, N., Errors of the Eng. P. 173.

Bible: History of, and Introductions.

Bagster S., Bible of Every Land, 1851.

Chevreau, Premières Leçons, 1855.

Dissertation, canon, authority of, 1732.

Duruy, Histoire Sainte, 1856.

Eichhorn, Inleiding in het Oude Testament, 1789. B. C.

Gleig, History of the Bible, 1831. B. C.

Hawes, J., Lectures on, 1833.

Horne, T. H., Introd. to the Holy Scriptures, 1826.

Hug's Introduction to N. T., 1836.

Jahn, Introd. to the Old Testament, 1827. B. C.

Jones, J., Canon of the N. Test., 1798.

*The references in Italics denote headings under Bibliography.

Bibliography (continued).

AMERICAN HISTORY, ETC., BOOKS ON.
Allen, E., Cat. of Books, 1856, 58.
Almon, Cat. of Books, 1776.
Antonio, Bibliot. Hispana.
Asher, Bib. Essays, New Netherland, 1867.
Bibliotheca Americana: Homer, 1789.
Bœhmer, Bib. Script. Hist. Nat.
Boucher, Bibliot. des Voyages.
Brown, J. C., Catal. of Books in Library of, 1493-1800.
Coolidge, Hist. of New England.
Drake, S. G., Cat. of Lib. Ant. of America.
Du Parc d'Avagour, Aut. sur Guyane.
Gowans's Catalogues.
Gurley, Cat. of Books on, at auction.
Haven, Archæol. of U. S., Bibliog.
Hotten, Tracts on America.
London Institution, Cat. v. 2.
Ludewig, Lit. of Amer. local history.
Mondidier, Cat. of Library of.
Muller, F., Cat. of Books on.
Norton's Literary Letter, 1858.
Rich, Biblioth. Americana, etc.
" Catalogue of Spanish books on America.
" Cat. of Sp. MSS. on.
" Gen. Cat. 1837.
" Books relating to.
Smith, J. R., Books on Sale. Lond.
Squiers, Cat. on Central America.
Stevens, Amer. Bibliographer, 1857.
" Amer. Nuggetts, 1857.
Ternaux, Bibliothèque Américaine.
Trübner, Cat. of Books on Sale, 1857.
Warden, Biblioth. Americana, 1820, 1831, 1840.

AMERICAN LIBRARIES, *See Libraries in America*; *Catalogues of*.

AMSTERDAM. Bibliot. der Stad, 1858, 60.
See Dutch.

AMUSEMENTS. Le Verrier, L'ecole de la Chasse.
See Angling; Chess.

ANA. Artigny, Mémoires.
Peignot, Répertoire de Bibliog.

ANATOMY. Douglas, J., Bib. Anatomicæ spec., 1734.
Vigiliis. Bibliot Chirurgica. 1781.
See Medical.

ANGLING. Smith, J. R., Books on.

ANONYMOUS AUTHORS. Baillet, Auteurs Déguisés.
Barbier, Dict. des Ouvrages Anon. 1827.
Chardon, Mélanges, V. 3, Revue de Barbier.

Bibliography: ANONYMOUS AUTHORS (continued).
Dict Bibliographique, V. 3.
Hamst, Fictitious names, 1868.
Le Long, Bib. Hist. de la France, V. 5.
Manne, Dictionnaire anon. et pseud., 1862.
Notes and Queries, index.
Quérard, Litt. Franc. Contemporaine.
" France Littéraire, 1864.

ANTIQUITIES. Lerouge, Cat. Paris, 1853.
Letronne, Cat. de la Bibliot. de.
Reimann, Idea Systematis, etc.
Soc. of Ant. Newcastle, Eng., Cat.
Soc. of Antiquaries, Lond., Cat.
Warmholtz, Bibl. Hist. Sueo-Gothica.
See American History, Books on.

ARABIC. Bavaria, Roy. Lib. Col. Arabicos.
Casiri, Bibl. Arabico-Hisp. Esc.
Herbelot, Bibliot. Orientale.
Leyden, Univ. Catalogus.
Schnurrer, Bibliot. Arabica.
See Oriental; Asiatic.

ARCHITECTURAL. Evans, Cat. of Works on, 1851.
Malberg, Literatur des Bau-und Ing.-wesens.
Weale, Cat. of Books for sale.

ARTS, MECHANIC. Blumhof, Bibliot. Ferri.
France: Ecole des Ponts et Chaussées.
Schubarth, Repert. der Tech. Literatur.
Weigel, Catalog.
See Architectural; Engineering.

ASIATIC LANGUAGES. Astor Library, Linguistics.
Burnouf, Cat. de la Bibliot.
Clarke, A., Bibliot. Misc.
Klaproth, Verz. der Chines, Bucher.
Rask, Cat. of MSS. Zend, etc.
See Oriental; Manuscripts.

ARMENIAN. Cat. de l'imprimerie arménienne.
Somal, Storia letteraria di Armenia, 1829.

AUCTION SALES, AMERICAN. Allan, J., Catalogue of library, sold N. Y., 1864.
Bangs Brothers & Co., N. Y.
Bérard, Lib., West Point.
Bouton, Cat. of lib., sold 1868.
Brady, H. A., Lib., N. Y., 1851.
Campbell, J. N., Cat. of lib. sold N. Y., 1864.
Choate, R., Library, 1859.
Colman, W. A., Lib., N. Y., 1850.
Conway, F. W., N. Y., 1854.
Corwin, E. B., Lib., N.Y., 1856, priced.

Bibliography: Auction Sales, American (continued).

Dean, Amos, Catalogue, 1868.

Griswold, R. G., Lib. sold, N. Y., 1859.

Gurley, Sales, 1846-48.

Hall, Fitz-Edward, Lib. sold Boston, 1867.

Hunt, F., Lib. sold N. Y., 1859.

Ingraham, E. D., Lib. N. Y., 1855.

Ingraham, J. W., Lib., Boston, 1848.

Jarvis, S F., Lib., N. Y., 1851.

Ludewig, Lib. sold N. Y., 1858.

Philadelphia Trade Sales, 1848-57.

Pickering, J., Lib., Boston, 1846.

Rice, sale cat., N. Y., 1870.

Roche, R. W., Sale N. Y., 1867.

Romeyn, J. B., Lib., N. Y., 1825.

Stevens, H., Bibliot. Historica, 1870.

Town, I., Cat. of Library sold, N.Y., 1847.

Townsend, R., Library sold, N. Y., 1868.

Turner, W. W., Library sold, N. Y., 1860.

Wight, Cat. of Lib. sale, N. Y., 1864.

Auction Sales, Dutch. Coster, Bibl. Delphis, 1718, priced.

Lennep, Van., 1855.

Major, Bibliot. Mechlin, 1767, priced.

Meermann, Bibl., Hague, 1824, priced.

Servais, Bibliot., Malines, 1808, priced.

Verbeyst, Lib., Bruxelles, 1852.

Water, De, Lugd. Bat., 1823.

Auction Sales, English. Akers, E.F., Lond., 1820.

Askew, Bibliot. lib. raris., 1775, priced.

Bacon, T. S., Catalogue, 1736.

Barrett, J. T., London, 1851.

Beauclerk, Lib., London, 1781.

Beckford, Fonthill Abbey, Lib., 1823.

Bennett, Cat., 1723.

Bindley, J., London, 1818.

Bird, G., Lond., 1856.

Bohn, J., Lond., 1855.

Booth, W. H., Lond., 1837.

Borromeo, Cat. Nov. Ital., Lond., 1817.

Boucher, J., Lib., Lond., 1806.

Brit. Mus., Cat. of Duplicates, priced.

Brockett, J. T., Lond., 1823.

Clarke, Repert. Bibliographicum.

Combes, W., Lond., 1837.

Crowningshield, Lond., 1860.

Dallaway, J., Lond., 1841.

Dibdin, The Director.

" Decameron, v. 3.

Evans, Lond., 1831-39.

Farmer, R., Lib., Lond., 1798, priced.

Folkes, M., Lib., Lond., 1756.

Bibliography: Auction Sales, English (continued).

Francis, Sir P., 1838.

Gancia, 1856.

Gardner, J. D., London, 1854.

Garrick, D., Lib., Lond., 1823, priced.

Harding & Lepard, 1838.

Harley, R., Bibliot., Lond., 1743.

Hawtrey, C., Lib., London, 1854.

Heber, Bibliot., London, 1837.

Hibbert, Lib., London, 1829, priced.

Hill, T., 1811.

Lang, R., Lond. 1828.

Lansdowne, Lib., Lond., 1806, priced.

Lawford, E., Lond., 1855.

Libri, Library sold, July, 1861.

Marchmont, Lond., 1830.

Mathias, T. J., Lond., 1841.

Maturin, Lond., 1841.

Mondidier, Lib., Lond., 1851.

Montagu, Lib., Lond., 1733, 40, priced.

Mead, Bibliot., Lond., 1754, priced.

Paris de Meyzieux, Lib., Lond., 1791, priced.

Parr, S., 1827.

Paul, Sir G. O., Lond., 1828.

Payne & Foss, Lond., 1848.

Penrose, Lib., Lond., 1851.

Pierson, T., Lond., 1815.

Perry, J., Lib., Lond., 1822, priced.

Pinelli, Bibliot., Lond., 1789, priced.

Puttick & Simpson, 1849, 54.

Raine, Lib., Lond., 1812, priced.

Reed, I., Lib., Lond., 1807.

Roscoe, W., Lond., 1816.

Rose, H. J., Lib., Lond., 1840.

Roxburghe, Duke of, Lib., Lond., 1812, priced.

Skegg, Lib., Lond., 1842.

Sotheby, Lib., Lond., 1841, 56, priced.

Southey, R., Lib., Lond., 1844, priced.

Stirling, 1839.

Strettell, Lib., Lond., 1820, priced.

Sussex, Duke of, Lib., Lond., 1844.

Tooke, J. H., Lib., Lond., 1813, priced.

Towneley, J., Lib., Lond., 1814, priced.

Turner, D., Lib., Lond., 1853.

Wakefield, S., 1835.

Watt, 1838.

Willett, R., Lond., 1813.

Williams, T., Lib., Lond., 1827.

York, Duke of, Lond., 1827.

Auction Sales, French. Bearzi, Bibli., Paris, 1855.

Bossange, Librairie, Paris, 1853.

Brunck, M., Bibliot., Paris, 1853.

Dallerange, Bibliot., Paris, 1851.

Bibliography: Auction Sales, French (continued).
Emméry, Cat. des MSS., etc., Metz, 1849, priced.
Gouttard, Cat., Paris, 1781.
Jacob, Bibliot. Cat., 1839, priced.
Langlès, Bibliot., Paris, 1825.
Lerouge, Cat., Paris, 1833.
Letronne, Bibliot., Paris, 1849.
Libri, Bibliot., Paris, 1847.
Louis Phillippe, Bibliot., Paris, 1852.
MacCarthy-Reagh, 1817.
Nodier, Descr. d'une Collect., Paris, 1844, priced.
Peignot, Bibliot., Paris, 1852.
Perrot, Bibliot., Paris, 1775, priced.
Raoul-Rochette, Bibliot., Paris, 1855.
Renouard, Bibliot., Paris, 1854.
Suard, Bibliot., Paris, 1817.
Vanackere, Lille, 1854.
Verny, E., Strasbourg, 1855.

Auction Sales, German. Carpzovius, Bibliot. Carpzoviana, 1700.
Gesenius, Bibliot., Halæ, 1843.
Julius, Bibliot., Berlin, 1850.
Kloss, Library of, Lond., 1835.
Krohn, Bib., Hamb., 1796.
Lippert, Halle, 1846.
Mertens, F. K., Bremen, 1833.

Auction Sales. *See Prices; MSS.*

Augsburg. Braun, Notitia Hist. Lit.
Krauth, Augsburg Confession Bibliog.
Mezger, Augs. älteste druckdenkmale.
Veith, Orig. typ. in Aug. Vind.
Zapf, Ann. typ. Augustanæ.

Bamberg. Jaeck, Beschreibung der Bib.
Laborde, Débuts de l'impr. à.

Belgium. Acad. de Belgique, Stassart, Cat. de la bibliothèque, 1863.
Belgium, Chambre. Cat. de la bibliothèque.
Bibliophile Belge, 1845-64.
Foppens, Bibliotheca Belgica, 1739.
Hennebert, Bibliologue de la Belgique, 1831.
Kervin, Bibliophiles Flamands, 1853.
Lambinet, Recherches Historiques, 1798.
Major, Bibliot., Mechlin, 1767, priced.
Namur, Hist. des Bib. de la, 1840.
Néve, Append. à la Bibl. Douaisienne.
Provincial Genoot. Noord Braband, Cat.
Reiffenberg, Ann. Bibliot. royale, 1840-51.
Reume, Variétés Bibliog., 1847.
Vandermeersch, Cartes aux archives de la Flandre, 1850.
See Libraries in Belgium; Dutch; Auction Sales.

Bibliography (continued).

Belles Lettres. *See Literature.*

Beuerberg. Hupfauer, Druckstucke aus dem xv jahrhundert.

Bible (Editions of the). American Bible Soc. Cat. of Lib.
Anderson, Annals of English, 1845.
Bagster's Catalogue, 1838.
Beloe, v. 3, English editions.
Biblical Student's Asst., 1844.
Butler, C., Horæ Biblicæ.
Classical Collector's Vade mecum.
Darling's Cyclop. Part II. Commenta.
Dibdin, Bibliot. Spenceriana, v. 1, 5.
" Introd. to Classics, v. 4.
Horne, Manual of Bib. Bibliog.
O'Callaghan, Amer. Editions of.
Orme, Bibliotheca Biblica
Paitoni, De' volgarizzamenti della Bibbia.
Panzer, Von dem allerältesten deutschen Bibeln.
" Gesch. der Nurnberg Ausgaben.
" Der Augspurgischen Ausgaben.
Pellicer, Traducciones en Castellano.
Pettigrew, Cat. of Duke of Sussex's Library.
Platt, Cat. of Ethiop. MSS.
Rive, Chasse aux Bibliog, 1789-88.
Schinmeier, Schwedischen Bibel Uebersetzungen.
Shea, Catholic editions, U. S.
Steigenberger, Zwo allerälteste deutsche Bibeln.
Stewart, Catalogue of Bibles on sale.
Sussex, Duke of, Library sold.

Bibliographical Books, Catalogues of.
Hibbert, Cat. of Library of.
Labbe, Bibliot. Bibliothecarum.
Major, Bibliotheca, 1767.
Munsell, Cat. of Lib. for sale, 1857.
Namur, Bibliog. paleog. dipl. Bibliol.
" Man. du Bibliothécaire, 1834.
Peignot, Répert. Bibliographique, 1812.
Renouard, Cat. de sa Bibliothèque.
Tessier, Catalogus Auctorum, 1688.
Tross, Cat., Paris, 1855.
Trubner, Cat. of Books on sale, 1857.
Warmholtz, Bibl. Hist. Sueo-Gothica.
See Typography.

Bibliographical Dictionaries. *See Dictionaries.*

Bibliographical Miscellanies. Aldine Magazine, 1838-9.
Analectabiblion, 1836.
Artigny, Mémoires, 1749-56.
Bibliog. Miscellany, London, 1830.

Bibliography: BIBLIOGRAPHICAL MISCELLANIES (continued).
Burton, The Book Hunter, 1862.
Dibdin, Bibliog. Decameron.
" Bibliography, a poem.
" Bibliomania.
" Cat. of books, 15th century, Lib. Cassano.
" Library Companion.
" Rare editions of the Classics.
" Bibliophobia.
" Reminiscences of a Lit. Life.
Mencke, De Charlataneria.
Nodier, Mélanges, 1829.
Rive, Chasse aux Bibliographes.
Savage, The Librarian, 1808, 9.
See Books ; Periodicals.

BIBLIOGRAPHY, ELEMENTARY. Branca, Cat. Introd.
Clarke, A., Bibliog. Dictionary, Essay.
" Bibliog. Misc., V. 2.
Constantin, Bibliothéconomie, 1841.
Dibdin, Decameron.
Diction. Bib., Cailleau, V. 3.
Guild, Librarian's Manual, 1858.
Horne, Introduction to, 1814.
Namur, Manuel du Bibliothécaire.
Peignot, Dict. de Bibliol, 1804.
Pseaume, Dict. Bibliog. V. 1.
See Classification ; Libraries, Administration of.

BIBLIOGRAPHY. *See Booksellers ; Fifteenth Century ; Rare Books ; Libraries.*

BIOGRAPHICAL BIBLIOGRAPHY. Œttinger, Bibl. Biog. supp.

BIOGRAPHIES OF BOOKSELLERS AND PRINTERS. *See* Typography; *Booksellers.*

BOCCACCIO. Bearzi, Cat. de Livres Rares.

BOOK-KEEPING. Foster, B. T., Works on.

BOOKS. *See Prices; Rare Books.*

BOOKSELLERS' CATALOGUES. *See Law; Manuscripts; Auctions.*

BOOKSELLERS' CATALOGUES, AMERICAN. Amer. Publishers' Circular.
Appleton's Bulletins, etc.
" Library Manual, 1847, 52.
Bartlett & Welford, N. Y.
Blake, A. V., Booksellors' trade list, 1847.
Butler, E. H., Phila., 1843.
Carter, R., 1858.
Catalogues, Miscellaneous, 76 vol.
Doyle's Cat., N. Y., 1840-50.
Eastburn, Cat., N. Y., 1818, 19, 24.
Gowans, N. Y., 1840-64.
Harper and Brothers, 1847.
Library Reporter, 1854.

Bibliography: BOOKSELLERS' CATALOGUE (continued).
N. Y. Trade Sales, 1845-51. Cat. 39-43.
Norton, Bibliot., Amer., 1857.
Norton's Literary Advertiser, 1851-54.
Philadelphia Trade Sales, 1850, 55. Cat. 42, 73.
Putnam, G. P., For. and Am. 1850.
" Book-buyer's Manuel.
Roorbach, O. A., Bibl. Am., 1820–61.
Trade Circular, N. Y., 1871.
Wiley & Putnam, N. Y., 1842-47.

BOOKSELLERS' CATALOGUES, DUTCH. *See Dutch Books; Belgium.*

BOOKSELLERS' CATALOGUES, ENGLISH.
Bent, R., London Cat. 1814-39.
Bent, Adver., London,. 1846-53.
Bibliotheca Londinensis. 1814–46.
Blackwood, Edinburgh, 1812.
Bohn, H. G., Cat., 1841-56,
" Catalogue, 1848, pp. 1841.
" General Catalogue, 1850-67.
Catalogues of Secondhand Books, Cat. V. 3. 6, 7, 21, 23, 27, 28, 46, 47, 65, 71, 77, 79, 88.
Chapman's, Lond., 1842–56.
Denis, Bookseller's Cat. Lond., 1789.
Hodgson, T., Books published in Great Britain, 1814-51.
Kerslake, 1823-53.
Leslie, Cat. Eng. and For. Theol.
Lilly, J., Lond., 1848, 49.
Longman, Old Books, 1816-53.
Low, S., Brit. Cat, 1837-52, 1835-62,
" Amer. Cat., 1856.
" Index to Cat., 1858.
Montague, R., 1733, 40.
Nattali. Cat. with prices, Lond., 1842.
Nutt, D., Theol. Books, Lond,, 1837.
Pamphlets, Vol. 602.
Payne & Foss, Lond., 1848.
Publishers' Circular, 1855-69.
Quaritch, Catalogues, classified, 1864, 69, 70.
Rich, O., Lond., 1831-46.
Rodd, relating to America.
Smith, J. R., Bibliotheca Americana, 1853.
" Catalogue 1865, 1871.
Stevens & Haynes, 1870.
Stevenson, T. G., Edinb., 1853.
Stewart C. J., Cat. of bibles. etc., Lond. 1849.
Thorpe, T., Curious books, 1842, 1843.
Weale, Lond., 1836–44.
Willis, G., Lond., 1844-62.
Willis & Sotheran, 1855-69.
See London Catalogues; English Books.

Bibliography (continued).

BOOKSELLERS' CATALOGUES, FRENCH. Bachelier, Paris, 1830–53.
Bossange, M., 1830–55.
Bossange, Sale catologues, 1845–50.
Delalain, Cat., Livres Class. Fr., 1858.
Goddé, Ca. de livres relatifs aux arts.
Hachette, 1854–58.
Reinwald, Lib. Française, 1858.
Tross, Cat., Paris, 1855, 71.
See French Books, etc.

BOOKSELLERS' CATALOGUE, GERMAN. Asher & Co., Berlin, 1844-54.
Eylert, 1854.
Hinrichs, 1835-67.
Weigel, R., Lipsiæ, 1832–43.
Weigel, Apparat. lit., 1832.
" Cat. Sammlung von Buchern.
See German Books and Authors.

BOOKSELLERS' CATALOGUES, ITALIAN. Bibliog. Italiana.
Branca, Cat. Della Libreria.
Molini, Firenze, 1853.
Renuccini, Milano, 1850.
Scapin, Padova, 1839.
See Italian Books.

BOTANICAL. *See Natural History.*

BOURGOGNE. Barrois, Biblio, des Ducs de.
Bock, Liber Guidonis.
Bourgogne, Inventaire des MSS.
La Serna Santander, Mém. sur la Bib. de.

BRITISH MUSEUM. Brit. Mus. Catalogues.
" Catalogue of letter A., 1841. f°.
Cumberland, Essay, prints in.
George III, Bibl. Regiæ Catalogus.
Great Britain, Reports of Comm. of House of Commons, 1850.
Hargrave, Cat. of MSS. of Library of.
Simms, Handbook of Lib. of Brit. Mus.
Stevens, Cat. of Amer. Books in.
Waagen, Treasures of Art in G. B., V. I.

BRUSSELS. *See Libraries; Belgium.*

BRY, T. DE. Bure (De), Bib. Instructive.
Camus, Mém. sur la Collection de.
Tièle, Mém. Bibliographique, 1867.

CAMBRAI. Coussemaker, Notices sur la Biblioth. de.
Le Glay, MSS. de la Bibl. de.

CAMBRIDGE UNIVERSITY. Cranwell Trin. Coll. Cat.
Halliwell, MS. rarities at Univ. of Cambridge.
Hartshorne, Book Rarities of.
Parker, M., Cat. Lib. MSS.

Bibliography (continued).

CANADA. Canada, Cat. of Lib. of Parliament, 1857, 58.
" Parl. lib., Index, 1862.
" Books relating to America.

CATALOGUES. Bunau, Cat. de la Bibliot.
Catalogues, 97 vols., miscellaneous.
Catalogues, Pam. vols. 212, 602, 1218. B. C., 38, 39, 40.
Feurlein, Supellex Libraria.
Jewett, Construction of Catalogues.
Observations on Cat. of Brit. Museum.
Panizzi, Letter, 1838.
Peignot, Repert. Bib., List of.
Royal Society, on Panizzi's notes.
Techener, Consid. sur la Bibl. Royale.
See Auction Sales; Booksellers; Classification; Bibliography; Libraries, Catalogues and Administration of; Priced Catalogues.

CAXTON, W. *See* Typography.

CHEMISTRY. Bochmer, Bib. Script. Hist. Nat.
Zuchold, Bibliot. chemica, 1840-58.

CHESS. Game of chess, W. Caxton, 1474. Lond., 1865.
Vogt, Principal Works on.

CHINESE. Klaproth, Cat. des Imprimés.
Klaproth, Verzeichniss der Chinese und Mandschu Bucher.
Trubner, Oriental record, 1865-67.

CHURCH FATHERS. Cleaver, List of Books.
Darling's Cycl., Art. Bibliotheca.
Dibdin, Introd. to Classics.
Dodwell's Cat. of Church authors.
Lennep, D. J. Van. Cat. de la bibliot.

CHURCH HISTORY. Jablonowski, Biblioth.
See Theology; Roman Cath. Church; Protestantism.

CLASSICS, EDITIONS OF GREEK AND LATIN.
Baillet, Jugemens, vol. 3, 4.
Bibliot. Gr. et Lat. (Reviczky).
Books, Rare, etc., Boston, 1815.
Botfield, B., Prefaces to First ed. of Classics, 1861.
Clarke, A., Bibliographical Dict., 1804.
Classical Collector's Vade Mecum, 1822.
Dibdin, Introduction to editions of.
Engelmann, Bibliot. Philol., 1853.
Fabricius, Bibliotheca Latina, 1703.
Fournier, Dict. de Bibliog, 1809.
Greswell, Early Greek Press.
Harless, Notitia Litt. Græcæ.
Hebenstreit, Dict. ed. Classicorum, 1828.

Bibliography: CLASSICS, EDITIONS OF GREEK AND LATIN (continued).

Hoffman, S. F. G., Lexicon Scriptorum Græcorum, 1832.

Jacobs, F., Bibliotheca. *Cat.*

Iriarte, Bibl. Matritensis, Gr. MSS.

Lennep, D. J. Van, Cat. de la Biblioth.

Moss. J. W., Manual of Classical Bibliog., 1837.

Paitoni, Autori Gr. e Lat. Volgarizzati.

Pointer, Miscellanea, 1718.

Peignot, Repert. Bibliog., 1810.

Smith, Dict. of Gr. and Rom. Biog.

Tarlier, Traductions de Persius.

See Manuscripts.

CLASSIFICATION OF BOOKS. Alembert, Système des Conn. Humaines.

Chaudon, Dict. V. 20.

Constantin, Bibliothéconomie.

Fortia d'Urban, Syst. de Bibliog. Alpha.

Great Brit. Report Brit. Mus., 1835.

Palermo, Classazione dei libri à Stampa.

Peignot, Dict. de Bibliol, 1804.

See Bibliography, Elementary; Catalogues; Libraries.

COISLIN, H. C. De C. Montfaucon, Bib. Coisliana.

COLOGNE. Hartzheim, Bibliot. Coloniensis.

COTTON, R. B. Brit. Mus. Cat. of Cott. MSS.

DALMATIAN. *See Slavic.*

DANISH. Worm, Lexicon over Danske laerde Maend, 1783.

DANTE. Bearzi, Cat. de Livres Rares.

Colomb, Bibliog. Dantesca, 1845.

DEVONSHIRE, ENG. Davidson, Bibliot. Devoniensis, 1852.

DICTIONARIES OF BIBLIOGRAPHY. Allibone, S. A., Dict of Engl. Lit. & Brit. & Amer. Authors, 1859-71.

Bauer, Bibliot. Libr. Rar., 1770-72.

Brunet, Manuel du Libraire, 1842-44.

" " 5e. éd., 1860-65.

Bure, G. F. De, Bibliot. Instructive, 1763-69.

Chaudon, Dict. Univ. Hist. et Bibliog., 1810-12.

Clarke, A., Bibliograph. Dictionary, 1802-4.

Clement, Bibliothèque Curieuse, 1750-60.

Dictionnaire bibliographique, Cailleau, 1790, 1802.

Ebert, Gen. Bibliog. Dict., 1837.

Fournier, Dictionnaire de Bibl., 1809.

Georgi, Allge. Europ. Bucherlexicon, 1750-58.

Gesner, Bibliotheca, 1574.

Hain, Repertorium Bibliog., 1826-38.

Bibliography: DICTIONARIES OF BIBLIOGRAPHY (continued).

Hallevord, Biblioth. Curiosa, 1678.

König, Bibliot. Vetus et Nova, 1678.

Laire, Index Librorum... ad an. 1500.

La Serna Santander, Dict. Bibliog., 1805-7.

Lowndes, Bibliog. Man. of Eng. Literature, 1834.

" Bohn's ed., 1857-64.

Maittaire, Annales Typographici, 1719-41, 1789.

Osmont, Dict. typog. hist. et crit., 1768.

Panzer, Annales Typographici, 1793-1803.

Pseaume, Dict. Bibliographique, 1824.

See Fifteenth Century Editions; Bibliography, Elementary.

DICTIONARIES OF AUTHORS, OF LITERARY HISTORY, ETC. Allibone, Dict. of Brit. and Amer. authors, 1859-71.

Aprosio, Bibliot. Aprosiana.

Brunet, Manuel du Libraire, 1865.

Chaudon, Dict. Univ. Hist. et Bibliog., 1812.

Darling, Cyc. Bibliographica.

Ladvocat, Dict. Hist. et Bibliog., 1789.

Lowndes, Bibliog. manual, (Bohn), 1857-64.

Oettinger, Bibliog. Biog. Univ., 1854.

Sarrut, Biog. des Hommes du Jour, 1841.

See American; English; French, etc.

DIPLOMATICS. Bossange, Catalogue.

Christ, Abhandlungen, 1776.

Maffei, Letter to Countess of Seefeld.

Namur, Diplo-Bibliol., 1838.

Peignot, Dict. de Bibliol., 1804.

Silvestre, Universal Palæography.

See Bibliography, Elementary; Writing; Manuscripts; Alphabets.

DISSERTATIONS. Boekeren, Cat. Theol. Dissertationum, 1853.

Marklin, Cat. Diss. Acad. Scandinaviæ.

Muller, Cat. Diss. Juridicarum.

Weigel, Corpus Diss. Theol., *for sale.*

DOUAI. Nève, Appen. à la Bib. Douaisienne.

Duthillœul, Cat. des MSS. de la Bib. de.

DRAMATIC AUTHORS. Baker's Bibliot. dramatica, 1812.

Barker's List of plays, 1814.

Burton, W. E., Bibliot. dram. Auct. sale, N. Y., 1866.

Egerton's Theatrical Remembrancer, 1788.

Garrick, Cat. of Library of, 1823.

Heinsius, Allg. Bucher Lexicon, v. 4.

Langbaine, Lives of Eng. Dram. Poets, 1698.

Bibliography: Dramatic Authors (continued).
Reed, Bibl. Reediana, 1807.
Riccoboni, Hist. du Théatre Ital.
Roxburghe Library Cat., 1812.
Soleinne, Bibliot. Dramat., 1845.
See Shakespeare.

Dresden Lib. Bunau, Cat. Bib. Bunavianæ.
Ludewig, Zur Bibliothekonomie.

Dutch Authors and Books. Abkoude, Naamregister: Nederduitsche boeen, 1600–1761.
Asher, Bib. Essay....New Netherland, 1867.
Bon, Theol. lib. for sale, Amsterdam.
Dutch catalogues, Pam. vols. 38, 39, 40. B. C.
Exposition Univ., Cat. de Livres publiés en Hollande.
Friesch Genootschap, Catal., 1848.
Jaarboekje voor den Boekhandel, 1839-1843.
La Rue, Geletterd Zeeland, 1734.
Meulman, Catalogus, 1500-1688, 1867.
Maatschappij van Ned. Lett. Cat.
Meerman Uitvinding, etc., Ed. Visser,
Muller, Cat. Diss. Jurid. Neerlandiæ.
Pauw, Cat. Bibliot. Hagæ, 1654.
Provincial Genootsch, N. Braband.
Revue Bibliog. des Pays Bas, 1822-30.
Schotel, Archives en Hollande.
Tiéle, Mém. Bibliog sur les journaux des Navig. Néerlandais, 1867.
Servais, Cat. de la Biblioth., 1808.
Vereeniging des Boekhandels, Cat. Lib.
Voorst, Bib. de Théol., 1859.
See Belgium; Auction Sales; Gand; Alost; Elzevir; Libraries.

Early Editions. *See Fifteenth Century Editions.*

Educational. Barnard, List of works on.
Cat., V. 57, 59, 60.
Delalain, Cat. Livres d'éducation, 1858.
Hachette, Cat. Livres d'éducation.
Soc. for Encour. of Arts, Cat. of Educ. Exhib.
South Kensington Museum, 1860.

Elzevir Editions. Jaarboekje voor den Boekhandel, 1839-42.
La Faye, Traités Imprimés par.
Nodier, Mélanges, 1829.
Pieters, Annales de l' Impr. Elsév.
Reume, Recherches sur, 1847.

Engineering. Blumhof, Bibliot. Ferri, 1803.
France: Bridges, Catal., 1856.
Malberg, Literatur des Bau. und Ingenieur Wesens, 1852.
Schubarth, Repertorium Techn.

Bibliography: Engineering (cont'd).
Weale, Cat. of Books on, for sale.
Williams, J., Works on, for sale.

English Books and Authors. Berkenhout, Biog. Lit., 400-1600.
British Critic, 1793-1818.
Bryges, Censura Literaria, 1815.
" Restituta, 1816.
" Brit. Bibliographer, 1814.
Cole, Bibliog. Tour to a Library.
Critical Review, 1756-98.
Darling, Cyc. Bibliograph., 1854.
Fry, Bibliog. Memoranda, 1816.
Goodhugh, Engl. Gent's Library.
Literary Blue Book, 1830.
Low, Brit. Cat., 1837-57.
Lowndes, Bibliog. Man. of Eng. Lit.
Reuss, Register of Authors of G. Brit.
Savage, The Librarian, 1808, 9.
Wright, Biog. Britan. Literaria.
See Booksellers, English; Great Britain; Scotland; Dictionaries.

English History, General and Local.
Bohn's Cat. 1841, Index. *Local.*
Chalmers, G., Cat. of Lib. for sale.
Davidson, Bibliot. Devoniensis.
Farmer, R., Cat. of Lib., 1798.
Great Britain, Lib. of H. of Commons.
Halliwell, Notices of English histories.
Leland, Comm. de Script. Britannicis.
Macray, Man. of Bri. historians to 1600.
Newman Cat. County hist. for sale.
Nichols, Cat. of County hist. for sale.
Nicolson, Engl. hist. library, 1714.
Roxburghe library Cat.
Smith, Bibliot. Cantiana, 1837.
Soc. of Ant., Newcastle, Cat., 1839.
Soc. of Ant., Lond., Cat., 1816.
Towneley, Auction sale of lib., priced.
Upham & Beet, Books on topog. for sale.

English Libraries. Botfield Cathedral Libraries, 1849.
British Museum.
Clark, Repertorium Bibliog., 1819.
Dibdin, The Director, Folkes', etc.
" Northern tour, and other works.
Merryweather, Dibdin, Middle Ages.
See Libraries in England, Catalogues of; Cambridge; Oxford; London.

English Poetry. Beloe, Anecdotes.
Brydges, Restituta, etc.
Farmer, Cat. of Lib.
Greene, A. G., Auction catalogue, 1869.
Halliwell, Account of Vernon MSS.
Longman, Bibl. Anglo-poetica.
Malone, Cat. of Early Eng. Poetry.
Perry, J., Lib. at Auction, 1822.

Bibliography: ENGLISH POETRY (continued).
Reed, I., Cat. of Lib., 1807.
Rimbault, Bibliot. Madrigaliana.
Ritson, Bibliot. Poetica, 1802.
Strettell, Cat. of Library of.

ERLANGEN, Irmischer, Handschriften Kat.

ESCURIAL LIBRARY. Casiri, Bibliot. Arab.

EUROPEAN. Berlin Royal Library.
Bibliotheca Uffenbachiana MSS.
Christern, Bulletins of For. Lit., N.Y., 1855–67.
Frieschgenootschap, Cat. der Bibliothek.
Georgi, Allg. Bucher Lexikon, V. 5.
Gesner, Bibliotheca, redact. per J. Simlerum, 1574.
Gryphius, De Script. sec. xvii.
Heinsius, Allg. Bucher Lexikon.
Palm (Van der), Lib. ac. MSS. Bib. Schultensianæ, 1841.
Thott, Cat. Bibliot., sold, 1791.
See Dutch; French; German; Bookseller's Catalogues.

FATHERS OF THE CHURCH. *See Church.*

FIFTEENTH CENTURY EDITIONS. Bauer, Bibliot. Lib. Rar., 1774.
Berlin, Lib. Incunab., 1851.
Boutourlin, Cat. de la Bibliot.
Braun, Notitia Hist. Lit., 1788.
Catalogus Lib. Rarissimorum.
Clarke, A., Bibliog. Misc., V. 2.
Clement, Bibliot. Curieuse, 1760.
Cranwell, Engl. books, Trin. Coll.
Crevenna, Catalogue, 1776.
Denis, Supp. to Maittaire.
" Merkwurdigkeiten, etc., 1780.
Gand, Recherches Historiques, 1845.
Hain, Repertorium Bibliog., 1838.
Holtrop, Cat. Bib. Haganæ, 1856.
Hupfauer, Druckstucke..in Beurberg.
Kloss, Cat. of Library of, 1835.
Laire, Index Librorum ad an., 1500.
" Spec. Typ. Romanæ xv sec.
La Serna Santander, Dict. du Quinzième Siècle, 1807.
MacCarthy Reagh, Cat. de vente.
Maitland, Index of Lib. at Lambeth.
Maittaire, Annales typograp., 1789.
Meerman, Uitvinding, etc. Ed. Visser.
Murr, Memor. Bibliot. Norimb., 1791.
Nyerup, Spicil. Bibliog., 1784.
Pinelli, Bibliot. Pinelliana, 1790.
Panzer, Der Buchdruckerkunst in Nurnberg, 1789.
" Annales typographici, 1803.
Seemiller, Incunab. Bib. Ingolst.
Servais, Cat. de la Bibliothèque.

Bibliography: FIFTEENTH CENTURY EDITIONS (continued).
Sussex, Duke of, Library sold, 1845.
Towneley, Library sold, Lond., 1814.
Visser, Boeken in de Nederl. voor MD.
Wurdtwein, Bibliot. Moguntina.
Zapf, Ælteste Buchdruckergesch.
See Dictionaries; Festivals; Typography.

FIFTEENTH CENTURY EDITIONS IN THE LIBRARY.
Æneas Sylvius, Historia, 1477, f°.
" " Abbreviatio Blondi, 1484.
Albertus Magnus, Liber secretorum, 1496, 4°.
Aristoteles, Lib. Predicamento., 1484.
" Libri physicorum, 1482, f°.
Articella, Thes. operum medicorum veterum, 1491.
Donati, ed. minor, 1494.
Ficinus, M., Epistolæ, 1495, f°.
Game of Chess, Caxton, 1474. Fac sim., 1865.
Gerson, J., Opera, 4 v., 4°, 1478-1502.
Gouvernayle of helthe, 1483. Fac. sim.
Juvenalis, Satyræ, 1486, f°.
Leonardus de Utino. Sermones aurei, 1473, f°.
Picus mirandula, J., Heptaplus, 1479, f°.
Plotinus, Opera, 1492, f°.
Plutarchus, De viris clariss., 1473, f°.
Rosa anglica medicinæ, 1492, f°.
Schedel, H., Chronicon Nurimb., 1493, f°.
Socrates, Sozomenus et Theodoricus, 1472, f°.
Statius, P. P., Sylvæ, 1494, f°.
Suidas, Lexicon Græcé, 1488, f°.
Thebaïs. *See Statius.*
Theramo, Belial, 1472, f°.
" " 1484, 4°.
Thomas Aquinas, Catena aurea, 1470.
Trithemius, De Scriptoribus eccles., 1492.
Vincentius, Speculum historiale, 1494.

FINE ARTS. Immerzeel, Bibliothek.
Raoul-Rochette, Cat. Bibl. Artistique.
Schlegel, Kat. der Bucher Sammlung.
Taylor, Cat. of library sold, 1853.
Weigel, Cat. von Kunstsachen, for sale, 1840.
See Engraving; Fine Arts.

FLEMISH. Kervin, Bibliophiles Flamands.
See Belgium.

FLORENCE. Biscioni, Bibliot. Med. Laur. MSS., 1752.

Bibliography (continued).

FRENCH BOOKS AND AUTHORS, Annonces de Bibliog., 1790.

Baillet, Jugemens, vol. 4, 5, Poëtes.

Baudry's Catalogues, 1845–49,

Bibliog. de la France, Journal de l'imprimerie et de la librairie, 1820–40; 1859–63.

Bossange, Catalogues, 1836, 45, 47, 53,

Delalain, Paris, 1858.

Georgi, Allg. Europ. Bucherlexicon, V. 5, 1750-58.

Goujet, Bibliot. Françoise, 1740-56.

Leber, Bibliothèque de *Litetrature.*

Lerouge, Local and Revolutionary Hist.

Lorenz, Librairie Française, 1840–65.

Raynal, Anecdotes Littéraires.

Quérard, La France Littéraire, 1827-1864.

" Litt. Fran. Contemporaine, 1827–57.

Sarrut, Biog. des Hommes dujour.

Soleinne, Bibl. Dramatique *et po tique.*

Techener, Annuaire Pibliographique.

Ventouillac, The French Librarian.

See Bookseller's Catalogues; Auctions.

FRENCH HISTORY AND LITERATURE. Baillet, Jugemens des Savans.

France, Bibliot., Imp. Cat. de l'hist. de la France, 1855-65.

Frère, Bibliog. Normand, 1860.

Gouget, Bibliot, Françoise.

Jacob, Biblioth. Cat. 1839.

Leber, Cat. de sa Bibliothèque.

Le Long, Bib. Hist. de la France.

Monfalcon, Bibliog. de Lyon, 1851.

FRENCH LIBRARIES. Bordeaux, Bibliothèque de la ville.

Bure, Bibliot. de M. le Duc de la Vallière.

Coussemaker, Bibliot. du Département du Nord, 1843.

Dibdin, Bibliog. Tour in France.

France, Bibliot. Impériale, 1859-62.

" Bibliot. de la Marine et des Colonies, 1843.

Larénaudière, Cat. de livres de sa Bibliothèque, 1846.

Le Glay, Bibliot. du Nord, 1841.

Manuscripts in public Libraries in France. *See* Law Library.

Petit-Radel, Recherches, sur les Bibliot. anc., 1819.

Prousteau, Bibliothèque Publique, fondée par, 1777.

Voyage Littéraire de deux Bénédictins, 1724.

See Libraries in France, Catalogues of; Paris; Douai; Aix; Cambrai; Lille; Orleans; Lyon.

Bibliography (continued).

FRENCH MANUSCRIPTS. *See Manuscripts.*

FRIENDS. Smith, J., Cat. of books by Soc. of Friends, 1867.

GAELIC. Reid, Bibliot. Scoto-Celtica.

GEOGRAPHICAL. Boucher, Bibliot. des Voyages, 1808.

Engelmann, Bibliot. Geog., 1858.

Pinelo, Bibliot. nautica et geografica.

See Maps; Voyages.

GEOLOGICAL. Austria, Kat. Bibl. Min. Cabinetes, 1851.

Agassiz, Bibliog. Geologiæ., 1854.

Boehmer, Bibliot. Hist. Naturalis.

See Scientific.

GERMAN BOOKS AND AUTHORS.

Aretin, Beyträge, 1807.

Bingner, Lit. über Baden, 1854.

Boekeren, Cat. theol. dissertationum.

Brockhaus, Leipzig, 1853.

Bucherschatz der Deutschen nat. litt.

Catalogues, v. 22, 30, 32, 34, 35, 48, 67, 68, 86, 91.

Engelmann, Bibliot der neueren Sprachen, 1842.

" Bibliot. Juridica, 1840.

" Bibliot der schönen Wissenschaften, 1846.

" Bibliot. Philologica, 1853.

Ersch, Bibl. handbuch der phil. lit.

Feuerlein, Supellex libraria, 1768.

Georgi, Allg. Europ. Bucherlexicon.

Heinsius, Allg. Bucherlexicon.

Hinrichs, Verzeichniss, 1832-58, 1862, 1866.

Jordens, Lexikon deutscher dichter und prosaisten, 1811.

Kayser, Index lib. 1750-1846, in German.

Kirchhoff, Gesch. des deutschen buchhandels, 1857.

Koehler, Catalog., 1851.

Meusel, Das gelehrte Teutschland.

" Lex. der lebenden teutsch. schriftsteller, 1806-34.

Muller, Cat. Diss, jurid. Germaniæ.

Panzer, Annalen der ältern deutschen litt., 1788.

Schubarth, Repert. der tech. literatur.

Trömel, Litt. der deutschen mundarten.

See Booksellers' Catalogues; Auction Sales; Baden; Manuscripts.

GHENT. Voisin, Bibliot. Gandavensis.

GRAMMARS. Engelmann, Bib. der Neueren Sprachen, Bib. Philologica, 1853.

Estienne, Thesaurus, 1825.

See Philological.

Bibliography (continued).

GREAT BRITAIN Cooper, C. P., Account of Records in, 1832.

See England; Scotland; Ireland; Libraries; Booksellers.

GUICHARD. Vries, A. De, Speculum hum. salv., 1843.

GUIDES IN SELECTION OF BOOKS. *See Libraries; Books.*

GUTENBERG, J. *See* Typography.

GUYANA. Du Parc d'Avagour, Liste d'auteurs sur.

HAWAII IS. Hunnewell, Bib. of Hawaiian Is., 1869.

HEBREW BOOKS AND TYPOGRAPHY. Affo', Vita di V. Gonzaga, 1780.
Bartolocci, Bibliotheca Rabbinica.
Biscioni, Cat. Medic. Laurent, 1752.
Bowyer, Hist. of Printing, Hebrew.
Buxtorff, Bibliot. Rabbinica nova.
Krafft, Cod. Hebraici Bib. Vind.
Rossi, De Heb. Typ.... Editionibus.
" Ann. Hebræo. Typog., 1799.
See Bible.

HERALDRY. Bohn's Cat., 1841.
Moule, Biblioth. Heraldica, 1822.

HISTORICAL. Bunau, Cat. Bibliothecæ.
Bure, Bibliog. Instructive.
Crevenna, Catalogue, 1776.
Dupin, Bibliot. Univ. des Historiens.
France, Bibliot. Impér., Catalogue de l'Hist.
Gryphius, Script. Hist. Seculi xvii.
Le Long, Bib. Hist. de la France.
Lenglet du Fresnoy, Méth. pour étudier l'histoire, Catal. des Historiens.
See English; French; American.

HOLLAND. *See Belgium; Dutch; Auctions.*

HORTICULTURAL. Felton, Eng. Authors on.
Johnson, Hist. of Eng. Gardening.
Séguier, Bibl. Botanica.
Weston, Cat. of Eng. Authors on.
See Agricultural.

HULSIUS. Tiele, Mémoires bibliog. de la coll. de.

HUNGARIAN. Koehler, Catalog. 1861.

ICELANDIC. Möbius, Cat. Lib. Island., 1856.
Worm, Lexicon over Isl. Laerde Mænd.
See Swedish.

ILLUMINATED MSS. Humphreys, Middle Ages, 1849.
Waagen, Treasures of Art, 1854.
Wright, Art in the Middle ages.
See Manuscripts; Writing.

INDIA. Elliot, Bibliog. index to Historians of.

Bibliography (continued).

INDIAN (AMERICAN) LANGUAGES. Am. Phil. Soc., Catal. of MSS. on.
Clavigero, Cat. of Mexic. Grammars.
Ludewig, Literat. of Am. Abor. Lang.
Schoolcraft, Bib. Cat. of books in.

INGOLDSTADT. Seemiller, Incunab. Bib. Ingolst., 1789.

INSURANCE. N. Y. Insurance report, List of books on, 1868.
Pocock, List of books on.

IRISH AUTHORS. Berkenhout, Biog. Lit. 400-1500.
Hiberno-Celtic Soc. Cat. (O'Reilly).
Reuss, Reg. of Authors on, 1770–1803.

IRON. Blumhof, Bibliot. Ferri, 1803.

ITALIAN BOOKS, AUTHORS, LIBRARIES, TYPOGRAPHY. Aprosio, Bibliot. Aprosiana, 1734.
Argelati, Bibliot. Scriptorum, 1745.
Azara, Bibliotheca, 1806.
Bibliog. Italiana, 1839, 40.
Bibliog. Class. Italiani, 1814.
Blume, Iter Italicum, 1824-36.
Boutourlin, Cat. de la bibliot.
Borromeo, Catalogo, 1817.
Branca, Cat. della libreria, 1844.
Capponi, Cat. della libreria, 1747.
" Cat. dei manoscritti *istorici.*
Colle, Storia lit. sci. di Padova, 1824.
Coulomb, Bibliog. Dantesca.
Crapelet, Progrès de l'imprimerie en.
Fontanini, Bibl. dell' eloquenza ital.
Ginguéné, Hist. litt. d'Italie, 18 4.
Haym, Bibliot. Italiana, 1741.
Hoffman, Imprimerie en Italie.
Lechi, Tipog. Bresciana, 1854.
Libri, Cat. de la Bibliot., 1847.
Marsand, Bibliot. Petrarchesca, 1826.
Melzi, Bibliog. dei Rom. e Poemi....
Molini, C. F., Cat. of Books on sale, Lond., 1848.
Molini, L., Cat. de Libri....vendibili, Firenze, 1853.
Morelli, Cod. volgari, Naniana, 1776.
Muston, Bibliog. of Vaudois hist.
Osmont, Dict. bibliographique.
Paitoni, Bibliot. autori ant. volgarizzati.
Pasinus, Cod. MSS. Taurin. Athenæi.
Pinelli, Bibliot. Pinelliana, 1790.
Renuccini, Libreria, Milan, 1850.
Riccoboni, Hist. du Théatre ital.
Saxius, Hist. lit. typ. Mediolan., 1745.
Toppi, Biblioteca Napoletana, 1678.
Valentinelli, Bibliog. del Friuli, 1861.
Valéry, Voy. historiques en Italie.
Zacharia, Bibliot. Pistoriensis, 1752.

Bibliography: ITALIAN BOOKS, AUTHORS, LIBRARIES, TYPOGRAPHY (cont'd).
Zanetti, D. Marci bibl. codicum.
Zeno, Dissertazioni Vossiane, 1752.
See Libraries (Catalogues of) in Italy; Auction Sales; Booksellers; Rome; Milan; Venice.

JUNTA EDITIONS. Dibdin, Decameron, v. 2.
Ebert, Bibliog. Dict., v, 4.

JAPAN. Charlevoix, Liste d'Auteurs sur.

JESUIT WRITERS. *See Roman Catholic.*

JOURNAL DES SAVANS. Camusat, Hist. des Journaux, 1734.

JEAN, ROI. Barrois, Bibliot. de, 1830.

KENT, ENG. Smith, Bibliot. Cantiana.

LATIN AUTHORS. *See Classics.*

LANGUAGES. *See Philology; Grammars; Indian Lang.*

LAW BOOKS, CATALOGUES OF. Bossange, Catalogue, 1845.
Brooke, Bibliot. Leg. Angliæ, 1788.
Butterworth, Catalogues, Lon., 1854.
Camus, Biblioth. des liv. de droit, 1819.
Crevenna, Catalogue, 1776.
Engelmann, Bibliot. Juridica, 1840.
Muller, Cat. Diss. Juridicarum, 1840.
New York State Law Lib., 1855, 65.
" Law Institute, Cat.
Pickering, J., Lib. Boston.
Struve, Biblioth. Juris., 1714.
U. S. Library of Congress, Cat. on Law, 1861, 69.
Voisin, Bibliot. Gand. Cat.
Worrall, Biblioth. Leg. Angliæ.
See Booksellers' Catalogues, etc.

LEYDEN UNIV. Hamaker, Spec. Cat. MSS. Orient. in, 1820.
Leyden Univ. Cat. 1741.

LIBRARIES, SELECTION OF BOOKS FOR.
Barbier, Bibliot. d'un Homme de Gout, 1817.
Bossange, Ma bibliothèque, 1855.
Chaudon, Bibliot. d'un Homme de Gout, 1772.
Churton, Book Collector's Hand-book.
Dana, Biblioth. Probata, 1857.
Dibdin, Library Companion.
Goodhugh, Eng. Gent's Library.
Kett, Elem. of General Knowl.
La Borde, Organisation des Biblioth.
Livermore, G., Remarks on public libraries.
Moore, What to read and how to read, 1870.
Manchester Lib., Books for Purchase, 1851.
Oakley, Course of Engl. Reading.

Bibliography: LIBRARIES, SELECTION OF BOOKS FOR (continued).
Observations on forming a Library.
Park, R., Select Cat. on all subjects.
Peabody Institute, Cat. of books for purchase, 1861.
Potter, Hand-book for readers, 1847.
Stevens, My English Library, 1853.
Ventouillac, The French Librarian.
See Books.

LIBRARIES, HISTORY OF. Account of Celebrated Libraries, 1739.
Berlin, Royal Library, 1839.
Clarke, Repertorium Bibliog., 1819.
Delandine, Hist. des Bibl. de Lyon.
Edwards, E., Memoirs of Lib., 1859.
Eichhorn, Geschichte der Litteratur.
Great Britain, Report, Comm. of H. of C.
Guild, Librarian's Man N. Y., 1858.
Jewett, Notices of Libraries in U. S.
Lomeierus de Bibliothecis.
Morhof, D. G., Polyhistor, 1808.
Namur, Hist. des Bib. de la Belgique.
Peignot, Dict. de Bibliol.
Petit-Radel, Recherches sur les Bibliot.
Rees, Manual of, in the U. S. A.
Wynne, Private Libraries in New York.

LIBRARIES, ADMINISTRATION OF, ARCHITECTURE OF, ETC. Budik, Verbereitungstudien.
Boston, Public Lib. Annual reports 1855-67.
Clark, A., Bibliog. Misc., V. 2.
Constantin, Bibliothéconomie.
Cotton, J. B., Des Devoirs du Biblioth.
Critical Account, 1739.
Gibbs, Bibliotheca Radcliviana.
Gr. Brit., Reports Comm. of H. of C.
Guild, Librarian's Manual.
Horne, T. H., Introd. to the study of Bibliog.
Jewett, Construction of Catalogues.
Laborde, Organisat. des Bibliothèques.
Lehmann, Stadtbibliothek.
Le Gallois, Traitte des Bibliot. de l'Europe.
Le Prince, Essai sur la Bibliot du Roi.
Namur, Man. du Bibliothécaire.
Panizzi, Supply for readers.
Papworth, Museums and Libraries.
Porter, Plea for.
Shurtleff, Decim. Syst. of Arrangement.
Techener, Amélioration des Anc. Bibl.
See Bibliography, Elementary; Classification.

LIBRARIES IN AMERICA, CATALOGUES OF.
Albany Library, 1821.
Amer. Antiq. Soc., 183

Bibliography: LIBRARIES IN AMERICA, CATALOGUES OF (continued).

Amer. Bible Society, 1855.
Amer. Philos. Soc., 1824.
Amherst College, 1855.
Apprentices' Library, N. Y., 1860.
Apprentices', Phila.
Astor Library, N. Y., 1857, 61, 66.
" " Index, 1851.
" " Oriental Languages, 1854.
Boston Public Library, 1854, 58, 66.
Boston Athenæum, 1827, 40.
Bowditch Library, 1841.
Bowdoin College Cat., 1863.
Brady, H. A., N. Y., 1851.
Brookline, Ms., Pub. Lib. 1865.
Brooklyn Atheneum, 1855.
California State Lib., 1860, 1871.
Cleveland, Ohio, Ass'n.
Cincinnati, Public Library, 1871.
Conway, F. W., N. Y., 1854.
Farnham, Private Libraries.
Georgia State Lib., 1869.
Groton, Mass., 1855.
Indiana State Lib., 1859.
Jewett, C. C., Notices of Pub. Lib. in the U. S., 1851.
King, Hist. of Redwood Lib. Newport, 1860.
Library Comp. of Phila., 1856.
Loganian Library, Philadelphia.
Lyceum of Nat. Hist. N. Y., 1830.
Maine State Lib., 1856.
Mass. State Library, 1846, 58.
Massachusetts Hist. Soc., 1859, 60.
Mercantile Lib. Asso., Boston, 1848, 50, 69.
Merc. Lib. Asso., Cincinnati, 1855.
Mercantile Lib. Assoc., N. Y., 1856, 1865-6, 69.
Mercantile Lib. Comp., Philadelphia, 1851-56.
Merchants' and Clerks', N. Y., 1857.
Michigan State Lib., 1855.
Minnesota State Lib., 1850.
Newark Lib. Assoc., 1857.
New Bedford Pub. Lib., 1856, 58, 69.
Newburyport, Mass., 1857.
New Jersey State Lib., 1853.
New Hampshire State, 1857.
New Haven Y. M. Inst., 1841.
New Orleans Lyceum.
New York State Lib., 1855, 58, 61.
" " Annual Reports to 1871.
New York Maps and Surveys, 1851, 59.
New York City Lib. Assoc.
New York Hospital Lib., 1845.
New York Hist. Soc., 1859.

Bibliography: LIBRARIES IN AMERICA, CATALOGUES OF (continued).

New York Law Inst., 1843.
New York Society Library, 1850.
Norton's Lit. and Educ. Reg., 1854.
Ohio State, 1859.
Oswego, N. Y., 1858.
Pamphlets containing Library Associations' Reports, Vols. 169, 170, 209, 275, 276, 512, 1237, 1692.
Peabody Institute, Balt., Cat., 1861.
Pennsylvania State Lib. 1857.
Portland Atheneum, 1852.
Prince, T., Catalogue of Library of, 1868, 70.
Prot. Ep. S. S. Union Library.
Providence Atheneum, 1853.
Queen's Coll., Toronto, 1853.
Redwood Lib., Newport, 1860.
Rochester Atheneum, N. Y., 1850.
Rochester City Lib., 1839.
Salem Atheneum, 1842, 58.
Soc. of Friends, Phila., 1853.
St. Paul's, Minn.
Society of Friends, Library.
Syracuse, Central Lib., 1860.
Tennessee State Lib., 1855.
Troy Y. M. Assoc., 1859.
U. S., Lib. of Congress Catalogues, 1812, 15, 30, 40, 52-53, 61.
" Catalogue of Authors, 1864-69.
" Index of subjects, 1869
" Mil Acad. Lib., 1860.
Univ. of Pennsylvania, 1829.
Van Rensselaer, Cat. of Lib., Albany, 1834.
Vermont State Lib , 1858.
Virginia State Lib., 1856.
Voice from the people, 1838.
Worcester Free Public Lib. Reports, 1861-70.
Worcester, Mass., Lyceum.
Yale College, Cat., 1743.
Yale College, Soc. Lib., 1836, 46.
Yonkers Lib. Assoc., N. Y., 1856.
Young Men's Assoc., Alb., Cat., 1853.
" " Reports, 1857-67.
" Assoc., Buffalo, 1848.
" Assoc., Cincinnati, 1855.
" Assoc., Milwaukee, Cat., 1855, 61.
" Assoc., Rochester, N. Y.
" Assoc., Utica, N. Y.
" Institute, Hartford, 1844.
" " Reports, 1840-68.
" Lib., Worcester, Mass.
" Merc. Assoc., Cincinnati, 1855.

See American Books; Law.

Bibliography (continued).

LIBRARIES IN BELGIUM AND NETHERLANDS, CATALOGUES OF. Amsterdam, Biblioth. der stad.

Bourgogne, Inventaire des MSS.

Holtrop, Cat. Bib. Haganæ, 1856.

La Serna, Bibliot. de Bruxelles.

Leyden, Univ. Cat., 1741.

Namur, Hist. des Bib. de la Belgique.

Pauw, Cat. Bibliot. Hagæ, 1654.

Provinciaal Genootschap, 1841.

Voisin, Bibliotheca Gandavensis.

" Hist. des Bibliot. en Belgique.

See Belgium.

LIBRARIES IN ENGLAND AND SCOTLAND, CATALOGUES OF. Advocates' Library, Edinb., 1863, 64.

Athenæum of London, 1845-51.

Beauclerck, Cat. of Lib., 1781.

Beckford, Fonthill Abbey, 1823.

Bibliot. Chethamensis (Manchester).

Brand, J., Cat. of Lib. for sale, 1807.

Brit. and For. Bible Soc.

British Museum: Letter A.

Cat. Lib. MSS. Angeliæ, 1697.

Dibdin, The Director, Askew's Lib.

" Bibliot. Spenceriana.

East India Comp. Cat.

Edinburgh Select Subs. Lib.

Edwards, E., Lib. in England.

" Memoirs of Libraries, 1859.

Geol. Soc. of London, Library.

George III, Bibl. Regiæ Catal.

Gibraltar Garrison Lib., 1793.

Great Britain, Library of House of Commons, 1830.

Halliwell, MSS. in Library at Plymouth, Eng.

Lincoln's Inn, 1835.

London, Lib. of the Corporation, 1859.

London Library Cat., 1847.

London Institution Cat., 1835-52.

Macray, Annals of Bodleian Library, 1868.

Maitland, Index of Books, Library at Lambeth.

Manchester Free Library Cat., 1791, 1826.

" Reference Cat., 1864.

" Reports, 1860, 67.

Minerva Library, Liverpool.

Oxford Univ. Cata., 1620, 74, 97.

Parr, Bibliot. Parriana.

Royal Asiat. Soc. Cat. 1830.

Russell Institution Cat., 1837.

Salford Borough Cat., 1851.

Stowe, The, Catalogue, 1848.

Williams, Red Cross St. Lib. Cat.

See London: English Libraries; Auctions.

Bibliography (continued).

LIBRARIES IN FRANCE, CATALOGUES OF.

Bordeaux, Chambre de Commerce.

Delandine, Cat. de la Bibl. de Lyon.

Dibdin, Bibliog. Tour, 1829.

France: Ecole des Ponts et Chaussées.

Le Glay, MSS. de la Bibl. de Cambrai.

" Bibl. pub. de Nord de, 1841.

Louis Philippe, Bibliothèque, 1852.

Prousteau, Bibliot. Publique, 1777.

Rouard, Bibliothèques d'Aix, 1831.

Voyage Littéraire, 1717.

See Lyons; Paris; Lille; Douai; Aix; French Books; French Libraries.

LIBRARIES IN GERMANY, ETC., CATALOGUES, ETC. Bavaria, MSS. Biblioth. à Munich.

Berlin Royal Library, 1821-51.

Braun, Not. de Bib. ad SS. Udal. et Afrae, 1788.

Bunau, Cat. Bibliothecæ, 1750.

Dibdin, Bibliog. Tour, 1829.

Galitzin, Catalogue, 1866.

Hamburg Library, 1844, 56.

Irmischer, Bibliot. zu Erlangen.

Jablonowski, Bibliotheca, 1755.

Murr, Memorab., Norimb., 1786-91.

Petersen, Hamburg Bibliot., 1838.

Strauss, Bibliot. in Rebdorf, 1790.

See Munich; Vienna; Augsburg.

LIBRARIES IN ITALY. Biscioni; Cat. Bib. Medico-Lauren, 1752.

Blume, Iter Italicum, 1824-36.

Capponi, A. G., Catalogue, 1845.

Pasinus, Cod. MSS. Taurinensis Ath.

See Rome; Milan; Padua; Venice; Italian.

LIBRARIES. For other libraries see various towns, *Manuscripts*, etc.

LILLE. Le Glay, Cat. des MSS. de la Bib. de la Ville, 1859.

LITERATURE. Bure, G. F. De, Bibliog. Instructive, 1763.

Crevenna, Catalogue, 1776.

Dallerange, Cat. de sa Biblioth., 1851.

Delandine, Cat. de la Bib. de Lyon.

Eichhorn, Geschichte der Litteratur.

Engelmann, Bibliot. der schönen Wissenschaften, 1837.

Jordens, Lexikon Deutscher Dichter und Prosaisten, 1806-11.

Quaritch, Catalogue of Literature, 1864, 69.

Renouard, Cat. de la Bibliothèque.

See French; English, etc.

LONDON LIBRARIES AND CATALOGUES.

British Museum.

Bent, Cat. 1814-39.

Bibliography: London Libraries and Catalogues (continued).
Christie, Scheme of London Library.
East India Company.
Lincoln's Inn.
London City Corporation.
London Institution Cat.
London Library Cat., 1852.
Low, British Cat., 1835-57.
Maitland, Ind. of Archiep., Palace Lib.
Royal Asiatic Soc.
Russell Institution.
Soc. of Antiquaries.
See Libraries in England.

Lorraine. Emmöry, Cat., des MSS. relatifs, 1849.

Louvain. Namur, Hist. des Bibl. de.

Lyon. Delandine, MSS. de la Bib. de Lyon.
" Cat. de la Bib. de Lyon.
Dolet, E., Vie de, 1779.
Lyon, Cat. des Doubles, 1831.
Monfalcon, Le Nouveau Spon, 1856.
" Bibliog. de Lyon, 1851.

Madrid. Casiri, Bibliot. Arab. Hisp. Escu.
Iriarte, Codices Greci MSS.
See Spanish.

Manuscripts, Essays on Knowledge of, etc. Delandine, Mem. Bibliog.
Dibdin, Bibliog. Decameron.
Humphreys, Art of Illumination.
" Illum. MSS. of Mid. Ages.
Langlois, Calligraphie du Moyen Age.
Maitland, The Dark Ages, Essays.
Merryweather, Bibliog. Mid. Ages.
Namur, Bibliog. Paleog. Dipl. Gén.
Peignot, Dict. de Bibliog.
Waagen, Treas. of Art in Gr. Brit.
Wright, Illuminated MSS.
See Writing; Illum. MSS.; Alphabets; *Diplomatics.*

Manuscripts in Libraries, Catalogues of. Arwidsson, K., Bib. Stockholm.
Barrois, Bibliot. Protypographique.
Bavaria: Cat. MSS. Bib. Monacensis.
" Bib. Bavar. Cat. MSS. Gr.
Bibliot. D. Marci Græc. MSS.
" Lat. et Ital. MSS.
Biscioni, Bib. Mediceo-Laurent. *Greek and Oriental.*
Black, Ashmole MSS.
Blume, Iter Italicum.
" Bib. MSS. Ital.
Bock, Liber Guidonis.
Bourgogne, Inventaire.
Boutourlin, Cat. de la Bibliot.
British Museum, Catalogues of.

Bibliography: Manuscripts in Libraries, Catalogues of (continued).
Capponi, Cat. dei Manoscritti dal.
Casiri, Bibliot. Arab. Hisp. Escur.
Catalogi Lib. MSS. Angliæ.
Cocchi, Diarium Phillippi III, 1301.
Coussemaker, Coll. à Cambrai.
Delandine, MSS. de la Bib. de Lyon.
" Mém. Bibliographiques.
Duthillœul, Cat. de la Bibl. de Douai.
Fortunatus, Com. de Alcobacensi MSS.
Haenel, Cat. MSS. in Bibl. Europæ.
Halliwell, Vernon MSS.
Hardt, MSS. Græcorum Bib. Bavariæ.
Hargrave, Cat. of MSS. of Library of.
Iriarte, Bib. Matrit. Græci MSS.
Irmischer, Handsch. Kat. Erlang., etc.
Jaeck, Beschreibung der Bib. zu Bamberg.
Joursanvault, MSS. concernant l'Hist. de la France.
Kloss, Cat. of Library of, 1835.
La Croix, Not. des MSS. sur la France.
Leber, Cat. de la Biblioth. de.
Le Glay, MSS. de la Bibl. de Cambrai.
" MSS. de la Bibl. de Lille.
Leyden Univ,, Cat. *Oriental.*
Libri, Collection of, 1859.
Mengarelli, Græci Cod. MSS. apud Nanios.
Montfaucon, Bibl. Coisliniana. *Greek.*
Morellius, Cod. MSS. Bib. Nanianæ, Venet.
Notice des Bib. des Départements Fr.
Nys, Les Archives d'Anvers.
Ochoa, MSS. Españols en Bibl. de Paris.
Oxford Univ. MSS. in Bodleian Llbrary.
Paris, MSS. de la Bibl. Impér.
Parker, M., Cat. MSS. Cantab.
Pasinus, Cod. MSS. Gr. Taurin. Athenæi.
Paulinus, Musei Borgiani Cod. MSS.
Pettigrew, Bibliot. Sussexiana.
Rask, Cat. of MSS. Zend, etc.
Russia, Cat. de la Bibliot. *Oriental.*
Soc. of Antiquaries, Lond., Cat.
Vienna Imp. Lib. Cat. Manuscriptorum.
Zacharia, Bibliot. Pistoriensis.
Zanetti, D., Marci Bibl. Cod. Fr. Lat. et Ital.

Manuscripts priced. Bell, Cat. of MSS. on sale, 1850, 56.
Cochran, Cat. of MSS. for sale, 1837.
Meermann, Biblioth., v. 4, priced.
Quaritch, Cat. of MSS., 1870, 71.
Thorpe, Cat. of MSS. on sale, 1843.
Upcott, Cat., 1836.
See Booksellers' Catalogues.

Bibliography (continued).

MAPS. Asher, On Maps of New Netherland.
Crelle, Catalogue, Berlin, 1856.
George III, Bibl. Regiæ Catal., v. 6.
Grattan, Cat. of cheap maps. P. 1331.
Johnston, W., List of maps by, 1857.
Kohl. On anc. American Rep., (Smithson), 1856.
" Altesten general Karten von Amerika, 1860.
Laurie & Whittle's Maps, 1800.
New York State Catalogue of maps at Albany, 1859.
New York State Lib. Cat., 1856.
Robiquet, Catalogue des Cartes, 1842.
Schumacher, Cat., des Cartes, 1855.
Stanford's Catal. of maps. P. 1331.
Uricoechea, Mapoteca Colombiana, 1860.
Vandermeersch, Cartes aux Archives de la Flandre, 1850.

MASONIC. Cat. of Books on Masonry (Gassett), 1852.
Gowans, Catalogue, 1858.
Lerouge, Catalogue, Paris, 1833.

MATHEMATICAL. Bachelier, Catalogues, Paris, 1830–53.
De Morgan, Arithmetical books, 1847.
" English Math. Writers.
Libri, Catalogue of Math. Hist. and Bibliog. library, 1859.
Schumacher, Livres de la Bibl., 1855.

MEDICAL. Baillière, Catalogues, 1833–56.
Boehmer, Bib. Script. Hist. Nat.
Edinb. Univ. Cat. Lib. Med., 1798.
Haller, Biblioth. Medicinæ, ad 1775.
Méding, Biblioth. du Paris Médical.
Rosenbaum, Additam. ad Bibl. Med. 1842.
Roy, Cat. Med. Bibl., 1830.
Vigiliis von Creutzenfeld, Bibl. Chir.
See Anatomy.

MEJANES. Rive, Chasse aux Bibliographes.
Rouard, Bibliot. de, à Aix.

MELBOURNE. Library Cat. 1861.

METHODIST. Decanver, Catalogue: Works against Methodism.

MEXICAN. Andrada, Bibliotheca Mejicana, Auction, 1869.
Bibliotheca Mexicana, Auction, 1868.
Catalogue de la Bibliothéque, Maximilien, 1869.
Clavigero, Cat. of Authors in New Spain.
Cotton, Typ. Gazetteer.

MILAN. Argelati, Bibliot. Scriptorum.
Saxius, Hist. Lit. Typ. Mediolan.
See Italian; Libraries.

Bibliography (continued).

MILITARY. Anselin, Catalogues, Paris.
Corréard, Cat. 1841.
Doisy, Bibliologie Militaire, 1824.
Du Maine, Librairie Mil. Paris.
United States Mil. Acad Lib. Cat.
Van Nostrand, N. Y., 1861–66.

MONOGRAMS. Brulliot, Dict. des Monogrammes, 1835.

MORIN, M. Frère, De l'imprimerie à Rouen.

MUNICH LIBRARY. Aretin, Beyträge zur gesch. und literatur, 1807.
Bavaria, Biblioth. à Münich, Cat. Cod. MSS.
" Gall., Hisp., Angl. etc., 1858.
" " Cod. Persian, Frank, 1814.
" " Cod. Germanicorum, 1866.
" Renseignements sur la Bib.
Dibdin, Bibliog. Tour.
Frank, Morgenl. Handsch. der Bibliot.
Steigenberger, Hist. Versuch von der Bibliot, 1784, 87.

MUSICAL. Coussemaker, Col. Musicales à Cambrai, 1843.
Moore, J. W., Encyc. of Music, 1854.
Rimbault, Bibliot. Madrigaliana.

NAMES, FICTITIOUS. Barbier, Dict. des ouv. anon. et pseudonymes, 1822.
Hamst, Fict. names of authors, 1868.
Manne, Ouvrages anon. et pseudonymes, 1862.
See Anonymous.

NAPLES. Blume, Iter Italicum.
Paulinus, Mus. Borgiani Velitris.
Toppi, Biblioteca Napoletana.
See Italian.

NATURAL HISTORY. Agassiz, Bibliog. Zoölogiæ.
Baillière, Catalogues, 1833–56.
Boehmer, Bib. Script. Hist. Nat.
Bohn, Catalogue, 1847, 56.
Quaritch, Lond., 1869.
Scheuchzer, Bibl. Script. Hist. Nat. Helvet. et Galliæ.
Seguier, Bibl. Botanica.
Warmholtz, Bibl. Hist. Sueo-gothica.
See Zo logical; Scientific.

NETHERLANDS. *See Belgium; Booksellers; Dutch; Libraries.*

NEWSPAPERS, HISTORY OF. Camusat, Hist. des journaux, 1734.
Fifty Years Recollections, 1837.
Gt. Britain, Report on Newsp. Stamps.
Hunt, F. K., The Fourth Estate, 1850.
Mitchell, Newspaper Press Directory.
Rowells, Amer. Newsp. Directory, 1870.
Timperley, Encyc of Typ. Anecd.
See Periodicals; Newspapers.

Bibliography (continued).

NUMISMATICAL. Bunau, Cat. Bibliothecæ.
Hearne, Cat. of Numism., books for sale.
Labbé, Bibliot. Nummaria, 1672.
Lincoln & Son, Lond., 1856.
Lipsius, Bibliot. Nummaria, 1801.
Selden, De Nummis (Labbe), 1675.

NUREMBERG. Murr, Memor. Bibl. Norimb.
Panzer, Deutschen Bibeln, in Bibliot.
" Geschichte der Ausgaben.
" Aelteste Buchdruckergeschichte in, 1789.

ORIENTAL. Clarke, A., Bibliog. Miscellany.
East India Co., Catalogue, 1851.
Elliot, Bib. Index to Historians of India, 1849.
Fraehn, Indications Bibliographiques.
Frank, Morgenl. Handsch. in Munchen,
Garcin de Tassy, Littérature Hindoui, 1839, 47.
Gesenius, Bibliotheca Geseniana.
Hamaker, Spec. Cat, MSS. Orient.
Herbelot, Bibliothéque Orientale.
Klaproth, Cat. des Livres de la Bib. de,
König, Bibliot. Vetus et Nova, 1678.
Langlès, Cat. de la Bibliot.
Leyden, Univ. Catalogus.
Marsden, Bibliot. Philol. et Orient.
Ouseley, Cat. of MSS. in Orient. Lang.
Platt, Cat. of Ethiop. MSS.
Paulinus, Mus. Borgiani MSS. Indostani.
Royal Asiat. Soc. Cat.
Russia, Cat. MSS. Orient. de la Bibliot.
Sacy, S. de, Cat. de sa Bibliot., 1842.
Stewart, Cat. of Lib. of Tippoo Sultan.
Trubner, Books on sale, 1853.
" Am. and Oriental Literary Record, 1865–67.
Zenker, Bibliot. Orient., 1846, 61.
See Manuscripts; Sanskrit; Asiatic; Arabic.

ORLEANS. Prousteau, Bibliothèque Pub. de.

OXFORD UNIVERSITY. Black, Ashmole MSS.
Douce, Library Bequeathed to.
Gibbs, Bibliotheca Radcliviana.
Macray, Annals of the Bodleian Lib., 1868.
Malone, Cat. of Early Eng. Poetry.
Oxford, Bodleian Lib. Cat., 1620.
" Cat. impressorum Lib., 1674.
" Cat. Lib. manuscriptorum, 1697.
Singer, Account of Book Printed, 1468.
Waagen, Treasures of Art in G. B., v. 3.

PAMPHLETS. Almon, Cat. of Publications, 1770.

Bibliography: PAMPHLETS (continued).
Boon, Sale Cat. of Pams., N. Y., 1869.
Halliwell, Tracts of Capt. Cox's Lib.
Hamilton, Cat. of Tracts for sale, 1844.
Hotten, Tracts on America, Lond.
London Institution, Cat., v. 2.
Pamphlets relating to Bibliog., vols. 470, 1015, 1226.
Rodd, Catalogue of 24,000 Pamphlets, 1819.
Smith, J. R., Cat. of 25,000, for sale.

PARCHMENT. *See Vellum.*

PARIS LIBRARIES, ETC. Barrois, Bib. Prototypog.
Dibdin, Bibliog. Tour.
France, Bibliot. Impérial. Catal., 1859.
Greswell, Early Greek Press, 1833.
" Parisian Typography, 1818.
Jacob, Bibliot. Parisina, 1643–6.
Le Prince, Essai sur la Bibliot.
Montfaucon, Bib Coisliniana, Bib. Roy.
Ochoa, MSS. Españoles existentes Bib. Roy.
Paris, MSS. de la Bib. Impér.
Platt, Cat. MSS. Ethiop. Bib. Roy.
Praet, Cat. Livres sur vélin de.
Techener, Considérations sur la Bib. R.
See French Libraries; Libraries; Typography.

PERIODICALS, RELATING TO BIBLIOGRAPHY OR LITERARY HISTORY. Aldine Magazine, 1839.
American Literary Gazette, Phila. 1863–1870.
Amer. Publishers' Circular, N. Y., 1855–61.
Archæologist, The, Lond., 1842.
Bibliog. de la France, 1820–40, 1859–63.
Book Buyer, Scribner, 1867-70.
Booksellers' Medium, N. Y., 1858–60.
British Critic, 1793-1818.
Bulletin du Bibliophile, Techener, 1834-53.
Critical Review, 1756-98.
Gazette Litt., Amst., 1768–70.
Hennebert, Bibliologue de la Belgique.
History of the Works of the Learned, 1699-1709, 37, 38.
Literary World, Crocker, Boston, 1870-71.
Miller, J., Fly-Leaves, Lond., 1854-5.
Monthly Review, 1749–1806.
Norton's Lit. and Edu. Register, 1854.
Notes and Queries, Lond., 1849-71.
Philobiblion, v. I, II, N. Y., 1862, 63.
Poole, Index to Reviews and Periodicals,
Publishers' Circular, Lond., 1839–69.
Retrospective Review, 1820-28.

Bibliography: Periodicals, Relating to Bibliography or Literary History (continued).
Revue Bibl des Pays Bas, 1822-30.
Revue de Bibliographie analytique. 1840-45.
Savage, The Librarian, 1808-9.
Techener, Annuaire Bibliog., 1851.
Willis, Current Notes, Lond., 1851-64.
See Booksellers' Catalogues.

Periodicals, Catalogues of, History of, etc. Astor Library, List of.
Camusat, Hist. des Journaux.
Eichhorn, Geschichte der Litteratur.
Fifty Years' Recollections.
France, Bib. Imp. Cat. de l'Hist.
Longman, Cat. of London Period.
Namur, Bibliog. Bibliologique.
Timperley, Encyc. of Typ. Anecd.
See Newspapers; Societies for Printing.

Persian. Frank, Pers. MSS. Bibliot. in Munchen.
Ouseley, Cat. of MSS.
Stewart, Lib. of Tippoo Sultan.
See Oriental.

Petrarch. Bearzi, Cat. de Livres rares.
Marsand, Biblioteca Petrarchesca.

Philological. Burnouf, Catalogue de la Bib. de.
Engelmann, Bib. der Neueren Sprachen.
" Bib. Philologie, 1853.
Ersch, Bibl. Handbuch der Phil. Lit.
Jacobs, F., Bibliotheca, Cat., 1849.
Marsden, Bibliot. Philol. et Orient.
Pickering, J., Cat. Lib. Boston.
Trömel, Litt. der Deutschen Mundarten.
Trubner, Catalogue, 1857.
See Grammars; Indian Lang.

Philosophical. Hachette, Cat. Librairie, Paris, 1851.
Struve, Bibliot. Philosophica, 1714.
See Scientific.

Pistoria. Zacharia, Bibliot. Pistoriensis.

Poetry. *See* English Poetry; French Lit.

Polish. Hoffmann, De Typog. in Reg. Poloniæ, 1740.
Jablonowski, Bibliotheca, 1755.

Political Economy. McCulloch, J. R., Literature of, 1845.

Portuguese. Adamson, Bibl. Lusitana.
Barbosa, Summario da Bibl. Luzitana.
Fortunatus, Comm. de Alcobacensi MSS.
Oliveyra, Mémoires: Bibliot. des écrivains sur le Portugal, 1743.
Southey, Cat. of Library, 1844.
See Spanish.

Bibliography (continued),
Prices of Books. Azara, Bibliotheca.
Beloe, Anecdotes, vol. 5.
Bibliog. Miscellany.
Brit. Mus., Cat. of Duplicates.
Clarke, A., Bibl. Dictionary.
Corwin, E. B., Cat. of Books, 1856, priced.
Delandine, Cat. de la Bibl. de Lyon.
Dibdin, The Director.
" Biblioth. Spenceriana, vol. 7.
" Decameron, vol. 3.
Dodd, J. W., Library, and prices at the sale, 1797.
Haym, Bibliot. Italiana.
Hoyois, Ouvrages de 1000 Piastres.
Lafontaine, Bibliot., Montreal, 1860, priced.
Leclerc, Bibl. Amer., 1867, priced.
Major, Bibliot. Mechlin, 1767.
Meerman, Bibliot., 1808.
Morell, T. H., Cat. Am. books, 1859, priced.
Norton's Lit. Advertiser, N. Y.
Pinelli, Bibliot. Lond., 1789.
Stevens, H., Bibliot. Historica, Bost., 1870, priced.
See Auctions; Booksellers; Dictionaries; Manuscripts.

Printers. *See* Typography.

Prisons. Julius, Cat...de Disciplina Pauperum, 1850.

Privately Printed Books. Martin, Bibliog. Cat. of, 1854.

Prohibited Books. Oettinger, Bibliog. univ.
Rom. Cath. Ch. Index Lib. Prohib.

Proverbs. Gowans, W., Cat. of Books of, 1853.
Nopitsch, Handb. der Sprichwörter. 1833.

Pseudonymes. *See Anonymous; Names.*

Rabbinic. *See Hebrew.*

Rare Books Noticed. Analectabiblion.
Aprosio, Bibliot. Aprosiana.
Azara, Bibliotheca.
Bauer, Bibliot. Libr. Rar.
Beloe, Anec. of Literature.
Bearzi, Cat. de Livres Rares.
Beauclerck, Cat. of Library of
Beyer, Memoriæ Lib. Rar., 1734.
Bibliog. Miscellany, 1830.
Blaufus, Vermischte Beyträge.
Brydges, Restituta, 1814–16.
" Brit. Bibliographer, 1810–14.
" Censura literaria, 1815.
Bulletin du Bibliophile, 1834-53.
Burton, J. H., The Book-Hunter, 1862.

Bibliography: Rare Books Noticed (continued).
Clarke, A., Bibliog. Misc.
Clement, Bibliothèque Curieuse, 1760.
Dibdin, Bibliog. Tour.
Fischer, Beschreibung typ. Seltenheiten, 1804.
Freytag, Adparatus Literarius, 1753.
Hallevord, Biblioth. Curiosa, 1676.
Hartshorne, Rarities of Cambridge.
Hoyois, Ouvrages de 1000 Piastres.
Murr, Memor. Bibl. Altdorf.
Nyerup, Spicil. Bibliog.
Paris, Bibliot. Parisina, 1791.
Peignot, Reportoire de Bibliog.
" Catalogue, 1852.
Strauss, Opera rar. in Bibliog. Rebdorf.
Vogt, Cat. Hist. Crit. Lib. Rariorum.
See Fifteenth Century Editions; Prices; Dictionaries of Bibliography.

Rebdorf. Strauss, Opera rariora in Bib.

Republics. La Faye, Cat. des Républiques, 1842.

Roman Catholic. Alegambe, Bibliot. Script. Soc. Jesu, 1608-42.
Backer, Ecrivains des Jésuites, 1853–1861.
Catalogue of Books against Popery, 1669-1688.
Dolman, Cat. Lond., 1843, etc.
Foppens, Bibliot. Belgica, 1839.
Gratianus, Script. Ord. S. Augustine.
Molanus, Bibliot. Cath. SS. Interp.
Ribadeneira, Cat. Scr. Soc. Jesu.
Rom. Cath. Ch., Index Lib. Prohib.

Rome. Blume, Iter Italicum.
Papponi, Cat. della Libreria.
Laire, Spec. Typ. Romanæ.
Quirini, Liber de Edit. Romæ.
See Italian Books; Libraries in Italy.

Rouen. Frère, De l'Imprimerie à.
" Bibliographe Normand, 1858.
Leber, Cat. de la Bibliothèque,

Russian. Otto, Hist. Russ. Literature.
Galitzin, Cat. de sa Bibliothèque, 1866.
Russia, Cat. Bibliot. Horti. Imp.
" Cat. MSS. et Xylographes.

Sales. *See Auctions; Prices; Books.*

Sanscrit. Burnouf, Cat. de la Bibl. de.
Chambers, Cat. of Sanskrit MSS.
Gildemeister, Bibliot. Sanskritæ.
Paulinus, Mus. Borgiani MSS.
Royal Asiat. Soc Cat.
See Oriental; Asiatic.

Scientific. Bachelier, Paris.
Baillière, Catalogues, 1833-56.
Boehmer, Bib. Script. Hist. Nat.

Bibliography: Scientific (continued).
Crelle, Catalogue, en vente, 1856.
Dana, J. D., Mineralogical Bibliography, 1837.
Koen. Baier. Ak. Verz. Druckschriften.
Konink. Akad., Amsterdam, 1858.
Ray Soc. Bibliog. Zoölogiæ, Agassiz.
Schubarth, Repert. der Techn. Literatur, 1856.
Schumaker, Livres de la Bibliot., 1855.
Smithson. Cont. vol. 7, List of Trans. of Sci. Societies.
" Vol. V, IX, N. Amer. Conchology.
Weale, Cat. of Books on.
See Engineering; Arts; Philosophical; Natural History.

Scientific Societies. *See Societies; Periodicals.*

Satires. Baillet, Jugemens, V. 7.

Scotch. Ames, Typog. Antiq.
Berkenhout, Biog. Lit. 400-1600.
Dibdin, Typog. Antiquities.
" Northern Tour.
Reid, Bibliot. Scoto-Celtica.
Watson, Hist. of Printing.
See English.

Shakspeare. Bohn's Lowndes' Manual, vol. 4.
Burton, Bibliot. Dram., 1860.
Halliwell, J. O., List of Works on, 1867.
Sillig, Die Shakespeare Literatur, 1854.
Wilson, Shaksperiana, 1827.

Slavic. Storch, Antiq. Katal., 1858.
Talvi, Lit. of Slavic Nations.
Valentinelli, Spec. Bibliog. de Dalmat.
" Bibliog. del Friuli, 1861.

Societies, (Bibliography of Scientific and Printing). Agassiz, Bibliographia.
Astor Library, Cat. Periodicals.
Bossange, Liste, 1845.
Hume, Learned Societies of Gr. Brit.
Lilly's Catalogues.
Longman, Cat. of London, Transactions of, 1849.
Low, Index, 1858.
Smithson. Contr., List of Publications.
See Periodicals.

South African. Pub. Lib. Cat., 1862.

Spanish. Antonio, Bibliot. Hispana.
Diosdado, De Prima Typ. Hispaniæ.
Escurial Lib. Bib. Arab. Hisp.
Hispaniæ Bibliotheca, 1608.
Majansius, Spec. Bibliot. Hisp.
Pellicer, Bibl. de Traductores Esp.
Southey, Cat. of Library.
See Portuguese.

Bibliography (continued).

STATISTICS. Julius, Cat. de Statistica.

STOCKHOLM. Arwidsson, R. Bibliothek. Holmia Literata, 1701.

SURGICAL. *See Medical; Anatomy.*

SWABIAN. Zapf, Buchdruckergesch. Schwabens, 1791.

SWEDISH. Alnander, Artis Typog. in Sveciæ, 1725.
Arwidsson, K., Bibliot. Stockholm. Holmia Literata, 1701.
Marklin, Cat. Diss. Acad. Scandinaviæ.
Möbius, Cat Lib. Isl. et Norvegicorum, 1856.
Schinmeier, Schwedischen Bib. Uebersetzungen, 1778.
Stiernman, Biblioth. Suio-Gothica.
Upsal University, Cat. of Lib., 1814.
Warmholtz, Bibl. Hist. Sueo-Gothica.
Worm, Lexikon, Skrifter, 1783.

THEATRICAL. *See* Dramatic.

THEOLOGICAL. Biblical Student's Asst.
Bray, Biblioth. Parochialis, 1707.
British Librarian, Relig. and its history (Lowndes), 1839.
Bure, G. F. De, Bibliog. Instructive.
Carpzovius, Bibliot. Carpzoviana.
Coster, Bibl. Costerana, 1718.
Crevenna, Catalogue, 1776.
Dana, Biblioth. Probata, 1857.
Darling, Cyc. Bibliographica, 1854.
" Cyc. Bibliog. Holy Scriptures, 1859.
Decanver, Works on Methodism, 1846, 1868.
Einem, Intro. in Bibl. Ecclesiasticam.
Eysengrein, Cat. Testium Veritatis.
Gratianus, Anastasis Augustiniana.
Horne, Manual of Bib. Bibliog.
Krohn, Cat. Bib....Ad Theol.
Leslie, Cat. of Eng. and For. Theology, Lond., 1844.
Malcom, H., Theolog. Index, 1868.
Nutt, Cat. of Foreign Theol. for sale, 1845–57.
Parr, Bibliot. Parriana.
Peirson, T., Auct. Cat., 1815.
Sacy, Silvestre de, Cat. de sa Bibliot., 1842.
Smith, J., Catalogue of books written by Friends, 1867.
Weigel, Corpus Diss. Theol. for sale.
See Church Fathers; Roman Cath.

THERESIAN LIB. Denis, Die Merkwurdigkeiten der.

TOLERATION. Arranged Catalogue of pub. on toleration, Lond., 1790.

TRAVELS *See Voyages.*

Bibliography (continued).

TROIS EVECHES. Emméry, Cat. des MSS. relatifs.

TURIN. Pasinus, Cod. MSS. Athenæi.

TYPOGRAPHY. *See* Typography.

ULM. Hassler, H., Buckdrucker Gesch. Ulm's, 1840.

UPSAL. Marklin, Cat. Dissertationum. Upsal, 1820.
Upsal, Univ. Cat., 1814.

UNITED STATES. *See American.*

VELLETRI. Paulinus, Musei Borgiani, MSS.

VELLUM. Dibdin, Decameron, vol. 2.
Praet, Van, Cat. de Livres sur.
See Manuscripts.

VENICE. *See Libraries; Italian.*

VIENNA LIBRARIES. Austria, Gesch. Druckerei, Wien, 1851.
Denis, Merkwurdigkeiten der Bib. am Theresiana, 1780.
" Wiens Buchdruckergeschichte.
Dibdin, Bibliog. Tour, 1829.
Krafft, Cod. Hebraici, 1847.
See Germany.

VOYAGES. Boucher, Bibliot. des Voyages.
Cat. of Voyages and Travels.
Kerr, Cat. of, 1822, V. 18.
Pinkerton, J., Cat. of Books of Voy. and Trav.
Tièle, Journaux des Navig. Néerlandais réimprimés, 1867.
See American History, etc., Geographical; Maps.

WALDENSES. Muston, Bibliography of Hist. of, 1857.

WALPOLE PRESS. Lemoine, Typog. Antiq.

WELSH. Longman, Cat. V. 36.

ZOÖLOGICAL. Agassiz, Bibliog. Zoölogiæ.
Allman, Bibliog. of the Polyzoa, Ray Soc., 1856.
See Natural History.

NOTE.—For other sources, see Literary History; Typography.

Bickersteth, E. Birks, T. R., Memoir of, 1851.

Biddeford, Me. Folsom, G., Hist. Sketch of, 1830.

Biddle, N. Waldo, S. P., Life of, 1823.

Bigelow, H. Young, E. J., Death of 1866.

Bigelow, R. Thomson, E., Sketches.

Bigelow, T. Hersey, C., Reminiscences of.

Bigg, T. Belsham, T., Sermon on.

Bilderdijk, W. Immerzeel, Works of.

Bill. Family History, 1867.

Billerica, Ms. 200th Annsversary, 1855.
Farmer, J., Hist. Memoir of, 1816.

Binghamton, N. Y. Directory, 1869-70.
Wilkinson, S. B., Annals of.

Bingley, Eng. M'Kaeg, Baptist Ch. at.

Binns, John. Recollections, 1854.

Biography. *See* Painting; Architecture; Autobiography; Dramatic, etc.

Biography, General and Miscellaneous. Adamus, Vitæ Germ. jureconsultorum.
Adamus, Vitæ Germ. Medicorum.
" Vitæ Germ. Theologorum.
Aikin, General Biography, 1799-1815.
Appleton's Cyclopædia of, 1856.
Arago, Œuvres, vol. 1, 2, 3, 1854.
Biographie Nouvelle, (Arnault), 1820-1825.
Biographie Etrangère, 1819.
Biographie Universelle, 1811–62.
Biog. of Self-taught men, 1846.
Biog. Dict. of Soc. U. K., vol. 1-4, 1842–44.
Blake, J. L., Gen. Biog. Dict., 1839, 1856.
Bruce, James, Classic and hist. portraits, 1854.
Chalmers, Gen. Biog. Dict., 1812–17.
Characteristics of Men of genius, 1847.
Cox, S. H., Interviews memorable and useful, 1853.
Crespin, Galerie Chrétienne, 1837.
Davenport, R. A., Dictionary of, 1832.
Despaze, The Five Men, 1793.
Dict. of Contem. Biog., 1861.
Fabricius, Bibliot. Latina.
Flower of the Jacobins, 1797.
Francis, G. H., Orators of the age: Biog., etc., 1847.
Godwin, Hand-book of Univer. Biog. (Putnam).
Goodrich, S. G., Curiosities of human nature.
Hall, J. E., Memoirs of eminent persons, 1827.
Hardie, New Univ. Biog. Dict., 1805.
Harsha, Eminent Orators and Statesmen, 1855.
Harwood, E., Biog. Classica, 1778.
Hazlitt, W., Spirit of the age; or Contem. portraits, 1825.
Historic Gallery, 1807-11.
Hoffmann, J. J., Lexicon Universale, 1698.
Johnson, G. W., New and Gen. Biog. Dict., 1795. 8 v.
Johnson, S., Works, vol. 9, Lives of Eminent Persons.

Biography, General and Miscellaneous (continued).
Jovius, Vitæ illust. Virorum, 1596.
Koenig, Bibliot. Vetus et Nova, 1678.
Ladvocat, Dictionnaire Hist., 1777-79.
Lempriere, Universal Biography, 1825.
Library E. K., Biog. of Eminent Men, 1847.
Lives of the British Dramatists, 1846.
Martineau, H., Biog. Sketches, 1869.
Men of the Time, 1852, 1868.
Oettinger, Bibliog. Biographique, 1854.
Pamphlets, Biographical, vols. 390, 471, 601, 670–675, 899, 1227-1232, 1490-1494, 1659, 1761, 1856. B.C.44.
Pilkington, M., Gen. Dict. of Painters, 1840.
Priestley, J., Chart of Biography.
Rose, Biographical Dict., 1850.
Seward, W., Anecdotes of distinguished Persons, 1795.
" Biographiana, 1799.
Seymour, Self-made men, 1858.
Sigourney, Examples, 18th, 19th Cent., 1857.
Smith, W., Classical Dictionary, 1851.
" Dict. of Gr. & Rom. Biog., 1849.
Soc. Diff. Use. Knowl. Biog. Dict. A., 1829.
Timbs, School Days of Eminent men, 1862.
Tuckerman, Biog. Essays, 1857.
Universal Biog. Dict. (Baldwin), 1826.
Vapereau, Dict. des Contemporains, 1858.
Vasari, Lives of the most eminent Painters, etc., 1850-52.
Watkins, Biog. Hist. and Chron. Dict., 1807.
Willis, N. P., Famons Persons, 1854.
You Have Heard of Them, N. Y., 1854.
See AUTOBIOGRAPHY, and under the names of individuuls; Sermons, Funeral; Eulogies.

Biography, American. Adams, J. Q., Lives of Statesmen, 1846.
Allen, W., Amer. Biog. Dictionary, 1809, 32, 57.
Amer. Bapt. Memorial, Period, 1855, 6.
Amer. Military Biog., 1825.
Bailey, J., Amer. Naval Biog., 1815.
Baldwin, J. G., Party Leaders sketches, 1855.
Bartlett, D. W., Amer. Reformers, 1855.
Belknap, American Biography, 1794, 1841.
Berrian, Recollections, 1850.
Binney, Leaders of Old Bar, 1859.
Biographia Americana, N. Y., 1825.
Blake, M., Hist. Mendon Ass'n., 1856.

Biography, American (continued).
Bogart, W. H., Who goes there, 1866.
Bradford, A., Biog. of disting. men of N. E., 1842.
Brown, W. H., Portrait Gallery of Am. Citizens, 1845.
Bungay, Off-hand takings, 1854.
" Portraits N. Y. Leg., 1857.
Campbell, J. H., Georgia Baptists, 1847.
Campbell, J. W., Biograph. Sketches, 1838.
Coffin, C., Lives and Services, 1845.
Cooper, J. F., Lives of Naval Am. Officers, 1846.
Corwin, Manual of Reformed Dutch Church, 1869.
Crosby, Annual Obituary, 1858, 9.
Curwen, Ward's Notices of Am. Loyalists, 1775-84.
Davidson, J. W., Living writers of the South, 1869.
Delaplaine, Lives of Disting. Amer., 1816-18.
Drake, S. G., Biog. of Indians of N. A., 1845.
Duyckinck, Cyclopedia of Amer. Lit., 1855-66.
" National Portrait Gallery, 1862.
Dwight, Theod., Signers of Dec. of Independence.
Edwards's Great West, 1860.
Eliot, J., Biographical Dictionary, 1809.
Ellet, Pioneer Women of the West.
Everest, Poets of Connecticut, 1847.
Fisher, Physicians of Westchester Co., N. Y.
Flint, T., Indian Wars of the West, 1833.
Fowler, H., Amer. Pulpit (Living), 1856.
Gorrie, Lives of Methodist Ministers, 1852.
" Lives of Mem. of Black River Conference, 1852.
Glyndon, Notables in House of Repr., 1862.
Griswold, R. W., The Repub. Court, 1853.
" The Biographical Annual, 1841.
" Writers of America, 1847.
Gross, S. D., Amer. Physicians and Surgeons, 1861.
Hamersly, Biog. of Liv. Officers, U. S. N., 1870.
Hampden Co. As'n of Cong. Ministers, 1854.
Hardie, The Am. Remembrancer.
Hart, Female Prose Writers of Amer., 1852.

Biography, American (continued).
Harvard Memorial Biographies, 1867.
Herring, Portrait Gallery of Americans, 1834.
Homes of American Authors, 1853.
Homes of American Statesmen, 1854.
Hunt's Lives of Am. Merchants, 1856.
Hunt, W., Amer. Biog. Sketch Book, 1848,
" Amer. Biog. Panorama, 1849.
Indiana, Legislature of, 1861.
Jenkins, J. S., Lives of Governors of N. Y., 1851.
" Lives of Generals of War of 1812.
Jones, A. D., Am. Portrait Gallery, 1855.
" Illust. Amer. Biog., 1853-'55.
Judson, L. C., The Sages and Heroes of, 1852.
Kilbourne, Litchfield, Co., Conn., 1851, 59.
Knapp, S. L., American Biography, 1833.
" Biographical Sketches, 1821.
Knickerbocker Gallery, 1855.
Lanman, Dict. of Congress, 1859, 64, 69.
Lester, Gallery of illust. Americans, 1840.
" The Artists of America, 1846.
Livingston, Biog. of Am. now living, 1853.
" Am. Portrait Gall., 1854.
Loring, 100 Boston Orators.
Lossing, Eminent Americans, 1857.
" Sketches of signers of Decl. of Independence, 1848.
Magoon, Orators of the Am. revolution, 1848.
" Living Orators of Am., 1849.
Maury, Amer. Statesmen of 1846.
Memoirs of disting. Amer., 1853, 54.
Moore, J. B., Lives of American Governors, 1846.
Moore, F., Heroes of Amer., 1861-62.
Morgan, H. J., Celeb. Canadians, 1862.
Murphy, N. Y. Legislature, 1858-62.
New England Biographies, Pam. vol., 1857.
New York Biographies, Pam. vol., 1858.
Officers of Union Army, 1861.
Ohio Legislature, 1862.
O'Neall, Bench and Bar of S. Carolina, 1859.
Parsons, Officers on L. Erie, 1812-14.
Peterson, Hist. of Am. Navy, 1852.
Pierson, Missionary Memorial.
Powell, Living Authors of Am., 1850.
Q., O. P. Sketches N. Y. Press, 1844.
Robinson, F., Lives of disting officers U. S. A., 1848.

Biography, American (continued).
Rogers, T. J., American Biog. Dict., 1824.
Sanderson, J., Biog. of Signers to Decl. of Independence, 1820–22.
Savage, Living repres. men, 1860.
Schussèle, Am. Inventors.
Shanks, Recoll. of generals, 1866.
Shea, The Fallen Brave, 1861.
Sigourney, Examples, 19th Century, 1857.
Simpson, Eminent Philadelphians, 1859.
Smalley, Worcester, Mass., Pulpit, 1851.
Smith, J., Hist. of Jeff. Coll., 1857.
Sprague, W. B., Annals of Am. Pulpit, 1857–68.
Stowe, H. B., Men of our time, 1868.
Street, A. B., New York Coun. of Revision, 1859.
Summers, Meth. ministers, South, 1859.
Taylor, Biog. of Bapt. ministers.
Thatcher, B. B., Indian Biog., 1848.
Tuckerman, H. T., Book of the Artists, 1867.
" Sketches of Am. painters, 1847.
U. S. Commer. Register, 1852.
Updike, Memoirs of Rhode Island bar, 1842.
Washington and the Generals of the Am. rev, 1847.
Watterston, Gallery of Portraits, 1830.
Wealth and Biog. of wealthy citizens of N. Y., 1846. P. 45. B. C.
Wheeler, H. G., Hist. of Cong., biog., 1848.
Whittier, J. G., Old portraits, 1850.
Willard, S. D., Albany Co. Physicians, 1857.
Williams, S. W., Med. Biog., 1845.
Willis, W., Lawyers of Maine, 1863.
Wilson, Illinois officers, 1861, 62.
Wilson, T., Heroes of Rev. and late Wars, 1817.
Winslow, S. N, Phila. Merchants, 1864.
Wynne, Lives of eminent Lit. men in America, 1850.
Yale College, Class Histories.
See Genealogies, American; New York Biographies.

Biography, British. Almon, J., Biog... Anecdotes, 1797.
Annual Biog. and Obituary, 1817–37.
Annual Necrolooy, 1790-97.
Aubrey, J., Lives of eminent men.
Barlow, Sketches....Cheshire.
Berkenhout, Biog. Lit. 400–1600.
Biogr. Magazine, 1776.
Biogr. Dict. of Living Authors, 1816.

Biography, British (continued).
Biographia Britannica, 1766.
Blore, Monumental Remains.
British Histor. Biographies, 1502-1634.
Brook, Lives of Puritans, 1813.
Brougham, Sketches of Statesmen in Geo II, III, 1839. B. C.
" Lives of Men of Lett. and Science, 1845, 46.
Brydges, Censura Literaria, 1815.
Burke, Romance of the Aristocracy.
Calamy, Nonconformist's Memorial, 1802.
Campbell, J., Lives of the Admirals, 1750.
Carlyle, Alex., Autobiog. Memorials of the Men of his Time, 1861.
Catalogue of 500 Authors, 1788.
Catalogue (New) of Living English Authors, 1799.
Chambers, Dict. of Scotsmen, 1847.
Chancellors of England, 1712.
Characters, Lond., 1777.
Charnock, Biog. Navalis, 1660-1798.
Clark, S., Lives of Eminent Persons, 1683.
Coleridge, Worthies of Yorkshire and Lancashire, 1836.
" Biog. Borealis, 1833.
Cooper, C. H., Athenæ Cantabrigienses, 1500–1609.
Craik, G. L., Romance of the Peerage, 1849, '50.
Cunningham, A., British painters and Sculptors, 1832. B. C.
Dodd's Annual Biography, 1842.
Drake, N., Essays Biog., etc., 1814.
East India Military Calendar, 1823.
Fauconberge, Memorial.
Forster, J., Eminent Statesmen, Lardner's Cyc.
Fox, J., Book of Martyrs.
Fuller, T., Worthies of England, 1684, 1830.
Gallery of Portraits, with Memoirs, 1833–37.
Georgian Era, 1832-34.
Gleig, Eminent Brit. Mil. Commanders.
Granger, J., Biog. Hist. of England, 1804.
Harris, J., The Selector, 1814.
Hist. Gallery of Portraits, 1811.
Howitt, Homes of the Poets, 1847.
Hunt, L., Works, Vol. 1, 2, 1854.
James, G. P. R., Lives of For. Statesmen, Lardner's Cycl.
Jockey Club, 1792.
Johnson, Hist. of Eng. Gardening, 1829.
Johnson. S., Works, vol. 6, 7, 8, Lives of the Poets.
Kay, J., Portraits and Biog., 1842.

Biography, British (continued).
Kippis, A., Biographia Britannica, 1778, 89.
Kirby's Wonderful Museum, 1820.
Leland, Comm. de Script. Britannicis.
Lit. and Biog. Magazine, 1788-94.
Literary Blue Book, 1830.
" Memoirs of Living Authors, 1798.
Lives, Essex, Suffolk and Norfolk Co's., 1820.
Lives of the English Saints, 1844, 45.
Lives of Scottish Poets.
Lodge, E., Portraits of personages of Great Britain, 1835.
McClure, Authors of Engl. Version of Bible.
M'Crie, Miscellaneous writings, 1841.
Mackenzie, W. S., Lives of 1000 Irishmen.
Manley, Secret Memoirs, 1709.
Manning, Lives of Speakers of the House of Commons, 1850.
Marshall, S., Royal Naval Biog., 1835.
Miller, W., Sketches fr. Geo. IV, 1826.
Morison, Fathers of Lond. Mis. Society.
Naunton, R., Favorites of Elizabeth.
Nichols, Lit. anecd. of the 18th century, 1812.
" Illust. of Lit. history of 18th century, 1817-58.
O'Byrne, Naval Dict. of Living officers, 1849.
Parry, Cambrian Plutarch.
Philippart, Royal Military Calendar, 1812, 13.
Powell, T., Living Authors of Eng., 1849.
Prince, Worthies of Devon, 1701, 1810.
Public Characters, 1798–1810.
" " 1828.
Reid, J., Memoirs of Divines of Westminster Assembly.
Reuss, Register of authors of Gt. Brit. 1770-90.
Roscoe, H., Lives of Brit. Lawyers, Lardner's Cyc.
Sandford, P. P., Wesley's Missionaries, 1843.
St. John, J. A., Lives of Travellers, 1832. B. C.
Scott, Sir W., Biographies, 1840.
Sheil, R. L., Sketches of the Irish bar, 1844.
Smiles, S., Brief Biographies, 1860.
Smith, Gol., Three English Statesmen.
Southey, R., Lives of uneducated Poets, 1836.
" Lives of British Admirals, Lardner's Cyc.
Sprague, W. B., Visits to Europ. Celebrities, 1855.

Biography, British (continued).
Stephen, Sir J., Essays on Eccl. Biog., 1849.
Suppressed Facts, 1843.
Taylor, W. C., Mod. Brit. Plutarch, 1846.
Walpole, Cat. of Royal and Noble Authors, 1842.
Walton, I., Lives, 1848.
Watt, Biblioth. Britannica, 1824.
Welsby, Lives of English Judges, 1846.
West, Sketches of Wesleyan Preachers, 1848.
Willis, B., Survey of St. Asaph, 1801.
Wodrow Society, Biographies, 1845, 47.
Wood, Athenæ Oxonienses, 1691, 92.
Wordsworth, C., Eccl. Biog., 1818.
Wright, T., Biog. Britan. Literaria, 1846.

Biography, French. Alembert, Eulogies, Fr. Academy.
Annales Biographiques, 1825.
Annuaire Nécrologique, 1826, 7.
Arago, Œuvres: Notices Biograph. 1854.
Baillet, Jugemens, vols. 4, 5, Poëtes, 1732.
Blanc, Peintres des fêtes galantes, 1854.
Bouillet, Dict. d'histoire, 1858.
Bush, Queens of France, 1847.
Cormenin, Orators of France, 1847.
Flower of the Jacobins.
Houssaye, Men of 19th Century.
Lamartine, Hist. des Girondius.
La Sarthe, Notice des Hommes Distingués, 1806. P. 608.
Lyon, Almanach historique, 1828.
Quérard, La France littéraire, 1827-57.
" Litt. Fran. Contemporaine, 1842-64.
Raynal, Anecdotes littéraires, 1752.
Robin, Galerie des gens de lettres, 1848.
Sarrut, Biographie des Hommes du jour, 1835-41.
Shelley, Mrs., Lives of Em. Frenchmen, Lardner's Cyc.
Société Montyon et Franklin, Hist. des Hommes utiles, 6 vols.
Vapereau, Dict. des Contemporains, 1858.

Biography of Physicians. Adamus, Vitæ Germ. Medicorum.
Davis, N. S., Am. Med. Assoc'n.
Fisher, Westchester Co., N. Y.
Gross, American Physicians.
Jackson, J., Mem. of his Son.
Jeaffrerson, Book about Doctors, 1861.
Parsons, U., Rhode Island Physicians.
Pettigrew, Mem. of Distinguished Physicians.

Biography of Physicians (continued).
Physic and Physicians, 1839.
Spilman, Kentucky Medical Biography.
Thacher, American Med. Biog., 1828.
Willard, S. D., Albany Co. Physicians.
Williams, S. W., Amer. Medical Biography, 1845.

Biography of Printers, Booksellers, etc. Almon's Memoirs, 1790.
Amoretti, Lett. s. d'Aldo, 1804,
Baillet, Jugmens des Savans, 1722.
Beloe, v. 3, Early Printers, 1807.
Blancken, Bildnisse, 1725.
Buckingham, Personal Mem., 1852.
Chalmers, Life of Ruddiman, 1784.
Cras, Elogium Meermanni, 1817, B. C.
Dibdin, Bibliomania, 1842.
" Typog. Antiq. Eng. Printers, 1810.
Dolet, E., Vie de., 1779.
Dunton, Life and Errors, 1818.
Falkenstein, Gesch. der Buchdruckerkunst, 1840.
Fifty Years' Recollections, 1835.
Foppens, Bibliot. Belgica, 1739.
Franklin, B., Autobiography, 1818, 68.
Gent, The Life of, 1832.
Greswell, Early Greek Press, 1833.
Hansard, Biog. of L. Hansard, 1829.
Hartzheim, Bibliot. Coloniensis, 1747.
Hillard, Mem. of J. Brown, 1856.
Hutton, Life of, by himself, 1816.
Iseghem, Biog. de Martens, 1852.
Johnson, Typographia, 1824.
Kerr, Life of Smellie, 1811.
Kervin, Bibliophiles Flamands, 1853.
Knight, Biog. of Caxton, 1844.
Lackington, Confessions of, 1804.
La Serna Santander, Dict. Imprimeurs, 1805–07.
Lewis, Life of Caxton, 1737.
Maittaire, Hist. typog. Parisiensium, 1717.
Malaspina, Cat. di Stampe, 1824.
Nichols, Illustrations, v. 8.
" Lit. Anecdotes, v. 3, 1812.
" Anecdotes of W. Bowyer, 1782.
Nodier, Vie de: Par Wey, 1844.
Oettinger, Bibliog. biographique univ., 1854.
Perthes, C. T., Memoirs of, 1856.
Reume, Imprimeurs Belges, 1848.
Saxius, Hist. Lit. Typ. Mediolan, 1465.
Teissier, Catalogus auctorum, 1686.
Timperley, Encyc. of Typ. Anecd., 1842.
Weld, Franklin's Autobiog., 1848.
Winaricky, Jean Gutenberg, 1847.
See Coster; Gutenberg; Typography.

Biography, religious, individual.
Adams, S. W., Bishop, J. P., Mem. of, 1866.
Adorna, Catharine, Upham, Life of.
Baldwin, A. G., Utica, 1814.
Boston, T, Memoirs.
Boyse, Writings, 1839.
Bowles, J., 1802.
Branagan, Pleas. of contemplation, 1818.
Bruyère, J. B., Montreal, 1859.
Bunting, Miss, Memoirs.
Charma, Saint Anselme.
Clark, J., 1855.
Clough, Mrs., Life, 1829.
Crabtree, W., Memoirs, 1815.
D., A., A Brief Account, 1743.
Davies, Arabella, Diary, 1788.
Dow, L., History of Cosmopolite.
Emerson, Eleanor, N. Y., 1817.
Evans, W., 1823.
Fletcher, J. W., Appeal, 1814.
Graham, Isab., Correspondence, 1838.
" Life of, 1816.
Holcombe, H., The first fruits, 1812.
Landers, A., Narrative of.
Lee, Mem. of Preble.
Military criminal, 1849.
Mitchell, R., 1859.
Moody, J., 1809.
Morris, T. A., Miscellany, 1854.
Nicolas, A., Conversation with God, 1749.
Original Memorials, 1822.
Othen, N., 1757.
Page, H., Hallock's memoir of.
Payson, Rev. E., 1830.
Peck, P., Utica, 1848.
Peet, Rev. J., 1854.
Perry, J., Conv. from Popery, 1819.
Pope, M., Life and death, 1709.
Raynsford, Lord's Dealings with, 1837.
Richards, Miss L., 1842.
Scott, T., Force of Truth.
Smith, L. E., Martyrs, etc., of missions.
Spicer, T., Autobiography, 1860.
Taylor, J. B., 1838.
Temple, D., Life of, 1855.
Thomson, A., Great Missionaries.
Thomson, E., Sketches Biographical, 1856.
Turner, Mrs. J., N. Y., 1827.
Vaughan, R. A., Memoir of.
Wagner, G., Simpkinson, Mem. of.
Wilder, S. V. S., Life of, 1865.
Wren, W., Account of, 1784.
Wyer, M., Lond., 1823.

Biography, religious, individual (continued).
Yale, E., Wood, Life of, 1854.
Young, Z., Autobiography, 1847.
See Autobiography.

Biography, Scientific. Alembert, Eulogies of the French Academy.
Arago, Notices Biographiques.
Audubon, Life of.
Barnard, H., Educat. Biogr.
Boyle, R., Life of, Birch.
Brewster, Martyrs of Science.
Brightwell, Heroes of the Laboratory, 1862.
Brougham, Philosophers of Time of George III.
Darlington, W., Memorial, 1863.
Dunham, Lives of Sci. and Lit. Men in G. B., Lardner's 35.
Ed. Cab. Cyc., Lives of Zoölogists.
Edwards, Biog. Hist. of Fr. Academy.
Foucaud, Book of Illustrious Mechanics, 1846.
Galilei, Life of.
Howe, H., Disting. Amer. and Europ. Mechanics, 1847.
Lives of Shoemakers.
Macgillivray, Lives of Eminent Geologists. Edin. Cab. Lib. 16.
Montgomery, J., Lives of European Scientific men. Lardner's 55, -57.
Renwick's Lives of Fulton, Rittenhouse, Rumford.
Schüssele, Amer. Inventors.
Shelley, Mrs., Lives of Sci. and Lit. Men.
Smiles, Lives of Boulton and Watt.
" Life of G. Stephenson.
Stuart, Civ. and Mil. Engineers of America, 1871.
Wilson, G., Mem. of E. Forbes, 1861.
Wilson, T. B., Mem., Phila. P. 1492.
Wynne, Em. Sci. and Lit. Men of Ame., 1850.

Biography, Theatrical. Baker, D. E., Biographia Dramatica, 1782.
Bell, R., Lives of Eng. Dramatists, Lardner's 1.
Boaden, Life of Kemble and Siddons.
Clapp's Boston Stage.
Dunham, Lives of Eng. Dramatists, Lardner's 1, 2.
Dunlap's Amer. Theatre, 1832.
Fennell, J., Life of, 1814.
Garrick's Life and Corresp.
Genest, Acct. of Engl. Stage, 1832.
Houssaye, Philos. and Actresses.
Ireland, J. N., The N. Y. Stage, 1867.
Lives of British Dramatists, 1846.
Wemyss, Chron. of Am. Stage, 1852.

Biography, Theatrical (continued).
Wood, Personal recollections, 1855.
Young, C. M., Memoirs, 1871.
See other individual names and Dram. Lit.

Biography of Women. Atkinson, Queens of Prussia.
Brantome, Vie des dames galantes.
Clarke, M. C., World-noted women.
Costello, L. S., Eminent English women.
Doran, Lives of the Queens of Eng., 1855.
Ellet, Women of the Am. revolution.
" Pioneer women of the West.
" Women Artists.
Eminent women of the age, 1869.
Forrest, Women of the South in literature, 1865.
Green, M. A. E., Letters of illus. ladies of G. B.
Griswold, Female poets of America, 1849.
Hale, S. J., Sketches of all disting. women, 1853.
Hart, Female prose writers of Am.
Hist. litt. des femmes françoises, 1765 (La Porte).
Houssaye, Men and Women of the 18th century, 1852.
James, G. P. R., Biog. of celeb. women.
Jameson, A., Beauties of Court of Charles II, 1838.
" Memoirs of the loves of the poets.
Kavanagh, English women of letters.
Knapp, S. L., Female biography.
Sainte Beuve, Portraits de femmes.
" " Celebrated women, 1868.
Starling, Noble deeds of woman.
Strickland, Queens of England.
Wharton, Queens of Society (by Thomson).
See Woman.

Biology. *See* Life; Man; Population.

Bird. Family genealogy.

Birds. Beckstein, Cage and chamber birds.
Browne, D. J., Bird fancier.
Canary Bird fancier, 1842. P. 616.
See Ornithology; Poultry.

Birmingham, Eng. Hutton, W., Life of, 1816.

Birmingham riots. Kenrick, T., Spirit of persecution, 1791.
Priestley, Appeal on the riots, 1791.

Birney, J. G. Green, B., Life and writings of, 1844.

Biron, A. L. S. De. *See* Lauzun.

Bishop, M. Life of, 1744.

Bishops in America. Chandler, T. B., Appeal, 1767.
" Appeal defended, 1769.
Chauncy, C., Appeal, 1768.
Masères, Essays, 1809.
Mayhew, J., Remarks, 1764.
Sharp, G., Life of Hoare.

Bismarck, Von. Hesekiel, Life of, 1870.

Bissell. Family geneal. (Stiles).

Black Friars' Society, N. Y. Clinton, D. W., Oration, 1795.
Watkins, J. W., Oration, 1792.

Black Hawk. Life of, by himself, 1834.
Drake, B., Life of, 1850.
Smith, E. H., Hist. of, 1846.

Blackhead, S. Sprat, T., A Relation of, 1692.

Black Sea. Arrianus, Ponti Euxini Periplus.
Dearborn, Commerce of, 1819.
Taitbout de Marigny, Voyages en, 1836.

Blackstone, W. Blackstone Mon't Assoc'n, 1855

Blackwood's Magazine. Hypocrisy unveiled, 1818.

Blagdon controversy. P. vol. 1938.

Blair, F. P. McClurg, Speech on, 1864.

Blair, H. Hill, J., Account of Life of, 1808. B. C.

Blair, Rob. Wodrow Society, Life of.

Blake. Family genealogy, 1857.

Blake, J. E. Simison, B.D., Correspondence with, 1837.

Blake, W. Gilchrist, Life of.

Bland, T., jr. Bland papers, 1843.

Blaregnies. Kennett, W., Sermon, Victory at, 1709.

Blasphemy. Mulock, Not to be repressed, 1819.

Blast furnace. Schinz, Researches, 1870.

Bleeding. Campbell, J., Letter on, 1746.

Blennerhassett, H. Safford, W. H., Life of, 1853.

Blessington, Countess of. Madden, R. R., Life of, 1855.

Bligh, Gen. Exam. of a Letter of, 1758.
Letter to His Excellency, 1758.

Blind. Almanac for the Blind, 1847.
Alston, Spec. of printing for.
Asyle de Lausanne, Reports, 1850-53.
Atlas for the blind, 1837.
Connecticut, Reports on, 1851.
De Kroyft, Mrs., A place in the memory, 1850.

Blind (continued).
Guide to devotion: for the use of, 1846.
Guillié, Instruction des aveugles.
Indiana Institut., Reports, 1854-65.
Johnson, Tangible typography.
Kitto, The lost senses.
Mahony, Musical notation for, 1853.
Milburn, Rifle, Axe, etc., 1857.
Moon's Printed books.
N. Y. Institute for the Blind, Reports, 1845-70.
Ohio, Reports, 1850–65.
Pamphlets relating to, vols. 218, 473.
Pennsylvania Insti., Reports, 1846, 67.
Perkins Instit. and Mass. Asylum for, 1834-60.
" Guide to Devotion, *and* Atlas, 1837, 46.
Reynolds, Address Eye and Ear infirm., 1850.
School...in St. George's Fields, 1857.
Taylor, W., Printing for the blind, 1837.
Tennessee, Asylum Reports, 1851.

Bliss, J. C. Parker, J., Tribute to.

Blockbooks. Russia, Cat. Xylographes, 1852.
Sotheby, Principia Typographica, 1858.
Varusoltis, Xylographie Troyenne, 1859.
See History and Engraving.

Blood. Barry, Mouvement du sang., 1825.
Brander, Sanguinis distributio.
Davies, R., Human blood.
Delany, Of abstinence from.
See Physiology.

Blumenbach, J. F. Life of, Anthrop. Soc.

Boardman, G. D. King, A., Life of, 1836.

Boardman, J. Sprague, W. B., Serm., Death of, 1853.

Boddily, J. Dana, D., Discourse on.

Boden, J. Muir, J. H., Sermon on, 1841.

Bodleian Library. *See* Bibliography; Oxford.

Boerhave, A. Burton, W., Life of.
Schultens, A., Lykrede, 1739.

Bogardus Family. *See* Yale.

Bohemia. Bowring, Cheskian Anthology.

Bohun, E. Diary and Autobiog., 1853.

Boileau, N. Alembert, Eulogy on.

Bokhara. Burnes, Travels into, 1833.
Khanikoff, Amir. and People of, 1845.
Moorcroft, Trav. in Himalayan Provinces and, 1841.
Wolff, J., Researches, 1837.
" Mission to, 1843-5.

Bolingbroke, H. St. John, Lord.
Articles d'accusation, 1715.
Bulkley, Notes on Writings of, 1765.
Cooke's Memoirs of, 1835.
Goldsmith, O., Life of.
Heathcote's Philosophy of.
Jesse's Memoirs of the Court.
Pye, Moses and Bolingbroke.

Bolivar, S. Morillo, Gén., Mémoires du Gén Morillo, 1826.
Holstein, Memoirs of, and his Generals, 1829.

Bolles, L. Sharp, D., Discourse on.

Bolling. Family Memoir, 1868.

Bolton, Mass. Evangelical Church at, 1830.

Bombay. Murray's Handbook.
See India.

Bonaparte Family. Gregorovius' Corsica, and Hist. of the Bonapartes, 1855.
Napoleon Dynasty, by the Berkley Men, C. E. Lester, 1852.
See Napoleon I, III.

Bond, G. Lothrop, Sermon on.

Bonin Is. Perry, Paper on, 1856.

Bonneville. Irving, W., Adventures of, 1850.

Book-Binding. Churton, Hand-book of.
Cundall, Orna. Book-binding, 1847.
Dibdin, Decameron, V. 2, 1817.
Exposition Univ., Rapports du Jury, etc., 1856.
Hannett, Art of.
Nicholson, Manual of the Art, 1856.
Walker, E., Hist. of.
" The Art of Bookbinding.
Woolnough, Art of Marbling, 1854.

Book-keeping. Bertrand, Tenue des livres.
Burnham, L. W., Its rules. P. 1295.
Colt, J. C., Science of, 1844.
Cory, J. P., Practical treatise on accounts, 1840.
Cotheal, On accounts.
Crittenden, Treatise on, 1859.
Edwards, Book-keeper's atlas, 1834.
Goddard, T. H., Practical accountant, 1837.
Marsh, C. C., Science of, 1854.
Merchants' Manual of, 1810.
Palmer, J. H., First lessons in, 1853.
" Treat. on, 1853. P. 606.
Preston, L., Treatise on, 1854.
See Arithmetic; Finance; Tables.

Book of Judgment. Wilson, E. S., 1853.

Books. Anecdotes of Books, 1836.
Baillet, Jugemens, v. 1, 1730.
De Bury, Philobiblion, 1832, 1861.
Dibdin, Bibliomania.
" Library companion.
Jewett, Duties on, 1846. P. 17.
Knight, The old printer.
Le Gallois, Traitte des Bib. de l'Europe, 1697.
Merryweather, Bibliomania, 1849.
Spizelius, Infelix Literatus, 1680.
" Literatus Felicissimus, 1685.
See Bibliography.

Books: Guides in the Selection of.
Atkinson, W. P., B. and reading.
Bossange, Ma Bibliothèque française.
Chaudon, Bibliot. d'un homme de gout, 1772.
Churton, Book Collector's hand-book, 1845.
Dana, Biblioth. Probata, 1857.
Dibdin, Library companion, 1825.
Goodhugh, Eng. Gent's library, 1827.
Kent, Course of Reading, 1840.
Kett, Elem. of general knowl., 1803.
Manchester Library, Books for purchase, 1851.
Moore. C. H., What to read, Classif. list, 1871.
Oakley, Course of Engl. reading, 1853.
Observations on forming a library, Pamphleteer 2.
Park, R., Select Cat. on all subjects, 1841.
Potter, Handbook for readers, 1847.
Stevens, My English library, 1853.
Ventouillac, The French librarian, 1829.
See Libraries, administration of; Bibliography.

Booksellers. Beloe, Sexagenarian.
Dibdin, Bibliophobia, 1832.
Dunton, Religio Bibliopolæ, 1720.
Dupont, Hist. de l'imprimerie, 1854.
Kirchoff, Gesch. der Deutschen Buchhandels, 1851.
Lackington, J., Memoirs of, 1830.
Nichols, Literary Anecdotes, v. 3, 1812.
Statist. Soc. Lond. III. Meidinger.
See Bibliography; Typography.

Book Trade, American. Freedley, Leading pursuits.
Trade circular annual, 1871.

Boone, D. Bogart, W. H., Dan'l Boone, etc., 1854.
Boone, D., Adventures, 1844.
Bryan, The Mountain muse, 1813.
Flint, T., Biog. memoir of, 1833.

Boone, D., (continued).
Hill, G. C., Biography of, 1860.
Metcalf, S. L., Narratives, 1821.
Peck, J. M., Life of (Sparks, 23).

Bordeaux. Nouveau conducteur, 1851.
Bordes, Hist. des monumens de, 1845.
Chambre de commerce de, Mémoires, etc., 1850-57.
Cocks, Bordeaux, its wines, 1846.
Costello, Bearn and the Pyrenees, 1844.
Guilhe, Histoire de, 1835.

Borgia, Lucrezia. Gilbert, Life of, 1869.

Borneo. Beeckman, Voyage to, Pinkerton, 11.
Brooke, J., Narrative of events in, 1848.
Chamerovzow, Borneo Facts, 1850.
Keppel, H., Expedition to Borneo, 1846.
Low, H., Sarawak, its inhabitants, 1848.
Marryatt, Borneo and Indian Archipelago, 1848.

Boscawen, N. H. Price, E., Chronol. register of, 1820.

Bossuet, J. B. Alembert, Eulogies.

Boston, T. Memoirs of.

Boston, Mass. Ballard's Old South Church.
Boston Almanac, 1836–58, 64.
Boston Common, 1842.
Boston, City Documents, etc., 1838-53.
Boston, Directories, 1820-69, not complete.
Boston, Munic. Register, 1856–61, 65.
Bowen, Picture of, 1838.
Bridgman, Copp's Hill epitaphs, 1851.
" Memorials of dead, King's Chapel, 1853.
" Pilgrims of Boston, Granary Burying ground.
Clapp, Letter on Growth of, 1853.
Dana, J. F., Geology of: and vicinity, 1818.
Dearborn, N., Boston notions, 1630–1847.
" Reminiscences of Boston, 1851.
Drake, S. G., Hist. and antiq. of, 1630-1670.
Dunton, J., Letters from N. E., 1686.
Eliot's New North Church, 1822.
Emerson, W., Hist. First Church in, 1812.
Federal Street Church, History.
Frothingham, Siege of, 1849.
Greenwood, Hist. of King's Chapel, 1833.
Hales, J. G., Survey of, 1821.

Boston, Mass. (continued).
Hancock, J., Oration, March 5, 1774.
History of, (R. Carver).
Hollis Street Society, 1841.
Jarvis, S. F., Of St. Paul's Church, 1825. P. 502.
Knapp's Ali Bey's journal, 1818.
Lothrop, S. K., Hist. of Brattle street Church, 1851.
Nason, E., Frankland's life or Boston in colonial times.
New Engl. Meth. E. Hist. Soc., Trans.
Old South Church History.
Palfrey, Brattle Street Church Hist., 1824. P. 485.
Parkman, F., New North Church.
Prince, T., Revival in, 1740-43.
Pulsifer, Guide to, 1868.
Quincy, J., Centennial Discourse, 1830.
" History of, to 1830.
Robbins, Hist. of Second Church, 1852.
Rowe Street Baptist Church.
Shattuck, Report on census, 1845.
Shaw, Description of, 1817.
Simonds, Hist. of South Boston, 1857.
Sketches of Boston and vicinity, 1851.
Snow, C. H., History of, 1828.
Sumner, W. H., Hist. of East Boston, 1858.
Wisner, Hist. of Old South Church, 1830.
Warren, The great tree.
Wines, Trip to Boston, 1838.
See Earthquake of 1727; Newspapers of New England.

Boston Athenæum. Quincy, J., Hist. of, 185C.

Boston Massacre, 1770. Boston, Short Narrative, 1770. P. 114.
Boston Orations on, 1771-82.
Clark, J., Sermon on, 1776.
Kidder's, History of, 1870.
Loring, 100 Boston Orators.

Boston, Eng. St. Botolph's church.

Boswell, James. Letters to A. Erskine.

Botany. Barton, B. S., Mat. Med., U. S., 1810.
Barton, W. P. C., Floræ Philad. Prod., 1815.
" Veg. Mat. Med. U. S., 1825.
" Account of Holcus bicolor, 1816.
Baster, Voorteeling der dieren en Planten, 1768.
Berkeley, Cryptogamic Bot., 1857.
Bliss, Sale cat. of flower seeds, 1870.
Bonaparte, C. L., Progress of Botany, *Ray Soc.* Pub.
Bordley, Queries of B. of agr. answered, on veg. phys., 1797. P. 39.

Botany (continued).

Bourne, Florist's manual, 1833.
Brunet, Plantes de Michaux.
Candolle, Alph de, Géog. Botanique, 1855.
" Geograph. Botany. P. 3, 4°.
Candolle, Aug. de, Philosophy of plants, 1821.
" Various memoirs, 1819-21.
" Veget. organography, 1841.
Catalogues of Botan. Libra. P. v, 188.
Clayton, Connubia Florum, 1791.
Coxe, J. R., Agaricus atramentarius.
Darlington, Lecture on study of, 1844.
" Agricultural Botany, 1847.
Darwin, Botan. Garden, Notes, 1795.
Dict. des Sciences naturelles, 1816–30.
Don, Hist. of Dichlamydeous plants, 1841.
Dresser, Manual of, 1860.
Eaton, A., Botanical Dictionary, 1817.
Eberle, Bot. terminology, 1818.
Féburier, Phénomènes de la végétation, 1812.
Feuillée, Obs. bot. sur l'Am. méridionale et l'Inde occ., 1714.
Germain, Conseils sur l'étude de.
Griffith, R. E., Medical Botany, 1847.
Grisebach, Botanical Geog., 1842, 43.
Henfrey, Botan. and Physiol. Mem., Ray Soc.
Hill, John, History of Plants, 1752.
Humboldt, Des Melastomacées, 1833.
Henslow, Desc. and Physiological Botany, Lardner's, 44.
Jussieu, Cours d'hist. nat., 1860.
" Elements of, 1858.
Knight and Perry, Coniferous Plants.
Koenigl. Ak. der Wiss., Gefässpflanzen.
Lefébure, Méthode...à l'étude du nom des plantes, 1814.
Linnæus, Systema plantarum, 1779.
Lincoln, Mrs., Familiar lectures, 1831.
Lindley, Orchidearum sceletos, 1826.
" Introd. to natural system of, 1831.
" The Vegetable Kingdom, 1846.
Link, Prog. of Physiological Bot.
Loudon, J. C., Trees and shrubs of Great Britain, 1838.
" Encyc. of Plants, 1836.
Macmillan, First forms of vegetation, 1861.
Martius, Bot. Erforschung des k. Bayern, 1850.
Massachusetts Survey, reports on, 1840.
Mercklin, Prothallium der Farrnkrauter, 1850.
Meyen, Outlines of geog. of plants. Ray Soc.

Botany (continued).

Munting, Oeffening der Planten, 1672.
Nageli, On vegetable cells. Ray Soc.
Oliver, D., Elem. Botany, 1864.
Pamphlets on Botany, vols. 188, 961.
Paxton, Magazine of Botany, 1835, 39-49.
" Flower Garden, 1850–1.
Persoon, Synopsis Plantarum, 1805.
Pinnock, Catechism of.
Pultney, Prog. of Bot. in Eng. 1790.
Rogues, Hist. des champignons.
Rowden, Poet. introd. to, 1801.
Salmon, English Herbal, 1710.
Schleiden, Principles of Scient. Bot., 1849.
Schrenk, Enumeratio plantarum novarum, 1841.
Schultze, Ueber den organ. der Polythalamien, 1854.
Schwægrichen, Species Muscor. Frondosorum, 1830.
Séringe, Mélanges botariques, 1818-26.
Smith, E., In Orr's Circle, 1854.
Smyttère, Phytologie Pharmaceutique, 1829.
Stark, L. G., Aphorismi Botanici, 1821.
Sullivant, Icones Muscorum, 1864.
Sweert, Florilegium, 1620.
Teysmann, Rafflesias Rochusenii.
Unger, Botan. Letters, 1853.
Vinton, Hunt Garden Address, 1855.
Vriese, W. H. de, Het gezag van Kaempfer en anderen, 1836.
Vrolik, Ziekte der Aardappelen, 1846.
Waterhouse, The Botanist, 1811.
Waterman's Flora's Lexicon, 1840.
Withering, Syst. Arrangement of Brit. plants, 1801.
Wydler, Genre Scrofularia, 1828.
Zuccarini, Morphology of the Coniferæ. Ray Soc.
" Vegetationsgruppen, Bayern, 1833.
See Physiology; Flowers.

Botany, Various Collections and Localities. Aiton, Hortus Kewensis.

Aldinus, Descr. Plantarum Romæ, 1625.
Barton, W. P. C., Floræ Phil'æ Prodromus, 1815.
Beck, L. C., Bot. of the U. S. North of Va., 1848.
Bentham, G., Plantes des Pyrénées, 1826.
Berkeley, Brit. Fungology, 1860.
Bigelow, J., Florula Bostoniensis, 1814, '40.
Blume, Orchidées du Japon, 1858.

Botany, Various Collections and Localities (continued).

Brereton, Floræ Columbianæ Prodromus, 1830.

Browne, D. J., The Trees of America, 1846.

Bruinsma, Flora Frisica.

Christener, Die Hieracien der Schweiz.

Darby, Botany of the Southern States. 1855.

Darlington, Plants of West-Chester, 1826.

" Flora, Chester Co. Penn., 1853.

Dewey, Herbaceous Plants of Mass., 1840.

Donn, Hortus Cantabrigiensis, 1807,'45.

Eaton, A., Manual of, for Northern States, 1817.

" Manual of, for N. America, 1829.

Eaton, H. H., Plants near Troy, 1832.

Elliott, S., Bot. of South Carolina, 1821.

Emerson, G. B., Trees and shrubs in Mass., 1846.

Emory, Mexican Boundary survey.

Fischer, Sertum Petropolitanum.

Flora Napolitana, 1811-36.

Florula Columbiensis, 1819.

Gay, C., Chile. Botanica, 3 v.

Gibbes, Plants near Columbia, S. C., 1835. P. 188.

Graham, Plants R. Bot. Garden, Edin., 1825-33.

Gray, A., Chloris Boreali-Americana, 1846. P. 1003.

" Man. of Bot. of the U. S., 1848.

" The Genera of the Plants of U. S., 1849.

" Plantæ Wrightianæ Texano-Neo-Mexicanæ.

" Plants from Chile.

Gray, S. O., British Sea-weeds.

Griffith, W., Plants of India, 1837-41.

" Palms of India, 1850.

Hartinger, Paradisus Vindobonensis.

Harvey, W. H., British Algæ, 1849.

" Marine Algæ of N. A.

" Sea Side Book, 1854.

" Australian Sea-weeds, 1858.

Hasskarl, Cat. Pl. in Hor. Bot. Bogoriensi, 1844.

Henslow, Cat. of British plants, 1835.

Hitchcock, Cat. of Plants near Amherst Coll., 1829.

Hooker, Flora Boreali-Americana, 1833.

" Botany of Capt. Beechey's voy., 1825-28.

" Flora of South America.

Botany, Various Collections and Localities (continued).

Hough, F. B., Plants of Lewis Co., N. Y. P. 188.

Houghton, D. D., Plants from Northwest Expeditions, 1831.

Humboldt, Plantes Equinoxiales.

Irvine, The London Flora, 1838.

Jardin d' Hiver, Catalogue des Serres.

Johnston, G., The Eastern Borders, 1853.

Landsborough, Hist. of British weeds, 1851.

Laterrade, Flore Bordelaise, 1846.

Lawson, P., Veg. Prod. of Scotland.

Lee, C. A., Med. Plants growing in New York, 1848.

Loudon, J. C., Trees and shrubs of Britain, 1838.

Lowe, R. T., Flora Maderæ, 1831.

M'Murtrie, Florula Louisvillensis, 1819.

Marshall, H., Arbustrum Americanum, 1785.

Martius, Botan. Garten in München, 1852.

Meyer, Flora-Hannover, 1837.

Michaux, Flora-Boreali Americana, 1803.

" Hist. des chênes de l'Am. Septentrionale, 1811.

" Oaks of U. S.

" North American Sylva, 1819.

Mueller, Plants of Victoria, 1865.

" Australian Mosses, 1864.

" Veget. of Chatham Is., 1864.

Muhlenberg, Cat. of Plants in N. Am. 1813.

" Gram. et Calamar. Amer. Septen., 1817.

" Gram. et Plant. Calam. Am. Septen., 1817.

New York Nat. Hist., J. Torrey.

Nuttall, Genera of N. A. plants, 1817.

" North Am. Sylva, 1849.

Oeder, Icones Plantarum Daniae et Norvegiæ, 1766-70.

Olney, S. T., Cat. of Rhode Island plants, 1844.

Pesneau, Plantes de la Loire Inférieure, 1837.

Plants, Bot. Garden Edinburgh. P. 188.

Plants of New Castle Co. Del., 1844.

Plants near Yale College, 1831.

Plumier, Nova plant. Amer. genera, 1703.

Provancher, Flore Canadienne.

Providence Frank. Soc., Cat. of Plants in R. I., 1844.

Pursh, Flora Amer. septentrionalis, 1814.

Rafinesque, Flora Telluriana, 1836.

Brewing. Baverstock, Obs. on the state of the Brewery. Pamphl'r 2.
Booth, D., Art of Brewing, Lib. U. K.
Byrn, Practical Brewer, 1852.
Corbett, Cottage economy.
Coppinger, J., Amer. Practical Brewer, 1815.
Denneston, Frauds of the Brewers, 1713.
Discourse on.... Malt Liquors, 1733.
Dissertation conc. Barley Wine, 1750.
Hughes, Treatise, 1796.
London Brewer, 1758.
Ploughman, Family Brewer, 1800.
Randall, W., Hop Plantations, 1800.
Taylor, J., Ale, by J. Savage.
Worth, W. Y., Art of, 1692.

Brewster, James. Addresses, N. Haven, 1857.

Brewster, Joseph. Smith, A. D., Sermon on, 1851.

Brewster, W. Steele, A., Life of, 1857.

Briberies. Bacon, F., Case of, considered, 1721.
Collection of the debates, 1695.
Crosfield, Corrupt Practices, 1694.
Gr. Brit. Debates on, 1773. P. 1021.
Isaacson, Electoral Reform.
Remarks with Suggestions.
Russell, Earl, J., Speech, 1820. P. 703.

Bricks. Dobson, Manuf. of, 1850.

Bridge at Albany. New York, Bridge at Albany, 1841. P. 493.
Seward, W. H., Argument, 1858.
Van Santvoord, G., Speech, 1856.
Van Valkenburgh, Speech, 1856.
Wheeler, O. B., Speech, '859.
See Law Libr. Catalogue.

Bridges. Annales des ponts et chaussées, 1831-65.
Buck, Oblique Bridges, 1839.
Clark, E., Britannia Tubular Bridges, 1850.
Dempsey, Iron Girder Bridges, 1850.
Drewry, Suspension Bridges, 1832.
Ellet, Suspension Bridge, St. Louis; Middletown, Conn., 1840, '48.
Hann, Architecture of Bridges, 1839.
Haupt, Theory of construction, 1853.
Hawksmoor, London Bridge.
Internat. Bridge Co., N. Y., 1858.
Jackson, T., Britannia Bridge.
Latham, Wrought Iron Bridges, 1858.
Lehardy de Beaulieu, Ponts en fonte, 1845.
Lentze, Brucken uber d. Weichsel, 1855.
London Bridge, 1823.
Long, S. H., Plans for, 1841.

Bridges (continued).
Montreal Railway, Bridge over the St. Lawrence, 1853.
Niagara Falls Suspension.... Co., 1855.
Pamphlets relating to Bridges, v. 493.
Poncelet, On draw-bridges.
Pope, T., Treatise on Bridge Architecture, 1811.
Pring, Menai Bridge, 1827.
Robinson, S. W., Suspension bridges.
Theory, Pract. and Arch. of, (Weale), 1843.
Theory of; Supp., 1853, (Weale).
Town, I., Improvement in construction of, 1839.
Whipple, S., On Bridge Building, 1847.
White, A., Wooden Sus. Bridge of, 1852. P. 205.
See Military B.

Bridgewater, Mass. Mitchell, N., History of, 1840.
200th Anniversary, 1856.

Bridgeton, Me. Bram, Hist. address, 1852.

Briggs, G. N. Richards, W. C., Memoir of.

Brigham family. Morse, A., geneal. of.

Brigham, J. C. Adams, W., Disc. on.

Bright family of Suffolk, Eng. Geneal. hist.

Bright, Gen. M. Trial of, Phil., 1809.

Brighton, Eng. Brighton, New hist. of.
Brighton and its environs.
Stranger's guide.

Brimfield, Mass. Morse, J., Annals of the Church, 1856.
Vaill, J., Memorial Sermon, 1864.

Brinsmade, J. E. Coit, T. W., Sermon on, 1860.

Brissot de Warville. Life of, 1794.

Bristol, Eng. Britton's views, 1829.
Bristol Statist. Soc., 1838.
" Tabernacle Centenn., 1854.
" and West of Engl. Archæol. Mag., 1843.
Buck, C., Sermon, fires in, 1831.
Chillcott's guide.
Corry, J., History of, 1816.
Hanserd Knollys Society, Broadmead Church, 1640-87.
Rose, J., Disturbances at, 1793.
Shiercliff, Guide to, 1793.
Talbot, W., Narrative, 1772.

Bristol Co., Ms. Directory, 1868.

Britain. *See* Great Britain.

British. *See* English; Great Britain; Bibliography.

British and Foreign Bible Society. *See* Bible So ieties.

British Colonies in America. Andrews, I. D., Report on Comm. of, 1853.

Bray, T., General view of, 1699.

British Empire in America, 1741.

Buckingham, Travels in, 1841.

Burton, R., Eng. Empire in Am., 1711.

Bury, Exodus of the Western nations, 1865.

Colonial Policy considered, 1816.

Colonising, 1774.

Dilke, Greater Britain, 1869.

Douglass, W., History of, 1755.

Durham, Dispatches concerning, 1839.

Edwards, Hist. of Brit. West Indies, 1806, 10, and 19.

Hypocrisy unmasked, 1776.

Martin, M. R., Hist. of Brit. Colonies.

Pamphlets relating to British Colonies, vol. 434.

Relation of....New England, 1689.

Representation on Amer. trade, 1721.

Review of Rise of New England, 1774.

Walsh, Appeal from the judgments, etc.

Wynne, Brit. Empire in America, 1820.

Whitworth, State of trade, 1776.

See United States; Canada; New England; West Indies; North America, British; Virginia; Australia.

British Columbia. Knight's Handbook, 1864.

Lennard, Travels in, 1862.

Lowe, On the independence of. Pamphleteer, v. 21, 22.

Macdonald, Account of, 1863.

Milton, Northwest passage, 1865.

See Vancouver's Island.

British Museum. Biblioth. Amer., Homer, MSS. in.

Boyle, Curiosities of, 1791.

British Museum, Synopsis of contents, 1837, 1851.

" Catalogue of MSS., Record Pub. *See* Law Lib.

" Books of reference, 1859.

" Catalogue, Letter A.

Cumberland, Essay, prints in.

Ellis, Townley Gallery in, Lib. E. K.

" Elgin marbles in, Lib. E. K.

George III, Bibl. regiæ catalogus.

Great Britain, Brit. Mus. Reports of Comm. of House of Commons, 1850.

Hargrave, Cat. of MSS. of Lib. of.

Sims, Hand-book of the Library, 1854.

Stevens, Cat. of Amer. books in.

Waagen, Treasures of Art in G. B.

See Bibliography; Law Library.

British North America. *See* North America; British Columbia; Hudson's Bay; Canada; Arctic, etc.

British India. *See* India.

British Pamphlets, Vols. 123–141, 452, 841, 1106, 1107, 1846, 1847, 1848, 1851, 1857, 1876.

British Parliamentary Pamphlets. *See* Parliamentary.

British Political Pamphlets, vols. 123-141, 407–422, 442, 443, 445–448, 450, 451, 572, 573, 591, 640, 700, 701, 709, 735, 738, 743, 745, 756, 757, 811–815, 817, 896, 917, 1011, 1026, 1047, 1108, 1116, 1117, 1394-1406, 1544-1547, 1729–1731.

British Topographical Pamphlets. Pam. vols. 1478, 1573, 1754-57.

Brittany, France. Gourcy, Voyage en, 1862.

Pitre-Chevalier, La Brétagne, anc. et mod.

Robidou, Histoire d'un beau pays, 1861.

Trollope, F., Summer in, 1840.

Brock, Gen. Sir I. Correspondence on monument to, 1841.

Tupper, F. B., Life of, 1845.

Brodhead, J. Sermon, historical, 1851.

Memorial of, 1855.

Brodie, H. Mathieson, A., Sermon, Death of, 1852. P. 555.

Broglie, Duchess of. Baird, R., Memoirs of, 1839.

Broke, Adm. P. B. V. Brighton, Life of, 1866.

Bronaugh, Dr. Coles, Letters of.

Bronte, C. Gaskell, E. C., Life of, 1857.

Bronte, Theod. Bayne's Essays.

Brooke, H. Brookiana, 1804.

Brooke, J. Keppel, H., Extracts from Journal of, 1846.

Brookfield, Mass. Foot, J. I., Hist. discourse, 1828.

Stone, M., Hist. Sermon, 1851.

See North and West Brookfield.

Brookline, Ms. Town documents, 1855–1863.

Directory, 1868.

Pierce, J., Hist. disc., 1817. P. 111.

" Century Discourses, 1811, 37.

" Hist. Discourses, 1845, 47.

Brooklyn, N. Y. Manual of Common Council, 1859.

" Water-works, reports, 1854–61.

" Prospect Park, reports, 1866-70.

Brooklyn Directories, 1839, 48–66, 70.

" Record, 1855.

Field, T. W., Historic scenes, 1868.

Buckingham, Jas. S. Autobiography, 1855.
Sketch of life of, 1830.

Buckingham, Joseph T. Personal memoirs, 1852.

Buckinghamshire, Eng. Berry, County genealogies.
Beauties of England and Wales.

Buckle, H. T. Essays and life.

Buckminster, J. Parker, N., Discourse, Death of, 1812. P. v. 214.

Buckminster, J. and J. S. Lee, E. B., Lives of, 1849.

Buddhism. Bird, J., Origin and principles of, 1847.
Cunningham, Buddhist monuments, 1854.
See Hindoos; India.

Budgett, S. Arthur, W., Life of, 1857.

Budington, E. L. Blagden, G. W., Discourse on, 1855.

Buel, J. Dean, A., Eulogy on.

Buell, Samuel. Life of, in Narrative of revival, 1808.

Buenos Ayres. Andrews, Journey from, to Cordova, 1827.
Archivo Americano, 1850.
Beaumont, J., Travels in, 1828.
" Authen. descr., 1806.
Conder, Brazil and B. Ayres, 1831.
Five Years residence in, 1820–25.
Funez, Victoria de Ayacucho, 1825.
Gerstäcker, Travels, 1850.
King, A. J., Argentine Republic, 1846.
Monarchical projects of the Bourbons, 1820.
Nunez, Esquisses Historiques, 1826.
Parish, Descr. of, 1852.
Rio de Janeiro, Almanac, 1843.
S * * E. de G., La République de, 1825.
Whitelocke, Gen., Trial, 1808.
See La Plata; Argentine Confed.

Buffalo, N. Y. Barton, J. L., Commerce of the Lakes, 1845, 46.
Bedini, Lettres, St. Louis Church.
Buffalo, various city Docts , 1836–58.
" Female Academy Cat., 1852–66.
" Directories, 1832, 35-40, 58–69.
Clinton, G. W., Hist. Address, 1862.
First Presb. Church, 1838, 1852.
First Unitarian Church Hist., 1861.
Henderson's Trade of, 1853, 54.
Ketchum, History of, 1865.
Lord, Dead of the War.
Pamphlets concerning, v. 474, 475.
Reply to speech of Babcock on St. Louis Church.

Buffalo, N. Y. (continued).
St. Louis Church, Docts. and History, 1853. P. 1435.
Thompson, M. L. P., Sermon, Deaths in, 1850.
Timon, Bp., Hist of Diocese.
Young Men's Asso. Quart. Cent. Celeb., 1861.

Bugeaud. Galerie des Contem., Vie de, 1845.

Building. Alderson, on Kyan's Process.
Dearn, improved Method of, 1821.
Glover, G., Lodging houses.
Leadbeter, J., Art of Measuring, 1769.
Warren Roofing Co.
Wilson, Builders' Price Book.
See Carpentry.

Building Assoc. Building Soc. Dalhousie, Canada, 1848. P. 520.
Franklin, W., Buil. Assoc. Examined, 1856.
Kenyon, R., Errors of, 1846.
Mutual Benefit Association.
Scratchley, Benefit B. Soci., 1851.
Soc. for Improved Dwellings of Poor, Gore, M.
South Kensington Museum, 1859.
See Mutual Aid.

Bulgaria. Keppel, Journey in, 1829.
Paton, Researches, 1862.
See Turkey.

Bulkley, M. Adams, E., Sermon on.

Bulkely, R. *See* French Prophets.

Bull, W. M. Rudd, Elegiac Essay.

Bullard, C. Wright, L., Fun. Sermon, 1806.

Bullions, A. Biog. of, 1858. P. 1856.

Bullions, P. Sprague, W. B., Sermon on.

Bulwer, E. Lytton. Westmacott, Letter to, 1833.

Bumsted, D. Pawson, J., Sermon on, 1797.

Bunbury, Sir H. Corresp. with Hanmer, 1838.

Bundling. Stiles, H. R., Origin of.

Bunker Hill battle. Bradford, A., Account of the battle, 1825.
Bunker Hill Mon. Assoc'n, Report, 1832; Warren Statue, 1857.
Clarke, J., Narrative of Battle, 1775.
Coffin, Bat. of Breed's Hill.
Dawson, H. B., On Israel Putnam.
Ellis, G. E., Oration on.
Emmons, C. P., Sketch of the bat. on, 1843.
Everett, E., Oration 75th Anniv., 1850.

Bunker Hill battle (continued).
Fellows, Notice of Swett's sketch of battle, 1843.
Frothingham, Battle of, 1849.
Humphreys' Putnam's Life, 1818.
Knickerbocker Mag., 1841, Sketch of.
Packard, Hist. of Monument, 1853.
Panoramic view from.
Putnam, Phalanx.
Swett, S., Hist. of, 1827.
Webster, D., Oration, 1825.
See Charlestown, Mass.

Bunsen, C. C. J. Life of, 1868.

Bunting, H. S. Memoir of, 1837.

Bunyan, J. Cheever, Lect. on Pilgrim's Progress, etc., 1845.
Ivimey, Life of.

Buonaparte. *See* Bonaparte; Napoleon.

Burdett, Sir F. Adam, W., Speech on.
Erskine, Opinion of.

Bure, G. De. Rive, Chasse aux Bibliog. 1788, 89.

Burges, T. Bowen, H. L., Memoirs of, 1835.

Burgess, T. & D. Family memorial, 1865.

Burgess, T. Lear, F., Sermon on.

Burghley, Lord. Nares, E., Memoirs of administration, 1828.

Burgoyne, J. Brief Examination, 1779.
Burgoyne, Gen. J., State of the Exped., 1780.
" Letter, 1779.
" Reply to letter, 1779.
" Letter on the exped., 1780.
" Speeches, 1778.
" Orderly Book, 1797. Munsell's Hist. Ser., 7.

Burk, J. D. Campbell, C., Life of.

Burke, E. Correspondence, 1744-97.
Bisset, R., Life of, 1800. B. C.
Leadbeter papers.
McCormick, C., Memoirs of, 1797.
Miles, W. A., On Letter of, 1796.
Pamphlets containing answers to, vol. 754.
Philo-Theodosius, Character of, 1770.
Priestley, Letters to, on France, 1791.
Prior, J., Life of, 1825, 54.
Second Thoughts on Letters to Bristol, 1777.

Burlesque. *See* Humor.

Burlington, Vt. First Cong. Church, Jubilee, 1867.
Ingersoll, G. G., Address 1st Cong. Soc., 1844.

Burlington Coll., N. J. Doane, G.W., Lecture on, 1848. P. 286.

Burmah. Griffith, W., Travels in, 1847.
Malcom, H., Travels in S.E. Asia, 1839.
Thévenot, Relations, v. 1.
See India; China; Asia (South).

Burnet, Bp. Braddon, L., Burnet's Hist. on Arthur, Earl of Essex, 1725.
Edwards, J., On an Exposition by, 1792.
Gregory, Preface to History (Swift), 1713. P. 340.
Higgons, Remarks on.

Burnet, Jacob. Fisher, S. W., Sermon on, 1853. P. 268.

Burney, C. Arblay, F. B. d', Mem. of, 1832.

Burnham family. Geneal., 1869.

Burnham, A. Noyes, D. J., Fun. disc.

Burnham, M. C. Tompkins, I., Sermon on.

Burns, A. Bowditch, Rendition of.
Stevens, C. E., History of, 1856.

Burns, R. Carlyle, T., Life of.
Chambers, R., Life of, 1851-2.
Cunningham, A., Life and land of, 1841.
Kingsley, C., Essays.

Burnside, A. Woodbury, A., Ninth army corps.

Burr, Rev. A. Livingston, W., Eulogium on, 1758.

Burr, A. Adams, J. Q., Report on J. Smith, associate, 1808.
Cheetham, Letters on his defection, 1803. P. vol. 17.
Clark, D., Proofs against Wilkinson, 1809.
Clinton, Letters of Marcus, 1810.
Daveis, President's conduct, 1807.
Davis, M. L., Memoirs of, 1836.
Examination of charges against. P. vol. 22.
Knapp, S. L., Life of, 1835.
Narrative of the suppression, 1802.
Parton, J., Life of, 1858.
Safford, W. H., Life of Blennerhassett, 1853.
" Blennerhassett papers.
Victor, Hist. of Am. conspiracies.
View of the pol. conduct of, 1802.
Wood, J., Full exposition, 1802.
See Law Library.

Burrillville, R. I. Keach, Description of.

Burritt, E. Thoughts and things, etc., 1854.

Burroughs, Stephen. Memoirs, 1798.

C.

California, Congressional Debates on (continued).
Benton, T. H., Speeches, 1849, 50.
Clarke, C., Speech on, 1850.
Hall, W. P., Speech on, 1850.
King, J. A., Speech, 1850.
McLane, R. M., Speech, 1850.
Morse, I. E., Speech, 1850.
Mullin, J., Speech, 1849.
Spaulding, Speech on, 1850.
Thurston, S. R., Speech, 1852.
Winthrop, R. C., Speech, 1850.
See Compromise Measures.

Calisthenics. *See* Gymnastics.

Calixtus, G. Dowding, Life of.

Calvados, France. Annuaire, 1839, 1840, 48.

Calvert, G. Kennedy, J. P., Discourse of the life of. P. 22.

Calvert, L. Burnap, Life of, (Sparks).

Calvin, J. Audin, Histoire de la vie de, 1843.
" History of the Life of. B. C.
Beza, T., Life of, 1836. B. C.
Burgess, S., Pol. Principles of.
Calvin, J., Letters.
Henry, P., Life of.
Merle d'Aubigné, Hist. de la Réformation of J. Calvin.
Waterman, Memoirs of, 1813. B. C.

Calvinism. Catton, Mercy and Reprobation.
Contrast between, 1824.
Contrast with Christianity and C.
Dialogue, 1786.
Dickinson, M., Inquiry, 1750.
Ely, Cal. and Hopkinsianism.
Emmons, E., Hopkinsian-Calvinism.
Gill, J., Cause of God.
Hill, R., Finishing Stroke, 1773.
Holcombe, Defence of, 1818.
Horsley, S., Polit. Principles of, 1790.
Hunter, J., Calvinism of Ch. of Eng., 1841. P. 327.
Huntington, J., Calvinism improved, 1796.
Knight, W. B.. Considerations on, 1822.
Nichols, J., C. and Arminianism.
Osgood, S., Three Letters.
Pearson, E., Remarks on.
Remarks on Two Particulars, 1811.
Reply to Academicus, 1803.
Rouquet, 17th Art. of C. of Eng.
Ryland, J., Writings.
Smith, D. D., False Testimony.

Cambaceres. Langon, Evenings with, 1837.

Cambodia. Mouhot, Travels in, 1859.

Cambrai. *See* Bibliography.

Cambridge, Mass. Adams, G., Directory, 1848.
Harris, T. W., Epitaphs from Burying Ground, 1845.
Holmes, A., History of. Mass. Hist. Soc. Coll.
Hoppin, Hist. Christ Church.
N. Eng. Hist. Register, July, 1871.
Newell, W., Hist. Discourse, 1846.
See Harvard University; Mt. Auburn.

Cambridge, Eng. Brown, J., Sixty Years' Gleanings, 1859.
Cambridge Univ. Hist., 1721.
Concise Descr., 1790.
Cooke's Topog. Lib.
Frend, W., Proceedings against him, 1893.
Fuller, T., History of, 1840.
Halliwell, The Rarities of, 1841.
Lekeux, Buildings of Univ. and Town, 1845.
New Cambridge guide, 1804. P. v. 1573.

Cambridge University, Eng. Beverly, Corrupt State of, 1833.
Browne, T., Exam. of Calumnies.
Cambridge University, 1790.
Cooper, Athenæ Cantabrigienses, 1500-1586.
Dyer, Hist. of the Univ., 1814.
" Academic Unity, 1827.
Everett, W., On the Cam, 1869.
Inquiry into the Right of Appeal, 1751.
Malden, King's College.
Miller, On Trinity College, 1710.
Opinion of an Em. Lawyer, 1751.
Remarks on the actual, 1830.
Remarks on the Enorm. Expense, 1788.
See Bibliography.

Cambridgeshire, Eng. Beauties of Eng. and Wales.
Cooke's Topog. Library.

Cambridgeport, Mass. Stearns, W. A., Sermons, 1852, '54.

Camden, Me. Chase's Hist. Disc., 1855.
Locke, J. S., History of, 1859.

Camden, N. J. Fisler, History of.

Camden and Amboy Railroad Co.
Reports and Pamphlets on.

Camel. Marsh, G. P., The Camel, 1850.
Savi, Della vescica, 1824.

Camoens, L. de. Adamson, Memoirs of.

Camp, H. W. Trumbull, H. C., Life of, 1865.

Campan, Mme. Maigne, Journal anecdotique de, 1825.

Campaigns. Gleig, Light Dragoon, 1852.
Guillemard, Adven. of a Fr. Sergeant, 1805-23.
See Battles; Sieges.

Campbell Family. House of Argyll.

Campbell, Alex. Jennings, O., Debate on, 1832.
Rice, N. L., Rise of Campellism.
Stiles, J. C., Letter to.

Campbell, Arch. Sprague, W. B., Sermon, Death of, 1856.

Campbell, D. Sprague, W. B., Sermon, Death of, 1851.

Campbell, G. Detection of the Dangerous, 1781.

Campbell, Sir J. Autobiography.

Campbell, J. N. Memorial of, 1864.

Campbell, J. W. Sketches of.

Campbell, Thos. Beattie, W., Life and Letters of, 1850.
Irving, W., Life of, 1841.

Campton, New Hamp. Centen. Celebration.

Canaan, Me. Hanson, History of, 1849.

Canada, History and Politics. Account of Proceedings at Quebec, 1775.
Anderson, D., Canada, Importance of, 1814.
Apology for Great Britain, 1809.
Barnard, D. D., Of the Caroline, 1841.
Barthe, Canada Reconquis, 1855.
Beauclerk, Mil. operations in, 1839.
Beyard, Actions of the French at Canada, 1693.
Bibaud, Hist. de, sous la France, 1837.
Brasseur de Bourbourg, Hist. du, 1852.
Brief von einem Herrn, 1795.
British American League, 1849.
Brooks, J., Speech, Reciprocity, 1850.
Brown, J. B., Views of, 1851.
Bury, Exod. of the Western Nations, 1864.
Canada, Various Public Documents, 1850-67.
Canadian Freeholder, 1777-79.
Cavendish, Parl. Debates, 1774.
Christie, Hist. of Lo. Canada, 1848-53.
Climax of Protection, 1836.
Consid. on the importance of, 1759.
Creuxius, Hist. Canadensis, lib. x, 1656.
Dessaulles, L'Annexion aux Etats Unis. 1851. P. 503.
Dreuillette, Recueil, 1648.
Drew, Colored Fugitives in, 1856.
Duane, W., Canada and Continental Congress, 1850. P. 504.

Canada, History and Politics (continued).
Dunkin, Discours, sur les droits des seigneurs, 1833.
" Address, of, Seignories, 1853.
Dussieux, C. sous la domination Française.
Ferland, Hist. du, 1534-1663.
Garneau, Histoire du Canada, 1845.
" History of, Bell, 1866.
Gaspé, P. A. De, The Canadians of old, 1865.
Gérin, Catéchisme politique, 1851.
Glenelg, Dispatches to Sir F. B. Head, 1839.
Great Britain: Canada, 1839. P. 1103.
Grèce, Facts respecting, 18 9.
Haliburton, Bubbles of Canada.
Heriot, History of Canada to 1804.
Hogan, J. S., Canada, An Essay, 1855.
Hough, Statist. of Population, 1857.
How I came to be Governor in, 1852.
Journal Expéd., du St. Laurent, 1759.
Journal of Education, 1848-69.
Justice and Policy of Parl't, 1774.
Kennedy, Sir J. S., Mil. defence of, 1865.
Kierzkowski, Seignorial tenure in, 1852.
La Potherie, Histoire du, 1722.
Laroche-Heron, Communautés Relig. des Femmes, 1855.
Le Clercq, Relation de la Gaspérie, 1691.
Le Moine, Maple Leaves. Three series.
Lescarbot, Hist. de la nouvelle, France, 1609.
Little, O., Trade in the Northern Colonies, 1748.
Lyon, C., Wright's Narrative, battle of Prescott, 1844.
Masères, Proceedings of Protestants in, 1775.
Morgan, H. J., Sketches of celeb. Canadians, 1862.
Narrative of Occurrences, 1817.
N. Y. Hist. Soc. Coll., ser. 2, vol. 3.
O'Callaghan, Relations des Jésuites, 1850.
Official Documents, war of 1759-60.
Pamphlets relating to Canada, vols. 12, 143, 503, 567, 1265, 1660-61.
Parkman, F., Pioneers of France in New World, 1865.
" Jesuits in North Am., 1867.
" Hist. of conspir. of Pontiac, 1851, 70.
Perrault, Abrégé de l'histoire de, 1833-1843.
Political and Hist. account of, 1830.
Present State of, 1787.
Rameau, La France aux Colonies, 1859.

Canada, History and Politics (continued).
Relations des Jésuites, 1611-72.
Relations, 1696–1702.
Review of Leg. proceed., 1831.
Roebuck, J. A., Existing difficulties in, 1836. P. 12.
Roy, Hist. of, for schools, 1850.
Roger, C., Rise of.... to Wealth, 1856.
Russell, W. H., Defences of.
Sagard, Histoire du C., 1615.
St. Alban's Raid, 1864.
St. Valier, Estat de l'église de la Nouvelle France, 1688.
Scrope's life of Lord Sydenham, 1844.
Sewell, J., Jurid. hist. of France in Canada, 1824.
Short, Gesta Americana.
Siege of Quebec, 1759.
Sillèry, Etudes Biog. sur, 1855. P. 254.
Smith, W., Hist. to 1791.
Smyth, Wars in, 1755–1814.
Soc. litt. et hist. de Quebec, 1838–43.
Stone, E. M., Invasion of, in 1775.
Taché, J. C., Esquisse (économiste) sur le Canada, 1855.
Thévet, La France antarctique, 1558.
Urquhart, Case of M'Leod, 1841.
Walker, Sir H., Late exp. to Canada, 1720.
Warburton, Conquest of Canada, 1850.
See Jesuit Missions; North America; British Colonies; Nova Scotia; United States.

Canada, Travels in. Albert, Prince, Tour, 1860.
Beavan, Visit to Indian missions, 1846.
Bigsby, The Shoe and the Canoe, 1850.
Bonnycastle, Canada in 1846.
Bouchette, Brit. Dom. in N. Am., 1832.
" Descr. of Lower and Upper, 1815.
Buckingham, Travels in, 1843.
Canada: Crown Lands Commr's Maps, 1857.
Canada and the Colonists, 1844.
Canada in 1849.
Canadian Guide Book, 1849.
Canadian Tourist, 1856.
Carroll, C., Visit to, 1776.
Cartier, Voyages, 1534–35.
Champlain, Voy. de la Nouvelle France, 1632.
" Œuvres, 6 v., 1869.
Charlevoix, Voy. to North Am., 1761.
Crespel, Voyage dans le Canada, 1742.
De Veaux, Traveler's own book, 1843.
Dièreville, Voyage de l'Acadie, 1710.
Duncan, J. M., Travels in, 1818.
Everett, Journey through, 1855.

Canada, Travels in (continued).
Excursion through, 1823.
Ferguson, Tour in Canada, 1834.
Foster, V., Guide to Emigrants.
Finan, Voyage to Quebec, and war of 1812, 13.
Galt, J., The Canadas, 1836.
Gray, H., Letters from Canada, 1806.
Griffin, C., Letter on his miss'y labors, 1828. P. 143.
Hall, F., Travels in Canada and the U. S., 1818.
Harmon, Voyage, 1820.
Head, Sir F. B., The Emigrant, 1847.
" A Narrative, 1839.
Henry, A., Travels in, and the Indian territories, 1760-76.
Heriot, G., Travels through the Canadas, 1807.
Howison, Sketches of Upper Canada, 1822.
Hunter, W. S., Ottawa Scenery, 1855.
" East. Townships Scen., 1860.
Hutton, W. Guide to, 1853.
Jameson, Mrs., Rambles in, 1839.
Johnston, J. F. W., Notes on North America, 1851.
Kingston, W. H. G., Western Wanderings, 1856.
Lambert, J., Travels through, and the U. S., 1806-8.
Landmann, Adventures of, 1852.
Lanman, Tour to the Saguenay, 1848.
Le Beau, Avantures; descr. du Canada, 1738.
Lillie, Canada, Physical, etc., 1855.
Mackay, C., Life in America, 1857–8.
Mackay, Stranger's Guide to, 1854.
Mackenzie, E., Descr View of, 1819.
Mackenzie, W. L., Sketches of, 1833.
Mactaggart, Three Years in Canada, 1826-28.
Magrath, Letters from Upper Canada, 1833.
Marryatt, Settlers in Canada.
Martin, R. M., Brit. Col. Lib., V. 1.
Milton, Viscount, N. W. Passage by land, 1865.
Monts, De, Descr. of New France, 1604.
Moodie, Mrs., Roughing it in the Bush, 1852.
Morris, A., Can. and Resources, 1855.
Murray, A., Letters from, 1856.
Notes upon Canada, 1832–40.
Oliphant, Minnesota and, 1855.
Preston, T. R., Residence in, 1837-39.
Prevost, Gen., Public Life in the Canadas, 1823.
Richardson, Major, Eight Years in, 1847.

Canada, Travels in (continued).
Russell, Red River Country, 1869.
Ryerson, Missionary Tour, 1855.
Sagard, Voyage du Pays des Hurons, 1630.
Sansom, J., Sketches of Lower Canada, 1817.
Sarrasin, M., Notes sur., 1856. P. 254.
Selkirk, Red River Settlement, 1817.
Sketches for Settling, 1822.
Sleigh, Pine Forests, etc., 1853.
Smyth, D. W., Top. descr. of Upper Canada, 1799.
Smith, M., Description of 1813.
Stoddard, Expedition to, 1851.
Strachan, J., Visit to Upper Canada, 1820.
Talbot, E. A., Five Years Residence in, 1824.
Taylor, H., Journal of a Tour, 1840.
Theller, Canada in 1837.
Tunis, Guide, 1859.
Viaggio di un Livornese, 1827.
Weld, J., Travels through, 1855.
See Geology.

Canada: Registers and Statistics. Boucher, P., Productions de la nouvelle France, 1663.
Bouchette, Dict. of Lower C., 1832.
Buchanan, Industry of, 1864.
Canada Census, 1851, 1861.
Canada Directory, 1811, 1837, 57.
Canada Dominion Directory, Lovell, 1871.
Canada Year Book, 1867.
Canadian Almanac, 1855.
Caroline Almanac, 1840.
Dunlop, W., Statist. Sketches of Upper, 1832.
Exposition de 1855, Paris.
Gazetteer of Upper C., 1813.
Gourlay, Statist. acct. of Upper Canada, 1822.
Le Brun, T., Statis. des Canadas, 1835.
Liste des Evèques, 1834.
M'Gregor, British America, 1832.
Pamphlets on Canada Emigration, vol. 1265.
Smith, D. W., Gazetteer, 1813.
Smith, W. H., Canadian Gazetteer, 1846.
Stewart, C., Eastern Townships, 1815.
Sussex Emigrants, 1833.
Traill, Backwoods of.
See Montreal; Quebec; Toronto.

Canals. Armroyd, Internal Navig. of the U. S., 1830.
Barlow on the Strain of Lock-Gates.
Belgium, Canal Navigation, 1834-39.

Canals (continued).
Belly, Percement de Panama, 1858.
Canada, Public Works, Reports on, 1851-65.
Canada, St. Lawrence Navigation, 1856.
Carey, M., Brief view of System of Penn'a, 1831.
Chapman, W., On Canal Navigation, 1797.
Chesapeake and Del. Co. Reports, 1853, 55.
Clinton, Hampshire Canal, Mass., 1828.
Davis, C. H., Iuteroceanic C., 1867.
Dearborn, H. A. S., Internal Improvements West, 1839.
Dehay, Canal des Pyrénées, 1834.
Delaware and Raritan, N. J., Report, 1831, 56-58.
Doin, Canal à la Garonne, 1835.
Fox and Wisconsin Imp. Co., 1856.
Frisi, On Rivers and Torrents, 1818, 61.
Fulton, R., Canal Navigation, 1796.
Gallatin, Report on Roads and Canals, 1808.
Genet, Address on Rivers and Canals, 1825.
Georgian Bay Canal.
History of Canals, 1779.
Hist. of Canal Navigation in Penn'a, 1795.
History of Bridgewater's canal.
Illinois and Michigan, 1847.
Indiana Canal Co., 1856. P. 953.
Iowa, Report on Des Moines R.
Keefer, The Canals of Canada, 1850.
Kennebec Locks Co., Me., Rep., 1837.
Lachine Canal, Docks, 1854.
Lesseps, De l'isthme de Suez.
Letter to the Proprietors, 1785, Lond.
Maryland, Report, 1825.
Massachusetts, Canals from Boston to Conn. River, 1826.
Memorial, Welland and Oswego, 1845.
Molineau, Jonction du Danube au Rhin, 1836.
New Jersey, Reports on, 1824, 56, 57.
Ohio, Documents, 1828, 48.
Pamphlets on Canals, vols. 145, 223, 477, 953, 1825, 1859.
Penn'a, Reports, 1854.
Pennsylvania Soc., Report, 1826.
Phillips, C., Hist. of Inland navigation, 1803.
Philpotts, Canal nav. in Canada.
Priestley, Hist. of Canals of G. B., 1831.
St. Mary's Falls Ship Canal Co., 1858.
Sandy and Beaver Co., 1835.
Schuylkill Nav. Comp. Report, 1840, 54, 56.

Caricatures. Album pour rire.
B., H., Political Sketches, 1830-38.
Gillray, J., Works.
Grose, Rules for Drawing.
Hogarth's Prints.
Spain Vindicated.
Wright, T., Account of Gillray's Works, 1851.
" Hist. of Caric. under House of Hanover, 1848.

Carleton, Sir Dudley. Letters, 1615-20.

Carlile, Rich. Marriott, J., On his Trial, 1819.

Carlyle, A. Autobiography, 1861.

Carlyle, T. Blackwood *v.* Carlyle, 1850.
Brimley, Essays, 1868.

Carmichael, Dr. Gordon, W. B., Rebuke of.

Carnahan, J. Macdonald, Serm. on.

Caro, Annibale. Lettere.

Caroline, Queen. Character of.
Diary, with original Letters of, 1838, 1839.
Gadsby, W., Serm., of Marriage, 1820.
Guernsey, Countess of, Confessions.
Horne, M., Crisis of England, 1820.
Huish, Life of.
Reply of the People, 1821.
Wilks, J., Memoirs of, 1822.

Caroline Matilda, of Denmark. Keith's Memoirs.

Caron, R. E. Draper, W. H. Correspondence with, 1846. P. 503.

Carpentry. Builders' Dictionary, 1734.
Bury, Modêles de, 1855.
Nicholson, P., Carpenters' Ass't, 1815.
" " New Guide, 1818.
Tredgold's Carpentry, 1837.
See Architecture; Arts; Building.

Carr, Sir J. My Pocket Book.

Carriages. Adams, W. B., English Pleasure Carriages, 1837.
Cook's Catalogue, N. Haven.

Carrickfergus, Ireland. M'Skimin, Hist. of, 1811.

Carroll, C. Sergeant, J., Eulogy on, 1832. P. 268.

Carroll, J. Brent, J. C., Biog. Sketch of, 1843.

Carson, Mrs. A. History of, 1822.

Carson, C. Peters, Adventures of, 1858.

Carson, J. Revealer of Grievances, 1811.

Carter, Mrs. E. Letters to Mrs. Montague, 1755-1800.
" Poems and Life.
Pennington, Memoirs of.

Carthage. Perry, A., Carthage and Tunis, 1869.

Carthagena. Journal of the Expedition to, 1744. P. 131.
Account of Expedition, 1743.
New Granada Canal Co., 1855.

Cartier, J. Voyages au Canada, 1534-6.

Cartwright, Edmund. Life of.

Cartwright, John. Cartwright, F. D., Life of, 1826.

Cartwright, Rev. P. Autobiography, 1856.

Carver, Capt. J. Centenary, 1867.

Cary, H. F. Cary, H., Memoirs, 1847.

Cary, Lott. Gurley, R. R., Life of, 1839.

Cary, R., Earl of Monmouth. Mem., 1808.
Allestree, Sermon, Defeat of, 1685.
Interest of the Three Kingdoms, 1680.

Cary, T. Andrews, G., Sermon on, 1808.

Casault, L. J. Larue, Eloge de.

Case, I. Thurston, D., Sermon on.

Cashmere. Hügel, Travels in.
See Himalaya Mts.

Caslo, A. Life of, 1846.

Caspian Sea. Holmes, W. B., Sketches of, 1845.
Hanway, J., Acct. of Caspian trade, 1753.
Hommaire de Hell, Travels.

Cass, L. Jarvis, R., Facts and Arguments, 1848.
Schoolcraft, H. R., Outlines of the life of, 1848.
Smith, W. L. G., Life of, 1856.
Young, W. T., Sketch of, 1852.

Cassano, Duke of. Dibdin, Bib. Spenceriana, vol. 7.

Caste. Bowers, Prize essay on Hindu caste.
Muller, Chips from a German, 1867.
Small, Mythol. and castes.
Tappan, L., Letters on.

Castle, A. L. Armstrong, R., Sermon on, 1841.

Castleman, M. A. M'Chord, Serm. on.

Castlereagh, Mar. of Londonderry. Letters.

Castorland, N. Y. Stephens, W. H., Notes, 1868.

Castriot, G. Moore, C. C., Life of, 1850.

Casuistry. Casus Conscientiæ, 1749.

Catalogues of Academies. *See* Academies.

Caxton, W. Dibdin, Bibl. Spencer, v. 4.
" Typ. Antiq., v. 1.
Knight, Biography of Caxton, 1844.
Lewis, Life of, 1737.
Library U. K., Life of.
See Bibliography; Typography.

Cayenne. Aimè, Déportation to Cayenne, 1800.
Biet, Voyage en l'Isle de Cayenne, 1652.
Chautard, Escape from, 1857.
Pitou, Voyage á, 1807.
Préfontaine, Maison Rustique de, 1763.
Vignal, Coup-d'œil sur, 1822.
See Guyana.

Cayuga Co., N. Y. Directory, 1868.

Celibacy. Lea, H. C., Hist. of Sacerdotal Celibacy.

Cecil, Sir R. Correspon. (Camden Soc).

Cecil, Sir W., Lord Burghley. Peck's Desiderata curiosa.

Cellini, B. Memoirs, 1823.

Celtic Nations. Betham, Etruscan & Iberno-Celtic languages.
Holtzmann, Kelten und Germanen.
Logan, Scottish Gael, 1833.
Prichard, Eastern origin of.
Ritson, Celts or Gauls, 1827.
Toland, Hist. of Celtic Religion.
See Druids; Language; Ethnology.

Cements. Davy, On artific. foundations, 1839.
Dobson, Foundations and concrete, 1850.
Higgins, Art of composing, 1780.
Pasley, Observ. on, 1838.
Sandusky Manufac. Comp. P. 298.
Simms, F. W., Mastic of Seyssel, 1838.
Totten, On hydr. and common mortars.
Vicat, Treatise on mortars, 1837.
Wright's treatise, 1845.

Cemeteries. Albany Rural Cemet. Association, Rules, 1846.
Alden, T., Coll. of Amer. epitaphs, 1814.
Barnard, D. D., Address.
Bigelow, J., Hist. Mt. Auburn, 1860.
Bliss, G., Hist. of Springfield Cem.
Boston Rural Cemetery, 1850. P. 237.
Bridgman, T., Inscriptions at Northampton, etc., 1850.
Camden, Remaines, 1637.
Clark, B., Kensal Green Cem.
Clinton, N. Y., Addresses, 1857. P.478.
Cochet, La Normandie Souterraine, 1854.
Congdon, Address, Oak Grove.
Dale Ceme. Rules.

Cemeteries (continued).
Erie Ceme. Rules.
Forest Hills, Roxbury, Reports, 1850–1856.
Forest Lawn, Buffalo, 1856. P. 478.
Godwin, W., Essay on Supulchres, 1809.
Gosden, Churchyard Monuments. MS.
Graceland Ceme. Rules
Great Britain: Ceme., 1850. P. 478.
Green Lawn Ceme.
Green Mount, Baltimore, Rep., 1848.
Greenwood illustrated, 1848.
Greenwood Cemetery, 1850.
Hints on interments, Phila.
Kinnersley, Sepulchral curiosi., 1823.
Laurel Grove Ceme.
Laurel Hill Ceme., 1854.
London Necropolis, 1849.
MacDonald, A. J., Monuments and gravestones, 1848. Muns. P. 9.
Madden, Shrines and Sepulchres.
Maliphant, Monuments.
Malone, N. Y., Cemetery.
Mayo, A. D., American Ceme., Disc., 1858.
Memoirs of the dead, 1806.
Mount Auburn illustrated, 1848.
" Catalogue, 1857.
Mount Vernon, Abingdon, Report, 1853.
Muret, Rites of Funeral, 1683.
Oakwood, Syracuse, 1860.
Pamphlets on, vols. 478, 955, 1662.
Parr, S., Works, vol. 4, Inscript., 1828.
Peabody, W. B. O., Address.
Pine Grove Ceme.
Pittsfield, Mass., 1850.
Poughkeepsie Ceme.
Putnam, Add., Forest Hill Cemetery, 1848.
River-side Cem., Gouverneur, N. Y., Rules, 1858.
Rome, N. Y., Ceme.
Roxbury, Report on, 1847, 56.
Sargent, Dealings with the dead, 1856.
Savage, Memorabilia.
Spring Grove Cemetery.
Stearns, J. F., Address.
Story, J., Address, Mount Auburn.
Troy Cemetery.
Walker, H. D., Address, Mount Vernon, 1853.
Weaver, Anc. Fun. Monuments.
Woodlawn Cemetery, Chelsea, 1856.
See Antiquities; Monuments; Epitaphs.

Cenci, B. Whiteside's Italy.
Notes and Queries, Jan. 1853.

Censuses. *See* Statistics; Population.

Central America. Baily, J., Central America, 1850.
Byam, Wild Life in, 1849.
Cassani, Historia de Granada, 1741.
Catherwood's Views in Central Amer., 1841.
Clayton Convention, 1850.
Cockburn's Journey from Honduras, 1735.
Coup-d œil sur. P. 1001.
Crowe, Gospel in.
Cullen, Darien Canal.
Davis, A., Antiquities of, 1841. P. 77.
Douglas, S. A., Speech on Treaty, 1853.
Dunn, H., Guatemala, 1828.
Edwards, B., Hist. West Indies, vol. 4, 1806.
Gallatin, Indians of Central America.
Geog. (Royal) Soc. Jour.. vols. 3, 5, 11, 14, 15, 23.
Gisborne, The Isthmus in 1852.
Greytown, Bombardment of, 1854.
Hale, J., Six Month's Residence in, 1826.
Henderson, Account of Brit. Honduras, 1811.
Hodgson, Account of Mosquito Territory, 1822.
Hughes, G. W., Intermarine Communication, 1850. P. 103.
Juarros, Hist de la Cuidad de, 1808–18.
" Statist. and Comm. Hist. of, 1823.
La Bastide, Passage de la Mer du Nord à la Mer du Sud, 1791.
Mémoire Statistique sur, 1840.
Mexico and Guatemala, 1825.
Molina, Costa Rica and N. Granada, 1853.
Mosquito Kingdom.
Oviedo, Histoire du Nicaragua.
Pamphlets relating to, vol. 1266.
Pitman, Of a Ship Canal, 1825.
Poyais, Const. de la Nation, 1825.
Proposed Oceanic Commun. P. 258.
Rio, Ruins near Palenque, 1822.
Roberts, O. W., Narrative of Voyage, 1827.
Sampson, M. B., Cent. America, 1850.
Sealsfield, Scenes in, 1852.
Seward, W. H., Speech, 1856.
Squier, E. G., The States of, 1858.
" Authors on, 1861.
" Mosquito Quest. Whig Rev., Feb., Mar., Nov., 1850.
" Nicaragua, and Interoceanic Canal, 1852.
" Notes on Cent. Amer., 1855.
" Dem. Review, Nov., Dec., 1852.
Stephens, John L., Incidents of Trav. in, 1841.

Central America (continued).
Strangeways, Sketch of Musquito shore, 1822.
Tempsky, Journey, 1853–5.
Thompson, G. A., Official visit to Guatemala, 1829.
Tomes, Panama in 1855.
Trautwine, Interoceanic Canal, 1854.
U. S. Cong. Docts., 1855, Mason's Report on Ruatan.
United States, Documents, 1854.
Velasquez, Mem. of an Expedition, 1850.
Villagutierre, Conquista de el Itza, 1701.
Wafer's Voy. to Isth. of Darien, 1699.
Waikna, or Adven. in Musquito, 1855.
Wells, W. V., Cent. Am. War, 1855.
" History of, 1857.
Young, T., Musquito shore, 1839–41.
See Guatemala; Honduras; Greytown; Nicaragua; New Granada.

Central America Steamer. Mayo, A. D., A Discourse, 1857.
Rogers, E. P., Discourse, 1857.

Century Club. Constit. N. Y., 1858, 71.
Gourlie, J. H., Origin of, 1856. P. 253.
See Verplanck, G. C.

Ceremonies, Religious. Cérémonies Religieuses, Picard, 1783.
Rom. Cath. Church, Man. of Ceremonies.

Certosa. Visita alla Certosa, 1836.

Ceylon. Baker, S.W., Rifle and Hound in.
" Eight Years' Wanderings.
Baldæus, Description of, 1670.
Colombo Bible Society.
Farrington, Speech on, 1851.
Forbes, Maj., Eleven Years in Ceylon, 1841.
Hoffmeister, Travels in, and Continental India, 1848.
Marshall, H., Description and History, 1846.
Pridham, C., Hist. and Polit. account of, 1849.
Tennent, Account of, 1859.
Upham, E., Sacred and Hist. Books of Ceylon.
See India; Voyages, India.

Chaldæa. Loftus, Researches in, 1849.
Rawlinson, Hist. of five Monarchies, 1862–67.
See Mesopotamia.

Chalmers, T. Life of, Cummings.
" Correspondence.
Edwards, B. B., Discourse on.
Hanna, W., Memoirs of, 1850–52.
Sprague, W. B., Discourse on, 1847.

Chase, Bp. P. Reminiscences, 1st and 2d ed.
Norton, J. N., Life of.

Chase, S. Mattison, H., Sermon, death of, 1843. P. 554.

Chase, S. P. Stowe's men of the time, 1868.

Chastellux, Marq. De. Remarks on travels of, 1787.

Chastity. Cobden, Sermon, 1749.

Chateaubriand, F. R. de. Mémoires d'outre tombe, 1849–50.

Chateaugay, N. Y. *See* Adirondack.

Chatterton, T. Maitland, Essay on.

Chaucer, G. Canterbury Tales (Percy Soc).
Godwin, W., Life of, 1803.
Saunders, Tales from.

Chauncey, C. Boardman, Discourse on.

Chaunceys, The. Fowler, Memorials of, 1858.

Chauncy, J. *See* Drake's Hist. of Boston.

Chautauqua Co., N. Y. Foote, E. T., Early Mail routes.
Warren, E. F., History of, 1846.

Checkley family pedigree.

Cheever, E. Barnard, H., Biog. of, 1856.

Cheever, G. B. Deacon Giles' Distillery.
Church of the Puritans.

Chelsea, Ms. Boston Directory, 1869.
Langworthy, Farewell Discourse.

Cheltenham, Eng. Guide, 1834.
Davies, H., Guide, 1834.

Chemistry. Abel, Manual of, 1857.
Accum, Essay on Chemical re-agents, 1817.
Albineus, Bibliotheca, 1653.
Anderson, T., Agric. Chemistry.
Beck, L. C., Manual of, 1831.
Bergman, Usefulness of, 1783.
Berthollet, Laws of Chem. affinity.
Berzelius, Inorganic Bodies, 1833.
" Of the Blow-pipe, 1845.
Blair, D., Grammar of, 1827.
Boerhave, Elementa Chemiæ.
Bolley, Technical Analysis, 1857.
Booth, J. C., Improvements in the Chemical Arts, 1851.
" Encyclop. of Chemistry, 1850.
Bowman, J. E., Introd. to Pract. Chemistry, 1849.
" Med. Chemistry, 1850.
Boyle, R., Works, v. 1.
Brande, W. T., 10 Lec. on Organic Chem.
" Arts of organic Chemistry.

Chemistry (continued).
Brande, W. T., Prog. of Chemical Philosophy, 1829.
Brard, Dictionnaire, 1855.
Cahours, Chimie Générale, 1860.
Chandler, Misc. Researches, 1857.
Columbian Chem. Soc., Phil'a, Memoirs, 1813.
Conversations on Chymistry, 1806. B. C.
Cooke, J. P., Chemical Physics, 1860.
Croockewit, Specimen Chemicum, 1848.
Daniel, J. F., Chemistry.
Daubeny, Inaugural Address, 1823.
Davy, Sir H., Works, v. 2, 3, etc.
" Elem. of Chem. philosophy, 1812.
Donovan, Treatise on Chemistry.
Draper, J. W., Introd. Lectures, 1841.
" Text-book in, 1846.
Dumas, La Chimie appli. aux arts, 1828-46.
Eaton, A., Chemical Instructor, 1822.
" Agric. Chem., 1847.
Ewell, T., Plain Dicourses, 1806.
Faraday, Non-metallic Elements.
" Chemical Manipulation, 1831.
Forsten, De æthere et naphthis, 1832.
Fownes, Elementary Chemistry, 1847.
Fresenius, Quantitativen Chem. Analy.
Fuchs, Einfluss der Chemie, 1824.
Gerhardt, Traité de Chimie organique. 1853, 54.
Gibbs, Ammonia Cobalt Bases.
Gmelin, Handbook of Chemistry, 1848–66.
Gorup Besanez, Zoöchemischen analyse.
Gregory, W., Organic Chemistry, 1852.
Griffiths, Agric. of the 4 Seasons, 1853.
Hare, R., Course of Instruc. on, 1824.
" Organic Chem.
" Animal Chem.
" On the Explosiveness of Nitre.
Henry, W., Epit. of Exper. Chemistry, 1810.
Hoefer, Hist. de la Chimie, 1842.
Horsford, E. N., Publications, 1846-48.
Horsley, Cat. of Chym. Philosophy.
Jahres-Bericht, (Wagner), 1861.
Johnston, J. F. W., Report on Progress of, 1832.
" Agricultural Chemistry.
Kane, R., Elements of Chemistry, 1841.
Kirwan, R., Essay on Phlogiston, 1787.
Knapp, F., Chemical Technology, 1848-1851.
Kopp, Geschichte der Chem., 1847.
Laurent, Méthode de Chimie, 1854.
Lavoisier, Oeuvres, 1862-68.
" Mémoires, 1862.

Chemistry (continued).
Le Docte, Mémoire sur la Chimie, 1849.
Lehmann, Zoöchemie, 1858.
" Physiol. Chemistry, 1856.
Liebig, Agricul. Chemistry.
" Organic Chemistry, 1831.
" Familiar letters on, 1851.
" Organic Analysis.
Lindauer, Der Hütten-chemie.
Mac Neven, W. J., Atomic Theory of Chemistry, 1819. P. 1004.
Macquer, Elements of, 1775.
Malaguti, Chimie agricole.
Miller, W. A., Elements of Chemistry, 1855, 67.
Nava, Caglio Vitellino, 1857.
Nesbit, Agricul. chem.
Noad, Lectures on, 1843.
" Chemical Manipulation, 1852.
Normandy, Commercial Hand-book of chem. anal., 1850.
Orfila, Pract. Chemistry, 1818.
Pamphlets on, v. 1500. B. C. v. 34.
Parkes, S., Chymical Catechism, 1807.
" Chemical catechism, 1821.
Parnell, Applied Chemistry, 1844.
Payen, Précis de la chimie industrielle, 1851.
Pearson, G., Papers.
Pélouze, Traité Générale, 1865.
" General notions of chemistry, 1854.
Pettenkofer, Die Chemie und Physiologie, 1848.
Phillips, R., Lectures, 1822, 31.
Porter, J. A., First Book of, 1857.
Rammelsberg, Krystallographischen Chemie, 1855.
Regnault, Elements of, 1856.
Regodt, Applic. aux usages de la vie, 1858.
Renwick, J., Application to arts, 1851.
Rèpertoire de chimie appliquée, 1858–1860.
Répertoire de chimie pure, 1858–60.
Richter, R., Leitfaden......analyt. Chemie, 1853.
Rochleder, Chem. der Pflanzen.
Roscoe, H. E., Lessons in elem. C., 1868.
Rose, H., Chemical Analysis, 1848, 49.
Scoffern, Elem. Chemistry, 1854.
Silliman, Elements of, 1830.
Silliman, B., jr., First principles of, 1847. B C.
Smith, T. P., Revolutions in, 1748.
Solly, E., Rural Chemistry, 1852.
Stammer, Chem. Rechenaufgaben, 1855.
Stockhardt, Principles of, 1850.

Chemistry (continued).
Stockhardt, Chem. of Agric., 1855.
Thomson, R. D., Dictionary of, 1850.
Thomson, T., System of, 1802.
" History of, 1830.
Topham, Chem....for agriculturists.
Turner, E., Elements of, 1835.
Ure, Dictionary of, 1824.
" Spurious Chemistry, 1843. P. 79.
Valerius, Fabrication de la fonte, 1851.
Vogel, Laboratorium Muenchen, 1851.
" Der Vegetation, 1852.
Watson, R., Chemical essays, 1784-87.
Watts, H., Dictionary of, 1866-69.
Will, H., Chemical analysis, 1855.
Woehler, Anal. Chem. Assistant, 1852.
Wolff, Chem. Untersuchung, 1857.
Youmans, Class-book of, 1852.
See Natural Philosophy; Agriculture; Dyeing: Photography, etc.

Chemung Co., N. Y. Directory, 1868-9.

Chemung Valley, N. Y. Cheney, Hist. Sketch of.

Chenango Co., N. Y. Directory, 1869.
Clark, H. C., History of, 1850.

Cherokees. Bell, J., Report, 1840.
Bowles, W. A., Authen. memoirs, 1791.
Relations....with U. S. Government, 1830. P. 75.
See Indians.

Chesapeake, Ship. Brighton, Adm. Broke's Life.
Lawrence, Capt. James, Funeral of.

Chester Co., Pa. Darlington, Flora Cestrica, 1826.

Cherry Valley, N. Y. Campbell, W. W., Centen. celeb., 1840.
Hosmer, P. H., Kate Clayton, 1855.

Cheshire, Eng. Directory (Pigott), 1829.
Barlow, T. W., Lit. Illustrations and Biog. Sketches, 1855.
Beauties of Eng. and Wales.
Cooke's Typog. Library.
Holland, View of Agric. of, 1808.

Chess. Carrera, Treatise on, 1822.
Chess Monthly, 1857.
Game of Chess, (Caxton), 1474.
Hoyle's Chess.
Morphy, Exploits in Europe, 1859.
" Games of, 1860.
Philidor, Studies of.
Philidorian, The, 1838.
Staunton, Chess Tournament, 1852.
" Chess-player's Companion.
" Chess-player's Hand-book, 1847.
Trübner, Bibliot. Scaccariana

China (continued).
Huc, Journey through China, 1855.
Hunt's Library, Commerce of.
Ides, Travels in, 1706.
Kircher, A., Tooneel van China, 1668.
Lay, The Chinese as they are, 1843. Muns. P. 7.
Livres Classiques, 1784-86.
Ljungstedt, Portuguese Settlement in, 1836.
Macfarlane, Chin. Revolution, 1853.
Mackenzie, K. S., Second Campaign in, 1842.
Majoribanks, Intercourse with, 1833.
Martinius, Atlas Sinensis, 1655.
Medhurst, China, its state and prospects, 1838.
" Interior of, 1850.
Mendoza, Hist. of, 1853, 54.
Murray, H., Hist. and descr. of.
Nieuhoff, Description of, 1673.
Olearius, Travels, 1633-39.
Oliphant, Elgin's Mission, 1860.
Oriental, Newspaper, 1855.
Orléans, P. J. d', Two Tartar Conquerors of, 1854.
Pamphlets on China, vol. 1234.
Perry, Narr. of Expedition, 1852-54.
Picturesque representations, (Alexander), 1814.
Pumpelly, Across America, 1870.
Reinaud, Voyages des Arabes, 9e siécle.
Renaudot, Travels of two Mohammedans.
Ripa, Memoirs at the Court.
Rubruquis, Voyage, 1253.
Shuck, G. L., Chinese State papers, 1840.
Sketches by a Trav., 1830.
Smith, G., Visit to the Consular Cities, 1844-46.
Staunton, Sir G., Brit. Embassy to, 1798.
Staunton, British Relations with, 1836.
Tiffany, O., The Canton Chinese, 1849.
Timkowski, Travels through Mongolia, 1827.
U. S., Chinese Correspondence, 1860.
Waln, R., View of, 1823.
White, C. A., Student's Mythol.
Williams, H. D., Year in C., 1864.
Williams, S. W., The Middle Kingdom, 1848.
Williamson's Journeys in North China, 1870.
See Asia, Southern.

hinese Language. *See* Language.

hipman, N. Chipman, Life of, 1846.

hippewa. Treat, Vindication of Conduct in Battle of, 1815.

Chirography. *See* Writing.

Chisholm, The. Clark, A., Sermon on.

Chittenden, D. Chipman, Memoir of.

Chivalry. Beltz, Order of the Garter.
Digby, K. H., Broad Stone of Honor.
James, G. P. R., History of, 1832.
Maffei, Della Scienza Cavalleresca.
Michelet, Procès des Templiers.
Mills, C., History of, 1826.
St. Palaye, Memoirs of Ancient Chiv.
Scott, W., Essay on.
See Crusaders; Knights.

Chloroform. *See* Etherization.

Choate, R. Works and Memoir.
Parker, E. G., Reminiscences of, 1860.
Parsons, T., Address on, 1859.

Cholera. Acad. de Médecine, Rapport sur, 1831.
Adamson, J., Cure of, 1851.
Alfriend, Cholera infantum.
Allen, T., Treatment of, 1848.
Asbury, Treatise on, 1833.
Asiatic Cholera, 1848.
Ayre, J., Letter on, 1854.
" Treatment of, 1859.
Batchelder, J. P., Causes, etc., 1849.
Beck, L. C., Report on, 1832.
Becker, Chol. in Russia, 1832.
Boddy, Diet and Cholera, 1848.
Boston, Health Comm., Report on, 1849.
Broussais, Clinical Lectures, 1832.
Bryson, Origin of, 1851.
Bureaud-Riofrey, Du Choléra, 1847.
Caspar, De Verhandeling der, 1832.
Clanny, Chol. at Sunderland, 1832.
Coventry, C. B., Hist. and Treatment, 1849.
Dubrueil, Choléra dans le midi de la France, 1835.
Etienne, Mémoire sur le Choléra, 1835.
France, Report on, in Paris, 1849.
Gazette Médicale de Paris, 1852.
Gérardin, Choléra en Russie, etc., 1831.
Granville, A. B., Catechism.
Gr. Br., Reports on, 1831, '50, '56.
Hamilton, F. H., Vegetable Malaria, 1852. P. 271.
Hawthorne, G. S., Pathol. Nature of, 1845. P. 405.
Heidler, Die Epidemische Cholera, 1848.
Joslin, Homœop. Treatment of.
Kingsley, C., Four Sermons.
Kirk, J. B., Observations on, 1832.
Knapp, M. L., Cure of, 1855.
McLoughlin, Premon. Diarrhœa, 1854.

Christ, Divinity of (continued).
Edwards, J., Exposition of Bp. Burnet, 1792.
Hind, T., Sermon, John i, 14, 1717.
Horne, G., Christ God, a Sermon, 1775.
Hughes, T. S., St. Paul's Doct., 1828.
Ibbetson, Sermon, 1 Tim. iii. 16, 1712.
Kennicott, Sermon, Immanuel, 1765.
Lardner, Of the Logos, 1759.
Law, E., A defence of, 1816.
MacWhorter, Yahveh Christ, 1857.
Mitchel, J., Sermons on, 1830.
Moore, J., Defence of, 1721.
Peck, F., Four discourses.
Pitkin, J. B., Two natures of.
Priestley, Early opinions respecting, 1786. B. C.
Riedel, Diss. theologica, 1852.
Robinson, R., Plea for, 1776.
Rogers, J. M., Discourse on, 1814.
Sharp, G., Divine dignity of, 1806.
Smith, T., On 1 Tim. 3:16.
Stephens, W., Sermon of, 1722.
Supreme deity of, 1757 (Burr).
Tulloch, On Renan's life of C.
Wilson, S., Deity of, asserted, 1747.
Wynpersse, Godhead of, 1795.
See Trinity; Unitarian.

Christ, Resurrection of. Benson, G., Evidence of, 1754.
Brief defence, 1710.
Bush, Resurrection of, 1845. B. C.
Evidence for, 1730.
Evidence of, 1744.
Holdsworth, Locke examined, 1720.
Impartial Examination, 1730.
Lushington, Res. vindicated, 1741.
Pamphlets regarding, vol. 309.
Perry, R., Harmony on, 1765.
Resurrection of Jesus (Annet), 1743.
Sermon, 1 Cor. xv. 35, 1757.
Sherlock, Trial of the Witnesses, 1729.
Sykes, Enquiry on, 1757.
Tilly, Serm., Phil. iii. 10, 1718.
Tyrwhitt, Resurr. through, 1787.
Wilson, T., Serm., Matt. vi. 21, 1711.

Christ, Second Advent of. Bates, J., 7th day Sabbath, 1848.
Chapman, J., Proofs of, 1846.
Churchill, Midnight Cry, 1858.
Cumming, J., Lecture on, 1853.
Dissertation on the Millenium, 1792.
Dowling, Exposition of W. Miller.
Evans, F. W., The Second Appearing, 1853.
Fessenden, C. P., The Second Advent, 1843.
Folsom, N., Dissertation on.

Christ, Second Advent of (continued).
Hawley, S.... Vindicated, 1843.
Hooper, J., Doctrine of, 1829.
Mandell, Six Sermons, 1817.
Marsh, W., Thoughts on.
Millenial Church, 1829.
Miller, W., Evidences for, 1843, '46.
Pelly, J. K., Poem on, 1837.
Prior, W. M., On Wm. Miller, 1862.
Proud, J., Proofs of, 1792.
Putnam, E., Crisis, or Last Trumpet, 1847. B. C.
Review of Miller, 1844. P. 866.
Spaulding, J., Sentiments concerning, 1796.
Voice in New Hampshire, 1842.

Christian Associations. *See* Young Men's C. A.

Christian Denominations. Clough, S., Account of, 1827.
Evans, Denominations of the Christian World, 1832. B. C.
See United States; Religion.

Christian Union. Bacon, L., Sermon on, 1845.
Chalmers on the Evan. Alliance, 1846.
Christian Alliance, N. Y., 1843.
Conference on, Liverpool, 1846.
Eaton, D., Famil. Conversation, 1803.
Evangel. Alliance, Conferences, 1845-1858.
Evan. Alliance. P. v. 495.
Goode, W., Commun. with foreign Prot. Churches.
Greatheed, S., Recommended, 1798.
Haweis, T., Plea for Peace.
Hints for, 1820.
M'Master, G., Thoughts on, 1846.
Maimbourg, Un. of Prot. and Catholics, 1686.
Osborn, G., Evang. Faith, 1794.
Pax redux, 1689.
Ranney, The Evangelical Ch., 1849.
Sectarianism the law, etc., 1846.
Shepherd, R., No False Alarm, 1808.
Sherlock, W., Discourse on, 1688.
Tabaraud, Histoire des Projets, 1824.
Tracts on Catholic Unity, 1852.
Turkey.... Evang. Alliance, 1856.
Tyng, S. H., Plea for, 1844.
" Union Principle, 1855.
Wainright, Plea for Unity, 1850.

Christianity. Abbott, The Young Christian.
Bowdler, Practical Christ'y, 1845.
Britannus and Africus.
Bunsen, E. de, Hidden wisdom of Christ, 1865.

Christianity, Evidences and Defences of (continued).

Grotius, Truth of the Chr. Rel., 1825.
Guillon, Exam. de Gibbon, Strauss et Salvador, 1841, 42.
H. W., Spirit of Prophecy, 1679.
Hall, C., Sermon, Matt. xxviii. 20, 1756.
Hall, R., Works, vols. 4, 5, 6, 1832.
Halley, E., The Pantheism of Germany, 1850.
Halliwell, J. O., Introduction to, 1859.
Hamburgisch Ministerium.
Hardwick, C., Parallelisms of, with other Systems, 1863.
Haviland, Fitness of the Times.
Hincks, T. D., Letters on Age of Reason, 1796. P. 355.
Historic Doubts on Shakespeare, 1853.
Hollis, J., On Scepticism, 1790.
Hooker's Weekly Miscellany, 1738.
Hudson, C., Doubts on Battle of Bunker's Hill.
Hughes, T. S., Defence of St. Paul, 1823.
Jackson, J., Address to Deists, 1762.
Jacob, Jew turned Christian, 1679.
Jortin, Truth of Chr. Religion, 1746.
Kenrick, Obs. on Jenyns, 1776.
Kneeland, A., A review of, 1830.
Lackington, J., Confessions, 1804.
Lardner, N., Works, 1788.
Lavington, Nature of a Type, 1724.
Law, E., On the state of the World, 1745.
Leaming, J., Evidences, 1785.
Lectures on.... Prot. Ep. Ch., 1853–4.
Leeke, Serm., Acts vii. 37, 1728.
Leland, J., View of Deistical writers of England, 1754.
" Reflections on Bolingbroke, 1753.
" Remarks, 1744.
Leslie, Deism Refuted, 1755.
Locke, Reasonableness of, 1695.
" Works, vol. 7, 1823.
Loftus, Reply to the Reasonings of Gibbon, 1778.
Lyttelton, Conversiou of Paul, 1747.
Malebranche, Recherche de la vérité, 1749.
Mann, E., Anatomy of a Christian, 1843.
Mannynham, Two Discourses, 1681.
Marin, Il Barone van Hesden, 1841.
Maurice, F. D., What is Revelation?
Middleton, C., Letters to Waterland and Bentley, 1755.
" Variations of the Four Evangelists, 1755.
Minutius Felix, The Octavius.

Christianity, Evidences and Defences of (continued).

Mitchel, O. M., Astron. of the Bible.
Moral Demonstration, 1775.
Neal, J., One Word More, 1854.
Nelson, D., Cause and Cure of Infidelity.
Nisbett, N., An Attempt, 1807.
Norton, A., Internal Evidences.
Onderdonk, On Objections to, 1838.
Origen *vs.* Celsus.
Orr, Theory of Religion, 1762.
Owen, R., Debate on, with A. Campbell, 1829, B. C.
Oxford Young Gent., Reply, 1743.
Pamphlets on, vols. 332-335, 686, 805, 1271–1274, 1503, 1762.
Paley, Works, vols. 1, 2, 1830.
Parkinson, Hulsean Lectures, 1837.
Peabody, A. P., Chr'y, Religion of Nature.
Phillips, C., Defence of.
Pianezza, Truth of Chr. Rel., 1703.
Plain Discourse, 1752.
Priestley, Discourses on the Evidences of, 1794, B. C.
Randolph, T., Essays, 1744–52.
" Propagation of, 1777.
Rawlins, on Heretical Opinions, 1772.
Rawlinson, G., Hist. Evidences, 1860.
Reinhard, Plan of founder, 1831, B. C.
Remarks on additional Letters, 1814.
Richardson, W., Four Sermons, 1730.
Robinson, T., Discourses, 1819.
Rogers, H., Defence of Faith.
Rogers, J., Neces. of Revelation, 1740.
Rose, H. J., Brief Remarks.
Rotheram, Arg. from Prophecy, 1753.
" The One Argument, 1754.
Salvianus, Opera, 1684.
Sharpe, G., Rise and Fall of Jerusalem, 1765.
" Want of Universality of, 1766.
Simpson, D., Plea for Religion.
Smith, S. S., Lectures on the evidences, 1809. B. C.
Southwick, S., Letter to Herttell, 1834.
" Layman's apology, 1834.
Stebbing, H., Miscellanies, 1718–46.
Stillingfleet, Mysteries Vindicated, 1691.
Sumner, Vérité du Christianisme.
Swain, Levi answered, 1787.
Taggart, S., Evidences of, 1811. B. C.
Taylor, H. B., View of, 1848.
Taylor, J., Restoration of Belief.
Tracts for Priests and People, 1861.
Trollope, Gentile Opposition, 1822.
Tupper, Probabilities.

Church Extension (continued).
Rivington, Extension in St. Pancras, 1801-51.
Wordsworth, C., Church Extension, 1843.
See Missions, Home.

Church Fathers. Apostolical Fathers, 1810. B. C.
Athanasius, Opera, 1686.
Augustinus, Les Confessions, 1688.
" Opera, 1700.
Bear, J., De Patrium Auctoritate, 1748.
Blunt, J. J., Lectures on, 1840.
Butler, A., Lives of.
Cave, W., Lives of.
Chrysostomus, De Virginitate, 1562.
Cyprianus, Opera, 1726.
Cyrillus Alexand., Opera, 1528.
" Hom-in Jeremiam.
Daillé, Right use of.
Damascenus, Sanct. imag. oppug., 1554.
Dionysius, Opera, 1502.
Epiphanius, Contra 80 Hæreses, 1543.
Eusebius, Theophania, Trans.
" Eccl. Hist., 1833. B. C.
Fulgentius, Opera.
Grabe, Spicilegium Patrum.
Greek Eccl. Historians, 1845, 46.
Gregorius Nazianzenus, Opera, 1850.
" Sermons, 1693. Fren.
Gregorius Nyssenus, De Virginitate, 1562.
" Comm. in Hexæmeron, 1553.
Hieronymus, Opera, 1823, 4.
Irenæus, Fragmenta Anecdota.
Isidorianæ Collationes, 1670.
Justinus, Opera, 1742.
Socrates Sozomen, Eccl. History, 305–445.
Tertullianus, Opera, 1584.
Theodoretus, Opera, 1573.
Theophylactus, Opera, 1754–63.
See Bibliography.

Church Government. Bowden, Apostolic Origin of Episcopacy, 1806.
Chauncy, View of Episcopacy, 1771.
Corbet, Remaines, 1684.
Cotton, The Keyes, 1644.
Deems, Speech, Trial of W. A. Smith.
Hobart, Apology for Apostolic Order, 1844.
Homes, W., Proposals on....Church government, 1732.
Hooker, Ecclesiastical polity, 1849.
Jarvis, S. F., The Church of the Redeemer, 1850.
King, P., Const. of Primitive.
Milton, J., Works, Of Prelatical Episcopacy, 1851.

Church Government (continued).
Noel, Union of Church and State, 1849.
Pamphlets, vol. 1291.
Parker, R., De politeia Ecclesiastica.
Pradt, Les quatre concordats, 1818.
Rutherfurd, Surveys of Hooker's discipline, 1658.
Wigglesworth, Sober Remarks, 1724.
Wilson, J., Apostolic Church Govt., 1798.
See Church of England; Presbyterian; Church of Scotland; Congregat.

Church History. Andrews, Review of Fox's Book of Martyrs.
Apostolical Fathers, 1810. B. C.
Armenian Church, Liturgie, 1851.
Baluzius, Nova collectio, concil., 1683.
Batavia Sacra, 1714.
Bennett, J., History of, 1831.
Bourne, G., Lectures: Church of Christ.
Boyle, I., Hist. of Council of Nice, 1836.
Brady, Clavis Calendaria, 1815.
Burnet, Hist. of Ref. of Ch. of Eng., 1781.
Campbell, G., Lectures on, 1807. B. C.
Coleman, Antiq. of Christ Church, 1841.
Collier, Eccl. Hist. of Great Britain, 1708–14.
Duykerius, Korte Verhandeling, 1686.
Erskine, J., Sketches and hints of, 1790–97.
Eusébe, Lett. à Morénas sur l'hist. de Fleury, 1757.
Eusebius, Eccle. History, 1833. B. C.
Flaccus Illyricus, Cent. Magdeburgensis, 1624.
Fleury, Mœurs des Chrétiens, 1754.
Giannone, Anecdotes Ecclésiastiques.
Goodrich, Eccl. Class-book, 1839.
Greek Eccl. Historians, 1st-6 cent.
Gregory, G., Hist. of the Chris. Ch.
Gieseler, Text-book of.
Gillies, Historical Collections.
Hales, J., Remains, Letters from Dort.
Hardwick, C., History of Middle Age.
Hase, Hist. of the Christian Church.
Haweis, Reply to Dean of Carlisle, 1801.
Hawks, Cont. to Eccl. Hist. of U. S. A.
Hetherington, Westminster Assem. of Divines.
Jones, W., History of.
Jortin, J., Remarks on.
Kip, W. I., Early Conflicts of Christianity.
Labbeus, Sacrosancta Concilia, 1671–2.
Maitland, The Dark Ages, 1853.

Church History (continued).

Martini, Staatsreligion durch Constantin, 1813.

Mass. Hist. Soc., series I, Church Hist. of N. E.

Mather, J., Disquisition on Councils, 1716.

Maurice, F. D., Lect. on I and II Cent.

Milman, H. H., Hist. of Christianity, 1840.

" Hist. of Latin Christianity.

Miræus, De Statu Religionis, 1619.

Morénas, Abrégé de l'Hist. de Fleuri, 1752.

Mosheim, Eccl. Hist. by Murdock, 1824. B. C.

" Hist. Comm. for 325 years, 1852.

Naldini, Corographia ecclesiastica, 1700.

Neander, A., Hist. of Christ. rel. and Church, 1847–54.

" Memorials of Christian Life, 1852.

" Planting and Training of the Ch., 1851.

Nicephorus, Eccl. Hist. lib. 18, 1566.

Odespun, L., Concilia Galliæ, 1646.

Papendrecht, Eccl. Ultrajectinæ, 1725.

Pastorini, Gen. Hist. of Christ. Ch., 1807. B. C.

Pelletreau, Abridgment of.

Priestley, Gen. Hist. of the Church, 1790.

" History of Corruptions of Christian, 1793. B. C.

Pupils of St. John.

Riddle, Eccl. chronology, 1840.

Ruffner, Origin of Monkery.

Sage, J., Cyprianic age.

Schaff, Hist. of the Church, 1–311, 1859.

" What is Ch. History?

Schott, The Augsburg Confession, 1530.

Scott, T., Synod of Dort, 1831.

Seabury, Continuity of the Church of England, 1853.

Sewell, History....to Nice, 1860.

Sirmond, Concilia Galliæ, 1629.

Sleidan, De Statu Religionis, 1785.

Smith, H. B., Science of C. H., 1851.

Socrates Scholasticus....to 445, 1853.

Southey, R., Book of the Church.

Sozomen, Hist. A. D. 324–440, 1855.

Spotswood, Church of Scotland, 1677.

Stebbing, H., Hist. of Christ. Church, Lardner's Cyc.

Stilling, H. Jung, Siegsgeschichte der.

Stillingfleet, Origines Britannicæ.

Storia della rivoluzioni, 1803.

Church History (continued).

Strype, Reformation in Eng., 1736-38.

Thackeray, F., Eccl. state of Ancient Britain, 1843.

Theodoret and Evagrius, 322-594, 1854.

Turrettin, J. A., Different fates of, 1708.

Union Theol. Sem., Hitchcock's Address.

Usher, De Ecclesiarum in Occidentis partibus.

Valerot, Journ. de la France, 1722.

Vergilius, De rerum inventoribus, 1546.

Vitalis, Eccl. Hist. of England and Normandy, 1853, 54.

Waddington, History of the Church.

Waylen, Eccl. reminiscences of, 1846.

Willtsch, Hand-book of Ch. geography.

Westminster Assembly of Divines, 1841.

Ypeij, Nederlandsche Hervormde Kerk, 1819–27. B. C.

See Great Britain, Church History; Martyrs; Protestantism.

Church Members. Cobbet, Vind. of covenant, 1642.

Emmons, E., Qualifications for.

Fish, Primitive piety.

James, J. A., Church member's Guide, 1830.

Stoddard, S., Right of Saints to, 1709.

See Communion.

Church Missionary Society. Church her own Enemy, 1818.

Considerations on the probable effects, 1818.

Defence of, 1818.

Terrot, Bp., Correspondence, 1844.

Church of England, History, Polemics, etc. Anderson, J. S. M., History of, in the Colonies, 1856.

Address to the Bishops, (Disney), 1790.

Advice to Confuter of Bellarmin, 1687.

Altham, Vindication of, 1687.

Andrews, T., Vindication of, 1799.

Answer to a late seditious, 1689.

Apol. for adherence, 1801.

Appeal to Common Reason, (Jones), 1850.

Bedford, Blazon of Episcopacy, 1858.

Barrington, Bp., Charges, 1792–1810.

Baxter, R., Petition for peace, 1661.

Beda, Historia Eccl. Gentis Anglorum. (E. Hist. Soc).

" Eccl. Hist. of Eng., 1847.

Best, S., Deans and Chapters, 1837.

Beverley, Corrupt state of, 1831.

Black-book, The, 1835.

Blandford, Episc. Property, 1853.

Church of England, History, Polemics, etc. (continued).

Bowtell, Sermon to dissenters, 1711.

Brand, Philanth. Society, 1806.

Browne, E. H., Expos. of the 39 Articles.

Burges, G., Address to Stanley, 1838.

Burnet, Exposi. of xxxix Art., 1842.

Case of Ch. of Eng., 1834.

Catholicism without popery, 1699.

Cave, Discourse concerning, 1684.

Chamberlain, C., Position of our Ch., 1859.

Christmas, Hampden controversy, 1848.

Church of England vind., 1739.

Church Pastoral Aid Society, 1837, 55.

Church Questions, 1855.

Church Reviewed, Lond., 1835.

Claims of, Lond., 1815.

Cobbett, Legacy to Parsons, 1845.

Cole, H., Modern Dissent, 1839.

Coming Conflict, 1851.

Considerations of Present use, 1682.

Cooper, C. P., Tracts Concerning, 1850, 51.

Cosin, De la foi et rites de, 1857.

Davys, G., On the Doctrines of.

Dealtry, W., Charges, 1830-43.

Defence of Doctrines of, (Wake), 1686.

Defence of the Doctrine, 1807.

Dilemmas of a Churchman, 1838.

Discourse, Troubles at Frankfort, 1554.

Dow, Innovations of, 1637.

Do not be Duped, 1850.

Ecclesiast. Almanack, 1842.

Evils of the Policy, 1849.

Falkland, Speech on Episcopasie, 1641.

Forby, R., Letter to Bp. of Norwich, 1815.

Fullwood, True Churches, 1652.

Goodman, Sisterhoods of.

Gordon, T., Cordial for Low Spirits, 1763.

Gorham (The great) case, 1850.

Gresley, W., Church Clavering.

" Real Danger of, 1846.

" Short Treatise on, 1845.

Gray, J., The Capitular Comm., 1853.

Grey, W. H., Church Leases, 1851.

Grosseteste's Epistolæ, (Chron. G. B.)

Grueber, The One Faith, 1850.

Hall, Robert, Works, v. 4, 5, 1832.

Hamilton, W. R., Cathedral Commission, 1853.

Hampden, R. D., Writings.

Hardwick, Hist. of Articles of Religion.

Hickes, G., Vindication of, 1687.

High Church Politics.

High Flown Epis. Claims, 1737.

Hill, Sir R., An Apology for, 1798.

Hook, W. F., Sermons, 1838-42.

Hunt, J., Religious thought in, 1871.

John Search's Last Words, 1839.

Keble, Tracts, 1833-54.

Keith, G., Two Sermons, 1700.

Kenn, Expostulatoria.

Kingscote, Wants of the Church, 1846.

Knight, The Parochial System, 1854.

Landor, Popery, English and Foreign, 1851.

Laud, Abp., Speech, 1637.

Lawson, Hist of Epis. Ch. in Scotland.

Layman's Vindication.

Le Grice, Sermon, Matt. xiii, 18, 1812.

L'Estrange, Relapsed Apostate, 1661.

Letter, Respectfully Addressed, etc., 1835.

Letter to the Rt. Hon. Sir R. Peel, 1832.

Letters on Church Matters, 1851, 2.

Lingard, Hist. of Anglo-Saxon Church, 1845.

Maclear, On Catechism of.

Madan, Upon the 39 Articles, 1772.

Maltby, E., Charges, 1834-49.

Marriott, H., Survey of, 1826.

Maskell, On High Church Party, 1850.

Meyrick, J.,....n'est point Schismatique, 1855.

Miller, J., Claims on Estates, 1831.

Milton, J., Civil Power in Eccl. Caus., 1839.

Modern Puritanism, 1843.

Morres, Duty of Communion with, 1817

Muscutt, Hist. of Lands of, 1851.

Newland, Seasons of the Church.

Nourse, P., Homilies fitted for Common use.

Pamphlets relating to, vols. 128, 322-331, 687-691, 722, 734, 775, 776, 933, 1270, 1276-1293, 1499, 1501, 1502, 1628.

Parker Society, Publications.

Pelling, E., Good Old Way, 1680.

Peril of being zealously affected, 1709.

Persuasive to Comm. with, 1683.

Phillpotts, H., Letters on the Edin. Rev., 1850, 52.

Plan for the Coöperation, 1848.

Preservative against Separation, 1721.

Puritan Discipline Tracts, 1843-45.

Questions and Answers, 1723.

Raikes, Sermons and Charges.

Real Advantages, (Welles), 1762.

Reply to Reasons of...Clergy....1687.

Rhenius, C. T. E., Review of "The Church," 1834.

Civil War in the United States, 1861-1865 (continued).

Hanson, J. W., Hist. of 6th Mass. Regt.
Harris, W. C., Prison Life in Richm'd, 1862.
Haynes, Hist. of Vt. 10th Regt., 1870.
Headley, History of, 1863.
" Mass. in the Rebellion.
Helper, H. R., No joque, 1867.
Hepworth, The Gulf Department, 1863.
Historicus, Letters, Lond., 1863.
Hosmer, Thinking Bayonet.
Hospital Transports, 1863.
Hotchkiss, Chancellorsville Battle.
Hough, Hist. of Duryee's Brigade, 1864.
Howard, P., Barbarities of the Rebels.
Hunnicutt, Conspiracy Unveiled, 1863.
Hunt, Shenandoah Cruiser.
Huntington's Stamford, Conn. Soldiers.
Illinois, Adj. Gen's Reports, 1861–67.
Indiana, Adj. Genl's Reports, 1861–69.
Iowa, Adj. Gen's Reports, 1863–65.
Iron Platform, 1863, 4.
Jackson, T. J., Life of.
Jacobs, M., Invasion of Maryland, 1864.
Joinville, Army of the Potomac.
Judd, 33d N. Y. Volunteers.
Junkin, Political Fallacies, 1863.
Kellogg, Rebel prisons.
Kelso, Stars and Bars in Missouri, 1863.
Kennedy, J. P., Ambrose's Letters.
Kettell, History of.
Kidder, F., First N. H. Regt.
Kirke, Down in Tennessee, 1864.
Laugel, The U. S. During the War, 1866.
Laurie, T., Sermon, 1861.
Lecomte, Swiss Mil. Report, 1863.
Leslie's Pictorial History of.
Life in thê Union Army, 1863.
Lord, J. C., Sermon, Buffalo, 1862.
Loring, C. G., Correspondence, 1861.
" Remarks on Historicus, 1864.
Lossing, B., History of the War.
Love, Wisconsin in the War.
McClellan, G. B., Report, 1861–62.
McClenthen, Campaign in Va.
McKinstry's Vindication, 1862.
MacPherson, Polit. Hist. of, 1864, 66.
Mahony, The Prisoner of State.
Maine, Adj. Gen's Report, 1861.
Marks, Campaign in Va., 1864.
Massachusetts Register, 1862.
" Adj. Gen's Reports.
Mass. 58th Regiment, 1865.

Civil War in the United States, 1861-1865 (continued).

Melville, H., Battle pieces, 1866.
Memoirs of Nullifier, 1860.
Merrell, Five months in.
Moore, F., Rebellion Record, 1861-65.
" Heroes and Martyrs.
" Lyrics of Loyalty.
" Political Ballads.
Moore, James, Kilpatrick and Cavalry.
Moreau, Politique Française, 1864.
Morse, F. W., Perso. Experiences.
Myers, 192 Penn'a Vols., 1864.
My Life in Vicksburg, 1864.
Nation's Sin, 1864.
Nemo, Mrs., Our Present Men, 1863.
New Gospel of Peace.
N. Y. Army List, 1862.
" County Enrollment Lists.
" *See* New York, Civil War.
Nicholas, S. S., Conservative Essays.
Nichols, G. W., Sherman's March.
Noel, The Rebellion in 1863.
Nott, C. C., Sketches of the War, 1863, 5.
" Sketches in Prison Camps, 1865.
Noyes, G. F., The Bivouac, 1863.
Old (The) Guard, (Period.), 1863-66, N. Y.
Oneida Volunteers.
Owen, R. D., Wrong of Slavery.
Paige, Address, 1862.
Pamphlets relating to the War, vols. 1534–1593, 1819, 1839, 2504, 2505.
Pamphlets containing Sermons on, vols. 1594, 1595, 1617. *See* Sermons, Political.
Patterson, R., Campaign of the Shenandoah, 1861.
Pelleton, Au roi Coton, 1863.
Penn'a, Prisoners of Andersonville, 1864–65.
Petersen, F. A., Campaign in Virginia, 1862.
Peyton, J. S., Am. Crisis, 1867.
Phelps, Mrs. L., Our Country, 1864.
Pittenger, Daring and Suffering, 1864.
Police Record, Tennessee, 1863.
Pollard, E. A., Southern History of, 1862–5.
" Secret Hist. of the War, and Davis's life, 1869.
Quint, Potomac and Rapidan.
" Second Mass. Infantry.
Rawlins, Amer. Disunion.
Redpath, Echoes of Harper's Ferry.
Red Tape and Pigeon-hole Generals, 1864.
Reid, Ohio in the War.
Rejected Stone, 1861.

Civil War in the United States, 1861-1865 (continued).

Reynolds, E. W., The Barons of the South, 1862

Richardson, A. D. Field, Dungeon and escape, 1865.

Rhode Island, Registry, 1866.

Rogers, W. H., Hist. of 189th Reg't of N. Y.

Rosecrans, Battle of Murfreesboro.

Russell, W. H., Diary North and South, 1863.

Sabre, War Prisons.

St. Andrews' Society, Sanitary Fair, Albany, 1864.

Schalk, Campaigns of 1862-3.

Schouler, Massachusetts in the War.

Schuylkill County, Memorial.

Semmes, Cruise of the Alabama.

Sergeant's Mem. (Thompson).

Shaffner, The War in America, 1862.

Shanks, Recoll. of Disting. Generals.

Shea, J. G., The Fallen Brave, 1861.

Soldier's Bible.

Soldiers.... Half-dime Tales, 1868.

Soldiers' Letters, 1865.

Songs of the War, 1863.

Southern Generals, (Snow.)

Spence, J., The American Union, 1862.

" Recog. of the Confederation.

Spencer, C. P., Last Days in N. Carolina.

Sprague, J. T., Treachery in Texas, 1861.

Stars and Stripes in Rebellion, 1862.

Stanton, R. L., The Church and the R.

Stevens, G. T., Army of the Potomac, Sixth Corps.

Stewart, A. M., Army of the Potomac, 1865.

Stillé, Fair at Phila., 1864.

Stone, E. W., Rhode Island in, 1864.

Strong, R. M., Life of.

Swinton, Army of the Potomac.

Sypher, Penn'a Reserve Corps.

Tenney, W. J., Mil. and Nav. Hist.

Tharin, Arbitrary Arrests.

Tomes, R., Hist. of the War with the South.

Trip of the Oceanus to Fort Sumter, 1865.

Trumbull, H. C., Camp's Life.

" Manning's Life.

Tucker, Partisan Leader, 1836.

U. S., Harper's Ferry invasion.

" Corresp. on Foreign Affairs, 1861-1864.

" Fort Pillow Massacre.

" General Orders, 1861-63.

" Reconstruction, P. v. 1839.

Civil War in the United States, 1861-1865 (continued).

U. S., Rolls of Honor.

U. S. Christian Commission Reports, 1863-66.

U. S. Sanitary Commission Bulletin, 1863-65.

U. S. Reporter, 1863-65

U. S. Service Maga. Period., 1864-6.

Victor, History of, 1862, 63.

Western San. Comm. History, 1864.

Whiting, War Powers of U. S.

Willson, 126th N. Y., Regt.

Wilson, H., Hist. of Anti-Slavery Congress Measures.

Woodbury, Burnside and 9th Army Corps, 1867.

See Confederate States; Slavery.

Claflin, A. L. Warren, W., Sermons on, 1853.

Claggett, T J. Norton, Life of.

Clap, Roger. Memoirs of.

Clapham, Eng. Directory, 1859.

Clapp, Rev. T. Autobiography.

Clare, T. G. Coleridge, W. A., Serm. on.

Clarendon, E. Hyde, Earl. Life of, 1759.

Letters of.

Lister, H., Life of, 1838.

Clarendon, T. V. Hyde, Earl. Mountain, Sermon on, 1824.

Clark, Dr. Fenwick, Letter to, 1802.

Clark, D. A. Biog. Sketch of.

Clark, H. Newman, J., Eulogy on.

Clark, H. Descendants, 1640-1866.

Clark, J. Hall, B. M., Life of, 1857.

Clark, Rev. J. Sketches of, (Peck), 1855.

Clark, J. L. Descendants, (Sims), 1870.

Clark, G. L. Clark, J., Descendants of, 1870.

Clarke, A. Clarke, J. B. B., Life of.

Etheridge, Life of, 1859.

Clarke, E. D. Otter, Life and Rem. of, 1827. B. C.

Clarke, G. Voyage of, 1703, N. Y. Colon. Tracts.

Clarke, M. Neal, O., Sermon on.

Clarke, M. S. Huntington, F. D., Discourse on.

Clarke, T. Descendants, 1623-97.

Classical Literature. Adler, G. J., Notes on.... Aeschylus.

Anthon, Classical Dictionary, 1841.

" Manual of Greek Lit., 1853.

Arnay, Private life of the Romans.

Classical Literature (continued).

Begerus, Ulysses Sirenes prætervectus, 1703.

Bentley, Works, vol. 1, 2, 1836.

Bonstetten, Voyage sur la scéne de l'Enéide, 1804.

Botfield, Editions of the Classics.

Brumoy, Greek Theatre, 1759.

Cælius, Antiquæ lectiones.

Campagnol, Thèmes Latins, 1853.

Classical Journal, Lond., 1826–28.

Cleveland, First Lessons in Latin, 1831.

Coleridge, H. N., Study of Greek Poets, 1831. B. C.

Coray, Greek Class. Criticisms, 1812.

Corderius, Colloquies, 1783. B. C.

Crombie, Gymnasium sive sym. crit., 1838. B. C.

Cuperus, Observationes, 1670.

Damm, Lexicon Etymol., 1765.

Dissertation ....Greek Accents, 1755.

Docen, Ueber die Ursachen, etc., 1815.

Donaldson, J. G., Constr. Græcæ praecepta, 1845.

Donaldson, J. W., Varronianus, 1860.

Dunlop, G., Hist. of Roman Lit., 1827.

Eschenberg, Classical antiq., 1837.

Eusebius, Actual state of, 1826.

Felton, C. C., Lectures on Greece, 1867.

Fosbroke, Arts of Greeks and Romans.

Gellius, Attic Nights, 1795.

Græviue, Lectiones Hesiodæ, 1667.

Grifolus, Ciceronis defensiones Celii disquis., 1546.

Güthe, Ueber den Astrios, etc., 1809.

Haldeman, Elements of Latin pronunciation, 1851.

Harpocration, De Vocibus liber, 1696.

Harwood, Biographia classica, 1802–4.

Heeren, A. H. L., Gesch. des studiums der Griechischen, 1797.

Heyne, Opuscula Academica, 1785–88.

Krabinger, Die klassischen studien, 1853.

Linacre, De emendata structura lat. serm., 1557.

Lobeck, Questionum Ionicarum liber, 1850.

Lyne, R., Latin Primer, 1801. B. C.

Manutius, Orthographiæ ratio collecta, 1566.

Middleton, C., Works, vol. 4, 1755.

Millin, Dizionario delle favole, 1804.

Mnemosyne, period, 1852–61.

Monboddo, Origin of Language.

Montfaucon, Antiquity explained.

Moore, N. F., Pronunc. of Greek, 1819.

Muller, K. O., Hist. lit. of anc. Greece. Lib. U. K.

Mure, Lang. and lit. of anc. Greece, 1867.

Classical Literature (continued).

Museum Criticum, Cambridge, 1826.

Observations on, 1753.

Occasional Thoughts, 1762.

Olivet, J., Comm. in Ciceronis Opera, 1819.

Outhof, Cebes den Thebaner, 1727.

Pamphlets, vols. 692, 693, 1294, 1504, 1764.

Parr, S., Works, vol. 3, 1828.

Pierron, Hist. Lit. Rom., 1857.

Porson, R., Tracts, 1815.

Preston, W., Ancient Amatory Writ., 1797.

Pye, H. G., Life of Tyrtæus.

Quintus Calabrus, Prætermiss. ab Homero, 1734.

Ramsay, Travels of Cyrus, 1814.

Rapin, Critical Works.

Roth, Ueber Thucydides u. Tacitus, 1812.

" v. d. Class. Gelehrsamkeit, 1825.

Schoell, Hist. Lit. Romaine, 1815.

Schomann, Assemblies of the Athenians, 1838.

Schweighaeuser, Lexicon Herodoteum.

Sigonius, Scholia Livii Historiæ, 1555.

Smith W., Gr. and Roman Geography.

" Classical Dictionary, 1851.

Sophocles, E. A., Hist. of Greek Alphabet, 1848.

Thomas, De vocis atticis, 1757.

Turner, D. W., Notes on Herodotus, 1853.

Vitringa, De Protagoræ Vita, 1852.

Waddington, Carmen Græcum, 1819.

Wakefield, Corres. with Fox, 1795–1801.

Weld, B. H., Latin lessons, 1847. B. C.

Wellendarffer, In Aristot. Comment, 1509.

Wheeler, Anal. of Thucydides, 1855.

Wyttenbach, Of Greek Literature.

See Antiquities; Greek; Latin; Bibliography; Cicero; Homer, etc

Classical Studies. Atkinson, Class. Studies, 1865.

Brooks, M. C., Address, 1840.

Clarke, J., Usefulness of Translations, 1734.

Essays on a System of, 1829.

Essays on a Liberal Ed., 1868.

Keynes, Class. Instruction, 1816.

Malden, H., Study of, 1851.

Merrill, T. A., Essay on Study of Latin.

Pillans, Order of Study.

Ray, R., Two Lectures, 1826.

Sears, etc., Classical studies, 1843.

Urquhart, On Classical Learning.

Verplanck, Use of Liberal Studies, 1833.

Classification of Books and Knowledge. Bibliog. Miscel., (Clark.)
Bulletin du bibl., 1840, Syst. de Daunou, 1834-52.
Charma, A., Nouv. Class. des Sciences, 1859.
Chaudon, Dict., v. 20, 1812.
Constantin, Bibliothéconomie, 1841.
Edwards, Memoirs of Libraries.
Fortie d'Urban, Syst. de Bibliog. Alpha., 1822.
Great Brit., Report Brit. Mus., 1835.
Horne, Introd. to Bibliog., 1839.
Middleton, Bib.Canta.ordin.methodus.
Palermo, Classazione dei libri à stampe, 1854.
Park, R., Pantology.
Peignot, Dict. de Bibliol. 1802.
See Bibliography, elementary; Catalogues: Libraries, scientific.

Claverack, N. Y. Zabriskie, History of the Church in.

Claxton, T. Memoirs of a Mechanic.

Clay, Anne. Jones, C. C., Life of.

Clay, H. Anspach, Discourse on, 1852.
Ashland Text-book.
Baldwin, N. B., Discourse, 1852.
Barstow, H , Club House, Detroit.
Clay, H., Life and Speeches (Mallory).
Colton, Correspondence of; Life of, 1855–6.
Green, W., Address to Club, 1844.
Lathrop, J. H., Eulogy on, 1852.
Leavitt, J., The Great Duelist, 1844.
McJilton, Sermon on, 1852.
N. Y. State Aux. Clay Mon. Ass'n.
New York City, Funeral Ceremony of, 1853.
Prentice, G. D., Biography of, 1832.
Sargent, E., Life and Services of, 1848.
Scott, W. A., Docts. on Calumnies, 1845.
Sketches of Public Services of, 1823.
Sketch of Several, etc.
Smith, S. L., Eulogy on.
U. S. Congress, Eulogies on.

Cleaveland, E. Misrepresentations corrected, 1859.
Clarke, E., Discourse on.
Woods, L., Address on, 1860.

Cleghorn, G. Lettsom, J. C., Memoirs of.

Clement, XIV. Caraccioli, Life of.
" Leven van, 1778.
Ganganelli, Letters of.

Clergy. Academia Speculum, 1830.
Admonition to the younger ...1764.
Advice to a Son....1725.

Clergy (continued).
Advice from a Bishop, 1759.
Arnold, W. H., Licentious Clergymen, 1828.
Beverley, Of a human Priesthood, 1839.
Brooks, C., Salaries in N. Eng., 1854.
Cambridge, G. O., Charges to, 1837, 38.
Canada, Report on support of, 1835.
Chapman, Charge to, 1746.
Christian Deacon.
Clerical Papers, 1852.
Christian Temple, Lond., 1849.
Clarke, A., Letter to Preacher, 1812.
De Lancey, W. H., Sermon, Rev. ii. 10, 1843.
" Charges, 1846, 55.
Dissuasive from....orders, 1723.
Drake, S., Concio, 1724.
Ducard, Vicarages of Canterbury.
Eachard, Contempt of the, 1705.
Evans, H., Sermon on, 1773.
Free and apposite Obs., 1782.
Gerard, The Pastoral Office, 1760.
Goddard, C., Ordin. Service defended, 1846.
Goddard, W. S., Visitation Sermon, 1811.
Gordon, T., Cordial for low spirits.
Grimshawe, Wrongs of....Peterborough, 1822.
Harris, H., Essay on Priesthood.
Hickeringill, Lay Clergy, 1695.
Hone, Parson's Horn-book.
Howitt, W., Of Priestcraft.
Jackson, W., Of Supporting themselves, 1821.
James, J. A., Minist. duties, 1816.
Langley, W., Persecuted Minister, 1655.
Latham, Difficulties of, 1736.
Laurence, R., Charges, 1822.
Lecture, Folly of Servants, 1842.
Leechman, Sermon, Duty of, 1744.
Letter to Brougham, 1823, (Rennell).
Lodington, Honor of, vindicated, 1674.
Loehner, Bib. Man. Concionatoria.
Mason, J., Letter on Entrance, 1753.
Mather, C., Manductio ad ministerium, 1726.
" Student and Preacher.
Maurice, P., Causes of Contempt of, 1729.
Messer, Sermons, 2 Pet. i. 13, 1773.
Miller, S., On Cler. Manners.
Napleton, J., Advice on Duties.
Non-residency, 1710.
Occasional Paper, 1703.
Orton, J., Letters to a Young C.
Owen, J., Plea for Ordination, 1694.

Confederate States (continued).
Jones, C. C., Chatham Artillery.
Pollard, Histories of the War, 3 vols.
" Life of Jeff. Davis, 1869.
Richmond Enquirer, Feb. 1863,—Dec. 1864.
Richmond Examiner, Feb. 28, 1861,—May, 1861; May 14, 1863,—Mar. 31, 1865.
Richmond Sentinel, Jan. 1864,—Mar. 1865.
Stephens, A. H., The war between the States, 1868, 70.
Stevenson, W. G., In the Rebel Army, 1862.
Warder, Manasses battle, 1861.
Weekly Register, Lynchburg, Va., 1864.
See Civil War, 1861–65.

Confession. Auricular confession.
Confessional, The, Lond., 1858. P.1277.
Disc. conc. Auricular....1648.
Hogan, Auricular confession.
Instructions for confession, 1730.
Lasteyrie, Histoire de la.
Maskell, Letter to Pusey.
Mutter, G., Lecture, 1828.

Confirmation. Allen, J. M., Apostol. Confirmation, 1858.
Baxter, R., Its nature, 1658.
Friendly conversation, 1824.
Piers, O., Conf. proved, 1841,
Smyth, T., C. examined, 1845.
See Church of England.

Conformity. Bicheno, Engl. Non-conformity, 1798.
Bristow, Non-Conf. recommended, 1817.
Calamy, E., Sermons.
Case of great use, 1677.
Case of lay communion, 1683.
Charge of Scandal, (Hesketh), 1683.
Corbet, Remaines, 1682.
De Laune, Plea for the non-conformists, 1712.
Dissertation against joining, 1716.
Letter to a Clergyman, 1704.
Principle of Prot. Reformation, 1704.
Principles of an occasional, 1718.
Repeal of the Act, 1717.
Serious Inquiry, London, 1704.
Short Surveigh, 1663.
Some considerations, 1683.
See Dissenters; Toleration.

Congar, Capt. O. Autobiography, 1851.

Congregational Churches. Allen, J., Worcester Association Hist.
Am. Cong. Union Report, 1861.
Amer. Cong. Year Book, 1854–59.

Congregational Churches (continued).
Backus, Church Hist. of New England, 1690–1804.
Bacon, L., Letters to G. A. Calhoun.
Beecher, L., Rights of Churches, 1826.
" Local Churches, Serm., 1819.
Bowdoin St. Church, Boston, 1833.
Brief narrative, 1645.
Bulmer, J., Government of, 1813.
Cambridge platform, 1648.
Cawdrey, Independencie a great schism, 1657.
Christian Witness, vol. 2, Lond., 1845.
Clap, T., Doctrines of the Churches of New England, 1755.
Clark, J. S., Sketch of Ch. of Mass.
Congreg. Almanac, 1846.
Congregational Board, 1854–58.
Congr. Calendar, Lond., 1841.
Cong. Churches, Eng., Minutes, 1838.
Cong. Ch. Eng., Decl. of Faith, Lond., 1659.
Congregat. Churches, Testimony, 1743.
Congregational Churches, U. S., Connecticut, Illinois, Maine, Massachusetts, New York and Vermont, Minutes of Associations.
Congregational Quarterly, Boston, 1859–69.
Congregational Union, Eng., 1834–45.
Cong. Year-book, Lond., 1855–8.
Connec. Evang. Magazine, 1800–08.
Cotton, J., Way of Cong. Ch. Cleared, 1648.
" The Way of the Churches of N. E., 1645.
" The Keyes, 1644.
Cummings, Dict. of Congregationalism.
Davidson, D., Manual, 1833.
Fairchild's Life, 1855.
Emery, Ministry of Taunton, 1853.
Evangel. Magazine, Lond., 1793–1854.
Felt, Eccl. Hist. of N. E., 1855.
" First Church, Salem.
First Cong. Ch., Albany, 1853.
First Ch., Cambridge, Mass.
First Congr. Ch., Hartford, 1851.
First Ch., Worcester, 1820.
Genesee Consociation.
Hall., J., Against Brownists, 1610.
Hanbury, Hist Mem's of, to 1660.
Harris, W., Church Fellowship, 1823.
Hinton, Lectures.
Homes, W., Proposals on Eccl. Gov., 1732.
Hooker, T., Way of the New England Churches, 1648.
Horton, T. G., Theory of Church, 1854.
Inquiry into....Ch. of Mass., 1816.
Keep, J., Congregationalism, 1845.

Conventions. Jameson, J. A., Hist. of Consti. Conventions, 1867.

Convicts. Boston Society for Discharged Convicts, 1847–57.
Bucquet, Jeunes libérés, 1853.
Carpenter, Mary, Our Convicts, 1864.
Convict Treatment, 1847.
Hints for the regulation of, 1782.
Mudie, J., Treatment of C. Servants.
Murray, J. P., on Transportation, 1857.
Palmer, T. F., Sufferings on Voyage, 1794.
Pamphlets Relating to Conv's. P. v. 822.
Pocock, Z. P., Discipline of.
Reed, T. S., Ticket of Leave, 1857.
See Punishmerts; Prisons; Crime.

Conway, Ms. Centen. Celeb., 1867.

Cook, Mrs. Manning, E., Serm. on, 1826.

Cook, D. P. Brown, W. H., Memoir of, 1857. P. 494.

Cook, E. Robbins, T., Sermon, Death of, 1823. P. 104.

Cook, James. Forster, G., Voy. with, 1774.
Ellis, W., Narr. of Voy. of, 1776–80.
Hawkesworth, Account of his Voyages, 1773.
Kippis, A., Vie de, 1789.
Ledyard, J.. Journal of his last Voy., 1776–79.

Cook, Rev. J. M. Bacon, H., Review of Memoir, 1851. P. 488.

Cook, Hon. J. M. Memoir of, 1869.

Cooke, H. Cogan, E., Sermon on.

Cookery. *See* Domestic Economy.

Cooley, T. M. Sprague, W. B., Discourse on.

Coombs, W. Dana, D., Discourse on.

Cooper, Sir A. Cooper, B. B., Life of, 1843.

Cooper, A. A. *See* Shaftesbury, Earl of.

Cooper, J. F. Memorial of, 1832.
Greeley, H., Trial, 1851.
Greene, G. W., Biog. Studies.
Livermore, S. T., Sketch of, 1862.

Cooper, S. Clark, J., Sermon on, 1784.

Coöperation. *See* Labor; Trades.

Cooperstown, N. Y. Cooper, J. F., Chronicles of, 1838.
Livermore, S. T., History of, 1862.

Coos County, N. H. Powers, G., Hist. Sketches of, 1754–85.

Copper Companies. Hafod Works, Smelting, 1833.
Montreal Mining, 1853.
Montreal River Co., 1846.

Copper Companies (continued).
N. Y. & Lake Superior, 1846.
Pamphlets, vol. 1802.

Copway, G. Life of, 1847.

Copyright. *See* Literary Property.

Coral Islands. Darwin, C., Journal, 1832.

Corcoran, H. Caldicott, Narrative of Conversion of, 1853.

Corder, W. Hyatt, C., Sermon, Execution of, 1828. Pam. 380.

Corea. Du Halde, Description of, 1738.
Hall, B., Voy. to West Coast of, 1818.
Hamel, Dutch Travels in, (Pinkerton).
M'Cleod, Voyage, 1818.
Williamson, A., Journeys, 1870.

Corfu Island. Quirini, Primordia Corcyræ.
See Ionian Islands.

Cork, Ireland. Tuckey, F. H., Remembrance, 1837.

Corn, Indian. Banks, Disease in Corn, 1805.
Brown, On Maize.
Cobbett, A Treatise on, 1828.

Corn Laws. Byrne, Letters on, 1851.
Day, G. G., Anti-Corn Law League, 1843.
Fitzwilliam, Addresses on, 1839.
France, Légis. de céréales, 1859.
Free Trade in Corn, 1828.
Great Britian; Commerce, 1806.
Greg, R. H., Pressure of, 1842.
Greg, W. R., Prize Essay. Pam. 424.
Hall, G. W., Observations, Lond., 1822.
Lauderdale, A Letter on, 1814.
National Anti-Corn Law League.
Malthus, Restriction of Trade, 1815.
Obs. on the prop. measure, 1842.
Pamphlets relating to the corn laws, vols. 424, 779, 1297.
Peel, R., Papers on, 1845.
Représentations aux magistrats, 1769.
Ricardo, On Protection, 1822. P. 424.
Sheffield, Remarks, 1800.
Thompson, T. P., Fallacies.
Tyrconnel, Address to the People, 1840.
See Free Trade; Tariff.

Corneille, P. Guizot, Corneille and his times, 1852.

Cornelius, E. Edwards, B. B., Life of, 1833.

Corning, J. Memorial of, 1870.

Cornplanter, Chief. Snowden, Sketch of.

Cornwall, Conn. Obookiah's life.

Costa Rica. *See* Central America.

Coster, L. J. Kortebrant, Lof der drukkunst, 1740.
Lennep, Carmen, auctore H. Bosscha, 1817.
Linde, A. van der, The Haarlem legénd, 1871.
Loosjes, Gedenkschriften, 1823.
Scriverius, Laurea L. Costeri, 1609.
Vries, A. De, Notice sur le Speculum, 1823.
See Harlem; Typography.

Costumes. Album des costumes des Pays Bas.
Ambert, Armée Française.
Costumes of Turkey, 1814.
Costumes Suisses.
Encyc. Méthodique: Antiquités.
Ferrario, Costume, 1831–37.
Glen, Habits du monde, 1601.
Hope, Costume of the Ancients.
Kinsey, Portugal, illustrated.
La Belle Assemblée, 1810–33.
Malcom, London, twelve plates.
Mazuy, Types Anciens, 1841.
Musée Belge populaire, f°.
Nicholas, Orders of Knighthood.
Observateur en Espagne, 1822.
Picturesque representations of China, Turkey, Austria, Russia, 1814.
Pinelli, Italian costumes.
Pitre, La Brétagne.
Planche, British Costumes. Lib. E. K.
Semple, Netherlands.
Shaw, Dress of middle ages.
Solvyns, Costume of Indostan.
Stone, Mrs., Chronicles of fashion.
Strutt, English Dress, 700–1800.
Stuart, Costume of the Clans.
Trollope, Brétagne.
Voy. du Roi à Windsor, f°.
See Costumes.

Cote d'Or, France. Annuaire, 1820–28.

Cotes du Nord. Annuaire, 1845.

Cotton, Father. Du Moulin, Answer to, 1615. P. 1425.

Cotton, John. M'Clure, Life of.

Cotton, R., Family. Drake's Hist. of, Boston.

Cotton, Sir R. Brit. Museum, Cat. of Mss.

Cotton. Arnold, R. A., Cotton famine, 1861–64.
Atkinson, E., Report, 1862.
Bazley, Lectures on, 1852.
Bishop, Hist. of Am. manufactures.
Bronson, Manufacture of.
Calais, Industrie tullière à, 1851

Cotton (continued).
Chapman, J., Cotton of India, 1851.
Cordova, Cultiv. of, in Texas.
Cotton is King, 1855.
Dudley, J. G., Paper on Cotton, 1853.
Fibrilia, (Vattemare).
History of silk, cotton, wool, etc., 1845.
Johnson, W., Nugæ georgicæ.
Lawrence, A. A., Prospects of American, 1849–50. P. 273.
Loring, F. W., Cotton culture, 1869.
Montgomery, J., Cotton man. of U. S. and G. B. compared, 1840.
Olmsted, The Cotton Kingdom, 1861.
Remarks on, in Alabama, 1850. P. 69.
Tryon, Merchants' instructor, 1701.
Un. St., Duties on Am. Cotton, 1856.
Ure, A., Cotton....in Great Britain, 1861.
Ure, Manufact. of, in Great Britain, 1836.
Vaillant, Culture du....en Algérie, 1854.
Woodbury, L., Tables on cult. and trade in, 1836.
See Manufactures; Tariff.

Councils. *See* Church History.

Counterfeiting. Assoc'n of Banks, Reports, 1857–64.
Collection of counterfeit bills, MSS.
Ormsby, W. L., Cycloidal config., 1862.
" Pres. syst. of note engraving, 1852.
Society for Encour. of Arts, Report, 1819.
Thompson, Autog. counterf. detector, 1849.
" Coin Chart Manual, 1853.
See Engraving.

Courten, Sir W. Several remarkable passages, 1673.

Courthope, J. Rose, G., Serm. on, 1845.

Covenants, Scripture. Deakin, Treatise on, 1816.
Colman, G., State of differences, 1768.

Covent Garden Theatre. Covent Garden Journal, 1810.
Harris, T., Narrative, 1768.
Rebellion (The), 1809.

Coventry, C. B. Batchelder, Reply, 1829.

Coventry, Conn. Tolland Co. Assoc'n, 1812.

Coventry, Eng. Coventry guide, 1824.
Shakespeare Soc., 1841, The Coventry mysteries.

Coventry, Vt. White, P. H., Hist. of, 1859.

Cow. Milburn, M. M., The Cow.

D.

Davy's Lamp. *See* Safety lamp.

Day, R., Family, of Hartford, descendants.

Day, T. Keir, Account of.

Days. Times' Telescope, 1814–1834.
See Chronology; Calendars.

Dayton, A. O. Memorial of, 1858.

Dayton, Ohio. Hall, B. F.. Sketch of, 1849.
Lyford's Directory, 1837.

Dead Sea. Lynch, W. F., Exploration of, 1852.
Saulcy, Journey round, 1850–1.

Deaf and Dumb. Am. Asy. for, Hartford; Reports, 1819–45.
Am. Annals of the Deaf and Dumb, 1848–51.
Amer. Instructors' Conventions, 1856.
Clerc, L., Address, Hartford, 1818.
Connecticut Asylum for, 1817, 18.
Connecticut, Reports on, 1851.
Convention of Instructors of, 1850, 51.
France, Statistique, 1861.
Gallaudet, Addresses on, 1817, 21, 28.
Glasgow Society for Education of, 1840.
Illinois, Asylum for. P. 167.
Indiana Instit. Reports, 1853.
Instituut voor Doofstommen, 1845–50.
Kitto, The Lost Senses.
Lieber, Vocal Sounds of L. Bridgman.
N. Y. Institution, Reports, 1828–69.
Ohio Asylum Reports, 1843–1864.
Pam. vols., 167, 168, 218, 235, 473.
Peet, Statistics of, 1852.
" Report on Education of.
" Address, North Carolina, 1848.
Pennsylvania Inst. for, Reports, 1844–1862.
Puybonnieux, Mutisme et surdité, 1846.
Tennessee, Asylum Reports, 1853.
Turnbull, Recoveries of, 1849.
U. S. Public Lands for, 1848.
Wisconsin, Reports of Institute.

Deane, J. Bowditch, Address on.

Deane, L. Family genealogy.

Deane, S. Papers Relating to, (Seventy-six Soc. Pub.)
" Theodosius, Anecdotes of.

Dearborn, H. Coffin, C., Life of, 1845.

Dearborn, H. A. S. Putnam, G., Address on. P. 1857.

Death. Charron, Of Wisdom, 1729.
Dodd, W., On death.
M'Gowan, Death, A Vision.
N. A. Review, Jan. 1834.
Reid, John, Philoso. of Death, 1841.

Death (continued).
Sormani, Morti repentine, 1834.
Struve, Suspended animation, 1803.
Vigne, Morte apparente, 1841.
Woodward, J., Warnings, 1758.
See Soul; Future State.

Debating. *See* Elocution.

De Berdt, E. Reed, W. B., Life of.

Debt. Address to Prince of Wales, 1783.
Beaumont, Abolition of Imprisonment for, 1836.
Ellis, C, M., Law betwixt Debtor, etc., 1857.
Martin, H., Twenty Reasons Against.
Whitmore, Serm., Running in Debt, 1800.
Stephen, J., Considerations on imprisonment, 1771.
See Great Britain, Debt of.

De Candolle. *See* Candolle.

Decatur, S. Life of, (Sparks Biog.)
Waldo, S. P., Life of, 1821.

Decency. Dissertation concerning, 1751.

Decimal Currency. Bowring, J., Decimal System, 1854.
Decimal Assoc. Tracts.
Liverpool Fin. Ref. Assoc'n, 1855.
Nation. Curr. Ref. Assoc'n, 1850.
Pamphlets relating to, vol. 1504.

Decoration. *See* Architecture; Arts.

Decretals. Gregory IX, Pope, 1585.

Dedham, Ms. Dedham Pulpit, 1840.
Haven, J., Hist. disc., 1796.
Haven, S. F., Hist. Address, 1836.
Lamson, Hist. of 1st Parish.
Mann, H., Annals of, to 1847.
Worthington, E., History of, 1635–1827.

Dee, John. Diary, 1554–1601, (Camden Soc.)

Deerfield, Mass. Bradford Club Pub., Papers concerning, 1859.
Taylor, John, Cent. Sermon, 1804.
Willard, S., Eccl. Council at, 1807.
Williams, J., Redeemed Captive, 1776.
Williams, S. W., Memoir of Rev. J. Williams, 1837.

De Foe, D. Life and newly discov. writings, Lee, 1869.
Chalmers, G., Life of, in Works.
Scott, W., Memoir of.
Wilson, W., Life of, 1830.

Deformity. Hay, W., Essay on, 1754.

Dehon, T. Gadsden, C. E., Life of, 1833.

Deism. Account of Growth...(Stephens), 1691.
Brown, G., Philos. and Atheism, 1797.
Christianity true Deism, 1762.
Dissertation on the Unreasonableness, 1725.
Fox, W. J., Duties to Deists, 1819.
Halyburton, T., Nat. Religion, 1812.
Morgan, The Moral Philosopher, 1738.
Letter to a Deist, (Balguy), 1730.
Ogden, Antidote, 1795.
Reflections upon a Pamphlet, 1696.
Remonstrance...to the Clergy, 1731.
Rogers, H., Greyson Letters, 1857.
See Natural Theology; Infidelity.

Deitz, Capt. Brice, Captivity of.

De Lancey Family. Holgate's Genealogies.

Delany, Mrs. M. G. Autobiography, and Corresp., 1861–2.

Delaroche, P. Galerie des cont., Notice sur, 1845.

De Laune, T. Plea and Sufferings, 1733.

Delaware. Baltimore, Articles, 1760.
Booth, Geolog. Survey, 1841.
Delaware Register, 1838–9.
Scott, J., Geog. descr. of, 1807.
See Wilmington; Pennsylvania.

Delaware Co., N. Y. Gould, J., History of, 1856.

Delaware Co., Penn'a. Smith, G., History of, 1862.

Delft. Beschrijving der, 1729.
Gribius, Redenvoeringen, 1831.
Oosterland, Delfshaven, Serm., 1746.

Deluge. Catcott, A., Treatise on, 1751.
Fairholme, G., Geol. of Scripture, 1833.
Harcourt, Doctrine of the Deluge, 1838.
Harris, On Nat. History of the Earth, 1697.
Whitehurst, Orig. State of the Earth, 1792.
See Cosmogony; Geology.

Delusions. Apocatastasis, 1854.
Barnum, P. T., Humbugs.
Boismont, Hallucinations.
Brown, T., Works, Vulgar errors.
Christmas, Cradle of the Twin giants, 1849.
Defoe, Hist. of apparitions, vol. 13.
" Syst. of Magic.
Keightley, Fairy Mythology, 1850.
Mackay, Mem. of popular delusions, 1841.
Madden, R. R., Phantasmata, 1857.

Delusions (continued).
Polydorus, De rerum inventoribus, 1546.
Salverte, The Occult Sciences, 1847.
Southcote, History of.
Whittier, Supernaturalism of N. E., 1847.
See Witchcraft; Mythology; Magic.

Demerara. M'Donnell, Negroes in, 1825.

Democracy. Barruel, Hist. du Jacobinisme.
Byrdsall, Hist. of the Locofoco party, 1842.
Camp, G. S., Democracy, 1845.
Carey, M., The Olive Branch, 1814, 16.
Cobbett, W., New Years Gift, 1796.
" Hist. of Jacobinism, 1796.
Consolatory Odes, 1799.
Democratic Conventions, 1852, etc.
Dumas, A., Progress of, 1841.
Guizot, Democracy in France, 1849.
Jones, W. D., Mirror of Modern, 1864.
Macauley, Cath., Loose Remarks, 1769.
National Dem. Conv., 1851.
N. Y. Dem. Ass'n of Washington, 1856.
Representative Govt., 1863.
Tappan, M. W., Speech, 1856.
Tocqueville, A. De, Dem. in America, 1836, 38.
" Mem. and Remains, 1862.
See Republics; Liberty; Government; Revolution; United States, Politics.

Demoniacs. Church, T., Vindication, 1750.
Critical Dissertation, 1738.
Dissertation on, 1775.
Dixon, T., Christ's Temptation.
Farmer, R., An inquiry, 1765.
Pegge, Examination of, 1739.
Thacher, J., Essay on, 1831.
Woodwarn, T., Demon. Possession, 1849.

Denmark. Berlien, Der Elephanten-Orden, 1846.
Biernatzki, The Sheep-Fold.
Boisgelin, Trav. Through, 1810.
Crichton, History of.
Dunham, History of.
Geffrey, Histoire de, 1851.
Hamilton, Danish Isles, 1852.
Harris, Voy. vol. 1, Danish East Ind. 1744.
Keith, R. M., Mem. of Queen Matilda of, 1849.
" Correspondence, 1861.
Laing, Observations, 1851.
Leavitt, Den. and its relations, 1864.

Denmark (continued).
Letters on the Sound-dues, 1855. P.
Lövenörn, Navig. of the Cattegat.
Marryat, Residence in, 1862.
Nicholls, W., Serm. Death of Pr. George, 1708. P. 364.
Non-intervention, 1864.
Remarks on the Injustice, etc., 1807.
Sinding, Hist. of Scandinavia, 1866.
War of the Gaedhill (Chron. G. Brit.).
Wheaton, H., Hist. of the Northmen, 1831.
Who is to Blame, 1849.
Wraxall, N. W., Tour, 1807.
See Sweden; Scandinavia.

Dent, J. Bray, T., Sermon on.

Dentistry. Allen, J., Of Dentures, 1854.
Baltimore College of, 1855.
Brown, W. S., Treatise, 1847.
Clark, F. Y., Dental Monitor, 1856.
Dwinelle, On Watts' Crystal Gold, 1855.
Family Dental Journal, 1854.
Gidney, Treatise, 1824.
Howard, Loss of Teeth.
N. Y. College of Dental Surgery, 1851.
Penn'a Coll. of Den. Surgery, 1856.
Phil'a Col. of D. Surg., 1855.
Potter, E., Dissertation on.
Putnam. C. S., The Forcep, 1857.

Depravity. *See* Sin; Evil.

De Quincey, T. Bayne, Essays.

Derby, Earl. Era in the Life of, 1857.

Derbyshire, Eng. Beauties of England and Wales.

DeRham, W. M. M'Vickar, Address on, 1834.

Dervishes. Brown, J. P., Oriental spiritualism.
See Mystics.

De Saumarez, James, Lord. Ross, Mem. and corresp. of.

Des Moines. Iowa, Descr. of Central Iowa, 1858.

Despotism. Mirabeau, Essai sur.
Spirit of Despotism, (V. Knox), 1795.
See Government.

Despreaux. *See* Boileau.

Detroit, Mich. Darby, Tour to, 1818.
Detroit Directory, 1858.
Hough, Siege of, 1763, (Muns. Hist. Series.)
Trowbridge, C. C., D. past and present, 1864. P.

Deux Ponts, Count W. De. My campaigns in America, 1780–81.

De Veaux, J. Gibbes, R. W., Memoir of, 1846.

Deventer, Neth. Jaarboekje, 1857.

Devereux, Earls of Essex. Lives and letters, 1540–1646.

Devonshire, Eng. Beauties of England and Wales.
Davidson, Bibliot. Devoniensis, 1852.
Delabeche, Geology of.
Moore's Hist. and topog. of, 1829.
Prince, The Worthies of Devon, 1701, 1810.
Shortt, Antiquities of, 1850.

Devotional. Clergyman's Companion.
Companion for sick room.
Possinus, Thes. asceticus.
See Prayers; Religious.

Dewees, W. P. Hodge, H. L., Eulogium on.

D'Ewes, Sir S. Autobiography and letters.

Dewey, D. L. Memorial of, 1864.

De Witt, J. Barnwell, R. G., Life of.
James, G. P. R., Life of, 1837.

D'Wolf, A. A. Cooley, T. M., Serm. on.

Dexter, S. Reminiscences of, 1857.

Dexter, Tim. Knapp, S. L., Life of, 1838.

Dial. Descr. of d. of the seasons.
See Calendars; Chronology.

Dialling. Ferguson's Lectures, 1814.
Lacroix, App. of trigonometry.
Moxon's Mechanical exercises, 1703.
Oughtred, Dialling, 1652.

Dialogues. Corderius, Centur. Colloquia, 1743.
" Colloquies, 1743.
" Les colloques, 1646.
Erasmus, Colloquia, 1810.
Familiar dial. in Gr., Arm., Eng. and Fr.
Fénélon, Dial. des morts.
Infernal conference, 1795.
Landor, Imaginary conversations.
Leone, Dialoghi d'amore, 1545, 52.
Lovell, J. E., School dialogues, 1851.
Lucianus, Select dialogues of, 1785.
Lyttelton, Dialogues of the dead.
Plato, Works.
Swift, Polite conversations, v. 22.
See Elocution.

Diamond. *See* Brazil; Gems; Precious Stones.

Diamond Necklace. La Motte, Life of.

Dictionaries of Languages: DUTCH (continued).

Lemans, Heb.—Nederduitsch, 1831.

Meyer, L., Woordenschat, 1745.

Marin, Pierre, Dict. Franc-Hollandois, 1793.

Martin, H., Beredeneerd Nederd. Woordenboek, 1836, B. C.

Polyglott, Dutch, Eng., Fr. and Germ.

Sewell, W., Eng. and Dutch, 2 parts.

Werninck, Pocket Dict., Dutch and English.

Wilcocke, Pocket Dict. of English and Dutch.

EGYPTIAN. Bunsen, Egypt. hieroglyphics.

ENGLISH. Ash, J., 1775.

Bailey, N., Univ. Etym. Eng. Dict., 1755, 59, 66, 93.

" English and German, 1792.

Bartlett, Dict. of Americanisms, 1859.

Bolles, W., Phonographic Dict., 1845.

Booth, D., Analyt. Dict. of English Lang., 1836.

Bulloker, An English Expositour, 1680.

Burhans, Expositor, 1827.

Cobb, L., Abridgement of Walker, 1828.

Cooper, Thesaurus ling. Rom.-Britan., 1584.

Dialect of Craven, 1828.

Dict. of Modern slang, 1860.

Dyche's New, 1759.

Eastwood, Bible word-book, 1866.

Franke, Technological Dict., 1855.

Gallaudet, School Dict., 1844.

Glossographia Anglicana, 1719.

Glossary of Herefordshire.

Grimshaw, Gentleman's Lexicon, 1830.

" Etymological Dict., 1821.

Grose, Prov. glossary, 1811.

Halliwell, Dict. of Archaic....words, 1855.

Hearne, Langtoft's Chronicle, 1810.

Holloway, Gen. Dict. of English provincialisms, 1839.

Holyoke's, T., 1677.

Johnson, S., English Dict. 4 vol. 8vo. and 2 vol. 4to, 1818, 19.

" Improved by Todd, 1828.

Jones, S., Sheridan improved, 1802.

Lemon, English Etymology, 1783.

Manipulus vocabulorum, 1570, Levins. Camden Soc.

Mason, G., Supplement to Johnson's, 1800.

Minsheu, Guide into tongues, 1627.

Nares, Glossary of obscure words, 1867.

New critical Dict., Burlington, N. J., 1813.

Oswald, Etymolog. Dict. of Eng., 1832.

Phillips, E., World of words, 1700.

Dictionaries of Languages: ENGLISH (continued).

Polyglott Eng., Fr., Ger. and Dutch.

Richardson, C., Eng. Dict., 1838–1846.

Rowson, S., Boston, 1807.

Sternberg, Dialect of Northamptonshire, 1851.

Tolhausen, Technolog. Dict., 1854, 55.

Trench, Glossary of changed tenses.

Webster, N., 1806, 1st ed.

" Am. Dict. of Eng. lang., 1828.

" Unabridged, 1865.

" English, 1859.

Webster, W. G., Elementary Dict.

Wedgwood, Dict. Engl. Etymol., 1862.

Wiggins, N. Y. Expositor, 1844.

Worcester, J. E., Universal Dict. of English, 1847.

" English Dict., 1860.

Wright, T., Dict. of Provincial Eng., 1857.

See Bibliography; Language; Grammars.

ESKIMAUX AND ENG. VOCAB., (Washington's.)

FLEMISH. Ende, Gazophilace, Françoise et Flamande.

FRENCH. Académie Française, Dict. de la langue, 1814, 35.

Barré, Complément du Dict. de l'Acad., 1847.

Blanche, Dict. d'Administration, 1857.

Boyer, A., French Dict., Boston, 1841.

Court de Gébelin, Dict. Etymol.

Dict. Fran., All., Anglais, 1836.

Fleming, Complete Fr. and Eng. Dict., 1844.

Landais, Dict. gén., 1843.

Polyglott Lex. French, Dutch, German and Eng., 1848.

Wilson, J., French and Eng. Dict., 1850.

GAELIC. Highland Soc. of Scotland, Dict. Gaelic, 1828.

Jamieson, Etym. Dict. of the Scottish, 1840–41.

GEORGIAN. Klaproth, Vocab. de la Langue Georgienne, 1847.

GERMAN. Adler, Germ. and English Dict., 1849.

Birlinger, Schwabisch Wörterbuch.

Dictionnaire Allemand-François, 1762.

English-German Dict., Phila., 1834.

Flugel, Dict. of Germ. and English, 1845.

German-Eng....and Eng-Ger. Dict., Muhlenberg, 1812.

Grieb, Eng. and Germ....Ger. and Eng., 1866.

Grimm, Deutsches Wörterbuch, 1854–62.

Dictionaries of Languages: German (continued).

Kaltschmidt, Germ. dict. Leipsic, 1837.

Kilianus, Etymologicum Teutonicæ Linguæ, 1777. B. C.

Meidinger, Dict. Etym. langues Teuto-Gothiques, 1833.

Polyglott, German, Fr., English and Dutch.

Greek. Alexandre, Dict. Grec-Français, 1857.

" Dict. Français-Grec, 1856.

Apollonius, Lex. Græcum, 1773.

Burke, W., Gr. Eng. Dictionary, 1806.

Court de Gébelin, Dict. Etymol.

Damm, Lex. Etymol.... Homer. et Pindar., 1765.

Donnegan, Greek and Eng. Lexicon, 1839.

Estienne, Thesaurus Græcæ Linguæ, 1572, 1816–25.

Gesner, Lexicon Græco-Latinum, 1545.

Hedericus, Lexicon Man. Gr. Latinum, 1825. B. C.

Hesychius, Lexicon.

Lexicon Græcum, Antverpiæ, 1592.

Lowndes, Eng., Modern Greek, 1827.

" Modern Greek—English, 1837.

" Hebrew—Modern Greek, 1842.

Morell, T., Lex. Gracco—Prosodiacum, 1815.

Parkhurst, Gr. and Eng. to the N. T., 1825.

Photius, Lexicon, (Porson), 1822.

Pickering, John, Greek and English Lexicon, 1829.

Reineccius, Manuale Biblicum, 1734.

Robinson, E., Gr. and Eng. Lex., 1825.

Scapula, Lex. Gr.—Latinum, 1816.

Schleusner, Lex. Gre.—Lat. in Nov. Test., 1814.

Schrevelius, Lex. Manuale Gr. Lat., 1670, 1818.

Schweighaeuser, Lexicon Herodoteum.

Sophocles, Rom. and Byzantine, 1870.

Suidas, Lexicon, Græce, 1498.

Hebrew. Gesenius, Heb. and English, 1844.

Goldenthal, Clavis Talmudica, 1847.

Lex. Græc. Thes. Heb. Pagnino, 1572.

Lowndes, Heb. and Modern Greek.

Parkhurst, Heb. Lex. and Grammar, 1792.

Hindustani. Shakespear, Hindustani and English.

See Tamil; Oordu.

Italian. Antonini, Dict. Fran. Lat. et Ital., 1766.

Baretti, Dict. of Eng. and Ital., 1839.

Dictionaries of Languages: Italian (continued).

Mandosio, Vocab. Italiano-Latino, 1818.

Millhouse, Engl. and Ital.,—Ital. and Eng.

Pianzola, Dizionarie Ital. Greca é Turca.

Latin. Ainsworth, R., Lat. and Eng., 1818, 1823.

Andrews, E. A., Lat. Lex. of Freund, 1851.

Calepinus, Dict. Latinum, 1521.

" Dict. undecim ling, 1511.

Cellarius, Lat. lib. Memorialis, 1709.

Cicero, Epitheta, 1570.

Ciceronianum Lexicon, 1743.

Cooper, Thesaurus Ling. Rom.-Britan, 1584.

Court de Gébelin, Dict. étymol.

Dictionarium Latinum.

Du Cange, Glossarium ad scrip. medii ævi.

Entick, Latin English Dict., 1826. B. C.

Facciolati, Totius Latinitatis Lexicon, Lond., 1828.

Holyoke, T., Lat. and English, London, 1677.

Leverett, New Lexicon, 1850.

Martinius, M., Lex. Etymologicum, 1623.

Quicherat, Dict. Lat.—Français, 1858.

" Dict. Fran.—Latin, 1858.

" Thes. Poet. Ling. Latinæ, 1857.

Riddle, J. E., English-Latin Lexicon, 1849.

Salmon, Etymol. Lat. Dict., 1796.

Malay. Eysinga, Maleisch en Nederduitsch, 1825.

Marsden, Malai, Holland., Fran., 1825.

Persian. Angelus, Gazophylacium ling. Pers., 1684.

Burhani Kati, Calcutta.

Polynesian. Mosblech, Vocab. océanien.

Portuguese. Vieyra, Dict. of Portug. and English lang., 1840.

Roman. Raynouard, Lexique Roman.

Roquefort, Langue Romaine, 1808.

Russian. Dictionary, English and Russian, 1855.

Spanish. Taboada, Fran-Espan., Espan-Fran.

Velasques, Span. and Eng. Dict., 1852.

Swedish. Dictionary, Eng. and Swedish.

Syriac. Uhlemann, Gram. and Dict. Syr., 1855.

See Chaldaic.

Tamil. English and Tamil, 1842.

Dictionaries of Languages (cont'd).
TURKISH. Arménien-Turc-Français.
Bianchi, Turc, Arabe, Français.
Knight, W., Eng. and Turk. Vocab.

URDU. Thompson, Oordoo and English.

WELSH. Owen, W., 1793, 1803.
Richards, English-Welsh.

Dictionaries of Geography and History. Anthon, Classical Dict., 1841.
Blanche, Dict. de l'administration, 1857.
Bayle, Dict. Hist. et Crit. Fr. and Eng., 1740.
Bouillet, Dict. d'Hist. et de Géog., 1845, 58.
Collier. *See* Moreri.
Crabb, Dict. of General Knowledge, 1830.
Dozy, Dict. des Vêtements Arabes, 1843.
Evans, Denominations of the Christian World, 1832.
Fosbroke, Encyc. of Antiquities, 1825.
Glossary of Heraldry, 1847.
Hall, B. H., Collection of College words, 1851, 56.
Hoffman, J. J., Lexicon Universale, Hist. Chron., 1698.
Hook, Church Dictionary, 1854.
Kitto, Cyclopædia of Bib. Literature, 1846.
Ladvocat, Dict. Hist. Portatif, 1755.
La Martinière, Le Grand Dict. géog. hist. et crit., 1739–41.
Lemprière, Classical Dictionary, 1816.
Luiscius, Alg. hist. geog. Woordenboek, 1724–27.
Millin, Dizionario delle favole, 1804.
Moreri, Grand Dict. historique, French and English, 1698.
Murray, H., Encyc. of Geography, 1834.
Nuttall, P. A., Dict. of Nations of Antiquity, 1840.
Political Dictionary, 1845, 46.
Smith, W., Classical Dict., 1851-54.
See History; Geography; Gazetteers; Encyclopædias.

Dictionaries of Science and Arts.
Appleton, Dict. of Mechanics, 1852.
Beeton, S. O., Dict. of Universal information, 1865.
Brown, D. J., Etymol. Encyc. of arts, 1832. B. C.
Chambers, E., Cyclopædia of, 1784–6.
Crabb, Univ. Technological Dict., 1823.
Dict. des Sci. Naturelles, 1816–30.
Falconer, Univ. Marine Dict., 1830.
Franke, Technolog. Dict., 1855.

Dictionaries of Science and Arts (continued).
Gardner, Farmer's Dictionary, 1846.
Glossary of Architecture, 1850.
Gregory, G., Dictionary of Arts and Sciences, 1815–16.
Gwilt, Encyc. of Architecture, 1867.
Harris, Lexicon Technicum, 1710.
Hebert, Engineer's and Mech. Encyclopædia, 1837.
Hubner, Kouranten-Tolk; and Kunst-Woorden-boek, 1748.
Humble, Dict. of Geol. and Mineralogy, 1843.
Johnson, G. W., Dict. of Mod. Gardening, 1847.
Lomax, Encyc. of Architecture.
McCulloch, Dictionary of Commerce, 1834, 40 and 69.
Nichols, J. P., Cyc. of Phys. Sciences, 1857.
Nicholson's British Encyclopædia, 1809.
Nieuwenhuis, Woordenboek van Kunsten, 1826.
Ogilvie, Imp. Technolog. and scientific, 1851.
Stuart, Dict. of Architecture.
Tolhausen, Technological Dict., 1864.
Tomlinson's Cyc. of useful Arts, 1852.
" Supplement, 1868.
Ure, Dictionary of Chemistry, 1824.
" Dictionary of Arts, etc., 1840, 45.
" Supplement, 1863.
Weale, Dict. of civil and naval Arch., 1849, 50.
See Encyclopædias; Sciences; Arts.

Diet; Dietetics. *See* Health; Food; Domestic Economy.

Digby, Sir K. Private Memoirs, 1827.

Digby, Simon, Lord. Kettlewell, Sermon on, 1686.

Dighton rock. Moreau, Pierre de Taunton.

Dignities. Ashmole, Order of the Garter.
British compendium, 1721.
Dodd, Book of Dignities.
Haydn, Book of Dignities, 1851.
Murray, Hand-book of church and State.
Nicolas, Hist. of orders of Knighthood, 1842.
" Precedency of Peerage.
Pancirolus, Notitia dignitatum, 1608.
Pegge, Curialia.
Selden, Titles of Honor.
Tomkins, Sketches of aristocracy.
See Heraldry; Officers; Rank.

Dike, T. Hill, J., Answer to, 1818.

Dikes. Deventer, Memorie.
Nanninga, Deichbauverbesserung.

Dillaye, S. D. Pittsburgh case, 1860.

Dimmick, L. F. Withington, Memorial, 1860.

Dinsmore, J., Family genealogy, 1867.

Diplomacy. Adair, Negotiations, 1808, 1809.
Avaux, Négociations, 1754–55.
Capefigue, Diplomat. of Europe, 1842.
Chateaubriand, Congress of Verona, 1838.
Coalition (La) et la France, 1817.
Demeunier, Economie diplomatique.
Estrades, Lettres et Négociations, 1743.
Flassan, Hist. de la Dipl. Française, 1811.
France, Négociations dans le Levant.
" Négociations avec l'Autriche, 16me siècle.
Goertz, La Neutralité armèe, 1801.
Grotius, Rights of War and Peace, 1814. B. C.
Guines, De, Ambassade, 1775.
Hill, R., Diplom. Correspond., 1845.
Koch, Hist. des traitès de paix, 1796, 1797.
Lyman, T. jr., Diplomacy of the U. S., 1828.
Martens, Guide diplomatique, 1832.
Portfolio, Lond., 1843.
Pradt, Congress of Vienna, 1816.
Torcy, Négotiations from the treaty of Ryswick, 1757.
Traité diplomatique, 1833. B. C.
Trescot, The Diplomacy of the revolution, 1852.
Warden, D. B., Consular establishments, 1813.
Wheaton, H., International law, 1836.
See Consuls.

Diplomatics. Abella, Noticia Col. dipl. Espagna, 1795.
Bartlett, Preservation of archives.
Bossange, Catalogue, 1845, 47, 50, 53.
Christ, Abhandlungen, 1776.
Encyc. Méthodique.
Great Britain, Record commission rep., 1857–59.
Maffei, Letter to Countess of Seefeld, 1730.
Martens, Bibliographie diplomatique.
Namur, Bibliog. diplo-bibliol., 1838.
Peignot, Dict. de bibliol., 1802, 04.
See Bibliog. Elementary; Alphabets; Writing; Manuscripts; Charters.

Diptheria. Copeman, Essay on.
Cotting, Diptheritis, 1859.
Paine, H. D., Essay, 1859.

Diptheria (continued).
Pamphlets, vol. 1361.
Willard, S., Diphtherite, 1859.

Directories. *See* Towns by name; Joint Stock.

Discoveries. *See* Geographical: America, Discovery in.

Disease. Bigelow, J., Enquiry into origin of, 1859.
" Nature in Disease, 1854.
Jackson, J., Letters to a young Physician, 1856, 61.
Holmes, O. W., Currents and Countercurrents, 1861.
See Medical; Health.

Disney, G. Life of, 1692.

Disney, J. Jervis, T., Serm., Death of, 1817. P. 382.

Dispensaries. Boston Dispensary, 1856, 1858.
Bury Dispensary, 1790.
Demilt, N. Y., Reports, 1856, 57.
Eastern Dispen., N. Y., 1853.
N. Y. Dispensary, 1846, 57.
N. Y. Homœop. Dispensary, 1852.
Northern Dispensary, N. Y., 1851, 55 and 59.
Public Disp., Lond., 1838.
Williamsburgh, N. Y., Report, 1855, 1858.

D'Israeli, I. Corney, Review of Curiosities of Literature, 1838.

Dissenters. Abrabanel, Complaint, 1736.
Address to.... on Regium Donum, 1774.
Apostolic Conformity, 1703.
Bogue, History of, to 1808.
Brown, J. B., Brougham's Education bill, 1821.
Calamy, E., My Own Life.
" Church and D. compared, 1719.
" Letter to Echard, 1718.
Campbell, J., Anal. of Binney, 1856.
" Non-conformist theology, 1856.
Canne, J., Separation from Ch. of Eng.
Case of Dissenters, 1703.
Case of Dissenters in Carolina, 1706.
Case of the Dissenters, 1833.
Chandler, Letter to, 1748.
Collins, R., Advice to, 1733.
Conder, Political Position, 1853.
Conscientious Nonconformity, 1737.
Consid. on a Comprehension, 1748.
Dissenters to the Queen, 1714.
" Statement of Case, 1827.
" Apology, 1739.
Dissenting Gent's Answer, 1748.
Dorrington, T., D. Ministry Censured, 1703.

Domestic Economy. A., L. E., La Cuisinière de la campagne, 1851.
Art of cookery. 1854.
Bibra, Getreidearten, 1860.
Brillat-Savarin, Physiologie du gout.
" Physiology of taste.
Buchoz, Manual alimentaire, 1771.
Carter, S., Frugal housewife, 1760.
Cobbett, Cottage Economy.
Donovan, Domestic Economy. Lardner's, 17, 18.
Evans's Expense-book.
Gilman, Lady's Annual Register, 1838, 1839.
Green, W., Plans of Economy, 1802.
Hints on the abuses.
Hollandsche Keuken-Meid.
Leslie, Lady's House book.
Markham, Engl. Housewife, 1683.
Pamphlets relating to, vol. 1768.
Patissière, La, de la campagne, 1825.
Robert, La grande cuisine, 1845.
Rosny, Parfait œconome, 1710.
Rumford, Essays, 1797.
Skinner, American book of, 1850.
Society of Antiquaries, Receipts, 1790.
Sayre, History of Food, 1853.
Stafford's Receipt book, 1857. P. 515.
Stone, R., Family book, 1836.
Sylvester, C., Philosophy of, 1819.
Timbs, J., Dom. Science.
Viart, Cuisinier Royal, 1838.
Webster, T., Encyc. of domestic econ., 1845.
Wittenmyer, Milit. kitchens.
See Confectionery; Receipts.

Dominica Is. Atwood, T., History of, 1791.

Dominique, St. Caro, E., Vie de.

Doncaster, Eng. Miller, E., Hist. of, 1804.

Doniphan, Gen. Edwards, F. S., Campaign of, in Mexico, 1848.

Doolittle, W. M. Wood, N. N., Serm., Death of, 1842.

Dorchester, Mass. Allen, W., Hist. discourse, 1848. P. 233.
Blake, J., Annals of, 1750.
Codman, Hist. Sermon, 1846.
Davenport, D., Cemetery Memo., 1826.
Dorchester Antiquarian Soc., 1859.
Dorchester Directory, 1868.
Dorchester Epitaphs, 1869.
Dorchester Town Documents, 1850–53.
Drake, S. G., Early History of, 1851.
Harris, T. M., Mem. of First Church, 1830.
" Discourse, 1799.

Dordogne, France. Annuaire, 1802, 45.

Dordrecht. Outrein, Intreeds-reden, 1703.
Wall, De, Handvesten, Privilegien, Costumen, 1770–83.

Doria, A. Durazzo, Elogio, 1781.

Dorr, T. W. Frieze, Hist. of Suffrage in.
King, D., Life of, 1859.
U. S., Report on Rh. Is. affairs, 1844.
Waterman, H., Fun. Address.

Dorsetshire, Eng. Beauties of Engl. and Wales.
Cooke's Topog. Library.

Douai. Duthillœul, Biographies des hommes de, 1844.
See Bibliography.

Doubs, France. Annuaire, 1845.

Douglas, Sir H. Fullom, Life of, 1863.

Douglas, S. A. Polit. Record.
Addresses in Congress on his death, 1861.
Marshall, H., Speech on, 1852.
Schurz, C., Speeches.
Sheahan, Life of.
Wright, J. A., Eulogy on.

Douglas, T. *See* Selkirk, Earl of.

Douglass, D. B. Hale, B., Sermon on, 1849.

Douglass, Fred. My Bondage, etc.
Stowe's Men of the Time.

Dow Family, Genealogy. *See* Stranahan.

Dow, L. History of Cosmopolite, 1859.

Dow, N. Marsh, J., Sketches of, 1852.

Downam, G. Answer to a sermon of, 1609.

Downing, Jack. Davis, C. A., Letters of, 1834, 36.

Dowse, T. Mass. Hist. Soc. Proc., 1859.

Dracut, Ms. Gould, W., Farewell Discourse.

Drainage. Banister, Letter, 1853.
Donald, J., Land Drainage.
France, Lois sur le drainage, 1854.
Green, R., Under Draining, 1832.
Hawkins, Dra. of London, 1848.
Johnston, J., Experiments in. P. 205.
Morton, J., Whitfield Farm.
Rawlinson, R., D. of towns, 1854.
Wood, T. L., Thames embankment, 1857.
See Sewers.

Drake, D. Mansfield, E. D., Memoirs of, 1855.
Thomson, E., Sketches.

Drake, Sir F. Burton, R., Account of, 1687.
Maynard, Voy. of, (Hakluyt Soc. Pub).

Dramas, American. Bailey, J. J., Waldimar, 1834.
Brackenridge, Death of Montgomery, 1777.
Calvert, Arnold and André.
Dunlap, W., Dramatic Works, 1806.
" The Archers, 1796.
Featherstonhaugh, Death of Ugolino.
Fayette in Prison, 1802.
Hillhouse, J. A., Dramas, 1839.
Howe, J. W., The World's Own, 1857.
Ioor, Independence, 1805.
Lord, W. W., André, 1856.
Miles, G. H., Mohammed.
Owen, R. D., Pocahontas, 1837.
Paulding, American Comedies, 1847.
Ritchie, A. C. M., Plays and Tales.
Rush, J., Hamlet, 1834.
Sargent. E., Velasco, 1839.
Tarnation Strange. P. 396.
Taylor, C. W., Goblet of Death, 1847.
Warren, Mrs. M., Poems, dramatic, 1790.
Willis, N. P., Bianca Visconti.
" Tortesa, 1839.
See Literature; Poetry.

Dramas, Dutch. Bruhl, De Burgemeester, 1789.
Dutch Dramas, 1711–40.
Engelant, Tooneel-Poezy, 1730.
Holberg, L., Blyspelen, 1747–66.
" De Maskarade, 1766.
Hooft, P. C., Werken, 1671.
Loghem, Krispyn, 1725.
Müller, Admirael Piet Hein, 1832.
Pool, Adeka, 1834.
Tafereel, De, etc., 1720.
Treuerspelen, 1728–45.
Vondel, Treuerspelen, 1660–62.
" Jerusalem.
" Palamedes, 1707.
Wiselius, Adel en Mathilda, 1817.
See Poetry, Dutch.

Dramas, English, and Translations.
Addison, J., Cato, 1761.
Æschylus, Tragedies, 1834.
Antonio Foscarini, 1836.
Aristophanes, Comedies, 1853.
Armstrong, J., Misc. The Forced Marriage, 1770,
Baillie, J., Dramatical Works, 1851.
Banim, Damon and Pythias. P. 621.
Beaumont and Fletcher, works, 1840.
" Finest scenes of, 1855.
Beaumont, The Chances. P. 396.

Dramas, English, and Translations (continued).
Becket, Dram. Miscellanies.
Bride of Abydos, 1818.
Buckston, J. B., 1833–38.
Burgoyne, J., Dramatic Works, 1808.
Butler, F. A. K., Francis the First, 1833.
" Star of Seville, 1837.
Byron, G. N., Manfred, 1817.
Carey, Honest Yorkshireman. P. 396.
Centlivre, Mrs., Comedies.
Cibber, Works.
Coleridge, S. T., Remorse, Zapolya Wallenstein, (Schiller).
Collection of Farces, 1792.
Colman, G., jr., 1788–1808.
Congreve, Dramatic Works, 1840.
Cumberland, R., 1775–1804.
D'Avenant, Sir Wm., 1669–77.
Dennis, J., Appius and Virginia.
Dibdin, T., Miscellany.
Dodsley's Collection of old Plays, 1827.
Dryden, Works, 1808.
Edgeworth, M., Comic Dramas, 1817.
Euripides, Tragedies, 1834–5. B. C.
Fabian, Trick for Trick, 1761.
Farquhar, Dramatic Works, 1840.
Fielding, Works, vol. I, 1810.
" Don Quixote, 1733.
" Pasquin, 1736.
Ford, J., Dramatic Works, 1827.
Garrick, D., Misc. Plays.
Glengall, Irish Tutor, 1847.
Goldsmith, Miscellaneous Works, 1839.
Gregg, Edward VI.
Halliwell, The Poetry of Witchcraft, 1853.
Hart, Bell-ringer of St. Paul's.
Hey, R., Captive Monarch.
Holcroft, T., Road to Ruin. P. 396.
Home, J., Works: Agis, Douglas, etc., 1822.
Johnson, S., Works,
Jonson, B., Works.
Jones, T. P., Firmilian, 1855.
Killigrew's, Works, 1663–4.
Knowles, J. S., Select Dramatic W'ks, 1835.
" [Plays collected.]
" The Hunchback, 1832.
Lamb, C., Specimens of Eng. Dram. Poets, 1854.
" Works, vol. I, 1818.
Lillo, G., Dram. Works, 1810.
" George Barnwell, 1761.
Lilly, J., Dramatic Works, 1858.
Marston, J., Works, (Halliwell), 1856.

Dramas, English, and Translations (continued).
Massinger, Plays, 1840.
Maturin, Bertram, 1816.
Middleton, T., Works, (Dyce), 1840.
More, H., Sacred dramas.
Morgan, Lady, Dramatic scenes.
Murphy, A., Works, 1756–73.
Newton, C., Arnold, 1856.
O'Keefe, J., Plays collected, 1789–1800.
Orphans, (The), 1814. P. 1725.
Pamphlet volumes containing Dramas, vols. 396, 621, 639, 643, 697–699, 739, 740, 782, 783, 936, 1020, 1301, 1302, 1510, 1511, 1622, 1623, 1769, 1860, 2522.
Penn, J., Battle of Eddington.
Pilon, F., Plays, 1769–93.
Pictcairns, Assembly, 1692.
Plautus, Comedies, 1852.
Racine, The Victim.
Reynolds, F., 1793–1808.
Rowe, N., Works.
Schiller, Works, 1846–49.
Scott, W., Halidon Hill, 1822.
Select Plays, Baltimore, 1802–1804.
Shakespeare's Plays, 1623, 1664, 1795, 1819, 42, 44, 45, 47, 50, 51, 54, 57-1859.
Shakespeare Soc., Contin. of Dodsley's Collection.
Sheridan, R. B., Dram. Works, 1848.
" The Critic, 1781.
Sophocles, Tragedies.
Southey, Wat Tyler, 1817.
Steele, R., Conscious Lovers, 1755.
Suckling, J., Poems, 1646.
Talfourd, Athenian Captive.
Taylor, Philip Van Artevelde.
Terentius, Comedies.
Vanbrugh, 1840
Vortigern, (Ireland's).
Whitehead, W., Creusa, 1754.
Wiseman, N., Hidden Gem.
Wycherley, 1840.
Wynne, G., Three Plays, 1853.
See Literature; Poetry.

Dramas, French. Alvin, Beausire, Education à la mode, 1809.
Beaumarchais, Œuvres, 1837.
" Barbier de Séville.
Boissy, Œuvres de Théatre, 1837.
Chalory, Répert. des écoles.
Chamfort, La Jeune Indienne, 1777.
Collet, L'Isle déserte, 1758.
Corneille, Œuvres, 1838.
" Théat. choisi.
Crébillon, Œuvres.
Delavigne, Les Comédiens, 1834.

Dramas, French (continued).
Destouches, Œuvres, (Regnard).
Ducancel, Esquisses dramatiques.
Ducange, Calas, 1819.
Gherardi, Le Théatre Italien, 1701.
Kailaz, ou les Jeunes Sauvages, 1770.
Le Blanc, Manco-Capac, 1782.
Lucas, Tháatre Espagnol, 1851.
Mars, Cadet Roussel, 1834.
Mendès da Costa, Le Dey d'Alger.
Molière, Œuvres, 1739. B. C.
" Théatre choisi.
Montrose et Amélie, 1783.
Perrot, Esmeralda, 1856.
Phillippe II, Portrait de, 1785.
Piron, Fernando Cortès, 1756.
Poëmes sur l'Amérique, 1756.
Racine, Œuvres, 1737.
" Théatre choisi, 1847.
Raynouard, Les Templiers, 1805.
Regnard, Œuvres, 1837.
Rozoi, Azor ou les Péruviens, 1770.
St. Evremond, Mélange curieux, 1726.
Sauvigny, Hirza, 1767.
Scribe, Les Huguenots, 1838.
" Guido et Ginevra, 1838.
" Bertrand et Raton, 1834.
Viollet le Duc, Anc. Théatre Français.
Voltaire, Œuvres, 1785–89.

Dramas, German. German Theatre, (Thompson), 1811.
Goethe, W. J. von, Faust, B. Taylor's trans., 1871.
" Faust, Hayward's trans., 1851.
" Faust, Swanwick's translation, 1850.
" Dramatic Works, 1850.
Kotzebue, Translations.
Lessing, Nathan the wise, 1868.
Ludvigh Kossuth, 1853.
Rosenthal, Theater fur die Jugend.
Schiller, F. von, Werke.
" Die Räuber.
" Wilhelm Tell, 1850.
" Maria Stuart, 1851.
" Historical dramas, (Bohn).
" Early dramas, (Bohn).

Dramas, Italian. Alfieri, Tragedie.
" Rosamunda.
Guarini, Il Pastor Fido, 1590.
Manzoni, A., Tragedie, 1825.
Metastasio, P., Opere, 1813.
" Dramas, 1800.
Monti, V., Opere, 1835.
" Aristodemo, 1833.
Pistucci, F., Marozia, 1837. P. 992.
Polcastro, Opere, vol. I, 1832.

Dramas, Italian (continued).
Teatro Moderno, 24 vol., 1838–41.
Varano, A., Opere Scelte, 1818.

Dramas, Miscellaneous. Pamphlets, vols. 396, 621, 639, 643, 697-699, 739, 740, 782, 783, 936, 1020, 1301–1305, 1510, 1511, 1622, 1623, 1769.

Dramatic Biography and Literature.
Adolphus, Bannister's life.
Aikin, S. C., Sermon on Theat. exhib., 1825.
Baker, Biog. Dram., 1782, 1812.
Barker, J., List of Plays.
Bernard, J., Retrospection of the Stage, 1830.
Betterton, T., Hist. of Eng. Stage, 1814.
Betty, Life of, 1804.
Boaden, Life of Kemble.
Brayley, Prynne's Defence, 1825.
British Theatre and Church of England, 1804.
Bunn, The Stage.
Calcraft, Defence of the Stage, 1839.
Cibber, C., Apology for the Life of, 1822.
Clapp's Boston Stage, 1853.
Collier, Immorality of the Eng. Stage, 1698.
Colman, G., Covent Garden, 1768.
Covent Garden Journal, 1810.
Cowell, Thirty Years among Players, 1844.
Cradock, J., Literary Memoirs, 1828.
Defence of the Drama.
Dibdin, T., Reminiscences.
Dickens, Grimaldi's Life, 1838.
Destrem, Projet de réforme théatrale, 1846.
Diss. on Anc. Tragedy, (Francklin).
Dumesnil, Mémoires de, 1798.
Dunlap, W., Hist. of Amer. Theatre, 1832.
Edwards, S., Hist. of Opera, 1862.
Egerton's Theatrical remembrancer, 1788.
Felix, Rachel, Memoirs, 1858.
Ford, Lives of Brit. dramatists.
Garrick, D., Correspondence, 1831, 32.
Genest, Account of Engl. stage, 1832.
Girardin, Lectures on, 1849.
Hazlitt, Essays of the Eng. stage, 1851.
" Dram. Lit. of Queen Elizabeth's age, 1845, 46.
Hodgkinson, J., Old American Comp., 1792–97.
Hone, Miracle plays.
Houssaye, Philosophers and Actresses, 1852.
Hunt, L., Works, vol. 1, 1854.

Dramatic Biography and Literature (continued).
Ireland, J. N., New York stage, 1867.
Kelley, Reminiscences, 1826.
Langbaine, Lives of Dram. Poets, 1698.
Lawrence, J., On the state of the Theatres. Pamph'lr. 2.
Lives of British Dramatists, 1846.
Lives of Dramatic Poets, 1698.
Macklin, C., Memoirs of, 1804.
Macready, Mrs., Life of, 1855. P. 471.
Manzoni, Teoria dell dramma tragico.
Mathews, C., Memoirs.
Mirror of Taste, Balt., 1811.
Montes, Lola, Reply, 1851. P.
O'Keefe, Recollections, 1827.
Peake, R. B., The Colman family.
Riccoboni, Hist. du Théatre Ital., 1660.
Ritchie, A. C. M., Autobiography.
Robinson, Mrs. M., Autobiography.
Schlegel, A. W., Lectures on, 1846.
Scott, W., Essays on.
Shakespeare Society Publications.
Smith, E., The Theatre, 1841.
Smith, S., Management, West and South.
Taylor, J., Records of my Life, 1833.
Vandenhoff, Reminiscences.
Wallack's Life.
Wemyss, Chronol. of the Amer. Stage, 1752–1852.
Witherspoon, Effects of the Stage, 1812.
Wood, W. B., Recollections of the Stage, 1855.
See Amusement; Bibliography; Covent Garden; Shakespeare.

Drawing. Cavé, Cours de Dessin.
" Le Dessin sans Maitre, 1850.
Clarke, H., Practical Perspective, 1776.
De Witt, S., Elements of Perspective, 1813.
France: Education: Ecole de Dessin, 1857. P. 499.
" " Modèles de Dessins, 1857.
Goubaud, Human Figure.
Ignatius, (Perspective, in Armenian), 1814.
Le Bealle, Dessin Linéaire.
Minifie, Lectures on.
Montesson, Art de lever les plans, 1775.
New Treatise on Perspective, 1810.
Nicholson's Treatise of Projection, 1840.
Peale, R., Graphics.
Pyne, G., Treatise on Perspective, 1851.
Rowbotham, Sketching from nature.
Ruskin, Elements of, 1857.

Dunbar, R. Dunbar, R., Phren. character of. Muns. Pam. 12.

Dunbarton, N. H. Stark, C., History of, 1860.

Dundonald, T. Cochrane, Earl. Autobiography, 1860.

Dunkers. Conyngham, On the Dunkers.

Dunkin, M. Townsend, J., Serm., fun. of, 1806.

Dunkirk. Case of Dunkirk, 1730.
Dunkirk or Dover, 1713.
Steele, R., Importance of, 1713.

Dunnel. Family Genealogy.

Dunstable, N. H. Fox, C. J., History of, 1846.

Dunton, J. Life and Errors.

Du Ponceau, S. Dunglison, Commem. Discourse on, 1844.

Dupuytren, G. Galerie des Contem. Vie de, 1845.

Du Quesne, Fort. Régistre, baptêmes à, 1753–6.
Beaujeu, Relations sur la bataille, 1755.
See Braddock; Pittsburg.

Durand, J. R. Life and adven. of, 1820.

Durer, A. Scott, W. B., Life of.

Durham, Conn. Fowler, W. C., History of.

Durham, Eng. Bagg, Antiquities of, 1866.
Beauties of Eng. and Wales.
Cooke, Topog. Library.
Liddel, Speech, 1840.
Raine, History of North Durham.
Westmoreland and Durham illust., (Allom.)

Dutch. *See* Dramas; Language; Literature; Netherlands; Poetry; etc.

Dutch Church. *See* Reformed (Prot. D.) Church.

Dutch Colonies. *See* Indian Ocean; Guyana; Voyages to India; Java; Sumatra; Netherlands.

Dutch East India Co. Begin ende Voortgangh, 1646.
Boom. Nederl. Oost Indie, 1864.
Dubois, Vie des gouverneurs gén.
Montanus, Embassy to China and Japan, 1670.
Nieuhoff, Embassy to China, 1673.

Dutch History, etc. *See* Netherlands.

Dutch Pamphlets, in vols. 107–110, 568, 569, 633, 634, 966, 1782, B. C. 30, 31, 32, 35.
See Literary; Miscellaneous; Poetical; Political; Theological.

Dutch Voyages. Tiele, Mémoire bibliographique, 1867.

Dutch West India Co. Consideratien, 1629.

Dutchess County, N. Y. Davis, S., Moravians in, 1858.

Dutens, Rev. L. Memoirs, 1806.

Dutton, A. Bacon, L., Sermon on.

Duty. *See* Moral Philosophy.

Duxbury, Ms. Winsor, J., Hist. of, 1849.

Duy, A. W. Clark, S. A., Mem. of, 1847.
Cutler, B. C., Sermon on, 1846.

Duyckinck, E. A. Griswold, Cyclopædia, etc., 1856. P. 266.

Dwight, B. W. Life of, 1862.

Dwight, F. Biog. of, 1858.

Dwight, Mrs. E. B. Dwight, H. G. O., Memoir of.
Goodell, Sermon on.

Dwight, Rev. L. Jenks, Memoir of.
Prison Discipl. Soc. Reports, 1846–54.

Dwight, M. S. Fisher, S. W., Sermon on, 1845. P. 554.

Dwight, T. Incidents in Life of, 1831.
" Theology and Life of.
Chapin, Sermon on.
Silliman, B., Eulogium on, 1817.
Sprague, W. B., Life of.

Dyckman, J. Ducachet, H. W., Tribute to, 1823.

Dyeing. Bancroft, E., Researches on Perman. Colours, 1813.
Berthollet, Elements of the Art of, 1824.
Bronson, Manufac. Assistant.
Dyer and Color Maker, 1850.
Lasteyrie, Treatise on Pastel or Woad, 1816.
Napier, J., Art of Dyeing, 1853.
Persoz, Impression des tissus, 1846.
Smith, D., Dyer's Instructor, 1853.
Treatise on, 1846.
See Colors.

Dyspepsia. Culverwell, Hints to the Nervous.
Peppercorne, Remarks on, 1851.
See Health.

E.

Ear. Buchner, For the deaf, 1770.
Curtis, J. H., Hearing Trumpets.
Du Verney, Treatise on, 1737.
Lighthill, On Deafness.
Neill, H., Report on Deafness, 1841.
Soemmering, De l'organe de l'ouie, 1825.
See Deaf and Dumb.

Echard, Dr. Calamy, E., Letter on his Hist. of Eng., 1718.
" Answers to Calamy, 1718.

Economy. Observations, 1669.
See Domestic Economy.

Ecton, Eng. Cole, J., Hist. of, 1865.

Ecuador. Bollaert, Researches in, 1860.
Orton, J., The Andes, 1870.
See Brazil; New Granada; Peru.

Eddy, T. Knapp, S. L., Life of, 1834.

Edgeworth, R. L. Memoirs by himself, 1844.

Edinburgh. Anderson's History of.
Britton's Views of Mod. Athens, 1829.
Creech, Fugitive pieces, 1815.
Edinburgh Almanac, 1822, 41.
Grant's Castle of Edinburg.
Kay, J., Portraits and biog. Sketches, 1842.
Lockhart, Peter's Letters, 1819.
Memorial of Catholics, 1779.
Peddie, J., Sermon, Fire in, 1824.
See Scotland.

Edinburgh Review. Reviewers Reviewed, 1816.

Edinburgh University. Bower, A., History of, 1817, 30.
Edinb. Univ., Catalogue of graduates, 1858.
" Catal. of Med. graduates, 1846.
" Uuiv. Calendar, 1859, 67.
" Med. Dissert., 1778—1819, 127 vols.
Great Britain, Report on Univ. of Scotland, 1837.

Edmonds, H. A. Willard, S. D., Eulogy on, 1857.

Edmonton, Eng. Robinson, W., History of.

Edmundson, W. Journal of, (Friends' Library.)

Education, Treatises, Method, etc.
Abbott, J., Mt. Vernon School.
Anderson, G., Ed. of working classes.
Baines, E., Writings, 1843–56.
Batchelder, J. P., Life and matter and Ed., 1845.
Bell, Mutual Instruction, 1807.
Booth, What to learn.
" National education, 1847.
Bouillon, Objet moral de l'éducation, 1802.
Braun, T., Principes d'Education.
Bristed, C. A., Lett. to Horace Mann, 1850.
Brougham, Speeches, etc.
" Pract. observations on, 1826.

Education, Treatises, Method, etc. (continued).
Burgh, Dign. of human nature, 1816.
Burrowes, Sch. Architecture, 1855.
Campe, Leerstelsel van Opvoeding, 1785, 86.
Castalio, Dial. Sac. lib. iv, 1722.
Castille, Nouvel Eraste, 1808.
Chapman, G., Treatise on, 1790.
Chambers, Educa. Course, 1837–41.
Clarke, W. B., Sermons on, 1838.
Cobb, L., Corporal punishment.
Colquhoun, for Labouring People, 1806.
Common School Assistant.
Condit, Discourse, 1849.
Consequences of a Sci. ed., 1826.
Cornelius, Jacotot's System.
Crandall, Talks with the People, 1853.
Edgeworth, M., Practical education.
Educational aphorisms.
Foster, Review of Wyse, 1837.
Fox, W. J., Lect. on National Education, 1840.
Genlis, Adéle et Théodore, 1782.
Girard, Meth. Instruc. in the mother tongue, 1847.
Goodrich, S. G., Sow well and Reap well, 1846.
Gordon, R. A., Village Schools, 1850.
Gresley, Church Clavering.
Hall, B. R., Teaching, a Science, 1848.
Hall, S. R., Lectures on.
Hart, J. S., In the School room, 1870.
Hecker, J., Sci. basis of Ed., 1867.
Helvetius, On man, 1810.
Henry, J., The family and school monitor, 1852.
" Address on Education in Common Schools, 1843.
Hill, F., Prospects of national education, 1836.
Hinton, J. H., Essays.
Hitchcock, Enos, Bloomsgrove family, 1790.
Holbrook's School Apparatus.
Hook, W. F., National educ., 1847.
Hoppus, Crisis of, 1847.
How can the church educate, 1844.
James, Fam. and school monitor, 1852.
Jardine, G., Outlines of Philosophical education, 1818.
Johonnot, Country School-houses, 1859.
Kames, Loose hints, 1782.
Lancaster, J., Improvements in, 1807.
Locke, J., Works, vol. 9, 1823.
Mann, H., Lectures and reports.
Mansfield, E. D., Am. education, 1851.
Martineau, H., Household educa., 1849.
Means, Duties of Parents, 1852.

Education, Treatises, Method, etc. (continued).

Mercer, C. F., Disc. on popular educ., 1826.

Mill, J., Lancastrian Schools.

Modern, The, theme, 1847.

Neat, J. W., Christ. ed. in India, 1846.

Nesbit, A., Essay on, 1841.

Nova Scotia, Report, 1857.

Olin, Works, vol. 2, 1852.

Panton, Guardian's instruction, 1688.

Parr, S., Discourse on.

Parson, B., Educ. as it ought to be.

Pears, Mind and body, 1855.

Peers, American Education, 1838.

Pemberton, R., Mind-formation, 1858.

Phillips, J. T., Of Teaching lang., 1750.

Phillips, R., New theories of ed., 1835.

Pillans, Ed. for the Orders of Society, 1836.

Pole, T., History of adult School.

Poole, J., Village School, 1812.

Popular Educator, 1853, 54.

Preston, S., Ed. in the 19th Century, 1846. P. 1704.

Publication of Books at the public expense.

Randall, S. S., Princ. of pop. Ed.

" Mental and Moral Culture.

Richson, Pauper education.

Rollin, Method of teaching Belles-lettres, 1749. B. C.

" New thoughts, 1738.

Rousseau, J. J., Emilius and Sophia.

Schmidt, H. J., Hist. and Plan, 1848.

Schoolmaster (The), from Ascham, etc., 1836.

Seward, W. H., Discourse on, 1837.

Shuttleworth, Public educa., 1846–52.

Simpson, J., Necessity of pop. education, 1834. B. C.

Smith, S. H., Remarks on, 1798.

Soc. for the Encouragement of Arts: Educat. Exhibition, 1854.

Spencer, H., Essays on, 1861.

Spurzheim, Elemen. principles of, 1833.

Styles, J., Lancastrian System, 1812.

Surtees, Ed. for the People, 1846.

Symons, J. C., School Economy, 1852.

Taylor, J. O., The District School.

Temple, Sir W., Works, 1720.

Thompson, D. W., Day Dreams of a Schoolmaster, 1864.

Thoughts on domestic, 1806.

Todd, Student's Manual, 1835.

Tweed, D., Teacher's and Pupil's assistant, 1820.

Vincent, On Public Education, 1802.

Wordsworth, Public Education, 1844.

Education, Treatises, Method, etc. (continued).

Youmans, Culture of Modern life, 1867.

See Children; Academies; Military Ed.; Object Lessons; University Ed.; Self-culture.

Education, Teachers and Normal Schools, Addresses. Abbott, J., Address.

Addresses. P. vols. 969, 1669.

Babington, View of Christian E., 1818.

Barnard, H., Papers for the Teacher.

" Normal Schools, 1851.

Bates, J., On T. Arnold, 1852.

Benedict, E. C., N. Y. Normal School Address, 1858.

Board of Nat. Education, Report, 1848, 52–57.

Bond, T. E., Dickinson Inst., 1837.

Brown, J., Mech. Assoc., Oswego, Ad., 1841.

Burgess, R., Serm., National Educ., 1839.

Calthrop, Lecture, 1859.

Clinton, G. W., Normal School Address, 1856.

Conolly, Lecture on, 1836.

Garnett, J. M., Address, Richmond, Va., 1830.

Hagar, Supervision of Schools, 1851.

Hall, S. R., On School-keeping, 1832.

Huntington, F. D., Home and College.

Indiana State Teachers' Assoc., 1854.

Jones, R. D., N. Y. Teachers' Assoc., 1855.

Kennedy, B., On School Discipline, 1842.

Keyes, E. W., N. Y. Teachers' Assoc., 1858.

May, S. J., Normal Asso., Ad., 1855.

Normal Schools. Pam. vol. 994.

Oliver, Lect., Teachers' Morals, 1851.

Onondaga Teachers' Institute, 1851, 52.

Page, D. P., Theory of Teaching.

Penn'a State Convention, 1850.

Perez, Inoculacion del Entendimiento, 1789.

Perkins, F. B., Conn. Normal School Address, 1858.

Phelps, W. F., N. J. Normal School Address, 1857.

Rogers, E. P., Normal School Address, 1857.

Russell, W., Ass'ns of Teachers, 1830.

" Normal Training.

Sands, Philosophy of Teaching, 1869.

Shepard, D., Colchester Ed. Asso., 1843.

Sinclair, W., Baltimore Coll.

Sweet, S. N., Temporary Normal Sch's, 1848.

Education, Massachusetts (contin'd).
Taunton, Reports, 1851-2.
Twistleton, E., Schools in Mass., 1854.
West Roxbury, Reports, 1854.
Wightman, J. M., Boston Primary Schools, 1818-55.

Education, New York. Academies of N. Y., Catalogues. Pam. v. 456, 7, 9, 596-99, 850-853.
Albany, Reports of Free Academy, 1868, 9.
Boese, T., Ed. in the City of N. Y., 1869.
Bourne, Hist. Pub. Sch. Soc. in N. Y. City, 1870.
Brooklyn Reports, 1856-68.
Buffalo Female Academy, Proc. and Catalogues, 1852-56.
Hawley, G., Instructions, 1819.
High School Society, 1828.
New York, Reports of Com. Schools, 1839-69.
" Code of Public Inst., 1856.
" Decisions of Sup't, 1837.
New York City, Board of Education, Reports, 1851, 54.
" Free Academy, College of N. Y., Registers to, 1863.
New York Normal School Reports, 1845-68.
N. Y. State Teachers' Assoc. Advocate, 1845-50.
New York Teacher, 1854-67.
Oswego, Board of Education, (Object lessons), 1863.
" Reports, 1854-62.
Public Sch. Soc. N. Y. Reports, 1832, 1835, 42.
Randall, S. S., Digest of N. Y. System, 1844, 45.
" Hist. Sketch of, 1851.
" Hist. of, in N. Y., from 1795-1871.
Russell, A., Account of New York Schools, 1847.
Rochester, Board of Education, Reports, 1858-67.
Schenectady, N. Y., Reports, 1856.
Seton, Manual of primary, 1830.
Stone, W. L., On the Board of Educ. of New York, 1843.
Syracuse, Educ. Reports, 1852-61.
Troy, Manual of Board, 1869, 71.
University of N. Y., Regents Reports, 1823-1870.

Education, Pennsylvania. Morgan, G., Report on, 1836.
Penn'a Reports, etc., 1848-57.
Common School Laws, 1870.
Phil'a Charity Schools.

Education, Pennsylvania (continued).
Phil'a, Reports, 1841-58.
Union Schools, Phil'a., 1847.

Education, United States. Amer. Ass'n for, 1852-6.
Allston, System in S. Carolina, 1847.
Andrews, C. C., Reflections on, 1853.
Bangor, Me., Report, 1854.
Baltimore Reports, 1851, 52.
Bushnell, Rom. Cath. Demands, 1853.
California, Reports, 1856, 65, 68, 69.
Charleston, S. C., Report on Schools, 1859.
Chicago, Supt's Reports, 1866-69.
Cincinnati, Supt's Reports, 1833-56.
Cleveland, O., Supt's Reports, 1853-56.
Connecticut, Reports on, 1850-58.
Convention of Friends of, 1830.
Education dans les Etats Unis, 1812.
Education Reports, 1829-54. Pam. vol. 171, 174, 190.
Illinois School Reports, 1859, 61-62, 65, 67, 69.
Indiana, Supt. Reports, 1855, 57.
Iowa Reports, 1854.
" School Laws, 1856.
Kentucky, Reports, 1855, 59, 63.
Louisiana, Supt's Report, 1853.
Maryland, Lands for Schools, 1823.
" Report, 1821.
" Washington Coll., 1784.
" Univ. of Maryland.
Michigan, Rep. on Pub. Ins., 1859-69.
" School Laws, 1864, 70.
Nashville, Tenn. Report, 1858.
New Hampshire, Supt's Reports, 1847, 59, 60.
N. J. Reports on, 1848, 55-57.
New Orleans Public Schools, 1858.
Ohio, Comm'rs Reports, 1854-59, 62-66.
Penn'a, Reports of Superintendent.
Phil'a, Reports of Public Schools.
Phil'a Soc. for Charity Sch.
Report on Ragged Schools, Phil'a.
Rhode Island, Supt's Reports, 1845, 48, 53-57.
San Francisco, Cal., Report, 1855.
Smyth, T., Parochial Schools, 1849.
Tucker, J., N. Y., Appeal for Free Schools, 1850.
U. S., 1st Report, (Barnard), 1868.
" 2d Report, 1870.
Vermont Report, 1857-60.
Virginia School Laws, 1842.
Virginia Report, 1842.
Watson, A., Bible in Schools, 1846.
Wisconsin, Supt's Rep., 1852, 53, 58, 59.
" School code, 1867.

Education, England. Baines, Strictures, 1853.

Barnard, H., English Pedagogy.

Boone, J. S., National Ed., 1833.

" Educ. Economy in Eng., 1838

Bristed, Five Years in an Eng. Univ., 1852.

British and Foreign School Society, 1818.

Buckler, Views of 60 Grammar Schools.

Central Soc. of Education, Papers, 1837-39.

Christ's College, Brecon, 1853.

Close, F , Writings.

Great Britain, Council of Education, Minutes, 1840-53.

Hamilton, H. P., Church of England Schools, 1850. P. 388.

Harrow, Prolusiones, 1850.

Hinton, J. H., Manchester Educationists, 1852. P. 388.

Huber, English Universities, 1843.

Hughes, T., School Days at Rugby, 1858.

Ingestre, Meliora, 1852, 53.

Irish School System.

Longman, School-books by Gov't., 1851. P. 388.

National Society, England.

Obs. on Brougham's bill, 1821.

Packard, F. A., Schools in, 1841.

Philanthropos, Letters, Lon., 1841.

Potter, J. P., Proposed Systems, 1828.

Pound, W., Church Education Society, 1852, 53.

Rapier, Education for Private Gentlemen, 1842.

Reed, A., Review of Ed. Commission of the Privy Council, 1852.

Shrewsbury School List, 1838. P. 387.

Slaney, Reports to Parliament, 1838.

South Kensington Museum, Educ. Division, 1860.

Staunton, Great Schools of England, 1865.

University Coll. of London, 1845-47.

Westminster School, Letter on, 1831.

Wickham, G., Hertford School, Eng.

See University Education; Cambridge; Oxford.

Education, French and European. Annuaire de l'Instr. Publique, 1851-58.

Arnold, M., Schools and Univ. in Europe.

Bache, Education in Europe, 1839.

Barnard, H., Nat. Ed. in Europe, 1854.

" German Schools.

Barrau, Educ. Privée, 1857.

" Lois en vigueur, 1853.

Education, French and European (continued).

Barrau, Conseils, 1852.

" Direction Morale, 1855.

Belgium, Instruc. Primaire, 1830-40.

" Instruc. Moyenne, 1842-48.

" Etat de l'enseignement, 1842.

Buddingh, Jaarboekje, 1846.

" Kerk, School en Wetenschap, 1853.

Charte (La) Vérité, 1844.

Cousin, Instruction en Hollande, 1838.

" Instruction in Prussia, 1835.

France: Education, 1851, 52, 54, 57.

" Rapport par A. Thiers.

" Plan d'études des lycées, 1852.

" Statis. de l'enseign. supérieur, (Duruy), 1865-68.

Gelliers, Trap der Jeugd, 1715. B. C.

Greuve, Volkslees, 1807-8.

Henry, P., Manuel des Maitres, 1854.

Heun, Briefe an Jünglinge die auf Universitäten, etc., 1792.

Hickson, Dutch and German Schools.

James, G. P. R., Educ. Institutions of Germany, 1835.

Jourdain, Le Budget de l'Instr. Pub., 1857.

Julien, Méthode d'éducation de Pestalozzi, 1842.

Lorain, Man. de l'Enseig. Prim., 1858.

Maes, Schriftuurlyk School-boekje.

Manuel Général, Jour. hebdom., 1832-1857.

Neigebauer, Preussischen Gymnasien, 1835.

Netherlands, Verslagen, 1840-51.

Pamphlets, relating to Education in France, vols. 657, 784.

Prévost, Du Rôle de la Famille, 1857.

Rendu, Enseigne. obligatoire, 1853.

Roman States, Organisation des Universités, 1847.

Saint Marc Girardin, Instruction intermédiaire, 1835.

Steffens, Deutsch. Prot. Universitäten 1820.

Stowe, C. E., Instruction in Europe, 1838. Pam. 490.

Taylor, J. O., Digest of Cousin's Report, 1836. B. C.

Thèry, Conseils....1853.

Thiers, Instruction secondaire, 1844.

See University Education.

Educational Biography. American Journal of Education.

American Annals of Education.

Barnard, English pedagogues.

" Educ. Biography.

" Pestalozzis Life.

Emmet, R. Madden, Life of, 1857.

Emmet, T. A. Haines, C. G., Memoir of, 1820.

Madden, Memoir of, 1857.

Mitchill, S. L., Discourse on, 1828.

Emporium Co. Smith, J. F., Details, 1857.

Emmons, N. Cox, S. H., Interviews, 1853.

Williams, T., Character of.

Encyclopædias of Knowledge. Allgemeine Deutsche Real-Encyk., 1848.

American Annual Cyclopedia, 1861–70.

Beeton, Dict. of univ. information, 1865.

Bouillet, Dict. des Sci., des Lettres et des Arts, 1845, 58.

Browne, D. J., Etymol. Encyc. of technical words, 1832.

Chambers' Cyclopædia, 1786.

Chambers' Encyclopedia, 1868.

Collier, Historical Dict., 1701.

Crabb, Univ. Hist. Dict., 1825.

" Dict. of Gen. Knowl., 1830.

" Univ. Technolog. Dict., 1823.

Dictionnaire de l'Indus. Manuf. Comm. et Agr., 1833–41.

Dict. Univ. de Trévoux, 1740.

Edinburgh Cab. Lib , 1835–44.

Edinburgh Encyclopædia, 1832.

Encyclo. Americana, 1829–47.

Encyclo. Britannica, 1853–60.

Encyclo. Dobson, Phil'a, 1798–1803.

Encyclo. Metropolitana, 1845.

Encyclopédie, (Diderot), 1778.

Encyclo. Méthodique, 1782–1832.

Encyclo. Populaire, 1848–50.

Faber, Thes. Erudit. Scholast., 1696.

Iconographic Encyclopædia, 1851.

New Amer. Cyclopædia, Appleton, 1860–64.

Nichol, Cycl. of Phys. Science, 1857.

Nicholson's Brit. Encyclopædia, 1809.

Nieuwenhuis, Alg. Woordenboek, 1829.

Ogilvie's Imper. Dictionary, 1851.

Penny Cyclopædia, 1833–46.

Rees, A., Cyclopædia.

Soc. pour l'éman. intell., Encyc. pop., 1848–50.

Standard Library Cyclopædia, 1858.

Tomlinson, Cycl. of Useful Arts, 1852. Supplement, 1868.

Ure, Dict. of Arts, Man. and Mines, 1840.

" Supplement to Dict., 1845, 63.

Vincentius, Speculum Majus, 1494.

Waterston, Cyclopædia of commerce, 1843.

Encyclopædias of Knowledge (continued).

See Dictionaries of Sci., Hist., etc.; Sciences; Arts; History; Bridges; Railroads.

Engel, Mary. Memorial, 1860.

Enghien, Duc d'. Savary, Memoir relative.

Engineering, Civil and Mechanical.

Aeneæ, Verhand om afstanden te metem, 1812.

Alexandria aqueduct, 1837–38.

Annual retrospect, 1861.

Appleton's Dict. of Mechanics, 1852.

Annales des Ponts et Chaussées, 1831–1859.

Barlow, On the strength of timber, 1826.

Belgium, Des Inondations, 1844.

Byrne, Model Calculator, 1852.

Chapman, W., Reports, 1792–1832.

Civil Engineer's Journal, 1838–68.

Clark, E., Britannia tubular bridges, 1850.

Cole, G., The Contractor's Book, 1855.

Cresy, Encyclopædia of Civil Engin., 1847.

Davy, Artificial foundations, 1839.

Downes, Marine Railway.

Eaton, A., Direct. for Surveying and, 1830.

Ecole R. des Ponts et Chaussées, 1827.

France, Bridges and Roads, 1856.

Frazer, W. A., Algemeene voorwaarden, 1857.

Galbraith, Surveying and Railway engineering, 1842.

Gillespie, Treat. on Land surveying, 1855.

Gurley, Instruments for Engineering.

Hebert, Engineer's and Mech. Encyc., 1837.

Henz, Anleitung zum Erdbau.

Hoppus, Tables for measuring, 1823.

Illinois and St. Louis Bridge Company, Report, 1868.

Institution of Civil Engineers, Transactions, 1836–40.

Konink. Inst. van Ingen., Verhandelingen.

Kraijenhoff, Opérations géodesiques en Hollande, 1827.

Long, J. H., Cadet engineer.

Mahan, Elementary course of, 1848.

Millington, J., Elements of Civil engineering, 1839.

Moseley, Mech. Principles of, 1856.

Mount Cenis tunnel.

N. Y. State Inst. of Civil Engineering, Transactions, 1849.

Nicholson's treatise on projection, 1840

Engineering, Civil and Mechanical (continued).
Pamphlets relating to Engineering, vol. 493; B. C. 36.
Rankin, Manual of, 1863.
Rennie, Rivers and Harbors of Great Britain.
Roads, Railroads and Bridges, 1839.
Routledge, Sliding rule.
Sganzin, Elementary Course of, 1828.
Simms, F. W., Public Works of Great Britain, 1838.
Smeaton's Reports, 1812.
Stuart, C. B., Naval Dry-Docks of U. S., 1852.
Tomlinson, Cyclopedia, 1852, 68.
Weisbach, Mechanics of Engineering, 1847, 48.
Weissenborn, American Engineering, 1858, 59.
Whewell, Mechanics of, 1841.
Zusto, Estrazione della Nave La Fenice, 1789.
See Railways; Bridges; Steam Engine; Machinery; Military Science; Croton Aqueduct; Cements; Drawing.

England, Antiquities. *See* Great Britain; Antiquities.

England, Church of. *See* Church of Eng.

England: History: General. Baker, Sir R., Chron. of the Kings of, 1679.
Barlace, Prog. of Knowl. in Eng.
Buckle, Hist. of Civilization in, 1858.
Camden, Rerum Ang. annales, 1639.
Camden Society publications, 1838-69.
Catechism of, 1842.
Chronicles and Memorials of G. B., (Rolls Pub.), 80 vols.
Chronicle of the Kings. P. 1708.
Clarke, S. R., Vestigia Anglicana.
Craik, G. L., Pict. Hist. of, 1849.
Doleman, Succession to the Crown, 1681.
English Histor. Soc. Publications, 1838-56.
Farr, School History, 1848.
Goldsmith, O., History of, to 1802.
Granger, J., Biog. Hist. of, 1769, 1804.
Green, W., Chron. Epitome of.
Hardy's Catalogue of Materials, (Chro. G. B).
Hume, D., History of Eng. to Rev. of 1688.
Kennett, W., Hist. to Death of William III, 1719.
Leland, De rebus Britann. Collectanea, 1774.
Lingard, History of, 1826-31.
" Vindication of his Hist. of, 1826.

England: History: General (cont'd).
Lloyd, T., Gen. Hist. of, 1764.
McMasters, Index to Hume.
Millar, J., Hist. View of Eng. Gov. to 1688.
Markham, Mrs., History of.
Mortimer, T., History of, 1764.
Nicolson, Engl. Hist. Library, 1714.
Pearson's Hist. of the Early and Middle Ages of, 1867.
Rapin, Hist. of Eng., 1728-31.
Rhymes for Youthful historians.
Sanford, Governing Families of.
Strickland, Lives of Queens of, 1848.
Tindal, Summary, to George II, V. 3.
Thompson, Municipal Hist. of, 1867.
Towers, On Hume's History, 1778.
Turner, Hist. of Anglo-Saxons, 1828.
White, J., History of, to 1858.
See Great Britain; Bibliography.

England, History: Early Chronicles, etc. to Henry VIII. Abingdon, Chron. Monasterii, (Chron. G. B.).
Adamus Murimuthensis, Chronica sui temporis, (E. Hist. Soc.).
Anglo-Saxon Chron., (Chron. G. B.).
Annales Monastici, (Chron. G. B.).
Arnold's Chronicle, 1811.
Arthur, History of, 1858.
Bacon, Lord, King Henry VII, 1824.
Bede, Eccl. Hist. of Eng., 1847.
" Opera Historica Minora, (E. Hist. Soc.).
Berington, Hist. of Henry II, 1154-1216.
Blondell, Narr. of Expulsion of Eng. from Normandy, 1449, 50, (Chron. G. B.).
Brady, Hist. to Henry III.
Brougham, History of, 1861.
Camden Soc. Publications.
Capgrave, J., De Illust. Henricis, 1858.
" Chronicle of England, 1858.
Chronicles of Great Britain, 1863-69.
Cobbe, Norman Kings of England.
Cotton, B. de, Historia Anglicana, (Chro. G. B.).
Domes-Day Book, Liber judicialis.
Du Fresnoy, Chron. tables.
Edward, King, Lives, 1858.
Eulogium Historiarum, (Chron. G. B.).
Fabyan, New chronicles, 1811.
Florence of Worcester, Chronicle.
Florentius Wigorniensis, Chronicon, (E. Hist. Soc.).
Geoffroy of Monmouth's Brit. History, 1848.
Gildas, Opus de Excidio Britanniæ, (E. Hist. Soc.).

England, History: Early Chronicles, etc. to Henry VIII (continued).

Giustinian, Four years at Court of Henry VIII, 1815–19.

Gloucester, Cart. Monast. S. Petri Gloucestriæ, (Chron. G. B.).

Gonzalez, Docts. from Simancas, 1568–15.

Grafton's Chronicle, 1189–1558.

Halsted, Richard III, as Duke and King.

Harding's Chronicle to Henry VIII.

Hearne, Curious Discourses.

Henrici Quinti Gesta cum Chronica Neustriæ, (E. Hist. Soc.).

Henry of Huntingdon, Chronicles, 1853.

Higden, R., Polychronicon, (Chron. G. B.).

Hyde, Liber monasterii de Hyde, (Chron. G. B.)

History of Eng. and France, 1852.

Hopkins, S., The Puritans, Edw. VI and Eliz., 1859.

Hoveden, Annals of, 732–1201.

Ingulph, Chron. of Abbey of Croyland, 1854.

Johannes de Oxenedes, (Chron. G. B.).

Johannes de Trokelowe, Chronica Monasterii S. Albani, (Chron. G. B.).

John de Wavrin's Chronicles, (Chron. G. B.).

Kemble, J. M., Codex Diplomaticus Aevi Saxonici, (E. Hist. Soc.).

Langtoft, P. de, Chronicle to Edward I, (Hearne, and Chron. G. B.).

Lappenberg, Under Anglo-Sax. Kings, 1845.

Leland, De rebus Britannicis, 1774.

Letters of the wars of, with France, in Henry VI, (Chron. G. B.).

Livere (Le) de Reis de Brittanie, (Chron. G. B.)

Lyttelton, Hist. of Henry II, 1767.

Matthew of Paris, Historia Anglorum, (Chron. G. B.).

" Eng. Hist., 1235–73.

Matthew of Westminster, Chronicle to 1307.

Melsa, Chron. Monast. de Melsa, (Chron. G. B.).

Miller, T., History of the Anglo-Saxons, 1848.

Monumenta Franciscana, 1858.

Monumenta Historica Britannica, (Petrie), 1848, f°.

More, Sir T., Reigns of Edward V, and Richard III.

Nennius: Historia Britonum, (Eng. Hist. Soc.).

Palgrave, Hist. of Normandy and, 1851, 57, 64.

Rise and Prog. of Eng. Commonwealth, 1832.

England, History: Early Chronicles, etc. of Henry VIII (continued).

Paston Letters, 1840.

Pauli, Life of King Alfred, 1852.

Polydorus, Anglica Historia.

Richard I, Chron. of the reign of, (Chron. G. B.).

Richard II, Chronicque de la Traïson, (E. Hist. Soc.).

Richard of Cirencester Speculum Historiale, (Chron. G. B.).

Ricardus Divisiensis: Chron. de Rebus gestis Ricardi I, (E. Hist. Soc.).

Rishanger's Chron. Monast. S. Albani, (Chron. G. B.)

Roberts, E., Hist. of York and Lancaster.

Roger de Wendover, Chronica, (Eng. Hist. Soc.)

" Flowers of Hist. to 1235.

Six Old English Chronicles, 1848.

Stapleton, Rot. Scaccarii Normanniæ, 1840.

Stephen: Gesta Stephani, Reg. Angl., (E. Hist. Soc.).

Thierry, History of Conquest by Normans, 1847.

Thomas of Elmham's Hist. Monast. Cantuar., (Chron, G. B.).

Thomson, R., Hist. of Magna Charta, 1829.

Trivetus, (F. N.), De Ordine Fratrum prædic., (E. Hist. Soc.).

Turner, S., Hist. of, during Middle ages, 1825.

Tyler, J. E., Mem. of Henry of Monmouth, 1838.

Tytler, P. F., Reigns of Edward IV and Mary, 1839.

" Life of Henry VIII.

Verstegan, Restitution, 1634.

Walsingham, T., Historia Anglicana, (Chron. G. B.).

Walter de Hemingburgh.... Chron. de Gestis Regum, (E. Hist. Soc.).

William of Malmesbury, Gesta Regum Angl., (E. Hist. Soc.).

" Chron., 1847.

Willelmus Parvus, Hist. Rerum Anglicarum, (E. Hist. Soc.).

Zurich Letters, 1537–58.

See Great Britain; Parliament; Names of the Sovereigns.

England, History to 1688. Aikin, L., Mem. of C't of Elizabeth, 1819.

" Mem. of Court of James I, 1822.

" Mem. of Court of Chas. I, 1833.

Bell, R., Memorials of the Civil War, 1849.

Birch, T., Times of Charles I, 1848, 49.

Carrel, A., Counter-Rev. in: Charles II, 1846.

England, History to 1688 (continued).

Cary, Civil War in, 1646–52.
Caulfield, High Court of Justice, 1820.
Charles I., Bibliot. Regia, 1659.
Clarendon's Life, 1759.
Clarendon, Earl of, Hist. of Rebellion, 1641.
" State Papers, 1621–45.
Coll. of Proclam. of the Pretender.
Coll. of State Tracts, Rev. of 1688.
Cromwell, O., Letters and Speeches, 1845.
Dahlman, Hist. of the English Rev., 1844.
Description....des Guerres, 1668.
Echard, Hist. of Rev. to 1688.
Ellis, H., Original Letters, Illustrative of, 1824.
Ellis, J., Correspondence, 1686–88.
Evelyn, J., Memoirs and Diary, 1641–1706.
Fox, C. J., Hist. of James II, 1808.
Froude, J. A., From fall of Wolsey to Death of Elizabeth, 1856–70.
Godwin, W., Hist. of Commonwealth, 1824.
Goodman, G., Court of James I, 1839.
Guizot, Hist of Eng. Rev. of 1640.
" Hist. de la Républ. d'Angleterre, 1649–58.
Henrietta Maria, Letters.
Historical Collections, 1674.
Hallam, Constitutional Hist. of, 1829.
Hamilton, A., Mem. of Count Grammont, 1811.
Hayward, J., Reign of Elizabeth, 1849.
Hobbes, T., Works, v. 6, Civil Wars, 1839.
Howard, Earl of, Life of.
Johnson, G. W., Fairfax Corresp., 1848.
Le Clerc, On Clarendon's History.
Leycester, Civil War of, 1641–48.
Lodge, E., Illustrations of Brit. Hist. Henry VII, to James I, 1838.
Ludlow, E., Mem. of Charles I, 1771.
Macaulay, T. B., History of, from Jas. II, 1849.
Mem. of God's last 29 Years of Wonders, 1689.
Milton, J., Literae, 1676.
Nalson's collection of State Papers. 1639–50.
Nickolls, Letter, to Cromwell, 1743.
North, R., Examen. Vind. of Charles II, 1740.
Orléans, P. J. d', Révol. d'Angleterre, 1723.
Peacock, List of Roundheads and Cavaliers.
Peck's Desiderata Curiosa, 1779.

England, History to 1688 (continued).

Political poems and Songs Relating to, (Chron. G. B.).
Plot of 1679.
Prynne, Opening of the Great Seale of, 1643.
Rushworth, Hist. Collections, 1721.
Sadler, Sir Ralph, State Papers, 1809.
Salmasius, C., Defensio Regia, 1649.
Secret Hist. of Reigns of Charles II, and James II, 1690.
Sidney, H., Diary of Times of Charles II, 1843.
Slingsby, Memoirs of Civil War, 1806.
Somers, Coll. of Tracts, v. 1–9.
Somerville, T., From Rest. of Charles II, to William, 1793.
State Tracts, 1660–93.
Stiles, Hist. of Three of the Judges, etc., 1794.
Stoughton, Eccl. Hist., 1640–50.
Strafford's Dispatches.
Sydneys, Memorial and State Papers.
Temple, Sir W., Works, 1720.
Thurloe, Coll. of State Papers, 1742.
Vaughan, R., Revolutions in English History, 1860.
" Protec. of Cromwell, 1839.
" Hist. under the Stuarts, 1603–88.
Vicars, England's Worthies, 1642–47.
Walker, C., Hist. of Independency of Parl., 1640–1660.
Ward, R. P., On the Revolution of 1688.
Welwood, Mem. for last 100 years, 1700.
Whitlock, Memoir of the English Affairs, 1732.
Wiffen, Mem. of House of Russell, 1833.
York, Duke of, Mem. of Eng. Affairs, 1660–73.

See Names of the Sovereigns.

England, History of, 1688 to present time. Account of the Young Chevalier.

Adolphus, Hist. of, to death of George III, 1840–45.
Aikin, J., Annals of George III, 1760–1820.
Amer. and Brit. Chron., 1773–83.
Auberteuil, Admin. of Lord North, 1784.
Baring, Orders in Council, 1808
Belsham, W., Chron. George III, IV, 1828.
" Mem. of Kings of H. of Brunswick, 1800.
" Reign of George III, 1801–5.
Birch, T., Reign of Queen Eliz., 1754.
Bisset, R., Reign of George III, 1820.

England, History of, 1688 to present time (continued).

Buckingham, Court of George III, 1853–54.
" Court of Engl., 1811–20.
Bunbury, French War, 1799–1810.
Burke, E., Works, 1826, 27.
Burnet, Hist. of his own time, 1818.
Butler, C., Hist. of Brit. Catholics, 1822.
Caroline, Queen, Character of, 1738.
Cavendish, Parl. Debates, 1768–74.
Cole, State Papers, 1697–1708.
Cockburn, Mem. of his time, 1856.
Devereux, Lett. of the Earls of Essex, 1540–1646.
Dodington, Diary, 1749–61.
Doubleday, Finan. and Statis. History of, 1688–1847.
Dutens, L., Etablissement d'un Régence, 1788, 89.
Eustace, Lettres sur les crimes de George III, 1794. Pam. 33.
Fonblanque, Eng. under 7 administrations, 1837.
George, Prince of Wales, Tracts concerning, 1795–1816. Pam. 141.
Great Brit., Parl., Rebell., 1722.
Hamilton, Lady, Secret Hist. of reign of George III, IV, 1832.
Hervey, Reign of George II, 1848.
Historical Memorial, 1761.
Holland, Lord, Mem. of the Whig Party, 1852–54.
Holt, E., Life of George III, 1820.
Intercepted Letters, 1804.
Jesse, J. H., From 1688 to death of George II, 1843.
" Memoirs of the Pretender, 1846.
King, W., Polit. and Lit. Anecdotes, 1818.
Lexington Papers, 1694–1698.
Macaulay, T. B., Hist. from James II.
Mahon, Lord, Insurrection of 1745.
" Hist. of Eng., 1713–83.
Marchmont, Events from 1685–1750.
Marlborough, Duke of, Letters, 1702–1712.
Massey, Hist. under George III, 1855.
Martineau, H., Hist. of, 1816–54.
" Introd. to Hist. of Peace, 1800–15.
Mém. des Commissaires du roi, 1755–57.
Mémoires touchant le gouvernement de, 1764.
Neale, E., Life of Edward, Duke of Kent, 1850.
Nicholls, Public Affairs under George III, 1822.
Parkin, Invasion by William.
Pitt, W., Anecdotes of Life of, 1736–94.
Roebuck, J. A., History of Whig Ministry, 1830–52.
Rolt, Hist. of War, 1739–48.
St. John, Lord Bolingbroke, Works.
Smollett, T., History of, 1758–61.
Somers, Collection of Tracts, v. 10–13, 1809–15.
Sophia, Consort of George I, Memoirs.
Steele, Sir R., Political Works, 1715.
Stuart, The, Papers, 1847.
Thomson, A. T., Memoirs of the Jacobites, 1715–45.
" Life of Sarah, Duchess of Marlborough, 1839.
Tindal's Hist. of Eng. from 1688–1747.
Turner, Modern Hist of Eng., 1828.
Vernon, Letters, 1696–1708.
Waldegrave's Memoirs, 1750–58.
Walpole, H., Mem. of George II.
" Mem. of George III, 1845.
Walpole, R., Crit. Hist. of his administration, 1743.
" Rapport du Comité secret, 1715.
Walsh, Sir J., Chap. of Contemporary History, 1836.
William III, Letters.
Wraxall, Hist. Mem. of his time, 1836.
" Posthumous Memoirs, 1836.
Wright, T., Eng. under House of Hanover.

England, Manners and Customs.

Andrews, The 18th Century.
Brief Remarks on, 1816.
Brookes, Man. and Cust. of.
Brown, J., Estimate of Manners, 1757.
Ellis, Daughters of.
" Mothers of England.
Female Jockey Club.
Goldsmith, O., Citizen of the World.
Goodman, Social Hist. of G. B., to 1688.
Kay, Social condition of, 1863.
La Belle Assemblée, 1810–33.
M'Elheran, Woman in Gothic Nations.
Merryweather, Glimmerings.
Saunders, English Life.
Stone, Mrs., Chron. of Fashion, 1846.
Thornbury, Shakespeare's England.
Thrupp, Anglo-Saxon Home, 1862.
Wright, Superstit. of Middle Ages.

England, Registers and Almanacs.

Almanacs, 1679–1800.
Annual Register, 1758–1769.
Army List, 1757–1850.
British Almanac, 1828–69.

England, Registers and Almanacs. (continued).

Chamberlayne, Present state of, 1676, 1735, 43, 55.

" Staat van, 1743.

Clergy List, 1841-50.

Dietrichsen's Royal Alm., 1842, 44, 52.

Englishman's Alm., 1852.

Gilbert's Clergyman's Alm., 1836-8.

Great Britain, Census, 1851.

" Registrar Gen., Births, Marriages and Deaths, 1839-53.

Gutch, Lit. Register, 1845, 7, 8.

Hull and Yorkshire Almanac, 1852.

Martin's Statesman's Year-book, 1865-1871.

Price, R., Population of, from 1688.

Royal Blue Book, 1855.

Royal Calendar, 1763-1855.

Whitaker's Almanac, 1867, 71, 72.

See Great Britain.

England, Topographical, Travels, etc. Angleterre, L', en 1800.

Account of the Manors, 1787.

Archæol. Inst. of G. B., 1851.

Austin, Letters from London, 1804.

Baker's Northamptonshire, 1822-41.

Beauties of England and Wales, 25 v.

Bray, W., Tour, Derbyshire and Yorkshire.

Brayley's Surrey, 1850.

Britannia....Chorog. Descriptio.

Bulwer, England and the English, 1833.

Cooke's Topog. Library.

Coxe, A. C., Impressions, 1856.

Dibdin, C., Obs. on a Tour, 1801.

Dickinson, A., My First Visit to Europe, 1851.

Drew, Glimpses in, 1851.

Elmham, Hist. Monast. S. Augustini, 1858.

Emerson, English Traits, 1856.

Etat de l'Angleterre, 1822, 23.

Fisher, Bedfordshire, 1812-36.

Gilpin, W., Observations on England, etc., 1808.

Gœde, C.A.G., Foreigner's Opinion of, 1822.

Gourcy, Quatrième Voyage en.

Granville, The Spas of England, 1841.

Great Brit., County Boundaries, 1832.

Howitt, Rural Life in.

" Visits to Remarkable Places.

Items, (Todd), 1855.

Johnson, W., England as it is, 1851.

Lee, Hist. of Lewes, 1795.

Lester, C. E., Condition and Fate of.

" Glory and Shame of, 1841.

England, Topographical, Travels, etc. (continued).

Lewis, S., Topog. Dictionary of, 1831, 1838.

Lowe, J., Present State of, 1824.

Mackenzie, A. S., The Amer. in, 1835.

Magna Britannia, 1720.

Mézaque, Bilan général de l'Angleterre, 1600-1761.

Miller, H., First Impressions of, 185'.

Mirabeau, Letters from, 1832.

Misson, Memoirs in his Trav. in, 1719.

Montgaillard, Situation of, in 1811.

Moritz, Travels in.

Nash's Worcestershire, 1781, 82.

Olmsted, F. L., Walks of an American Farmer, 1852.

Pamphlets, vols. 1478, 1573, 1754-1757.

Patterson, Cross Roads in.

Pegge, Curialia.

Raumer, F. Von, England in 1835.

Reresby, Memoirs and Travels, 1813.

Rogers, Three Years in, 1694.

Rose, Westmorland, Cumberland, Durham, Northumberland, 1833.

Rush, R., Memoranda of a Residence, 1833.

Salisbury Guide, 1830.

Sedgwick, T., Public and Private Economy, 1836.

Shebbeare, Letters on the English Nation, 1756.

Sherburne, Tourist's Guide, 1847.

Silliman, B., Travels in, 1805-6, 1820.

Smith, J. T., A Book for a Rainy Day, 1845.

Society of Antiquaries, Lond.

Sorbière, Voyage to, 1709.

Southey, R., Letters of Espriella from, 1808. B. C.

Topographer and Genealogist, J. G. Nichols, 1846-58.

Tuckerman, H. T., A Month in Eng., 1853.

Tymms, Family Topographer.

Tyng, Recollections of Eng., 1847.

Uncle Tom in England, 1852.

Voltaire, Letters, 1733.

Ward, Matt. F., English Items, 1833.

See also the following: Anglesea; Berwick; Cheshire; Cumberland; Durham; Edmonton; Ecton; Gravesend; Guernsey; Hackney; Islington; Jersey; Kent; Liverpool; London; Man Is.; Newcastle; Norfolk; Norwich; Oxfordshire; Reading; St. Saviour's; Salisbury; Smithfield; Sussex; Tottenham; Upminster; Uxbridge, Wales; Windsor; Whitby; Worcestershire; Wight; Wiltshire; York; and other counties and towns.

Engraving, History of, etc. (cont'd).
Donlevy, The Graphic arts, 1854.
Gilpin, Essay on Prints, 1802.
Exposition Univ., Rapports du Jury, 1856.
Fielding, The Art of Engraving, 1844.
Fournier, Orig. de l'Art de Graver, 1758.
Granger, Biog. Hist. of England, 1804.
Heineken, Idée d'une Coll. d'Estampes, 1771.
Jackson, Treatise on wood-engraving, 1839.
Jansen, Origine de la Gravure, 1808.
Joubert, Man. de l'Amateur d'Estampes, 1821.
Landseer, Lectures on the art of, 1807.
Menapius, Statera Chalcographiæ. *See* Wolf.
Ormsby, Bank-note Engr., 1852.
Ottley, Early use of wood engr., 1863.
Peignot, Répertoire de Bibliog., 1810.
" Recherches sur les Danses des morts, 1826.
Sotheby, Principia Typographica, 1858.
Spooner, Dict. of Engravers, 1853.
Strutt, Biog. Dict. of Engravers, 1785, 1786.
Waagen, Treasures of Art in Great Britain, 1854, 57.
Walpole, H., Catalogue of Engravers.
See Cards; Typography; Fine Arts.

Enoch. Brake, Character of, 1839.

Enthusiasm. Chauncy, Sermon, 1742.
Green, T., Diss. on, 1755.
Henry, G. W., Shoutings in the Church, 1859.
Lavington, Enthusiasm of Methodists, 1749.
Milman, H. H., Sermon, 1826.
Reflections upon a Letter on, 1709.
Taylor, J., Natural History of, 1830.
See Revivals; Methodist; Moral Philosophy.

Entomology. Abbot, S., Lepidopterous Insects of Georgia, 1797.
Adams, H. G., Insects of the Month.
Agassiz, Classification of Insects, 1849.
Boisduval, Lepidoptères de l'Amér. Septentrionale.
Burmeister, Manual of, 1836.
Candèze, Des Elatérides.
Chenu, Coléoptéres.
Curtis, John, British Entomology, 1823–49.
Cuvier, Animal Kingdom.
Duncan, J., Introd. to; Beetles, Nat. Lib.
" Brit. Butterflies and Moths, Nat. Lib.

Entomology (continued).
Duncan, J., Foreign Butterflies and Moths, Nat. Lib.
" Transformations of, 1871.
Encyc. Mèthodique, Entomologie, (Olivier; Latreille), 1818, 9 v.
Entomologists' Annual, 1855.
Episodes of Insect Life, 1851.
Fitch, A., Noxious Insects, 1855, 56, 1859.
" Hessian Fly, Winter Insects of N. Y., 1846. Muns. P. 5.
Guérin, Des Insectes, 1852–54.
Harris, M., Engl. Moths and Butterflies, 1840.
Harris, T. W., Insects injurious to Vegetation, 1842, 62.
" Entomol. Corresp., 1869.
" N. A. Coleopterous insects.
Hope, F. W., Coleopterist's Manual, 1838.
Humphreys, H. N., Butterfly Vivarium, 1858.
Jaeger, Life of North Amer. Insects, 1854.
Jardine, Naturalist's Lib., 1833–40.
Kirby, W., & W. Spence, Introduc. to Entomol.
Kollar, Insects Injurious, 1840.
Lacordaire, Coleop. Subpentamères.
Library of Ent. Knowl., Rennie, 1848.
Melsheimer, Cat. of the Coleoptera of U. S., 1853.
Morris, Lepidoptera of N. America.
Nederlandsche Entom. Vereeniging.
Newport, Sawfly of the Turnip.
New York: Nat. Hist., Emmons.
Phillippi, Orthoptera Berolinensia, 1826. P. 1003.
Raumer, Konst om Tamme-vogelen optebrengen, 1751.
Richardson, Pests of the Farm.
Sacken, Diptera of N. America.
Say, T., Amer. Entomology, 1824–28.
Selys-Longchamps, Several Publica.
Smithsonian Institute, Misc. Contr., Catal.
Snellen, Nederl, Insekten. P. 523.
Stephens, J. F., Illus. of British Ent. 1828–46.
Swainson, W., Hist. and Nat. Arrangement of.
Uhler, Hemipteræ.
Westwood, Classification of, 1839.
" Arcana Entomologica, 1845.
" Entomologist's Text-book, 1838.
See Bees; Insects; Zoölogy; Zoöphytes.

Eon de Beaumont. Kirby's Museum.
Lettres, Mémoires, 1763.

Epidemics. Hooper, R., Observations, 1803.
Marchant, Causes des, 1836.
Martin, E., Ep. in Maryland, 1813.
Vingtrinier, Epidem. à Rouen, 1850.
Willard, M., Fever in Albany, 1809.
See Cattle; Diptheria; Cholera; Medicine; Plague; Yellow Fever.

Epigrams. Booth, Epigrams, 1865.
Martialis, Epigrammata.
" Epigrams.
See Maxims: Proverbs; Poetry.

Epiphany. Maurice, F. D., Sermons on.

Episcopacy. Address by Plain Truth, 1827.
Answer to a Sermon, 1609.
Baynes, P., Diocesan's Tryall, 1621.
Beman, Episc. Exclusive, 1856.
Bolles, J. A., Episc. Defended, 1843.
Bowden, J., On Chauncy's View, 1789.
Brittan, Apology for.
Bunsen, Church of the Future, 1847.
Butler, C. M., Old Truths, 1850.
Cave, W., Gov't of the Church.
Church and the Sword, 1847.
Collection of Essays on, 1806.
Defence of the Vindication, 1695.
Discourse about Novelty, 1685.
Discourse Showing, 1698.
Dixon, Exam. of Catechism, 1845.
Emmett, Of the word Bishop, 1836.
Episcopacy Examined, (Gallagher), 1849.
Hobart, Companion to Festivals and Fasts, 1804.
" Candidate for Confirma., 1816.
Ives, L. S., The Trials of a Mind, etc., 1854.
" Pastoral Letter, 1846.
Letter from Congregationalist, 1820.
M'Vickar, Dr. Hook's History of, 1838.
Miller, S., Const. and Order of the Ministry, 1807. B. C.
Newman, J. H., Suffragan Bishops, 1835.
Onderdonk, H. U., Tested by Scripture.
Pamphlets, vols. 622, 857, 866, 877, 999, 1000, 1201, 1202, 1281, 1282, 1673, 1861.
Pearson, Opera Posthuma.
Smith, E., Epis. Examined.
Stanley, W., Faith of a Churchman, 1688.
Wainwright, No Church Without a Bishop.
White, W., On Episcopacy, 1859.
See Authority; Church of England; Church Government; Apostolical Succession.

Episcopal Church Brotherhoods.
Brotherhoods of P. E. C., 1853, 56.
Fitch, C. W., James the Lord's Brother.
Prot. Epis. Church, U. S.

Episcopal Church, England. *See* Church of England.

Episcopal Church, Ireland. *See* Irish Church.

Episcopal Church, Scotland. Lawson, History of, 1844.
Low, D., Charge, 1826.
See Scotland.

Episcopal Church, United States.
Address from Clergy, N. Y , 1771.
Address to the Ministers, 1790.
Allen, E., Clergy of Maryland.
Anderson, Hist. of, in the Colonies.
Appeal to the Members, 1826, (Phil'a).
Barnes, A., Evang. Party in, 1844.
Beardsley, Hist. of, in Connecticut.
" Address, Cheshire, Conn.
Blackburne, F., On Bishops in Amer., 1770.
Brief Directory.
Candid hints concern., 1858.
Caswall, Synodical action in.
Catholic Work, 1855.
Chandler, T. B., Appeal, 1767.
" Appeal defended, 1769.
" Appendix to Secker's Life, 1774.
Chase, Bishop, Reminiscences, 1847.
Chauncy, C., Appeal answered, 1768.
Christ Prot. E. C., New York, 1845.
Church Almanac, 1851–66.
Churchman's Almanac, 1830–46.
Churchman's Year-book, 1870.
Clark, J. A., Letters on the Church, 1839.
Clark, O., Principles of, vindicated, 1818.
Clark, S. A., Hist. of Ch., Elizabethtown, N. J., 1703–1857.
Comment. of F. Blackburne, on Bishops in America, 1770.
Consid. on the Eastern Diocese, 1837.
Conversation with a Churchman, 1858.
Croswell, W., Letter to Bp. of Mass., 1845.
Defence of the Conv., 1832.
Doane, G. W., Collection of publications on, 1836–52.
Explanation of Common Prayer, 1834.
Fitch, James the Lord's brother.
Gallagher, M., True Churchmanship, 1851.
Greenwood, Hist. of King's Chapel, 1833.

Episcopal Church, United States (continued).
Hawkins, E., Mission of Ch. of Eng. in America, 1845.
Hawks, Epis. Ch. in Virginia, Maryland, 1836, 39.
Hoare, Life of G. Sharp, 1820.
Hobart's Writings.
Hobart, N., Epis. Sep. in N. E.,1751.
Hoffman, M., Penal Law of, 1853.
Hopkins, J., Letters to the Bishops, etc., of, 1844.
Is the Diocese vacant ? (N. Y.), 1850.
Letter to the Clergy, (N. Y.), 1850.
Letter to the Rev. J. N. Campbell, 1844.
Letters to Editor of Essays in Albany Centinel, 1806.
Letters to the Laity, 1843.
Lewis, W. H., Consid....On Daily Service, 1853.
Mayhew, J., Obs. on Soc. Prop. the Gospel, 1763.
Memorial Papers, 1857.
Narrative of Occurrences, (N.Y.),1851.
Norton, Lives of Bishops of.
Odenheimer, On the Prayer-book.
Onderdonk, Hist. of, in N. Y. City, 1843, 44.
Perry, Hist. Collections, vol. I, Virginia; II, Pennsylvania.
Pamphlets relating to the, vols. 541, 543, 678, 679, 690, 699, 942, 999, 1000, 1201, 1202, 1552.
Present State of the Quest., (N. Y.), 1838.
Protestant Episcopal Brotherhoods. Pam. vol. 656.
Prot. Epis. Church, Jour. of Conv., 1785-1867.
" Journals of Conventions in Connecticut, Maine, Massachusetts, New York, Western York, New Jersey, Pennsylvania, Vermont.
Remarks upon Bp. M'Coskry's Sermon, 1853.
Response to Bp. Potter, 1858.
Right of Eastern Diocese, 1837.
Secker, Bishops in America, 1750-1.
Sherlock, T., Some Considerations, 1750.
Smith, W., Answer to Blatchford, 1798.
Smyth, Eccl. Republicanism, 1843.
Sprague, Annals of Am. Pulpit, 1857-1869.
Swords's Eccl. Register, N. Y., 1816, 21-27, 56-59.
Tremlett, Botolph Ch., Boston, 1851.
Trinity Church, N. Y., Pamphlets, 1836-57. 4 vols.
Two Letters, (Bowden), 1807.

Episcopal Church, United States (continued).
Trapnell, Trial of, 1847.
Vindication of N. England, 1691.
Vital truth, 1853.
Waylen, Eccl. Reminiscences, 1846.
White, W., Memoirs of.
" Two addresses, 1826.
Whittingham, Division of the Diocese, (N. Y.), 1838.
Wilberforce, S., History of, 1846.
See Trinity Church.

Episcopal Societies. Pam., vol. 542.

Episcopius, S. Calder, F., Memoirs of.

Epitaphs. Abbey of Kilkhampton, 1780.
Alden, Coll. of American, 1814.
Bridgman, Granary Cemetery, Boston.
" King's Chapel, Boston.
" Copps' Hill Cemetery, Bos.
" Mem. of the Dead, Northampton.
Camden, Remains, 1637.
Davenport, D., Dorchester Cemetery, 1826.
Dingley, History from marble, (Camden Soc.).
Dorchester, Epitaphs, 1869.
Epitaphs and Epigrams, (Palmer), London, 1869.
Gosden, Fun. Monum., Lond.
Gruterus, J., Inscriptiones.
Harris, W. T., Cambridge, Mass.1845.
" From Watertown, 1869.
Kinnersley, Sepul. curiosities.
Memoirs of the Dead, Balt., 1809.
Parr, Works, vol. 4.
Pettigrew's Collection, 1857.
Walker, G. A., Gatherings from,1839.
Weever, Funerall Monuments, 1631.
Cemeteries; Monuments.

Epithets. Jermyn, Book of Epithets, 1849.

Equador. *See* Ecuador.

Equator. Spilsbury, Nautical shaving

Erasmus, D. Butler, C., Life of.
Erasmus, Epistolæ, 1521.
Jortin, J., Life of, 1808.
Seebohm, F., Oxford Reformers, 1867.

Ericsson, J. Braithwaite, Voyage of Victory, 1835.
Coles, Cupolas and Turrets, 1864.

Erie, Pa. Slie, War of the gauges.

Erie Canal. Beach, S. B., Against Continuing, 1819.
Fact and Observations, 1825.
Fulton, R., Correspondence with G. Morris, 1814.

Essays, Critical, Historical, Moral, etc. (continued).
Johnson, S., Works, vol. 2, 3, 4, 1823.
Judson, L. C., The Probe, 1846.
Knox, V., E. moral and literary, 1792.
Lamb, Charles, Essays of Elia, 1851.
Lounger, The, 1789. B. C.
Lunt, G., Three eras, 1857.
Macaulay, T. B., Crit. and Hist., 1841.
M'Crie, Miscel. Writings, 1841.
Martineau, H., Life in a sick room, 1844.
" Miscellanies, 1836. B. C.
Melancthon, Select. declamationum, tom. 5, 1544, 1590.
Mercier, Fragments of politics, etc., 1795.
Meré, Œuvres, 1701.
Mill, J. S., Dissertations and discussions, 1859–67.
Miller, Hugh, Essays, Hist. and Biog., 1865.
" Witness papers, 1863.
Montaigne, M., Essais, 1745. B. C.
" Essays, Wight's ed.
Montesquieu, Œuvres: Essais, 1842.
Ossoli, M. Fuller d', At home and abroad.
Oxford Essays, 1855, 56, 57.
Oxford prize essays, 1830.
Pamphlets, vol. 606.
Parker, T., Crit. and Misc. writings, 1843.
Pictures of men, manners, 1779.
Playfair, Works, vol. 4, 1822.
Prescott, W. H., Biog. and Crit. Misc., 1845.
Roberts, Looker-on.
Sampson, E., Brief remarker, 1855.
Sands, R. C., Writings, 1835.
Sargent, L. M., Dealings with the dead, 1856.
Saunders, F., Salad for the solitary, 1853.
Shaftesbury's Characteristicks, 1733.
Simms, W. G., Egeria, 1853.
Smith, Sydney, Works, 1840.
Sorbière, Lettres et Discours.
Southey, R., Essays, Mor. and Polit.
Spencer, H., Essays, Sci., Pol., and Speculative, 1864.
Stephen, Sir J., Crit. and Misc. Ess., 1843.
Sterling, John, Essays and Tales, 1848.
Story, Joseph, Misc. writings, 1852.
Talfourd, Crit. and Miscel. Essays.
Tatler, The, 1786.
Tucker, G., Essays on Subjects of taste, 1822.
Tuckerman, H. T., The Optimist, 1850.

Essays, Critical, Historical, Moral, etc. (continued).
Tuckerman, H. T., Essays, Biog. and Crit.
Whipple, E. P., Essays and reviews, 1848.
" Success and its conditions, 1871.
Witherspoon, Misc. Works, 1803.

Essex, Earl of. Elizabeth, Secret Hist. of the Queen. B. C.

Essex, Earls of. Devereux, Letters.

Essex, Eng. Beauties of England and Wales.
Berry, County genealogies.
Wright, T., History of, 1836.

Essex, Mass. Crowell, R., History of.
Felt, J. B., History of, 1834.

Essex Co., Mass. Newhall, Essex Memorial.

Essex Co., N. J. Boyd's Directory, 1870–1.

Essex Co., N. Y. Cook, Home Sketches, 1858.
Watson, W. C., History of, 1869.
See Champlain.

Estienne, R. Crapelet, Nouvelles Recherches, 1839.

Etherization. Anstie, Stimulants and Narcotics, 1864.
Channing, On Etherization, 1849.
Edwards' Reports on Morton's discov.
Ether Controversy, a collection.
Forsten, Responsio de æthere, 1832.
Gay, M., Claims of C. T. Jackson, 1847.
Jackson, C. T., Manual of, 1861.
Lord, J. L., Defence of Jackson, 1848.
Morton, W. T. G., Rep. in Cong. on, 1852.
" Claim as discoverer, etc., 1853.
Pamphlets, vol. 1674.
Rice, N. P., Trials of a benefactor.
Sédillot, Chloroforme et Ether, 1848.
Smith, T., Exam. of claims, 1858.
Stanly, E., Vind. of Jackson's Claims, 1852
United States Reports on Dr. Morton's Claim, 1849.
Wells, H., Use of, in Surg. operat., 1850.

Ethics. *See* Moral Philosophy; Morals.

Ethiopia. Geddes, Church History of.
Lepsius, Denkmaeler aus, 1842–45.
Ludolfus, Historie van Abissinien.
Santos, History of.
See Abyssinia; Egypt; Nubia.

Ethnology. Agassiz, Origin of the human races, 1850. Pam. 74.
American Ethn. Soc. Trans., 1845, 48.
Bartlett, J. R., Prog. of Ethnology, 1847.
Brace, C. K., Races of the Old World.
Bronson, Unity of the Race, 1831.
Coles, Crit. on Nott and Gliddon, 1857.
Donaldson, Ethn. of Anc. Italy, 1860.
Earl, Races of Indian Archipelago, 1853.
Ethnological Journal, 1848, 49.
Gobineau, Inégalité des Races, 1855.
" Diversity of Races, 1856.
Gœrres, Die Japhetiden, 1844.
Gliddon, Types of Mankind, 1854. *See* Nott.
Hale, H , Ethnography, U. S. Exp., 1838–42.
Haxthausen, Tribes of Caucasus, 1855.
Hodgkin, On Inquiries into the Races, 1841.
Holtzmann, Kelten und Germanen, 1855.
Klaproth, Tableaux Hist. d'Asie.
Knox, R., Races of Men.
Lang, Polynesian Nations.
Latham, R. G., Germania of Tacitus, 1851.
" Varieties of the Race.
" Prog. of Ethn. Philol., 1847.
" Races of Russia, 1854.
" Essays, 1860.
" Ethnol. of the Brit. Col., 1851.
Massy, Tribes of Britain and Ireland.
Mastman, Deutsch und Weltsch, 1843.
Maupertuis, Œuvres.
Maury, Terre et l'Homme, 1857.
Meigs, Catal. of Human Crania.
Morgan, L. H., Systems of Consanguinity and affinity of the Human Family (Smithson. Contrib. v. 17.).
Morton, S. G., Pigmy Race of the Mississippi. P. 74.
" Crania Egyptiaca, 1844.
" Crania Americana, 1839.
Nicholas, T., Pedigree of Eng. People.
Niebuhr, B. G., Lectures on.
Nott, J. C., Indigenous Races, 1857.
" Types of Mankind, 1854.
" Bib. and Phys. Hist. of Man, 1849.
Palma, Della Nazionalitá.
Pickering, C., The Races of Men, 1851.
Potocki, Astrakan, 1829.
Pouchet, Plurality of the Race.
Prichard, J. C., Nat. Hist. of Man, 1855.
" Applicat. of Philol. Researches to, 1832.

Ethnology (continued).
Prichard, J. C., Ethnog. of High Asia.
" Celtic Nations, 1831.
Pruenr, Der Altägyptisch. Menschenrace, 1846.
Reid, M., Odd People, 1861.
Ritson, Celts and Gauls, 1827.
Schoolcraft, Algic Researches, 1839.
" Oneota, 1844.
Smith, S. S., Variety in the Species, 1787.
Smyth, T., Unity of Races Proved, 1850.
Taylor, I., Words and Places, 1865.
Van Amringe, Nat. Hist. of Man, 1848.
Vaughan, L, Revolutions of Race, 1860.
Walker, A., Physiognomy.
See Philology; Indians (American); Man.

Etiquette. Amer. Chesterfield, 1827.
Brown, D. M., Young Ladyism.
Butler, C., The Amer. Gentleman.
Calvert, G. H., The Gentleman.
Chapone, Mrs., Works, 1818. B. C.
Chesterfield, Practical Morality.
" Prin. of Politeness.
Chevigni, La Science des Personnes de la cour, 1725. B. C.
Dinocourt, Cours de Morale Sociale, 1839.
Dodd, C. R., Manual of Etiquette, 1842.
D'Orsay, Etiquette, 1843.
Friswell, The Gentle Life.
Galateo, or Treatise on Politeness, 1811.
Gayot, Esprit des Convers. Agréables, 1731. B. C.
Gracian, L'Homme Universel, 1723.
Habits of Good Society, 1860.
Laws of Etiquette, 1836. B. C.
Nash, R., Life of, 1762.
Pamphlets, vol. 1793.
Parisian Etiquette.
Wagstaff, Collection of Conversations, 1738.
William R., Gov't of the bed-chamber.
Young Man's own book.
See Customs; Gentleman; Manners.

Eton College. Creasy, Memoirs of Etonians, 1850.
Jesse, E., Favorite haunts, 1847.
Staunton, Great Schools of Eng., 1865.

Etruria. Betham, Etruria-Celtica.
Byres, Sepul. caverns of.
Disney, Museum Disneianum.
Ferrario, Costume.
Gray, Mrs., Sepulchres of.
Janssen, Inscriptiones, 1840.
See Tuscany.

Europe, Politics of (continued).
Frœlichius, Biblioth. sive Cynos. Peregr., 1643.
Genlis, Memoirs of, 1825. B. C.
Gentz, Vindication, 1803.
Heeren, Man. Hist du système politique de, 1821.
" Hist. of the Pol. System of, 1829, 34, 46.
Holland, Lord, For. Reminiscences, 1850.
Hughes, T. S., Political System of, 1855.
James, G. P. R., Hist. of Chivalry, 1832.
Kossuth, Future of Nations.
Laing, Notes on France, Prussia, etc., 1842.
Letter to the Craftsmen, 1734.
Linguet, Pol. and Phil. Speculations, 1788.
Memoirs of the most Chr. Brute, 1747.
Musgrave, Balance of Power in.
Oracle de ce siécle, 1743.
Pamphlets, vols. 817, 1320–1322, 1513, 1852.
Portfolio, Period., 1835–7, 1843.
Present Measures...Balance of Power, 1743.
Present State of Europe. v. x, 1699.
Pres. State of Politics of, 1739.
Private conference, 1744.
Révision de la carte de, 1854.
Rousset de Missy, Les intérêts présens des puissances, 1741.
Schmidt-Phiseldek, Europe and Amer., 1820.
Society Inst. in London for Relief of Sufferings by War, 1814.
Thérémin, Des intérêts des puiss. continentales, 1794.
Tucker, J., Cui Bono? 1781.
Urquhart, D., Myst. of the Danube, 1851.
" La Crise, 1840.
Zimmerman, Political Survey of, 1787.
See Diplomacy; Great Britain; France; Spain.

Europe, Registers, etc. Almanach de Gotha, 1856–72.
Annual Register, 1854–69.
Annuaire des Deux Mondes, 1856–62.
Edinburgh Ann. Register, 1808–26.
Historical Register, 1714–38.
Lesur, Annuaire Historique, 1818–24.
Lowrie, Geog. and Stat. Chart, 1835.
Martin's Statesman's Year-book, 1866–1870.
Schnitzler, Statist. générale, 1846.

Europe, Travels in. American Wanderer, 1783.

Europe, Travels in (continued).
Baird, R., Visit to Northern Europe, 1840.
Baker, P. C., Early Recollections.
Bartol, C. A., Pictures of Europe, 1855.
Benedict, E. C., A run through, 1860.
Benjamin, Rabbi, Trav. through, to China.
Bernard, R. B., France, Switzerland, etc., 1814. B. C.
Breckenridge, Memoranda of for. trav., 1845.
Brooks, C., Remarks on Europe, 1846.
Browne, E., Travels on Continent.
Bruen, M., Essays....on scenes in, 1823. B. C.
Bryant, W. C., Letters of a Traveler, 1850.
Brydges, Sir E., Recoll. of for. trav., 1825.
Brydges, E., Letters, 1822.
Buckingham, Belgium, Switzerland, etc.
Budget of Letters, (Eames), 1847.
Burnet, G., Travels in.
Burr, Aaron, Jour. of resid. in, 1838.
Butler, Mrs. F. K., Year of Consolation, 1847.
Calvert, Scenes and thoughts in, 1846.
Carr, J., Trav. in Northern Europe, 1804.
Carter, N. H., Letters from, 1825–27.
Catlin, Eight years residence in, 1848.
Chishull, Trav., 1747.
Clinton, C. A., A Winter from Home, 1852.
Clarke, J. F., Eleven weeks in, 1852.
Colman, H., Eur. Life and Manners, 1849.
Colton, W., Notes on Fr. and Italy, 1851.
Cooper, J. F., Recollections of, 1837.
Copway, G., Running sketches, 1851.
Corson, Loiterings in, 1848.
Coryat, Crudities, 1776.
Cox, S. S., A Buckeye abroad, 1852.
Coxe, W., Trav. in Russia, Sweden, etc., 1787.
Derby, Two Months Abroad, 1843.
Desultory Reminiscences, 1838.
Dewey, O., Old World and New, 1836.
Dodge, R., Sketches in Eur. tour, 1847.
Doré, by a Stroller, 1857.
Douglas, Bp., Works, 1820.
Durbin, Observations in, 1844.
Dutens, Routes les plus fréquentéos, 1783.
Echard's Gazetteer, 1741.

Europe, Travels in (continued).
Fetridge's Hand-book, 1862.
Fisk, W., Travels in, 1843.
Furniss, The Old World, 1850.
George, W. C., A Year Abroad, 1852.
Granger, J., Letters, 1805.
Granville's St. Petersburgh, 1809.
Greeley, H., Glances at, 1851.
Griscom, A Year in, 1818, 1819.
Haight, Letters from the Old World, 1840.
Headley, J. T., Rambles and Sketches, 1851.
Holthaus, Wanderings, 1824.
Humphrey, H., G. Britain, France, Belgium, 1835.
Jacob, W., View of the Agr. Man., etc., 1820.
Johnson, James, Change of air, 1831.
Jousiffe, Hand-book, 1846.
Keatinge, Trav. in Eur. and Afr., 1816.
Keysler, Trav. in Germany, Hungary, Bohemia, 1758.
Kimball, R. B., Romance of student life, 1853.
Kirkland, Mrs., Holidays abroad, 1849.
Laing, S., Notes of a traveller, 1854.
La Motraye, Travels, 1732.
Lester, C. E., My Consulship, 1853.
Le Vert, Souvenirs of, 1859.
Lithgow, Travels, 1609.
Matthews, H., Diary of an invalid, 1835.
Mitchell, D. G., Fresh Gleanings, 1847.
Mitchell, J., Notes from over sea, 1843, 44.
Moore, J., Soc. and manners in Fr., etc., 1820.
Mott, V., Travels in Europe and the East, 1842.
Murray's, J., Hand-books, 1836–49.
Murray, N., Men and things..in, 1854.
Noah, M. M., Travels, 1819.
Ossoli, At Home and abroad, 1856.
Piozzi, Obs. on Journey.
Pollnitz, Trav. through Poland, Germ., Eng., etc., 1739.
Prime, S. I., Travels in Eur. and the East, 1855.
Ray, In Harris, vol. 1.
Rives, Residence in, 1842.
Rockwell, C., Sketches of, 1842.
Rolamb, N., Jour. to Constantinople, 1657.
Salvo, Travels, 1806.
Sansom, J., Letters from, 1801, 02.
Schroeder, Shores of the Mediterranean, 1843–5.
Sedgwick, C. M., Letters from abroad, 1841.

Europe, Travels in (continued).
Sherburne, Tourist's guide, 1847.
Sherlock, Lettres d'un Voyageur Anglais, 1781.
Smith, Sir J. E., Tour on the Cont., 1786, 87.
Smith, J. J., Jaunt across the water, 1846.
Stephens, J. L., Incidents of Tr. in Turkey and Russia, 1844.
Talfourd, T. N., Vacation Rambles, 1841, 42, 43.
Taylor, B., Views a-foot, 1848.
Thackeray, W. M., Cornhill to Cairo, 1846.
Tour in Germany, Eng., etc., 1826–28.
Upham, T. C., Letters from, 1855.
Wall St. Bear in, 1855.
Wallace, H. B., Art and Scenery in, 1855.
Ware, W., Sketches of Eur. capitals, 1851.
Watson, E., Travels, 1777–1842.
Weed, T., Letters, 1842–62.
Wikoff, H., Roving diplomatist, 1857.
Wilson, Sir R., Journal, 1812–14.
Wilson, W. R., Records of a route through, 1835.
Wraxall, Tour in Northern, 1807.
Wright, E., Tr. in France, Italy, etc., 1720–22.
Wyndham, Travels through.
See Travels in the several countries of.

Eusebius. Greek Eccl. Hist., Life of.

Eustis, Gov. W. Barnaby, J., Fun. Sermon, 1825.
Sharp, D., Sermon on.

Evangelical Alliance, Conferences, 1845–57.
Pamphlets, vol. 495.
See Christian Union.

Evangelical Lutheran Church. Proceedings, 1858–67.
Mayer, Semi-Centennial Disc., 1756.
Pamphlets, vols. 1675, 1676.
Sprague's Annals of the Am. Pulpit.
See Lutheran.

Evangelicals. Church Parties, (Conybeare), 1854.
Hints to the Public, (Sedgwick), 1810.
Jephson, W., Bp. of Peterborough's Questions, 1821.
Lorimer, Old Orthodox Faith, 1847.
Merewether, Thoughts, 1824.
Minton, On "Church Parties," 1859.
Obs. on Death Bed Scenes.
Remarks on a Charge.
Truth Against Error, 1828.
See Dissenters; Church of England.

Evans, C. Stennett, S., Serm., Death of, 1792.

Evans, Rev. P. Death of, 1679.

Evarts, J. Spring, G., A Tribute to, 1831.
Tracy, E. C., Life of, 1845.
Woods, L., Serm., Death of, 1831.

Evelyn, John. Diary and Corresp.
Hone, R. B., Life of, 1833.

Everett, E. Bartol, C., Sermon on.
Boston, Memorial to, 1865.
Bunker Hill Mon't Associa., on his Death.
Dana, R. H. jr., Address upon, 1865.
Davis, T. T., Eulogy on.
Massachusetts Hist. Soc. Pro., Tribute to, 1865.
New Eng. Hist. Geneal. Soc., Tribute to, 1866.

Evertsen, J. and C. Jonge, Levens-Beschrijving, 1820.

Evesham, Eng. Chronicon Abbatiæ, (Chron. of G. B.).
Tindal, Antiquities of, 1794.

Evidences. *See* Christianity; Bible.

Evil, Origin of. Blood, B., Optimism, 1860.
King, W., Origin of, 1731.
Philosophy of Evil, Phil'a, 1845.
Proclus, Essay on Subsistence of.
See Sin.

Ewing, C. J. Southard, S. L., Eulogy on.

Ewing, G. Wardlaw, R., Serm., Death of, 1828.

Examination Questions. Annual Calendar, Lond., 1857.
Answers to 300 Questions, 1839.
Booth, Exam. by the State.
Bristed's, T., Five Years in University.
Camb. Univ. Ex. Papers, 1830.
" Calendar, 1867.
Dalton, Arith. Examples, Lond.
Dublin University Calendar, 1867.
Edinburgh Univ. Calendar, 1867.
France: Programmes des Examens, 1857, 59.
Lincoln's Inn Exam., 1857.
London Univ. Cat., 1867.
N. Y. Free Acad. Exam., 1854, 58.
Oxford Univ. Calendar, 1869.
Parkinson, Government Examinations.
Pluck Exam. Papers, 1836.
Sargent, J. Y., Passages for trans. at Oxford.
Snowball, Camb. Course of Nat. Phil.
Three hundred ordin. quest., 1838.
Un. of Toronto, Ex. Papers, 1858, 60.

Exchange. Considerations on Protested Bills.
James, System of, N. Y., 1800.
See Finance; Currency; Banking.

Excise. Appeal to Landholders, 1733.
Bagot, Observations, 1853.
Denneston, A Scheme for Excise, 1713.
Devon, Eng., Case of the County, 1763.
Gr. Br. Parl. Protest. on Act, 1743.
Letter from a Member, 1733.
Maddox, J., Sermon, 1750.
Nicholson, R., Sale of Beer, 1854.
Prynne, Protestation, 1654.
Rise and Fall of, 1733.
Remarks on the Horrible Oppressions, 1706.
Scott, N., Proposals, 1705.
Some Observations, 1733.
Some Observations, Bost., 1754.
True Discovery.... Wine Project, 1641.
See Taxation; Customs; Temperance.

Exeter, N. H. First Congr. Soc. Council.
Nason, Events of 1861.

Exhibitions of Arts and Industry.
Académie de l'Industrie, 1836.
Amer. Inst., of City of N. Y., 1842–1853.
Art Journal, Illus. Cat. Lond. Exhib., 1851.
Art Treasures, Manchester, 1857.
Association...of Industry, N. Y., 1853.
Cox, J., Mechanism and Jewelry, 1773.
Dilke, Cat. of Works on, 1851.
Dublin International, 1865.
Exhibition of London, 1851, Catalogues.
" Reports of Juries.
Exhibition of London, 1861.
Exhibition, N. Y., 1853.
Exposition Universelle, 1851.
Exposition de 1855, Paris.
Exposition des Prod. de l'Ind. Franç., 1834, 39, 44.
Exposition Universelle de Paris, 1867, 15 vols.
France: Algeria, Catalogue, 1855.
Great Britain: N. Y. Exhib. of 1851.
Gr. Brit. Reports on Paris Ex. of, 1855.
Greeley, H., N. Y. Exhib. of 1853.
Hoyt, U. S. Commrs. Report, 1867.
Hunt, R., Synopsis of Ex. of 1851.
Internat. Ex. of 1862. Lond. Ill. Cat.
" Report of Juries.
Italy, Espos. Internaz. del, 1862.
" Exp. à Parigi, 1867.
Johnson, B. P., Report on London Exhib., 1851.

F.

Fiction. Dunlop, J., History of Fiction, 1814.

Dutens, Héros des Romans. P. 1824.

Forsyth, On the Novels of the 18th Century, 1870.

Ogilvie, J., Philosoph. Essays, 1816.

Pamphlets containing, Vols. 496, 497, 971, 1323, 1677, 1678, 1706, 1707, 2506.

Scott, Sir W., Essay on.

Senior, N. W., Essays on, 1864.

Wheeler, W. A., Dictionary of Noted Names in Fiction, 1865.

Fiction, American. Algerine Captive, (Tyler).

Allston, W., Monaldi.

Arthur, T. S., Old Man's Bride.

Beecher, H. W., Norwood.

Benjamin, S. G. W., Choice of Paris, 1870.

Brackenridge, Modern Chivalry, 1801.

Brainard, J. G. C., Fort Braddock Letters, 1830.

Brown, C. B., The Novels of, 1827.

Brownson, O. A., Charles Elwood.

Buccaneers, The, 1827.

Burdett, Margaret Moncrieffe.

Carlotina, 1853.

Chubbuck, C., Charles Linn.

Clare, The Trial, 1851.

Cooper, J. F., Novels and Tales, 1823–1851.

Curtis, G. W., Potiphar Papers, 1853.

" Prue and I.

Curtis, N. M., Bride of the Northern Wilds, 1843.

Dana, R. H., Prose Writings, 1850.

Debtor's Prison, 1834.

Dickinson, A. E., What Answer?

Dixon, C. H., Scenes in Practice, 1855.

Eastman, Aunt Phillis's Cabin, 1854.

Ewer, Nights of Aug. 20, 21, 1855.

Fanatic, (Brisbane).

Flint, T., Shoshonee Valley, 1830.

Fay, Countess Ida.

Garangula, 1857.

Gebel Teir, Mountain of birds, 1829.

Grahame, 1850.

Greene, Am. Nights Entertainments.

Hall, B. R., Frank Freeman's Barber's Shop, 1852.

Hall, J., Wilderness and War-path, 1846.

" Legends of the West, 1832.

" The Soldier's Bride, 1833.

" Harpe's Head, 1833.

" Tales of the Border, 1835.

Hawthorne, House of the seven gables, 1851.

The Scarlet Letter, 1850.

Fiction, American (continued).

Hawthorne, The Blithedale Romance, 1850.

" Twice-Told Tales, 1852.

" Mosses from an Old Manse, 1846.

" Marble Faun, 1860.

Hermit of Aleova, 1857.

Highlands, The, 1826.

Hildreth, Archy Moore.

Hitchcock, Enos, The Farmer's Friend, 1793.

" Bloomsgrove family, 1790.

Hoffman, C. F., The Greyslaer, 1849.

Hoffman, D., Chron. of Cartaphilus, 1853.

Holland, J. G., The Bay Path, 1857.

Holmes, O. W., The Professor at the breakfast table.

" Autocrat of breakfast table.

Hopkins, S., Youth of the Old Dominion.

Huntington, Miss, Sea-Spray, 1857.

Hypocrite, The, 1851.

Ingraham, J. W., Lafitte.

" Montezuma.

Irving, J. T., The Attorney, 1853.

" Harry Harson, 1853.

Judd, S., Margaret, 1857.

" Richard Edney.

Judson, E., The Kathayan Slave, 1853.

Kelroy, 1812.

Kennedy, J. P., Quodlibet.

" Rob of the Bowl, 1855.

" Swallowbarn. 1851.

" Horseshoe Robinson, 1852.

Kimball, R. B., Saint Leger, 1853.

Kip, L., Aenone, 1867.

" The Volcano Diggings, 1851.

Knapp, S. L., Tales of the Garden of Kosciusko, 1834.

Knickerbocker Ms., 1824.

Leggett, W., Naval Stories, 1835.

Lippard, Writings.

Locke Amsden, or the Schoolmaster, 1847.

Locke, R. A., Discov. at Good Hope.

Longfellow, Kavanagh, 1853.

" Hyperion, 1851.

Longstreet, A. B., Georgia scenes, 1854.

M'Henry, J., Waltham, 1823.

Mary Hollis, 1822. P. 5. B. C.

Mayo, W. S., Romance Dust, 1851.

" The Berber, 1850.

" Kaloolah, 1849.

Melville, Mardi, 1849.

" Moby Dick, or the Whale, 1851.

" White Jacket.

Fiction, American (continued).

Midsummer's Day Dream, 1847.
Mitchell, S. T., Spirit of the Old Dominion, 1827.
Motley, Merry-Mount.
Murdock, Dominie of the Catskills.
Neal, J., Rachel Dyer, 1828.
" Errata, 1823.
" True Womanhood.
New England's Chattels.
Old Fort Du Quesne.
Otis, Barclays of Boston, 1854.
Otiska, 1832.
Page, J. W., Uncle Robin, 1853.
Pamphlets, Vols. 496, 497, 971, 1323, 1706, 1707, 1863.
Parmelee, Mrs., Little Ellis.
Paulding, The Dutchman's Fireside, 1831.
" The Old Continental, 1846.
" The Puritan and his Daughter, 1849.
" Konnigsmarke, 1836.
" Wise Men of Gotham, 1839.
" John Bull in America.
Poe, E. A., Works, v. 1, 1850.
Porter, W. S., Quarter Race in Kentucky, 1850.
Read, T. B., Paul Redding.
Robinson, S., Hot Corn, 1854.
Roe, Long Look Ahead.
Rowson, S., The Inquisitor, 1796.
" Charlotte Temple, 1802.
" Reuben and Rachel, 1798.
Ruth Hall, 1855.
Scenes at Washington, N. Y., 1848.
Sedgwick, C. M., Redwood, 1850.
" Home, 1850.
" New England Tale, 1822.
" The Traveller, 1825.
" Hope Leslie, 1827.
" Clarence, 1830.
Sedgwick, T., Alida, 1844.
Shady Side.
Simms, J. R., Amer. Spy, 1857.
Simms, W. G., Confession.
" Vasconcelos.
" Border Beagles.
" Guy Rivers.
" Lily and the Totem.
" Southward Ho! 1854.
" The Maroon, 1854.
" Richard Hurdis, 1855.
" The Yemassee, 1835.
Sixty Years of Jeremy Levis, 1831.
Smith, J. H., Gilead, 1863.
Stone, W. L., Ups and Downs, 1836.
" Tales and Sketches, 1834.

Fiction, American (continued).

Stowe, H. B., Mayflower, 1844.
" Uncle Tom's Cabin, 1852.
" Dred, 1856.
" Minister's Wooing, 1859.
" Pearl of Orr's Island, 1862.
" Oldtown folks, 1869.
" Pink and White Tyranny, 1871.
" My Wife and I, 1872.
Spectre of the Forest, 1823.
Talvi, (Robinson), Life's Discipline.
Tayler, The Merchant's Clerk, 1848.
Taylor, B., John Godfrey's Fortunes, 1864-6.
Tucker, B., Partisan Leader, 1861.
Tucker, St. G., Hansford, 1857.
Walworth, M. T., Stormcliff.
" Lulu, 1863.
" Hotspur.
" Warwick, 1869.
Ware, W., Aurelian, or Rome in third Cent., 1848.
" Letters from Palmyra, 1837.
" Julian, or Scenes in Judea, 1841.
Warner, S., Hills of the Shatemuc, 1856.
Warren, C. M., The Gamesters.
Watterston, The Lawyer, 1829.
Week in Wall St., 1841.
White, The, Slave, 1845. B. C.
Whittier, Leaves from M. Smith's Jour., 1678.
Williams, C. R., Religion at Home.
Willis, N. P., Paul Fane.
" Inklings of adventure.
Winkfield, Unca E., 1814.
Wirt, Letters of the British Spy, 1832.
Wood, G., Modern Pilgrims, 1855.
Young, The, Emigrant, 1830. B. C.
Young Parson, 1863.
Young Patroon in 1690.
See Literature.

Fiction, English. Aguilar, Home Influence.

Ainsworth, W. H., Crichton.
" Windsor Castle, 1844.
Alexis, or the Young Adventurer, 1746.
Almacks.
Arblay, D', Evelina.
" Camilla.
" The Wanderer, 1814. B. C.
Arthur, King, Actes of.
Austen, Miss, Pride and Prejudice.
Beckford, W., Vathek.
Borrow, G., Lavengro, 1851.
" Romany Rye.
Bouchier, Eveling Lodge, 1847. P.619.
Braddon, Eleanor's Victory.

Fiction, English (continued).
Braddon, John Marchmont's Legacy.
Brontë, Jane Eyre, 1837.
" Shirley, 1850.
" Wuthering Heights, 1848.
" Villette.
Brooke, The Fool of Quality.
Brunton, Self-Control, 1811. B. C.
Bulwer, Pilgrims of the Rhine, 1846.
" Harold, 1848. B. C.
" Alice.
" Zanoni.
" The last of the Barons.
" Rienzi.
" The Caxtons.
" My Novel.
" The Disowned.
" Peer's Daughter.
" Leila.
" Pelham.
" Paul Clifford.
Bulwer, Lady, Cheveley, 1839. B. C.
Bunyan, Pilgrim's Progress.
Carleton, Traits of Irish Peasantry, 1833, 34.
Charlesworth, England's Yeomen.
Children's Week, 1830. B. C.
Classic Tales.
Cobbold, Margaret Catchpole.
Collins, After Dark.
Confessions of an Etonian, 1846.
Cottage and its Visitor, 1860.
Cunningham, J. W., World without Souls, 1815. B. C.
" Velvet Cushion, 1815.
" Pneumanee, 1815. B. C.
Day, T., Sanford and Merton, 1833.
De Foe, Works, 1840–41.
De Quincey, Klosterheim.
" The Avenger.
Destiny, (Ferrier), 1831.
Devotee, The, Marriott, 1823.
Diary of Lady Willoughby, 1845, 48.
Dickens, C., Barnaby Rudge.
" Martin Chuzzlewit.
" Hard Times.
" Great Expectations.
" Battle of Life, 1847. B. C.
" Oliver Twist, 1840.
" Bleak House, 1853.
D'Israëli, B., Venetia.
" Young Duke.
" Contarini Fleming.
" Tale of Alroy.
" Coningsby.
" Sybil.
" Vivian Grey.
" Lothair

Fiction, English (continued).
D'Israëli, Henrietta Temple.
D'Israëli, I., Romances.
Edgeworth, M., Belinda, 1814. B. C.
" Castle Rackrent, 1814.
" Patronage, 1814. B. C.
" Harrington, 1817. B. C.
" Rosamond.
Elton, P. S., The Piedmontese envoy, 1852.
Evans, Rectory of Valehead.
Evenings at Haddon Hall.
Female Foundling, 1802.
Fielding, H., Works, 1806.
Friarswood Post-Office, (Yonge).
Galt, J., Annals of the Parish, 1844.
" Ayrshire Legatees, 1844.
" Sir Andrew Wylie, 1854.
" The Provost and other tales, 1850.
" The Entail, 1850.
Gaskell, North and South.
" My Lady Ludlow.
" A dark night's work.
Gaspé, Canadians of old, 1864.
Gaudentio Di Lucca, Memoirs, 1737.
Gerund, History of Friar, 1772.
Godwin, Mary W., Wrongs of Woman, 1798.
Godwin, W., Fleetwood.
" Caleb Williams, 1832. B. C.
Goldsmith, Vicar of Wakefield.
Gore, Mrs., Banker's wife.
" Agathonia.
" Abednego.
Grattan, T. C., Agnes de Mansfield, 1836.
Gresley, Church Clavering.
Grey, Mrs., Novels, 3.
Griffin, Tales of my neighborhood.
Guernsey, Death-bed Confessions, 1822.
Gurney married, 1839.
Haliburton, T. C., The Attaché, 1856.
" Wise Saws, 1853.
" Nature and Human Nature, 1855.
" The Old Judge.
Hamilton, Eliz., Memoirs of Modern Philosophers, 1804.
Hawkstone, A tale of England, 1848.
Haywood, Cleomelia, 1727.
Helen's Fault.
Henri Quatre, (Mancur.).
Hesitation, 1819. B. C.
Hofland, Daughter-in-law.
" Son of a Genius.
Hogg, J., Tales and Sketches, 1836.
Hook, T., Sayings and Doings, 1836.

Fiction, English (continued).

Hope, T., Anastasius, 1831.

Howitt, Our Cousins in Ohio, 1849.

" Stories of Engl. and For. life, 1853.

" Traditions of the most Ancient Times, 1839.

" Hall and Hamlet.

Hunt, R., Panthea, the Spirit of nat., 1849.

Independent, The. 1784. B. C.

Ingelo, Bentivolio and Urania, 1682.

James, G. P. R., Morley Ernstein.

" Agnes Sorel.

" Old Dominion.

" The Commissioner.

" Gentleman of the old School.

" The Forgery.

" Margaret Graham.

" Old Oak Chest.

" False Heir, etc.

" The Gipsy.

" The Jacquerie.

" The Huguenot.

" Mary of Burgundy.

" Attila.

" Rose d'Albret, 1844. B. C.

Johnson, S., Rasselas, Works, vol. 5, 1823.

Justina, or the Will, 1823. B. C.

Kingsley, C., Alton Locke, 1850.

" Westward Ho! 1857.

" Yeast.

" Hereward.

" Hypatia.

Kingsley, H., Ravenshoe.

Landon's Prose Works.

Lawrence, Brakspeare.

" Maurice Deering.

Lever, C., Sir Jasper Carew.

" Fortunes of Glencore.

" Maurice Tiernay.

" Gerald Fitzgerald.

" Charles O'Malley.

" The Daltons.

" Harry Lorrequer.

" Jack Hinton.

" Roland Cashel.

" Tom Burke of "Ours."

" The Dodd family abroad.

Lewis, M. G., Tales of wonder.

" The Monk.

Lights and Shadows of German life, 1833. B. C.

Lockhart, J. G., Reginald Dalton, 1849.

" Passages in the life of Adam Blair, 1849.

Lover, S., Handy Andy, etc.

Fiction, English (continued).

Mackenzie, H., Man of feeling; Julia de Roubigné.

McLeod, Pynnshurst, 1852.

Marriott, W. M. S., Royal promise, 1824.

Marryatt, Novels, 1856, 7.

Marsh, Mrs., Mount Sorel, etc.

Martineau, H., Deerbrook.

" Times of the Saviour, 1832.

Mason, J., Fact and fiction.

Maturin, Fatal Revenge, 1808. B. C.

Maxwell, W. H., Captain O'Sullivan.

Melville, Good for Nothing, 1861.

Meredith, G., Emilia in England, 1864.

Miller, Hugh, Tales and Sketches.

Moir, Life of Mansie Wauch, 1853.

Moore, J., Zeluco, Works, v. 5, 1820.

" Edward, Works, vol. 6, 1820.

" Mordaunt, Works, vol. 7, 1820.

Moore, T., Epicurean, 1839.

More, H., Cœlebs, 1809. B. C.

Morgan, Lady, The O'Briens.

Morier, Hajji Baba.

Mulock, Miss, Ogilvies.

" Life for a Life.

Munchausen, Gulliver revived.

Murray, C. A., The Prairie Bird.

" Trapper's Bride.

Old English Baron, 1805.

Oliphant, Madonna Mary.

" Miss Marjoribanks.

Opie, Mrs., Adeline Mowbray.

" Father and Daughter.

" Madeline.

" Valentine's Eve.

" Temper.

Pardoe, Confessions of a pretty Woman.

Parismus, 1725.

Peacock, Headlong Hall; Night-mare Abbey, 1845. B. C.

Pickerlng, E., The Fright.

" Agnes Serle.

" The Expectant.

" Merchant's Daughter.

Porter, A. M., Honor O'Hara.

Priest's Turf Cutting Day.

Radcliffe, A., The Italian.

Reade, Love me little, etc.

" Griffith Gaunt.

" Foul Play.

Reid, Mayne, The Wood Rangers.

" Osceola.

" Rifle Rangers.

Richardson, S., Pamela.

" Clarissa Harlowe.

" Sir Charles Grandison.

Roche, Children of the Abbey, 1822–28.

Fiction, English (continued).
Rotchfords, The, 1786.
Rouè, The.
Royall, A., The Tennessean.
Sandwith, Hekim Bashi.
Scott, Sir W., Novels, 1852–53.
Sealsfield, Works, 1844.
Shelley, M., Frankenstein.
Sherwood, Indian Pilgrim.
Sidney, Pembroke's Arcadia.
Simpkinson, The Washingtons.
Sir Ralph Willoughby, (Brydges.).
Sir Roger de Coverley, 1850.
Smollett, T., Works, 1796.
Sterne, Laurence, Works, 1847.
Swift, J., Works, 1812–13.
Sydenham, 1833.
Tales of Passion, 1829.
Tales of the Genii, (Ridley), 1857.
Thackeray, Wm., The Newcomes, 1855.
" The Luck of Barry Lyndon, 1853.
" Fatal boots.
Things by their right names, 1812.
Thinks-I-to-myself.
Thoms, Early prose romances.
Trollope, He knew She was right.
" Miss Mackenzie.
Tupper, M. F., Works, 1851.
Uncle Tom in England. P. 199.
Walker, G., The Three Spaniards, 1831.
Walpole, Castle of Otranto.
Ward, R P., Illust. of human life, 1838.
" De Clifford.
Warren, S., Ten Thousand a Year.
" Merchant's Clerk.
" Works, 1854.
Watkins, L., Henry and Eliza, 1823.
Whitty, Knaves and Fools.
Wilson, J., Margaret Lyndsay.
" Lights and Shadows of Scottish Life.
Wiseman, *Card.*, Fabiola, 1855.
Yonge, Dove in the Eagle's Nest. *See* also Friarswood.

Fiction, French. About, E., Madelon.
" Germaine.
" Trente et quarante.
" King of the Mountains.
Adeline et Solignac, 1802. B. C.
Arlincourt, D', De Pelgrim, 1842.
Balzac, Les Petits Manêges, 1845. B. C.
" César Birotteau.
Beaumont, Marie: l'Esclavage, 1840.
Berthet, E., Garde-Chasse: Chauffeurs, 1853, '57.
Capendu, Chasseur de Panthêres.

Fiction, French (continued).
Capendu, Marthe de kerven.
" Le Pré Catelan.
Chateaubriand, Atala, Fr. and Eng.
" The Martyrs, 1812, Fr. and Engl.
" Les Natchez, 1827.
Cleveland's Life, (Prevost).
Cottin, Exiles of Siberia, .853.
Chauveau, Charles Guêrin, 1853.
Diable, Le, diplomate, 1825.
Dudevant, Mme., Jeanne, 1844. B. C.
" Mont Revêche, etc. 1853, 54.
" Jean de la Roche.
" Consuelo, Engl.
" Elle et Lui.
" Famille de Germandre.
" Marquis de Villeneuve.
Dumas, Les Mêmoires d'un Medecin.
" Les Mohicans de Paris.
" Hist. d'un Casse-noisette.
" La Batard de Mauléon, 1846.
" Vingt Ans Après, 1846.
" Le Comte de Monte Christo, 1846, Fr. and Eng.
" Les Louves de Machecoul.
" Black.
" L'Horoscope.
" Les Compagnons de Jéhu.
" Le Chasseur de Sauvagine.
" Edmond Dantès.
" Three Musketeers, Trans.
Duplessis, Les Mormons.
Entretien des Beaux Esprits. (Engl.).
Femmes, Les, Militaires, 1739.
Fénélon, Aventures de Télémaque.
" Adventures of Telemachus.
Feuillet, O., Jeune homme pauvre, etc.
Féval, Le Bossu.
" Bouche de Fer.
" Les Habits Noirs.
" Le Champ de Bataille, etc., 1854.
" Madame Gil Blas, 1857.
Gasparin, Tristesses Humaines.
Gautier, Le Capitaine Fracasse.
Genlis, Alphonsus, 1809, B. C.
" The Rival Mothers.
Gilbert, ou le Poëte malheureux, 1840.
Gleizés, Séléna, 1838.
Gomez, La Belle Assemblée, Engl., 1736.
Gondrecourt, Les pretendans de Cathérine, 1853.
" Mém. d'un Vieux Garçon, 1855.
" Une vraie Femme 1856.
" Le prix du sang.

Fiction, French (continued).
Gondrecourt, L'Anaia.
" Le Bon Homme.
Gracien, B., Le Héros, 1725.
Hoffman, Contes fantastiques.
Horizons célestes, (Guizot).
Hugo, V., Les Misérables.
Kock, Madeleine, 1842.
" Edmund and his Cousin.
Lamartine, Les Confidences, 1849.
" Geneviève, (Engl.).
" The Stone Mason, (Engl.).
" Fior d'Aliza.
" Raphael, 1849, (Engl.).
La Motte-Fouqué, Undine, etc.
" Wild Love.
Le Brun, History of Tekeli, 1815.
Le Sage, Gil Blas, 1831,(Fr. & Engl.).
" Asmodeus, 1850, (Engl.).
" Le Diable Boiteux, 1785.
" Bachelor of Salamanca.
Liaisons dangéreuses, 1722.
Libertin, Le, devenu vertueux, 1777.
Maquet, La Belle Gabrielle, etc.,1854.
" L'envers et l'endroit.
" Dettes de cœur.
Margaret, Heptameron, (Engl.), 1855.
Marmontel, Les Incas, 1817.
Mayer, Asgill, ou les désordres des guerres civiles, 1784.
Méry, J., Le Dernier Phantome, etc., 1854.
Mille et une Faveurs, (Mouhy), 1783.
Mouhy, La Paysanne parvenue, 1749.
Musset, A., Lui et Elle.
Nouvelles de l'Amérique, 1679.
Pain, Voyage au hasard, 1819.
Petit, Vertueux Ouvrier.
Pigault Le Brun, Œuvres.
Princesse, La, de Cléves, 1719.
Puymaigre, Aquarelles, 1842.
Rabelais, Works, 1849.
Reid, M., Les Chasseurs....1854.
" Les Tirailleurs....1855.
Relation d'un Voyage du Pole, 1721.
Reybaud, Pierre Mouton.
Romagnesi, Coll. des Romances, etc.
Rousseau, J. J., Œuvres, 1801.
" Eloisa, (Engl.).
" Letters of a Nun.
Saint-Georges, Les Princes de Maquenoise.
St. Pierre, J. H. B., Paul et Virginie.
" Voy. of Amasis.
Scarron, Le Roman comique.
Scudery, Clelia, (Engl.).
Semaine Littéraire, (Collection), 1844–63, 31 vols.

Fiction, French (continued).
Sethos, Life of, (Terrasson).
Soulié, Au jour le jour.
" Huit jours au Chateau.
" La Lionne, 1858.
Soupirs d'Euridice, 1770.
Souvestre, Philosophe sous les toits.
" Au bord du lac.
Stael, De, Corinne, 1848, (Fr. and Engl.).
Sue, E., Le juif errant, (Fr. and En.).
" Martin, l'enfant trouve.
" Les Sept péchés capitaux.
" Fernand Duplessis.
" Les Mystères du peuple
" Commander of Malta, etc.
Ulbach, Pauline Foucault.
Vigny, Cinq Mars.
Villedieu, Les Exilez, 1695.
Voltaire, Romances, etc., 1794.

Fiction, German, Dutch, Italian, Latin, etc., and translations.
Aleman, Guzman de Alfarache.
" Life of Lazarillo De Tormes.
Amadis of Gaul of Lobeyra, 1803.
Andersen, H. C., Improvisatore.
" Only a fidler.
" O. T.
Arabian Nights Entertainments, Scott's and Lane's editions.
Azeglio, Ettore Fieramosea.
Bandello, Novelle.
Barclay, J., Argenis, 1621.
" Euphormion.
Bocalini, Advertisements from Parnassus.
Bremer, F., Works, 1852, 53.
" The Bondmaid.
Calcar, De Zoon v. d. Klepperman, 1854.
Capella, M., Satyricon.
Carlen, E., John.
" Louise, 1854.
Carlyle T., German romances, trans. 1841.
Cervantès, Don Quixote, 1852, (Sp. and Engl.).
" Exemplary Novels, 1855.
" La Galatea.
Chamisso, Peter Schlemihl, 1824.
Collier, Selima and Azon.
Florian, Guillaume Tell.
" Eleazar and Naphtali, 1830.
" Novelas Nuevas.
Goethe, Wilhelm Meister, 1855, Engl.
" Hermann und Dorothea, 1829.
" Sorrows of Werther.
" Novels and tales, 1854.

Fiction, German, Dutch, Italian, Latin, etc., and translations (continued).
Hauff, the Jew Suss, 1737.
Hebrew tales, (Hurwitz).
Holberg, Iter subterraneum, 1766.
" Onderaardsche Reis van Klim, 1741.
" Journey under the ground, 1844.
Janhen, De Dienstmeid.
La Motte Fouqué, Undine.
Meinhold, Amber-witch.
Montgomery, Bernardo del Carpio.
Muntz, C. (Muhlbach), Henry VIII.
" Joseph I.
" Marie Antoinette.
" Louisa of Prussia.
" Empress Josephine.
Palmerin of England, 1555.
Petrarca, Le Sage resolu, 1644.
Pulszky, Tales of Hungary, 1852.
Quevedo, Works.
Richter, Titan, (Engl.).
Rivera, Life of Alonzo.
Roscoe, Italian Novelists.
Ruffini, Doctor Antonio, 1857, (Engl.).
" Vincenzo, 1863, (Engl.).
Schiller, The Ghost seer.
Spindler, C., Arch. Werner.
" The Invalide.
" The Jew.
Tyll Uilenspiegel, Leven van.
" Marv. Adventures of Tyll Uilenspiegel.
Wieland, Socrates, (Engl.).

Field, G. P. Williams, W. G., Disc., interment of, 1847. Pam. 494.

Fielding, H. Scott, W., Memoir of.

Fife & Kinross. Maclaren, Geology.
Sibbald, History of.

Fiji Is. Arthur, W., What is Fiji?
Dix, Customs of; Wreck of the Glide.
Oliver, Recollections, 1848.
Rowe, Hunt's life.
Williams, T., Account of, 1859.

Filibusters. *See* Buccaneers; Privateers.

Fillmore, J. Biog. of, 1848.

Fillmore, M. Brooks, J., Defence of, 1856.
Fillmore, M., Biography of, 1856.
Taylor, Z., Life of, 1847.

Fillmore Co., Minn. Bishop, Hist. of.

Financial. Banker's Magazine, N. Y., 1846–65.
Barker, Jacob, Life of.

Financial (continued).
Boston Stock Board, 1844.
Bristed, J., Bankruptcy of Gt. Brit., 1809.
Browne's Bank. and Merc. Table, 1794–1901.
Chevalier, M., Fall of Gold, 1859.
Cohen, Compendium of, 1822.
Cory, Treatise on Accounts, 1840.
Dew, Law of Credit, 1840.
Dict. de Comm., Banque, etc., 1805.
Elliott, J., Funding System of U. S. and G. B., 1845.
Fonfrède, Œuvres, v. 7, 1845.
France: Finances, 1809.
Francis, J., Chron. of the Stock Exchange, 1850.
Gallatin, A., Consid. on the Currency, 1831.
" Sketch of Finances of U. S., 1796.
Grenville, G., Admin. des Finances d'Angleterre, 1768.
" On a Sinking Fund.
Jœrres, Equation of Payments, 1843.
Johnson, A. B., An inquiry, of Capital, 1813.
Joplin, W., Panics, 1854.
Josseau, Crédit foncier et agricole, 1851.
Koster, Trade in Bullion, 1811.
Laurent, Cours des receveurs des communes.
McCulloch, Principles of taxation, 1848.
Mass.: Auditor's Reports, 1860–62.
Martin's Boston Stock Market, 1835–56.
Morgan, W., Review of Dr. Price, 1795.
National, A, Exchange, 1842.
Necker, Finances of France, 1781.
Nolte, Fifty years in both hemispheres, 1854.
Pamphlets relating to Finance, vols. 252, 427, 498, 786, 787, 931, 972, 1324–1326, '514, 1864.
Parnell, H., Finan. Reform, 1830.
Patterson, Science of Finance, 1868.
Preston's Interest Tables.
Price, R., Funds, 1795
" National debt, 1775.
Rosaz, Elémens .... des changes étrangers, 1810.
Rowlett's Interest Tables, 1842.
Sedgwick, T., What is Monopoly? 1835. P. 29. B. C.
Société Gén. de crédit mobilier.
Tate, Modern Cambist, 1852.
Trotter, Observations on Public debt of the States, 1839.
Turgot, Œuvres, 1808–11.
Usury Explained. Pamphr. 11.

Fine Arts (continued).
Mason, G. C , Applic. to Manufactures, 1858.
Mêmes, Hist. of Sculpture, Painting and Architecture, 1831 B C.
Mercey, Etudes sur, 1855.
Monuments of art, Kugler, 1862.
Moor, J., Essays, 1759.
Morse, S. F. B., Discourse on, and Reply, 1827, 28.
Muller, C. O., Anc. art and its remains.
Müller, E., Donaustauf und Walhalla, 1847.
Mulvany, Fine Arts in Ireland, 1847.
Musée de Bordeaux, 1787.
Musée du Louvre, 1830, B. C.
Musée du Luxembourg, 1842.
Musée de Peinture, etc. de Belgique, 1846.
Nat. Acad. of Design, N. Y., Exhibitions, 1832–60.
Nat. Gallery, London, 1846, B. C.
Netherlands, Schilderijen van het K. Kabinet, 1826-40.
N. Y. Hist. Soc., Cat. of Museum, 1868.
Norfolk and Norwich Museum, Eng.
Painter's Primer.
Palgrave, F. T., Essays on Art, 1866.
Pamphlets relating to, vols. 69, 400, 489, 499, 607, 659, 787, 788, 973, 1015, 1022, 1036, 1235, 1515, 1679 2509. B. C. vol. 20, 52.
Parkes, M., Art monopoly, 1850.
" The Bowyer collection.
Paterson, M. C., Address, Am. Acad. 1826. Pam. 71.
Perry statue.
Perugino, L'Ascension.
Peters, W., Nude Human Beings.
Price, U., On the Picturesque, 1796.
Profess. Sketches of Mod. Artists.
Quatremère de Quincy, Essai sur l'Idéal, 1837.
" Essay on the Fine Arts, 1837.
Rembrandt, L'Œuvre, 1858.
Reynolds, Sir J., Literary Works, 1835.
Ripley, Hand-book of Lit. and.
Rossi, G. B. De, Roma sotterranea, 1864, 67.
Ruskin, Political Economy of, 1857.
" The True and the Beautiful, 1868.
" Modern Painters, 5 v.
" Lectures on, 1870.
Samber, Rome illustrated, 1721.
Schlegel, Letters on Christian Art, 1849.
" Descr. of Paintings in Paris and Netherl., 1802–4.

Fine Arts (continued).
Seroux d'Agincourt, History of Art, 1847.
Shaw, H., Catalogue of Illuminated Drawings.
Soc. of Artists of U. S., 1811.
South-Kensington Museum, 1860.
Stothard, Life of.
Sulzer, J. G., Alg. Theorie der Schœnen Kunste, 1792–94.
Taine, Philos. of Art. 1865.
Taylor, Condition, in Great Britain, 1841.
Trumbull J., Encouragement of, 1827.
Tuckerman, H. T., Book of Artists.
Verplanck, Add., Am. Acad., 1824.
Vignon, Exposit. de 1855.
Visconti, Œuvres; Musée Pie Clémentin, 1818.
" Monumens du Musée Chiaramonti, 1822.
Waagen, Treasures of Art in G. Brit., 1854,57.
Wallacc, H. B,. Art in Europe, 1855.
Walpole H., Painting in England.
Washington Exhibition, 1853.
Wechniakof, Economie des travaux ésthetiques, 1870.
Whitmore, On P. Pelham.
Winckelmann, Hist. of Anc. Art., 1849.
" Werke, 1808–20.
Works of Eminent Masters, Lon., 1854.
See Engraving; Drawing; Gems; Music; Painting; Taste; Sculpture; Museums.

Fine Arts: Sale Catalogues. Abraham, R. For sale, New York, 1830.
Hone, P., Catalogue, N. Y., 1852.
Pamphlets, vols. 996, 1679.
See Bibliography.

Finistere, France. Annuaire, 1845.

Finland. Acerbi, Travels, 1797–99.
See Russia.

Finley, J. B. Pioneer Life.

Finley, R. Brown, I. V., Biog. of,1857.

Finney, C. G. Perkins, E., Bunker Hill Contest.
Rand, New Divinity Tried, 1832.
See Oberlin.

Fire-Arms. *See* Military.

Fire Departments. Albany, F. D. Rules, 1350.
Boston, F. Dep. Report, 1855.
Buffalo, Report, 1858.
Cincinnati Reports, 1854, 56.
Fire Engine Companies, 1839–58.

Fourier, C. Gal. des Contem. vol. 10, Vie de, 1840.
Pellarin, C., Life of, 1848.

Fowler, O. Life of, 1862.

Fowler, W. Descendants, 1870.

Fowls. *See* Poultry.

Fox, C. J. Speeches, 6 v.
Correspondence, 4 v.
Green, W., Portrait of.
Letter to a Country, &c., 1784.
Letter to the Electors of Westminster, 1793.
Parr, S., Character of, 1809.
Rogers, Recollections.
Russell, Life of, 1859.
Tooke, J. H., Two Portraits, 1788.
Trotter, Memoirs of.

Fox, E. Revolutionary Adven.

Fox, G. Friends' Library, v. 1, Journal and Life.
Tallack, Notes on.
Wood, E. R., Essay on Writings of.

Fox, James. Hay, C. A., Discourse on.

Fox, John. Andrews, Review of Book of Martyrs.
Maitland, Townsend's Ed., 1841.

Foxborough, Ms. Williams, T., Ded. Sermon, 1823.

Foxcroft, S. Moseley, E., Sermon on.

Fox Hunting. Radcliffe, The Noble Science, 1839.

Framingham, Ms. Barry, W., History of, 1640–1847.

France, Almanachs, Registers. Almanach du Commerce, 1818.
Almanach de France, 1855.
Almanach du Marin, 1855.
Almanach Royal, 1738–1854.
Annuaire de l'instruction publique, 1851–56.
Annuaire de l'Université, 1830.
Annuaire de la Société de l'hist. de la France, 1837.
Annual Registers of Departments: *See* Aisne, Ardèche, Aube, Brest, Calvados, Cantal, Corrège, Corse, Cote d'or, Costes du Nord, Creuse, Dordogne, Doubs, Finistère, Gard, Gers, Garonne, Haute Marne, Herault, Landes, Loire, Lot, Lozère, Lyon, Manche, Marne, Meurthe, Meuse, Montpelier, Morbihan, Moselle, Nièvre, Nord, Puy de Dôme, Pyrenées, Rhin, Sàone et Loire, Seine et Marne, Sèvres (Deux), Somme, Tarn, Vienne, Vosges.

France, Colonies of. Bury, Exodus of the Western nations, 1865.
Compagnie des Indes, 1765–69.
Depons, Commerce avec les deux Indes, 1807.
Exposé de la situation actuelle, 1822.
Jeffery, Hist. of Sp. and Fr. dominion in America, 1760.
Malouet, Mém. sur l'administration de, 1801.
Mémoires des Commissaires, 1755–57.
Petit, Sur le gouv. des esclaves, 1777.
Recueil de différentes pièces, 1785.
Recueil dipl. du commerce, 1784.
See French war, 1743-63; Colonies; Guyana; St. Domingo; Voy., etc.

France, General Histories. Crowe, History of, Lardner, 12, 13, 14.
Duruy, Histoire de, 1858.
Gaultier, Histoire de F.
Lacretelle, Histoire de, 1844.
Mignet, Hist. of, to 1814.
Millot, Histoire de....à Louis XIV.
Ranken, A., Hist. of, 1801.
Ségur, Le Comte de, Hist. de, 1830.
Smedley E., Hist. of France.
Stephen, J., Lectures.

France, History from early period to 1789. Adams J., Discourses on Davila, 1790.
Aubigné, Histoire, 1552–1601.
Avaux, D', Négotiations, 1754–55.
Barante, Hist. des Ducs de Bourgogne, 1836.
Bassompierre, Mémoires, 1765.
Blondel, Expulsion of the English, 1449–5.
Bush, Memoirs of the Queens of, 1847.
Cayet, Guerre sous Henry IV, 1608.
" Hist. de la Paix, 1605.
Charrière, Négotiations dans le Levant, 1848.
Choisy, Mémoires de Louis XIV, 1725.
Chronicles of Great Britain, Letters and papers of the wars of the English with.
Collezione di Carte, Venezia, 1806–07.
Commines, Memoirs, Louis XI, Charles VII, 1757.
Comyn, Hist. of the Western Empire, 1841.
Costello, Jacques Cœur.
Cuvelier, Chron. de Bertrand du Guesclin, 1839.
Dangeau, Memoirs of the Court, 1684–1720.
Davila, Hist. of Civil Warres of, 1647.
Depping, Correspondance sous Louis XIV.
Du Bouchet, Seconde et troisième ligne royale, 1646.

France, History from early period to 1789 (continued).

Du Hausset, Private Memoirs of, 1827.

Du Monstier, Neustria pia, 1663.

Espernon, Life, from 1598.

Estrades, Lettres et Négotiations, 1743.

Etat actuel, 1756–63. MS.

Fabyan, New Chronicles, 1811.

Flassan, Hist. de la Diplomatic Française, 1811.

Formeville, Canonniers de Caen.

Fortoul, Versailles et Louis XIV.

France, Documents inédits sur l'Histoire de, 1839–69.

Freer's Henry IV.

Gaillard, Rivalité de: et de l'Angleterre, 1771.

Godwin, P., Hist. of Ancient Gaul, 1860.

Golnitz, Itinerarium Belgico-Gallicum, 1655.

Guilhe, De Bordeaux, de l'Aquitaine et de la Guienne, 1835.

Haton, Mémoirs, 1553–82.

Hist of Eng. and France under House of Lancaster, 1852.

Hotoman, Franco-Gallia.

Hunter, J., Agincourt.

James, G. P. R., Lives of Henry IV and Louis XIV, 1847, 51.

Jamison, Life of De Guesclin.

Kremer, Des Rheinischen Franziens, 1778.

Louis XIV, Memorials, 1688.

" Œuvres.

Mably, Obs. sur l'Histoire de, 1794,95.

Maintenon, Secret Correspondence.

Mariobert, L'Espion Anglois, 1782–84.

Margaret de Valois, Memorials, 1664.

Martin, H., History of France, 1866.

Michelet, History of, 1847.

Montluc, Commentaries, 1520–57.

Mornay, P. de, Histoire de la Vie de, 1647.

Noailles, Rome and the Constitution, 1728.

Notice....des Assassins, 1804.

Ossat, Lettres, 1594–1604.

Palgrave, Hist. of Normandy and Eng., 1851–64.

Pardoe, Louis XIV and the Court of, 1847.

" Court of Francis I, 1849.

" Life of Marie de Medicis.

Phillippe d'Orléans, Régent, 1736.

Rathéry, Hist. des Etats Généraux.

Read, Charles, Henri IV.

Retz, Card., Memoirs.

Richlieu, Mémoires.

France, History from early period to 1789 (continued).

St. Simon, Mémoires...regne de Louis XIV.

Satyre Ménippée, 1726.

Soc. de l'Hist. de France, 1837.

Soulavie, Hist. Mem. of Louis XVI, 1802.

Stapleton, Rot. Scaccarii Normanniæ, 1840.

Sully, Duke of, Memoirs, 1856.

Taylor, W. C., Mem. of House of Orleans, 1850.

Thierry, Hist. Ess., Scenes of 6th Century, 1845.

" Prog. of the Tiers Etat, 1855.

Thou, Hist. sui Temporis, 1543–1607.

Tocqueville, The Old Régime, 1856.

Tommaseo, Relations....au xvi siècle.

Turgot, Œuvres, 1808–11.

Varin, Archives, Ville de Reims.

White, Queens and Princesses in.

William III, Letters of Louis XIV.

Wraxall, History, 1574–1610.

" Hist. under House of Valois, 1364–1574.

France, Pamphlets Political, to 1789. Allies, The, defended, 1711.

Belleisle, Letters, 1759.

Candid Enquiry, 1770.

Duvergier, Politique de la, 1841.

Examination of a Letter, 1758.

Great Bastard Protector, 1689.

Historical Memorial, 1761.

Impartial Narrative, 1758.

" " of Belleisle, 1761.

Journal of Campaign, 1758.

Letter from a Mem. of Parl., 1758.

Modest Vind. of French King, 1703.

Needham, Christianissimus, etc., 1678.

Sherlock, W., Letter on Invasion, 1692.

Sketch of, 1735.

France, History, 1789–1830. Abbott, J. S. C., French Revolution, 1859.

Abrantès, Duchesse d', Memoirs, 1833–1835.

Adolphus, Hist. of, 1790–1802.

Baines, E., Hist. of the Wars of, 1817.

Barlow J., Writings.

Barruel, Mem. on Hist. Jacobinism, 1799.

Barruel, Hist. du Jacobinisme.

" Storia del Clero di Francia, 1794.

Beauharnais, H., Memoirs.

Blanchard, Clergé Fr. à Londres, 1808.

Bonaparte, L., Œuvres, Works, 1848.

Bonaparte, N., Correspondence, 1855.

France, History, 1789-1830 (cont'd).

Bonaparte, N., Istoria di Napoleone, 1807.

Bouillé, Memoirs relating to, 1797.

Bowles, French aggression.

Brissot, Life of.

Brune, Campagne en Batavie, 1800-1.

Burke E., Reflections on, 1791.

Calonne, De l'état de....à venir, 1790.

" State of Europe, 1796.

Campan, Court of Marie Antoinette, 1850.

Carlyle, T., French Revolution, 1837.

Cartwright, Letter to D. of Newcastle, 1792.

Chronologist, 1790-98.

Clavière, France et les Etats Unis, 1787.

Clubb, Narr. of sufferings.

Cobbett, Bloody Buoy, 1823.

Collection of Addresses, 1793.

Cooke, J. H., Narrative of Events in, 1814-15.

Dechaumereix, Esprit en Brétagne, 1795.

Ducancel, Exquisses Dramatiques.

Dugardier, De la Constit. de l'an 8.

Dumas, A., Democracy in France, 1841.

Dumas, Count, Memoirs of his own Time, 1838.

Dumouriez, Correspondance avec Pache, 1792.

Essai phil. pol. sur les états généraux, 1791.

Fantin, Hist. Phil. de la Rev. 1797.

" Hist. de la Répub., 1797.

Fasti della Rivol., 1799.

Giguet, Rév. du 18 Fructidor.

Gourgaud, Gen., Memoirs, History of.

Grouchy, Campagne de 1815.

Guizot, Democracy in, 1849.

Harper, R. G., Works; U. S. and Fr., 1797, 98.

Headley, J. T., The Imp. Guard of Napoleon, 1852.

Histoire Pitt. de la Convention, La Mothe, 1833.

Holstein, Baroness, Appeal against the Continental System, 1813.

Ivernois, D', Reflections, 1798.

" Préparatifs de Guerre, 1804.

" Budget, Au XIII.

Jal, Mém. sur les trois couleurs nationales.

Knox, V., Narr. of Transactions, 1793.

Lamartine, Hist. des Girondins, 1847.

" History of the Girondists, 1847.

" History of Restor. of the Monarchy, 1851.

France, History, 1789-1830 (cont'd).

Langon, Evenings with Cambacères, 1837.

Laroche Jaquelein, Mém. de la Vendée, 1816.

" Memoirs of La Vendee, 1816.

Lavalette, Pers. Memoirs.

Le Sur, Annuaire Historique, 1818-24.

Lettres de l'Armée en Egypte, 1779.

Lloyd's Hamburgh, 1813.

Loménie, Beaumarchais....1856.

Louis XVI., Trial, 1793. Pam. 454.

Louis-Philippe d'Orléans, Correspondance, 1800.

Louvet, J. D., Quelques notices, 1793.

Mackintosh, Sir J., Fr. Revol. defended.

Mallet Du Pan, Hist. du Républicanisme Français, 1796.

" Considérations on, 1793.

" Mem. and Corresp. illustrative of, 1852.

Michelet, Hist. View of Fr. Rev., 1848.

Mignet, History of Fr. Rev., 1827.

Moleville, Hist. de la Rév., 1803.

Money, History of Campaign of 1792.

Moniteur, Le, Newsp., 1789-1836.

Montgaillard, Etat de la France, 1794.

Moore, J., Causes and Progress of, 1820.

Narrative of Invasion, 1806.

New and Concise History, 1794.

Normandie, Misfortunes of the Dauphin, 1838.

Paine, T., Answer to the Attack of Mr. Burke.

Philipppart's Bernadotte, 1815.

Playfair, History of Jacobinism, 1796.

Pradt, La Restauration en 1814.

" Les Quatre Concordats, 1818.

Priestley, Letters on the Rev., 1798.

Proyart, Louis XVI décapité, 1800.

Puisaye, Mémoires, parti royaliste.

Rabaut, Précis Historique de, 1813-15.

Ramel, Journal, 1799.

" Anecdotes, 18 Fructidor.

" Nar. of deportation to Cayenne.

Recueil de Pièces officielles, 1815.

Reflections on Peace, 1793.

Reign of Terror, 1826.

Renée, Louis XVI, 1858.

Siborne, Hist. of War, 1815.

Sketch of, and of Napoleon, 1792-1815.

Sketch of Military System of, 1812.

Smyth, Lectures on Fr. Rev., 1855.

Somerville, W. C., Letters on Fr. Rev., 1823.

Stael, Mme. de, Considerations on Events of Fr Rev.

France, History, 1830–71, Pamphlets. Amer. Claims on France. 1836.
Audifret, Le Budget, 1841.
Bonaparte, L., Au Confessional, 1853.
Caldwell, J., Sermon, 1830.
Causeries sur les affaires, 1831.
Considérations sur la crise, 1830.
Etudes Politiques et historiques, 1836.
Girardin, Des 52, 1849.
Hunter, R. M., Speech, Spoliations of, 1851.
Pamphlets of this period, vols. 789, 1327–1330, 1516.
Romand, Dictature de Paris, 1848.
Sinclair, G., Reflections, 1859.

France, Navy. Bonfils, Hist. de la Marine Française, 1845.
France: Ordinance, 1689.
Grasse, Combat Naval du 12 Avr. 1796.
Joinville, Naval forces of.
La Serre, Essais sur la Marine de, 1661 à 1785.
Letter from an Officer, 1798.

France, Society and Manners.
Aristocratie en France, 1834.
Beaumanoir, Coutumes du Beauvoisis.
Berry, Social Life in Eng. and France, 1844.
Bulwer, H. L., France, social, 1834.
" Monarchy of the Middle Ages, 1836.
Chéruel, Dict. Hist. de la France, 1855.
Costello, Bearn and the Pyrenees.
Houssaye, Men and Women of 18th Century.
Lauzun, Mémoires, 1747–83.
Récamier, Mme., Sketch of.
Renneville, Coutumes Gauloises, 1823.
See France; Travels.

France, Travels in and Descriptions.
American Wanderer, 1783.
Angoulême, Voy. de Louis XVI, 1824.
Berrian, W., Travels in, and Italy, 1817, 18.
Blessington, Countess, Idler in France, 1841.
Breval, Tr. through, and the Low Countries, 1726.
Carr, J., Stranger in France.
Cass, L., Its King, Court, etc., 1840.
Chiniac, La Religion Gauloise.
Cobbett, J. P., Ride of 800 miles, 1824.
Cobbett, J. M., Letters from, 1825.
Cooper, J. F., Residence in, 1836.
Coste, Voyage...sur le littoral, 1855.
Costello, Bearn and the Pyrenees, 1844.
" Valley of the Meuse.
Cradock, J., Lit. Mem., Trav. in, 1828.

France, Travels in and Descriptions (continued).
Ditson, Para papers, 1858.
Donelan, My trip to, 1857.
Dumas, Pictures of Travel in.
Faber, Sketches of France, 1813.
Few weeks in Paris, 1814.
Gentleman's guide, 1768.
Inglis, The Pyrenees.
James, J., Sketches of Travel in Italy and, 1820.
Jefferys, Maps of Maritime parts, 1761.
Johnston, D., Charity in, 1829.
Letters concerning the French, 1769.
Letters descriptive of, (Cushing), 1832.
Letters from Geneva and France, 1819.
Louis XVIII, Voyage à Bruxelles, 1791.
Meissas, Quest. sur la carte, 1858.
Mérimée, Voy. dans l'Ouest de, 1836.
" Voyage en Auvergne, 1838.
Moore, J., Jour. of Residence in, 1792.
Overbury, Sir T, Observations on, 1609.
Pardoe, The River and the Desert, 1838.
Pinkney, Col., Tr. in South of, 1807.
Rombise, Itin....Galliæ, 1639.
St. John, Letters from, 1787.
Simpson, J., Paris after Waterloo, 1853.
State of France, 1760.
Stearns, S., Tour from London to Paris, 1790.
Steffens, Adventures, 1813, 14.
Taylor, J. N., Sketch of, 1815.
Thicknesse, Journey through, 1789.
Trollope, Summer in Brittany, 1840.
Vatout, Résidences Royales, 1845.
Willard, E, Journ. and letters from, 1833.
Young, A., Trav. in, 1787.
See Europe, Travels in; French.
See also Avignon, Bazas, Bordeaux, Brittany, Lillebourne, Lyon, Nevers, Normandy, Paris, Rheims, Rouen, Toulon.
See also Antiquities, Genealogy, Heraldry, Literature, Language, Protestantism, Typography, etc.

France, Isle of. *See* Mauritius.

Francis, B. Ryland, J., Discourse on.

Francis, C. Newell, W., Memoir of, 1866. P. 1857.

Francis, Sir P. Burke, E. H., "Not Junius."
Parkes, J., Memoirs of, 1867.
Taylor, J., Identity of Junius, 1816.
See Junius.

Franciscus, S. Bourchier, De Martyrio Francisci.

Franck, A. H. Life of.

Frankland, Sir C. H. Nason, E., Life of.

Franklin, B. Autobiography, Bigelow, 1868.
" Vie de, Paris, 1791.
" Life of, by himself, cont. by W. T. Franklin, 1818.
" Life and Writings, (Sparks), 1840.
Boston, Inaug. of Statue of, (Shurtleff), 1857.
Fauchet, Eloge de, 1790.
Franklin, B., Letters by his family, 1859.
Gilpin, H. D., Address on, 1857.
Green, S. A., Of his Autobiography, 1871.
Histoire d'un pou, 1779.
Holley, O. L., Life of, 1848.
Mignet, Vie de, (Inst. de France; Ac. Mor. v. 7).
Parton, J., Life of.
Smith, W., Works, Eul. on, 1803.
Tuckerman, H. T., Biog. Essays.
Weems, Life of, 1835.
Weld, H. H., Narr. of his life, 1848.
Winthrop, R. C., Speech, Statue of, 1856. P. 242.
Wynne's Lives, 1850.

Franklin, Sir J. Kennedy, W., Voy. of the Prince Albert, 1853.
La Roquette, Notice Biog. sur, 1857.
Osborn, Fate of, 1860.
Weld, C. R., The Search for, 1851.
See Arctic Voyages.

Franklin, W. Whitehead, W. A., Life of, 1763–1776.

Franklin, Conn. Nott, S., Half Century Serm.
Woodward, Congr. Church Centenn.

Franklin Co., Ms. Holland, Western Massachusetts.
Packard, Hist. of Churches in.

Franklin Co., N. Y. Gazetteer, 1862.
Hough, B. F., History of, 1853.

Franklin Co., Ohio. Martin, W. T., History of.

Fraser, H. Rosewell, J., Discourse on.

Fraunhofer. Thiersch, Biog. Nachrichten, 1852.

Frazer, S., Lord Lovat. *See* Lovat.

Frederica, Margravine of Bareith. Memoirs, 1828.

Frederick. *See* York, Duke of.

Frederick I of Prussia. Jablonski, Memoriæ ...Monumentum, 1713.
Kugler, F., Campaigns of, 1845.

Frederick II of Prussia. Abbott, J. S. C., Life of, 1871.
Carlyle, History of, 1858, 62, 64, 65.
Dover, Lord, Life of, 1832.
Frederick II, Œuvres, 1846-53, 23 v.
" Hist. de mon temps.
" Recueil de lettres, de 1757.
Grimm et Diderot, Correspondance, 1753–1790.
Mirabeau, Secret Hist. of the Court.

Frederick William III, of Prussia. Towers, Life of.

Frederick, Md. Zacharias, Centen. Sermon, 1847. Pam. 267.

Free Communion Brethren. Wauby, Sermon, 1811.

Freedmen. *See* Civil War; Negro races; Slavery.

Free Masonry. *See* Masonry.

Free Soil. *See* U. S. Territories; Slavery.

Free Thinking. *See* Natural Religion; Deism.

Free Trade. Agricola, Letters on, 1845.
Agriculture, Commerce, 1826.
Alison, A., F. T. and Currency.
Assoc. Belge, Liberté commerciale, 1846, 47.
Atkinson, S., Effects of, 1829.
Badnall, Letters, 1830.
Bastiat, Sophisms of the protect. pol.
" Popular fallacies, 1849.
" Harmonies économiques, 1860.
Brown, C. B., Address to Congress.
Carey, H. C., Principles of Social Science, 1858.
" Dinner to, 1859.
" Letters to the President, 1858.
" [Writings collected].
Carey, M., Views on the Lib. System, 1826.
Chaptal, Impost duties, 1821. P. 153.
Commercial facts, 1855.
Dunckley, A., The Charter of the Nations, 1854.
Essay, 7th, P. Webster, 1785.
Essay on, 1825. P. 153.
Finch, Town dues....free trade, etc., 1850.
Free Trade Convention, 1831. P. 55.
Fonfrède, Œuvres, v. 8, 1845.
Gladstone, Intended repeal of the Corn laws, 1846.
Greeley, H., Essays of Polit. Econ., 1870.
" Protect. of industry. P. 290.
Lee, H., An Exposition, 1832.
Letter to the Electors, 1848.
Lherbette, De la liberté commer. P.10.

Free Trade (continued).
Maitland, Export. of Wool, 1818.
Morton, J , Protection on Agriculture, 1846. P. 424.
Necessity of Comm. treaty with France, 1787.
Pamphlets relating to, vols. 153, 424.
Pearson, R., A reply, 1850.
Raguet, Principles of, 1840.
Report of Comm. of Citizens of Boston, 1828.
Review of H. G. Otis's Speech, 1831.
Stewart, A., Review of Walker.
Turgot, Œuvres, Liberté du comm. des grains, 1808–11.
Urquhart's Turkey.
Webster, P., Essays, 1785.
Young, G. F., F. T. Fallacies, 1852.
See Tariff; Corn Laws; Monopoly; Commerce; Polit. Econ.

Free Will. *See* Necessity; Will.

Free Will Baptists. F. W. B. For. Miss. Soc., 1855. P. 604.
F. W. B. Register, 1847–59.
Treatise of Faith of.
Mark's Life.
Stewart, History of.

Frelinghuysen, T. Campbell, W. H., Sermon on, 1862.
Chambers, Life of.

Fremont, J. C. Life of, 1856.
" Explorations.
" Trial, etc., 1848.
" Claims, U. S. Sen., 1848.
Bigelow, J., Life of, 1856.
Fish, H., Reason for support, 1856.
Fremont, J. B., Story of the Guard, 1863.
Hall, B. F., Republican Candidates, 1856.
Headley, J. T., Letter on, 1856.
Lord, O. P., His Principles, 1856.
Pam., v. 537, Pres. Election, 1856.
Steele, A., Letter on, 1856.
Willard, E., Late Amer. Hist., 1856.

French Judiciary. Floquet, L'Echiquier de Normandie.

French Pamphlets. Vols. 523, 608, 747, 748, 789, 1109, 1783; B. C. 41. *See* Political; France.

French Prophets. Bulkeley's Answer, 1708.
Calamy's, E., Life and times, vol. 2.
" Caveat against, 1708.
" Bulkeley's remarks considered, 1708.
Luttrell, v. vi, 307, 571.
Pamphlets, vol. 2516.

French Spoliations. Clayton, J. M., Speech on, 1846.
Hunter, R. T. M., Speech on, 1851.
Spoliations of Am. Commerce.
See France, Hist., 1789–1830; Neutrals.

French Wars in America, 1744–63.
Banvard, Tragic Scenes.
Beaujeu, Bataille du Malangueulé.
Bradstreet's expedition, 1759.
Brief view of Penn'a, 1756.
Chauncy, Braddock's defeat, 1755.
Clarke, W., Obs. on conduct of the French, 1755.
Comparative importance, 1762.
Craig, N. B., Washington's first Campaign, 1848.
Dobson, Chronol. of the war, 1755–63.
Drake, S. G., History of French war.
Evans, L., Letter on Fort Frontenac, etc., 1756.
Gardiner, Exped. to W. Indies, 1759.
Gibson, Siege of Cape Breton, Louisburg, etc., 1747.
Knox, J., Jour. of campaigns in N. America, 1757–60.
Le Moine, Maple leaves, 1864.
Letter to the people of England, 1756.
Lettres d'un François, 1755.
Livingston, Review of operations.
Loudon, Conduct of a commander reviewed, 1758.
Mante, History of the late war, 1772.
Mémoire contenant le précis des faits, 1756.
Mémoires des commissaires du roi, 1755–1757.
Memoirs of the war from 1744.
Mitchell, Contest in America, 1757.
Niles' Hist. of, (Mass. Hist. Soc. Coll.).
Parsons's Hill family.
Peuple, Le, Juge, 1756.
Pouchot, Memoir upon, Trans. 1866.
Poullin, Hist. de la guerre, etc., 1759.
Proposals for uniting the Colonies, 1757.
Rég. Baptêmes à Fort Du Quesne, 1753–56.
Reminiscences of the French war, 1831.
Review of the Military opera., 1753–56.
Rogers, R., Journals, 1765.
Sabine, Hist. address, 1859.
Sargent, W., Braddock's expedi., 1855.
Serious Consid., (Kennedy), 1754.
Shirley, Gov., Conduct of, 1758.
" Louisbourg Siege, 1746.
Smyth, Sir J. C., Wars in Canada, 1755–1814.
Washington, G., Journal to Ohio, in 1752.
Wright, J., History of, 1865.
See France.

Friesland. Cate, Doopsgezienden in Friesland.
Eekhoff, Geschiedenis van, 1846.
Friesland, Toestand, 1859.
Hedendaagsche Historie, 1785.
Leeuwen, J. Van, Kronyk, 1834.
Schik, Geschiedenis der staaten, 1581–1795.
Sjoerds, Jaerboeken van.
Winsem, P., Rerum sub Philippo II, 1646.
See Netherlands.

Frignano. Tondini, Mem. della vita, 1782.

Frisbie, L. Writings and Life, 1823.

Froissart, J. La Curne, De, Life of, 1801.

Froment-Coste, A. Labretonnière, Notice sur, 1846. P. 230.

Frontenac, Fort. Bradstreet's expedition, 1759.

Fronto, M. C. Epistolæ.

Fruits. Am. Pomological Soc., 1854.
Baily, Catalogue, 1859.
Downing, Fruit Trees of America, 1847.
Forsyth, Management of Fruit Trees, 1803.
Hovey, C. M., The Fruits of America, 1847–56.
Knoop, Pomologia, 1758.
Lindley, Pomologia Britannica, 1841.
N. Y. Nat. Hist., (Emmons).
North Am. Pomolog. Convention, 1849.
North-Western Fruit Growers, 1852.
Thomas, J. J., Am. Fruit-culturist, 1849.
Vermont Fruit Conv., 1848, 50. P. 52.
See Agriculture; Horticulture.

Fry, Caroline. Autobiography, 1849.

Fry, Elizabeth. Journals and Letters, 1847–8.

Fryeburg, Me. Davies, C. S., Address, commem. at, 1825.

Fuel. *See* Ventilation; Warming.

Fuller, Andrew. Works and memoir of.
Observations on.

Fuller, Arthur. Life of.

Fuller, J. Descendants of, 1869.

Fulton, R. Cartwright's, E., Mem. of, 1843.
Chapman, W., On his wheel-boats, 1797.
Clarkson, Biog. Hist. of Clermont.
Colden, C. D., Life of, 1817.
" Vind. of Steamboat right, 1818.
Duer, W. A., Letter to C. D. Colden on his life of, 1817.

Fulton, R. (continued).
Fulton, R., Corresp. with G. Morris, 1814. P. 145.
Latrobe, The Lost chapter, 1871.
Livingston, Petition respecting steamboats, 1814. P. 9. B. C.
Reigart, Life of, 1856.
Renwick, J., Life of, (Sparks 10).
Tuckerman, H. T., Biog. Essays.
Wynne's lives, 1850.
See Steam.

Fulton Co., N. Y. Directory, 1869.

Fulton St. Prayer Meeting. Chambers, Account of, 1858.

Funeral Sermons. *See* Sermons; Eulogies.

Funerals. Madden, Fu. Customs.
Maitland, P., Burial Service.
Muret, Rites of Funeral, 1683.
See Cemeteries.

Fungi. *See* Botany; Microscope; Mildew; Mushrooms.

Furniture. Attingham Catalogue, 1827.
Normand, Decorations.
Shaw, H., Spec. Anc. Furniture, 1836.
See Architecture; Domestic Economy.

Furman, R. Sommers, Life of.

Fur Trade. Neill, Dahkota Land.
See Hudson's Bay Co.

Future Life and State. Æneas, De immortalitate.
Alger, Hist. of the Doctrine, 1864.
Athenagoras, De mort. resurrec.
" Jews on resurrection.
Blanchard, J. P., An Examination, 1858.
Cobbold, An Essay, 1793.
Coleridge, Words of Instruction, 1834.
Coxe, R. C., Death Disarmed, 1848.
Craven, W., Sermon, Gal. vi. 9, 1775.
Cruickshank, W., No Intermediate Place, 1839.
Dorr, B., Recognition in, 1839
Edwards J., Justice of God, 1773.
Fiddes, Serm. on the Judgment, 1707.
Fisk, W., Future Rewards, 1823.
Friendship in Death, 1733.
Future Punishment. P. 296.
Gould, G. B., Origin of relig. belief, 1869.
Gray, J. T., Immortality, 1847.
Hopkins, S., State of those dying in Sin.
Hudson, C. F., Debt and Grace, 1858.
Huidekoper, Christ in the under world, 1854.
Human Nature, 1844.

Genealogies, American (continued).
Dow. *See* Stranahan.
Drake's Hist. of Boston, Pedigrees.
Drake Family, 1845.
Dudley, D., Dudley Geneal., 1848.
Dudley, R. *See* Drake's Boston.
Dunnel and Dwinell Family, 1862.
Durrie, Bibliog. Geneal. Americana, 1868.
Dutton Family, Cope, 1871.
Earle, R., and Descendants, 1860.
Eliot. *See* Drake's Boston.
Eliot Family, 1854.
Fairfaxes of England and Amer., 1868.
Farmer, Geneal. of Settlers of N. E., 1829.
Fessenden, Bradford Family, 1850.
Field, Geneal. of Brainerd Family, 1867.
Fiske, W., Family of N. H., 1867.
Fitch. *See* Stranahan.
Fitz Family, 1869.
Flint, T., Gen. Register, 1860.
Fletcher Family, 1871.
Foot Family, Supp., 1867.
Forster, J., Family, 1870.
Fowler, W. C., Mem. of the Chaunceys, 1858.
Fowler, W., 1870.
Fuller, J., Descendants, 1869.
Gale family, 1866.
Giles Memorial, 1864.
Gilman family, 1864.
Gilman, J., of N. H., 1869.
Gilpin family geneal., 1870.
Glover genealogies, 1867.
Goddard, E., Genealogy of, 1833.
Goodwin. N., Olcott descendants, 1845.
" Gen. notes of Conn. settlers, 1856.
Goulding family. *See* Morse.
Grant family. *See* Marshall.
Greene, T., family, 1858.
Greenleaf, J., 1854.
Grout family. *See* Morse.
Guild family, 1867.
Hallock, J. & M., Ancestry, 1863.
Harklakenden pedigree.
Harris, R., 1861.
Hastings Memorial, 1866.
Hatch family, 1850.
Haven, R., Geneal. of, 1859.
Hayden, W., 1859, (Stiles Geneal.).
Heacock family, 1869.
Heraldic Journal, (Whitmore), Boston, 1865–68.
Herrick, J., Gen. Reg., 1846.
Hill, Lloyd family, 1854.

Genealogies, American (continued).
Hinman, Descendants, 1856.
Hinman, Settlers of Conn., 1846, 52–56.
Hodges Family, 1633–1853.
Holgate, Geneal. chart, 1838.
" American Genealogy, 1848.
Holt family, 1864.
Hoyt, D. W., Gen. Hist. of J. and D. Hoyt, 1857, 1871.
Hudson, Lexington MS., families.
" Hist. of Marlborough, Ms.
Hull, R., Descendants, 1869.
Hunt family, 1862–3.
Huntington family, 1863.
Hutchins, L., Autobiography, 1865.
Hutchinson, W., Notes, Chester, 1866.
" Ancestry of, (Whitmore), 1866.
Hyde family, (Walworth), 1864.
Janes family, 1868.
Josselyn. *See* Stranahan.
Judd, T., Judd and descendants, 1856.
Judd's Hist. of Hadley.
Kellogg family, 1858.
Kellogg, A. S. *See* White, J.
Lathrop family, 1867.
Laurence family, 1858.
Lawrence, J., of Watertown, 1857.
Lee family, of Va., 1868.
Leland Magazine, 1850.
Leverett family, 1856.
Leverett, T. *See* Drake's Boston.
Lincoln families, 1865.
Livermore Association.
Lloyd family of Penna., (Hill.).
Locke, J. G., Locke family, 1853.
Loomis family, 1870.
Lyman, Dickinsons and Partridges, 1865.
Lyman, R., family, 1865.
McKinstry family. *See* Willis.
Macy family, 1868.
Marshall's Grant, 1869.
Marvin family, 1848.
Mather family, 1848.
Messinger family, 1863.
Minshell family, 1867.
Montgomery family, 1863.
Moody, Moody family, 1847.
Morgan, James, family, 1869.
Morse, A., Grout, Goulding, Brigham, Hapgood, Cutler, Pettee, Hewins, Frary, Willis, Richards families, 1859–67, 4 vols.
" Geneal. of Towns of Sherborn and Holliston, 1856.
Mudge family, 1868.
Munsell family, (From Stiles).
Nason family, 1859.

Genealogies, American (continued).

New Eng. Hist. Geneal. Soc. Register, 1847–71.

Olcott. *See* Goodwin, 1845

Oliver, T., Ancestry. *See* Hutchinson.

Olmsted family, 1869.

Otis, H. N., Family of R. Otis, 1851.

Ott family.

Paine family register. 8 Nos., 1857–58.

Parsons, Hill family, 1854.

Peabody family, 1867.

Pease, F. S., Gen. of I. Lawrence, 1848.

" Descendants of J. Pease, 1847.

Peck, Descendants, 1868.

Phelps, O., St Catharines, 1862.

Pitman, G. *See* Thurston.

Plummer family. *See* Salem Atheneum, 1857.

Poor, A., Gen. of Merrimack Valley, 1857, 58.

Pope, J., Family.

Pope, W., family, 1862.

Pratt, S., Pratt Memorial.

Pratt, W., family.

Pratt Memorial, Chapman, 1864.

Pratt, Z., Genealogy, 1857.

Preble family, 1850, 1870.

Prescott Memorial, 1870.

Preston family, 1864.

Quincy family, 1857.

Rawlins, or Rollins family, 1870.

Rawson, E., family, 1849.

Read, J., Descendants, 1859.

Redfield family, 1860.

Redfield, T., family, 1839.

Reed family, 1861.

Reed, W. D., Leonard family, 1851.

Rice family. *See* Ward, A. H., 1858.

Richards families, 1861.

Ripley, H. W., family, 1867.

Robinson family, Pittsburgh, 1867.

Robinson, E., Mem. of W. Robinson, 1859.

Rockwood family, 1856.

Rollins. *See* Rawlins.

Root family, 1600–1870.

Salem Ath., Plummer family, 1857.

Salkeld family, 1867.

Sanborn family, 1856.

Savage, J., Geneal. Dict. of New England, 1860, 62.

Sawin, T. E., family, 1866.

Scranton, E. J., Scranton family, 1855.

Sears, Pictures of the family.

Sewall, H. *See* Drake's Boston.

Shattuck family, 1855.

Shattuck, L., Syst. of family registration, 1841.

Genealogies, American (continued).

Shippen family, (Balch).

Sigourney family, 1854.

Sill family, 1859.

Slafter, E. F., Discourse on, 1870.

Slafter, John, Memorial, 1869.

Smith, N., Family, by D. Smith, 1849.

Smith, T., Journal, Portland, Me., 1849.

Spotswood family, 1868.

Stafford family, 1870.

Steele, J. and G., family, (Durrie), 1859, 62.

Stickney family, 1869.

Stiles, H. R , Mass. family of Stiles, 1863.

" Windsor, Conn. families, 1859, 1863.

Stoddard, A., Family, 1849.

Stranahan families, 1868.

Strong family, (B. W. Dwight), 1871.

Sumner, R., 1854. *See* Drake's Boston.

Taft pedigree.

Tainter family, 1859.

Tappan, Mrs. S., Memoir.

Thayer, E., Family Memorial, 1835.

Thomas, J., Descendants, 1850.

Thurston, C. M., Descendants, 1868.

Todd, A., family, 1867.

Townsend, J. H. and R., Descendants, 1865.

Turner, J., Fam. of H. Turner, 1852.

Vail, Questions for a family record.

Van Brunt family, 1867.

Vassall, J., Geneal. Sketch, 1862.

Vinton, J., Descendants of, 1858.

Vinton, J. A., Giles Memorial, 1864.

Waldo family, 1863.

Waldron. *See* Gale.

Walker Memorial, Plymouth Co., 1861.

Ward, A. H., Rice, E., Family, 1858.

" Ward family, 1857.

Warren, J. C., Warren family.

Weaver, Anc. Windham, Conn., genealogy, P. I, 1864.

Wentworth, W., Descendants of 1850.

Wetmore family, 1861.

White, J., Memorials of, 1860.

Whiting, W., Address, Hist. Gen. Soc., 1853.

Whitmore, F., Family, 1855.

Whitmore, W. H., Medford families, 1855.

" Lane, Reyner, Whipple families, 1857.

" Temple family, 1856.

" Am. Genealogist, 1862, 68.

" Elements of Heraldry.

Genealogies, American (continued).
Whitmore, W. H. *See* Heraldic Journal; Hutchinson.
Whitney's Champney, 1855.
" Park fam., 1855.
Willard, S., Descendants, 1858.
Williams, S. W., Williams family, 1847.
Willis, W., McKinstry family, 1858, 66.
Winchell family, 1869.
Winegar family, 1859.
Winsor, J., Hist. of Duxbury, 1849.
Wolff, C. & A., Memorial, 1863.
Woodman, E., Descendants of, (Coffin), 1855.
Worcester, W., Descendants, 1856.
Wynkoop family, 1866.
Yale family, 1850.
Young. *See* Gale family.
See Heraldry.
See also the town histories.

Genealogical, British. Beatson, Political Reg. of Great Brit., 1786.
Berry, W., Berkshire, Buckinghamshire, Hampshire, Hertfordshire, Kent, Surrey, Sussex Counties, Genealogies, 1830–37.
Biographical Peerage, England, Scotland and Ireland. (Brydges), 1808–17.
Bridger, Index to printed pedigrees.
Bridgman, J., Sackville & Dorset families, 1821.
Burke, J. and J. B., Dict. of extinct Baronetcies.
" Dict. of extinct Peerages, 1831, 1861.
" Geneal. hist. of landed gentry, 1838, 48.
" Geneal. Dict. of Peers and Barons, 1841, 61.
" Royal families of Eng., 1848.
" Encyc. of Heraldry of G. B., 1847.
" Hist. Lands of Engl., 1849.
" Family Romance, 1853.
" Romance of the Aristocracy, 1855.
Burn, J. S., Parish Registers of England.
Camden Soc. Publications, 1838–68.
Chronicles of Great Britain, Livere de Reis de Brittaine et Engletere.
Cole family.
Coleman, Index to printed pedigrees.
Collectanea Topog. et Geneal., 1834–43.
Collins, A., Peerage of Engl., 1756, 1812.
Comberbach family.
Craik, G. L., Romance of the Peerage, 1849–50.

Genealogical, British (continued).
Davidson, Holte family.
Drummond, (Malcolm, D.), family.
Forster pedigree, 1871.
Foster, J., pedigree of.
Gordon, Sutherland family.
Grace family.
Gun & Co., Advertisements for kin.
Hale, Sir M., Law of hered. descents.
Lodge, E., Peerage of the Brit. Emp., 1845.
Lower, English surnames, 1842.
Nichols. *See* Collectanea Topographica.
" Collec. of Royal wills, 1780.
O'Kelly, Familles d'Irlande, 1837.
Playfair, British family antiquity, 1809–11.
Pocock, Tufton family.
Pollard, Stanley's of Knowsley.
Shirley, Nobles and gentlemen of, 1866.
Sims, Genealogist's Manual, 1856.
" Index to Pedigrees, 1849.
Stirling Peerage.
Sutherland, Countess, case of.
Thoms, W. J., The Book of....the English gentry, 1845.
Topographer and geneal., 1846, 53, 58.
Tracy pedigree, 1854.
Travers Pedigrees.
Tymms' Family Topographer.
Walford's County families, 1869.
Waldo family, (Jones), 1863.

Genealogical, European. Anderson, J., Royal Genealogies, 1732.
Beeldsnijder, Verbond....Nederl. Edelen.
Fitzgerald, Kings of Europe.
Forstemann, Alt. deutsches Namenbuch, 1856.
France, Docts. inéd., Du Cange, Familles d'outre mer.
Hartland, Chart of Royal houses.
Hauterive, Annuaire de la noblesse, 1868.
Hozier, D., Armorial général de la France, 1737–1768.
Jurisprudentia Heroica, (Chrystin), 1616, 68.
Lastborn, Geneal. of noblemen of Swea and Gotha since 1720, 1842, 43.
Lavoisne, Atlas..Royal families, 1834.
Nesle, L'imposture de, 1756.
Poplimont, La Belgique héraldique, 1867.
Siebmacher's Grosses u-allgem. Wappenbuch, 1865–70.
Spener, Opus heraldicum, 1717.
Wall, De, Handvesten, Privilegien, etc., ...Dordrecht, 1770–83.
See Heraldry.

Geography, Discovery. Buache, Découvertes....mer du sud, 1753.
Burney, Hist. of N. E. Discov., 1819.
" Hist. of Dis., South Seas.
Clarke, J. S., Prog. of Maritime discovery, 1803.
Cooley, W. D., Hist. of Marit. discov.
Edinburgh Cab. Lib., vols. 5, 9, 21, 34.
La Popellinère, Les trois mondes, 1582.
L'Isle, Nouv. cartes des mers septen., 1753.
Retrospect of the Origin of.
Robinson, C., Discoveries in the West to 1519.
Stevenson, W., Hist. of, 1824.
Traité de la Nav. et des voy. de descouvertes, 1629.
Tytler, P. F., Progress of disc.
United States Exploring Expedition, 1855.
See Voyages; America, Discovery of.

Geography, Elementary for Schools. Bond, R., Popular Geog., 1853.
Campe, Bibliothèque Géog., 1804.
Cortambert, Leçons de, 1856.
Dwight, N., Short System of, 1801.
Elementos, N. Orleans, 1818.
Free, J., Tyrocinium Geog., 1789.
Gaultier, Géog., 1859.
Gonzalez, Elementos de, 1852.
Grandpré, Abrégé élém., 1825.
Guyot, A., Primary Geog. Series, 1866.
" Second Series, 1866.
Hart, J. C., Exercises on Maps.
Hughes, W., Scholar's Atlas, 1854.
Mitchell, S. A., School Geog.
" New Intermediate, 1868.
Monteith's Intermediate, 1863, 1866.
Morse, J., Geog. made easy, 1796.
Muenscher, Outlines, 1827.
Olney, Introduction to.
" Practical System of, 1835.
Pinnock. *See* Williams.
Sanis, Leçons de.
" Petite Géog., 1855.
Scott, J., Elem. of Geog., 1807.
Smith, R. C., Geog. for Schools, 1848.
Spafford, H. G., General Geog., 1809.
Stewart, K. J., Palmetto Geog., 1864.
Thayer, W. A., Compendium, 1816.
Willetts, J., School Geog., 1838.
Williams, E., System of Modern, 1835.
Woodbridge, W. C., System of Universal.
Worcester, J. E., Elem. of, 1829.

Geography, Biblical. Calmet's Dictionary, (Robinson).
Fleming, W., Essay on.

Geography, Biblical (continued).
Fleming, W., Scripture Gazetteer.
Jenks' Bible Atlas, 1847.
Kitto's Cyclop. of Bib. Lit.
Parish, E., Sacred Geography, 1813.
Robinson's Researches in Palestine.
" Geog. of Holy land, 1865.
Sanson, N., Geog. Sacra, 1665.
Scripture Atlas, Lond., 1813.
Smith, W., Dict. of the Bible.
" The Same, (Hackett), 1870.
Spanheim, Introd. ad Sac. Geog., 1686.
Wells, Geog. of the Bible, 1721–34.
Willtsch, Church Geog., 1868.
See Bible; Palestine.

Geography, Atlases of Maps. Atlantic Neptune.
Bannister, Maps of Land and Sea, 1849.
Blaew, Atlas, America, Africa, 1662.
Bradford, T. G., Atlas, 1835.
Brender à Brandis, Zak-en Reis-Atlas
Bromme, Atlas zu Von Humboldt's Kosmos, 1851.
Burr's new univ. atlas, 1833.
" New York Atlas, 1829.
Cartes du monde, 1660, 61.
Charts, Admiralty office, Lond., 1775-1809.
Colton's Atlas of the World, 1855, 6.
Colton's Geog. cards, 1856.
Cortambert, A. de, Géog. Moderne 1850.
Delisle, Atlas, 1700–1750.
Encyclopédie méthodique, 1787.
Gage, L., Modern Hist. Atlas, 1869.
Giustiniani, El Nuevo atlas, 1755.
Jeffery's Amer. Atlas, 1776.
Johnson's Atlas of the World, 1863.
Johnson's Physical Atlas, 1848.
Lavoisne, Atlas.
Maps, misc., vol. 1–25.
Marine Atlas (Heather), 1802.
Martinius, Atlas Sinensis, 1655.
Mercator, Atlas, v. 2, 1636, f°.
" Atlas, Minor, 1607.
Mitchell, General Atlas, 1863.
Moll, H., Atlas Manuale, 1713.
Morse, Cerographic Atlas.
New General Atlas, Edinb., 1817.
Ortelius, Theatrum, 1570.
Robert, Atlas universel, 1759.
Sanson, L., Maps of the World.
Society diff. use. knowl., Atlas, 1844.
Steele's Marit. Atlas, 1814.
Vandermaelen, Atlas universel, 1827.
See Particular countries; *also* N. Y Catalogue of Maps in the Library

Geology, Elementary Treatises.
Ansted, Elem. course of min., geol., etc., 1850.
Beudant, Cours. d'hist. nat., 1859.
Dana, J. D., Manual of, 1863.
Foster, J. T., Introduction to, 1850.
Gray, A., Elements of Geology, 1853.
Hart, J. C., System of.
Houghton, Manual, 1866.
Hitchcock, Ed., Elem geol., 1847.
Jukes, J. B., Popular physical geol., 1853.
Lyell, Manual of, 1851.
Mather, W. W., Elements of Geol., 1833.
Mitchell, W., Manual of, (Orr), 1854.
Miller, Hugh, Sketch of popular Geol.
Page, D., Elements of Geology, 1848.
" Advanced book of, 1859.
" Introd. Text-book, 1860.
Phillips, Treatise on Geology, 1835.
" Manual of, 1855.
Playfair, Huttonian Theory.
Richardson, G. F., Introd. to, 1851.
" For Beginners, 1842.
St. John, S., Elements of, 1851.
Thomson, T., Outlines of, 1836.

Geology, Miscellaneous. Anderson, J., The Course of Creation, 1851.
Ansted, The Ancient World, 1847.
" Stone book of Nature, 1863.
Bertrand, A., The Revolutions of the Globe, 1835.
Boase, H. S., Treat. on Primary geol., 1834.
Bourrit, Glacières de Savoie, 1785.
Brainerd, Sandstone Conglomerate, 1852. P. 272.
Brasseur de Bourbourg, Quatre lettres sur le Mexique, (Glaciers).
Breislak, Geol. de Milano, 1822.
Buckland, Reliquiæ Diluvianæ, 1823.
Buckman, J., Stone steps, Gr. Brit., 1852.
" Straits of Malvern.
Conybeare, On progress of, 1832.
Cook, Subsidence of Land, 1857.
Cordier, Temperature of the Earth, 1828.
Cotta, Erzlagerstätten, 1859.
Cuvier, Theory of the Earth, 1818.
Dana, J. D., Addresses, 1847, 54, 55.
Darwin, C., Voy. of H. M. S. Beagle, 1840–42.
Davis, C. H., Deposit of flood tide.
Dawson, J. W., Writings.
De La Beche, Geol. of Cornwall, Devonshire, 1839.
" Geol. Memoirs, Selections, 1824.

Geology, Miscellaneous (continued).
De La Beche, How to observe Geology, 1836.
" Geological Observer, 1851.
Dixon, Geology of Sussex, Eng., 1850.
Dufrénoy, Exp. de la carte géol. de la France, 1841.
Eaton, Geol. Text-book, 1830.
Egloffstein, Geol. of Mexico, 1864.
Ehrenberg, Mikrogeologie, 1854.
Figuier, World before the Deluge, 1867.
Flurl, Gebirgsformationen, 1805.
Forbes, Theory of Glaciers.
Great Britain, Geol. Survey, Memoirs, 1846–48.
" Memoirs, Figures, Decade I-XII, 1846–66.
Greenough, Exam. of first prin. of, 1819.
Griffith, R., Address, Geol. of Ireland.
Hamilton, W., Researches in Asia Minor and Armenia, 1842.
Hand-book of, Lond., 1840.
Harting, De bodem onder Amsterdam, 1852.
Hartt, Sci. results of journey, 1870.
Haskins, R. W., Poisson on Temperature, 1837.
Hauer, Mines de l'Autriche, 1855.
Haughton, S., Sci. Papers, 1851–63.
Hayden, Geological Essays, 1820.
Hayes, J. L., Influence of icebergs on drift, 1843. P. 79.
Hiortdahl, Undersögelser i Bergens.
Hitchcock, E., Surface Geol.
" Geol. of the Globe, 1854.
" On Ichnolithology, 1858.
Holmes, F. S., The Horse, etc., 1858.
Hopkins, E., Geol. and Magnetism, 1851.
Hopkins, W., Resear. in Phys. Geol., 1839, 40, 42.
Humble, Dict. of Geol. and Mineral., 1843.
Johnston, Catech. of Agr. Geol., 1845.
" Agricultural Geol.
Junghugh, Cat. Geol. Samm. v. Java, 1854.
Kranz, Cat. of specimens for sale.
Lea, J., Contributions to, 1833.
Lee, C. A., Elements of, 1848.
Lyell, Sir C., Lectures on, 1842, 43.
" Principles of, 1850.
" Antiquity of Man, 1863.
McClelland, Geol. of Kemaon, India, 1835.
Maclaren, Geol. of Fife and Lothian.
MacCulloch, Memoir of Surv. of Scotland, 1836.
Manes, Mém. géologiques sur l'Allemagne, 1828.

Geology, Miscellaneous (continued).

Mantell, Excursions, Isle of Wight, and Devonshire, 1854.

" Geology of Sussex, 1827.

" Medals of Creation, 1844, 53.

" Wonders of, 1857.

" Petrifactions and their teachings.

Miller, H., Geology of the Bass Rock, 1851.

" Old Red Sandstone, 1842.

" The Foot prints of the Creator, 1850.

Murchison, The Silurian system, 1839.

" The oldest rocks with organic remains.

Netherlands, Verhandelingen, 1853, 54.

Orbigny, Géol. appliquée aux arts, 1855.

Osborn, A., Field Notes of, 1858.

Page, D., Geolog. terms.

Pamphlets relating to, vols. 790, 791, 974, 1517, 1866.

Phillips, J., Geol. of Yorkshire, 1835.

" Life on the earth, 1860.

Playfair, Works, 1, Huttonian Theory, 1822.

Portlock, Geol. of Londonderry, etc., 1843.

" Address, 1857, 58.

Ramsay, Geol. of Is. Arran, 1841.

Randall, S. S., Incentives to the study of, 1846.

Raspe, Basaltes, 1776.

Ray, J., Discourses, 1721.

Reynolds, Atlas of.

Rogers, H. D., Am. Geol. Assoc. Address, 1844. P. 92.

Rooke, J., Reclamation of land from sea, 1840.

Schafhäutl, Geognos. Untersuchunungen.

" Die Geologie in ihrem Verhältnisse, 1843.

Science of Geology, 1837.

Scrope, Volcanoes of Cent. France.

Sexe, Af Hardangerfjorden.

Silliman, P., Philos. of, 1839. P. 1517.

Sopwith, Treatise on Isomet. drawing, 1838.

Tjader, Stora Koppérbergs Grufwor.

Travanet, Physiol. de la terre, 1844.

Trimmer, Pract. Geol., 1841.

Tyndall, Glaciers of the Alps, 1861.

Vaughan, Phen. of World, 1856. P. 222.

Vestiges of creation, 1846.

Victoria, Austr., Notes sur.

Ville, Recherches sur....l'Alger, 1852.

Vose, Orographic geol., 1866.

Geology, Miscellaneous (continued).

Winchell, A., Sketches of creation, 1870.

Woodward, Nat. Hist. telluris, 1714.

See Cosmogony; Bibliography; Mineralogy; Earthquakes; Paleontology; Volcanoes.

Geology of North America. Surveys of United States, etc.

Akerly, Geol. of Hudson river, 1820.

Alabama, Reports of, by Tuomey, 1850.

" 2d Report, 1858.

Arkansas, Report, 1858.

" (Owen), 1860.

Blake, W. P., Fossils of California, 1855.

Booth, J. C., Survey of Delaware, 1841.

California, Tyson, Geology of, 1851.

" Reports of J. B. Trask, 1853, 54.

Canada, L. Superior and Red River, 1858.

" Rottermund's Survey of Lake Superior and L. Huron, 1856.

" Sir W. E. Logan's Reports, 1857, 58, 63, 66–69.

" Report, 1858.

Connecticut, C. U. Shepard's report, 1837.

Cozzens, J., Geolog. Hist., of Manhattan, 1843.

Dana, J. D., U. S. Expl. Exped., 1855.

Dana, J. F., Geol. of Boston, 1818.

Dawson, J. W., Acadian Geol., 1855.

Delaware, by Booth, J. C., 1841.

Dufrénoy, Survey of France, 1840.

Eaton, A., Index to Geol. of Northern States, 1820.

" Survey of Renss. and Albany Cos., 1822.

Eights, J., Hiatt Tract, Surry, N. C.

Emmons, E., The Taconic system, 1844.

" Bones of the Zeuglodon cetoides. P. 79.

" American Geology, 1855.

" Second Geol. Dist. N. Y., 1842.

" North Carolina Rep., 1856 58, 60.

Foster, J. W., Geol. of Lake Superior lands, 1850, 51.

Gesner, Geol. of Nova Scotia, 1836.

Hall, J., Key to Chart of geological formations, 1851.

" Niagara Falls, Geol. P. 74.

" *See* New York; Iowa.

Hayden, The Platte to Ft. Benton, 1857. P. 551.

Hitchcock, Economic Geol. of Mass.

Geology of North America (cont'd).

Hitchcock, Reports on the Geol. of Mass, 1833, 41.

Hovey, S., Geol. of St. Croix and Antigua.

Illinois Report, Norwood, 1858.

" Report, (Worthen), 1866.

Indiana, Reconnoissance, 1838.

Iowa Reports, 1856, 57, 70.

Kentucky, Report, 1854, 55.

" 4th Report, 1861.

Logan, W. E., Esquisse Geol. du Canada, 1855.

" *See* Canada.

Maclure, W., Geol. of the U. S., 1817.

Maine, 1st, 2d and 3d Reports, 1837–39.

Marcou, Geol. map of U. S. and Canada, 1853.

Maryland, Reports, 1834, 35, 40.

" 1st and 2d Reports, 1860, 62.

Mass. Surv. by E. Hitchcock, etc., 1833, 41.

Mass. Survey of lands in Maine, 1838.

Mather, Geol. of New York, 1842.

" Geol. New London, etc., Conn., 1834.

Mease, Geol. acct. of the U. S., 1807.

Michigan, Survey, (Houghton), 1838–1842.

Minnesota, Survey, (Owen), 1852.

Missouri, Survey, (Swallow), 1855.

New Brunswick, (Bailey), 1865.

New Hampshire, C. T. Jackson's rep., 1841.

New Jersey, H. D. Roger's reports, 1836, 40.

" Reports, 1855–57, 68.

New Orleans Ac. of Sci., 1858. P. 273.

New York, Reports, 1837–51.

" Nat. Hist. Four districts, 1853.

" Nat. Hist. Emmons Agric.

" Paleontology, (Hall).

Ohio, Geol. Surv., 1871.

" Reports of W. W. Mather, 1838.

Owen, Chippewa District.

" Kentucky Survey, 1854, 55.

" Arkansas Survey, 1858.

Penn., Rep. of H. D. Rogers, 1836–40, 1858.

Rhode Island Geol. Sur., 1840.

Rogers, H. D., Report on North Am., 1835.

Schoolcraft, Geology of Missouri, 1819.

South Carolina Geol. Survey, 1844, 48.

Swallow, S. W., Missouri, Pac. R. R., 1859.

Tennessee, Reports, 1856, 57.

" Rept. by J. Safford, 1869.

Geology of North America (cont'd).

Texas, (Buckley), 1866.

Tuomey, Pleiocene Fossils of S. C., 1855-57.

Tyson, P. T., Geol. and Indus. resour. of California, 1851.

United States, Exam. between Missouri and Red R., 1834.

" Report on California, 1850.

" Reports on Iowa and Michigan, 1847.

" Illinois, Minnesota and Nebraska.

" Lake Superior land districts, 1850, 51.

" Report of Geol. of Wisconsin, 1839.

" Pacific R. R. Explorations, 1856.

Van Rensselaer, J., Lectures on, 1825.

Vanuxem. *See* N. Y. Nat. Hist.

Vermont, Reports by C. B. Adams, 1845–48.

" Hitchcock's Reports, 1857, 1858, 61.

Virginia, Reports of, (Rogers), 1836, 1838, 40, 41.

Webster, M. H., Min. of N. Y., 1824.

Whitney, J. D., Metallic Wealth of U. S., 1824.

Whittlesey, C., Geol. of Ohio, 1848.

Wisconsin, Percival's Report, 1856.

" Report, (Daniels), 1854.

" Report, 1862.

See Gold; Iron; Mining, etc.

Geology, Periodicals and Societies.

Am. Jour. of Geol., Featherstonhaugh, 1832.

Assoc. of Am. Geol. and Nat., 1844.

Austria, Jahrbuch, 1850–56.

Geol. Soc. of Dublin, 1844–55, 62–64.

Geol. Soc., Lond., Transac., 1811–19, 1822–35.

" Proceedings, 1826–45.

" Journal, 1845–68.

Geol. Soc. of Penn'a, Trans., 1835.

Geologist, The, C. Moxon, 1842, 43.

" Mackie, 1862–64.

Jahrbuch fur, (Leonhard), 1830–57.

Kaiserlich Geol. Reichanstalt, Jahrbuch, 1850–66.

London Geological Journal, 1846, 47.

McClurian Lyceum, Contr.

Palaeontographical Society, Publication, 1848–69.

Société des Sci. Nat. de Strasbourg, 1862.

Soc. Géol. de France, 1844–52.

Zeitschrift fur Mineralogie, 1825–29, (Leonhard).

Georgia (continued).
Cherokee Land lottery, 1838.
Description of Georgia, 1741.
Georgia, Governor's Message, 1857.
Gorman, J. B., Med. acct. of, 1845.
Hewatt, Rise and progress of, 1779.
Impartial Enquiry, (Martyn), 1741.
Jones, C. C., Monumental remains of, 1861.
Longstreet, A. B., Georgia Scenes, 1854.
McCall, H., History of, 1811.
Miller, S. F., Bench and Bar of, 1790–1857.
Moore, F., Voyage to, 1735.
Narrative of the Colony, 1741.
New and Ac. Account, 1733.
New Voyage to, 1737.
Reasons for estab. the colony, (Martyn), 1733.
Richards, T. A., G. illustrated, 1842.
Sibbald, Pine lands of, 1801.
Sicilius, Sale of Western lands of, 1755.
Sherwood, Gazetteer of, 1837.
State of, London, 1742.
State of facts ....on lands, 1795.
Stephens, W., Proceedings from 1737.
Stevens, W. B., Hist. of, to 1798.
Strobel, The Salzburgers, 1855.
Tailfer, Pat., Narrative of, 1741.
Urlsperger, Nachrichten der Saltzburg. Emigranten, 1735–46.
" Amerikanisches Ackerwerk, 1756.
Von Reck, Journals of, 1734.
Voyage to Georgia, 1737.
Wesley, Journal, 1743–54.
White, G., Hist. Collections, 1854.
" Statistics of, 1850.
Whitefield, Works, V. 3.
" Journal, 1738.
Wright's Life of Oglethorpe.
See Florida.

Georgia: Trustees for Establishing the Colony of Georgia. Sermons before: 1734, Hales, S.; 1735, Watts, G.; 1737, Warren, R.; 1738, Bearcroft, P.; 1739, Berriman, W.; 1742, Best, W.; 1743, King, J.; 1743, Bruce, L.; 1746, Ridley, G.; 1748, Thoresby, R.; 1749, Crowe, W.; 1749, Harvest, G.; 1750, Francklin, T.

Gerando, J. M. De. Bayle, Eloge de, 1846. P. 238.

Gerard, J. W. Dinner to, 1869. P. 1858.

Geree, J. Penrose, T., Discourse, 1774.

German Books, Authors, Libraries. *See* Bibliography.

German Catholic Church. *See* Ronge; Treves.

German Language. *See* Language; Grammar; Dictionaries.

German Literature. *See* Literature.

German Pamphlets. Vols. 609, 842, 991, 999, 1109, 1784.

German Reformed Church. German Ref., Acts, 1841.
Harbaugh, The Fathers of, 1857.
Mayer, History of, 1851.
Tercentenary Monument.

German Typographical History.
Hupfauer, Druckstucke aus dem xv Jahrhund., 1794.
Panzer, Annales typographici, 1793–1803.
Wolf, Mon. Typog., 1740.
Zapf, Aelteste Buchdruckergesch., 1791.
See Augsburg; Bamberg; Beuerberg; Erlangen; Mayence; Nuremberg; under Typography.

Germans in America. Bokum, Discourse, 1836.
See Emigration.

Germantown Academy. Centennial, 1860.

Germany, History of. Almanach de Gotha, 1856–71.
Audiffret, Géog. Historique, 1694.
Blaze, Mem. of Princess Palatine, 1853.
Bunnett, L. Julianne and her times.
Butler, C., Revolutions of.
Capgrave's Book of the Illustrious Henries, (Chron. G. B.).
Caumont, Ant. de Trèves et Mayence.
Denina, Revoluzione della, 1805.
Draseke, Wiedergeburt, 1813.
Dunham, Hist. of the Empire.
Fessmaier, Des Oberdeutschen Städtebundes, 1819.
Fink, Einfluss jener Confoederationen, 1822.
Frederick II, Œuvres Hist., 1763–65.
Freyberg, Der Bayer. Landes-Gesetzgebung, 1834.
Gœrres, Prof., Germany and the Revolution. Pamphr. 15.
Hawkins, Germany, The Spirit of her History, 1838.
Heineccius, Antiq. Goslarienses, 1648.
Heintz, Pfalzgraf Stephan, 1823.
Hubner, Jahrbuch, 1852.
John of Austria, Leven van, 1737.
Kingsley, C., The Roman and Teuton, 1864.
Kohlrausch, History of, 1845.
Kremer, Zur Gulch-u. Berg. Geschichte, 1769–81.

Germany, History of (continued).
Kugler, Pict. Hist. of, 1845.
Lauresham, Codex Diplom., 1768–70.
Leopold I, Answer to France, 1688.
Leuckfeld, Rerum Germanic., 1707.
Macgregor, Germany under Fred. Wm. IV, 1848.
Marcus, L., Hist. des Wandales, 1836.
Meibonius, Rerum Germanicarum.
Menzel, History of, 1848, 9.
Mussato, Hist. Henrici VII, 1636.
Perthes, Memoirs of, 1789–1843.
Pfeffel, Droit Public d'Allemagne, 1776.
Revolution, W., The Real Crisis, 1735.
Schaeffer, Three Saxon Electorc.
Schiller, Hist. 30 years' War.
Schreiber, Taschenbuch, 1823.
State of the Palatines, 1710.
Urstisius, Germ. Historicorum...usque ad 1400.
Wraxall, Mem. of principal Courts, 1806.

Germany, Travels, &c. Adams, J. Q., Letters on Silesia, 1800, 1801.
Anthon, C. E., Pilgrimage to Tréves, 1844.
Daniel, Handb. der Geog., 1863.
Dwight, H. E., Trav. in North of, 1825–26.
Freytag, Pictures of Ger. Life.
Gleig, Germany and Bohemia, 1839.
Granville, Spas of Germany, 1837.
Heine, Pictures of Travel, 1863.
Hodgskin, Travels in North of, 1820.
Howitt, Art Student at Munich.
" German Experiences, 1844.
Hugo, The Rhine, 1845.
Jacquemin, L'Allemagne agr. indust. et pol., 1843.
Johnson, A., Peasant Life in, 1858.
Lights and Shadows of German Life, 1833. B. C.
Mansfield, Log of Water Lily, 1854.
Muller, Donaustaf und Walhalla, 1847.
Murray's Hand-book.
" Hand-book of Southern.
Planche, The Danube, 1827.
Reinbeck, Travels, 1805
Riesbeck, Travels, (Pinkerton).
Roese, F. A., Lectures.
Russell, J.; Tour in, 1820–22.
Samuelson, The Working Man of, 1869.
Spencer, E., Sketches of, 1836.
Stael, Madame de, Germany, 1814.
Tacitus, Manners of.
Tour in Germany, 1826–8.
Varnhagen von Ense, Sketches of German Life, 1847.

Germany, Travels, &c. (continued).
Wheaton, H., Address on Progress, 1847.
See Prussia; Austria; Saxony.

Gerry, E. Austin, J. T., Life of, 1828, 1829.

Gers, France. Annuaire, 1846.

Gettysburg, Pa. Doubleday, Battle of.
Everett, Oration at, 1863.
Penn'a, Soldiers' National Cemetery.
Pennsylvania College, Cat., 1848–50.
See Civil War.

Gholson, T. S. Collier, R. R., Reply to, 1847. P. 81.

Giant's Causeway. Dubourdieu, Antrim, 1812.

Gibbon, E. Chelsum, Remarks on two chapters, 1778.
Gibbon, Letters: Misc. Wörks.
" Mem. of Life, 1796.

Gibbons, T. Davies, B., Sermon on, 1785.

Gibraltar. Boland, On the Straits of.
D'Anverian History, 1731.
Drinkwater, Siege of, 1791.
Gr. Br., Charter for Civ. gov't, 1741.
James, T., History of the Herculean Straits, 1771.
Letter to the Indep. Whig, 1720.
Martin, R. M., Brit. Col. Lib., v. 7.
Newyear, Gib. or the Pretender, 1737.
Pamphlets relating to Gibraltar, v. 770.
Propriety of retaining, 1783.
Sayer, History of, 1865.
Urquhart, Pillars of Hercules, 1848.

Gibson, E. Letter to the Lord Bishop of London, 1750.

Gibson, J. B. Porter, On Life of, 1855.

Gifford, A. Rippon, Serm., Death of, 1784.

Gilbert, H. Lawson, C., Sermon on.

Giles. Family Memorial, (Vinton).

Gill, H. Lambert, G., Serm. on, 1784.

Gill, J. Stennett, S., Serm. on, 1772.

Gillies, R. P. Mem. of a Lit. Veteran.

Gilliland, W. Watson, W. C., Life of, 1863.

Gillray, J. Wright, T., Caricatures of, 1851.

Gilman. Family Genealogy, 1869.

Gilman, C. Recollections, 1838.

Gilmanton, New Hamp. Lancaster, History of, 1845.

Gipsy. *See* Gypsy.

Gold (continued).
Chevalier, Fall in value of, 1859.
Davidson, Discov. in Australia.
Fisher, Alcinda mine, 1839. P. 92.
Gold of St. Domingo, 1860.
Gold-und silber Währung, 1855.
Hittell, Mining in Pacific States.
Jacob, W., Consumption of precious metals, 1831.
Jukes, etc., Lectures on Gold, 1852.
Mariposa Company, 1863, 68.
Merritt, Mines of Veraguas, N. G., 1854. P. 255.
Neubauer, Refining of.
Nova Scotia, Gold Mines Reports, 1869, 70, 71.
" Gold fields. P. 1114.
Pedro, Exped. to El Dorado, 1560.
Pioneer Mills Mine, N. C., 1856.
Soyer, Modèles d'Orfévrerie, 1839.
Symons, W., On weighing gold, 1756.
U. S. Geol. Expl. 35°, 1870.
" Expl. 40th Parallel, 1871.
Victorian Exhibition, 1861.
See Australia; California; Currency; Metals.

Gold Mining Companies. Pamphlets, vol. 1802.

Golden Circle. Wright's Narrative of Knights of, 1864.

Goldoni, C. Memoirs of, 1828.
Copping, E., Life of, 1857.

Goldsmith, O. Forster, G., Life of, 1848.
Irving W., Life of, 1849.
Kalisch, Lectures on.
Prior, J., Life of, 1837.
Scott, W., Life of.

Gonzaga, V. Affo', Vita di, 1780.

Good, J. M. Gregory, Memoirs of.
Jerram, Serm. on, 1827. P. 382.

Goode, W. Wilson, D , Serm. on, 1816.

Goodhue, J. Bellows, Serm. on, 1848.

Goodrich, C. Stanton, R. L., Reply to, 1845.

Goodrich, S. G. Pers. recollections.

Goodrich Castle. Bonnor, T., Views of.

Goodwin, J. Jackson, T., Life of.

Goodwin Sands. Taylor H., Light on, 1796.

Gordon, G. Plain....Acc't of Riots, 1780.

Gordon, Mary J. Calhoun, J. S., Confession of, 1847.

Gordon, P. L. Personal Memoirs.

Gore family genealogy. (Whitmore's Heraldry.)

Gorges, Sir F. Maine Hist. Soc. Coll.
Popham celebration, 1863.

Gorham Case. Pamphlets, vol. 1270.

Gorham, Me. Pierce, J., History of.

Gorton, S. Mackie, J. M., Life of, (Sparks 15.).

Goslar, Sax. Heineccius, Antiq. Goslar et vic., 918–1648.

Gough, J. B. Autobiography, 1848, 1870.
Alliance Week. News, 1857.
Pound, J., Hist. of, 1845.

Gould, J. W. Private Journal, 1839.

Goulding, J. Vinall, J., Reply to, 1827.

Gout. *See* Medical.

Government. Ahrens, Das Naturrecht, 1846.
Alden, Young Citizen's Manual, 1867.
Aristotle, Politics and economics.
Barclay, G., Argenis, 1621.
Bathurst, Christianity and politics, 1818.
Bentham, J., Theory of Legislation.
" Fragment on Government.
Benton, T. H., Thirty years view.
Blanche, Dict. d'Administration, 1857.
Boccalini, New-found Politicke, 1626.
" Advertisements from Parnassus.
Bonaparte, L., Œuvres, Works, 1854–1856.
Boogert, Veiligheid van een Burgerstaat, 1762.
Brougham, Brit. Constitution, 1861.
" Political Philosophy, 1844.
Burgh, Political disquisition, 1775.
Calhoun, J. C., Disquisition on, 1851.
Cartwright, J., Rights of the Commonalty, 1777.
Catechism of Man.
Catholicism compatible with repub.
Chalmers, Sermon on, 1820. P. 288.
Chapter to the Engl. multitude, 1798.
Chipman, N., Principles of, 1793,1833.
Coleridge, J., Sermon on, 1777.
Consideratie van een vrye en geheymen Staets-regering.
Condorcet, Œuvres, 1847.
Conkling, A., Young Citizen's Manual, 1836. B. C.
Cousin, Œuvres; Discours, 1851.
Doleman, Conf. on Succession to the Crown, 1681.
Do States....tend....to Dissolution? 1830. P. 415.
Dove, P. E., Political Science, 1854.
Duganne, A. H. H., Hist. of govt's, 1860.
Eachard's Works, 1774.

Government (continued).
Three letters to a noble Lord, 1721.
Vind. of Bp. of Exeter, 1709.
Walsingham, Arcana Aulica, 1655.
Whiston, W., Government from the bible, 1717.
Wrottlesey, Thoughts on, 1860.
Young, A. W., Introd. to sci. of, 1842.
" Science of gov't, 1845.
" First lessons in, 1846.
See Officers; Republican; Authority; Great Britain; U. S. Government; Utopias.

Grace, S. Memoirs of the Family.

Grafton, Duke of. Belsham, T., Sermon on.

Grafton, J. Smith, S. F., Life of.

Graham, Mrs. I. Unpub. letters, 1838.

Graham, J. Quincy, J., Memoirs of, 1825.

Graham, Mary J. Bridges, Memoir of, 1834.

Graham, Gen. S. Memoir, 1779-1801.

Graham, Silvester. Lectures and Life of.

Grain. *See* Corn.

Grain in Distilleries. Bell, A., Prohibition of.

Grammar, General. Bentham, Works, vol. 8.
Barrett, Principles of, 1865.
Court de Gébelin, Le monde primitif, 1774, v. 2.
Harris, Hermes, or Univ. Gram., 1786.
Sacy, S. de, Gen. Principles of, 1837.
See Language.

Grammars:

AFRICAN. Gram. of Bakéle, 1854.
Gram. of Mpongwe, 1847.
Hanoteau, La Langue Tamachek.
Mackey, J. L., Benga Lang., N. Y., 1855.
Schreuder, Grammatik fur Zulu-sproget, 1850.

ANGLO-SAXON. Gwilt, Joseph, Anglo-Saxon, 1829.
Klipstein, L. F., N. Y., 1853.
Rask, Grammar of Anglo Saxon, 1830.
See Language.

ARABIC. Erpenius, Rudim. de, 1844.
L'homond, Gr. Fr., (Harairi), 1857.
Soyouti, De nom. relativis, 1840.
Taalibi, Syntagma Dictorum, etc., 1844.

ARMENIAN. Aucher, Gram. of the Armenian Lang.
Arm. English Grammar.
Riggs, Modern Armenian, 1847.

Grammars (continued).

ASSYRIAN. Ménant, 1868.

BASQUE. Eys, Langue Basque.

BOHEMIAN. Tham, K. I., 1798.

CELTIC. *See* Language.

CHALDEE. Harris, W., Elements of, 1823.
Palfrey, Chal. Syr. Samar. and Rabbinic, 1835.
Riggs, Chaldee Grammar, 1832.

CHINESE. Morrison, R., 1815.
Remusat, Elémens de, 1822.
Summers, Rudiments of.

CURDISH. Garzoni, Gram. e vocabulario, 1787.

DANISH. Deensche Spraakkunst.
Lund, H., 1860.
Rask, E. C., Gram. of, 1846.

DUTCH. Bolhuis, Spraakkunst, 1793.
Janson, B., Pract. Grammar of, 1803.
Murray, L., Engelsche.
Peplier, Gr. Françoise et Holl.
Pyl, Van der, Practical Gram.
Scherber, Taalregelen, 1845.

ENGLISH. Alexander, Caleb, 1814.
Alger, Israel, jun., 1824.
Allison, M. A., 1841.
Andrew, James, 1817.
Angel, Oliver, 1850.
Angus, William, 1807, 12, 25.
Arnold, Thomas K., 1841.
Ash, John, 1778, 94, 95, 98, 1802.
Babbit, A.
Bacon, C., 1823.
Baldwin, E., 1824.
Barnard, F. A. P., 1836.
Barnes, W., 1842.
Barrett, Solomon, jr., 1848.
Barton, J. G., Outline of, 1855.
Bell, J., 1769.
Blair, D., 1809.
Blair, John, 1831.
Booth, D., 1837.
Booth, L., 1819.
Brace, Joab, 1840.
Bradley, C., Grammat. Questions, 1816.
Brightland, John, 1714.
British Grammar, 1779, 1784.
Brown, Goold, New York, 1825, 26, 51.
" First lines of.
" Institutes of, 1863.
Brown, J., Difficulties in sys., 1819.
" An American Grammar, 1821.
Bucke, C., 1714.
Bullions, P., 1834, 37, 42, 44.
Burton, C. W., Grammatical trees.

Grammars: ENGLISH (continued).

Butler, Noble, 1846.
Cardell, W. S., 1826.
Champlin, J. T., 1850.
Chandler, J. R., 1847.
Churchill, T. O., 1823.
Clark, S. W., 1847.
" First Lessons.
Cobbett, W., 1818, 32, 37.
Cobbin, I , 1827.
Comic English Grammar, 1840.
Comly, J., 1832.
Cooper, J. G., 1828, 45.
Coote, C., 1788.
Corner, Miss, The Play Grammar.
Dale, W. A., Teacher's Assistant.
Dalton, J., 1803.
Davenport, B., 1830.
Dearborn, B., 1795.
Del Mar, C., 1842.
Devis, Ellen, 1825.
Doherty, H., 1841.
D'Orsey, Alex., 1842.
Dowd, J. N., 1830.
Dyche, T., 1736.
Earnshaw, Grammat. Remembrancer, 1817.
Elmore, D. W., 1830.
Elphinstone, The Principles of, 1765.
Emmons, S. B., Grammat. Instructor, 1832.
English Gram. for Classical Schools, 1838.
English Grammar in Persian.
Farnum, C., 1844.
Felch, C., 1817.
Felton, O. C., 1843.
Fenning, D., 1787.
Fisher, A., 1781.
Fisk, A., 1821.
Flint, A., 1813.
Flint, J., 1834.
Flower, M. and W., 1844.
Fowle, W. B., 1827, 28.
" Common School G., 1842.
Fowler, W. C., English Gram., 1855.
Frazee, B., 1845.
Frost, J., 1829, 42.
Gartly, G., 1830.
Giles, Rev. Dr., 1839.
Gilleade, G., 1816.
Gough, J., 1760.
Goodrich, J. and A,, 1828.
Grammar, A new, of, 1831.
Grant, J., 1813.
Gray, J., 1818.
Green, M., 1837.
Green, R. W., 1829.

Grammars: ENGLISH (continued).

Greene, C. R., 1830.
Greene, Sam'l S., Phil'a, 1848.
Greenleaf, J., Gram. Simplified.
Greenwood, J., Essay towards, 1729, 1753.
Guy, J., 1829.
Hall, S. R., 1832.
Hamlin, L. F., 1831, 32.
Harrison, R., 1792.
Hart, J. S., 1832.
Hazen, E., 1844.
Hiley, R., 1832, 35, 40.
Hornsey, John, 1816.
Hort, W. J., 1822.
Hubbard, A. O., Balt., 1827.
Hull, J. H., Lectures, 1829.
Inductive Grammar, 1829.
Ingersoll, C. M., 1822, 31, 35.
" Conversations on.
Irving, C., Lond.
Jenkins, System, Lect. on, 1836.
Johnson, S., N. York, 1750.
Juvenile, Boston, 1829.
Key to Murray, 1817.
King, W. W., Gramm. Chart, 1841.
Kirkham, S., 1824, 32, 36.
Latham, R. G., 1847.
Lennie, W., 1815, 34.
Leonard, S., The American, 1819.
Lowis, J., The Essentials of, 1828.
Little, The Grammarian, 1830.
Locke, J., Cincinnati, 1827.
Loughton, W., 1739.
Lovechild, Mrs., Parsing lessons, etc., 1832.
Lowth, R., 1794.
Lyle, J., Lexington, Ky., 1804.
M'Culloch, J. M., Prefixes, etc.
" Manual of, 1834.
MacGowan, James, 1825.
Marcet, Jane, Mary's Grammar, 1835.
Martin, T., 1824.
Mennye, J., 1785.
Millen, J., 1846.
Miller, The Misses, 1830.
Miller, Alexander, 1795.
Miller, F. H., Oral Grammar, N. Y.
Miller, G. B., Dansville Gram.
Milligan, George, 1831.
Morey, A. C., 1829.
Morgan, J., 1814.
Morley, Charles, 1830.
Mudie, George, 1840.
Munsell, H., Albany, 1851.
Murray, L., Abridgments.
" Eng. gr. 1823, 2 v.
Mylne, A., 1832.

Grammars: English (continued).

Newbery, John, 1787.
Nixon, H., 1853.
Oliver, James, 1807.
Oram, Miss E., 1846.
Palmer, Mary, 1803.
Parker, R. G., 1835.
Peirce, O. B., N. Y., 1839, 43.
Pengelly, E., 1840.
Pictorial Grammar.
Pinnock, W., 1830, 37, 39.
Pond, Enoch, 1832.
Priestley, Joseph, 1763, 72.
Productive Grammar, 1831.
Putnam, Samuel, 1816.
Putsey, Rev. W., 1829.
Rand, A., Teacher's Manual, 1832.
Reid, A., Rudiments of, 1837.
Ross, R., The Amer. Grammar, 1782.
Russell, J., London, 1835.
Ryland, J., 1767.
Sabine, H. A. M., London, 1802.
Sanborn, D. H., 1836.
Shatford, W., London, 1834.
Sheridan, T., Rhetorical Gram., 1783.
Simmonite, Self-teaching Gram., 1841.
Smart, London, 1811, 41.
Smith, C. J., London, 1846.
Smith, P., Edinburgh, 1826.
Smith, R. C., 1832, 1837.
Spencer, G., 1851, 1853.
Sullivan, R., 1843.
Sutcliffe, J., 1815.
Thring, E., Principles of, Oxf., 1868.
Tower, D. B., 1847, 55.
Turner, B., 1840.
Treatise on the Eng. tongue, 1767.
Usher, G. N., 1803.
Wallis, J., Gram. Ling. Angl., 1664, 1765.
Ward, W., York.
Webber, S., 1832.
Webster, N., 1807, 11, 31.
Weld, A. H., 1847.
" Parsing book, 1848. B. C.
Wells, W. H., 1846.
Wickes, E. W., 1840.
Williams, Mrs., 1830.
Willymot, W., English particles, 1789.
Wilson, J. P., Essay on Grammar, 1840.
Wilson, T., First Catechism of.
Wood, H., Gramm. read. book, 1841.
Wright, J. W., 1838.
Writer's and Student's Gram., 1838.

Flemish. Ende, Le Gazophilace Fran. et Flam., 1669.
Nouv. Gram. Flamand.

Grammars (continued).

French. Beauzée, Grammaire et Littérature.
Bœuf, J. and A., Gram. of the Fr., 1834.
Bolmar's Levizac, 1851.
Comenius, Janua aurea, 1668.
Duvivier, Gram. des Grammaires, 1822.
Génin, Grammaire de Giles de Guez.
Heusch, Practical French Grammar, 1796.
Holstein, H. V. S. D., Albany, 1836.
Lévizac, Abrégé, 1798.
L'Homond, Gramm. Franç., 1805.
" Elémens du Français.
Noël et Chapsal, Lond., 1848.
Nolan, Compendious Gram.
Perrin, J., Gramm. of, 1806.
Pinney, Pract. teacher.
Raynouard, Langue des Troubadours.
Rhasis, Gram. in Turkish.
Robertson's Method.
Rogissard, Nouv. Méth. pour apprendre, 1724. B. C.
Wanostrocht, Gramm., 1819. B. C.

Gaelic. Kelly, Gram. of the Manks Language, 1870.
See Irish.

Georgian. Klaproth, Gram. de la Lang. Georgienne, 1847.

German. Ahn, Pract. Method.
Bernay, Compendious, 1832.
Bokum, H., Introd. to Study of, 1832.
Follen, C., Gramm. of the German, 1828. B. C.
Grimm, Deutsche Grammatik, 1822, 26, 1831, 37.
Hartmann, Nouv. Méthode, etc., 1838.
Lemouton, Grammatik, 1833.
Meidinger, Nouv. Gram., 1804.
Stamm, Der Gothischen Sprache, 1851.
Woodbury, New Method, 1854.

Greek. Alexander, C., Worcester, Mass., 1796.
Bullions, P., New York.
Camden, Inst. Gr. Grammatices, 1763.
Campbell, Inst. Gr. Gram., N. Y., 1804.
David, La Langue Moderne, 1821.
Hachenberg, Elements of, Hartford, 1822.
Hickie, Gr. accidence.
Matthiæ, A., Bloomfield's ed., 1820.
Milner, J., Lond., 1740.
Moor, Elementa, 1780.
" Elements of, 1807, 1831.
Mynas, Grammaire Grecque, Anc. et Mod.
Nolan, F., A compendious, 1819.

Grammars: GREEK (continued).
Pianzola, Gramatiche Mod., 1801.
Smith, J., Grammar, Bost., 1809.
Valpy, Elements of, 1820.
See Classical Literature.

HEBREW. Bennet, T., Gramm. Hebræa, 1731.
Buxtorf, J., Epitome Heb. Gram., 1658.
Bythner, Lingua Eruditorum, 1650.
Danzius, Comp. Gramm. Hebræ., 1748.
Grammar in Hebrew.
Heinemann, Catechism of, 1823.
Johnson, S., 1767.
Kendrick's Ollendorff, 1851.
Lyons, I., Camb., Mass., 1812.
Mayer, I., Gram. and Chrestomathy.
Pamphlets, vol. 975.
Petit, P., Heb. Guide, 1752.
Probert, Elements of, 1832.
Seixas, Manual, 1834.
Smith, J., Heb. Gram., Boston, 1810.
Stuart, M., 1823, 1835.

HINDOSTANI. Shakespeare, J., London, 1843.
Peretti, On Tourner's Gram.
Pianzola, Gramatiche, 1801.
Vriend, Italiansche Spraakkunst, 1858.

HUNGARIAN. Csink, Grammar, 1853.
Lemouton, Grammatik, 1833.
Wekey, S., Gram. and spec. of poetry, 1852.

ICELANDIC. Marsh, G. P., Icelandic language, 1838.
Rask, Icelandic, 1843.

INDIAN, AMERICAN. Arenas, Langue Mexicaine.
Byington, Choctaw definer.
Cuesta, Mutsun Grammar, 1866.
Du Ponceau, Gram. of the Delaware.
Eliot, Indian Grammar.
English and Dakota vocab.
Hamilton, W., Ioway Grammar, 1848.
Howse, Gram. of the Cree and Chippewa, 1844.
Ludewig, H. E., Lit. of Am. Orig. Languages. List of Grammars, 1858.
Mengarini, Flat-head Gram.
Pandosy, Yakama language.
Riggs, S. R., Dakota Grammar, 1852.
Schoolcraft, Information on the tribes.
Shea's Library of Am. Linguistics, 13 v.
Smith, B., Heve language.
" Pima language, 1862.
Williams, R., Key to, 1643.
See Language; Dictionaries.

Grammars (continued).
IRISH. Furlong, Irish Primer.
O'Brien, Pract. Gram. of Irish, 1809.
Vallancey, Gr. of Iberno-Celtic, 1781.
See Gaelic.

ITALIAN. Barberi, Grammaire, 1825.
Grimani, Key to Grammar.

JAPANESE. Page's Grammaire Japonoise.
Rodriguez, Japanese Grammar, 1825.

LATIN. Adam, A., Cleveland's ed., 1836.
Andrews & Stoddard's, 1839.
Bullion's Principles of, 1843.
" Jacob's Lat. Reader, 1845.
Burr, Amer. Lat. Gram., 1794.
Cooper, J. G., New Latin Grammar, 1829.
Donati, Editio minor, 1494.
Grant, Instit. of Lat., 1823.
Introduction to the Latin, 1755.
Kenrick, J., Key to Zumpt's Gram., 1831.
Lily, Short Introduction, 1673.
Mair, Latin Syntax, 1779. B. C.
Milton, J., Works, vol. 6, 1851.
Nolan, F., Compendious Gr., 1825.
Parent's, The, Latin Grammar.
Putschius, Gram. Lat. auctores antiq.
Ramus, P., Grammatica, 1585.
Ruddiman, Rudiments of, 1807.
Scheller, Additions by Walker, 1825.
Smith, J., N. Hamp. Lat. Gram., 1802.
Tricot, Les Rudiments de la Langue Latine, 1777. B. C.
Turner, Exerc. on the verbs.
Westminster Grammar, 1643, 1741.
Zumpt, Grammar, 1829.

MALAY. Breugel, Maleische taal, 1823.
Marsden, Langue Malaie, 1812.

MARATHI. Marathi Grammar, 1854.

MEXICAN. Arenas, Langue Mexicaine.

PERSIAN. Altinghius, Synopsis, 1730.
Bleeck A. H., 1857.
English Grammar in Pers.
Jones, Sir W., Works, vol. 6, Persian Gram., 1807.

POLYNESIAN. Mariner, Tonga Islands, 1818.
Teichelmann, Australian.

PORTUGUESE. Tillbury, Gram. Portugueza.
" Arte Ingleza, 1827.
Vieyra, Portuguese Grammar, 1827.

RABBINIC. Altinghius, Synopsis, 1730.
See Hebrew.

RUSSIAN. Reiff, Engl.-Russ. Gram., 1853.

SAMARITAN. Altinghius, Synopsis, 1730.
Palfrey, Samaritan Gramm., 1835.

29

Great Britain, Government of (continued).

Leckie, Essay on practice and theory of, 1812.

Mann, A., Black-book, 1845.

May, Const. History of, 1760–1860.

Observations on the Brit. Cons., 1831.

Paine, T, Political Writings.

" Jests, 1796.

Principles of the Br. Const., 1793.

Pusey, The New Constitution, 1831.

Russell, Earl, Essay on, 1866.

Thoughts on Eng. Gov., (Reeves), 1803.

Toland, Memorial of England, 1705.

" Limitation of the Crown.

Trenchard, J., Tracts, 1751.

See Authority; Government; G. B., Political Pamphlets; Oath of Allegiance.

Great Britain, History of. Annals of, from Geo. III to Amiens.

Bartholomæus, Hist. Angl., 449–1298.

Baxter, R., Life and times.

Belsham, W., Hist. of, 1688–1802.

Bos, Hist. landbeschryvinge, 1685.

Bree, State of the kingdom, 1300–1400.

Brief and perfect journal, 1655.

Brief Hist. of the Succession, 1683.

Brief History of the Wars, 1797.

Brodie, Hist. of Brit. Empire, from Chas. I to the restor., 1822.

Buckingham, Courts of William IV and Victoria.

Calendars of State Papers, 1513–1667.

Carlisle, Three embassies, 1663–4.

Carr, Administrations of, 1801—69.

Carstare's State Papers, 1689–1709.

Cary, R., Memoirs.

Charles I, Reliquiæ Sacræ.

Constitution of 1688, 1709.

Cornwallis, Correspondence, 1859.

Cumberland, Duke of, Memoirs of, 1767.

Dalrymple, Memoirs of, and Ireland, 1771, 73, 88.

" Mem. and letters, 1766.

Etat Politique, 1757–59, Genest.

Fleury, Hist. de l'Angleterre.

Forbes, R., Mem. of Rebellion of 1745.

Forbes, State Papers, 1558–60.

Forster's Eliot's Life, 1590–1632.

" Grand Remonstrance, 1641.

Gardiner, Exped. to W. Indies, 1759.

Geoffrey, Brit. History.

Gildas, Epistle, A. D. 548.

Giles, Hist. of Ancient Britons.

Great Britain; Orders in Council, 1807, 1809.

" Rolls' Publications, 1857–66.

Great Britain, History of (continued).

Grosseteste, Epistolæ, 1225–1253.

Hardwicke, State papers, 1501–1726.

Henry III–VII, (G. B., Rolls, Chron.).

Henry, R., History of, 1771–96.

History of Prime Ministers, 1763.

Holinshed, Chronicles of England, Ireland and Scotland, 1587.

Impartial account, 1702.

John of Oxnead, 900–1290.

Leckie, Hist. Survey of Affairs of, 1810.

Leland, De Script. Britann., 1709.

" De rebus Britannicis, 1774.

Letter to a Friend....on King James, 1691.

Lewis, G. C., Admin. of, 1783–1830.

Lodge, Illust. of Br. Hist.

Luttrell, Diary of Affairs, 1678–1714.

Macpherson, J., Original papers, 1688–1715.

" Hist., to H. of Hanover, 1775.

" Introd. to Hist. of, 1772.

Massey, Hist. under George III.

Mentet, Hist. des troubles, 1643–49.

Mercurius politicus, 1716–20.

Milton, J., History of Britain.

Moleville, Chron. Abridg. of Hist. of, to 1763.

Monk, Letters on restoration, 1714.

Monumenta historica, (Petrie), 1848.

Oates, Narr. of Conspiracy, 1679.

Oldfield, Hist. of the Boroughs. 1794, 1797.

Ormonde, Campaign of 1712.

O'Sullivan, Agency of divine prov., 1816.

Palgrave, Hist. of Normandy and England, 1864.

Plowden, Hist. for 1794.

" Short History of, 1792, 93.

Present State of British Empire, (Goldsmith), 1768.

Rapin, Acta Regia.

Richard, Speculum, 447–871.

Rolls Publications, Calendars, 1603–62.

" Calendars of Colon. papers, 1574–1660.

Rushworth, Historical collections, 1721.

Somers, Coll. of tracts, (W. Scott), 1815.

Stanhope, Hist. of reign of Q. Anne, 1870.

Stow, English Chronicle, 1618.

Succinct Hist. of Regencies, &c., 1751.

Thomas, S. F., Historical notes, 1500–1711.

Thurloe, Coll. of State papers, 1742.

Toone, Chronol. of George III, IV, and William IV.

Great Britain, History of (continued).
United States, Corres., 1809, 56.
Vernon Letters, 1696–1708.
Wade, Brit. Hist. chron. arranged, 1841.
Walker, Sir E., Hist. Discourses, 1705.
Wallington, Notices of Events, 1869.
Welwood, Memoirs, 1588–1688.
Wilkins, Polit. Ballads, 1600–1700.
See England; Scotland; Ireland; British Colonies; Gunpowder Plot; and the several Kings.

Great Britain, Land. Danson, On Farming Agreements, 1855.
Great Britain; Waste Lands, 1795.
Greene, I. G. J., Present Laws, 1851.
Landed Interest, 1733.
Rainy, On Landed Property, 1851.

Great Britain, Military. Army Lists, 1757–1855.
Beatson, Naval and Mil. Memoirs, 1727–1783.
Bowles, W. C., National Defence, 1852.
Burton, Wars of, 1625–1660.
Campbell, J., British Army, 1840.
Cavalry Regulations.
Chesney, Royal Regiment of Artillery, 1849. P. 406.
Clode, Mil. forces of G. B., 1869.
Douglas, H., Defence of, 1859.
Grose, Mil. Antiquities of.
Harris, National Defences.
Hints for Ordering Militia, 1759.
Hist. Records of Brit. Army, (R. Cannon), 1834–66. 64 vols.
Macgregor, Plan for Militia, 1849.
MacKinnon, Coldstream Guards.
Military Defence of the Kingdom, 1852.
Napier, Defence by Militia, 1852.
National Regeneration, 1844.
Nugent, N., Case of, 1776.
Operations of the British Arms, 1744.
Reorganization of the Med. Dep't, 1855.
Royal Horse Artil., Instructions.
Smyth, R. C., Memorandum on defence of, 1852.
Stewart, Gen., Reform of, 1806.
Suggestions for Defence of, 1851.
Tayler, J. N., Def. of Coast, 1848.
Thomson, Mil. institutions of, 1855.
Treatise Concerning Militia, 1752.
Trenchard, Hist. of Standing Army, 1698. Pam. 416.
West, Col., Training for, 1859.
Wood, H., Military Education, 1847.
See French war in America; Waterloo.

Great Britain, Naval. Allen, J., Battles of the Brit. Navy, 1852.
Beatson, Naval and Mil. Memoirs, 1727–83.
Brenton, Naval History of, 1783–1834.
Byng, Fleet at Sicily, 1739.
Charnock, Biog. Navalis, 1660–1798.
Clavel, British Dominion of the Seas, 1665.
Dundonald's Autobiog., 1860.
Exposition of the Case of Surgeons, 1850. P. 406.
Field of Mars: Nav. and Mil. Engage. to 1801.
Great Britain; Navy Lists, 1811, 54, 1862.
" Steel's List, 1812, 13.
James, W., Naval history, 1793–1820.
Lediard, T., Naval Hist. of, to 1734.
Lestock, Engagement near Toulon, 1745. P. 391.
M., J., Campaign of 1778. P. 1113.
Manderson, Present State of, 1812.
Marshall, Royal Naval biog., 1823–35.
Miles, Epitome of R. N. Service, 1841.
Napier, The Navy, past and present, 1851.
Naval Chronicle, 1799–1818.
Naval Considerations, 1810.
Nelson, Lord, Dispatches, 1843, 46.
Nicolas, Sir N. H., History of Royal Navy, 1847.
Sainte Croix, Hist. de la Puissance navale, 1786.
Some observations, 1847.
Specimen of Naked Truth, 1746.
Standing Navy Economical, 1851.
Steel, Naval Chronologist, 1793–1801.
Tomlinson, R., Letters on Naval interests of, 1782.
United Service Journal, 1829–60.
Warning Voice of a Seaman, 1751.

Great Britain, Navigation. Collection of Reports, 1807.
Huskisson, Speech, 1827.
Obs. on the Manuf. of Rope, 1829.
Thring, Merch. Shipping Law, 1854.
See Gr. Br. Commerce.

Great Britain: Parliament. Black Book, 1826. P. 414.
Black Book, 1835.
Burdett, Power to imprison.
Burke, Speech, Independence of, 1780.
Christian, E., Lords in judicature, 1792.
" Privileges of Parl., 1810.
Cooper, C. P., Lords' Appeal.
Creevey, Formation of, 1826.
Essay on the power of, 1770.

Great Britain: Political Discussions and Pamphlets, to 1685 (continued).

Thompson, R., Sermon, Monmouth's Rebell., 1685.

Tory Plot, 1682.

Trimmer, The, 1683.

See Charles I, II; Authority, Church and Civil.

1685–1689.

Answer to the late K. James, 1687.

Coventry, Char. of a trimmer, 1689.

Dialogue, 1689.

Great Bastard Protector, 1689.

Higden, W., Rev. of 1688.

History of the desertion, 1689.

Important Questions, (Stephens), 1689.

Kippis, Serm. on Rev. of 1688.

Letter to a person of Quality, 1687.

Ludlow, E., Letter on Tyranny, 1688.

Proceedings of pres. Parl. justified, 1689.

Seventh Collection of Papers, 1689.

1689–1702.

Appeal to Heaven, (Stephens), 1691.

Consid. upon....Speaker, 1698.

Easie method, &c., 1691.

James II, Manifesto, 1697.

Johnson, S., Abrogation of K. James, 1692.

Last year's transactions, 1690.

Parable of the three jackdaws, 1694.

Persuasive to consideration, 1693.

Remarks on the Affairs of Eng., 1691.

Their Present Majesties, etc., 1691.

1702–1714.

Barrier Treaty Vindicated, 1712.

Bisse, P., Serm. on the Rebellion, 1711.

Brett, T., Serm. of the Rebellion, 1713.

Caveat against the Whiggs, 1710–12.

Character of a Popish Successor, 1712.

Evans, J., Serm., Victory in Brabant, 1706.

Faults in the Fault-finder, 1710.

Faults on both sides, 1710.

Gravenor, B., Sermon, Nov. 7, 1710.

Haversham's, Lord, Speech, 1707.

Learned Comment on Hare's Serm., 1711.

Letter to the Author, 1705.

Letter to the Examiner, 1714.

Nahash's Defeat, 1708.

Neck or Nothing....1713.

Norris, R., Thanksgiving Sermon, 1704.

Rehearsals, The, 1704–8.

Re-representation, The, 1711.

Revolution Principles, 1713.

Great Britain: Political Discussions and Pamphlets, to 1714 (continued).

Secret Hist. of Calve's Head Club, 1703.

Spademan, Serm., Victory in the Brabant, 1706.

Steele, R., The Crisis, 1713.

Toland, Memorial of England, 1705.

Wyvill, Serm., The Peace, 1713.

See Marlborough, Duke of.

1714–1727.

Browne, S., Sermon, 1716.

Clodius and Cicero, 1727.

Fleetwood, Serm., Rebellion, 1715.

Gibson, Serm. on Rebellion, 1716.

Greene, T., Sermon on Rebellion, 1715.

Harley, Impeachment of, 1715.

Kennett, Serm., 1715, 1716.

Lambe, Sermon, the Rebellion, 1715.

Letter to the Clergy, 1722, (Pearce).

Merchant, Peace and Trade, 1729.

Non-resistance, 1714.

Obs. upon a pamphlet, Lond., 1717.

Old Whig, On the Peerage, 1719.

Pearse, R., Sermon, 1716.

Plebeian, The, N. III, 1719.

Public Spirit of Whigs, 1714.

Sherlock, Sermon, Rebellion, 1716.

Some Observations, 1728.

See George I.

1727–1760.

Ancient and Mod. Liberty, 1734.

Answer to a Pamphlet, (Shebbeare), 1756.

Apology for the Conduct....1744.

Brief State....pedlars, 1730.

Burton, J., Serm., Rebellion, 1746.

Carr, Serm., Culloden Victory, 1746.

Characteristics of pres. pol. state, 1758.

Coleire, Serm., Rebellion of 1745.

Compleat List....votes on Septennial Act, 1734.

Compleat view of Politicks, 1743.

Conduct of the Ministry, 1759.

Conduct of the Opposition, 1734.

Consid. upon the present state, 1739.

Consolatory Letter, 1760.

Con-Test, Period., 1756-7.

Cooke, W., An enquiry, 1754.

Craftsman Extraordinary, 1729.

Dialogue, 1747.

Drapier's letters, 1730.

Dutch Reasoner, 1745.

Enquiry into Conduct, 1734.

Enquiry into the Reasons, 1729.

Essay on Polit. lying, 1757.

Great Britain: Political Discussions and Pamphlets, to 1760 (continued).

Examination of the Principles....of the two B....s, 1749.
Faction Detected, (Perceval), 1743.
False Accusers Accused, 1741.
Farther Vind.....Hanover Troops, 1743.
Fatal consequences, 1736.
First Letter, (Shebbeare), 1756.
Fitness... Septennial Act, 1740.
Fourth Letter to the People, 1756.
Free and Impar. Examiner, 1745.
French influence, 1740.
Full....answer to Fourth Letter, 1756.
Grand Accuser, 1735.
Hoadly, Enquiry into Reasons, 1728.
Huddesford, Sermon, Rebellion, 1745.
Hue and cry, 1739.
Important Question, 1755.
Lavington, Sermon, Rebellion, 1745.
Letter addressed to two great men, 1760.
" from a Gentleman, 1727.
" from Mem. of Parl., 1729.
" to a friend, 1755.
" to a Member, etc., 1729.
" " 1740.
" to C. D'Anvers, 1729.
" to the Craftsman, 1733.
" to the People of England, 1751.
" to the Whigs, 1748.
Ministry and Government of, 1734.
Miscellan. Thoughts, (Hervey), 1742.
Modest Enquiry, 1742.
New Miscellany for 1737–39.
Obs. on the Conduct of G. B., 1729.
Occasional letter, 1749.
Occasional writer, No. 4, 1738.
Ogden, S., Sermons, 1758.
Pasquin & Marforio, 1750.
Patriot, The, 1734.
Peuple (Le) instruit, 1756.
Polit. cabinet, 1745.
Political state, 1736.
Politicks on both sides, 1734.
Pres. state of Politics, 1739.
Proper Reply, (Pulteney), 1731.
Prussia, Motives of the King, 1752.
Question whether England....1745.
Reasons for the Neutrality, 1734.
Resignation, The, Discussed, 1748.
Richardson, A., Serm., Rebellion, 1745.
Roberts, S., Sermon, 1745.
Royal, The, Sin, 1738, (Croxall).
Seasonable Expostulations, 1742.
Serious Exhortation.... elections, 1740.
Shebbeare, Letters on the Eng., 1756.
Short View of the State....1730.
Sketch of French pol., 1735.
Sky, The, Rocket.
Some farther remarks, 1729.
Some of the Roman Hist. of Fabius, 1749.
Test, The, 1757. Period.
Warburton, Serm., Rebell. of 1745.
See Walpole, R.; George II; Scotland.

1760–1783.

Abbey of Kilkhampton, 1780.
Address to Prot. Dissenters, 1774.
Anticipation, 1779.
Appeal of Reason, 1763.
Auckland, Four letters, 1779.
Budget, The, 1764.
Campbell, J., Political Survey of, 1774.
Candid Thoughts, 1781.
Conduct of the Late Administration, 1767.
Consid. on the Dependencies, 1769.
Consid. on the Times, 1769.
Consid. on the Trade, etc., 1766.
Davis, G., Sermon, 1763.
Day, T., Reflexions, 1782.
" Letters of Marius, 1780.
Description of a Parliament, 1769.
Eleutheria, 1763.
Englishman Deceived, 1768.
Facts addressed to Landholders, Tooke, 1780.
Free Appeal, 1767.
Fugitive Polit. Essays, 1770.
Gordon, Cordial for low spirits, 1763.
Hardwicke, Original papers, 1763.
History of Lord North's Administration, 1782.
Hist. of the Minority, 1765.
Import. of Brit. Dominion in America, 1770.
Import. of Br. Dominion in India, 1770.
Letter to the Earl of Bute, 1771.
" to H. G., Duke of Grafton, 1768.
" to the Rt. Hon. C. T., 1763.
Letter to the Rt. Hon. the Lord Mayor, 1762.
Macaulay, C., Observations, 1770.
Political Essays concerning, 1772.
Political Tracts, Collection, 1764–73.
Pres. state of Nation, Grenville, 1768.
Principles of the late changes, 1765.
Right Honorable Annuitant, 1761.
Robinson, M., Peace the best policy, 1777.
Sandercock, Serm., Peace of 1763.

Great Britain: Political Discussions and Pamphlets, to 1783 (continued).

Shebbeare, Answer to the Queries, 1775.

Short Considerations, 1766.

Short Hist. of conduct of Ministry, 1765.

Some thoughts on..the Colonies, 1765.

Watson, R., Revolu. Vindicated, 1776.

See Revolutionary War.

1783-1820.

Adolphus, Rupture with France, 1803.

" Political state of, 1818.

Anti-Corsican, The, 1804.

Anti-Jacobin, 1800.

Answer to the inquiry into the State.... 1806.

Appeal to the head, 1798.

Appeal to the people, (Hawker), 1798.

Armata; Satire, 1817.

Atcheson, Amer. Encroachments, 1808.

Authentic Pieces ...Power of the Crown, 1780.

Beauties of Fox & Burke, 1784.

Berkeley, Sermon, English Rev., 1789.

Bowles, J., French aggression, 1797.

" Strictures, 1807.

Brief answer, 1803.

British Lion, (Penn), 1797.

British tocsin, 1795.

British Union Society, 1797.

Brougham, Speech, Orders in Council, 1808.

Burke, E., Letter to noble Lord, 1796.

Butler, Political fugitive, N. Y., 1794.

Callender, Political Progress of, 1795.

Campbell, D., Letter to Mar. of Lorn, 1798.

Cartwright, J., Letter, 1793.

Cause and cure, Reforms, 1817.

Chalmers, G., Peace of Paris, 1815.

Champion, Reflections on the Whigs, 1787.

Collection of Addresses, 1793.

Conduct of the present Parliament, 1789.

Considerations on public affairs, 1796-8.

Consid. on....sedit. practices, 1795.

Consid. on the Appr. Dissolution, 1790.

Consid. upon the State, 1796.

Countrymen, 1815.

Courtenay, T. P., State of the Nation, 1811.

Crambe repetita, 1799.

Crisis, The, 1785.

Datos sobre algunas Leyes Inglesas, 1807.

De Lolme, Obs. upon the..embarrassment, 1789.

Great Britain: Political Discussions and Pamphlets, to 1820 (continued).

Dumouriez, Specul. sketch, 1798.

Edwards, G., True Scheme of Economy, 1808.

Electors of Westminster, 1819.

Enquiry into the...Constitution, 1792.

Extracts from the Album....1788.

Few Cursory Remarks, (Bentley), 1803.

Fox, C. J., Speech on Peace, 1800.

Frend, W., Peace and Union, 1793.

Glover, Mem. of a cel. polit. character, 1813.

Grenville Agonistes, 1807.

Hartley, D., Address, York, 1781.

Heeren, Continental Interests of.

Hone, W., Miscellanies, 1817-20.

Inquiry into the state, etc., 1806.

Knox, W., Considerations, 1789.

Lister, Opposition dangerous, 1798.

Miles, W. A., Conduct of France, 1793

Morfitt, Observations, 1797.

Mornington's Speech, 1794.

Munkhouse, Thanksgiving Sermons, 1797, 98.

National Danger, (A. Young), 1797.

O'Bryen, D., Utrum horum, 1796.

Pax in bello, 1796.

Penn, J., Timely appeal, 1798.

People's Answer to, Wraxall, 1787.

Picture of the Times, 1795.

Political Letters, 1784.

Question as it stood, 1798, (Francis).

Randolph, F., State of the Nation, 1808.

Rennell, T., Thanksgiving Ser., 1798.

Reply to a Short Review, 1787.

Review of Mr. Roscoe's Considerations, 1808.

Review of Public Affairs, 1802.

Review of the Principal Proceedings, 1792.

Rights and Remedies, 1795.

Roscoe, Negotiations of, 1807.

" On the Present War, 1808.

Rose, G., Brief Examination, 1799.

Royal Register, 1788, 9.

Searcher, The, after Truth, 1817.

Short Review of state of, Wraxall, 1787.

Sins of the Government, (Barbauld), 1793.

Solemn appeal to Citizens, 1788.

Some Remarks on the....War, 1795.

Southey, R., Essays, 1811-16.

Stephens, Crisis of the Sugar Colonies, 1802.

Thelwall, J., Fraternity, 1795.

Thoughts on the relative, &c., 1806.

Great Britain: Political Discussions and Pamphlets, to 1820 (continued).

View of the History of, under North, 1782.

View of the relative ...1796.

Wakefield, Reply to Burke, 1796.

" Reply to Bp. of Landaff, 1798.

" Spirit of Christianity in, 1794.

War with France, (Rennell), 1794.

Waring, J. S., Letter to Burke, 1784.

Webster, N., Political Progress of, 1795.

Wellesley, Formation of Administration, 1812.

Whigs Unmasked, 1795.

Wilson, J., Letter....political, 1793.

Word to the Wise, 1790.

Wyvill, Defence of R. Price, 1792.

See George III.

1820-1867.

Balance of Power, 1831.

Boone, J. S., Political View, 1821.

Brougham, Speech, Reform bill, 1831.

Bulwer, Letter on Crisis, 1834.

" Letters to John Bull, 1850.

Burghley, England subsists by miracle, 1859.

Calm Statement, 1826.

Carlyle, Chartism.

Coalition Guide, 1854.

Cochrane, Who are Liberals? 1852.

Country without Government, 1830.

Countrymen, 1815.

Dallas, G. M., Letters, 1856-60.

D'Israeli, Crisis Examined, 1834.

Essays on Reform, 1867.

George IV, Letter, 1821.

Gladstone, W. E., Speech, 1853.

Grey, Earl, Policy of Russell's Admin., 1853.

Mullins, Magistracy of England, 1836.

Opinions as to the real state, 1823.

Pecchio, Osservazioni, 1827.

" Elezione di membri del Parl.

Perils of England, 1853.

Political Nomenclature, 1838.

Real Character of, 1833.

Russell, Prin. of Reform Act, 1839.

Short letter to Earl of Derby, 1852.

Tracts for the Times, No. 10, 1852.

Twiss, T., Letters of Pius IX, and Laws of England, 1851.

Whigs, The, 1847.

Whitehurst, Coalition, 1787 and 1853.

See England; Ireland; Church of England.

Great Britain, Registers, Almanacs and Statistics. Almanacs, 1679-1732.

Annual Register, 1758-1870.

Baert, Tableau de, 1800.

British Almanac, 1854-69.

Bristed, J., Resources of British Empire, 1811.

Catholic Directory, 1839, 49, 52, 54.

Colquhoun, Treat. on Resources of, 1815.

Court and City Register. *See* Royal.

Court Calendar, 1747. *See* Royal.

Chalmers, G., State of, 1815.

" Comp., strength of, 1782.

Chamberlayne, Present state of, 1674, 76, 1735, 43, 55.

Clergy List, 1841-50.

Dietrichsen's Almanac, 1842, 44, 52.

Etat Militaire, 1774.

Goldsmith, Almanach, 1852.

Great Britain, Official reg., 1728, 42.

Haward, Charges, 1647.

Haydn, Book of Dignities.

McCulloch, Statist. Account, 1837.

M'Queen, Statistics of, 1836.

Marshall, Digest of, 1799-1833.

Millan's Register. *See* Royal.

Murray, Hand-book of Church and State, 1852.

Owen's Book of Fairs, 1834.

Parl. Companion, 1836, 41, 52.

Parl. Directory, 1853.

Parl. Guide, 1837.

Rickman, Pop. account of, 1800.

Royal Blue Book, 1855.

Royal Kalendar, 1751-1855, not complete.

Watson's Almanacks, 1786, 99.

Will's Clerical Almanack, 1852.

See Almanacs.

Great Britain, Travels and Descriptions. Beauties of England and Wales, Brewer & Brayley, 1801-15.

Burke, Historic lands of England.

Camden, W., Britannia, 1772.

Carus, King of Saxony's Journey, 1844.

Colton, C., Four Years in, 1836.

De Foe, D., Tour through.

Gonzales, Voy. to Eng. and Scotland.

Gorton, Topog. Dictionary, 1833.

Great Britain: County Divisions, 1832.

Green, W., North of England, 1810.

Head, G., Tour through the United Kingdom, 1837.

Jones's Views of Mansions.

Kohl, J. G., Ireland, Scotland and England, 1844.

Long, Geography of.

Magna Brit. ant., (Cox), 1738.

Greece, Modern (continued).
Savary, N., Letters on Greece.
Slade, A., Sketches of travel, 1828–31.
Stephanini, Capture of Patras, 1829.
Strangford's Writings, 1869.
Strong, F., Greece as a Kingdom, 1840.
Taylor, B., Travels in, 1855.
See Turkey; Ionian Islands; Candia; Athens.

Greek Authors. Achilles Tatius, Clitopho, 1855.
Ælianus, Varia Historia, 1545, 1829.
" De natura aminalium.
Æneas Gazaens, De immortalitate.
Aeschylus, Tragedies, Graece, 1745.
" Tragedies; Translations.
Æsopus, Fabulæ, Fables.
Anacreon, Carmina; Gr., Eng. and Fr.
Andronicus Rhodius, Ethic. Nicom., Paraphrasis.
Antoninus Liberalis, Transform. Congeries, 1774.
Apollonius Dyscolus, Gr. and Lat.
Apollonius Rhodius, Argonauticorum, lib. IV, Gr. and Lat. and Eng. Trans.
Apollonius of Alex., Lexicon Græc., 1773.
Apostolius, Parœmiæ.
Aratus, Eratosthenes, etc., 1672.
Archimedes, Œuvres.
Aristides, A., Opera, 1829.
Aristophanes, Plutus, Gr. and Fr.
" Comedies, Eng.
Aristoteles, Works in Latin.
" Hist. des Animaux.
" Works, Translations.
Arrianus, Opera, 1792.
" Periplus.
" Exped. Alexandri.
Athenæus, The Deipnosophists.
Athenagoras, De Resurrectione, Lat.
Auteurs Grecs, Gr. and French.
Bion, with Sappho, in French, 1829.
Brumoy, Greek Theatre.
Callimachus, Gr. and Ital.
Cebes, Tabula.
" Tabula, (Outhof.)
Chronicon Alexandrinum.
Cory, Ancient Fragments.
Demosthenes, Gr., Engl.
" Discours sur la couronne.
" Orations, translated.
Diodorus Siculus, Biblioth. Historicæ.
Dionysius Halicarnas., Opera.
" Periegesis, trans.
Dioscorides, De Materia Medica.
Epictetus, Manuale, Trans. English, 1798.

Greek Authors (continued).
Epicurus, Morals.
Euripides, Τα Σωζομενα, Musgrave.
" Tragoediæ, Scholefield.
" Notae in, Lond., 1828.
" Translated by Potter.
" Alcestis, Trans.
" Hippolytus & Alcestis, Trans.
Eustratius, Comment. in Libros Aristotelis, 1536.
Heliodorus, Romances of.
Heraclides, Quae supersunt.
Herodotus, Gr. and Lat.
" Historiarum Lib. ix, Gr. and Engl.
" History of, Rawlinson's Trans., 1860.
Hesiodus, Gr. and Eng.
Hesychius, Lexicon.
Hierocles, On the Golden Verses.
Hippocrates, De Morbis Popularibus, 1717.
" Reliquiæ, 1859–64.
Homerus, Ed. Ernesti.
" Ed. Heyne.
" Ed. Ansse de Villoison.
" Iliad or Odyssey, Cowper's, Pope's, Derby's, Buckley's, Chapman's, Hobbe's, Bryant's, Herschel's Translations.
Isocrates, Opera, 1803.
Jacobs, Gr. Reader.
Koen. Baier. Ak., Theodosius.
Libanius, Præludia Oratoria.
Longinus, Greek and Latin.
" De Sublimitate, Gr. and Lat.
" On the Sublime.
Longus, Daphnis and Chloe, Engl.
Lucianus, Gr. and French.
" Translations.
" Dialogues, Trans.
Lycophron, Cassandra.
Lysias, Greek and Latin.
Manasses, C., Annales.
Maximus Tyrius, Dissert., Gr.
" Diss., Trans.
Meletius, Peri tes arches tou papa.
Menandri et Philemonis reliquiæ, 1823.
Mercurius, Pimandras, Gr. and Lat.
Montfaucon, Bibliot. Coisliniana.
Moschus with Sappho, in French.
Musaeus, Carmen.
Oratores Attici, Bekker.
Orpheus, Trans. of T. Taylor.
Outhof, Cebes, Tabula.
Passow, Pop. carmina.
Pausanias, Græciæ descriptio, 1829.

Greek Authors (continued).
Pausanias, Description of Greece.
Phalaris, Epistles, Trans.
Philemon. *See* Menander.
Philo Judaeus, Lucubrationes.
" Works, Translation.
Philostratus, Appollonius' Life, Trans.
Photius, Lexicon, (Parr).
" *Λεξεων συναγωγη.*
Pindarus, Ed. Heyne.
" Romæ, 1515.
" Odes, Translation.
Plato, Opera, Greek, Latin and Eng.
" Apol. Sokratous, Eng.
" Immortality.
Plotinus, Opera, in Latin.
" Select Works.
Plutarchus, Vitæ, Gr., Lat. and Eng.
" Apothegmata, Gr. and Lat.
Polybius, History; translation.
Proclus, Abp., Analecta, 1630.
Proclus, Platonist, Six books of, T. Taylor.
" Commentaries, Trans., T. Taylor.
" Select theorems. *See* Ocellus.
Quintus Calabrus, Praetermiss. ab Homero.
Sappho, in French.
Socratis et aliorum epistolæ.
Sophocles, Gr. and Lat.
Strabo, Rerum Geograph., Graece.
" Geog. Trans.
Taylor, T., Fragments of Archytas and Pythagoreans.
Themistius, Opera, 1534.
Theocritus, Bion and Moschus, Eng.
Theodorus, Rhodanthe et Dosicles.
Theophrastus, On stones, Gr. and Eng.
" The Characters.
Thucydides, De bello Pelop., (Bekker).
" Pel. War, Trans.
Tryphiodorus, Ilii Excidium, Gr., Lat. and Eng.
Wagner, Chronicon Parium, Gr. et Lat., 1832.
Winterton, Poetæ minores, 1684.
Wright, R. S., Treas. of Gr. poetry, 1867.
Xenophon, Opera, Edinb. 1811.
" Trans., Cooper, etc.
" Anabasis, (Owen).
" Minor Works, Trans.
See Antiquities; Classical Lit.; Bibliography.

Greek Church. Bodinus, De Officialibus.
Curzon, Monasteries in the Levant, 1849.
Eckardt, Greek Orthodox Church, 1870.

Greek Church (continued).
Great Britain, Turkey, 1854.
Greek Church identified, 1842.
Greek Church, A Sketch, E. S. A.
Irenæus, Liturgia Græca.
Meletius, Dissertatio.
Papal aggr. in the East.
Plato, Abp., Catechism of, in Turkish.
Proclus, Abp., Analecta.
Romanoff, Rites and Customs of, 1869.
Tuttle, Europ. and Eastern Churches, 1855.
See Greece, Travels in.

Greek Frigates Controversy. P. v. 12.

Greek Language. *See* Languages; Classical; Grammars; Dictionaries.

Greek Rom. Cath. Church. Selectæ preces, 1848.

Greeley, H. Reminiscences, 1870.
Hall, A. O., Dissected, 1862.
Parton, Life of, 1855.

Green, A. Jones, J. H., Life of, 1849.

Green, S. Storrs, R. S., Mem. of, 1836.

Green, T. Extracts from Diary, 1810.

Greenboro', Vt. Stone, J. P., Hist. of, 1854.

Greene, M. C. Hague, W., Disc. on, 1856. P. 268.

Greene, N. Caldwell's Life of, 1819.
Greene, G. W., Life of, 1867–71, and in Sparks's Biog.
Johnson, W., Life of, 1822.
Lee, H., Campaign of 1781.
Simms, W. G., Life of.

Greene, S. S. Bumpstead, Reply te, 1845. P. 513.

Greene, T. Family genealogy, 1858.

Greene, Z. Ordronaux, Life of, 1859.

Greene Co., N. Y. Juliand, Hist. Reminiscences of, 1858.
Rockwell, C., Hist. Discourse.

Greenfield, W. Calumnies of the Record, 1832.

Greenfield, Mass. Willard, D., Hist. of.

Greenland. Anderson, Efterretninger, 1748.
Cranz, History of, 1820.
Edin. Cab. Lib., vol. 28.
Edmond, Voyage, 1857.
Egede, Description of, 1745, 1818.
Graah, East Coast of, 1837.
Hakluyt Soc., No. 18, 1855.
Hayes, Arctic boat Journey, 1854.
Kane, E. K., Exp. for Sir J. Franklin, 1854.

Guatemala (continued).
Guatemala, Kalendario, 1805.
" Modern Traveler.
Montgomery, G. W., Journey to, 1838.
Palacio, D. G. De. *See* Squier.
Rio, Huehuetlapallan, 1822.
Squier, Description of, 1576.
Tempsky, Journey, 1853–5.
Thompson, Official visit to, 1819.
Ximenes, De los Indios.... de, 1857.
See Central America.

Guerin, Eugenie de. Letters.

Guernsey Is. Berry, W., History of, to 1814.
Hoskins, S. E., Climate of.
Keulen, Beschryvinge...Zee-kaarten.

Guesclin, B. De. Jamison, Life of.

Gueux, Les. Liefde, Founders of Dutch Republic.

Guiana. Bajon, Hist. de Cayenne et de la, 1777.
" Voy. à la, et à Cayenne, 1789.
Bancroft, On nat. hist. of, 1769.
Barbé-Marbois, Journal d'un déporté, 1797.
Barrère, La France Equinoxiale, 1743.
Bellin, Desc. Géographique de, 1758.
Bolingbroke, H., Voy. to the Demerary, 1807.
Boyer, Relation de Brétigny, 1654.
Brett, W. H., Indians of Guiana, 1852.
Catineau, La Guyane Française, 1822.
Cayenne, Official Documents, 1790–97.
Cazé, Compagnie de Colonisation, 1826.
Coll. of docts. on Gui. Fr., 1777–99.
Du Parc, La Guyane, 1852.
Essai sur Surinam, 1788.
Fermin, Description de Surinam, 1769.
Freytag, Memoirs of, 1824.
Giguet, Des Déportés à, 1799.
Grillet, Voyage dans, 1674.
Guiana, Brit., Contrib. to Exhib. of 1855. P. 1266.
Guisan, Terres de la Guiane, 1788.
Hancock, J., Clim. and Soil of, 1840.
Hartsink, Beschryving van, 1770.
Keyen, Von Neu Niederland und Guajana, 1672.
Labat, Voyages à Cayenne, 1725–27.
Le Blond, La Guyane Française, 1814.
Lescallier, Moyens d'Administrer la Guyane, 1791.
Malouet, Mém. sur l'Administration de la, 1801.
Martin, R. M., Brit. Col. Lib., V. 5, 1844.
Mém. sur la Guyane Française, 1803.
National Assoc., 1852.
Peck, N., Report on, 1840.

Guiana (continued).
Raleigh, Sir W., Discovery of, 1595.
Sack, Reize naar Surinamen, 1821.
" Voyage to, 1810.
Schomburgh, Descrip. of Brit. Guiana.
Scoble, J., Speech on, 1838.
Stedman, J. G., Expedition against Negroes of, 1772–1777.
" Voyage à Surinam, 1798.
Tableau de Cayenne, 1798.
Vignal, Coup-d'œil sur Cayenne, 1822.
See Cayenne; Amazon.

Guides. *See* Self-culture; Books.

Guides to Towns, &c. Pam. vols. 610.
See Topog., Emigrant's Guides.

Guidon. Bock, Liber Guidonis, 1850.

Guild. Family genealogy, 1867.

Guizot, F. Memoirs, 1858–61.

Gun Cotton. Gladstone, J. H., Of Gun Cotton. P. 402.
Maynard, J. P., Ethereal Solution of.

Gunn, W. Lintner, G. A., Memoirs of.

Gunning. *See* Shooting.

Gunpowder. Essays upon Saltpetre, 1776.

Gunpowder Plot. Everard, E., Depositions, 1679.
Jardine, Narrative of.
Pam., Vol. 600, Hist. of.
Plotters' Doom, 1680.
Prance, Narr. of Discovery, 1679.
Sherlock, W., Some Reflec. on, 1683.
True Narrative, 1679.

Gunpowder Plot, Sermons at Anniversary of. Adams, J., Dan. iii. 28, 1696.
Atterbury, F., Matt. xvii. 12, 1704.
Bradford, S., Gal. v. 1, 1713.
Burnet, G., Ps. xxii. 21, 1684.
" Micah vi. 5, 1689.
Butler, L., 1 Sam. xii. 23, 24, 1710.
Dalton, J., Sermon, 1747.
Dawes, Sermon, 1686.
Dove, H., Sermon, 1680.
Evans, C., Bristol, 1775.
Fleetwood, Sermon, 1700.
Forster, N., Sermon, Popery, 1746.
Hooper, G., Matt. xxii. 21, 1681.
Kennett, W., 1715.
Lamplugh, Lu. ix. 55, 56, 1678.
Lloyd, R. L., Is. viii. 10, 1712.
Lloyd, W., Sermon, 1678.
Newton, R., Sermon, 1713.
Pelling, 1681.
Pindar, W., Sermon, 1679.
Reynell, Bristol, 1730.

H.

Harrison, W. H. (continued).
Williams, T., Eulogium.
Wilson, H. N., Two Discourses.

Harrison, New York. Baird, Hist. of Rye, 1871.

Hart, J. Parker, J., Monument to.

Hartford, Duchess of Somerset. Correspondence.

Hartford, Conn. Beardsley, Trinity Coll., Hist., 1851. P. 241.
Bushnell, Hist. Disc., North Church, 1853, P. 267.
Convention of Delegates at, 1814.
Directories, 1851–55, 63.
Hartley, H., In Olden Time.
Hawes, Hist. of First Church.
" Centen. Address, 1835.
Porter, W. S., Hist. Notices of Conn. in 1640.

Hartshorne, J. Evans, Biog. Notice of, 1852. P. 64.

Hartz Forest. Behrens, Nat. Hist. of, 1730.

Harvard University. Catalogues and Reports to 1871, 13 vols.
Eliot, Hist. of 1848.
Everett, E., Speech on Memorial of, 1849.
Farmer, J., Memorials of the Graduates, 1642–1833.
Gray, F. C., Letter on, 1831.
Harvard Memorial biographies, (Higginson), 1867.
Hollis and others, Facts and Documents, 1829. P. 28, B. C.
Lowell, J. R., Fireside Travels.
Morse's Appeal, 1814.
Quincy, J., Hist. of, 1840.
Palmer, Deaths of Alumni, 1851–63.
Pierce, B., Hist. of, to 1776.
Popkin, J. S., Memorial, 1852.
Ticknor, Changes proposed, 1825.
See Cambridge, Mass.

Harvey, W. Coxe, J. R., Discovery Claims, 1834.

Harwinton, Conn. Chipman, History of, 1860.

Hasenclever, P. Case of, 1774.

Hasheesh. Ludlow, The Hasheesh Eater.

Hasselt, A. Van. Book, Liber Guidonis, 1850.

Hastings. Family Genealogy, 1860.

Hastings, W. Burke, E., Works, vol. 6, 7, Impeachment, 1826, 27.
East India Co., Proceedings, 1783.
East India Question, 1813.
Gleig, Memoirs of, 1841.*

Hastings, W. (continued).
Gr. Br., India Report, 1773.
" East India affairs, 1783, 5.
Letter to his Majesty, 1808.
Letter to the Hon. E. Burke, 1783.
Letters on Impeachment of, 1790.
Macaulay, T. B., Essays.
National Portraits.
Observations on Burke's Speech.
Parkes, Life of Francis, 1867.
Rumbold, Vindication, 1868.
Waring, J. S., The Conduct, etc., 1784.

Hastings, Eng. Osborne, H., Guide to.
Ross, Guide to.

Hatborough Monument. Belville's Address, 1862.

Hatch. Family Genealogy, 1850.

Hatch, J. Hist. Sketch of, 1850.

Hatfield, Mass. Bradford Club Publications, (Hough, Attack on, 1677).
Harris, S., Discourse, 1850.

Hatheway, S. G. Randall, H. S., Obit. of, 1864.

Hauser, C. Feuerbach, Account of, 1833.
See Stanhope, (Earl).

Havelock, H. Brock, Life of, 1858.
Headley's Life of.
Mursell, Lecture on.

Haven, N. A. Ticknor, G., Life of, 1828.

Haven, R. Geneal. of, 1859.

Haverhill, Ms. Directory, 1860.
Chase, G. W., History of, 1861.
Mirick, B. L., History of, 1832.

Hawaii. Account of the visit, &c., 1839.
Amer. B. of Missions, 1824–67.
Anderson, R., The Hawaiian Islands, 1864.
Baxley, What I Saw, 1865.
Bingham, Twenty-five years at, 1849.
Cook, Capt. J., Voyages, 1778.
Ellis, W., Narrative of a Tour through, 1827.
Gulick, Climate, etc. of, 1855. P. 272.
Hawaii, King's Accounts, 1854.
Hawaiian Club Papers, 1868.
Hawaiian Spectator, 1838.
Honolulu, 1848.
Hopkins, Condition of, 1862.
Jarves, J. J., History of, 1843.
" Scenes and Scenery in, 1840.
Mortimer, Voyage to, 1791.
Narrative of Five Youth, 1816.
Obookiah's Life.
Perkins, Na Motu, 1858.
Sandwich Is. notes, by a Haole, 1854.

Hawaii (continued).
Stewart, C. S., Visit to the South Seas.
Washburn, J., Speech, 1854.
See Polynesia; Pacific.

Haward, S. Newcome, P., Discourse on.

Haweis, Dr. Milner, I., Obs. on his history, 1803. P. 392.

Hawick, Scotland. Wilson, R., History of, 1825.

Hawker, R. Comb, Sermon on, 1827.
Lane, S., Sermon on, 1827. P. 382.
Mutter, G., Sermon on, 1827. P. 382.

Hawkes, M. Townsend, J., Disc., death of, 1808.

Hawkes, T. Townsend, J., Disc., death of.

Hawkins, J. H. W. Hawkins, W. G., Life of, 1859.

Hawks, F. L. Quarterman, Narr., 1844.

Hawley, W. Laurie, J., Sermon on.

Hayden Family. *See* Stiles.

Hayden, S S. Oviatt, G. A., Mem. of.

Haydn, J. Bombet, Life of.

Haydon, B. R. Taylor, T., Life of, 1853.

Hayes, I. Norton, S. H., Memorial, 1857.

Hayes, J. Earle, J., Sermon on, 1729.

Hay Fever. Smith, W. A., Observations, 1865. P. 1529.

Haynes, S. Cooley, T. M., Life of, 1837.

Hayti. *See* Saint Domingo.

Hazlitt, W. Lit. Remains, etc., (Bulwer & Talfourd).
" Memoirs, 1867.

Hazzard, D. Wallace, A., Memorial of.

Head, F. B. How I became Governor, 1852.

Health. Alcott, W. A., Tracts.
" Address, 1857.
Alexander, W., Vital Statistics of Halifax.
Armstrong, Art of Health, 1744.
Annales d'Hygiène, 1829–70.
Barton, E. H., Hygiène of Louis'a, 1851.
Becquerel, Hygiène privée et publ., 1851.
Beddoes, Essay on Hygeia, 1801–02.
Beecher, C., Letters to the People.
Belgium, Comm. de Salubrité, 1850.
" Hygiène Publique, 1850–51.
" Service Sanitaire, 1839.
" Service Méd. Rural, 1749.
Bélinaye, The Sources of Health, 1833.
Bell, J., Sanitary Measures, 1860.

Health (continued).
Beneficent Visits, 1817.
Bernard, Sir T., Comforts of Old Age, 1818.
Blake's Calendar, 1850.
Boston, Report on, 1848.
Bourdon, Hygiène Pratique, 1844.
Brigham, A., Influence of Mental Cultivation upon, 1832.
British Physician, 1716.
Buchan, Fleecy Hosiery, 1795.
Buffalo, N. Y., Reports, 1854.
Burnett, W., On Chl. of Zinc.
Chadwick, Interment in Towns, 1845.
Chevallier, A., Nettoiement de Paris, 1849.
Chloride of Zinc, 1850.
Churchman, The air we breathe, 1871.
Citizens' Assoc. of N. Y., Rep., 1865.
Clavel, Alm. de la Santé.
Combe, Principles of Physiology applied, 1834. B. C.
" Physiology of Digestion, 1836.
" Physiology and Health.
Cornaro's Guide to Long Life.
" Sure Means of. P. 18, 19.
Cuisine, La, de Santé, 1832.
Curtis, J., Sanitary Obs., 1856.
Cutbush, H. of Soldiers, 1808.
Cutter, Treatise on.
Day, G. E., Diseases of Advanced Life, 1849.
Duchatelet, Hygiène publique, 1836.
Duhring, Art of Living, 1843. B. C.
Easy Way to Prolong Life. P. 47.
Evans, T. W., San. Inst., Austr. Ital. Conflict, 1868.
Exposition de Paris, 1867. Tome 13.
Falconer, W., Diet and Regimen, 1778.
Fowler, O. S., Tight Lacing. P. 292.
France; Bains et Lavoirs, 1850.
Graham, S., Lectures on.
Great Britain, Report on Preserved Meats, 1852.
" Sanit. Commission, 1848.
Griscom, San. Cond. of Labor in N. Y., 1845.
Hall, W. W. Hygiene of the Night, 1870.
" Health and Disease, 1870.
" Coughs and Colds, 1870.
" Health by Good Living, 1870.
Halliday, Mortality in W. Indies.
Hammond, W. A., Treatise on Hygiene, 1863.
Harper, A., Œconomy of Health.
Hassall, Food and its Adulterations, 1851–54.
Hay, Deformity, An essay.

History, Dictionaries of (continued).
Hofmann, Lexicon Univ., 1698.
Ladvocat, Dict. Hist. Portatif, 1755.
La Martinière, Grand Dict. Géog. et Hist., 1739-41.
Luiscius, Alg. Hist. Geog. woordenboek, 1724-27.
Moreri, Grand Dict. Hist., 1701.
Nuttall, Dict. of Nations of Ant., 1840.
See Dictionaries; Encyclopedias; Geog.

History, General. Abrégé de, 1825.
Æneas Silvius, Historia Rerum, 1477.
" Decades Blondi, 1481.
Anquétil, Summary of Univ. Hist., 1805-9.
Art, L', de vérifier les dates, 1783.
Belle-Forest, Hist. Univ. du Monde, 1570.
Becmanus, Hist. Orbis Terrarum, 1865.
Bergomas, J. P., Hist. Omn. Repercussiones, 1506.
Bossuet, Disc. sur l'Hist Univ., 1836.
" Discourse on, 1731.
Bostwick, Lectures, 1838.
Coccius, M. A., Opera, 1538.
Cumberland, Origines gentium.
Ellis, T. F., Outlines of.
Eulogium Historiarum....ad 1366.
Feyjoo, Reflections on.
Goodrich, S. G., Parley's History.
" A Primer of, 1851.
Herbet, Leçons d'Histoire, 1849.
Herrera, Hist. Gen. del Mundo, 1606.
Histoire Universelle, 1747-92.
Hist. Catechism, 1784.
History in all ages, 1839.
Keightley, Outlines of.
Lambert, C. F., Histoire Générale de tous les peuples, 1750.
Lavoisne, Hist. Atlas.
Millot, Elements of, 1779.
Moke, Histoire Universelle.
Müller, J. Von, Univ. Hist., 1831, 2.
Muratori, Diss. Chorographica.
Ogilby, Hist. Collec., Africa, Asia, America, 1670-73.
Parker, R. G., Outlines of, 1848.
Petavius, Hist. of the World, 1659.
Piozzi, H. L., Review of 1800 years, 1801.
Prévost, Revue de l'Hist. Univ., 1854.
Puffendorf, Hist Gén. et Pol., 1743-45.
Raleigh, Sir W., Hist. of the World, 1614.
Ramsay, D., Univ. History Americanized, 1819.
Rotteck, Hist. of the World, 1840.
Roubaud, Hist. Gén. de l'Asie, Amér. et Afrique, 1770-75.

History, General (continued).
Salmon, Hedendaegsche Historie, 1729-1742.
Smith, G., Lectures on, 1866.
Taylor, W. C., Manual of ancient and modern.
Tytler, Elements of, 1828. B. C.
Vincentius, Speculum Historiale, 1494.
Vitriaco, Orien. et Occid. Historiæ, 1597.
See Bibliography.

History, Ancient. Bailly, Sur l'ancienne Hist. de l'Asie, 1779. B. C.
Bryant, J., Observations, 1767.
Cappele, De Regibus Pergamenis.
Chronicon Alexandrinum.
Drummond, Sir W., Origines, 1824.
Echard, Roman History, 1724-26.
Fosbroke, Arts of the Romans and Greeks.
Gibbon, History of Roman Empire.
Gillies, History of the World, 1809.
Guillemin, Hist. Ancienne, 1852.
Heeren, Manual of Anc. Hist., 1847.
Labbeus, Nova bibliotheca MSS. librorum, 1657.
Leland, T., Hist. of Philip of Macedon, 1806.
Lenormant, Manual of Oriental history, 1869, 70.
Rawlinson, Four Ancient Monarchies.
" Manual of Anc. Hist., 1869.
Riedel, Algem. geschied....der Oudheid, 1841-52.
Robinson, J., Summary of.
Rollin, History of Egypt, Carth. and Assyr., 1807, B. C.
Schomann, Assemblies of the Athenians, 1838.
Simson, Chronicon....ad A. D. 71.
Stackhouse, History of the Bible.
Volney, Recherches nouvelles, 1822.
See Antiquities; Man; Prehistoric.

History, Modern and Miscellaneous.
Arnold, T., Lect. on Mod., 1843.
Bav. Acad. of Sci., Mem., 1838-66.
Bigland, Letters on Modern.
Colvin, Historical Letters, 1821.
Ewald, Last Century of, 1868.
Gage, Modern Hist. Atlas.
Goodrich, Second book of.
Hist. Register, 1714-38.
Hübner, Kouranten Tolk, 1748. B. C.
James, G. P. R., Dark Scenes of.
Koch-Sternfeld, Betrachtungen, 1841.
Kœppen, A. L., World in the Middle Ages, 1854.
Le Sur, Annuaire historique, 1818-24.
Lieber, Great Events Described, 1847.

Hohenlohe, Prince. Badely, Extraordinary Cure by. Pamp'r 22.

Holberg, L. Autobiography, 1827.

Holcroft, T. Memoirs: Hazlitt, 1852.

Holden, Ms. Damon, History of.

Holland. *See* Netherlands.

Holland Lodge. Balestier, History of, 1862.

Holland Purchase. Turner, O., Pioneer Hist. of, 1849.
Erie Co. N. Y., Conv. on Holland Land Comp., 1830.

Holley, Horace. Caldwell, C., Discourse on, 1828.
Pierpont J., Sermon on, 1827. P. 62.

Holley, M. H. Smith's, G. Address, 1844. P. 504.

Hollis, Denzil, Lord. Memoirs (Masères, Tracts).

Hollis, J. Hunt, J., Sermon on, 1736.

Hollis, T. Memoirs, 1780.
Greenwood, I., Discourse on, 1731.

Holliston, Mass. Biglow's Sherburne.
Morse, A., History of, 1856.
" Geneal. of Holliston.

Holmes, E. Smith, T. M., Discourse on.

Holmfirth. Margoliouth, Sermon, 1850.

Holt. Family Genealogy, 1864, (Durrie).

Holt, J. Croker, T. C., Memoirs of, 1838.

Holyoke, E. A. Brazer, Serm., Fun. of, 1829. P. 214.

Holy Spirit. Ashdowne, Opera. of, 1798.
Brealey, Essay on, 1823.
Dissertation on "Angel," 1752.
Evans, C, Doctrine of.
Faber, G. S., Operations of the H. S.
Gospel, The Power of God, 1845.
Knowles, Answer to Clayton, 1753.
Ludlam, Two Essays, 1788.
" Four Essays, 1797.
Moncrieff, Hebrew Ruach.
Mulock, The Doctrine of, 1841.
S——y, Congrat. Letter, 1739.
Stephens, W., Sermon of, 1717. P. 361.
Waterland, Regeneration, 1829.
See Trinity; Baptismal Regeneration.

Holy Spirit Flower. Harper's Magazine, 1858.

Holy Week. *See* Rome.

Home, D. D. Incidents of my life, 1863.

Homer. Apollonius, Iliadis Metaphr.
" Lexicon Iliadis, 1773.
Benjamin, S. G. W., Choice of **Paris**, (Fiction), 1870.

Homer (continued).
Bonstetten, Voyage sur la Scène de l'Enéide.
Chandler, R., Hist. of Troy.
Damm, Lexicon Etymol.
Flaxman's Compositions.
Hobbes, T., Works, vol. 10, Trans.
Nimrod, (Apperley), 1826.
Oxford Essays, (Gladstone), 1857.
See Greek Authors.

Homer, H. Parr, S., Letter to Combe, 1795.

Homer, N. Y. Benson, G. R., Principles, 1859.
Keep, Narrative of Congreg. Church.

Homestead Bills. Cleveland, Speech on, 1852.
Cochrane, Speech, 1859.
Porter, G., Speech, 1852.
Sutherland J., Speech, 1852.

Homœopathy. Amer. Institute of, 1855, 1859.
Batchelour, F., Treatise on.
Becker, Allopathy and..1848. P. 271.
Blatchford, T. W., Illustrated, 1842.
Canadian Jour. of Homœopathy, 1856.
Chepmell, Domestic Homœop., 1849.
Epps, Constipation.
Forbes, J., Homœopathy and Young physic, 1846.
Geib, An Essay on, 1842.
Gray, J. F., Inaug. add., Hahnemann Acad.
Guidi, Letter on, 1824.
Homœop. Med. Soc. of N. Y., Proc., 1851, 56.
" Transact., 1863-70.
Hom. Oper. Pharmacy. P. 515.
Hom. Med. Coll. of Penn'a, 1849-57.
Hospital System of, London.
Humphreys, L., Materia Medica, 1851.
Lee, E. Animal Mag. and....1835.
Mabey, What is Homœopathy? 1858
Metcalf, J. W., Homœopathy, 1852.
Neidhard, Homœop. Delusions, 1842.
N. Y. Central Dispensary, 1857.
N. Y. City Alms House Dept., Report, 1858.
Pamphlets, vol. 1337.
Provincial Med. and Surg. Ass'n., Lond. 1851.
Quarterly Homœop. Journal, 1849.
Rhode Is. Homœop. Soc. 1850, P. 515.
Rosenstein, J. G., Treatise upon, 1836.
Sharp, W., Tracts on, 1856.
Sherill, Manual for prescribing, 1845.
Vanderburgh, An Appeal for, 1844.
Western Coll. of Hom. Med., 1854, 57.

Horticulture (continued).
Cutbush, Address, Hort. Soc. N. Y., 1831.
Downing, A. J., Treatise on Gardening, 1859.
" Landscape Gardening, 1841.
Duhamel, Culture des arbres, 1760.
Ecoles d'Horticulture, Belgium, 1850.
Essay on design in, 1768.
Felton, English Authors on, 1830.
Fessenden, Kitchen gardener, 1854.
" American gardener, 1858.
Florist, The, and Hort. Jour., 1853, 4.
Garden Companion, 1800.
Gardener's Chronicle, 1846–51.
Gardener's Magazine, 1828.
Greenhouses for the many.
Holley, M., Address, Geneva, 1828.
Hort. Soc. of London, Jour., 1846–50.
" Proceedings, 1838, 41.
Hort. Reg., J. Paxton, Lond., 1832–34.
" Fessenden, 1836–38.
Horticulturist, Downing, Albany, Rochester, 1846–54.
Horticulturist, Phil'a, 1855, 6.
Hosack, D., Inaug. Disc. N. Y. Hort. Soc., 1824.
Hovey, C. M., Fruits of America, 1847–56.
Hughes, W., The Flower Garden, 1683.
Johnson, G. W., Hist. of Engl. Gardening, 1829.
" Dict. of Modern gardening, 1847.
Johnson's, L., Flower gardener, 1854.
Kemp, Laying out a garden, 1858.
Knight, T. A., Hort. Papers, 1841.
Lawson, W., Orchard garden, 1626.
Lee, Z., Hort. Soc. of M'd, 1839.
Leuchars, Construction of hot-houses, 1851.
Lindley, J., Theory and Practice of, 1841, 1855.
Longworth, N., On the Strawberry, 1852.
Loudon, Encyc. of gardening, 1865.
" Cottage gardening, 1830.
Magazine of Hort. (Hovey), 1835–58.
Maling, In-door plants, 1861.
Marshall, C., Gardening, 1799.
Mass. Hort. Soc. Reports, etc., 1829, 30, 1839–48, 1861–66.
Miller, Dict. des Jardiniers, 1786.
Morren, Hort. de Belgique, 1851.
New Haven Co. Hort. Soc., 1847.
Pamphlets, vol. 69, 505, 1686.
" vol. 949, Addresses on.
Paxton, J., Mag. of Botany, 1839–49.
" Cottager's calendar.

Horticulture (continued).
Poiteau, Cours d'Hort., 1848.
Poynter, Cottage garden.
Ragonot, Alm. du Jardinage, 1855.
Revue Horticole, 1841–53.
Roessle, T., On Celery, 1860.
Sheppard, W. P., Hand-book, 1860.
Soc. Cen. d'Hortic., 1847–51, 55.
Vermont Hort. Soc. proceedings, 1850.
Watelet, Essai sur les jardins, 1764.
Wilkinson, Geometric gardens.
Wisconsin Fruit Growers' Ass'n, 1855.
See Agriculture; Fruits; Bibliography; Guano.

Horticulture, Catalogues. Booth, W., Cat., Balti., 1810.
Breck, Cat. of Dahlias, etc., 1845.
Crosman, Garden Seeds. P. 222.
Ellwanger & Barry, Trees, etc., 1850–55. P. 222.
Frost & Co., 1854.
Hooker, H. E. & Co., 1856. P. 505.
Manley & Br., Buffalo, 1853. P. 505.
Pamphlets, vol. 1218.
Parsons & Co., Flushing, 1845. P. 261.
Prince's Catalogue, 1823, 42–57.
Thompson, W., Flower Seeds, 1857.
Thorburn & Son, Cat., 1822.
Thorp & Co., Syracuse, 1858. P. 505.
Vibert, Rosiers et Vignes, 1847.
Watson's, B. M., Plymouth, Mass.
Wilson, J., Albany, 1857.

Hospitals. Albany Hospital, By-laws, 1852; Reports, 1857–67.
Barton, W., Marine Hosp., 1814.
Boston City Hosp., Rep., 1860–68, 70
Boston Free Hospital, 1861.
Brooklyn City, 1858.
Buffalo Gen. Hospital. P. 506.
Cabanis, De la médecine.
Christ Church H., Phil'a, 1856.
Cincinnati Township, 1851.
City of London Lying in Hospital.
Columbia Hosp., for women, 1866.
Coxe, W., In Russia, Sweden, Denmark, 1781. P. 403.
Dalton, J., Sermon, 1745, 1751.
Hallifax, J., Sermon, Lying in, 1755.
Hammond, W. A., Hygiene in military service.
Hayter, T., Sermon, 1759.
Herne, Domus Carthusiana, 1677.
Herring, Serm., Lond. Infirmary, 1747.
Hospital, P. E., Ch., Phil'a., 1858.
Madan, M., Sermon, 1764.
Maddox, Serm., Lond. Infirmary, 1743.
Malin, Of Penn'a Hospital, 1832.
Mass. Hospital, Rainsford, P. 243.

Hydrodynamics: Hydraulics, Hydrostatics (continued).
Hughes, Drainage of low lands.
" Hydraulic works of Holland, 1843. P. 36. B. C.
Jamieson, A., Mechanics of fluids, 1837.
Lacroix, Mech. of floating bodies, 1775.
Lardner, Treatise on hydrostatics.
Milligan, Hydraulics. Lib. U. K.
Mitchell, Penetrativeness of fluids.
Morin, Roues hydrauliques, 1836.
Pellizer, Syphon pump, 1790.
Phear, Elem. hydros., 1866
Prony, Archit. hydraulique, 1790, 96.
Rochester water owners, Memorials, 1846, 52, 53.
Russell, On waves, (Brit. Ass'n, 14th meet.).
Smith, B., Italian Irrigation, 1855.
Vacani, Della laguna di Venezia.
See Engineering; Canals; Croton Aqu.; Cements; Nat. Philosophy; Water for cities.

Hydrometers. Gilpin, G., Tables, 1794.
McCulloh, Sugar and Hydrom., 1848, 51.

Hydropathy. *See* Water Cure.

Hydrophobia. Blatchford, T. W., Origin, etc., 1856.
Chapman, N., Canine fever, 1801.
Thacher, J., Observations on, 1812.

Hydrostatics. *See* Hydrodynamics.

Hygrometer. *See* Meteorology.

Hymns and Psalms. Advent Harp, 1849.
Allen, W., Ps. and Hymns, 1835.
Am. S. S. Union, Hymns.
Ballou, Universalist Coll.
Baptist Hymn and Tune book, 1858.
Barlow, Dr. Watts' imitation of, corrected, 1786.
Barnard, J., New version of, 1752.
Bay Psalm book of 1640: repr., 1862.
Benedict, E. C., Mediæval hymns, 1867.
Berridge, Sion's Songs, 1785.
Bickersteth, E., Christ. Psalmody.
Brady, N., New version, 1755.
Brady & Tate, Psalms, Boston, 1770.
Catholic Hymns, Albany, 1860.
Cennick, Sacred Hymns, 1763.
Church of Scotland Psalms, 1815.
Church Psalmody, (Mason's), 1833.
Church Psalmist, 1845.
Cottle, J., New version, 1801.
Dickinson, W., Hymns, Passion week, 1846. Ps. v. 2.
Dwight, T., 181.

Hymns and Psalms (continued).
Erskine, Gospel Sonnets, 1798.
Esher Church Hymns.
Fawcett, Hymns, 1782.
Fitz, Amer. School H. Book.
Gibbons, T., Hymns, 1769.
Greenwood, F. W. P., Coll. of Psalms and Hymns, 1830. B. C.
Hamburgisches Gesangbuch, 1855.
Harris, T. M., For Lord's Supper, 1821.
Hastings, T., Spiritual Songs, 1836.
Hawaiian Is., Mission Hymns, 1834.
Hazen, Chris. Psalms and Hymns, 1849.
Hillman, The Revivalist, 1869.
Hymni ecclesiæ, E. Brev. Rom. et Par., 1865.
Hymns for the Army, 1862.
Hymns in Armeno-Turkish, 1850.
Jones, A., Melodies, 1832.
Kennett, B., Paraphrase of, 1706.
Langley, Sacred Hymns, 1776.
Löv, Geistelyke Gesangen, 1756.
Maltby, E., Psalms and Hymns, 1815.
Marburger Gesangbuch, Sauer, 1759.
Mather, C., Psalterium Americanum, 1718.
Medley, S., Hymns, 1800.
Merrick, J., Vers. of Ps., 1791.
Miller, E., Psalms, 1825. Ps. v. 3.
Milman, H. H., Selection, 1837. Ps. v. 3.
Mutter, G., Psalms, 1829. Ps. v. 3.
Needham, J., H. Devotional, 1768.
Nettleton, Village Hymns, 1824.
New England Psalm book, 1773.
Palmer, R., Book of Praise, 1864.
Parker Society: Devotional poetry, 1585.
Parkinson, A Selection, 1809.
Peabody, Springfield collection, 1835.
Pilsbury, A., Sacred Songster, 1825.
Prichard, R., Bedydd, 1848.
Prime, N. S., Collection, 1809.
Prot. Epis. Ch. Coll., 1827.
Psalms and Hymns, (collected in three vols.): Newington, 1817; Lond., 1813; Oundle, 1834;—for chanting: Lond., 1840; Lond. Miss. Soc., 1814; Islington, 1830; Isle of Wight, 1844, etc.
Psalms and Hymns: Boston, 1737.
Recueil de Psaumes, 1815.
Reformed (P. Dutch) Church version, 1769–91, 1814, 39.
Revival Melodies, Bost., 1843.
Relly, Christian Hymns, 1776.
Rippon's Selection.
Robert's Clavis Bib., 1665.
Sacred Songs, Am. Tr. Society.
Schaff, Hymns of all Ages, 1869.

Illinois (continued).
Illinois Directory, 1854.
Illinois in 1837.
Illinois Volunteers, 1846.
Jones, A. D., Illinois and the West.
Keokuk Directory.
Peck, J. M., Gazetteer of, 1834.
" Guide to, 1831, 37.
Reynolds, J., Pioneer Hist. of, 1852.
Rock River Country. P. 565.
Shepard, C. U., Geology of.
Welby, Visit to N. America, 1821.
Woods, J., Resid. at English prairie, 1822.
See Alton; Chicago; Joliet; Keokuk; Monticello; Ogle Co.; Randolph Co.; Rock Island; Wabash.

Illinois College. Catalogues, 1864, 7.
Hist. Sketch of, 1832.
Quarter Cent. Celeb., 1855.

Illinois Indust. University. Reports, 1868-70.

Illuminated Books and MSS. Dibdin, Bibliog. Decameron.
Humphreys, Art of Illumination.
" Books of the Middle Ages.
Jones, 1001 Initial Letters.
Silvestre, Universal Palæography.
Waagen, Treasures of Art, 1854.
Wright, T., Archæological Album, 1845.
See Manuscripts; Writing.

Immigration. *See* Emigration.

Immortality. *See* Future State; Soul.

Impey, Sir E. India, Min. of Council, 1781.

Impostures. *See* Delusions; Magic; Superstitions.

Impressment. Butler, C., Legality of. Pamph'r v. 23.
Essay on the pernicious practice of.
Impressments unlawful. Pam. 66.
Right and practice of. Pamphr. 14.
Taggart, S., Addresses, 1813.
Urquhart, T., Letter, 1816.

Imprisonment for Debt. *See* Prisons; Debt.

Income Tax. *See* Taxation.

Incunabula. *See* Bibliography.

Independents. *See* Congregationalists.

India, History, etc. Allen, D. O., India, Anc and Mod., 1856.
Anglo-Ind. Almanac, 1845.
Arthus, Hist. Indiæ, 1608.
Asiat. Soc. of Bengal, Bibliot. Indica, 35 Vols.

India, History, etc. (continued).
Bengal Directory, 1823.
Bird, J., Researches on the Buddha and Jaina religions, 1847.
British India Society, 1839.
Buist, Annals for 1848.
Castagneda, Histoire de l', 1553.
Chapman, J., Cotton and Comm. of, 1851.
Coorg and its Rajahs, 1857. P. 773.
Coppier, Hist. et Voy. des, 1645.
Cunningham, Buddhist Monuments, 1854.
Despatches....on the Sutlej, 1846.
Dirom, Campaign in, to 1792.
Dow, A., History of Hindostan, 1812.
Dufrène, De la Comp. des Indes, 1738.
East India Co., Nabob of Arcot, 1785.
East India Register, 1835-54.
Edinb. Cab. Lib., vol. 6, 8: Hist. accounts of.
Elphinstone, History of, 1841.
Elliot, Bibl. index to historians of.
Erskine, W., History of, 1854.
Garcilasso, Guerres des Espagnols dans, 1658.
Garcin de Tassy, Littérature Hindoui.
Great Britain: East India, 1783, 5.
" Parl. Pap., 1857.
Guyon, History of the East Indies, 1757.
Hist. Nat. y moral de las Indias. *Span., Eng. and Fr.*
History....Campaign on the Sutlej, 1846.
Holwell, Bengal and Hindostan, 1766.
Illustrations of the Thugs, 1837.
Indian Territories, Notes, 1852.
Inquiry on policy of conquests in, 1789.
Jefferys, S., Seat of War, 1754.
Kerr, Voy., vol. 2, Portuguese Discov.
Langlès, Fables Indiens.
Letter from an Officer, 1810.
Lutfullah's Autobiography, 1857.
Maffei, Historiarum Indicarum lib. 16, 1614.
Major, R. H., I. in the 15th Century, 1857.
Martin, R. M., Brit. Col. Lib., v. 10.
" History of Eastern India, 1838.
Martineau, Brit. rule in, 1857.
Maurice, T., Antiquities of Indostan, 1800-06.
" Hist. of Hindostan, Anc., 1795.
" Modern Hist. of Hindostan. 1802, 08.
Mill, J., History of, 1826.
Murray, H., Hist. and descr. acct. of.

India, History, etc. (continued).
Narrative.. Conquest of Mysóre.
Oakes, Tippoo's Prisoners, 1785.
Origin of the Pindaries, 1818.
Orme, R., Hist. Fragments of the Mogul Empire, 1805.
Oudo Gov't vindicated, 1857. P. 1312.
Palladius, De gentibus Indiæ.
Pococke, E., India in Greece, 1856.
Pownall, T., Duty of Government, 1781.
Raynal, Hist. of Trade in, 1777.
Reid, Chronol. Tables, 1835.
Retrospective View, 1783.
Ricards, Condition of, 1828.
Robertson, W., Histor. Disquisition, 1812.
Rumbold's Vindication, 1868.
Sleeman, Hist. of the Thugs.
Stanhope, P. D., Memoirs of Asiaticus, 1785. P. 432.
Symonds, Geog. and Hist. of, 1845.
Taylor, W. C., Anc. and Mod. India, 1851.
Tod, Annals of Rajasthan, 1829, 32.
War in India, 1845.
Welsh. Military Reminiscences, 1830.
Westmacott, G. E., Russian intrigue, 1838.
Wilson, H. H., History of, 1805–35.
Wytfliet, Hist. Universelle, 1611.
See Hindoos; Commerce; Pondichery.

India, Rebellion of 1857. Chettle, Indian Mutiny.
Duff, Indian Rebellion.
Frost, T., Narrative of, 1857.
Gardiner, G., Causes of Rebellion, 1858.
Kaye, Hist. of the Sepoy War, 1870.
Lay thoughts, 1858.
Mutiny in, 1857.
Mutiny of Bengal Army.
Narrative of....Bolarum, 1857.
Revolt of the Sepoys, 1858.
Richard, H., Future of, 1858.
Trevelyan, Cawnpore, 1865.
Wilson, J. L., The Great Revolt, 1857.
See Havelock.

India, Travels in, etc. Acland, A popular account of, 1847.
Badger, Education in, 1858.
Barbosa, O., On the East Indies, 1606.
Barr, W., Travels to Cabul and the Punjab, 1844.
Bontekoe, Journal van Ost-Indische Reize, 1618.
Broecke, Reysen, 1634.
Broughton, Customs of the Mahrattas.
Burges, B., Indostan letters, 1790.

India, Travels in, etc. (continued).
Burnes, J., Court of Sinde, 1831.
Chardin, Travels, 1686.
Considerations on Christianity in, 1808.
Coryat, Journey to Hindostan, 1824.
Cubero, Peregrinacion, 1688.
Dellon, Voyage, 1699.
Dubois, Desc. of the people of, 1818.
Fitch, R., Voy. to Ormus and E. Ind.
Forbes, Oriental memoirs, 1834.
Fraser, J. B., Himala mountains and sources of the Ganges, 1820.
Gama, V. de, First Voyage to.
Garcin de Tassy, Musulmanes de l'Inde.
Gerard, Koonawur in the Himalaya, 1841.
Godman, Coates' Voyage to India, 1833.
Groot, Reis in Nederl. Indie door Prins Willem, 1837.
Hamilton, F. B., Journey from Madras, 1800–03.
Harlan, Memoir of India and Avghaunistan, 1842.
Heber, R., Jour. in upper provinces of, 1828.
Herklots, Customs of Mussulmans of.
Hoffmeister, Contin. India and Nepal, 1848.
Hügel, Travels in N. W. India.
India, Pictorial, descriptive, 1854.
Jacquemont, Letters from, 1834.
Kaye, Corresp. of Metcalfe, 1854.
Kelly, Indo-Europ. tradition.
Lancaster, Sir J., First Voy. to.
Le Gentil, Voyage, 1761, 69.
Letter to a Friend....on Christianity in India, 1812.
Life in India, 1829.
Linschoten, Nav. in Lusitanor. Indiam, 1599.
" Voy. to, and West Indies, 1598.
Lloyd, Cawnpore to the Himalaya,
Lowrie, Two years in Upper, 1850.
Mackenzie, Mrs., Six years in, 1853.
Malcolm, Sir J., Memoir of Central, 1832.
Moorcroft, Travels in Himalayan Prov., 1841.
Mundy, Pen and Pencil sketches in, 1833.
Murray's Hand-book of.
Nieuhof, Zee-en lant reize, 1682.
Nieuhoff, Travels in, (Pinkerton, 7,14).
Oliphant, Journey to Nepaul, 1852.
Oriental Annual, 1834.
Orlich, Travels in India, Sinde and Punjaub, 1845.

Indians, American (continued).

Bowles, Ambassador of Cherokees to London, 1791.

Bradford, A. W., Origin and hist. of, 1841.

Brainerd, D., Journal among, 1748.

Brett, W. H., Indians of Guiana, 1852.

Brinton, Myths of the new World, 1868.

Bromley, Appeal for, 1820.

Brownell, C., Indian Races, 1854.

Buchanan, J., Hist. Man. and cust. of, 1824.

Bulkley's Pref. on rights of, to Wolcott's Poems, 1725.

Burder, Welsh Indians, 1797.

Case of the Seneca Indians, 1840.

Cass, L., Exam. of Ind. question, 1832.

Catlin, Notes on N. A. Ind., 1841.

" N. A. Indian Portfolio, 1845.

" Cat. of Portraits of, 1837.

" Mandan customs, 1867.

Church, Hist. of Philip's war, 1675, 76.

Clark, J. V. H., Lights and Lines of Character, 1854.

" Hiawatha Legend, 1856.

Clinton, D. W., Disc. N. Y. Indians.

Colden, C., Five Indian Nations, 1747, 1750, 55.

Colton, Tour of the Lakes, 1833.

Commuck, Indian Melodies.

Copway, G., Life, by himself, 1847.

" Sketches of the Ojibways, 1850.

Crawford, Descended from the ten tribes.

Cremony, Life with the Apaches, 1868.

Cusick, D., Hist. of the Six Nations, 1848.

De Forest, Indians of Conn., to 1850.

De Puy, H. W., Mishaps of an Indian agent, 1863. P. 1341.

Documents, Abor. Protec. Soc., 1829.

Drake, B., Life of Black Hawk, 1850.

Drake, S. G., Biog. and Hist. of, 1845.

" Catalogue of his library, 1845.

" Tragedies of the Wilderness, 1846.

" Old Indian Chronicle, 1836.

Eastman, Am. Aborig. Portfolio, 1854.

" Dahcotah legends, 1849.

Easton, King Philip's War, 1675, 76.

Edmonds, J. W., Claims of Potawatomies, 1837. P. 508.

Eliot, J., Brief narrative, 1670.

Enquiry into.... Delaware and Shawanese, 1769.

Events in Indian Hist. with Biog., 1812.

Ewbank, Remains in S. Amer., 1843.

Falconer, R., Voyages, 1764.

Fisher, W., Trav. among, from Lewis and Clark, 1812.

Indians, American (continued).

Flint, T., Indian Wars of the West, 1833.

Friends, Comm. on Civilization of, 1838.

Frisbie, Journal of Mission to, 1775.

Gale, G., Tribes of Upper Mississippi, 1867.

Gallatin, Indians of Mexico, etc.

" Synopsis of Tribes.

Garcia, Origen de los Indios del Nuevo Mondo, 1729.

Geddes, G., Onondaga Co. Indians, 1860.

Georgia, Controv. with Creeks, 1827.

Gookin, Indians of N. Engl., 1674.

" Doings and sufferings of New Eng. Indians, Am. Ant. Soc.

Halkett, Hist. Notes respecting, 1825.

Hall, J., Wilderness and War-path, 1846.

Hanson, Elizabeth, Captivity, 1782.

Hanson, J. W., Sketch of the Abnaquis, 1849.

Harrison, W. H., Aborigines of Ohio valley, 1838.

Hayes, D., Captivity by, 1707.

Heard's Sioux War, 1862.

Heckewelder, Morav. Mission among, 1820.

Henry, A., Travels....in the Indian Territories, 1760–76.

Hinman, Journal with the Sioux, 1869.

Hist. of Morav. Missions to.

Hopkins, S., Housatunnuk Ind., 1753.

Hough, F. B., Ind. Antiquities.

" Visit to St. Regis Ind., 1852.

Hoyt, Indian wars on the Connecticut, 1824.

Hubbard, W., Indian wars, 1609–77.

Hunter, J. D., Indians west of Mississippi, 1823.

Indian Advocate, 1846. P. 508.

Indian Board in N. Y. City, 1829.

Indian Narratives, 1854.

Indians, The, or Massacres in Wawasink, 1846.

Inquiries respecting Hist. of. P. 1003.

Iroquois, The, By Minnie Myrtle, 1855.

Irving, J. T., jr., Indian Sketches, 1835.

Jackson, H., Civilization of, 1830.

Jacobs, Nonantum and Natick, 1853.

Jarvis, S. F., Religion of, 1819.

Jogues, Captivity with the Mohawks.

Johnson, Sir W., Conferences with, 1755, 56.

Johnston, C., Capture and Ransom from, 1790.

Jones, C. C., jr., Sketch of Tomo-chichi, 1868.

Jones, J. A., Traditions of, 1830.

Indians, American (continued).
Journal of Sibley's Exped., 1863.
Kip, The Indian Council, 1855.
Kippis, A., Sermon, (Soc. in Scotland), 1777.
Knight and Slover's Narratives, 1782.
Kohl, Wanderings, 1860.
Laet, De, De Origine Gent. Am., 1643.
Lafitau, Mœurs des sauvages, 1724.
Lang, Visit to Tribes of, 1843.
Las Casas, Cruelties of Spaniards.
" Œuvres, vols. 1, 2, 1822.
Latrobe, Missions of Unit. Brethren among, 1815, 16.
Lee, N., Life with the Camanches.
Lefroy, Ind. Pop. of Brit. Amer., 1853. Pam. 508.
L'Estrange, Americans...Jews? 1652.
Lives of Celebrated Indians.
Long, J., Travels of an Indian Interpreter, 1791.
McCoy, Baptist Indian Missions, 1840.
McIntosh, Origin of, 1853.
McKenney, T. L., Tribes of N. A., 1844.
" Memoirs of Travels among, 1846.
Manheim, Captivity, 1794.
Manypenny, Rapport sur les hommes rouges, 1855.
Massachusetts, Instructions, 1762.
Mather, C., India Christiana, 1721.
Mather, I., Early Hist. of N. E., 1677.
" King Philip's War, (Drake's edition).
Maurault, Hist. des Abnaquis, 1866.
Mayer, Logan and Cresap.
Mayhew, Indian converts, 1727.
Megapolensis, J., Korte Antworp, 1651.
Menasseh, Spes Israelis, 1650.
Metcalf, S. L., Narra. of Warfare, 1821.
Milfort, Voy. dans la Nation Crêck, 1802.
Mitchill, S. L., Ethnology of.
Morgan, L. H., League of the Iroquois, 1851.
" Laws of Descent. P. 502.
" Systems of Consanguinity, Smithson. Cont. v, 17.
Morse, J., Rep. on Indian affairs, 1822.
Morton, S. G., Crania Americana, 1839.
" Inq. into Aborig. races, 1842.
Narrative of Seminole campaign, 1819.
New England's First Fruits, Repr.
N. Y., Commissioners, 1784-91. Munsell, Hist. Ser., 9, 10.
Pamphlets on, vols. 508, 1341.
Parkman, F., jr., Hist. of conspir. of Pontiac, 1851, 55.

Indians, American (continued).
Penhallow, Wars of New Eng. with, 1726.
Pidgeon, W., Traditions of De-Coo-Dah.
Plain Facts: Rights of, 1781.
Plummer, C., Capt. by the Camanches.
Riggs, Gospel among Dakotas, 1869.
Rights of the Indians, 1830.
Rowlandson, Mrs., Captivity by, 1676.
Sanders, Hist. of Indian Wars, 1812.
Schoolcraft, H. R., Thirty years residence among, 1812–42.
" Hist. and Statis. information, 6 vols., 1851–57.
" Notes on the Iroquois, 1846–47.
" Algic researches, 1839.
" Oneota, 1844.
" Indian in his wigwam, 1848.
Scouler, Observ. on Tribes of N. W. coast.
Seneca Ind. Controversy, 1840–48.
Seneca Indians, Doc'ts, 1857.
Shea, Hist. Cath. Miss. among, 1829–1854.
Shirley, Gov., Conferences with, 1742.
Smet, Residence among, 1843.
" New Indian sketches, 1863.
" Voyage aux montagnes rocheuses, 1859.
Smith, Col. James, Captivity with, 1755–59, 1831–34.
" Darlington's edit., 1870.
Society for Prop. the Gospel, 1819.
Some Observations on, 1784.
Speeches in Cong. on, 1830.
Squier, Aboriginal Monuments, N. Y.
" Ab. Mon., Mississippi.
Stanley, J. M., Portraits of, 1852.
Stone, W. L., Brant and Redjacket, 1838, 1841.
" Hist. of Wyoming.
" Uncas and Miantonomoh, 1842.
Stratton, Captivity among, 1858.
Strong, N. T., Appeal, 1841.
Swan, J. G., Indians of Washington Terr., (Smithsonian Contr., XVI).
Symmes, Lovewell's fight.
Tanner, J., Narrative of Captivity, 1830.
Treaty with the Creeks, 1790.
Thatcher, B. B., Indian Biog., 1848.
Thomas, W. H., Claims of, 1853.
Thorowgood, T., Jews in America? 1660.
Timberlake's Memoirs, 1762.
Traits of Amer. Indian life, 1853.
Tubbee, Choctaw, Life of.

Ireland, History, etc. (continued).
O'Connell, J., Recollections and Experiences, 1833–48.
" Argument for, 1844.
O'Connor, R., Address to the People, 1799.
O'Curry, MS. materials of anc. history, 1861.
O'Kelly, Familles d'Irlande, 1837.
Prendergast, Cromwellian settlement of, 1870.
Plowden, Hist. Review of the State of, 1805.
Revans, J., Evils, and Remedy. P. 11.
Ryan, Biog. Hibernica, 1822.
Sampson, W., Memoirs, 1807.
Savage, J., '98 and '48, 1856.
Smith, Gold., Ir., History and character, 1862.
Soc. of United Irishmen, 1791–94.
Taafe, Hist. from Engl. invasion, 1811.
Temple, Sir J., Hist. Rebell. in, 1641.
Thompson, R., Stat. Survey Co. of Meath, 1802.
Ticheborne, Siege of Drogheda, 1641.
War of the Gaedhill with the Gaill., (Chron. G. B.).
See Great Britain; England; Dublin.

Ireland: Travels, Descriptions, etc.
Balch, W., Ireland as I saw it, 1850.
Barrow, J., jr., Tour round, 1835.
Bigelow, Rambles in, and North Brit., 1817.
Carr, Sir J., Stranger in, 1805. B. C.
Cloncurry, Lord, Personal Recollections, 1849.
Croker, T. C., Researches south of.
Dewar, Observations on Manners, etc., 1812.
Dubourdieu, Survey of Antrim, 1812.
Forbes, R. B., Voyage of the Jamestown, 1847.
Foster, T. C., Condition of, 1847.
Hall, S. C., Sketches of....Character, 1855.
Heath's Annual, (Ritchie), 1838.
Irish abroad and at home, 1856.
Kennedy, P., Fireside Stories, 1871.
" Legends of the Irish, 1866.
Kohl, Travels in, 1844.
McElheran, Woman among the Celts, 1858.
McGee, Irish Settlers in N. A., 1850.
Maguire, The Irish in America, 1868.
Morgan, Lady S. O., Patriot. Sketches.
My Pocket-book, 1807.
Nicholson, Miss, Ireland's Welcome to the Stranger, 1844, 45.
Phillips, C., Emerald Isle, a poem.
Sketches of, 60 years ago, 1847.

Ireland: Travels, Descriptions, etc. (continued).
Smith, J., Irish diamonds.
Trench, W. S., Realities of Irish life, 1869.
Young, A., Tour in, (Pinkerton, 3).
Visit to Dublin, 1825.
Watkinson, J., Philosoph. survey of, 1777.
See Carrickfergus; Dublin; Londonderry; Meath; Roscommon; Waterford.

Irish Authors. Berkenhout, Biog. Lit., 400–1500.
Dibdin, Typog. antiquities, 1810.
Hiberno-Celtic Soc. Cat. to 1750, 1820.
O'Reilly, Acc't of Irish writers, 1820.
Reuss, Reg. of authors on, 1770–1803.
Ryan, Biog. Hibernica, 1822.

Irish Bible. Brief Sketch of Attempts, 1818. P. 395.
Hibernian Bib. Soc., 1823, 24. P. 467.

Irish Churches. Address to the Protestants of, 1829.
Cator, Letter on Nati'al Church, 1835.
Caulfield, Seals of the churches. P. 1344.
Colquhoun, Of reducing the Estab. Ch., 1836. P. 342.
De Foe, The Parallel, 1704.
Dickson, W., Narr. of Exile of, 1812.
Dublin, Debate, 1792.
Full and true relation, 1679.
Grattan, H., Life and times, 1839.
" Speech on Tithes, 1788.
Gregory XVI ad Epis. Hiberniæ, 1832.
Hales, W., Obs. on Tithes of, 1794.
Historical apology for, 1807.
Incor. Soc. in Dublin, 1735–73. P. 368.
Inquiry into penal laws.
Ireland, E. S., Political State of, 1837.
Ireland; Its Eccl. State, 1844.
Irish Evangel. Soc., 1824. P. 472.
Jebb, J., Irish Tithes, 1824.
Jones, W. T., Letter to Unit. Irishmen, 1792.
King, W., Protestants in, under King James, 1692.
Letter to the Rt. Hon. C. Grant, 1820.
MacDonnell, Principles of R. C. Ch., 1829.
M'Gee, T. D., Prot. reformation in, 1853.
Magee, W., Charge, 1826.
Mant's Hist. of the Church of, 1841.
Marrable, Missions to Catholics, 1852.
Milner, J., Inquiry, 1808.
Notes and Queries, Oct., 1866, on Irish Bishops.
Obs. on the State of, Dubl., 1822.

Italy: History (continued).
Maceroni, Col., Memoirs, 1838.
Machiavelli, Hist. of Florence and, 1847.
" Opere, 1811.
M'Crie, Prot. Reform in, 1855.
Mariotti. *See* Gallenga.
Muratori, Diss. Chorographica.
Mazzini, Royalism and Republicanism in, 1848.
Mussato, Hist. Henrici VII, 1636.
Newspapers of Rome and, 1848, 49.
Ossat, Card. d', Lettres, 1594–1604.
Pacca, Historical Memoirs, 1808–14.
Pamphlets, Italian, vols. 661, 842, 992, 1785.
Pagnoncelli, Gov. Municipali nelle citta.
Pepe, Memoirs, Events of Modern Italy, 1846.
Rome et le congrès, 1860.
Sanfermo, Condotto ministeriale, 1798.
Sismondi, Italian Republics, Lardner, 96.
Soc. of the Friends of, 1852.
Strictures on Ct. Dal. Pozzo, 1834.
Tiraboschi, Letteratura Italiana, 1805–1813.
Urquhart, Life of Sforza.
Volkman, Historie van, en Reisboek door, 1779.
Whiteside, Italy in the 19th Century.
Zeller, Histoire de, 1853.
See Rome; Florence; Naples; Sardinia; Tuscany.

Italy, Travels, Descriptions, etc.
Adalbert, Tr. in South of Europe, 1849.
Addison, J., Remarks on various Parts of, 1701, 2, 3.
Bakewell, R., Travels in the Tarentine, etc., 1820–22.
Beckford, W., Italy, with Spain and Portugal, 1835.
Berrian, W., Travels in.
Bremer, Life in the old world, 1860.
Butler, F. A. K., Year of consolation, 1847.
Chateaubriand, Voyage en, (Œuvres).
" Recollections of, 1816.
Ciceri, Portefeuille de.
Cooper, J. F., Excursions in, 1836.
Coste, Voyage....sur le littoral, 1855.
Dickens, C., Pictures from.
Eustace, Classical Tour through, 1821.
Ferber, Travels through in 1771, 72.
Ferrario, Costume, 1833.
Forbes, Four lectures, 1851.
Forsyth, J., Excursion in, 1802, 3.
Headley, J. T., Italy and the Italians, 1844. P. 43. B. C.

Italy, Travels, etc. (continued).
Hillard, Six months in, 1854.
Heare, Classical Tour, 1819.
Honan, Adven. of Correspond't, 1852.
Howells, Italian Journeys, 1867.
Jameson, Mrs., Diary of an ennuyée.
Jarves, J. J., Italian Sights, 1856.
Landscape Annual, Roscoe, 1832.
Laurent, Classical tour, 1822.
Letters from, 1770, 71.
Letters from North of, (W. H. Rose), 1819.
Lowell, J. R., Fireside travels, 1864.
Mahoney, Six years in the Monasteries, 1844. B. C.
Mendelssohn, Letters from, 1863.
Montfaucon, Travels, 1712.
Moore, J., Soc. and Manners in, 1820.
Morgan, Lady, Italy, Travels, 1821.
Murray, Hand-book of Northern I.
" Hand-book of Central I.
Peale, Notes on, a Tour, 1829, 30.
Raumer, F. von, Italy and the Italians, 1840.
St. John, B., Subalpine Kingdom, 1856.
Sansom, Letters during a tour, 1801–2.
Sardinia, Calendario, 1833, 34.
Spalding, W., Italy and the Italian Islands.
Turnbull, The Genius of Italy, 1849.
Tuscany, Almanac, 1846.
Valéry, Voy. Hist. et litt., 1826–28.
See Language; Literature; Bibliography.

Ithaca, N. Y. Cornell Uuiversity, Catalogues and Reports to 1871.
Goodwin, H. C., Ithaca as it is and was, 1853.
Ithaca, Views of its Environs, 1835.
King, H., Early History of, 1847.

Iturbide, A. Mémoires, (Quin).
Autobiography, (in Pamphleteer).
Beneski, Narr. of death of.
Gilliam, Tr. in Mexico; Life of, 1843, 1844.

Ives, L. S. Trials of a Mind, 1854.
Exam. of Doctrine of, 1849. P. 200.
Jay, W., Letter to, 1848.

Izard, R. Letters, 1774–1804.

J.

Jackson, A. Aristides, Invasion of Florida, 1827. P. 50.
Black, J., Eulogy on, 1845. P. 268.
Butler, W. O., Speech, his fine, 1843.
Cobbett, Life of.
Dusenbery, Twenty-five Eul. on, 1846.
Eaton, J. H., Life of, 1824.

Jesuits (continued).
Great Britain, Parl., 1663.
Hints to Protestants, 1826.
Jesuites, Les, dans l'Anc. et Nouveau Monde, 1759.
Jezuiten, De, de Troon der Nederlanden, 1841. P. 33. B. C.
Jouvancy, Epit. Historiæ Soc. J.
Kostka's Life.
La Martélière, Argum. against Jesuits.
Lockman, J., Travels of, 1743.
Mercure. Le, François, 1605–44.
Michelet, The Jesuits, 1845. B. C.
Michelsen, Modern Jesuitism, 1855.
Nicolini, History of, 1854.
Norbert, Mémoires Historiques, 1766.
Oates, T., Exact discovery, 1679.
Orleans, W., Travels.
Padilla, Hist. de Santiago de Mexico, 1625.
Palafox, Vie de, 1690.
Pamphleteer, vol. 9: Account of.
Pascal, Les Provinciales, 1823.
" Provincial Letters, 1828. B. C.
Procès contre, 1750. B. C.
Relation abrégée, 1758.
Rivet, A., Jesuita vapulans, 1635.
Secreta Monita, 1831.
Seymour, M. H., Mornings among, 1849.
Steinmetz, History of, 1848.
Taylor, Isaac, Loyola and the J., 1857.
Xavier, F., Novena, 1850.
See Ignatius; Roman C. Ch.

Jesuit Missions. Acosta, E., Rerum Gestarum in Oriente, ad 1568.
Assoc. de la Prop. de la Foi, Annales, 1828–52.
Avisi dall Indie Portogallo, 1558.
Epistolæ Indicæ, 1566.
" Japanicæ, 1570.
Histoire....de la Chine, 1624; Tibet, 1626.
" d'Ethiopie, 1824–26.
Lettres Edifiantes, 1717–76.
Lettres Nouvelles de la Chine et des Indes, 1818–23.
Litteræ Annuæ, 1584–1654.
" Japonenses, 1591–92.
" In Regno Sinæ, 1610, 11.
" In Prov. Peruana, 1604.
Ljungstedt, Roman Catholics in China, 1836.
Magistris, H. de, Relation de Maduré, Tanjeor, 1663.
Mémoires des Miss. dans le Levant, 1753.
Mercure, Le, François, 1605-44.
Muratori, Missions du Paraguay, 1754.

Jesuit Missions (continued).
Nouvelles des Missions, Amérique, 1827.
Murr, Reisen einiger Miss. in Amer., 1785.
Pelleprat, Miss. dans l'Amér. mérid., 1655.
Relation abrégée, 1758.
Stocklein, Brief Schriften von denen Miss., 1642-1731.
Tanner, M., Vita et Mors eorum, 1675.
Travels of several Learned Miss., 1714.
See Missions, Rom. Cath. Church.

Jesuit Missions; North America.
Biard, P., Relation 1616, Repr., 1872.
Bigot, J., 1684, 85.
Bigot, V., 1701.
Bressany, Rel. de quelques Missions, 1852.
Chaumonot, Vie de, 1688.
Copie de deux Lettres, 1656.
D'Ablon, Relations, 1670–79.
Dreuillette, Narré du Voy., 1650, 51.
Gravier, J., Relation, 1694, 1700.
Kip, W. I., Early Jesuit Missions in N. A., 1846.
Lalemant, Relation, 1545–48; 1662–64.
" 1659. *See* Copie de.
Le Jeune, 1634, 1635, 1656, 57, 1660, 1661.
Le Mercier, Relation, 1637, 38, 1653, 1654, 1664–65.
" 1665. *See* Copie de.
Marquette, Recit, 1673–75.
Mercure François, 1605–44.
Milet, Relation, 1690-1.
Mission du Canada, Relations, 1672–79.
Montigny, Miss. du Missisipi, 1700.
O'Callaghan, Relations des Jesuites, 1850.
Parkman, F., J. in N. America, 1867.
Ragueneau, Relation, 1649–51.
Relation, 1657–60.
Relation, 1676, 77. *See* Copie de.
Relation, 1676, 77. MS.
Relations des Jésuites, 1611–72, Montreal, 3 vols., 8°.
Relations, 1696–1702.
St. Vallier, Estat de la Nouvelle France, 1856.
Vimont, Relation, 1642–43, 1644, 45.

Jesus. *See* Christ.

Jewel, Bp. J. Letters, Parker Soc.

Jews. Adams, H., Hist. of, 1812.
Amer. Society for, 1818–47.
" Jewish Chronicle, 1845–7.
Ancient Hist. of, 1741.
Andrews, W. W., Heb. commonwealth, 1841.

Jews (continued).

Archives Israelites, 1853.

Berruyer, Histoire du peuple de Dieu, 1738.

Boon, C., Hist. ab exsilio Babylonico, 1834.

Boudinot, Star in the West, 1816.

British Society for, Report, 1843.

Brown, W., Antiquities of, 1826.

Burns, R., N. Y. Jewish Society arraigned, 1853.

Buxtorf, Operis Talmudici Recensio, 1616.

Christian, Cry from Turkey, 1854.

Clayton, R., Restoration of, 1751.

Cockayne, Civil History of, to Hadrian. 1841.

Collyer, W. B., Aspect of prophecy, 1829.

Creighton, J., Origin of Religion, 1803.

Cunæus, Republica Hebræorum.

Da Costa, History of, 1855.

D'Israeli, Genius of Judaism, 1833.

Drummond, W., Œdipus Judaicus, 1811.

Dusselthal Abbey Asylum.

Epistola ad Phil-Hebræos, 1743.

Essai sur Surinam: Colonie Juive, 1788.

Faudel, On Jewish Disabilities, 1848.

Faussett, Jew. Hist. Vindicated, 1830.

Female Soc. Boston for, 1818, 19.

Franck, A., La Kabbale, 1843.

Frey, J. S. C. F., Narrative, 1813.

" Converted Jews, 1847.

Further Considerations, 1753.

Galatinus, De Arcanis Cath. Veritatis, etc., 1550.

" Reuchlin, De Arte Cabalistica.

Gale, T., Court of the Gentiles, 1672.

Gawler, Emancipation of, 1847.

Goldsmid, Disabilities of, 1848.

Grant, A., The Nestorians or Lost Tribes, 1841.

" Les Nestoriens.

Hanway, J., Naturalization of, 1753.

Harby, Misc. writings, Charleston, S. C., 1829.

Hebrew Dedication, Phil'a. 1843.

Hebrew Y M. Lit. Ass'n, N. Y., 1852.

Herschfeld, P., Strictures, 1833.

History of, (Brownlee), 1842.

Hist. of the Hebrew Monarchy, (Newman), 1847.

Hoffman, D., Chronicles of Cartaphilus, 1853.

Isaacs, H., Ceremonies of, Lond.

Jahn, Biblical archæology.

" Hist. of the Hebrew Commonwealth, 1828.

Jews (continued).

Jarvis, S. F., Church of the Redeemed, 1850.

Jennings, D., Jewish Antiquities, 1837.

Jewish Admiss. in Parl., 1849. P. 321.

Jewish Chronicle, 1845-47.

Jews' Hospital, N. Y., 1865, 6.

Jones, C., Restoration of, 1855.

Josephus, F., Opera, Lat. and Eng., 1726, 1839.

London Society, Report, 1816. P. 321, 1859.

Longley, Serm. Epis. Jews' Chapel, 1841. P. 321.

Lyons, Jewish Calendar, 5164-5664.

Maatsch., Tot nut der Israelieten, 1849-54. P. 230.

Madden, F. W., Jewish coinage, 1864.

Magill, Claims of, 1851.

Maitland, S. R., On conversion of, 1828.

Margoliouth, Hist. of Jews in Great Britain, 1851.

" Israel's ordin'ces exam., 1844.

Martineau, Providence manif. through, 1833.

Mendelssohn, Ritual-Gesetze der Juden, 1778.

" Eccl. authority and judaism.

Michaelis, Laws of Moses. Law Lib.

Milman, History of, to the present, 1831. B. C.

Milman's History of: refuted, 1833.

Mt. Sinai Hosp., N. Y., 1867, 69.

Mulder, Orde v. de Feestdagen, 1843.

" Chron. Handboekje, 1846.

Myers, A. M., Jerusalem and the Jews, 1840.

Narr. of Miss. of Inquiry, 1839.

Naturalization of, Pamphlets, vol. 980.

Noah, On Restoration of the Jews, 1845.

" Trans. of Jasher, 1840.

Orobio, Israel avenged, 1839.

Oxford Essays, (Bridges), 1856, 57.

Palm, Van der, Apokryfe Boeken, 1829, 30.

Pamphlets relating to, vols. 321, 980, 981.

Peckard, Clamor agt., indefensible, 1753.

Phenix, The, 1707; Council of Jews in Hungary, 1656.

Prideaux, Old and New Test. Hist. connected, 1799.

Priestley, Comparison of the Institutions of Moses, 1799. B. C.

" Letters to Jews, 1794.

Prot. Epis. Ass'n, 1865.

K.

Kansas (continued).
Brewerton, The War in, 1856.
Byers, Gold fields of, 1859.
Emigrant Aid Comp., 1854. P. 565.
Fremont, Explo. on Kanzas River, 1843.
Gihon, Geary and Kansas, 1857.
Gladstone, The Englishman in, 1857.
Guide to the Gold Region, 1859. P. 610.
Hale, E. E., Kanzas and Neb., 1854.
Higginson, T. W., A ride through, 1856.
Hyatt's Appeal, 1860.
Kansas, Governors' Messages, 1861–68.
" Census, 1865. P. 1690.
" Memorial of Legis., 1856.
Kansas Aid Societies. P. 227.
Kansas and the Const., Cecil, 1856.
Kansas Border Ruffian Code. P. 537.
Kansas Democ. Conv. Address, 1857.
Kansas Herald of Freedom, 1855, 6.
Kansas State Rights, 1857. P. 560.
Kansas struggle of 1856 P. 259.
New Eng. Em. Aid Soc., 1857. P. 565.
Pacific Railroad Reports, 1853.
Pamphlets relating to, vols. 560, 561, 1690.
Parkman, F., The California Trail, 1849.
Phillips, W., Conquest of, 1856.
Redpath, Guide to, 1857.
Robinson, S., Kansas history, 1856.
Sage, R. B., Wild Scenes in, 1855.
Six Months in, 1856.
Three Years in, 1856.
U. S., Douglas' Reports, 1856.
" Investigation on Troubles, 1856.
" Indemnities for, 1855–6.
Walter, G., History of, 1854.
See United States, West.

Kansas, Debates on Affairs in. Bell, J., Speech, 1854, 58.
Benjamin, J. P., Speech, 1856.
Breckinridge, Speech, 1854.
Brown, G. M., Remarks, 1857.
Carpenter, D., Speech on, 1854.
Colfax, Speech, 1856.
Collamer, Speech, 1856.
Crittenden, Speech on, 1858.
Cullom, Speech on, 1854.
Dawes, H. L., Speech, 1858.
Diven, Speech on, 1858.
Dodge, A. C., Speech on, 1854.
Doolittle, Speech, 1858.
Douglas, S. A., Speeches, 1853, 56, 58.
English, W. H., Speech on, 1854.
Everett E., Speech on, 1854.
Farley, E. W., Speech on, 1854.
Green, J. S., Speech, 1858.
Hale, J. P., Speech on, 1856.

Kansas, Debates on Affairs in (continued).
Haskin, J. B., Speech, 1858.
Hatch, I. T., Speech, 1858.
Haven, S. G., Remarks, 1856.
Hughes, J., Speech, 1858.
Meacham, J., Speech, 1854.
Peckham, R. W., Speech, 1854.
Richardson, J. W., Speech, 1858.
Sage, R., Speech, 1856.
Seward, W. H., Speeches, 1854, 56, 58.
Simmons, G. A., Speech, 1854.
Simmons, J. F., Speech, 1858.
Sumner, C., Speech, 1856.
Stephens, A. H., Speech, 1856.
Taylor, J. J., Speech, 1854.
Thompson, J., Speech, 1858.
Walley, S. H., Speech, 1854.

Kars. Sandwith, H., Siege of, 1856.

Kay, J. Sutcliffe, T., Testimonial, 1846.

Kean, E. Life of, 1835.

Kearney, P. De Peyster, Hist. of, .869.

Keats, J. Life of, (Works).
Milnes, R. M., Life of, 1848.

Keble, J. Coleridge, J. T., Memoir of, 1870.
Remarks on tract of.

Keene, H. Dore, J., Sermon on.

Keene, New Hamp. Hale, S., Annals of, 1734–1815

Keeseville, N. Y. Old, The, Settler, 1847–56. Newsp.

Keith, Rev. G. Jour. of travels, 1706.
Prot. Epis. Hist. Soc., 1851.

Keith, Sir R. M. Memoirs and correspondence, (Smyth).

Keith, Tho. Memoir, 1824. P. 390.

Kellogg family meeting, 1858.

Kellogg, O. U. S., Obit. addresses, 1865.

Kelly, M. Reminiscences, 1826.

Kelly, R. Van Winkle, E. S., Tribute to, 1856. P. 80.

Kelly, T. Milne, R., Answer to, 1817.

Kemble, Frances. *See* Butler.

Kemble, J. P. Boaden's Life of.
Covent Garden Journal, 1810.
Rebellion, The..1809.

Kempis, T. à. Cancellieri, Notizie di G. Gersen, 1809.
Navarette, Diss., autore "De Imitat. Christi."

Kenilworth Castle. Laneham, Pageant at.
Nightingale, Account of, 1821.

Lafayette, G. M. (continued).
Lafayette, Life of. Pamph'r v. 26.
" Mémoires Historiques, 1793.
" Memoirs, vol. I, 1837.
" Memoirs, 1837, 3 v.
" Life of, 1837.
Levasseur, Reise durch Amerika, 1825.
" Lafayette in Am.
Mack, E., Life of, 1841.
Sarrans, L. et la révolution de 1830.
" Memoirs of, 1832.
Sprague, W. B., Oration on, 1834.

Lake. *See* Name of the Lake.

Lake Harbors. Graham, J. D., Report on, 1856.
Harbor and River Convention, 1847.
See Harbors.

Lakes. Agassiz, Lake Superior, 1850.
Gilpin, Lakes of Cumberland.
Lumsden, Scotch lakes.

Lally, Count T. A. Memoirs, 1766.

Lamartine, A. De. Les confidences.
" Memoirs of my youth.

Lamb, Charles. Letters and Life, 1837.
" Correspondence, 1868.
Procter, Memoir of, 1866.
Talfourd, T. N., Literary Sketches of, 1848.

Lamb, J. Leake, I. Q., Memoir of, 1850.

Lamb, R. Memoirs of his life, 1811.

La Marne, Fr., 1824. Pam. v. 608.

Lamarque, M. Bonaparte, L., Réponse à.

Lambrechsten, N. C. Citters, Lofrede op, 1824.

La Mennais, F. R. de. Gal. des Contem. vol 1: Vie de, 1845.

La Motte, Countess de. Life of, 1792.

Lanarkshire, Scotl. Cleland, Statistics, 1832.

Lamps. Barrachin, Lampe hydrostatique, 1828. P. 18.

Lancashire, Eng. Beauties of Engl. and Wales.
Cheshire & L., Hist. Collector, 1845.
See Liverpool; Manchester.

Lancaster, Jos. Life of, 1833.
Origin of system of Education of.

Lancaster and York Cos., Penn.
Rupp, Hist. of, 1844, 45.

Lancaster, Ms. Harrington, T., Century Serm., 1753.
Rowlandson, Narr. of captivity in 1676.
Thayer, W., Discourse, 1816.
Willard, J., Histor. address, 1853.

Lancaster, Pa. Evan. Luth. Church in.

Land Companies. Amer. Land Co.
Cabell, West Va., Description of 100,000 acres, 1864.
Canton Comp. of Baltimore.
Illinois Central R. R. Co's Lands, 1855–57.
Iowa Land Co.
McKean & Elk, Pa.
North West. Trans. and Land, 1858.
Pamphlets, vol. 69.
Pine lands of Michigan, 1856.
St. Mary's Falls Ship Canal Co., 1857–63.
Smith, G., Land Auction, N. Y.
See Great Britain, Lands; United States, Lands.

Landes, France. Annuaire, 1826.

Landon, L. E. Works and life.
Blanchard, L., Life of, 1841.

Landon, S. Fifty years in the ministry, 1868.

Landon, W. S. Forster, Biog. of, 1869.

Lands. Bulkley, Prof., On Indian rights. (Wolcott's Poems, 1725).
Greene, I. G. I., Laws relating to, 1851. P. 1548.
Howlett, J., Enclosures, 1787.
Humbert, C. F., Loans on land, 1855.
Karnebeek, De distrib. prædiorum, 1854.
Kent, J. H., Of small farms, 1844.
Letters to an editor, 1866.
Low, D., On landed property, 1856.
New South Wales, Disposal of.
Noakes, Aristocracy's rights, 1847.
Northumberland, Petition, 1831.
Pamphlets relating to, vols. 69, 1691.
Principles of freedom, 1852.
Rainy, A., On real property, 1852.
Savage, H., Canterbury Association, New Zealand.

Land Slides. Dwight, W. B., Paper in Am. J. of Science, 1866.
Perkins, G. H., In New Hampshire. A. J. of Sci., 1870.
Gardner, D., Treatise, Troy, 1837.
Roberts, G., At Lyme Regis.

Land Stewards. Hints on the duties of.

Lane Family. Whitmore, Memoranda, 1857.

Langdale, H. Hardy, T., Memoirs of.

Langdon, J. Memorial, 1870.

Langdon, S. Bradford, E., Strictures on, 1794.

Language and Comparative Philology. Adelung, Mithridates, 1806–17. B. C.

Adler, On W. Humboldt.

Am. Philol. Ass'n, 1871.

Bagster, Bible of every land, 1851.

Ballhorn's Grammatography.

Bilderdijk, Geslachten der Naamwoorden, 1818. B. C.

Bopp, Comparative Grammar.

Brerewood, Inquiry, 1635.

Bunsen, Phil. of Univ. Hist.

Charma, Essai sur, 1846.

Clifford, A., Learning of, 1827.

Court de Gébelin, Monde primitif, 1779.

Des Brosses, C. Formation mécanique, 1765.

De Vere, Outlines of Compar. Philol., 1853.

Doherty, Philos. of lang., 1835.

Dwight, B., Modern Philology, 1860, 64.

Fearn, J., Anti-Tooke, 1824.

Forster, C., The one primeval lang., 1854.

Ghirardini, A., Sulla lingua umana, 1869.

Goropius, Hieroglyphicorum lib. xvi, 1580.

Grimm, Ursprung der Sprache.

Hale, Philol., U. S. Expl. Exped.

Hapgood, G. R., Origin of, 1868.

Harris, Hermes, or Univ. Gramm., 1786.

Harrison, B., Study of, 1832. P. 1241.

Hazard, R. G., Language, 1836.

Herder, J. G., Origin of, 1827.

Jenisch, Vergleichung von 14 Sprachen.

Jenour, On Language.

Johnes, Philolog. proofs of Unity of race, 1846.

Johnson, A. B., Meaning of words, 1854.

" Treatise on, 1836.

Johnson, S., Works, Philol. Tracts, 1823.

Klaproth, Asia Polyglotta, 1831.

Kraitsir, Significance of the Alphabet, 1846.

" Glossology, 1854.

Latham, Essays, 1860.

Leibnitz, Collect. etymologica, 1717.

Lewis, J., Comp. Etymol. of European languages, 1828.

Meidinger, Dict. Etym. Langues Teuto-Gothiques, 1833.

Merian, Etude comp. des langues, 1828.

Michaelis, Influence of Opinions on, 1771.

Michel, Etudes sur l'argot, 1856.

Minsheu, Guide into tongues, 1627.

Language and Comparative Philology (continued).

Monboddo, Origin of, 1792.

Moore, N. F., Names of Anc. Minerals, 1834.

Muller, Max., Lectures, 1st and 2d series, 1862, 65.

Murray, A., Hist. of European Lang., 1823.

Nerses, Preces 33 linguis.

Philological Soc. Proc. and Trans., 1858–69.

Prichard, J. C., Celtic Nations.

Quatremère, Langue d'Egypte, 1808.

Rask, Afhandlinger, 1838.

Raynouard, Langue des troubadours comparée, 1844.

Rees, Influences of Christianity on.

Remarks on a Letter to Waterland, 1731. P. 353.

Schlegel, F., Philosophy....of Language, 1848.

Sherman, John, Philosophy of, 1826.

Smith, A., Origin of, 1853.

Taylor, I., Etym. of words and places.

Thornton, W., Cadmus; or Elements of written, 1793.

Tytler, A. F., Principles of Translation, 1813.

Webb, J., Primitive language.

Welsford, Mithridates Minor, 1848.

Whiter, Univ. Etym. Dictionary, 1800.

Whitney, W. D., Study of: 12 lectures, 1867.

Wilkins, Philosophical Lang., 1668.

Winning, Manual of compar. philol., 1838.

See Oriental Lit.; Classical Lit.; Alphabets; Translations.

See, besides, the languages below and under Dictionaries and Grammars.

Languages, African. Dict. Fran-Berbère.

Gram. of the Bakele, 1854.

Gram. of Mpongwe, 1847.

Benga Primer, 1855.

Hanoteau, Langue Tamachek.

Hayne, Hist. of the Greboes, 1860.

Smithson. Cont., Yoruba Lang., 1859.

Wilson, J. L., Comp. of language of, Bibliot. Sac., 1847.

See Bibliography.

Language, Anglo-Saxon. Aelfric Society, Aelfric's Homilies.

" Dialogues of Solomon.

Am. Syst. of Ed., Handbook of Ang. Sax.

Anglo-Saxon Chronicle, (Chron. of G. B.).

Beowulf, Poems of.

Language, Anglo-Saxon (continued).
Boethius, Alfred's version, 1864.
Bible: Anglo-Saxon gospels, (Thorpe).
Bosworth, Ang. Sax. Dictionary.
Conybeare, Anglo-Saxon Poetry, 1826.
Layamon's Brut, (Madden).
Miller, T., History of.
Monumenta historica Britannica, (Hardy), 1848.
North, S., Oration on.
Ormin, The Ormulum.
Rask, E. G., Grammar of, 1830.
See Dictionaries; Grammars.

Language, Arabic. Arabic Exercises, 1840.
See Arabic Authors; Oriental Lit.

Language, Armenian. Armenian exercises.
Ignatius, Untorinagoutiun, 1814.
Somal, Storia letterarîa di Armenia, 1829.
Upham, T. C., Mental philos., in Armenian.

Languages, Asiatic. *See* Oriental; Turkish; Persian; Sanscrit; Bibliography.

Language, Celtic. Chapin, A. B., The Study of, 1840.
Prichard, Orig. of Celtic nations, 1831.
See Gaelic; Irish; Welsh.

Language, Chinese. Andrews, S. P., Syst. of writing of.
" Discoveries in Chinese, 1854.
Confucius' works; text and trans., Serampore, 1809.
Du Ponceau, Diss. on Chinese Writing, 1839.
Klaproth, Asia polyglotta.
" Verzeichniss der Chin. und Mandschu Bücher, 1822.
Legge, J., Argum. for Shang Te, 1850.
Morison, View of, 1817.
Morrone, Vocab. of Cochin Chin., 1780.
Summers, Chi. language, 1864.
Webb, J., Chinese language, 1669.
See Grammars; Dictionaries; Bibliography.

Language, Coptic. *See* Hieroglyphics; Grammars.

Language, Dutch. Meyer, J. D., Verhandelingen, 1844, 46.
Mulder, Leesboekje, 1846.
Peel, Leerwijze der Engelsche, 1855, 6.
Quintus, Leerwijze der Engelsche, 1848.
Volks Letter-kunde, 1852.
See Bibliography; Literature; Grammars.

Language, English. Alford, Queens' English.
Amer. System of Ed., Hand-book of engrafted words.
Anti-Spelling-book, 1853.
Barclay, J., Sequel to Diversions of Purley, 1826.
Barrett, S., jr., Principles of Lang., 1837.
Bartlett, J. R., Dict. of Americanisms, 1848.
Bearcroft, Prac. Orthography, 1828.
Booth, D., Prin. of English Composition, 1833.
Camden, Remaines, 1637.
Cardell, Essay on Language, 1825.
Carey, Pract. Prosody and Versification, 1809.
Chambers, R., Hist. of, 1837. B. C.
Cobb, L., Webster's Orthog., 1831.
Coleridge, H., Index to lit. of 13th cent.
Crabb, English Synonymes, 1824.
Crombie, A., Etymol. and Syntax of, 1836. B. C.
Cumberland glossary.
Davidson, Difficulties of Eng. Gramm., 1839.
Dialect of Craven, 1828.
Dictionaries, (F. A. Poole).
Douglass, W., On Pronunciation.
Du Ponceau, English Phonology, 1818.
Elements of English Composition.
Elphinstone, The Principles of, 1836.
" Anal. of French and English, 1756.
Evans, Leicestershire Words, 1848.
Flügel, Literarische Sympathien, 1843.
" Philol. in Nordamerika.
Forby, Vocab. of East Anglia.
Fowler, W. C., Eng. Lang. in its Elements, 1850.
Gilchrist, Philosophic Etymol., 1816.
Girard, Meth. Instr. in Mother tongue, 1847.
Greene, R. C., Treatise on Structure of, 1848.
Grimshaw, Etymol. Dictionary, 1821.
Guy, Exercises in Engl. Syntax, 1829.
" Outlines.. in English Themes, 1828.
Haldeman, S. S., Affixes to words, 1871.
Halliwell, J. O., Hist. of Prov. dialects.
Harrison, M., Structure, etc., 1850.
Hiley, R., Treatise on Grammar, 1840.
Holloway, Gen. Dict. of provincialisms, 1839.
Hurd, S. T., Common Errors of Speech, 1847.
Ingersoll, C. M., Conv. on Etymol., 1822.

Language, English (continued).

Jamieson, J., Etymolog. Dict. with Supp., 1840–41.

Jermyn, Book of Epithets, 1849.

Kennion, Etym. and Synt. of Murray's Gram., 1842.

Ker, J. B., Archæology of our popular phrases, 1837.

Latham, R. G., The Engl. Lang., 1841.

" Hand-book of, 1852.

Lower, English Surnames, 1842.

Lynd, First Book of Etymol., 1856.

Lyon, C. J., Analysis of Parts of Speech of.

March, F. A., Meth. of philol. study of, 1868.

Marsh, G. P., Inaug. Ad. Columb. Col.

" Lectures on, 1860.

" Origin and Hist. of, 1862.

Matheson, J., Theory of Eng. Grammar, 1821.

Moon, The Dean's English.

Morris, R., Spec. of early English.

Mulkey, Treatise of Orthoepy, 1856.

Nares, Elements of Orthoepy, 1784.

Odell, J., On the Elements of, 1806.

Ormin's Ormulum.

Parker, R. G., Aids to composition.

" Engl. composition.

Peabody, A. P., Conversation, 1856.

Pegge, Anecdotes of Eng., 1844.

Pickering, J., Vocab. of Americanisms, 1816.

Philological Society, 1842–54.

" Transactions, 1854–67.

Quackenboss, First lessons in comp., 1856.

" Course of Comp., 1855.

Redesdale, Thoughts on prosody.

Reed, H., Lectures on English Literature, 1855.

Revis, B., Right words abused, 1857.

Robbins. R., Amer. Contr. to English language, 1837. B. C.

Rogers, H., Course of lectures.

Roget, Thesaurus of English Words, 1854.

Schoolmaster at home, Errors.

Sheridan, T., Dissertation, 1762.

Smith, C. J., Synonyms discriminated, 1871.

Smith, Wm. W., Etym. of Eng., 1867.

Soule, Eng. Synonymes, 1871.

Swan, W. D., On Worcester's Dict'ry.

Talbot, H. F., English Etymologies, 1847.

Thomas, J., First Book of Etymology, 1856.

Tooke, Horne, Diversions of Purley, 1806.

Language, English (continued).

Town, S., Analysis of Derivative Words, 1836. B. C.

Treatise on the Eng. Tongue, 1767.

Trench, R. C., On Study of Words, 1852.

" English, Past and Present,

" Deficiencies in Dictionaries, 1860.

" Glossary of changed senses, 1859.

Verstegan, Restitution, 1634.

Walker, Key to Pronunciation, 1804.

" Rhyming Dict., 1852.

Ward, J., Four Essays upon, 1758.

Webster, N., Obs. on Language, 1839.

Welch, A. S., The English Sentence, 1855.

Welsford, Ramifications of the Eng. Lang., 1845.

Whately, English Synonyms, 1852.

White, R. G., Words and their uses, 1870.

Whiter, Etymolog. Magnum, 1800.

Wilkins, J., Philosoph. Lang., 1668.

Wright, J. W., Hours of Idleness, 1843.

" Philol. lectures, 1844.

See Grammars; Rhetoric; Dictionar's.

Language, Eng. Punctuation. Brenan, Composition and P., 1849.

Burrow, J., De usu interpungendi, 1771.

Butterfield, Lessons in, 1846.

Greenleaf, B., System of, 1822.

Smallfield, Punctuation, 1838.

Wilson, J., Gram. punctuation, 1855.

Language, English, Spellers and Readers. Angell, Union Series, No. 1–6.

Bailey, R. W., Exercises in orthog. and deriv., 1866.

Barry, J., Spelling Book, 1814.

Bentley, R., Pictorial Reader, 1844.

Bingham, C., Am. Preceptor.

" Child's Companion, 1819.

Bullions, P., Parsing, 1852.

Burhans, Instructor, Spelling, 1836.

Chapin, A. B., Classical sp. book, 1845.

" Spelling book, 1841.

Cobb, L., N. American reader, 1844.

Comly, Reader, 1849.

Crandall, D., Spelling Book, 1831.

Emerson, Nat. Spelling Book.

Fowle, W. B., Common sch. Speller, 1849.

Frost, J., 500 Exercises in Parsing, 1827.

Gallaudet, Practical spelling book.

Language, English, Spellers and Readers (continued).
Good, P. P., Exercises, 1830.
Guide to Spelling, 1697.
Hart, Class-book of prose, 1845.
Hazen, The speller.
" Gram. reader, No. I, II.
Hopkins, H., Orthography, 1837.
Hubbard, J., Am. reader, 1807.
Hull, J., Guide to, 1818.
Leavitt, Joshua, Part II, Easy lessons.
McElligott, Manual of orthography, 1845.
McGuffey, Eclectic Reader, 1849.
Mandeville, H., Course of reading, 1851.
" 4th Reader.
Manual of orthoëpy.
March, F. A., A Parser, 1869.
Moral Amusement, 1808.
Murray, L., Eng. Reader, 1817.
N. Y. Reader, 1844.
New York Spelling book, 1813.
Northend, Exer. for dictation, 1862.
Parker, R. G., Nat. Fifth reader, 1862.
Pierce, O. B., Second Reader, 1849.
Pierpont, J., 1st, 2d, 5th Reader.
" Introd. to Nat. Read., 1835.
Pike, J., Columb. orthographer, 1808.
Randall, S. S., Educational R., 1845.
" Elem. reader, 1846.
Rickard, Class-book for Parsing, 1856.
Ryland, John, The Preceptor, Lond.
Sanders, Analysis of Words, 1859.
" Anal. definer, 1860.
Staniford, Art of Reading, 1816.
Swan, W. D., Primary Readers, 1844.
Torrey, Jesse, Mental museum, 1835.
" Pleasing companion, 1835.
Tower, D. B., Second reader, 1855.
Town, S., Spelling book, 1844.
" Third reader, 1854.
Webb, J. R., Normal reader, No. 1, 2, 4, 1848–51.
Webster, N., Pictorial Sp. book.
" American selection, 1799.
" The Teacher, 1836.
Wiggins, N. Y. Expositor, 1825.
Williams, D., Preceptor's Assistant, Lond., 1851.
Willson, Am. class reader, 1836.
Worcester, S., Third book, 1843.
" Fourth book, 1844.

Language, Finnish. Vogt, Bibbalhistoria.

Language, Flemish. *See* Literature.

Language, French. Art, L', de bien parler Français, 1730.
Bescherelle, Dict. des Verbes, 1843.
Binn's Exercises in False Engl., 1841.
Bossut, Word-book.
Elphinstone, Anal. of the French and English, 1756.
Génin, Eclaircissement de la Langue.
Gouin, French and E. Pronun., 1859.
Jullien, Cours Raisonné de Langue Française, 1851–56.
Lafaye, Dict. des Synonymes, 1858.
Laveaux, Dict. des Difficultés, 1857.
Lehman, Hand-boek ter beofening der Fransche taal, 1819. B. C.
Manesca, Course of Lessons in French, 1834. B. C.
Martinet, New Dialogues, French and English, 1815. B. C.
Meloy, Recueil de Lettres, 1856.
Michel, Etude de philol. comparée, 1856.
Monumenta historica (Hardy), 1848.
Palsgrave, Sur la Grammaire.
Pamphlets, vol., 1243.
Picard, Dict. of phrases.
Raynouard, Langue des Troubadours, 1844.
" Choix des poesies des troubadours, 1816–21.
Schutz, Eng. Franz. Rasirpiegel, 1830.
Soc. d'Emul. de Montbéliard.
Trav. Man. of Conv., Eng., Ger., French and Italian, 1840. B. C.
See Grammars; Dictionaries.

Language, French: Readers and Spelling books. Alphabet de Lecture.
Alvarez, Dictées normales.
Barbauld, Mrs., Leçons pour enfans.
Beléze, Enseignement Elémentaire pour les Enfants, 1855–59.
" Syllabaire.
Boniface, Lecture par Jour, 1851–2.
Damiette, Bibliothèque.
Delapalme, Exer. de Lecture, 1857.
Fénélon, Morceaux Choisis, 1857.
Frémont, Leçons de litt.
Gillet, Bibliot. de l'instr. primaire.
Guérard, La Corbeille.
Holstein, French Reader.
Monteith, A. H., Lessons in.
Oppen, French reader, 1864.
Perrin, J., Entertaining Exercises, 1801.
" Fables Amusantes, 1804. B. C., 1821.
" Conversation, 1839.
Picot, Hist. Narr. in Fr., 1845.
" Scien. Narr. in French, 1847
Pinney, French teacher.

Language, French: Readers and Spelling Books (continued).
Rècits Moraux, 1838.
Sanders, G. J. H., Student's First Book, 1848.
Sardou, Leçons de Grammaire.
Simon, Alphabets, des oiseaux, etc.
Vijver, Chrestomathie, French, 1826.
Wanostrocht, Recueil Choisi, 1820.

Language, Gaelic. Doddridge, Teagasg, etc.
Gaelic Soc., Dublin, v. I, 1808.
Grant, Mrs., Superstit., etc., trans. from G., 1811.
Ossianic Soc., vol. for 1857.
Soc. for the support of Gaelic schools, Edinb., 1824. P. 1550.
Stewart, Highland bards.
See Dictionaries; Grammars; Literature; Ossian; Irish.

Language, German. Adelung, Anweisung zur Deutschen Orthog., 1790. B. C.
" Worterbuch für die Aussprache, etc., 1791. B. C.
" Bernays, Lecture, London, 1831. P. 395.
Donatti, Germ. nouns.
Ertheiler, On study of, 1846.
Follen, C., Lesebuch, 1831. B. C.
Gibbs, J. W., Teutonic etymology, 1860.
Kinder Tafel. B. C.
Klauer, Deutsches Handbuch, 1840.
" German Exercises, 1843.
Krauth, Advantages of German.
Monteith, A. H., Lessons in.
Muhlenfels, Study of Germ., 1829.
Nevin, A Lecture on, 1842. P. 287.
Ollendorff, Méthode pour apprendre.
See Grammars; Dictionaries; Bibliography.

Language, Greek. Anthon, C., Manual of Greek Lit., 1853.
Apollonius, De Syntaxi.
Arnold, Greek reading book.
Boise, Gr. Prose composition, 1850.
Bos, L., Ellipses Græcæ, 1750.
Brooks, First lessons in, 1847.
Brumoy, Greek Theatre, 1759.
Chandler, H. W., Gr. accentuation, 1867.
Coleridge, H. N., Study of Gr. Poets, 1831. B. C.
Coray, Greek Class. Criticisms, 1812.
Crosby, A., Greek lessons, 1859.
Dalzel, Collec. Græca minora.
" Collec. Græca majora.
Damm, Lexicon Etymol., 1765.
Dissert.... Greek Accents, 1755.

Language, Greek (continued).
Dwight, T., jr., Lessons in, 1833.
Exempla Minora, 1821.
Gally, H., Pronunciation of accents, 1755.
Grævius, Lectiones Hesiodæ, 1667.
Greswell, Hist. of Greek press, 1833.
Gronovius, Thes. Gr. Antiquitatum.
Harkness, A., First Greek book.
Harpocration, De Vocibus liber, 1696.
Heeren, A. H. L., Gesch. des studiums der Griechischen, 1797.
Hemsterhuis, Anecdota.
Hodgkin, Greek penmanship, 1835.
Hoogeveen, Doct. Particu. Græcæ, 1769.
Jacobs's Greek Reader, 1827.
Kenrick, Gr. prose composition.
Lennep, Etymol. Ling. Græcæ, 1790.
Linwood, Lexicon to Aeschylus, 1847.
Moor, J., Tracts on the Cases, etc., of, 1830. P. 395.
Moore, N. F., Pronunciat. of Greek, 1819.
" Lectures on, 1835.
Neilson, Greek exercises, N. Y., 1810.
Outhof, Cebes, Tabula, 1727.
Pollux, J., Onomasticon, 1608.
Primatt, W., Greek Accent, 1764.
Quintus Calabrus, Prætermiss. ab Homero, 1734.
Ramsay, Travels of Cyrus, 1814.
Roth, Ueber Thucydides u. Tacitus.
Sophocles, E. A., Greek Lessons, 1843.
" Hist of Greek Alphabet, 1848.
Thomas, De vocibus Atticis, 1757.
Turner, D. W., Notes on Herodotus, 1853.
Veitch, Greek verbs, 1866.
Vigerus, De Idiotismis, 1813.
" Abridged in English, 1828.
Vitringa, De Protagoræ Vita, 1852.
Waddington, Carmen Græcum, 1819.
Wheeler, Anal. of Thuycidides, 1855.
See Classical Literature; Antiquities; Greek; Latin; Bibliography, etc.

Language, Greek, Modern. Biblos Kaloumene Euterpe, 1830.
Constantinos, Enchiridion, 1819.
Passow, Popularia carmina.
St. Pierre, B., Diegemata tessara.
" Tales, 1825. P. 615.
Wilson, S. S., Tou Klerou o odegos, 1829.
See Dict.; Gram.

Language, Gypsy. Paspati, A. G., Am. Orient. Soc. Journ., v. 7.
See Gypsies.

Language, Hebrew. Bartolocci, Bibliotheca Rabbinica, 1775–94.
Ben Sira, Proverbia, 1597.
Biscioni, Cat. medic. Laurent., 1752.
Bowyer, Hist. of Printing, Hebrew, 1776.
Buxtorf, De abbreviaturis Hebraicis, 1613.
Church of Engl. Prayer.
Conant, Defence of Heb. Grammar, 1847. P. 269.
Forster, C., One primeval language.
Groot, Exercitatio, 1767.
Jelf, Neglect of, 1832.
Koolhaas, Disser. Heb. Linguae, 1748.
Krafft, Cod. Hebraici bib. Vind., 1847.
Lowth, Hebrew Poetry, 1829.
Martinet, Heb. Chrestomathie, 1837.
Montanus, Communes Hebr. Ling. idiotismia, 1572,
Noah, Trans. of book of Jasher, 1840.
Pamphlets, vol. 975.
Reeves, Text of the Psalms, 1800.
Stuart, M., Heb. Chrestomathy, 1829.
Vienna, Imp. Lib. Cod. Heb. catal., 1847.
Withington, Solomon's Song.
See Bible; Bibliography; Jews; Grammars; Dict.

Language, Himyaritic. Forster, C., Geog. of Arabia, 1844.
" One primeval language, 1854.
Salisbury, E. E., On Forster's discovery, Bibliot. Sac., 1845.
Turner, W. W., Himyar. writing (Am. Ethn. Soc.).

Language Icelandic. *See* Bibliography.

Languages, Indian, American. Aiamie tipadjimoonin, masinaigan, 1859.
Allen, W., Wunnissoo, a poem.
Am. Antiq. Soc., Gallatin's Synopsis.
Am. Ethnol. Soc. Trans., vols. 1, 2, 1845, 48.
Am. Phil. Soc. Trans., v. 4, 3, 12.
" Trans. of Phil. & Lit. Com.
" Catal. of MSS. on.
Arenas, Guide, Langue Mexicaine.
Barratt, Lang. of New Eng., 1850.
Beatty, Two Months' Miss. Tour in Penn'a, 1768.
Belcourt, Langue des Sauteux, 1839.
Bible, N. T., St. John's Gospel in Mohawk, 1818.
" Bible, Chahta New Test.
Brasseur de Bourbourg, Lettres sur le Mexique.
" Popol vuh, Quiché.
Bruyas, Mohawk language.
Byington, Choctaw Definer, 1852.

Languages, Indian, American (continued).
Chahta Almanak, 1843.
Choctaw Hymn Book, 1851.
Church of Eng., Prayers in Mohawk, 1787.
Clavigero, Cat. of Mexic. grammars.
Cuesta, Mutsun language.
Dakotah Friend, Newsp , 1850-52.
Davies, J., Caribbian Vocab., 1666.
De Kay, Long Island names.
Dencke, John's Epist. in Delaware.
Du Ponceau, Gram. of the Delaware.
" Mém... sur les Langues de, 1835.
" Corresp. with Heckewelder, 1816.
Durocher, Catech. for the Montagnars, 1848.
Edwards, J., Obs. on Muhkeekaneew Lang., 1788. P. 28.
Eliot, J., Indian Bible, 1680.
" Indian Grammar, 1666.
English and Dakota Vocab., 1852.
Etudes philologiques, 1866.
Fisher, W , Travels, Dict. of Indian tongue, 1812.
Gabelentz, Der Tscherokesischen Sprache.
Gallatin, A., Notes Am. Ethn. Trans., 1845, 48.
Gallaudet, Scripture Biog. in Choctaw.
Hale, H., Ethnol. and Philol. of U. S. Expl. Exped., 1846.
Haven, S. F., Amer. Archæol., 1856.
Howse, Cree language and Chippewa, 1844.
Lang, Polynesian migrations.
Lieberkuhn, Hist. of Christ, in Delaware, 1821.
Long, J., Trav. of an Indian Interpreter, 1791.
Ludewig, Literature of Am. aborig. lang., 1846.
" Trübner's ed., 1858.
McKenney, Vocab. of Chippewa lang., 1827.
Marshall, Names at Niagara.
Mass. Hist. Soc., v. 10, (Pickering).
Morgan, L. H., Syst. of consang. of families, Smithson. Contr., v. 17.
Muskokee Hymns, 1859.
New York Hist. Soc., v. 3, Jarvis's Gramm.
Pickering, J., Notes on Ind. lang.
Préfontaine, Dictionn. Galibi, 1763.
Prot. Episc. Ch. Prayer-book in Mohawk, 1853.
Rhode Island Hist. Collec., Williams' Gram.
Rochefort, Vocab. Caraïbe, 1665.

Latin Authors (continued).
Nepos, C., Vitæ Imperatorum, 1773, 1786.
Obsequens, De Prodigiis, 1720.
Ovidius Naso, Opera, 1629.
" Metamorphoses, 1591.
" Excerpta, 1827, 1868.
" In English, Sandys, Riley, Dryden.
" Choix, In French, 1850.
" Werken, Dutch, Valentyn.
" Herschepinge, Vondel.
" Feestdagen, Hoogvliet.
Pamphlets, Latin, B. C., vol. 30.
Persius, Satiræ. *See* Juvenalis.
Petronius, Satyricon.
" Trans. *See* Propertius.
Phædrus, Fabulæ, 1727, 1824, 35.
" Trans. *See* Terentius.
Plautus, Comœdiæ, 1630, 1778.
" Trans., 1769, 1852.
Plinius, Historiæ Mundi, 1549.
" Nat. Historia, 1778–91.
" Natural History, 1855–57.
" 1st and 33d Books of Natural Hist., 1828.
Plinius, C. C., Epistolæ. 1800.
" Letters, 1805.
Poetæ Latini Minores, Wernsdorff, 1789.
Poetæ Latini Minores, Burmann, 1731.
Pollio, Valerian, Galienus, 1544.
Polybius, Folard's Fr. Trans. and Comm., 1727–30.
" Hampton's trans., 1823.
Porson, In Xenophontis Anabasin.
Propertius, Elegiæ, and in Eng., 1780.
" Petronius and Secundus: trans. 1854.
Prudentius, A., Opera, 1613.
Quintilianus, Institut. Oratoriæ, 1533, 1792.
" Inst. of oratory, 1856.
Rutilius Lupus, De Figuris Sententiarum, 1768.
Sallustius, Quæ extant, 1823.
" Bellum Catal. et Jugurth., 1521, 1774, 1831, 57.
" Trans. of Watson.
Scriptores Rei Rusticæ, 1787, 88.
Scriptores Romani, 23 vol. 1815–17.
Seneca, Opera Omnia, 1515, 1665.
" Epistolæ, 1509.
" Tragœdiæ, 1609.
" Tragedies, Sherburne's trans., 1702.
Sidonius Appollinaris, Opera, 1609.
Silius Italicus, Punica, 1798.
Statius, P. P., Sylvæ, Thebais, Achilleis, 1494.

Latin Authors (continued).
Suetonius, Opera, 1802.
" Lives of the Cæsars, 1796, 1855.
Symmachus, Q. A., Epistolæ, 1604.
Syrus, P., Sententiæ, 1726.
Tacitus, C. C., Opera, 1801, 1805.
" Libri v priores, 1581, 1823, 32.
" Works, 1794, 1813, 54.
" Le opere, Davanzati, 1832.
Terentianus, De literis, tractatus, 1531.
Terentius, P., Comœdiæ, 1726, 1837.
" Andria Adelphique, 1837.
" Comedies, Colman, 1768.
" Comedies, Riley, 1853.
" Trad. en Français, 1658.
Tibullus, Carmina, 1502, 1798.
" Trans. *See* Catullus.
Varro, M. T., Opera, 1573.
" De re rustica, 1787, 88.
Vegetius, De re militari, 1592.
Velleius, C., Paterculus, Hist. Romanæ, 1779.
Victor, S. A., Vita Imp. Romanorum, 1544.
Virgilius Maro, Opera, 1703, 17, 59, 1823.
" Ill. á C. G. Heyne, 1803.
" In English, Dryden's, Davidson's, Martyn's trans.
" In French: Delille.
" Lat. and F.: Sommer, 1858.
" In Dutch: Vondel, 1659.
Vopiscus, Hist. Romanæ, 1544.
See Poetry, Latin; Theology, Latin; Church-fathers; Bibliog'y; Language, Latin.

Latin Criticism. *See* Classical Literature.

Latitude Men. Brief account, 1662.

La Trappe. Lancelot, Tour, 1816.

La Tude, H. M. de. Memoirs of, 1834.

Laud, W. Heylin, Life of, 1668.
Prynne, W., Life of, 1645.

Laughton, Capt. Evans, G., Sermon on.

Laurence, P. Oxenham, Letter to, 1835.

Laurens, H. Correspondence, 1861.

Laurens, J. Bradford Club, Correspond. of, 1777.

Lauzun, Duc De. Mémoires, 1858.

Laval, M. Taché, Notice Historique, 1859.
Université Laval, 1857–59. P. 482.

Lavalette, Comte de. Memoirs of, 1831.

Lavater, J. C. Secret Journal.
" Mendelszoon, M., Brief van, 1770.

Law, John. Chimera, The, 1720.
" Hunt, F., Lib. of Comm., Mississippi Scheme, 1845.
Tafereel, De, 1720.
Thiers, Memoir of, 1859.

Law, J. O. Musgrave, Sermon, Death of, 1847. P. 494.

Law. Argyll, Reign of Law, 1867.
Barrister's Education, 1791, 2.
Blondeau, Enseignement du Droit en Hollande, 1846.
Blue Laws of New Haven, etc., 1838.
Butler, C., Horæ Juridicæ, 1808.
Closset, A. de, Droit civil, En. Pop.
Criticisms on the bar, 1819.
Cummins, Mankind and law, 1861.
Dissertations: Droit public des Colon., 1778.
Edward I, Year Book, (Chron. of G. B.).
Field, D. D., Practice of the Courts, 1847. B. C.
Fleury, Inst. au Droit ecclésiastique, 1688.
Gendebien, Droit commercial, En. Pop.
Gratama, Opuscula academica, 1821.
Grimké, Codes of Law, 1827.
Grotius, Rights of War and Peace, 1814. B. C.
Grün, Droit Général, 1844.
H., J., Of human laws, 1671.
Hogerbeets, Practijcke...in Hollandt, 1641.
Irving, D., Obs. on Civil law, 1815.
Jones, Sir W., Law of Bailments, Works, vol. 8, 1807.
Jottrand, Des Avocats en Belgique, 1850.
Justice to a judge, 1793.
Lapouyade, Contrat de Métayage, 1850.
Luzac, Du Droit naturel, civil et pol., 1802. B. C.
Meinesz, Staatsreglelijke bepalingen, 1856.
Pamphlets on Law and Legislation, vols. 799, 800, 907, 1524, 1776.
Puffendorff, De Jure Naturæ, 1698.
Rawle, W., Addresses to the Bar, 1824.
Sampson, M. B., Rationale of crime, 1846.
Sampson against the Philistines, 1805.
Sanford, H. S., Penal Codes in Europe, 1854.
Sheil, R. L., Sketches, legal and polit., 1855.
Story, Joseph, Misc. Writings, 1852.
Strictures on educat. for the Bar, 1792.

Law (continued).
Townsend, W. C., Lives of Twelve eminent Judges, 1846.
Univ. of Albany, 1851–69.
Univ. of City of N. Y., 1840, 52–59.
Updike, Mem. of Rh. Is., Bar, 1842.
Veder, De Antiq. juris notione, 1832.
" Hist. Phil. juris apud veteres, 1832. B. C.
Welsby, Lives of em. Eng. Judges, 1846.
Woodbury, L., Writings, judicial, 1852.
See International; Neutrals; and Law Library Catalogue.

Law Addresses. Butler, B. F., Law school, N. Y., 1835. P. 25. B. C.
Colquhoun, Suggestions for educat.
Dickinson, D. S., Hamilton Coll., 1858. P. 486.
Dwight, T. W., Columbia Coll., 1858.
Ferris, Univ. of City of N. Y., 1858.
Graham, D., Law school, N. Y., 1838.
Hopkinson, J., 1826.
Kent, J., Colum. Coll., N. Y., 1824.
Kent, W., Law School, N. Y., 1838.
Lord, J. C., Law Stud. Assoc., 1852.
Marvin, D., Law School, Albany, 1857. P. 514.
Noyes, W. C., Hamilton Coll., 1856.
Quincy, J., Dane Law College, 1832.
Story, Joseph, Harvard Univ., 1829.
Sullivan, W., Ad. to Suffolk bar, 1824.
Thacher, P. O., Suffolk bar, 1831.
Townsend, J. F., Law and Medicine, 1854. P. 204.
Van Santvoord, G., Albany, 1856.

Law Forms. Butts, I. R., Business man's ass't, 1847.
Christopher, N. Y. Business Man.
Clerk's Magazine, 1803.
Davis, A. S., Traveler's Legal Guide.
Jenkins, J. S., Clerk's assistant, 1846.

Lawes, J. Harrison, T., Fun. Serm. on.

Lawrence family. Holgate's geneal.
Hist. genealogy, 1858.

Lawrence, Abbot. Appleton, N., Memoir of, 1856 P. 494.
Everett, E., Remarks on, 1855, v. 3.
Prescott, W. H., Memoir of, 1856.

Lawrence, Amos. Gray, F. T., Serm. on, 1853. P. 555.
Hopkins, M., Discourse on, 1853.
Lawrence, W. R., Diary of.

Lawrence, I. Pease, Geneal. of, 1848.

Lawrence, Capt. J. Account of funeral, 1813.
Niles, J. M., Life of, 1821.
Voice of truth, 1807. P. 195.

Leyden Acad. Fabricius, Redenvoering.

Leydt, J. Ritzema, 1763.

L'Hopital, M. de. Butler, C., Life of.

Libel. Another Letter to Mr. Almon, 1771.
Dyer, G., Doctrine of.
Enquiry into the Doctrine, 1765.
Law of Libel, 1823. P. 800.
Letter concerning Libels, 1764.
See Press, Liberty of.

Liberal Christianity. *See* Unitarian.

Liberia. Constitution, etc., 1848.
Adventures in Africa.
Africa's Luminary, Liberia, 1839–46.
Alexander, Hist. of Col. in West Africa, 1846.
Amer. Col. Soc. Reports, 1818–65.
Ashmun, Life of S. Bacon, 1822.
Bacon, E., Journal, 1821.
Bacon, L., Life of Ashmun, 1828.
Brown, G. S., Life of, 1849.
Colonizationist, The, 1833, 4.
Gurley, R. R., Report on, 1850.
" Life of Ashmun, 1835. B. C.
Liberia: Tables of emigr., 1845.
Maryland Colon. Journal, 1841–43.
Mass. Col. Soc. Reports, 1844, 52, 53, 1863.
Miller, A., Liberia described, 1859.
N. Y. Col. Soc. Reports, 1823, 50, 52.
News from Africa, 1832.
Peterson, D. H., Life of, 1854
Putnam, L. H., On Liberia, 1859.
Wilkeson, S., History of, 1839.
See Africa, West; Colonization.

Liberty, Civil. Ancient and Modern Lib., Hervey, 1734. P. 418.
Bedenkingen over de vryheid, 1738.
Budgell, E., Liberty and property, 1732.
Considerations on.... warrants.
Defence ...on general warrants.
Eliot, S., The Liberty of Rome, 1849.
" Hist. of Early Christians, 1853.
Everett, E., Orat., Hist. of, 1828.
Experience preferable, 1776.
Griffiths, Autographs for freedom.
Grimké, Tendency of Free instit., 1848.
Guizot, Democracy in France, 1849.
Hey, R., Observations on, 1776.
Hotoman, Franco-Gallia, 1721.
Keith, Sir W., Collec. of Papers, 1749.
Knox, V., Spirit of Despotism, 1795.
Lacy, J., Peter's visitation. P. 299.
Letter from Candor, 1770.
Lieber, On civil liberty, 1853.
Martin, J., Remarks on, 1776.

Liberty, Civil (continued).
Miall, J. G., Footsteps of our forefathers, 1852.
Mill, J. S., On Liberty, 1863.
Milner, J., Essay, 1824.
Mirabeau, Essai sur le despotisme.
Naked truth, 1790.
Patton, C., Basis for, 1793.
Price, R., Obs. on the nature of, 1776.
Prinsterer, Vrijheid, Gelijkheid, Broederschap, 1848.
Protestant, The, Against Lowth.
Sacheverell, Serm., False notions of, 1713.
Shebbeare, Essay, 1776.
Vindication of Liberty, 1730.
Vindiciæ contra tyrannos (Beza), Trans., 1648.
Wilkes, J., North Briton, 1772.
See Authority; Government; Democracy; Toleration; Republics; Orations July 4.

Liberty, Religious. *See* Toleration; Persecution; Dissenters.

Liberty of the Press. *See* Press.

Libourne. Guinodie, Histoire de Libourne.

Libraries. Account of celebrated libraries, 1739.
Bartlett, Preserv. of Public Archives, 1824.
Botfield, Cathedral lib. of Eng., 1849.
De Peyster, F., Influence of, 1866.
Edwards, E., Memoirs of Libraries, 1859.
" Founders of Brit. Museum, 1870.
Eichhorn, Geschichte der Litteratur, 1805–12.
Encyc. Britannica, Art., Libraries, 1855–58.
Farnham, Glance at pri. lib., Boston.
Hints for Book Societies. P. 1781.
Horne, Introd. to bibliog., 1814.
Jewett, Pub. Lib. in the U. S., 1851.
La Borde, Organization des Bibliot., 1845.
Livermore, Remarks on Pub. Libraries, 1850.
Ludewig, Bibliothekonomie, 1840.
Mass., Report on State Lib., 1849.
N. Y. State Library, Reports, 1845–71.
Pamphlets, vol. 1237.
Rhees, Man. of Pub. Lib. in the U. S., 1859.
Schotel, Lettre à M. de Wal, 1850, 51.
Traice, Hand-book Catalogues of.
Wynne, Priv. Lib. of N. Y.
See Bibliography for other books on Libraries.

Literary Addresses (continued).
Curtenius, Oratio Inaug., 1754.
Davis, H., Inaug., Middlebury, 1810.
Demarest, D. D., Rutgers' Coll., 1855.
Dix, J. A., Geneva Coll., 1839. P. 264.
Draper, J. W., N. Y. Univ, 1853.
Emerson, R. W., Waterville, Me., 1841.
Everett, E., Orations and discourses.
Everett, A. H., Rutgers' Coll., 1838.
Felton, J. B., College of Calif., 1858.
Fisher, S. W., Inaug. Hamilton Coll., 1858.
Fitch, E., Baccalaureate, 1799.
Foote, T. M., Hamilton Coll., 1848.
Frelinghuysen, F. T., Rutgers' Coll., 1853. P. 100.
Forsyth, J., Rutgers' Coll., 1848.
Goddard, W. G., Phi Beta Kappa Soc.
Gourlie, Merc. Lib. Assoc., N. Y., 1839.
Grimké, T. S., Phi Beta Kappa, 1830.
Harrison, J. B., Hampden Sidney Coll.
Hemming, J., Mary-le-Bone Inst., 1835. P. 395.
Hillhouse, J. A., Phi Beta Kappa, 1826. P. 88.
Hitchcock, E., Inaug., Amherst, 1845.
Homes, W., Mer. Lib. Ass., St. Louis, 1854. P. 209.
Humphrey, H., Amherst Coll., 1823.
Kennedy, J. P., Univ. of Maryland, 1831.
Kent, J., Phi Beta Kappa, 1831.
Lunt, G., Three eras, etc., 1857.
Mann, H., Lectures, 1859.
Maxcy, J., Collegiate Addresses.
Mayer, C. F., Dickinson College, 1827.
Neal, J., Waterville Coll., 1830.
Pamphlets of, vols. 514, 887, 982–984, 1625, 1694. B. C. 10, 11, 19.
Parker, H. W., Hamilton Coll., 1851.
Parsons, T., P. B. K., Harvard, 1835.
Potter, A., Discourses, etc., 1858.
Raymond, H. J., Univ. of Rochester.
Russell, G. R., Phi Beta Kappa, 1849.
Savage, J., Mass. Lyceum, 1832.
Seward, W. H., N. Y., 1837, 44.
Shedd, Univ. of Vermont, 1845.
Sprague, W. B., 1829–65.
Southard, S. L., Nassau Hall, 1832.
Stanton, H. B., Williams Coll., 1850.
Stillé, C. J., Yale College, 1863.
Story, J., Phi Beta Kappa, 1826.
Sumner, C., Orations, 1845–60.
Van Santvoord, G., Discourses, 1856.
Verplanck, G. C., Columb. and Amh. Coll., 1833, 34.
Walker, T., Harvard Univ., 1850.
Wayland, J., Geneva Coll., 1845.
Wharton, G. M., Univ. of Penn'a, 1858.

Literary Addresses (continued).
Wheaton, H., N. Y. Athen., 1824.
White, A. D., Yale College, 1870.
White, D. A., Harvard Univ., 1844.
Whitehead, C. E., Delta Phi Soc., N. Y.
Williams, J., Inaug. at Trin. College, Hartford, 1849.
Winthrop, R. C., 1849–55.
Young, S., 1826–41.
See Speeches; Oration; Addresses.

Literary Criticism. Arnold, M., Essays in, 1865.
Atkinson, W., Books and reading, 1860.
Blount, T. P., Censura celeb. authorum, 1690.
British Essayists, 55 vol.
Chambers, Hand-book of Amer. lit.
De Bury, On the love of books, 1832, 1861.
D'Israeli, Lit. charac. illustrated.
Ernesti, Elements of interpretation, 1827.
Forsyth, Novels of the 18th Cent., 1871.
Gale, T., Original of human literature, 1669.
Hamilton, Sir W., Discuss. on philos. and lit., 1852.
Hazlitt, W., Writings.
Heron, Letters of literature, 1785.
Horne, R. H., New spirit of the age, 1844.
Johnson, Samuel, Works.
Macaulay, T. B., Crit. and hist. essays.
Ossoli, Papers on literature, 1846.
O'Reid, Reviewers reviewed, 1811.
Reed, H., Lectures on Eng. Lit., 1855.
Remarks on a late pamphlet. P. 1238.
Sears, B., Essays on anc. lit., 1849.
Stael, Mme. De, Influence of literature.
Tuckerman, H. T., Essays, biog. and critical, 1857.
Wallace, H. B., Literary criticisms, 1856.
Whipple, E. P., Lectures, 1850.
" Essays, 1848.
See Poetry; Books; Essays; Rhetoric; Classical Literature; Language.

Literary History. Allibone, S. A., Dict. of Engl. Lit., 1859–71.
Aretin, Beyträge zur Gesch. und Literatur, 1803–7.
Artigny, Mémoires, 1749–56.
Athenian Gazette, (Dunton), 1691.
Barbaro, F., Diatriba praelim., 1741.
Beloe, Recoll. of a Literary Life, 1818.
" Anec. of Lit. and Books, 1807–1812.
Berington, Lit. History of the Middle Ages, 1846.

Literary History (continued).

Blakey, Hist. of political literature, 1855.

Bouterwek, Hist. of Span. and Port. Lit , 1823.

Brimley, Essays, 1868.

Brydges, Censura Literaria, 1815.

Burnet, G., Reflexions on his travels, 1688.

Butler, C., Lit. Hist. of Netherlands.

" Life of Erasmus.

Camusat, Hist. Crit. des Journaux, 1734.

Chambers, Cycl. of Engl. Lit., 1859.

" Hist. of Eng. Literature, 1837. B. C.

" Robbins, American Literature, 1837. B. C.

Chardon, Mélanges, 1812.

Chasles, Am. Lit. and Manners, 1852.

Chaudon, Dictionnaire, v. 20, Tables.

Coggeshall, W. T., Western literature, discourse, 1858.

Colle, Storia Lit di Padova, 1824.

Collet, S., Relics of Lit., 1823.

Cradock, J., Liter. Memoirs, 1828.

Craik, Hist. of Engl. lit., 1863.

Dacier, Progrès de l'His. et de la Litt. Anc., 1789.

Delepièrre, Flemish literature, 1860.

Demogeot, Histoire de la Litt. Fran., 1857.

Denina, Revolutions of Lit., 1771.

D'Israeli, Quarrels of Authors, 1814.

" Amenities of Lit., 1841.

" Curiosities of Lit., 1824.

" Miscellanies of Lit., 1840.

Dunlop, J., History of Fiction, 1814.

Dunton, J., Life and Errors of, 1818.

Dutens, Memoirs of a Trav., 1806.

Eichhorn, Geschichte der Litt., 1812.

Fauriel, Hist. of Provençal Poetry, 1860.

Fry, Bibliog. Memoranda, 1816.

Garcin de Tassy, Litt. Hindoui.

Gazette Litt. de l'Europe, 1768-70.

Gilfillan, Sketches of Modern Lit., 1846.

Gillies, Mem. of Lit. Veteran, 1849.

Goujet, Hist. de la Litt. Fran, 1740-56.

Gravenweert, Hist. de la Litt. Néerlandaise, 1830. B. C.

Gruter, Lampas, sive Fax artium liberalium, 1602.

Hallam, Introd. to Lit. of Europe. 1837.

Halliwell, Pop. Engl. Histories, 1848.

Hamst, Fictitious names of authors, 1868.

Haneberg, Lehrwesen der Muhamedaner, 1850.

Literary History (continued).

Hart, J. S., Female Prose Writers of America, 1852.

Howitt, Lit. of Northern Europe, 1852.

Huet, P. D., Memoirs, 1810.

Hunt, L., Works, vol. 1, 2, 1854.

Ireland's, W. H., Confessions.

Jones, W. A., Essays upon Authors and Books, 1849.

Kay, J., Series of Orig. Portraits, 1842.

King, W., Polit. and Lit. Anecdotes, 1818.

Knapp, S. L., Lect. on Amer. Literature, 1829.

La Rue, Geletterd Zeeland, 1734.

Le Verrier, Ecole de la Chasse, 1763.

Libri, Réponse à M. Boucly.

Literary and crit. remarks, 1800.

Literary Blue Book, 1830.

Lockhart, Peter's Letters, 1819.

Lounger's Common-place Book, 1805-1807.

Maitland, The Dark Ages, 1853.

Mencke, Charlataneria erud., 1715.

Menzel, German Literature, 1840.

Miller, J., Fly leaves, 1854.

Mills, A., Literature and Lit. Men of G. B., 1851.

Mitford, Mary R., Recoll. of a Literary Life, 1852.

Mohedano, Hist. Lit. de España, 1768-1772.

Morhof, D. G., Polyhistor, 1708.

Morse, O. A., Rock me to Sleep, 1870.

Neal, J., Recollections, 1869.

Newnham, Disorders of Lit. Men.

Nichols, J., Lit. Anecdotes of 18th Century, 1812.

" Illustrations, Sequel to Anecdotes, 1817-58.

Nodier, Mélanges, 1829.

Norton, Literary Almanac, 1852-54.

Notes and Queries, 1849-70.

Patmore, My Friends and acquaintance, 1854.

Pegge, S., Anonymiana, 1818.

Pinkerton, J., Correspondence, 1830.

Puibusque, Hist. Comp. des Litt. Esp. et Franç., 1843.

Raynal, Anecdotes Littéraires.

Ripley, Hand-book of Lit. Putnam's Cycl.

Ritson, J., Life and letters, 1833.

Robinson, H. C., Diary, 1869.

Roscoe, W., Origin and viciss. of literature. Pamph'r 11.

Schlegel, F. von, Lect. on Hist. of Lit., 1818. B. C.

Simms, W. G., Views and Reviews, 1845.

Literature, American (continued).

Emerson, R. W., Conduct of life, 1864.
" Society and solitude, 1870.
Everett, E., Mount Vernon Papers, 1860.
Farrar, Mrs., Recollections, 1869.
Fay, T. S., Crayon sketches, 1833.
Ferguson, P. K., On Ugliness, 1852.
Forrest, M., Women of the South in lit., 1865.
Frost, Book of Amer. Lit., 1826.
Gallaher, Western Sketch Book, 1850.
Gardiner, M. L., Prose and Poetry, 1843.
Gem, The, 1848.
Gift, The, Annual, 1842.
Gilmer, F. W., Sketches, Essays, etc., 1828.
Goodrich, S. G., Recollections, 1856.
Greene, Amer. Night's Entertainm'ts.
Griswold, R. W., The Prose Writers of America, 1847.
Hale, E. E., Sybaris and other homes, 1869.
" Ingham papers, 1869.
Hammond, S. H., Hills, Lakes and Forest Streams, 1854.
" Country Margins, 1855.
Hand-book of, (Chambers).
Hart, Female Prose Writers of Amer., 1852.
Harte, Luck of roaring camp, 1870.
Hasheesh eater, (F. Ludlow).
Hawes, Sporting Scenes, 1842.
Hawthorne, Our old home, 1863.
" English note-book, 1870.
" Amer. Note-book, 1868.
" Italian Note book, 1872.
Hints to my Countrymen, 1826. B. C.
History of the Garret. P. 615.
Hitchcock, Ed., Phenomena of the seasons, 1850.
Hitchcock, Enos, Bloomsgrove family, 1790.
Hoffman, D., Viator, or a Peep into my Note Book, 1841.
" Thoughts on men, etc., 1841.
Hopkinson, F., Misc. Essays and Writings, 1792.
Irving, W., Knickerbocker's N. Y.
" Sketch book.
" Bracebridge Hall.
" Crayon Miscellany.
" Wolfert's Roost, etc.
" Spanish papers, 1866.
Jones, J., Prospect of Am. lit., 1839.
Jones, W. A., Characters, etc., 1857.
Judson, E., Trippings, 1846.
Ladd, J. B., Lit. Remains, 1833.

Literature, American (continued).

Legare, H. S., Writings, 1846.
Leslie, Miss, Pencil Sketches, 1833.
Locke, D. R., Swingin round the cirkle.
Longfellow, Outre Mer, 1846.
Lynch, W. F., Naval Life; Sketches, 1851.
Manhattan Souvenir, 1850.
Mayo, W. S., Kaloolah, 1850.
Mind among the spindles.
Mitchell, D. G., Reveries of a Bachelor, 1851.
" Wet days at Edgewood, 1865.
" My farm at Edgewood, 1863.
" Dream life, 1867.
Murray, N., Parish pencillings, 1854.
Neal, J. C., Charcoal sketches, 1843.
Nemo, Mrs., Series of appeals, 1863.
New Hampshire Book, 1844.
Nichols, W., Essays, N. Y., 1826.
Noah, Gleanings from a Gathered Harvest, 1847.
Ossoli, Life without, life within, 1864.
" Papers on literature, 1846.
Parthenon, Papers by Am. Authors, 1851.
Parton, Mrs. S., Fern leaves.
Paulding, J. K., Book of Vagaries, 1868.
" Letters from the South, 1817.
Phelps, Mrs. L., Our country, 1864.
Philadelphia Book, 1836.
Phœnixiana, Derby, 1856.
Portland Sketch Book, 1836.
Pratt, S. D., Inklings, 1852.
Pray, I. G., Prose and Verse, 1836.
Prentice, G. D., Prenticeana, 1860.
Rainbow, The, 1804.
Rhode Island Book, 1841.
Rush, B , Essays, 1806.
Salad for the Solitary, 1853.
Salmagundi, 1814.
Sands, R. C., Writings, 1835.
Sarmint agin Bull fights, 1860. P. 2504.
Scrap Table for 1831.
Scribblings, (Watmough), 1844.
Sedgwick, C. M., Facts and fancies, 1848.
Shahcoolen, Letters, 1802.
Shelton, F. W., Peeps from a belfry, 1855.
Shillaber, B. P., Mrs. Partington, 1859.
Sigourney, L. H., Water-drops, 1859.
" Pleasant Memories, 1844.
" Scenes in my native land, 1845.

Literature, American (continued).
Simms, W. G., Egeria, 1844.
Sketches by a traveller, 1830.
Spalding, Bp. M. J., Miscellanea, 1858.
Sprague, C., Writings, 1843.
Street, A. B., Woods and waters, 1860.
" The Indian Pass, 1869.
Talisman, The, 1828–30.
Tator, H. H., Essays, 1850. P. 606.
Taylor, B., At home and abroad, 1860.
" 2d series, 1862.
Taylor, J., Essays on various subjects, 1822.
Thompson, M., Hist. of Elephant club, 1857.
Thoreau, H. D., Excursions in Mass., 1863.
" Walden: life in the woods, 1854.
" Yankee in Canada, 1866.
" Cape Cod, 1865.
" Concord and Merrimac rivers, 1862.
Thorpe, T. B., Hive of the Bee-hunter, 1854.
" Mysteries of the back woods, 1846.
Token, The, 1828, 1832.
'Tother side of Ohio, 1818.
Tuckerman, H. T., Diary of a dreamer, 1853.
" The Optimist, 1850.
Tudor, W., Miscellanies, 1821.
Up Country Letters, 1852.
Verplanck, Disc. and Addresses, 1833.
Wallace, H. B., Lit. Criticisms, 1856.
Ware, H., Works, 1846.
Webber, Hunter Naturalist, 1851.
Webster, D., Beauties of.
Webster, N., A Collection of Essays, etc., 1790.
Western Souvenir, 1829.
Whipple, E. P., Lectures on, 1850.
Whitney, A. D. T., Real folks, 1872.
Whittier, J. G., Lit. recreations, 1854.
" Margaret Smith's Journal, 1849.
Willis, N. P., Dashes at Life, 1845.
" Rural Letters, 1849.
" Inklings of adventure, 1836.
" Letters from under a bridge, 1840.
" A l'abri, 1839.
" The Legendary, 1828.
" Hurry-graphs, 1851.
" Pencillings by the way, 1839.
" Fun-jottings, 1853.
" The Rag-bag, 1855.
" The Convalescent, 1859.

Literature, American (continued).
Wintergreen, The, 1844.
Wirt, W., The Old Bachelor, 1818.
Wright, Elizabeth, Lichen tufts, 1860.
See Fiction; Poetry; Essays; Literary, History.

Literature, Danish. Nordiske Literatur Samfund, 1847–51.

Literature, Dutch. Bowring, Batavian Anthology, 1824.
Diligentiæ Omnia Kunstgenootschap, 1774.
Douwama, Geschriften, 1849.
Duyse, Nederlandsche Versbouw, 1854.
Erasmus, Samenspraken, 1697.
Friesch Genootschap, 1856.
Genootschap, Dulces, etc., 1775.
God-geleertheid en dicht-kunden der Ouden. P 109.
Hagen, J., Verzameling van Bruiloftsverzen, 1835. P. 31. B. C.
Hemsterhuis, Œuvres philosophiques.
Hooft, P. C., Brieven, 1600–40.
Hoeven, A. Des Amorie v. d., Addresses, 1828. P. 30. B. C.
Jonckbloet, Op de Rym-Kronyk, 1840.
Kerkhistorisch Archief, 1857.
Kemper, Verhandelingen, 1835, 36.
Kolyn, K., Historia of Rym-chronik, 1745.
Letterkundig genootschap. Mengelingen, 1843–51.
Maatschappij der Ned. Letterkunde, 1846–50.
Maatschap., Tot nut van't Algemeen, 1790, 1804–12.
Maerlant, Rymbybel, 1859.
" Glossarium op. Rym Bibel.
" Spiegel Historiael, 1857–62.
" Alexanders Geesten, 1861.
Meyer, J. D., Verhandelingen, 1844, 1846.
Mulder, Letteryruchten, 1844.
Muller, P. L. S., Eenzame Nagt-gedagten, 1761.
Pamphlets, vol. 107.
Samenkomst der Geleerden, 1739.
Taal en Dicht, Mengelstoffen, 1776.
Tafereel, Het groote, der Dwaasheid, 1720.
Vereen. ter bervord. Oude Nederl. Letterkunde, 1844–48.
Vries, J. de, Nederduitsche Dichtkunde, 1808. B. C.
See Poetry; Drama.

Literature, English and Translations. Addison, Joseph, Works, 1809, 10, 56.
Amory, T., Life of Buncle, 1766.
Blanchard, L., Sketches from Life, 1846.

Literature, English and Translations (continued).

Boyd, A. H., Every day philosopher, 1863.
" Recreations of a country parson, 1861.
" Leisure hours in town, 1862.
" Graver thoughts, 1862, 63.
British Essayists: Spectator, etc.
Brown, J., Spare hours, 1862.
Browne, T., Works, 1836.
Brydges, Restituta, 1814–16.
" British Bibliographer, 1810.
" Censura literaria, 1815.
" Desultoria, 1815.
Buckingham, Duke of, Works, 1726.
Bulwer, Convers. with a Student, 1832.
Burton's Cyclopædia, 1858.
Camden Society Publications, 1838–69.
Carlyle, T., Sartor Resartus, 1837.
" On Heroes, 1841.
" Misc. essays, 1846.
Challenge sent by a young lady, 1697.
Chesterfield's Letters, 1777, 1865.
Coleridge, S. T., Works, 1854.
" Table talk, 1835.
Colman, G., Prose, 1787.
Comedian, The, No. 1–9, 1732.
Comforts of human life, 1807.
Cooper, A. A., Wit and Humour, 1709.
Creech, W., Edinb. fug. pieces, 1815.
Davy, H., Consolations in Travel, 1830.
Death of Cain, 1811.
De Quincey, Writings, 1851–54.
Desultoria, 1850, N. Y.
Doran, Habits and Men, 1855.
" Table Traits, 1854.
" Hist. of court fools.
Drake, N., Mornings in Spring, 1828.
Dunton, J., Athenian Oracle, 1791.
Earle, Microcosmography, Repr., 1867.
Elegant Extracts, 1818.
Evelyn, J., Misc. writings, 1825.
Fick, Elegant Extracts, 1804.
Fitzosborne's letters, 1814.
Froude, Short studies of great subjects, 1867, 1871.
Fry, C., The Listener, 1832.
Fugitive pieces, Dodsley, 1765.
Gibbon, Miscel. Works, vol. 3, 1796.
Godwin, Mary W., Posthumous Works, 1798.
Governayle of Helthe, Repr.
Gray, W., Hist. Sketch of, 1835.
Guileville, Pylgremage of the Sowle, 1483, Repr.
Hall, B., Patchwork, 1841.
Hallam, Remains, 1863.

Literature, English and Translations (continued).

Hanway, J., Journal of 8 days, 1756.
Hazlitt, Characteristics, 1837.
" The Plain Speaker, 1826.
" Winterslow, 1850.
" Table talk, 1846.
" Spirit of the age, 1825.
Head, F. B., Bubbles from the Brünnen, 1845.
Heath's Book of Beauty, 1836.
Helps, A., Companions in Solitude, 1857.
" Friends in Council, 1849.
Herbert, W., Works of, 1842.
Heron, Letters of Literature, 1735.
Hiffernan, Miscellanies, 1755.
Hood, T., Prose and verse, 1845.
" Whims and oddities, 1854.
Hook, T., Sayings and Doings, 1836.
Howitt, Pictorial Calendar of the Seasons, 1854.
Hunt, L., Works, 1854.
" Men, Women and Books, 1847.
" Table talk, 1851.
" Book for a Corner.
" The Seer, 1864.
Infernal conference, 1795.
Jackson, W., The Four ages, 1798.
James I, Workes.
James, G. P. R., Dark scenes of history.
Johnson, S., Works.
Keate, Sketches from nature, 1793.
Knight, C., Half-hours with Best Authors.
Knowles, J. S., Works.
Lamb, C., Works, 1818, 38.
" Elia, 1838.
Landor, W. S., Works, 1840.
" Imaginary convers., 1826–29.
" Exam. of Shakespeare, 1834.
Lorgnette, The, or Studies of the Town, 1850.
Lyttelton, G., Works, 1775.
" Dialogues of the Dead, 1797.
Mackinnon, Atlantic and Transatlantic Sketches, 1852.
Maginn, The Odoherty Papers, 1855.
" Fraserian Papers, 1857.
" Shakespeare Papers, 1856.
Meikle, J., Solitude sweetened, 1811.
" The Traveller, Life of, 1812, 1813.
Microcosm, Canning, etc., 1788.
Mill, J. S., Dissertations, 1864.
Miller, H., Essays, 1865.
" Tales and sketches, 1863.
Mitford, M. R., Our Village, 1848.

Literature, English and Translations (continued).

More, Hannah, Works.

Murphy, A., Works.

My Grandfather's farm, 1829.

Percy Society Publications, 1840–52.

Pinkerton, J., Letters on, 1785.

Polyanthea, Lond., 1804.

Prout, Reliques of, 1861.

Punch: miscellany, Lond , 1844–5.

Rickman, T. C., Evening walk, 1795.

Rogers, H., Essays from Ed. Rev., 1840, 55.

" Greyson Letters, 1857.

Rogers, S., Table Talk, 1856.

Rolliad, 1787, 90.

Roscommon, Letters for the press, 1832.

St. John, Lord Bolingbroke, Works, 1793.

Scenes in our parish, 1833.

Serious Inquiry, Lond., 1752.

Shaw, Manual of Eng. lit., 1867.

Sidney, Sir P., Misc. works, 1860.

" Pembroke's Arcadia.

Smith, H., Gaieties and Gravities, 1852.

Smith, Sydney, Wit and Wisdom of, 1856.

Southey, R., Omniana, 1812.

" Common-place Book, 1849, 1851.

" The Doctor, 1844.

Stephen, J., Crit. and Misc. Essays, 1860.

Sterne, L., Works, 1847.

Taylor, Jane, Writings.

Thackeray, W. M., Mr. Brown's Letters, etc., 1853.

" Paris Sketch Book, 1852.

" Early and late papers, 1867.

Tupper, M. F., Rides of Æsop Smith, 1858.

Turkish Spy, (Marana), 1736.

Vaughan, H., Works, (Grosart), 1870.

Vaughan, Sir W., Golden fleece, 1626.

Warburton, W., Lit. Remains, 1841.

Warren, S., Miscellanies, 1854.

" Diary of a physician.

Welsted, Works, 1787.

Wharton, Wits and beaux of Society.

Willmott, Journ. of Summer Time, 1852.

Wilson, J., Noctes Ambrosianæ, 1855, 1856.

" Dies Boreales, 1850.

" Recreations of, 1842.

Winter's wreath, Lond., 1831.

See Essays; Literary criticism and History; Fiction; Bibliography.

Literature, Flemish. Bibliophile Belge, 1845–64.

Delepierre, Hist. of Flemish lit., 1860.

Reiffenberg, Ann. Bib. Royale, 1840–1851.

Literature, French. Alembert, Mélanges de Litt., 1760.

Artiguenave, Morceaux choisis.

Beaumanoir, Coutumes des Beauvoisis.

Beaumarchais, Œuvres, 1837.

Besnier, Le Mexique Conquis, 1752.

Boileau, Works, Trans.

Boniface, Lecture par Jour, 1851, 54.

Brantome, Les Dames Galantes, 1834.

Brillat Savarin, Physiol. du gout.

" Physiol. of taste, 1854.

Buffon, Morceaux choisis.

Carraud, Maurice, 1858.

" La petite Jeanne, 1858.

Cartier, Mélange Curieux, 1767.

Chateaubriand, Œuvres, 1836, 37.

" Sketches of Engl. lit., 1836.

Chenier, Œuvres Diverses, 1816.

Chevreau, Œuvres Meslées, 1697. *See* Perron.

Condorcet, Œuvres, 1847.

Courier, P. L., Œuvres, 1837.

Du Fail, Discours d'aucuns propos, 1732.

Erasmus, L'Eloge de la Folie, 1715.

Estienne, Souvenirs, 1855.

Fauriel, Hist. of Provençal poetry, 1860.

Fénélon, Œuvres, 1836, 37.

Feugère, Morceaux choisis.

Fonfréde, Œuvres, 1844–47.

Genlis, Jeux champêtres.

Hist. Lit. des femmes françaises, 1769.

Jay, A., Le Glaneur, 1812.

La Harpe, Cours de Littérature, 1837.

Lamartine, Cours Familier, 1856.

" Les confidences, 1849.

Lambert, Marquise de, Œuvres, 1750.

Le Blanc, Lettres de Londres, 1751.

Le Brun, Lecture Courante, 1857.

" Etudes de Littérature, 1822.

Lemare, Cours de Lecture.

Maistre de Sacy, Journey round my room.

Masson, French classics.

Méon, Contes des xiie—xve Siècles.

Méré, Œuvres, 1701.

Montaigne, M. de, Essais de.

" Essays, Wight's Ed.

Ottavi, Recueil des Travaux de, 1843.

Perroniana, etc.

Revue des Deux Mondes, 1851–70.

Revue du Nouveau Monde, 1849–50.

Literature, French (continued).

Sainte Beuve, C. A., Portraits de femmes, 1858.

" Portraits of celeb. women, 1868.

St. Evremond, C. M. de St. D., Œuv., 1726. *See also* Perroniana.

St. Pierre, J. H. B., Œuvres, 1836.

Salm, La Princesse de, Œuvres, 1842.

Suard, J. B., Mélanges, 1803.

Théry, Cours de Litt., 1847.

Thou, De. *See also* Perroniana.

Turgot, Œuvres, 1808–11.

Vijver, Chrestomathie, 1826. B. C.

Villemain, Tableau de la lit. Fr.

See Language; Poetry, French.

Literature, German. Arnim, Armuth ....der Gräfin Dolores.

Eichhorn, Gesch. der Litteratur.

Gessner, Works.

Goethe, W. J von., W. Meister's apprenticeship.

Hedge, Prose Writers of Germany, 1848.

Korner, C. T., Tales, Poems, etc.

Lessing, Fabeln, 1857.

Literarische Verein, Nürnberg, 1841–1865.

Luther, M., Table Talk, 1857.

Schiller, F., Sammtliche Werke.

" Translations, Bohn's ed.

Schlegel, Æsthetic and misc. works.

Scholl, G. H., Geschichte der alt-und neu-deutschen Lit., 1845.

Wagenseil, Von der Meister-Singer, Anfang, etc., 1697.

Literature, Italian. Alfieri, V., America libera.

" Tragedies: Trans. Lloyd.

Boccaccio, Decamerone, 1825.

Collezione in dialletto Veneziano.

Dante, Le monde Dantesque, 1856.

Da Ponte, L., Storia della vita, 1807.

Doddridge, P., Principii, etc.

Foresti, Chrestomazia, 1851.

Ganganelli, L., Lettere, 1823.

Ginguené, Hist. Lit. d'Italie, 1824.

Giordani, Prose, 1827–29.

Leone, Dialoghi di Amore, 1545.

Machiavelli, Opere, 1811.

" Translations, Bohn's ed.

Maffei, S., Opere, 1790.

Manzoni, A., Tragedie, 1825.

" I promessi sposi, 1845.

Metastasio, P., Opere, 1813.

" Dramas, etc., Hoole,1800.

Monti, Opere, 1832–35.

Oration on Ital. works of imagination, 1832.

Literature, Italian (continued).

Pellico, S., Opere, 1835.

Pezzoli, L., Prose e Poesie, 1835, 6.

Polcastro, G., Opere, vol. 1, 4, 1832.

Roberti, G., Opere, 1831.

Rosetti, G., Discorso inaug., 1831.

Soave, F., Novelle morali, 1825.

Tasso, T., Opere, 1724.

" Translations, Bohn, 1854.

Tiraboschi, Letteratura Italiana, 1803, 1813.

Vannetti, C., Opere, 1826–31.

Villardi, F., Operette, 1832.

Literature, Latin, Modern. Barclay, J., Argenis, 1621.

" Euphormion, 1671.

Cælius, Antiquæ lectionis, 1616.

Goropius, J., Opera, 1580.

Gruter, Lampas, sive Fax lib. artium, 1606.

Larvina Satyricon, (Colardeau), 1619.

Politianus, A., Opera, 1553.

Sidonius, C. S., Opera, 1609.

See Poetry, Latin.

Literature, Russian. Bowring's Russ. Anthology.

Otto, Russ. Lit., 1839.

Talvi, Lit. of Slavic Nations.

Literature, Sanscrit. Asiat. Soc. of Bengal; Researches, 1812.

Asiatic Society of Bengal, Bibliot. Indica, 31 v.

Garcin de Tassy, Hist. litt. Hindoui.

Jones, Sir W., Works.

Lamartine, Cours de litt., 1856.

Mahawanso, Trans. of Turnour, 1837.

Ramchunder, Memorial, 1838.

Schlegel, Essays on Ind. literat.

Small, G., Sanscrit lit., 1866.

Stevenson, Trans. of the Sanhitá, 1842.

Yajnadattabada, Chàzy, 1826.

See Language, Sanscrit.

Literature, Spanish. Aleman, Vida del P. Guzman.

Botello, F., El nuevo mundo, 1701.

Cervantes Saavedra, M., Don Quijote, 1853.

" Galatea, 1784.

" Viage al Parnaso, 1784.

" Trabajos de Persiles, 1781.

Ercilla, La Araucana, 1776.

Feyjoo, Works, Trans.

Florian, Novelas nuevas, Trans.

Gallardo, El Criticon, 1836. P. 628.

Hita, G. P. de, Vandos de los Zegries ....de Granada, 1757.

Manrique, R., Coplas, 1779.

Mohedano, Hist. lit. de España, 1772.

Livingston County, N. Y. Directory, 1868.

Livingston Manor. Clarkson, Biog. History of, 1869.

Livonia. Account of, 1701.
Heath's Annual, (Ritchie), 1836.

Lobdell, H. Tyler, W. S., Memoir of.

Locke, J. Burnet, G., Preface on, 1732.
Grenville, Oxford & Locke, 1829.
King, Lord, Life of, 1830.

Locke, W. Locke, J. G., Geneal. Record of, 1853.

Lockhart, G. Lockhart papers, 1817.

Lockhart, J. G. Life of, in Spanish ballads, 1856.
Peter's Letters to his Kinsfolk, 1819.
Scott, J., Statement, 1821.

Locks. Chubb, Construction of.
Fichet, Notice sur les travaux de, 1855. P. 233.
Newell's Bank Lock, 1849. P. 298.
Tomlinson, C., Treatise on, 1853.

Lodging Houses. Great Britain, Lodging Houses, 1853. P. 472.
See Building Societies; Poor.

Loevenstein, H. Vollenhoven, Broeders gevangenisse, 1842.

Logic. Blakey, R., Hist. Sketch of, 1851.
Bouhours, Art of, 1728.
Brenan, Old and new logic, 1838.
Brerewood, Tractatus de Prædicalibus, etc., 1659.
" Elem. logicæ, 1668.
Burgersdicius, Instit. Logica., 1668.
Crousaz, J. P., Art of thinking, 1724.
De Morgan, Formal Logic, 1847.
Devey, Logic, 1854.
Duncan, W., Elements of, 1792. B. C.
Duns, Scriptum super 4° Sententiarum, 1520.
Fowler, T., Elem. of deduct. logic, 1867.
Hamilton, W., Lectures on, 1860.
Hamilton, W. G., Parliam. logick, 1808.
Hedge, L., Elements of.
Hornstein, Dialectica anal. imaginibus illust., 1779.
Lacrételle, Logique et Métaphysique.
Latham, R. G., Logic applied to Gram., 1847.
Lombard, Sententiarum lib. iv., 1634.
Melancthon, Erotemata Dialectices, 1577.
Mill, J. S., System of, 1846.
Milton, J., Works, vol. 5, 1851.
Mocenicus, Univ Instit. ad Hom. perfectionem, 1581.

Logic (continued).
Neil, S., Art of Reasoning, 1853.
Rogers, J. E. T., Lect. on Aristotle.
Tappan, H. P., Elements of, 1856.
Thomson, W., Laws of Thought, 1859.
Watts, I., Works.
Whately, R., Elements of, 1834.
Wilson, W. D., Elem. Treatise, 1856.
See Philosophy; Language; Mental Philos.

Loire, France. Annuaire, 1845.

Lollards. Netter, Fasciculi....1858.
See Wickliffe, J.

Lombardy. Barrow, J., jr., Tour in, 1840.
Kingsley, C., Roman and Teuton, 1864.
Smith, B., Italian irrigation, 1855.
See Certosa; Milan; Padua; Pavia; Venice; Verona; Vicenza; Italy.

London. Allen, T., Hist. and Antiq. of, 1837, 39.
Arnold's Chronicle, 1810.
Brayley, London and Middlesex.
Burton, Histor. remarks, 1681.
Calamy, B., Sermon on the fire, 1666.
" Sermon, 1685.
Cansick, Epitaphs in St. Pancras, 1869.
Change for Dickens's notes, 1843.
Cock, Dock Company, 1825.
Colquhoun, Commerce of the Thames, 1800.
Comparative statement, 1799.
Concanen's Southwark, 1795.
Cooper, J. F., Society in the Metropolis, 1837.
Crosby, Brass, Memoirs of,
Cunningham, P., Hand-book of, 1850.
Deering, Coal Whippers of, 1851.
De Foe, Works, Plague in.
Deykes, Pavement of the Streets, 1824. P. 139.
Elmes, Survey of Harbor of, 1838.
" Topog. Description of, 1831.
Emerson, G. R., How London grew.
Essay on increase of trade, 1749.
Estell, Commercial list, 1860.
Francklin, Serm. after the fire, 1748.
Gavin, Unhealthiness of, 1847.
Gerard, London and New York, 1853.
Gosden, Funer. Monuments in.
Grafton's Chronicle (List of Officers).
Grant, R., Great Metropolis, 1837.
Graunt, Nat. and pol. Obs. on, 1676.
Hawkins, T., Drainage of, 1848.
Herbert, 12 Great Livery Companies.
Hewitt, The Tower of.
Hogg, J., London as it is, 1836.

Mackintosh, Sir J. Macaulay's Essays, Life of.
Mackintosh, R. J., Memoirs of, 1836.
" Life of, in his History.

Macklin, A. Gray, J., Sermon on, 1859.

McKnight, J. Patton, J., Discourse on.

Macky, J. Mem. of secret services of, 1733.

McLagan, J. Davidson, A. D., Sermon on.

Maclaine, J. Allen, Dr., Behavior of, 1750.

McLean, J. Sprague, W. B., Disc. on.

McLeod. Urquhart, Case of, 1841.

McLeod, A. Wylie, S. B., Memoirs, 1835.

Macnaught, J. Lowe, J. B., Reply to, 1856.

M'Neale, J. Johnson, S. C., A Few Thoughts, 1843. P. 331.

Macomb, A. Richards, George H., Memoirs, 1833.

Macon, E. Cotten, Life of, 1840.

McPherson, J. Buist, On death of, 1806.

Macrea, Jane. *See* McCrea.

Macready. Rejoinder, Astor Opera House, 1849.

Macurdy, E. Elliott, D., Life of, 1840.

McVickar, J. In memoriam, 1868.

McWhorter, A. Griffin, E. D., Sermon on, 1807.

Macy, S. J. Genealogy of, 1868.

Madagascar. Boothby, R., Description of.
Cauché, Voyage à, 1651.
Copland, History of, 1822.
Drury's Adventures, 1807.
Ellis, W., History of, 1838.
" Three Visits to, 1859.
Everard, Sufferings near.
Jeffreys, K., Journal, 1827.
Madagascar, Past and Present, 1847.
Pfeiffer's, Visit to, 1861.
Relations Véritables, 1651.
Rochon, Voyage to, 1792.
See Africa.

Madeira Is. Bowdich, S., Excursions in Madeira, 1823.
Campden, C. G. N., British Chaplaincy, 1847. P. 238.
Dix, J. A., A Winter in, 1850.
Lord, J., Persecution at.
March, C. W., Sketches, 1856.
Steele, R., Tour, 1810.

Madiai family. Evang. Mag., 1852. Persecu. in Tuscany.

Madison, J. Adams, J. Q., Eulogy on, 1831.
Bacon, E., Address, 1844.
Barnard, D. D., Lecture on, 1837.
Jennings, P., Reminiscences of, 1865.
Lowell, J., Mr. Madison's war.
Madison, Papers, 3 v., 1840.
" Corresp., 1859, (Maguire).
" Letters, 4 v., 1865.
Rives, W. C., Life of, 1859–68.

Madison Co., N. Y. Directory, 1868.

Madison, Ind. Lyford's Directory, 1837.

Madison, Wis. Statistics, 1852.
Draper's Descr. of, 1857.

Madison University, N. Y. Catalogues, 1846–64.

Madras. Letter to a proprietor, 1750.
Lewin, M., Rupture with the Court, 1848.
Murray's Handbook.

Madrid, Spain. Descripcion, 1833.
Manual, 1833.

Maffitt, J. N. Elsemore, Life of, 1848.
Maffitt, Trial of, 1822.

Magaw, L. Bend, J., Sermon on, 1790.

Magdalens. Pam. vols. 985, 986.

Magee, J. Howe, F. S., Life of.

Magazines. *See* Periodicals.

Magellan Strait. Bry, J. De, Peregrin. Collectio.
Hacke, Wood's Voyage, 1699.
Pernety, Two voyages, 1763–64.
See Pacific voyages.

Magic. Boulton, Possibility of, 1722.
Brewster, D., Letters on
Collin de Plancy, Dictionnaire infernal.
De Foe, System of.
Ennemoser, History of, 1854.
Gentilis, S., In Apulei apologiam, 1607.
Godwin, Lives of the Necromancers, 1834.
Hauber, Bibliotheca Magica, 1739–45.
Horst, Zauber Bibliothek, 1821–26.
Leechdoms, Wortcunning, and starcraft of early Engl. (Chron. G. B.).
Madden, R. R., Phantasmata.
Maffei, Opere, Arte magica annichilata.
Porta, Magiæ Naturalis, 1607.
Salverte, E., Philosophy of, 1847.
Wright, T., Narr. of Sorcery and, 1852.
See Delusions.

Maginn, W. Mem., in Fraserian Papers.

Mammalia (continued).
Jardine, Felinæ, Ruminantia, Monkeys, Whales, (Naturalist's Lib.).
Macgillivray, British quadrupeds.
N. Y. Nat. Hist., v. 1, Mammalia.
Owen, R., Reports on Brit. foss. mammalia.
Smith, C. H., Mammalia.
" Dogs, Horses.
Swainson, Classification of quadrup.
" Nat. Hist. of quadrupeds.
Trimmer, Hist. of quadrupeds.
U. S. Expl. Expedition, Mammalogy, (Cassin).
" Mammalia, Peale.
Waterhouse, Hist. of Mammalia.
White, A., History of Mammalia.
Youatt, The horse, dog, sheep.
See Zoölogy; Natural History; Pygmies.

Mammoth Cave. *See* Caves.

Man. Anthropological Society, Transactions, 1858-69.
Atkinson, Lect. on Man's Nature, 1851.
Blanc St. Bonnet, De l'Unité Spirituelle, 1841. B. C.
Bory de St. Vincent, L'Homme, Essai zoölogique, 1827.
Boyne, L. S., Phys. and Mor. Hist. of, 1815.
Buffon, Hist. de l'Homme, 1750.
Bulkely, C., Apol. for human nature, 1797. P. 1787.
Burgess, Bp. S., Principles of vitality in, 1789.
Burgh, J., Dignity of human nature, 1816.
Cabell, Testimony on Unity of Race, 1859.
Caldwell, C., Thoughts on Unity, 1852.
Carter, Primitive State of, 1836.
Chalmers, Constitution of Man, 1833.
Charron, P. De, Of wisdom, 1729.
Coles, Crit. on Nott and Gliddon, 1857.
Combe, G., Constitution of man.
Comparative view, 1766.
Darwin, Descent of man, 1871.
Dunlap, S. F., Vestiges of Spirit History of, 1858.
Ewbank, Relation of: to the earth.
Forry, S., On the Position of Man, 1844. P. 272.
Fourier, Passions of human soul.
Goodrich, S. G., Curios. of human nature.
Gregory, J., Faculties of, and animals.
Guyot, The Earth and Man, 1849.
Harris, J., Man primeval, 1854.
Helvetius, C. A., L'homme et ses facultés.

Man (continued).
Helvetius, C. A., Treatise on man, 1810.
Hemsterhuis, Œuvres philosophiques, 1846.
Herder, J. G., Philos. of hist. of, 1803.
Home, H., Sketches of Hist. of, 1813.
Hugo, T., Dignity of the body, 1856.
Hunt, J., Addresses, 1863-67.
Johnes, Philolog. proofs of Unity of race, 1846.
Kidd, Adaptation of nature to, 1833.
Laurence, W., Lectures, 1848.
Liharzik, Law of increase, Vienna, 1862.
Lubbock, Primitive condition of, 1870.
Marsh, G. P., Man and nature, 1864.
" Uomo e la natura, 1870.
Marsh, H., Evolution of light from, 1842.
Maury, Terre et l'Homme, 1857.
Meigs, J. A., Catal. of human crania, 1857.
Moore, G., Man and his motives, 1848.
Morris, What is man? 1862.
Mudie, His physical, intell. and moral nature, 1839.
Neal, J., Man, an address, 1858.
Nott, J. C., Indigenous Races, 1857.
Quételet, L'homme et ses facultés, 1833.
Reid, M., Odd people, 1861.
Schouw, Earth and Man, 1852.
Smith, C. H., Nat. Hist. of, 1848, 59.
Spurzheim, Natural laws of man.
Tourtelle, Principles of health.
U. S. Sanitary Commission, Statistics, 1869.
Van Amringe, Nat. Hist. of, 1848.
Waitz, T., Introd. to anthropology, 1863.
Wanley, Wonders of the little world, 1806.
Warden, R. B., View of man and law, 1860.
See Philosophy; Soul; Ethnology; Mental Phil.; Physiology; Anatomy; Longevity; Life; Gentleman.

Man, Antiquity and Origin. Agassiz, Geog. distr. of animals.
Argyll, Primeval man, 1869.
Babbage, Remains of Human art with bones.
Clarkson, T., Antediluvian researches.
Darwin, Descent of man, 1871.
Davenport, A., Origin of, 1846.
Hale, Sir M., Prim. origination of.
Huxley, Man's place in nature, 1863.
Lesley, J. P., Origin and destiny of, 1868.

Man, Antiquity and Origin (cont'd).
Lubbock, Prim. condition of, 1870.
Lyell, Antiquity of man, 1863.
Poole, R. S., Genesis of man, 1860.
Quatrefages, A. De, Metamorphoses of, 1864.
Tuttle, H., Origin of, 1866.
Vogt, C., Lectures on, 1864.
See Geology; Pre-historic period.

Man, Isle of. Beauties of England and Wales.
Johnstone, Antiq. Celt. Normannicæ.
Man, Is., Letters from, 1847.
Robertson, David, Tour in.
Townley, R., Journal in.
Train, Hist. of Isle of Man, 1845.

Manche, France. Annuaire, 1828.

Manchester, Eng. Aikin, J., Descr. of country around, 1795.
Hulton, Case of Westhoughton, 1851.
Lee, J. P., Correspondence, 1849.
Manchester, Free Lib., Reports to 1870.
Manchester Chamber of Comm., 1839.
Manchester massacre, 1819. P. 795.
Manchester Lit. and Phil. Soc., Memoirs, 1785–98.
Manchester: Visitor's guide, 1857.
Philips, F., An Exposure, riot, 1819.
Pigot's Directory, 1829.
Prentice, A., Hist. Sketches of, 1792–1832.
Radical Monday, 1819.
Wheeler, J., History of, 1836.

Manchester, New Hamp. Directory, 1858, 64.
Potter, C. E., History of, 1856.

Manchuria. Williamson's Journeys, 1870.
See China; Tartary.

Mandeville, B. de. Law, W., Reply to.
True meaning, 1726.

Manet, M. Séchelles, Vie de.

Manley, Mrs. Nichols, Coll. of poems, v. 7.

Mann, H. Life of, 1865.
Bristed, Letter to, 1850.
Common School controversy. P. 175.

Manners and Customs. Arnay, Private life of Romans.
Berry, Social life in Eng. and France, 1844.
Brookes, J., M. and C. of the English, 1860.
Brown, J., Estimate of manners, 1757.
Bulwer, France, Social, 1834, 36.
Chasles, American manners, 1852.
Friswell, The Gentle Life, 1864.
Glen, Des habits...de l'Europe, 1601.

Manners and Customs (continued).
Hermit in London, 1819.
Malcolm, London to 17th cent.
" London in 18th cent.
Panton, Guardian's Instruction, 1688.
Planche, British costume, Lib. E. K.
Renneville, Coutumes gauloises, 1823.
Reviewers reviewed, 1815.
Sauzeau, Usages locaux dans les Deux Sèvres, 1846.
Shady Side, (Torrey), 1853.
Soc. lib. d'Agr. de l'Eure, Usages locaux, 1846–50.
Some doubts on Brown's Estimate of, 1758.
Strutt, J., Sports of England, 1801.
" English dress, 700–1800, 1842.
Trollope, Domestic manners of the Americans, 1839.
Tylor, On primitive culture, 1871.
Vergilius, De rerum inventoribus, 1546.
See Etiquette; Travels; Voyages; England, Manners.

Mannheim, F. Distresses of, 1794.

Mannheim. Acad. des Sciences, Collini, Discours, 1799.

Manning, J. Guild, R. A., Life of, 1864.

Manningham, J. Diary, 1602–1603, (Camden Soc.).

Mansfield, C. F. Memorial of, 1866.

Mansfield, Lord. Butler, C., Life of, 1817.
Holliday, J., Life of, 1797.

Mansfield, Conn. Sherman, J., Eccles. proceed. at, 1806.

Mantua, Italy. Description of, 1797.

Manufactures. Aikin, Illust. of the Arts and, 1841.
Barlow, P., Treat. on man. of G. Brit.
Bishop, History of American, 1861, 64.
Essex Comp., Lawrence, 1852. P. 266.
France, Enquête, Indust. Métall. et Textiles, 1861.
Great Britain: Patents, 1617–1867.
Hadley Falls Corpor., 1854. P. 298.
Journal of Design, 1849–53.
Lowell, Mass., Statistics, 1855. P. 192.
Macpherson, Annals of Comm., Manuf., etc., 1805.
Persoz, De l'impression des tissus, 1846.
Repertory of Arts and Manu. *period.* London, 1794–1848.
Society of Arts, Journal, 1852–70.
Strictures on Montgomery, 1841.
Tomlinson, Cyclopædia of 1852, 68.
Ure, Cotton Manf. of Gr. Brit., 1861.
See Cotton; Wool; Silk; Iron; Arts; Statistics; Exhibitions; Mechanics' Institutes.

Manures. Dana, S. L., Essay on, 1853.
Donaldson, Soils and manures. P. 667.
Dumas, On manure, (Stephenson, Book of the farm).
Emerson, G., Superphosphate of lime, 1859.
Johnston, J. F. W., Use of lime, 1849.
" Analysis of, 1855.
Kirwan, Essay on, 1796.
Martindale, J., Soils and manures, 1849. P. 667.
Morfit, C., On manures, 1848.
National fertilizers, 1858. P. 950.
Native guano, 1849. P. 1217.
Rendleb, Kein guano mehr.
Solly, Rural chemistry, 1852.
Stöckhardt, Chem. of agriculture, 1855.
See Agriculture; Guano.

Manuscripts, Essays on knowledge of, etc. Delandine, Mém. bibliog., 1817.
Dibdin, Bibliog. Decameron, 1817.
Humphreys, Art of Illumination, 1849.
" Illumina. MSS. of Mid. Ages, 1849.
Langlois, Calligraphie du moyen age, 1841.
Maitland, The Dark Ages; Essays, 1853.
Merryweather, Bibliomania in the Mid. Ages, 1849.
Namur, Bibliog. paléog. dipl. générale, 1838.
Peignot, Dict. de bibliol., 1802, 04.
Waagen, Treas. of Art in Gt. Brit., 1857.
Wright, Illuminated MSS.
See Writing; Alphabets; Illum. MSS; Bibliography.

Manutius, P. A. Epist. lib. xii, 1580.
Tre libri di lettere, 1556.

Manzoni, A. Gal. des Contem. vol. 6: Vie de, 1845.

Mappa, A. G. Specimens of Dutch type foundries.
Perkins, E., Bunker hill contest, 1826.

Maps, Geographical. Arrowsmith, Atlas, 1805.
Asher, On Maps of New Netherland, 1867.
Bible Atlas, 1832.
Blaew, America, Geographia, 1662.
Burr, County atlas of N. Y., 1829.
Carey, Amer. Atlas, 1802.
Catalogo de hidrografia de Madrid.
Catalogue of, (N. Hale's), 1862.
Crelle, Catalogue, Berlin, 1856.
Faribault, Catal. sur l'Amérique, 1837.

Maps, Geographical (continued).
Fitch, G. W., Mapping plates.
France, Hydrog. Française, 1847.
Gage, Mod. hist. atlas, 1869.
George III, Bibl. Regiæ Catal., v. 6, 1829.
Gr. Br., Crown lands: Maps.
Johnson, Family Atlas, 1862.
" Family Atlas of the world, and the U. S., 1872.
Keulen, G. Van, Atlas, Marine, 1710.
Koeppen, Authors on Geog. of Mid. Ages, 1854.
Kohl, On Maps of America, 1856.
Mackenzie, M., Survey, Coast of Ireland and Gt. Britain, 1776. 2 v. f°.
Martens, Cat. de cartes géographiques, 1837. L. L.
Mercator, Atlas, 1636, v. II.
Mitchell, S. A., Atlas, 1863.
New York, Cat. of Maps in the departments, 1851, 59.
N. Y. County maps, folded, 1851–60.
N. Y. State Lib., Catalogue of maps in, 1856, 61.
Ortelius, A., Teatro del mondo, 1608.
Pelton, Key to Maps, 1845.
Phelps, 100 cities, U. S., 1853. P. 565.
Picquet, Cat. Syst. de cartes anc. et mod., 1837.
Spruner, Hist. Geog. Atlas, 1846.
Steel's Marine Atlas, 1814.
Stevens, H., On the earliest maps of America, 1869.
Vandermaelen, P., Atlas Universel, 1827. 6 v.
Vandermeersch, Cartes aux archives de la Flandre, 1850.
Wyld, Cat. of, for sale, Lond., 1846.
See Bibliography; Geography.

Marathi. *See* Language.

Marble. Bury, Modèles de Marbrerie, 1855.
Hager, Marbles of Vermont, 1858.
Jervis, Min. of Central Italy, 1862.
Marble worker's Manual, 1856.
Roxbury, Vt., Verd Antique Co., 1857.
See Geology; Exhibitions.

March, A. Tribute to, 1870.

Marchmont, Earls of. Papers, 1685–1750.

Marcy, R. B. 30 years of army life, 1866.

Marcy, W. L. Allen, W. F., Address, Ham. Coll.
Jenkins, Lives of Gov. of N. Y.
Marcy, W. L., Funeral of. P. 1858.
Scott, W., Corresp. with, 1848.

Marriage (continued).
Pamphlets relating to, vols. 985, 986, 1526.
Reasons.. deceased wife's sister.
Religious courtship, (De Foe), 1777.
Robinson, E., Bibliot. Sacra, 1843, (Marr. with wife's sister).
Ross, F. A., On Bishop Colenso, 1857.
Sanchez, T., De Matrimonio, 1739.
Thelypthora, (Madan), 1780.
Thoughts on....from adultery, 1800.
Walker, A., Intermarriage, 1839.
West, M., Treatise, (Quaker), 1728.
Wilder, A., Intermarr. of kindred, 1870.
Young husband's book.
See Woman; Love; Social Questions, etc.

Marsden, J. Grace displayed; life of, 1814.

Marseilles. Berteaut, Marseille et les intérêts nationaux, 1843.
Julliany, Commerce de, 1834.
Marseilles, Journal of the plague, 1720.
Marseille, L'Hermès, 1826.

Marsh, E. G. Dwight, T., Discourse on.
Fowler, B., Oration on.

Marsh, H. Refutation of, 1822.

Marsh, J. Wheeler, J., Fun. discourse.

Marshall, A. West of Scotland arch-voluntary, 1835.

Marshall, C. Diary, 1774–77.

Marshall, H. Darlington, Memorial of, 1849.

Marshall, J. Binney, H., Eulogy on, 1835.
Story, J., Discourse on, 1835. P. 494.
Van Santvoord's lives of Chief justices.
Wynne's lives of eminent men, 1850.

Marshfield, Mass. Thomas, M. A., Memorials of, 1854.

Martens, T. Gand, Recherches sur la vie de, 1845.
Iseghem, Biographie de, 1852.

Martha's Vineyard Is. Mayhew, Indian converts, 1727.
Nantucket Papers, 1856.

Martial Law. Nicholas, S. S., Martial law, 1861.
See Civil War, 1861–65.

Martin, L. Keene, R. R., Letter to, 1802.

Martin, M. Captivity in Algiers, 1807.

Martinique. Bouton, Etablissement des Français dans, 1635.
Chanvalon, Voyage à, 1751.
Essai sur l'Etat actuel, 1817.

Martinique (continued).
Gardiner, Expedition against, 1759.
Sainte Croix, Statistique de, 1832.
See West Indies; French Colonies.

Martyn, H. Sargent, Memoir of.

Martyrs. Bourchier, T., Mart. Frat. Francisci, 1582.
Briefe collection, 1611.
Fox, J., Book of Martyrs, 1684, 1830.
Mall, History of, 1747.
Tanner, M., Soc. Jesu....mors eorum, 1675.
See Persecution.

Martyrs of Science. Brewster, D., Lives of.

Marvin family genealogy, 1848.

Marvin, A. Sprague, W. B., Sermon, Death of, 1858.

Mary, Blessed Virgin. Collin de Plancy, Legends of, 1860.
Gallagher, Regard due to, 1855.
Horne, T. H., Worship of, 1844.
Jameson, Legends of the Madonna, 1857.
Lambruschini, Treatise on Immac. conception, 1860.
Lowe, J. B., Worship of, 1851. P. 1554.
McCarthy, On the Devotion to, 1849.

Mary Stuart, Queen of Eng. Barnett, A., Sermon on, 1695.
Bates, W., Sermon on, 1695.
Bowber, T., Sermon on, 1695.
Bridgewater, Poem on, 1695.
D., J., Ode to, 1694.
Gould, R., Poem on, 1695.
Jenison, Serm. on, 1695.
Le Roy, Een predikatie, 1695.
Manning, F., Pastoral Essay, 1695.
Manningham, T., Sermon, 1695.
O., S., Epicedium, 1695.
Partridge, W., Poem, 1695.
Payne, W., Sermon on.
Procession, The, 1695.
Sherlock, W., Serm., Death of, 1694.
Tenison, T., Serm., Fun. of, 1695.
Urania, 1695.

Mary Stuart, Queen of Scots. Anderson, J., Collections, 1727.
Barnestaple, Maria innocens à cæde Darleana, 1588.
Bell, H. G., Life of, 1831. B. C.
Hays, Mary, Female Biography, 1803.
Labanoff, Lettres et mémoires de, 7 v., 1844.
Sadler's State papers, 1809. 3 v.
Scotus, R., Summarium de morte, 1588.
Whitaker, J., Queen vindicated, 1789.

Masonry, Free (continued).
Free Mason's Directory, 1851.
Free Mason's Magazine, Lond., 1855.
Gowans, Cat. of Books on, 1858.
Halliwell, Early hist. in England.
Harris, T. M., Discourses, 1801.
Hitchcock, E. A., Christ the Spirit, 1861.
Iris, period., N. Y., 1827.
Knapp, S. L., Oration, 1811. P. 1697.
Knights Templar, Pilgrimage to Virginia, 1859.
London Magazine, 1824, (De Quincey).
MacArthur, C. L., Address, Troy, N. Y., 1853. P. 287.
Mackey, A. G., Of Masonic Law, 1855.
Macoy & Sickels, F. Mason's Monitor, 1865.
Masonic charac. of Washington, 1830.
Masonic Mirror, Boston, 1825.
Masonic Mirror, Key to, 1819.
Masonry the same, etc., 1830. P. 184.
Michelet, Procès des Templiers.
Milnor, J., Oration on, 1811.
Moore, C., The Craftsman, 1854.
Mother, The, of Masons, 1831. P. 183.
Oliver, G., Hist. of, 1829–41.
" Symbol of Glory, 1855.
Pamphlets relating to Masonry, vols. 183, 184, 211, 550, 882, 1697.
Paine, Thomas, Origin of.
Parker, J., Sermon, 1779.
Pratt, L., A defence of, 1828.
Risley, H. A., Oration at Dunkirk, N. Y., 1858.
St. Andrews R. A. Chapter, Boston, By-laws; Biog. sketches, 1859.
Series of letters, 1815.
Soane's Curiosities of Lit., 1849.
Stanford, J., Discourse, 1800.
Storer, Free Masons in Connecticut, 1859.
Thacher, P., Address, Dorchester, 1797.
Town, S., A System of, 1818.
Vocal Companion, (with Names of lodges), Bost., 1802.
Webb, Free Mason's Monitor, 1816.
Yates, P. W., Addresses, Albany, 1783.
See Bibliography; Secret Societies.

Masonry, Controversy on Free.
Adams, J. Q., Letters on the Institution, 1847.
Address....by a Cit. of N. Y., 1830.
Address to Mass., 1832.
Anti-Masonic Almanac, 1829, 30.
Anti-Masonic Review, 1829.
Barruel, Hist. of Jacobinism, 1799.
Brown, H., Anti-Mas. Excitement in N. Y., 1826–29.

Masonry, Controversy on Free (continued).
Catalogue of books on, 1829.
Collection of Letters on, 1849.
Convention of Anti-masons, Leroy, 1828. P. 12. B. C.
Crary, J., Statement to Anti-masons, 1828. P. 67.
" Speech, N. Y. Sen., 1828.
Democratic Anti-Mas. St. Conv., Pa., 1822. P. 194.
Genesee Consoc., to J. Emerson, 1829.
Greene, The broken seal, 1870.
Letters of Rush, Adams, Wirt, 1831.
Marshall, J., Opinions on Free Masonry. P. 184.
Massa., Leg. Report on, 1834. P. 184.
Mass. Anti-Masonic Convention, 1830. P. 55.
Morgan, W., Rep. on his abduction, 1830.
" Narr. of kidnapping, 1827.
" Illust. of Masonry, 1829.
National Observer, Albany, 1826–31.
N. Y. Anti-Masonic State Conv., 1829.
Odiorne, J. C., Opinions on, 1830.
Payson, S., Proofs of illuminism, 1802.
Penn'a Anti-Mas. Almanac, 1830.
Phil'a Add. on Secret Soc., 1829.
Revelations in, 1827.
Rhode Is.; Legis. Investigation, 1831, 1832. P. 211.
Rhode Is. Anti-Masonic Conv., 1831. P. 211.
Ritner, Vind. of Washington, 1837.
Robison, Proofs of a Conspiracy, 1798.
Rush, R., Letter on, 1831.
Seward, W. H., Speech, Anti-Masonic Celeb., 1831.
Southwick, S., Oration, 1829.
" Warning against, 1829.
Sprague, W., Report, R. I., 1832.
Stearns, J. G., Inquiry and.....Dialogue on.
" Appendix, on Morgan, 1828. P. 624.
Stone, W. L., Letters on, 1832.
Sumner, C. P., Letter on, 1829.
Tatem, Reply to R. I. Chapter, 1832. P. 211.
Thacher, M., Address, Anti-Masonic Conv., 1832. P. 204.
United States Anti-Mas. Conv., 1830, 1832.
See Secret Societies.

Mass. *See* Communion; Roman Cath. Church.

Massachusetts. Addresses to, 1805, 06, 1810.
Allen, E., Claims of N. H. and Mass. Bay, 1780.

Massachusetts (continued).
Ames's Almanac, 1737–72.
Andrew, Gov. J. A., Speeches, etc.
Andros Tracts, 1689–90.
Answer of the Whig Members, 1840.
Barry, J. S., Hist. of, 1856, 7.
Bollan, Petitions presented by, 1774.
Bradford, A., Hist. of, 1764–1820.
Byfield, Revolution in N. E., 1689.
Capen, Mass. State Record, 1847–50.
Carpenter, W. H., Hist. of, 1853.
Chickering, Jesse, Stat. view of population of, 1765–1840.
Church, Hist. of Philip's war, 1675, 6.
Clark, J. S., Hist. of Cong. Churches, 1620–1858.
Congre. Churches; Results of three Synods, 1648, 62, 79, 80. 1725.
Congr. Churches of, Minutes, 1824–60.
Cooke, P., Century of Puritanism.
Crowell, Hist. of Essex Co , in the rebellion, 1865.
Cushing, Letters on First Charter of, 1839.
Dawson, H. B., Decl. of Independence by, 1862.
De Costa, Northmen in Maine, 1870.
Defense of the Legislature, 1804. P. 1698.
Derby, J. B., The Statesman Party, 1835.
Dickinson, Statist. view of, 1813.
Everett, E., Add., settlement of, 1830.
Felt, J. B., Who first Governor? 1853.
Fleet's Register, 1786–1800.
Forbes, A., Rich Men of, 1851.
Fowler's Fall River: On boundary.
Gorton, S., Simplicity's Defence, 1835.
Hallett, B. F., Oration, July 4.
Hanson, Hist. of 6th regiment, 1865.
Hayward, J., The Mass. Directory, 1835.
" Gazetteer of, 1847.
Holland, J. G., Hist. of West. Mass., 1855.
Hutchinson, T., Speeches in Assembly, 1773. P. 115.
" Letters sent to Gr. Brit., 1773.
" Hist. of the Colony of, 1765–69.
Masères, Essays, Charter of Ms., 1809.
Mass., Records, 1628–86.
" Case of boundary, 1764.
" Public documents, Hartford Conv., etc., 1815.
" Census, 1850, 55, 65.
" Civil List, 1630–1774.
" Election sermons, 1747–1869.
" Geol. Survey, Reports, 1838–53.

Massachusetts (continued).
Mass., Registration Reports, 1843–58.
" Speeches of Governors, 1765–75.
" Statistics of Industry, 1845, 55, 1865.
Massachusetts Annual Register, 1790–1870.
Massachusetts in the revolution, (Seventy-Six Society Pub.).
Mass. Hist. Society, Collections, 1806–1869.
Mass. Hist. of 58th Regt., 1863–5.
Mass. Manual, (Burdick), 1814.
Mauduit, Short view of, 1774.
Minot, G. R., Hist. of Mass. Bay, 1748–65.
" Insurrection in, 1786.
Moore, G. H., Hist. of Slavery in, 1866.
Moore, J. B., Lives of the Governors, 1620–1692.
N. E. Hist. Gen. Reg., vols. 22, 23, 24, Bibliog. of the towns.
Niles, S., Sermon, Mass. Missionary Society, 1801.
Oliver, Peter, The Puritan Commonwealth, 1856.
Otis, J., Vindication of, 1762.
" Appeal to the world, 1769.
Pamphlets containing town documents, vols. 590, 987, 1698.
Plymouth Col. Records, 1633–92, 10 v.
Quint, Second Mass. infantry in the civil war.
Rantoul, R., Speech, Coalition in, 1852.
Review of Rise of New Eng., 1774.
Sargent, Dealings with the Dead, 1856.
Savage, J., Address, Hist. of Const. of, 1832.
Schouler, History of, in the rebellion.
Scottow, Planting of the Colony, 1694.
Strong, Gov., Speeches, 1800–07.
Sullivan, J., Land titles in, 1801.
Sullivan, W., Address to the bar, 1825.
Thoreau, A week on the Concord and Merrimack, 1849.
Thornton, J. W., Landing at Cape Ann, 1854.
Thoughts upon the pol. situation, 1788.
Towle and Foster, Enlargement of State House, 1854. P. 99.
True State of Proc. of Parl., 1774.
Twistleton, E., Education in Mass., the religious quest., 1854. P. 1315.
Wood, W., New England's Prospect, (Young's Chronicles).
Young, A., Chronicles of the first planters, 1623–36.
See New England; Plymouth Colony; Puritans; Bunker Hill; Paper Money; Newspapers.

Massachusetts, Local History. *See* Abington; Acton; Ashburnham; Athol; Barnstable; Barre; Becket; Belchertown; Berkshire; Beverly; Billerica; Boston; Braintree; Bridgewater; Brimfield; Bristol County; Brookfield; Brookline; Cambridge; Cape Cod; Charlestown; Chicopee; Concord; Conway; Danvers; Dartmouth; Dedham; Deerfield; Dorchester: Dudley; Duxbury; Eastham; Easthampton; Essex; Fairhaven; Fall River; Fitchburg; Foxboro; Framingham; Franklin Co.; Granville; Great Barrington; Greenfield; Groton; Hadley; Hamilton; Hampshire Co.; Hanover; Hardwick; Hatfield; Haverhill; Hingham; Holden; Holliston; Hopkinton; Ipswich; Jamaica Plain; Lancaster; Lee; Leicester; Leominster; Lexington; Lowell; Lunenburgh; Lynn; Malden; Marlboro; Marshfield; Martha's Vineyard; Medford; Medw'y; Melrose; Mendon; Merrimac Val'y; Milton; Monson; Nantucket; Natick; New Bedford; Newbury; Newburyport; Newton; Northborough; North Bridgewater; North Brookfield; North Hampton; Norton; Orleans; Pepperell; Petersham; Pittsfield; Plainfield; Plymouth; Princeton: Quincy; Raynham; Reading; Rehoboth; Roxbury; Rowley; Salem; Scituate; Shelburne; Sherborn; Shrewsbury; Southwick; Spencer; Springfield; Stockbridge; Stoneham; Stoughton; Sturbridge; Taunton; Templeton; Topsfield; Upton; Ware; Watertown; Wellfleet; Wenham; Western; Westfield; Westhampton; Westminster; West Roxbury; West Springfield; Whately; Wibraham; Williamstown; Woburn; Worcester; Worthington; Wrentham.

Massie, N. McDonald, J., Biog. sketch, 1852.

Massillon, J. B. Alembert, Eulogy on.

Massinger, P. Coleridge, H., Life of, 1846.

Mastodon. Am. Quar. Journ. of Agr., 1845. P. 1866.

Cohoes Mastodon. P. 1866.

Richardson, Voy. of the Herald.

Warren, J. C., Mast. giganteus, 1855.

See Paleontology.

Materialism. *See* Matter; Natural Theology; Natural Religion.

Mathematics. Adams, J., Logarithms, 1796.

Æneæ, Verhandel., om afstanden te meten, 1812.

Alembert, D', Traité de Dynamique, 1750.

Mathematics (continued).

Alexander, J., Synopsis of Algebra, 1709.

Archimède, Œuvres, 1808.

Atkinson, H., Roots of equations, 1831.

Barlow, P., Theory of numbers, 1811.

Berkeley, Bp., Works, vol. 2, 1843.

Bézout, Elem. of Calculus, 1824.

Biot, Analytical geometry.

Blennerhassett, Longitude rules, 1750.

Blundeville, His exercises, 1622.

Bonnycastle, Algebra.

Bordinus, F., Math. disciplinæ, 1573.

Boscovich, R. J., Opera, 1785.

Bowditch, Mécan. Céleste of Laplace, 1829–39.

Bridge, B., Conic sections, 1831.

" Plane trigonometry.

Burrow, R., Apoll. Pergaeus, On inclinations, 1779. P. 1049.

Byrne, Model calc., Logarithms, 1852.

Chasles, Géométrie Supérieure, 1847.

Chauvenet, Trigonometry, 1860.

Church, Elements of the Calculus, 1855.

Clairaut, Gronden der, 1760.

Comte, Philos. of Mathematics, 1851.

Cowper, S., Parallactic angle, 1766.

Crambrook, Cat. of Math. puzzles, 1842.

Davies, C., Mathemat. Dict., 1855.

" Pract. Mathematics, 1852.

" Elements of Geometry.

Day, J., Algebra, 1814, 20, 38.

" Course of Mathematics, 1846.

Delambre, Progrès des, depuis 1789.

De Morgan, Mathematics. Lib. U. K.

" Calculus, 1847. Lib. U. K.

Des Cartes, Geometria, 1683.

Docharty, Algebra, 1867.

" Elem. of Geometry, 1867.

Dodd, J. B., Strictures on C. Davies, 1860.

" Elem. Algebra, 1853.

Donne, B., Mechan. Geometry, 1796.

Eaton, A., Art without Science, 1830.

Encyc. Méthodique, 1782–91.

Euclid, De ses eerste boeken, door La Bordus, 1752.

" Les Elémens d'Euclide, 1730. B. C.

" Editions of Blassière, 1762; Déchalles, 1753; Playfair, 1819; Todhunter, 1867; Van Lorn, 1738.

" Enunciations, etc., 1823.

Euler, In analysin infinitorum, 1797.

Flauti, Opere; Prospetto, 1860.

Fleming, P., Quadrature of the Circle, 1850.

Mathematics (continued).

Flint, A., System of Geom. and Trig., 1825.

Floryn, Grondbeginzels der Meetkunde.

Galloway, Treatise on Probability, 1839.

Gill, C., Angular Analysis, 1848.

Girault, C., Elém. de géométrie, 1858.

Graaf, De Wiskunst, 1706.

" De Verfulling van.

Gregg, Novum organum moralium, 1859.

Gregory, O., Math. for practical men, 1833.

Guilmin, Cours Elémentaire, 1856.

Hackley, Treatise on Trigonometry, 1853.

Halliwell, J. O., Rara Mathematica, 1841.

Hamilton, Bishop, Works, De sectionibus conicis, 1809.

Hann, Plane Trigonometry, 1849.

" Integral Calculus, 1850.

Harris, J., Treat. of Algebra, 1702.

" Spher. Trigonometry, 1706.

" Algebraist, 1818.

Hassler, Analytic Trigonometry, 1826.

" Geometry of Planes and Solids, 1828.

" Logarith. and Trigon. tables, 1830.

Haswell, Mensuration, 1858.

Hewitt, S., Key to Walkingame, 1856.

Hobbes, T., Works: Opera philosophica.

Huygens, Opera Varia, 1724.

" Exercit. Mathematicæ, 1833.

Introd. to Geometry, 1857, Bost.

Jackson, I. W., Conic sections, 1845.

Jones, C. A., Alg. exercises, 1867.

La Caille, Werktuig-kunde, 1764.

La Condamine, Voy. à l'équateur, 1751.

Lacroix, S. F., Trigonometry, 1826.

" Der Trigonometrie, 1839.

" Der Meetkunst, 1838.

" Der Stelkunst, 1825.

Ladies' Diary, 1767–1803. Questions.

La Lande, Mathématiques, Encyc. Méth.

La Place, Œuvres, 1843–47.

Lardner, Treatise on Geometry.

Lawrence, C. D., Treat. on algebra, 1853.

Lawson, J., Of triangles, 1773. P. 1049.

Lea, W., Equations in, 1811. P. 1049.

Leadbetter, C., Math. Companion, 1748.

Lobatto, Van de Statika....1857.

Mathemat. Monthly, Camb., Mass., 1858–59.

Meyer, A., Intégrales définies.

Mathematics (continued).

Miller, W. H., Differential calculus, 1833. P. 988.

Monge, Treatise on Statics, 1851.

Muller, J., Plane geometry, 1769. P. 989.

Myers, C. J., Differential calculus, 1827. P. 988.

Newton, Sir I., Principia, 1713.

Newton, T., Conic Sections, 1794. P. 989.

Orr's Circle of the Sciences, 1854, 5.

Oughtred, W., Opusc. Mathematica, 1677.

" The Key of the Mathematicks, 1647.

Pamphlets relating to, vols. 660, 766, 988, 989, 1527, 1778.

Pardies, Elem. of geometry, 1705.

Pascal, Cours de géométrie, 1853.

Pasley, Course of pract. geom., 1822.

Paterson, J., Calculus of Operations, 1850.

" Process of causation, 1858.

Payne, Wm., Introd. to Geometry.

Peacock, D. M., On Logarithms, 1812.

" Conic Sections, 1817.

" Fluxional calculus, 1819.

Peirce, B., Analyt. geometry, 1857.

" Elem. Geometry, 1858.

Perkins, G. R., Elements of Geom., 1848.

" Elements of Algebra, 1850.

" Plane and Solid Geom., 1855.

" Plane Trigonometry, 1852.

Piola, Meccanica Analitica, 1825.

Playfair, Works, 2, 3, Math. Science, 1822.

Quarterly Journal of....Lond., 1857.

Rheticus, Opus...de Triangulis, 1596.

Ray, J., Algebra, 1848.

Rigaud, On Newton's Principia, 1838.

Robinson, H. N., Math. recreations, 1851.

Ryan, J., Elem. algebra, 1824.

Schmidt, Beginselen der Statica, 1823.

" ....der Dynamica, 1825.

" ....der Hoogere Meetkunst, 1826.

Simms, F. W., Sectio-planography, 1837.

Smith, R., Opticks, 1778.

Smith, S., New elements of geometry.

Snowball, J. C., Spher. Trigonom. and logarithms, 1863.

Sopwith, Trea. on Isomet. drawing, 1838.

Stanley, A. D., Tables of logarithms, 1847.

Strachey, Early Hist. of Algebra.

Mathematics (continued).
Swinden, Theoremeta Geometrica, 1786.
Tait, On Quaternions, 1867.
Tillett, Key to Exact Sciences, 1824.
Todhunter, Algeb. for beginners, 1867.
" Elem. Trigonometry, 1866.
Tower, D. B., Intellec. Algebra, 1845.
Twisden, Planes; Spher. Trig., 1854.
Ward, J., Young Math. Guide, 1730.
Warren, S. E., Elem. Geometry, 1867.
Whewell, Doctrine of Limits, 1838.
Whitlock, G. C., Elem. of, 1849.
Wilkins, John, Math. works, 1802.
Wolf, C., Elem. Matheseos Univ., 1732–41.
Woodhouse, R., Plane and sph. trigonom., 1809.
Young, A., Quadrature of the circle, 1852. P. 79.
See Arithmetics; Astronomy; Dialling; Engineering; Natural Philos.; Navigation; Numbers; Surveying; Weights and Measures.

Mathematical Instruments. Coggeshall, Sliding rule, 1722.
Curtis, On Gunter's scale.
Douglas, Sir H., Reflecting semicircle.
Hadley's Quadrant.
Heather, Treatise on.
Jones, W., Catalogue of, 1793.
Ludlam, W., Hadley's quadrant, 1771.
McAllister's Catalogue, 1855.
Palmer, Cath. Planisphear, 1658.
Pennington, Descr. of Sector, 1780.
Phillips, G., Use and construction of, 1840.

Mather, C. Bishop, G., New England judged, 1702.
Drake, S. G., Memoir of, 1851.
Mather, C., Genealogy of, 1848.
Mather, S., Life of, 1729.
Peabody, Life of, Sparks, 6.
Poole, W. F., Essay on, 1869.
Stevens, H., The Mathers weighed, 1870.

Mather, I. Calamy, E., Life of, 1735.
Keith, G., Reply to, 1703.
Pond, E., Life of, 1847.

Mather, Nath. Mather, C., Life of, 1857.

Mather, Richard. Journal and Life.
Mather, I., Life of, 1670.

Mathew, Rev. T. Maguire, Life of.

Mathews, C. Memoirs, 1839.
" Trip to America, 1824.

Matter. Beale, L. S., Protoplasm, 1870.
Berkeley, Bp., Prin. of human knowledge.

Matter (continued).
Brewster, G., New philos. of, 1843.
Davy, Sir H., Works, Vol. 4.
Essay on, Phil'a, 1784. P. 1874.
Hazard, R. G., Existence of, 1869.
Schyanoff, A., Forces de la Matière, 1857.
Tyndall, Fragments of Science, 1871.
See Natural Philosophy.

Matthews, S. Thurston, S., Discourse, 1853.

Matthias, R. Stone, W. L., His impostures, 1835.
Vale, G., Fanaticism, 1835.

Maumee Valley, Ohio. Hosmer, Early history of, 1858.

Maupertuis, P. L. M. Anglieviel, Vie de, 1856.
Damiron, Mémoire, Inst. de France, Ac. mor. et pol., v. 10.

Mauritius Is. Arago, Freycinet's voy., 1820.
St. Pierre, Voyage à, (Œuvres).

Maury, J. W. Cummins, G. D., Fun. Disc. on.

Maxcy, J. Addresses, with memoir.

Maximilian II. Thiersch, Reden, 1849, 52, 53.

Maximilian, of Mexico. Hall, F., Life of, 1868.
Salm-Salm, F., Diary in Mexico, 1868.

Maxims. Æsopus, Fables of Æsop, 1844.
Atterbury, F., Maxims, reflections, &c. P. 1483.
Bartlett, J., Aphorisms, 1810.
Bennet, J., Collec. Sententiarum.
Britaine, Humane prudence, 1701.
Cato, D., Dicta Græca sapientium. P. 692.
Colton, C. C., Lacon, 1832. B. C.
Dictionary of Pop. quotations, 1831.
Erasmus, Adagiorum 4000, 1574.
Fénélon, Works, vol. 2, 1836, 37.
Galland, Maximes des Orientaux.
Halliwell, Dict. of Archaic words, 1855.
Hare, Guesses at truth, 1834, 47, 55.
Home, H., Art of thinking, 1813. B. C.
Jameson, Common-place Book, 1855.
Joannes, Summa de Exemplis, 1597.
La Bruyère, J. de, Works, 1776.
Laconics, 1829. B. C.
La Rochefoucauld, Réflexions, 1678.
" Moral reflections.
Lingrée, Réflexions et Maximes, 1827.
Luther, M., Table Talk.
Lycosthenes, Apothegmata ex optim. script., 1684.

Medicine: General and Miscellaneous (continued).

Balfour, Sol-lunar influence in India fevers, Asiat. Res.

Bancal, Lettres médicales, 1834.

Beck, J. B., Misc. Med. publications, 1817–42.

" Hist. of Med. before Am. revol., 1842.

Beck, L. C., Misc. and med. publications, 1824–50.

Beck, T. R., Misc. med. pub. 1811–40.

Beddoes, Abuses in medicine, 1808.

Besson, Æquilibrium Corporis, 1759. P. 612.

Beverwyck, Epistolicæ quaestiones, 1644.

Bigelow, J., Nature in disease, 1854.

" Rational medicine, 1858.

Blane, G., Medical Logick, 1825.

Blatchford, T. W., Dissertations, 1817–1856.

" On feigned diseases, 1817. P. 86.

Bleuland, Otium Academ., 1828.

Book about doctors, (Jeaffreson), 1861.

Booth, On Malaria, 1853.

Boucheron, Du Système pileux, 1837.

Bouillaud, Philos. Médicale, 1836.

Bowman, Med. chemistry, 1850.

Bowron, J. S., Planet influences in epidemics, 1850.

Breggen, Geneeskundige Bijdragen, 1842. P. 269

Bronson, Medical Reasoning, 1832. P. 786.

Broussais, Physiolog. Medicine, 1832.

Brown, R., Physiognomy in, 1807.

Brunet, C., Progrès de, 1697.

Buc'hoz, Médecine Pratique, 1771.

Cabanis, De la certitude, 1803.

Caldwell, Med. and phys. memoirs, 1801.

Cavallo, Properties of factitious airs, 1798.

Chevalier, Diss. Physico-Médicale, 1758.

Circular Letter, N. Y., 1829.

Conkling, Remarks, 1854.

Cours des Etudes Médicales, 1803.

Cronin, Med. no mystery, 1853.

Currie, Diseases of Un. States, 1792.

Da-Olmi, Hygiène Navale, 1828.

Desperrières, Fièvres de St. Domingue, 1780.

Dessaix, Thesis Medica, 1758.

Digestion, De la, 1712.

Donaldson's Review of systems, 1821.

Dunglison, Medical Lexicon, 1846.

Edelen, Theories of inflamm., 1815.

Medicine: General and Miscellaneous (continued).

Edinburgh Univ., Med. diss., 1778–1819.

Ewell, Improvements in, 1819.

Fenner, Southern Med. Reports.

Gallup, Epidemic diseases in Vt., 1815.

Gardner, D. P., Medical Chemistry, 1848.

Golleville, Maladies incurables, 1862.

Gr. Brit. Register: Statist. nosology, 1845.

Green, A., Nature of diseases, 1835.

Hale, E., Med. Prize dissertations, 1821.

Haller, Disputationes, 1757–60.

Hedges, P., Strictures on Dr. Brown's Work.

Herisson, The Sphygmometer, 1835. P. 87.

Herpin, Sur l'enfance et l'adolescence, 1826.

Heustis, Diseases of Louisiana.

Holmes, O. W., Currents and counter-currents, 1861.

Hosack, D., Misc. publications, 1812–1825.

Huff, Electro-physiology, 1853.

Jackson, James, Letter, Utility of, 1861.

" Letters to a young physician, 1856.

Joyand, Thesis Med., Hydropis, 1765.

Kuhn, Med. Græcorum Opera, 1821–30.

Leechdoms, Wortcunning, etc., of early England, (Chron. G. B.).

Leroy d'Etiolles, Lettres à l'Académie des sciences, 1842, 43.

Lettsom, Hints on temperance and med. science, 1801.

Mann, J., Med. sketches, war of 1812.

Manningham, R., Valetudo mulierum, 1756.

Mead, R., Medical works, 1762.

Merrett, C., Self-conviction, 1670.

Middleton, C., De Medicorum apud Vet. Rom. Cond. Diss., Works, vol. 4, 1755.

Miller, E., Med. works, N. Y., 1814.

Mitchell, J. K., Cryptogamous origin of epidem. fevers, 1849.

" Five essays, 1859.

Mitchell, T. D., Chem. and medicine, 1837.

Morel, Traité des maladies mentales, 1852.

Morris, C., Med. Hist. of Penn., 1826.

Musgrave, Gulstonian lectures.

Nature in disease, and her agents, Lond., 1859. P. 1713.

Newton, R. S., Eclectic treatise, 1866.

N. Y. Kappa Lambda Conspir., 1839.

Medicine: General and Miscellaneous (continued).

Pamphlets relating to, vols. 64, 86, 87, 89, 98, 196, 210, 235, 246, 271, 405, 515-517, 575, 579, 593, 611-614, 649, 650, 713, 802, 923, 945, 1040, 1351-52, 1354-1361, 1711-1714, 1528, 1529, 1779. B. C. 22.

Parrot, Epidémie de la suette miliaire, 1841, 42.

Pearson, C. H., Letter on med. ed. in Oxford Univ., 1858.

Pettigrew, Superstitions in, 1844.

Physic and its phases, B. T. Moore, 1858.

Pitcairn, Elem. Med. phys. math., 1717.

Pringle, Diseases of the Army, 1753.

Pugh, Nature in disease, 1804.

Pulvermachen, Hydro-electric chains, 1856.

Purple, Medical Observations, 1852, 54. P. 89.

Quincy, Lex. Physico-medicum, 1767, 1802.

Ramazzini, Maladies des Artisans, 1777.

Raymond, Maladies, dangereux à guérir, 1808.

Reply......on a new Corporation of Physicians, 1812. P. 37.

Retz, Epidémiques à Rochefort, 1784.

Roberton, On Medical Police, 1809.

Rowley, W., Essays, 1770-1800.

Rush, B., Med. inquiries on the mind, 1835.

" Sixteen Lectures, 1811.

Shecut, Med. and Phil. Essays, 1819.

Sherwood, Motive power, 1841.

Solly, S., The human brain: diseases of, 1848.

Soule, Science of Reproduction, 1856.

Spence, De vasis absorbentibus, 1790.

Swieten, Diseases of Armies, 1776.

Thomson, T., De Aëre atmosphærico, 1799.

Tissot, Moyens de Perfectionner, 1785.

Trnka, Hist. Haemorrhoidum, 1895.

Tucker, Med. Reg. of city of N. Y., 1862.

Turner, W., Triumphs of Young Phys., 1847. P. 89.

Uwins, D., Mod. Maladies. Pamp'r 13.

Whitlaw, New Discoveries in, 1847.

Willard, S. D., Col. writings, Albany.

Williams, S. W., Improvements of the half century, 1852. P. 1800.

See Anatomy; Asphyxia; Cholera; Climate; Consumption; Contagion; Death; Dispensaries; Drowning; Ear; Epidemics; Ether; Eyes; Homœopathy; Health; Hospitals; Hydrophobia; Insanity; Plague; Poison; Quackery; Quarantine; Small Pox; Surgery; Temperance; Teeth; Urine; Water-cure, etc.

Medicine: Legal. Accum, On poisons.

Beck, T. R., Elem. of Med. Jurisprudence, 1842.

Clark, H. G., Address on, 1868.

Esquirol, Des maladies mentales.

Hall, A. G., Inst. of med. jurisprudence, 1860.

Lobstein, Of the Eye, 1830.

Loomis, H., Trial, 1850.

Taylor, Poisons in relation to, 1859.

Webster, J., jr., Essays on, 1824.

Wharton, F., Invol. confessions, 1860.

See Insanity; Poisons, and Law Library Catalogue.

Medicine: Materia Medica. Acosta, Arom. et medic. in Orient. India, 1593.

Albertus Mag., De virt. herbarum.

Alderson, Rhus toxicodendron.

Allen, J. A., Pharmacology. P. 86.

American Chem. Inst., Manual.

Amer. Jour. of Pharmacy, 1832-68.

Amer. Pharmaceutical Assoc'n, Proceedings, 1851-69.

Anderson, A., Eupatorium, 1813. P. 64.

Barton, W. P. C., Veg. Mat. Med. of the U. S., 1818-25.

Bird, F., Sanguinaria Canadensis, 1822. P. 86.

Brandreth's Medicines. P. 515.

Brunfels, Onomasticon medicinæ, 1533.

Buchan's Balsam. P. 271.

Cartwright, S. A., Jussieua grandiflora, 1840. P. 98.

Chamberlaine, W., On Cowhage, 1792.

Christison, Hemlock and Conia, 1836.

Clark's Peruvian Syrup, 1854. P. 235.

Cutter, E., Veratrum viride.

Dale, Pharmacologia, 1737.

Deguise, Effets de l'acétat de Morphine, 1824. P. 86.

Dioscorides, De materia medica, 1822.

Edwards, H. M., Manuel de Mat. Méd., 1831.

Farvacque, Medecina pharmaceutica, 1741.

Forskal, Arabic Mat. Med.

Francis, J. W., On Mercury, 1811. P. 86.

Fuller, T., Pharmacopoeia, 1705.

Garcia, Medicamentorum apud Indos, 1593.

Hoffman, F., On Asses' Milk, 1754. P. 449.

Hooper, On Antimony, 1774.

Horsley, J., Cod liver oil, 1856.

Jacquet, De l'Antimoine, 1765. P. 612.

James, R., Pharmacopœia, 1764.

Labarraque, Use of Chlorides of soda and lime, 1851. P. 79.

Medicine: Materia Medica (cont'd).

Ledoyen's Disinfecting fluids, 1847, 1848.

Lemery, N., Verhand. der Enkele Droogeryen, 1743.

Magendie, Formul. de nouv. médicam., 1836.

Mass. Coll. of Pharmacy, 1851. P. 89.

Mead, Pharmacopœia, 1757.

Monardus, Remedies brought from Am., 1677.

Montot, Amidon de Santé, 1777.

Murray, J., Fluid Magnesia, 1840. P. 235.

Nat. Pharmaceut. Conv., 1852.

Norwood, Veratrum Viride, 1852. P. 515.

O'Shaugnessy, Preparations of Indian hemp. P. 1353.

Paine, M., Mat. Med., 1848.

Pamphlets relating to Materia Medica, vol. 1353.

Paris, Pharmacologia, 1833.

Patent Medicines. *See* Pam. V. 614; Alm. V. 38–40.

Percy, S. R., Veratrum viride.

Pharmaceut. Conv., 1852, 3.

Pharmacopoeia, Lond., 1758.

Pharmacopoeia chirurg., 1794.

Philip, Minute doses of Mercury, 1834. P. 210.

Pison, De medecina Brasiliensi, 1648.

Purple, S. S., On Cimaba Cedron, 1854. P. 89.

Quer, Uva-ursi.

Rafinesque, Medical flora, 1828–30.

Rayner, John, Cod-Liver Oil, 1849. P. 87.

Reece, R., Rhatany root, 1808.

Rogers, J. L., Catalogue, Mat. Med., 1826. P. 28. B. C.

Rougier, De la morphine, 1843.

Royle, Materia Med. and Therap., 1847.

Salisbury, J. H., Papers, 1862, 3, 7, 8.

Salmon, English Herbal, 1710.

Sauveur, De la vente des médicaments, 1846.

Schœpf, Mat. Med. Americana, 1787.

Slare, Bezoar Stones, 1715.

Smyttère, Phytologie pharmaceutique, 1829.

Steel, T. E., Digitalis purpurea.

Strobel, Med. Prop. of the Aralia spinosa, 1826.

Swaim's Panacea, 1829. P. 229.

Thacher, J., Am. New Dispensatory, 1813.

Thayer & Co., Fluid Extracts. P. 516.

Thomson, S., Botan. fam. physician, 1841.

Medicine: Materia Medica (cont'd).

Tilden & Co., Extracts, 1855.

Tournéfort, De la Mat. Médicale, 1717.

Treatise of..... Crust of Bread, 1756. P. 405.

Tully, W., Materia Medica, 1857, 8.

" On Sanguinaria canadensis. P. 86

" On Narcotine and Sulph. of Quinine. P. 86.

U. S., Adulteration of, 1848.

Yvan, Pharmacie en Chine, 1847.

See Pharmacy.

Medicine: Obstetrics, etc. Bacoffe, Plethora Menstrui, 1759. P. 612.

Bard, S., Compendium of Midwifery, 1812.

Barker, B. F., Puerperal Fever, 1857. P. 271.

Burns, Prin. of Midwifery, 1810.

" Observ. on Abortion, 1808.

Cleveland, Mrs., Address, 1858. P. 517.

Engeltrum, Waarneming, 1825.

Female Medical College, 1858. P. 517.

Freind, Emménologie, 1730.

Gregory, S., Man midwifery.

Krause, Der Geburtshülfe, 1853.

Letter to a young lady, 1764.

Maternal Physician, 1811.

Pechey, Compleat Midwife, 1698.

Pollard, Obstetrical Supporter, 1849.

Preston, Address, Fem. Med. Coll., 1858. P. 517.

Quackenbush, Add., Albany Med. Coll., 1855. P. 287.

Spratt, G., Obstetric Tables, 1850.

Medicine: Periodicals and Transactions. Albany Jour. of Neurology, 1843.

Amer. Jour. of Insanity, 1855–70.

Amer. Eclectic Med. Register, 1868.

Am. Ecl. Med. Review, 1866–69.

Am. Jour. of Med. Sciences, Phil'a, 1827–69.

Am. Jour. of Pharmacy, 1832–69.

Am. Med. Assoc., Trans. Phil'a, 1848–1868.

Am. Med. Monthly, N. Y., 1854–61.

Am. Med. Times, N. Y., 1860–63.

Annales d'Hygiène, 1829–70.

Anti-Lancet (Chron. Thermal), 1853. P. 196.

Archief van Geneeskunde, 1846.

Archives de Physiologie, etc., 1854.

Boston M. & Sur. Journal, 1835–37, 41–49.

Bouchardat, Annuaire de thérap., 1842-1846.

Braithwaite, W., Retrospect of Medicine, 1854–60.

Medicine: Periodicals and Transactions (continued).

Brit. and For. Med. Review, 1836-44.

Brit. and For. Med. Chir. Rev., 1854-1860.

Buffalo Med. Jour., 1845, 46.

Bulletin des Sci. Méd., (Férussac), 1829-31.

Edinburgh Med. & Phil. Jour., 1805-42.

" Med. Jour., 1855-60.

" Med. & Sur. Jour., 1855.

Esculapian, The, period., 1853. P. 4° 3.

Etat de Médecine, 1770, 77.

Fautes dans la Gazette de Santé, 1776. P. 612.

Foote, J., Med. Pocket Book, 1837, 40.

Gazette Méd. de Paris, 1859.

Jahrbuch, 1840, Wildberg.

Lancet, The, 1823-71.

Literarische Annalen, (Hecker), 1825-1830.

London Med. Gazette, 1831-51.

Magazin der Ausl. Lit. der Heilkunde, 1825, 30, 31, 34. P. 265.

Med. and Agric. Register, Bost., 1807.

Med. and Surg Journal, Phil'a, 1858-1863.

Medical Critic, (Winslow), 1861-63.

Medical Repository, 1800-24.

Med. Soc. of Pennsylvania, 1851, 2.

Medical Times, Lond., 1839-60.

Medico-Chirur. Review, 1820-44.

Méding, Bibliot. Paris Médical, 1855.

Miscellanea curiosa, (Serial), Lipsiæ, 1670-97.

Missouri Med. aud Sur. Jour., 1846. P. 196.

New England Jour. of Med. 1816.

New York Med. and Phil. Jour., Hosack, 1809-11.

New York Med. and Phys. Jour., Francis, 1822-30.

N. Y. Med. Magazine, (Mott), 1815.

Pharmaceutical Jour., 1841-59.

Pharmaceutical Repertory, 1844-46.

Phil'a University Jour. of Med., 1871.

Physo-Med. Jour., Cincinnati, 1851. P. 196.

Quarterly Homœop. Journal, 1849.

Smith, Am. Med. Alm., 1839-41.

Southern Med. and Surg. Jour., 1836-1839.

Southern Med. Reformer, 1854.

Medicine: Societies. American Med. Assoc., Transactions, 1848-68.

Amer. Pharm. Assoc. Proc., 1851-70.

Connecticut St. Med. Soc. 1852, 55. P. 89; 57-62.

Eclectic Med. Soc. of N. Y., Trans., 1865-70.

Medicine: Societies (continued).

Homœop. Med. Soc. of N. Y., Trans., 1863-70.

Illinois State Med. Society, 1860.

Impartial enquiry, etc., Lond., 1753.

Maine Med. Assoc., 12 and 13th meet., 1865.

Mass. Med. Soc., 1787-1854. P. 210.

" Diss., 1823-46.

" Communications, 1854-9.

Med. Assoc. of Southern N. Y., 1853-1857.

Med. Conv. of Va., 1846.

Med. Delegates, N. Hampton, Mass., 1827. P. 271.

Med. Soc. of N. Y., Trans., 1807-70.

Med. Soc. of Penn'a, 1851, 2.

Nat. Eclectic Med. Assoc., Transac., 1852.

National Med. Convention, 1846.

New Hampshire Med. Soc., Trans., 1854-61.

New Haven Co. Med. Soc., 1837.

New Jersey State Med. Soc., Trans., 1859, 62, 64.

N. Y. Acad. of Med., Trans., 1851.

Norfolk, Mass., Dist. Med. Soc., 1855. P. 615.

Provin. Med. and Sur. Assoc. Lond., 1839, 40, 47.

" On Homœopathy, 1851.

Soc. des Sci. Méd. de la Moselle, 1838-1852.

Vermont Med. Soc., 1852. P. 516.

Medicine: Therapeutics and Special Diseases. Ag., Le Médecin des campagnes, 1832.

Alibert, Maladies de la peau, 1822.

Alpini, De præsagienda Vita, 1733.

Amussat, Anus artificiel: tumeurs fibreuses, 1839.

Aretæus, Opera omnia, 1821-30.

Argolus, De Diebus Criticis, 1651.

Armstrong, Diseases of Children.

Articella, Med. treatises in Latin, 1491.

Astruc, De Morbis venereis, 1740.

Asylum for cure of scrofula, 1824. P. 98.

Aurelianus, De morbis acutis, 1709.

Averill, Disinfecting by chlorine, 1832. P. 86.

Bacher, L'Hydropsie, 1782. P. 613.

Banning, Chronic diseases, 1846.

Barry, D., De phlegmasia dolente, 1807. P. 86.

Baumes, Sur le vice scrophuleux, 1805.

" Science Méthod. des Maladies, 1801.

Beck, J. B., Infant Therapeutics, 1849.

Medicine: Therapeutics and Special Diseases (continued).

Beddoes, Nitrous acid in Ven. mal., 1797.

Bell, B., Treatise on Gonorr., 1814.

Bennett, J. H., Princ. and pract. of, 1863.

Bird, G., Chem. and Therapeutics, 1848. P. 402.

Blake, A., Delirium Tremens, 1834. P. 210.

Bliss, Strictures of the urethra, 1816. P. 86.

Boerhave, H., Study of physick, 1719.

Bouchard, Degen. of spinal cord, 1869.

Boudin, Traité des Fièvres intermittentes, 1845

Bouteille, Traité de la Chorée, 1810.

Bréra, Sopra i vermi del corpore umano, 1802.

" Mem. Medico-cliniche, 1816. P. 515.

Britt, W., Indigestion, &c., 1857. P. 1712.

Bright, R., Adhesions of the peritoneum, 1835.

" Obs. on jaundice.

Broussais, Inflam. Chroniques, 1808.

Bryson, Fevers of Sierra Leone.

Buchan, Domestic Med., 1828. B. C.

" On Venereal disease, 1797.

Cadogan, On gout and chron. diseases, 1772.

Carter, Vegetable Prescriptions, 1813.

Celsus, A. C., Of Medicine, 1756.

Cézan, Manuel Anti-Syphil., 1789.

Charpentier, Meningo-Céphalite, 1829.

Chavy, Sur la Goutte, 1774. P. 613.

Chevallier, A., Sur les empoissonnements.

Clark, H. G., Ship-fever, 1850.

Clark, J., Syph. disease in the East. P. 405.

Clark, T., Scarlatina anginosa, 1795.

Clossy, Diseases of parts of the body, 1763.

Cole, On Apoplexies, 1689.

Copeland, Diseases of the rectum, 1810.

Cotunnius, Hip gout, 1775.

Cox, D., Intermitting pulse, 1758.

Cullen, Practice of Physic, 1805.

Cunier, Maladies oculaires en Belgique, 1847.

Dana, S. L., Lead diseases, 1848.

Davey, J. G., Uterine hydatids, 1849.

Davis, C. S., Phlegmasia alba dolens.

Davis, N. S., Diseases of Spinal col., 1840. P. 86.

Dawson, Cases of rheumatism, 1776.

Dickson, S., Chrono-thermal system, 1845.

Disser. on gravel, 1733.

Doeveren, Sur les Vers, 1764.

Douglas, J., Diss. on gout.

Dubreuilh, De la nevrite, 1845.

Dumoulin, Du Rhumatisme, 1710.

Dupuy, De febre quotidiana, 1747. P. 612.

Eble, Maladies de la conjonctive, 1836.

Epps, Epilepsy, 1834.

Fallot, Médecine, (Encyc. Pop.).

Family Phys. and Surgeon, 1796.

Favarielle, De la Gale, 1807.

Fitzpatrick, Angina Pectoris, 1830. P. 405.

Flores, Spécifique pour la guérison du chancre, 1785.

Floyer, De l'Asthme, 1761.

Forbes, J., Cyclopædia of medicine, 1859.

Ford, H., Fevers of West Africa, 1856.

Fremery, Hydrop. ligam. uteri.

Gabucinius, De Comitiali morbo, 1561.

Galenus, Opera omnia, 1562.

Gales, Fumigations sulfureuses.

Gallup, J. A., Institutes of, 1839.

Gardane, Maladies Vénériennes, 1773. P. 611.

Garth, S., Works, 1769.

Giannini, Nature des Fièvres, 1808.

Good, J. M., Study of Medicine, 1826.

Gouraud, Etudes sur la Fièvre intermittente, 1842.

Granville, A. B., On Counter-irritation, 1839.

Halsted, On Motorpathy, 1853.

Haly filius Abbas, Liber medicinæ, 1521.

Hamersley, Phthisis pulmonalis, Diss., 1816.

Hand-book of Domestic Med., 1855.

Hawkins, C., Tumour of the liver, 1833.

Hecquet, Médecine des Pauvres, 1740.

Hees, C. C., De Ictero, 1829.

Hillary, W., Diseases of W. I. Is., 1811.

Hippocrates, Opera Omnia, 1695.

" Trad. des Œuvres médicales, 1801.

" .... Reliquiæ, 1859–64.

" De morbis popularibus, 1717.

Hollerius, De Morb. internis, 1571.

Hooper, J. H., On Phrenitis, 1815.

Hooper, R., Physician's Vade-mecum, 1809.

Hopkins, J., Of Epispastics, 1815.

Hosack, D., Emetics in constipation. P. 4.

Medicine: Therapeutics and Special Diseases (continued).

Hosack, D., Miscellaneous publica's, 1812–20.
" Essays on Medical subjects, 1824–30.
" Obs. on Contagious diseases, 1815.
" On Croup, 1811.
Hun, E. R., Trichina spiralis, 1869.
Imray, K., Cyclo of Pop. Med., 1842.
Jacksón, R., Fevers of Jamaica, 1795.
Jackson, S., Gangrene of the cheek. P. 6.
Jeffreys, J., The respirator, 1841. P. 1779.
Jenner, W., Acute specific diseases, 1853.
Johnson, F. G., Private Med. Companion, 1855.
Johnstone, J., Putrid sore throat, 1779.
Kelley's New System, N. Y., 1848.
Kirkland, T., Paral. and apoplexy, 1792.
Lee, W., Brandy and Salt for inflammation.
Levrat, Goutte, Rhumatisme, etc., 1850. P. 89.
Lommius, De.... Febris, 1562.
Long, St. John, Discoveries in healing, 1830.
Louis, P., On fevers, 1836.
Mahon, Médecine clinique, 1804.
Makellar, Black phthisis, 1846.
Malcomson, Of Beriberi, 1835.
" Rheumatism in India, 1835.
Mann, J., Cholera infantum, 1804.
Marchant, Sur la langue, 1841.
Médecin des Hommes, 1772.
Médecine Expèrimentale, 1755.
Menuret, Traité du Pouls, 1768.
Millar, J., Asthma and Hooping cough, 1769.
Milman, F., De Nat. hydropis, 1779.
" Scurvy and putrid fevers, 1782.
Morin, J., De Dolore, 1761. P. 613.
Morton, C., De tussi convulsiva, 1748.
Murchison, C., Gastro-colic fistula, 1857.
Murray, J. W. B., Essay on Neuralgia, 1816. P. 86.
Musgrave, On Worm fever, 1776.
Nonnus, De curatione Morborum, 1794, 1795.
Nouveau Recueil, 1744.
Olliffe, Sur la Méthode ectrotique, 1840. P. 1003.
Orr, W. S., Household handbook. P. 1779.
Osgood, Treatment of Fevers, 1848.

Medicine: Therapeutics and Special Diseases (continued).

Paine, M., Institutes of Med., 1860, 1867.
" Materia Med. and Therapeutics, 1848.
" Commentaries, Med. and phys., 1844.
Paré, A., Œuvres, 1585.
Parguez, De Inflammatione, 1758. P. 612.
Parker, E. H., Scarlet fever, 1859.
Pattison, J., Of Cancer, 1859.
Paul, G. O., Gaol fever, 187.
Pavy, F. W., On Diabetes, 1862.
Pemberton, C., Dis. of the viscera, 1806.
Perry, R., Silent friend.
Petit-Radel, Pyretologia, 1808.
Portal, De l'épilepsie, 1827.
Porter, W. O., Management of typhus, 1819. P. 1361.
Price, R., Sulphurous fumigation, 1821.
Ramadge, F., Curability of consumption, 1854.
Rees, G. O., Rheumatism and Lemons, 1849.
Reynal, Fièvres putrides, 1763.
Reynolds, J. R., On Vertigo, 1854.
Riolan, Ars Medendi, 1601.
Robertson, F., Chorea Sancti Viti, 1805. P. 516.
Rogerson, J., De sang. detract. abusu, 1786.
Rosa Anglica, Joan. Angliei, 1492.
Rose, J. S., Consumption curable.
Rossi, F., Médecine opératoire, 1806.
Rousseau, Remédes Eprouvez, 1718.
Roussel, De la pellagre, 1845.
Rowan, M., On Hepatitis, 1815.
Rowley, W., Medical essays, 1779.
Samuells, P. S., De Hæmoptysi, 1798.
Schroeder, Waarnemingen, 1852.
Schultz, De Entero-Mesenteride...... 1830. P. 210.
Seutin, Maladie syphilitique, 1843.
Some papers writ, 1670.
Spencer, T., Epidemic Diarrhœa, 1832. P. 87.
Taney, On Hydrocele, 1815.
Tanquerel, Lead diseases, 1848.
Taylor, C. F., Spinal irritation, 1866.
" Potts's Disease of the spine, 1863.
Teale, T. P., On Neuralgic diseases.
Thomas, R., Mod. Practice of Physic, 1811.
Triplet, On Apoplexy, 1798. P. 235.
Turner, W., Of Bleeding, 1851.
Underwood, Diseases of children, 1800.

Medicine: Therapeutics and Special Diseases (continued).
Upham, J. B., Typhus or ship fever, 1852.
" Typhus fever in G. B., 1858.
Van Solingen, Worms in the intestines, 1792.
Vingtrinier, Guérison de tétanos, 1845.
Viviand, Thesis, Regimen, 1762.
Vowell, On Dysentery, 1815.
Wadd, On Corpulence, 1822.
Wakeman, On Somnolency, 1815.
Warren, J. C., Diseases of the heart, 1809. P. 44.
Warton, Obstinate Constipation.
Waterhouse, On Hooping Cough, 1822.
Watson, W., Exper. in inoculation. P. 126.
Watt, De Scarlatina anginosa, 1803.
Whitney, D. H., The Fam. physician, 1834. B. C.
Wildrik, W., Kinderpokjes, Mazelen, Loop, etc., 1781.
Wilkins, H., Family Adviser, 1804.
Winslow, F., Diseases of the Brain, 1860.
Wilson, A. P., Febrile diseases, 1809.
Wilson, E., The heat cure, 1860.
Woodward, Camp diseases of the U. S. Armies, 1863.
Wyck, D., Redelyke Heelkonst, 1775.
Yates, Bilious fever of N. Y., 1813.
See References above under Medicine, General.

Mediterranean Sea. Colton, W., Land and lee, 1851.
" Sea and sailor, 1851.
Digby, Sir K., Voyage, 1628, (Camden Soc.).
Galt's Travels around, 1809–11.
Jackson, J., Commerce of, 1809.
Mahoney, S., Two years in the Mediterranean, 1844.
Records of Travel, Bost., 1838
Rockwell, C., Sketches of Travel, 1842.
Sandwich, Voyage, 1738–9.
Schroeder, F., Shores of the Med., 1844.
Torrey, F. P., Cruise of the Ohio, 1839–41.
Willis, N. P., Summer cruise in, 1853.

Medway, Mass. Wright, L., Century Sermon.

Meermann, J. Cras, Eulogium, 1817. B. C.

Meetings, Public. Fingerpost to, 1864.

Meggott, R. Sherlock, W., Sermon, Funeral of, 1692.

Meigs, R. J. Campbell's Biog. Sketches.

Meikle, J. The Traveller, or, Life of, 1812.

Melancthon, P. Epist. selectiores, 1565.
" Life of, 1830.
Kloss, Cat.... Annotations of, 1835.
Merle, History of the Reformation.
Sotheby, Observat. on handwriting of, 1839.

Melrose, Ms. Goss, M. Memorial, 1868.

Melvil, Sir J. Scott, G., Memoirs of, 1683.

Melville, Lord. Brief remarks on, 1805.
Letter to his Majesty, 1808.

Melville, A. M'Crie, Life of, 1819.
" Works, v. 2, 1855.

Memory. *See* Mnemonics; Mental Philosophy.

Menapii. De Peyster, Hist. of Carausius, 1858.

Mendelssohn, F. B. Letters from Italy, 1863.

Mendon, Ms. Centenn. celebration, 1868.
Blake, M., Hist. Mendon Assoc., 1851.

Menefee, R. H. Marshall, T. F., Life of, 1841.

Mengs, A. R. Works with Life of, 1796.

Mennonists. Acct of, 1727.
Rues, Staet.... der Mennoniten, 1745.

Mental Philosophy. Abercrombie, Inquiries, Intellect. Powers, 1833.
Bain, A., Mental Science, 1868.
Beasley, Search after Truth, 1822.
Blakey, R., History of, 1850.
Brodie, B., Mind and Matter, 1857.
Brown, T., Lectures on, 1826.
Buchanan, J., Phil. of Human Nat., 1812.
Consciousness, 1864.
Crichton, A., Phys. of the mind, 1798.
Crousaz, J. P., Art of thinking, 1724.
Edwards, J., Essay on Freedom of Will, (Watts), 1790, 1844.
Fearn, Physiol. of the Mind, 1829.
" Essay on External Perception. Pamph'r 5.
Gall, F. J., Origin of the faculties, 1835.
Gaskell, Sense and Sound, 1854.
Hamilton, W., Lectures on metaphysics, 1859.
" Discus. in Philosophy, 1852.
Hartley, D., Theory of the mind, 1775.
Helvetius, C. A., Treatise on map, 1810.
" Essays on the mind, 1810.

Methodist Churches and Doctrines (continued).

Cartwright, P., Autobiography, 1856.
Challoner, Caveat, 1803.
Chronol. list of preachers, Engl., 1814. P. 1363.
Church, T., Letter to Whitefield, 1744.
Church Meth. Soc., Const., Lon., 1826.
Clark, J., M. Inconsistency, 1814.
Clarke, A., Wesley family.
Clarke, J. B., Life of A. Clarke.
Coke, Dr. T., Journal in Amer., 1789.
Comparison between Ch. of Eng. and, 1741.
Conference reviewed, Lond., 1819.
Cooke, P., Century of Puritanism, 2d part, 1855.
Creamer, Meth. Hymnology, 1848.
Decanver, Works in refutation of, 1846, 68.
Deems, Annals of Southern Methodism, 1855, 1856.
" Speech, Trial of W. A. Smith.
Dialogue between a Meth. and, 1803.
Dixon, Tour in U. S., Hist. of Meth., 1849.
Downes, J., Meth. exposed, 1759.
Elliott, C., Life of Roberts.
" The Great Secession from, 1845.
Emory, Defence of, 1827.
Enquiry after New Lights, 1755.
Finley, Western Methodism, 1856.
Fly-sheets., Lond. P. 1364.
Fox and Hoyt's Quadren. Reg., 1852–1856.
Free, J., False Prophets, 1758.
Further Defence of Priestcraft, 1768.
Genesee Ann. Conference, 1855, 63.
Gorrie, Black River Conference, 1852.
" Episcopal methodism as it was and is, 1852.
Green, T., Diss. on enthusiasm, 1755.
Henkle, M. M., Life of Bascom, 1860.
Henry, G. W., Shoutings in the church.
Hill, Sir R., Logica Wesleiensis, 1773.
Hill, R., Pietas Oxoniensis, 1768.
Hodgson, F., Great iron wheel, 1848.
Huff, The Government of, 1852. P. 93.
Jackson, T., Vindication of, 1842.
Jobson, F. J., American methodism, 1857.
Lavington, Enthusiasm of, 1749. P. 262.
Lee, J., Hist. of Meth. in the U. S., 1766–1809.
Legacy to the World, (L'Estrange), 1762.
Letter to the Rt. Rev. Bp. of Exeter, 1748.

Methodist Churches and Doctrines (continued).

Love, B., Increase of ministers, 1847.
M'Caine, Mystery of M. Episcopacy, 1827.
M'Carter, Border Methodism, 1858.
Macgowan, Priestcraft defended, 1768. P. 603.
Mason, J. A., Conversion to Catholicism.
Mattison, H , Crisis on Slavery, 1860.
Meth. and Popery dissected, 1779. P. 1363.
Methodism displayed, 1770.
Methodist Almanac, 1835, 47–52, 54–1861.
Methodist Church in Canada, 1835. P. 91.
Methodist Conference minutes, Lond., 1813, 32, 41.
" Miss'y notices, 1816–25.
Methodist Epis. Church, U. S., minutes, 1773–1861.
" Missionary Society, Reports, 1844–51, 61, 62.
Meth. Ch. Property case, 1851.
Meth. Mag. and Quar. Review, 1822–1863.
Modern Wesleyanism, Lond., 1844.
Nature and fitness of things, 1742.
Nelson, J , Life of, 1745.
New Engl. Meth. Ep. Hist. Society, Transactions, 1859–61.
New Year's gift, Lond., 1822.
Observations upon the conduct, 1756.
Olin, S., Life and letters, 1853.
Pamphlets relating to, vols. 314, 519, 1363, 1364, 1701, 1715.
Parks, S., Troy Conference Miscel., 1854.
Peck, Of the Genesee Conference.
Perronet, Remarks on, 1749.
Perry, J. H., Reply to Mattison, 1856.
Phantom of Philo's, Lond., 1835.
Pocock, Ejectment, Bristol, Eng.
Pounder's Wesleyan Almanac, 1818.
Prince, J. H., Defence of, 1797.
Principles and practices, (Green), 1761.
Prindle, C., Memorial sermon, 1865.
Queries recommended, 1772.
Review of Robinson's Obs., 1824.
S——y, T., Reply to J. Bate, 1740.
Sandford, P. P., Wesley's Missionaries, 1843.
Scott, J., Wesleyan discipline, 1850.
Scott, O., Appeal to, 1838.
Shank, D., Meth. in Schoharie, 1863.
Sketches and incidents, 1844.
Sketches of an itinerant, 1851.
Southern Meth. Pulpit, 1849, 50.

Mexico (continued).

Humboldt, Vues des Cordillères, 1810, 1816.

" Essai pol. sur la Nouv. Espagne, 1811.

" Selections from his works on, 1824.

" Plantes équinoxiales, 1813.

" Narr. of travels, 1799–1804.

Iturbide, A., Mémoires autographes, 1824.

" Political life. Pamph'r 28.

Ixtlilxochitl, Cruautés des conquérants du, 1829.

" Hist. des Chichiméques, 1838–41.

Jordan, J., Danger to foreigners in, 1826.

Ker, H., Travels in U. S. and Mexico, 1808–16.

Kingsborough, Lord, Antiquities of, 1831–48.

Kingsley, V. W., French intervention, 1863. P. 1589.

Latrobe, The Rambler in, 1834.

Letter to a member of Parl., 1828. P. 1365.

Losa, Vie de Lopez, 1655.

Ludecus, Reise, 1834.

Lundy, Travels in, 1847.

Lyon, G. F., Residence in Mexico, 1828.

Maclure, W., Letters, (Opinions), 1831.

Mayer, B., Mexico, Hist., etc., Acc't, 1853.

" Mexico as it was and is, 1844, 1846.

" Mexican Archæology, Smithson. Contr., ix.

Mill, N., History of Mexico, 1824.

Niles, J. M., History of, 1839.

Norman, Rambles in Yucatan, 1844.

Ortiz, T., Mexico como independiente, 1832.

Padilla, Hist. de Santiago de Mexico, 1625.

Palafox, Abp. Juan de, Histoire de, 1696.

" Ist. della vita, 1773.

Pamphlets relating to, vols. 486, 1365, 1867.

Poinsett, Notes on Mexico, 1822.

Portilla, Mejico en 1856.

Poyet, C. F., Notices Géog., Jalapa, Orizaba, 1863.

Prescott, W. H., Hist. of Conquest of, 1843.

Ranking, Conquest of, 13th cent., 1827.

Reid, Mayne, The Rifle Rangers, 1851.

Robertson, W. P., Visit to, 1853.

Robinson, F., Mexico and her chieftains, 1847.

Mexico (continued).

Romero, M., Dinner to, N. Y., 1866.

Ruxton, Adventures in, and the Rocky Mountains, 1849.

Salm-Salm, My Diary in, 1868.

Santangelo, Claim on, 1841.

" Charges against commissioners, 1841.

Sartorius, Landscapes, etc., 1859.

Seatsfield, Scenes in, 1844.

Shepard, Two years in, 1859.

Simpson, J. H., Mil. Reconn. from New Mexico, 1852.

Smith, J., jr., Romanism in, 1844. P. 1365.

Smith, T., Phys. Char. of N. States, 1848. P. 486.

Sociedad Mex. de Geografia, Boletin, 1839–51.

Solis, Conquest of, 1783.

Stephens, J. L., Incidents of Tr. in, 1841.

Tacoteno estate, 1855.

Tempsky, Jour. in, 1853–5.

Thompson, W., Recollections of, 1846.

Ticknor, G., On Prescott's & Wilson's Histories.

Trip to Mexico, 1849, 50.

Triunfo mines, Lower California.

Tudor, H., Travels in, 1834.

U. S.: Corresp. of Sec. of State on present condition, 1862.

" Boundary and Map, 1855.

University of Mexico, Constituciones, 1775.

Van der Velde, C. F., La conquête du M., 1827.

View of South America and, 1826.

Villagutierre, Conquista de el Itza, 1701.

Voyage to, 1841.

Ward, H. G., Mexico in 1825.

Wilson, R. A., Mexico and its Religion, 1851–54.

" Hist. of Conquest of, 1859.

Wise, Los Gringos, 1849.

Wislizenus, Tour to Northern Mexico, 1846, 47.

Young, C. B., Catalogue of antiq. of.

Young, P., Hist. of, 1520–1847.

Zavala, Revoluciones de Megico, 1808–1830.

See New Mexico; Span. Col.; Texas; North America; Tehuantepec; Vera Cruz.

Mexico: War with the U. S. Allen, C., Speech on Indemnity, 1852.

Amer. Star, Newsp., 1847.

Ashmun, Speech on, 1847.

Benton, T. H., Speech on Treaty, 1854.

Military Science, History, General and Miscellaneous (continued).

Scott, H. L., Mil. Dictionary, 1861.

Series of letters on mil. Ethics, 1804.

Smith, F. H., Virginia Mil. Institute.

Swett, S., Rogniat's Art of War, 1817. P. 102.

Szabad, Modern War, 1863.

Texas, Army Regulations, 1839.

Thomson, Mil. Instit. of Gt. Britain.

Timour, Institutes, 1783.

Torcy, Des Remontes de l'Armée, 1842.

Travaux de Mars, 1684.

Tripler, Hand-book for Mil. Surg., 1862.

U. S. Army Regul., 1812, 41, 61, 63.

" Arsenal Stores, 1836. P. 102.

" Military Instruction, 1861.

" On National Foundry, 1835. P. 102.

U. S. Mil. Phil. Soc., 1806, 09.

U. S. Corps of Engineers, Pract. Papers, 1840.

Vacchiery, Wehrhaftmachung der Alten, 1785.

Vauban, Plans of Fortification.

Vegetius, De re Militari, 1592.

Vigny, Lights and Shades of Military Life, 1850.

Virginia Mil. Institute, 1854.

Whitman, Z. G., Hist. Anc. and Hon. Art. Comp., Bost., 1637–1842.

Williams, J., Fortifying the Narrows, N. Y. P. 2.

" Elements of Fortification, 1801.

Wolfe, J., Instruct. to young officers, 1768.

See Great Britain, Mil.; United States, Mil.; Waterloo; Battles; Sieges.

Military Arms, Artillery, Cavalry, Infantry. Adye, R. W., The Bombardier, 1804.

Aide-mémoire....artillerie, 1836.

Allix, Système d'artillerie, 1827.

Artillery for U. S. Land Service, Mordecai, 1849.

Beadle's Dime Drill book, 1861.

Beuscher, Handleiding....der Artil., 1836–44.

Brand, H. v., Taktiek, 1847.

Bruyn, Over de artillerie, 1835.

Burtchaell, Practical artillery, 1847. MS.

Campbell, Soldier's companion, 1798.

Casey's Infantry Tactics.

Cavalerie d'Afrique. P. v. 10.

Cavalry, British, Regulations, 1833.

Chambray, Fusil de guerre, 1839.

Colt's Firearms, 1857.

Conn., Volunteers of 1861.

Military Arms, Artillery, Cavalry, Infantry (continued).

Coppee, H., Battalion drill, 1862.

Coquilhat, Fabr. des bouches à feu en fonte, (Soc. de Liége).

Culmann, Military Projectiles. P. 102.

Darrow, P., The Artillerist, 1821.

Desbordéliers, Du Tir du fusil.

Duane, W., Hand-book for infantry, 1813.

Dundas, Sir D., Field Exercises of H. M's Forces, 1795.

Favé, Napoleon's field artill.

Forbes, H., Manual for the Volunteer, 1855.

Fulton, R., Torpedo War, 1810.

Gray, J., Treatise on Gunnery, 1731.

Gr. Brit.: Army, Cavalry riding.

" Patents of inven., 1857–59.

Greener, Science of Gunnery, 1841.

Hackett, W., Movements of Cav., 1841.

Hale, J., Arming with pikes, 1781.

Hall, J. H., Rifles, 1816, 1825.

Hardee, Rifle and Infan. Tactics.

Herries, Inst. for Volunteer Cavalry, 1811.

Hewes, Sword Exercise, 1812.

Holbrook, J., Mil. Tactics.

Honourable Artill. Co., Lond., 1849. P. 1113.

Hotchkiss, Projectiles, 1863. P. 1780.

Hubbard, W. W., Explosive shells.

Hubbell, Patent Firearms, 1844. P. 102.

Infantry Exercise, 93 plates, French.

Jenour, J., Spiral cartridges, 1827. P. 1532.

Kelton, Manual of the Bayonet, 1861.

Kosciusko, Manœuv. of Artillery, 1808.

Lallemand, Treat. on Artillery, 1820.

Libert, Carnet...de cavalerie, 1832.

McClellan, G. B., Bayonet exercise, 1856.

Manœuvres of Artillery, Metz, 1828. Lithog.

Memoir on Artillery, Metz, 1828. Lithog.

Mordecai, A., Mil. Commission to Europe, 1861.

Muller, J., Treatise on Artillery, 1779.

Pel, Beknopte handleiding, 1856.

Persy, On form of Cannon, 1832.

Pettibone, Bullet Mould, 1840. P. 102.

Roemer, Cavalry, uses, 1863.

Royal Horse Artillery, Instructions, 1835.

Scheel, Treat. of Artillery, 180

Schön, Rifled arms, 1855.

Scott, W., Infantry Tactics, 1846.

Military Arms, Artillery, Cavalry, Infantry (continued).
Smyth, A., Infantry Exer. U. S., 1812.
Stephens, T., Sword Exercise, 1844.
Steuben, Regula., U. S. Troops, 1794.
Stevens. E. A., Battery: Memorial, 1862. P. 1035.
Stevenson, R., Mil. Instr. for field. 1775.
Thackeray, Rifle Firing, 1853. P. 406.
Tone, Wolfe, School of cavalry, 1824.
Tousard, Am. Artillerist, 1808, 9.
Un. States, Cannon of Clarke, 1833.
" Navy, Dahlg'n Guns, 1850.
" War Department, Small Arms, Exper., 1856.
" Colt's Pistols, 1856.
" Infantry Tactics, 1825, 61.
" Cavalry Tactics, 1856.
" Artillery Exercise, 1829, 60.
" Field Artill., 1839, 60, 61.
" Ordnance manual, 1841.
Van Ness, W. W., Elem. mil. tactics, 1862.
Viele, E. L., Hand-book for service, 1861.
Wilkinson, H., On Swords. P. 406.
" Anc. and Modern Engines of war, 1841.
Woodbridge, W. E., Of Making Cannon. P. 102.
See Militia.

Military Orders. Clark, H., Hist. of Knighthood.
Hist. des Ordres Militaires, 1720, 21.
Historical view of. Pamph'r, 5.
Maffei, Della scienza cavalleresca.
Nicolas, Sir H., Battle of Agincourt, 1832.
Porter, W., Hist. of Knights of Malta, 1858.
Vertot, Knights of St. John and Malta.
See Knights: Malta.

Militia. Bustin, A Militia, 1847. P. 406.
Canada, Militia Laws, 1838. P. 521.
Dyckman, Militia Off. Manual, 1824.
Kinlock, Volunteer force, 1852.
Mansfield, Col., Application of, 1854.
Massachusetts, Adj. Gen's. Rep., 1851.
Military Ass'n of N. Y., Proc., 1853–1859, 60, 64, 65, 66, 69.
Military Gazette, N. Y., 1860.
New York: Adj. Gen's Reps, 1851–69.
" Militia, 1842–70.
Ohio, Gen. Regulations, 1859.
Palfrey, J. G., Plea for, 1835.
Para bellum, 1852.
Sumner, W. H., Importance of, 1823.
See Great Britain, Military; Army; United States.

Milizia, F. Lettere e vita, 1827.

Milk. Nava, Sul caglio vitellino.
Treatise on, 1825. P. 1521.
See Food.

Millennium. Lord, N., Essay, 1854.
Millenial Church, Lond., 1829.
Miller, W., Views of prophecies, 1842.
Priest, J., View of, 1828.
See Christ's Second Advent; Prophecy.

Miller, C. Kip, F. M., Memoirs of, 1848.

Miller, Mrs. E. Millar, D., Sermon on, 1733.

Miller, Hugh. Autobiography, 1854.
Bayne's Essays.
Brown, T. N., Life of, 1858.

Miller, J. Bradford, G. W., Memoir of, 1862.

Miller, M. S. Anthon, Serm., Death of, 1824. P. 268.

Miller, S. Boardman, H. A., Disc. on.
Presb. Mag., 1852, Biog. of. P. 1856.
Sprague, W. B., Serm., Death of, 1850.

Mills, S. J. Spring, G., Life of, 1820.

Miller, W. Views and life (Himes), 1842.
See Prophecies; Millenium; Christ, Second advent.

Millstone, N. J. Corwin, Hist. Disc.

Mill-work. Buchanan, R., Pract. essays on, 1823.
Evans, Young mill-wright.
Nicholson, J., Opera. mechanic, 1834.
See Engineering, Civil; Mechanics.

Milne, W. Philip, R., Life of, 1840.

Milner, J. Parr, S., Letter to, 1825.

Milnor, J. Stone, J. S., Memoir of.

Milton, J. Addison, On Paradise Lost.
Barber, A. D., Life and Opin. of, Bibliot. Sac., 1860.
Camden Soc., Papers illustrative of.
Channing, W. E., Essay on, 1826.
Cleveland, Index to Poetry of.
Douglas, J., Vind. from plagiarism, 1751. P. 1238.
Fry, A. A., Lecture on, 1838.
Godwin, Philips's Milton, 1815.
Hayley, W., Life of, 1797.
Hunter, Jos., Gleanings on, 1850.
Ivimey, J., Life of, 1833.
Keightley, T., Life of, 1855.
Macaulay, T. B., Essay on.
Masson, D., Life of, 1859, 71.
Nickolls, J., Papers of, 1743.
Richardson, J., On Paradise Lost, 1734.
Todd, H. J., Life of, 1809.
Toland, J., Life of, 1761.

Mineralogy (continued).
- Pinnock, Catechism of, 1828. P. 233.
- Romé de l'Isle, Essai de cristalloraphie, 1772.
- Russisch. k. Gesells. f. d. Gesammte Min., 1842.
- Schmeisser, System of, 1795.
- Schöpf, Miner. Kenntniss von Nord-Amerika, 1787.
- Shepard, C. U., Treatise on, 1835.
- Smith, J. L., Papers, 1850-53. P. 274.
- Söchting, Einschlüsse von Min. in Krystall. Min., 1860.
- Sowerby, Pop. Mineralogy, 1850.
- Thomson, T., Outlines of, 1836.
- Vanberchem-Berthout, Principes de, 1794.
- Volger, Min. der Talkglimmer Familien, 1854.
- Widenmann, des Oryktognostischen theils der Min., 1794.
- Williams, J., Nat. Hist. of Min. Kingdom, 1810.
- Zeitschrift für Mineralogie, (Leonhard), 1825-29.
- *See* Geology; Paleontology; Gold; Iron; Copper; Coal; Gems, etc.

Mines and Mining. Am. Bureau of Mines, Prospectus, 1866. P.
- Annales des Mines, 1860, 61.
- Beer, A. H., Erdbohrkunde, 1858.
- Berg-und Hüttenmanner....zu Wien, 1859.
- Berg-und Hüttenmänische Zeitung, Freiberg, 1860.
- Bodemann, T., Berg u. Hütt. Probierkunst, 1857.
- Browne, J. R., Min. resources of the U. S., 1867.
- Budge, Pract. Miner's Guide, 1845.
- Coal-Hill lead mines, Canada.
- Cornwall, its mines, 1855.
- Cotta, Gangstudien, 1860.
- France: Army. Ecole...du génie, Aêrage des mines.
- Gouin, L., Mines de Sardaigne, 1867.
- Instruction pratique sur les Lampes de sureté, 1824.
- Keating, Art of Mining, 1821.
- Kerl, B., Harzer Hütten Prozesse, 1857. P. 1797.
- Kimball, J. P., Our mineral interests, 1866. P.
- Leonhard, Bergbaukunde, 1852.
- Lottner, F. H., Bergbau und Hüttenkunde, 1859.
- Mariposa Comp., 1863, 68.
- " Browne's report, 1868.
- Mèrin, Mines in Hungary.
- Mines de cuivre, Lac Supérieur, 1861. P. 1802.

Mines and Mining (continued).
- Mining Magazine, N. Y., 1853-60.
- Mining Review, No. 9, 10, Lond., 1837.
- Mowry, S., Shall government seize? 1864. P.
- National School of Mines, Considerations, 1867. P.
- " Opinions of the press, 1868. P.
- Orton, J. W., Miner's Guide, 1849.
- Pamphlets relating to, vols. 69, 520, 1801, 1802.
- Phillips, J. A., Records of, 1857.
- Pract. Miner's Guide, 1858.
- Quarterly Mining Review, 1830-35.
- Raymond, R. W., Miner. resources of U. S., 1869.
- Richards vs. Smith, 1836.
- Tomlinson's Cyclopedia, 1868.
- U. S. Explor. Exped., 40th par., 1869.
- U. S. Mineral resources, 1868.
- Whitney, J. D., Metallic Wealth of U. S., 1824.
- Whitney, J. P., Silver mining, Colorado, 1865.
- Wilkes, Deep River, North Carolina.
- *See* Iron; Gold; Copper; Metallurgy.

Mining Companies. Albany and Boston, 1861, 4, 5, 6.
- Cleveland Min. Co.
- Cypress River Co.
- Fort Ann Hem. and Magn. Ore Co., 1869.
- Fort Fillmore Silver M. Co.
- Lake Superior Copper Co.
- " Iron Co.
- Mariquita and New Granada M. Co.
- Mendota Mining Co., 1864, 5.
- Nantahala and Tuckasege Land and Mineral Assocn., N. C., 1856.
- Pamphlets of mining comp., vol. 854, 1801, 1802.
- Phœnix Copper Comp., 1855.
- St. Mary's Copper M. Comp., 1863.
- Schoolcraft Iron Comp., 1865.
- Stephenson Mining Company, El Paso.
- Triunfo Silver M. Co., L. California.
- *See* Coal; Iron; Copper; Gold.

Minneapolis. St. Anthony, Sketch of.

Minnesota. Andrews, C. C., M. and Dacotah, 1857.
- Bishop, H. E., Floral home, 1857.
- Bond, J. W., Minn. and its Resources, 1853.
- Carver, J., Travels, 1766-68.
- " Centenary of, 1867.
- Donnelly, Minnesota, 1857.
- Eastman, Mary H., Dahcotah, 1849.
- Featherstonhaugh, Voyage up the Minnay Sotor, 1847.

Minnesota (continued).
Gale, G., The Upper Mississippi, 1867.
Heard, Hist. of Sioux war, 1862.
Hinman, Journal, Sioux Indians.
Keating, Exped. to source of the St. Peters, 1824.
Minnesota: Statistics, 1861, 70.
" Resources, 1870.
" Governors' Mess., 1859-68.
Minn., Its Advantages, 1867, 69.
Minn., As a Home for Emigrants, 1866.
Minnesota Hist. Soc. Annals, 1850-67.
Neill, E. D., History of, 1858.
Oliphant, Minnesota, 1855.
Parker, N. H., Hand Book, 1857.
Putnam, J. W., Description of, 1849.
Riggs, Among the Dakotas, 1869.
Saint Anthony and Minneapolis, 1857.
Schoolcraft, Residence of 30 years.
Seymour, E. S., Sketches of, 1849.
Sibley, H. H., Condition of, 1852.
Strickland, Northwest Almanac, 1858.
Taopi and his friends, 1869.
Williams, J. F., Bibliography of, 1870.
Winona and Southern M., 1858.
See United States, West; Red River; Mississippi R.; Wisconsin.

Minorca. Armstrong, J., Hist. of the Island, 1752.
Byng, Letter... case of, 1756. P. 391.
Foltz, Climate, Topography, 1843.
Full answer, 1757.

Minot, G. R. Adams, J. Q., Mass. Fire Soc., Address, 1802. P. 514.

Minshall Family Genealogy, 1867.

Mints. *See* Currency; Numismatics; U. S. Mint.

Mirabeau, H. G. R. Cabanis, Mort de.
Dumont, Recollections of, 1832.
Mirabeau, Mémoires, 1836.
" Œuvres, avec la vie de.
" Letters from England, 1832.

Miracle Plays. *See* Mysteries.

Miracles. Bowman, W., Answer to Woolston, 1721. P. 309.
Bullock, T., Defence of, 1728.
Chronicon Abbatiæ de Evesham, (Chro. G. B.).
Church, T., Vindication of First three centuries, 1750.
" Second Vindication of, 1751.
Clanny, W. R., Cure of M. Jobson, 1841.
Croly, G., Five Sermons.
Dodwell, Answer to Middleton, 1749. P. 350.
Douglas, Bp., Works, 1820.

Miracles (continued).
Girard, Defence against M. Cadière, 1732. P. 343.
Greenwell, Discourse on, 1842.
Jackson, J., Miraculous Powers, 1749.
Jenkin, Exam. of Middleton, 1750.
Lawton, J., A Remarkable Healing, 1821. P. 601.
Leckie, Rise of Rationalism, 1868.
Maillard, Wonderful Cure of, 1693. P. 601.
Morison, J., Serm., Modern Gifts, 1833. P. 377.
Myers, F., Hulsean Essay, 1831. P.
Myers, T., Norrisian Essay, 1833. P.
Newman, J. H., M. of the Early Ages, 1843.
Obsequens, De Prodigiis, 1720.
Owen, H., Intent of Script. Mir., 1755. P. 309.
Pamphlets relating to, vols. 309, 350.
Parker, W., Mir. of Early Ages, 1749. P. 370.
Pearce, Z., Mir. vindicated, 1749. P. 309.
Pearson, J. N., On Warburton's Moses.
Penrose, J., Of the use of, 1824.
Phlegon Examined, 1734.
Sykes, Two Questions, 1750.
Toll, Middleton's Free Enquiry, 1749. P. 350.
Townsend, G., Church of England and Gifts, 1839.
Turnbull, G., Mir. and Doctrines of Christ, 1739. P. 309.
Tyndall, J., Fragments of Sci., 1871.
View of the Controversy, 1748.
Vince, Answer to Hume, 1809.
Whiston, W., Cessation of Mir. Gifts, 1749. P. 262.
Whitaker, Doct. of Peter's Epistles, 1751. P. 350.
See Christianity, Evidences of; Natural religion.

Miranda's Expedition. Biggs, J., Attempts at Revolution, 1809.
Miranda's Exped. and Life, 1808.
Smith, M., Sufferings in, 1814.
See South America.

Mirth. Colman, The Government of, 1707.

Miscellaneous. *See* Pamphlets, Miscellaneous.

Misletoe. Colbatch, Dissertation on, 1720. P. 1353.

Missions. Amer. Miss'y Ass'n, N. Y., 1846-68.
Baptist Miss'y Magazine, 1845, 46.
Foss, Facts for Baptists, 1850.
Last Command. P. 525.
Maclear, Hist. of, in Middle ages, 1863.

Missions, Foreign (continued).

Haweis, T., Instructions for.

Hibernian Miss. Soc., 1823. P. 472.

Hopkins, M., Serm., A. B. C. F. M., 1845. P. 270.

Horne, M., Letters on, 1815.

Humphreys, Hist. of Soc. for Prop. the Gospel to 1728.

Heurnius, De Leg. Evangel. ad Indos, 1618.

Holmes, J., Missions of the United Brethren, 1818.

Hist. of Am. Miss. to the heathen, 1840.

Judson, E., Kathayan Slave, 1853.

Latrobe, Miss. U. B. among the Indians, 1815, 16.

Letter to the Rt. Rev. A. Potter, 1850.

London Miss. Soc. Reports, 1795, 96, 1807–51.

Lowrie, Expenditures of, 1851. P. 525.

" Man. of Miss. of Presb. Ch., 1854.

Lyman, H., Martyr of Sumatra.

McCoy, J., Baptist Indian Miss., 1840.

Malan, S. C., Letters to a Miss. in India, 1858.

Marsden, J., Narr. of Miss. to Amer., 1810.

Marshman, Christianity in India, 1813. P. 433.

Martyn, H., Journal and Letters, 1851.

Mason, E., Serm. and Report, 1850.

Mill, W. H., Sermons, 1828.

Missionary Manual, Phil'a.

Mission Schools, 1855.

Moore, E. D., Life Scenes from, 1857.

Nederl. Zendeling-Genootschap, 1821. P. 568.

Nestorians of Persia.

Newcomb, Cyclopædia of, 1854.

Niecampus, Hist. Miss. in India, 1737.

Orme, W., Hist. South Sea Missions, 1827, 29.

Pamphlets relating to Foreign Miss., Vols. 525, 1530, 1615.

Pamphlets relating to British Foreign Missions, Vols. 384, 715, 879.

Periodical Accounts, (Baptist), 1794.

Pierson, H. W., Amer. Missionary Memorial, 1853.

Presb. Ch., Board of Missions, 1835–1849, 54–63.

Prot. Episc. Ch., Spirit of Missions, 1836–47, 59–62.

Reed, A., Sermon, Lond. Miss. Soc.

" Case of Tahiti.

Scudder, J., Letters from the East, 1833.

Soc. for the Prop. of the Gospel, Lond., Reports and Sermons, 1711–1869.

Spirit of Brit. Miss., 1815.

Missions, Foreign (continued).

Stevenson, W., Prot. Miss., India, 1721.

Tappan, L., Am. Miss. Assoc., 1855. P. 630.

Turkey Miss. Aid Soc., 1855. P. 472.

United Breth. Miss. Intelligencer, 1828–30.

United Brethren: Missions, 1774, 97-1839.

United For. Miss. Soc., Amer. Miss. Register, 1822–25.

Ward, F. de, Miss. among the Hindoos, 1850.

Western For. Miss. Soc. Reports, 1833–1836.

Wilder, Schools in India, 1861.

Wiley, Cemetery at Fuh Chau, 1858.

Wilks, S. C., Missions vindicated, 1819. P. 384.

Williams, J., South Sea Missions, 1837.

Wilson, J., Voy. in the Pacific of the Duff, 1796, 7, 8.

Winslow, M., Hints on Miss., 1856.

Missions, Roman Catholic. Assoc. de la Prop. de la Foi, Annales, 1828–52.

" Annals, 1839–45.

Kip, Early Jesuit Missions in North America, 1846.

Lettres Edifiantes, 1717–76.

Lettres Edifiantes (Querbœuf), 1819.

Litteræ annuæ Soc. J., 1586–1654.

Parkman, F., Jesuits in North Amer., 1867.

Relations des Jésuites, dans la Nouvelle France, Québec, 3 v., 8°.

St. Valier, Estat de l'Eglise de la Nouv. France, 1688.

Shea, Miss. among the Indians, 1829–1854.

Smet, Residence with the Indians, 1843.

" Cinquante Nouv. Lettres, 1858.

Spalding, Early Cath. Missions, 1787–1827.

Vetromile, The Abnaquis and their history, 1866.

See Jesuit Missions; Rom. Cath. Ch.

Missisco. Sumner, History of, 1860.

See Mineral Springs.

Mississippi. Affeck's Almanac, 1854.

Darby, Geog. Description of, 1817.

Gravier, J., Relation, 1700.

Louisiana and Miss. Directory, 1871.

Meek, A. B., Romantic passages, 1857.

New Orleans Directory, Biog., 1855.

Mississippi River and Valley. Banvard, Panorama of.

Beltrami, Sources of the Mississippi, 1824.

Montaigne, M. de. Essais, 1745.
" Essays, 1603.
" Works, Hazlitt and Wight, 1861.
" Le Christianisme de. Par L.... 1819.

Montana. Boller, Eight years West, 1868.
Raymond, Mining resources, 1869.
U. S. Geol. Explor., Vol. iii.
See Rocky Mts.

Montcalm, Marquis de. Eloge historique de, 1855. P. 254.
Journal d'Instruc. Pub., 1858, 59, 63.
Stevens, H., Bib. Hist., 1870, p. 114.
Warburton, Conquest of Canada, 1850.
Wright, R., Life of Wolfe, 1864.

Montenegro. Krasinski, Montenegro, 1853.
Wilkinson, Dalmatia and Montenegro, 1848.
See Turkey.

Montes, Lola. Reply to Papon's Hist., 1851.

Montesquieu, C. De. Œuvres, Lettres familières.

Montevideo. Almanac del Commer. del Plata, 1851.
La Sota, Rep. Orient. del Uruguay.
Nuñez, Acc't of, 1825.
See Argentine; La Plata; Buenos Ayres.

Montgomery family genealogy, 1863.

Montgomery, J. Knight, H. C., Life of, 1857.
Montgomery, J., Memoirs and correspondence, 1856.

Montgomery, Gen. R. Entretiens, 1776.
Armstrong, J., Life of, (Sparks).
Smith, W., Oration on, 1776.

Montgomery Co., N. Y. Directory, 1869.

Montgomery Co., Penn'a. Buck, W. J., History of, 1859.
Richards, Sermon at Trappe.

Monticello, Ill. Baldwin, T., Hist. Add., 1855. P. 237.

Montluc, B. de. Commentaries, 1521–72.

Montpelier, Vt. Thompson, History of.

Montpellier, Fr. Annuaire, 1821.
Herault, Annuaire, 1819, 22, 46.

Monuments, Sepulchral, etc. Akerman, J. Y., Pagan Saxondom, 1855.
Begerus, Lucernæ sepulchrales, 1704.
Blore, E., Mon. remains..Gt. Britain, 1826.
Brit. Museum, Handy Book of Antiq. in, 1870.

Monuments, Sepulchral, etc. (cont'd).
Camden Society: Dingley, Hist. from marble.
Gosden, Church-yard Monuments. MS.
Græviua, Thes. Gr. Antiquitatum, v. 12.
Greenwood illustrated, 1848.
McDonald, A. J., Monuments, 1848.
Maliphant, G., Designs for, 1852.
Mount Auburn Cemetery illust., 1848.
Oderici, Dissertationes, 1765.
Weever, Anc. funeral monuments, 1631.
Wheildon's Life of Willard, with list of Mon. in Massachusetts.
See Epitaphs; Cemeteries; Antiquities; Sculpture.

Montreal. Bosworth, N., Hist. of, 1839.
Lachland, On Nat. Hist. Soc. of, 1852. P. 242.
Mackay, Montreal Directory, 1842–53.
Montreal, Annuaire de Ville-Marie, 1863, 68.
Montreal in 1856.
Montreal, Guide, 1857.
St. Andrew's Church, 1844–49.
See Canada.

Montrose, Earl. Napier, M., Life and Times of, 1840.

Moody Family. Sketches, 1847.

Moody, J. Narrative of, 1865.

Moore. *See* More.

Moore, Bp. B. Hobart, Bp., Serm. on.

Moore, Sir J. Charmilly, Correspondence.
Moore, J. C., Life of, 1834.
Napier, W. F. P., Reply, 1832.

Moore, Thomas. Memoirs, Journal and Corresp., 1853.
Croker, J. W., Corresp. with Russell, 1854.
Power, Notes from his letters, 1854.

Moore's Creek. Wright, J. G., Battle of, N. C., 1857. P. 504.

Moral Philosophy. Abercrombie, Phil. of the moral feelings, 1834. B. C.
Adams, J., Elements of, 1837.
Ahrens, Das Naturrecht, 1846.
Aristotle, Ethics, 1813, 50.
Ast, Epikur. Ethik, 1831.
Attempt to shew, 1836.
Bailey, S., Essays on the Pursuit of Truth, 1831. B. C.
Beattie, J., Elem. of Moral Science, 1807.
Bentham, E., Introduction to, 1746. P. 399.
Bentham, J., Principles of Morals, 1823. B. C.

Moral Philosophy (continued).

Bentham, J., Deontology, 1834. B. C.

Blakey, R., Hist. of Mor. Science, 1833.

" Essay, of good and evil, 1831.

Boyd, J. R., Eclectic Mor. Phil., 1846.

Buchner, Eth. Elem. in Rechtsprincip, 1848.

Burgh, Dign. of Human Nature, 1816.

Burton, Anatomy of Melancholy, 1826.

Butler, J., Works, 1827.

Catlow, Æsthetic Medicine, 1867.

Chalmers, T., Pol. Econ. in connexion with, 1832.

Chubb, T., Tracts, 1730.

Clap, T., Essay on.....Moral Virtue, 1765.

Cogan, T., On the Passions, 1821.

Coleridge, S. T., Works; The Friend, 1831.

" Aids to Reflection, 1839. B. C., 1854.

Combe, G., Lectures on, 1836. B. C.

" Moral Const. of Man, 1834. B. C.

Crombie, A., Philos. necessity, 1795.

Dana, J., Edwards on the Will.

Démon de Socrate, 1829.

Discours sur les déplaisirs.

Disc. concerning Virtue, 1735. P. 332.

Drummond, W., Academ. Questions, 1805.

Dyer, Theory of Benev. Pamph'r 14.

Dymond, Principles of Morality, 1836.

Enquiry on practice of virtue, 1725.

Ensor, G., Princ. of Morality, 1801.

Epictetus, Enchiridion.

Fairchild, J. H., Moral Phil., 1869.

Follen, Works, vol. 3: Lectures on, 1841. B. C.

Fourier, Passions of Human Soul.

Gambier, Study of Moral Evidence, 1824.

Geulings, Ethica, 1697.

Gioja, Elementi di Filosofia, 1835.

Gleïzès, Thalysie, 1840.

Godwin, W., Political Justice, 1793.

Gros, Treatise on, 1795.

Hall, E., On Hickok's Psychology, 1863. P. 1362.

Harris, J., Man primeval, 1854.

Hickok, System of, 1853.

Hildreth, Theory of Morals, 1844.

Holbach, P. P. von, System of nature, (Mirabaud).

Hopkins, M., Law of Love, 1869.

" On Moral Science, 1862.

Hutcheson, De nat. hom. socialitate, 1756.

" System of Mor. Phil., 1755.

Moral Philosophy (continued).

Illustrations of Hume on Necessity, 1795. P. 1369.

James, H., Moralism and Christianity, 1850.

" Nature of Evil, 1855.

Jarves, J. J., Why and What am I? 1857.

Johnson, A. B., Encyc. of Instruction.

Jouffroy, T., Introd. to Ethics, 1841.

Jouin, Elem. phil. moralis, 1865.

Lavater, Jour. of a self observer.

Law, W., Reply to Fable of the Bees.

Louvain, Phil. Moralis, 1820. P. 15.

Mackintosh, Sir J., Progress of Ethic. Phil.

Malebranche, De la Recherche de la Vérité, 1749.

" The search after truth, 1694.

Mandeville, The Fable of the Bees, 1806.

Moore, G., Body and mind, 1847.

More, H., Enchiridion Ethicum, 1712.

Mudie, Man as a mor. being.

Nash, Morality and the State, 1859.

New Estimate of Manners, 1760.

Origin of duty, 1796.

Paley, Moral philosophy.

" Analyses of.

Palmer, E., Principles of Nature, 1830.

Pamphlets relating to, Vols. 399, 1369, 1789.

Pavonius, Summa Ethicæ, 1668.

Payne, G., Elem. of Ment. and Moral Science, 1829.

Penrose, Discipline of human motives, 1820. B. C.

" Utilitarian theory, 1836.

Philosophy of evil, 1845.

Plutarch, Morals, Goodwin's ed., 1870.

Powers, G., Imagination and nervous system, 1828.

Price, R., Principal Questions in morals, 1769. B. C.

Remarks upon Dr. B's 6th Chap., 1737.

Rousseau, J. J., Œuvres, 1801.

Rush, Influence of Phys. Causes, 1786.

St. John, Innate Mor. Principles, 1752. P. 399.

Self Entertainment, (Whateley), 1751.

Senault, Usage des passions, 1664. B. C.

Shaftesbury, Characteris., 1733. B. C., 1837.

Simon, B. A., View of the human heart, 1825.

Smith, A., Theory of Mor. Sent., 1792.

Smith, J. A., Monograph on the moral sense, 1847. P. 46. B. C.

Smith, S. S., Lect. on, 1812.

Moral Philosophy (continued).
Spedalieri, Diritti dell' uomo, 1797.
Spirit of Humanity, 1835.
Stewart, D., Works, 1855.
Stewart, J., Mor. State of Nations, 1841.
Taylor, I., Nat. Hist. of Enthusiasm, 1849.
Tucker, A., The Light of Nature, 1831. B. C.
Wayland, F., Elements of Mor. Sci., 1843.
West, S., On Moral Agency, 1772.
Whewell, Four Sermons, 1837.
" Elements of Morality, 1845.
Witherspoon, Lectures on, 1810.
See Philosophy; Soul; Social Questions; Will; Necessity; Evil; Sin.

Morals, Practical. Alexander, J. W., The American Mechanic, 1847.
Austin, J. M., Voice to Youth, 1846.
Barrau, Morale Pratique, 1828.
Barret, Serm., Evil of Scandal, 1711. P. 365.
Beecher, H. W., Industry, 1850. P. 215.
Benef. Effects of Christian temper.
Brewer, D. R., Errors of ultraism, 1851.
Britaine, W. de, Humane prudence, 1701.
Britain's Remembrancer, 1747.
Broad Shadows, 1862.
Browne, T., Works, Religio Medici, 1686, 1836.
Caterpillars and Gooseberry bush, 1812.
Carey, M., Phil. of Common Sense, 1838.
Castilio, B., De Curiali, 1603.
Chapin, On Shameful Life, 1859. P. 558.
Chapone, Mrs., Works, 1818. B. C.
Charron, Of Wisdom, 1729.
Cicero, Offices, 1850.
Cobbett, W., Thirteen Sermons, 1834.
Combe, W., Letters, 1824.
Confucius, Morals.
Croiset, Réflexions sur la Morale, 1707.
De Foe, Works; Family Instructor, 1840–41.
Dewey, Mor. Views of Comm., Soc., and Politics, 1838. B. C.
Dialogues on Uses of For. Travel, (Hurd).
Dinocurt, Cours de Morale sociale, 1839.
Ecole de l'homme, Génard, 1752.
Edgeworth, Early Lessons, 1815. B. C.
Eldridge, J., Sermon on Mor. Reform, 1843.
Erasmus, Lingua, 1649.
Experimental Knowledge, 1849.

Morals, Practical (continued).
Felltham, Resolves, 1840.
Fénélon, Selections from, 1829. B. C.
Fowler, E., Vindication of Mor. Societies, 1692.
Fox, W. J., Lectures to the Working Classes, 1845, 46. B. C.
" Morality of the Scriptures, 1833. B. C.
Fragment, Phil'a, 1796.
Franklin, B., Works, 1836–40.
Friendly Instructor, 1811.
Fruytier, Salomons Raad.
Gracian, L'Homme universel, 1723. B. C.
Graham, S., To young men, on Chastity, 1838.
Graver thoughts, (Boyd), 1865.
Gregg, T. D., Novum organum moralium, 1859.
Guide du Bonheur, 1840.
Hanway, J., Journal, 1756.
Hooker, R., Weekly Misc., 1736.
Hopkins, S., Serm. of Mor. Reform, 1839.
Huarte, Exam. of men's wits, 1596.
Hunter, R., Cruelty to animals, 1835.
Hunter, T., On Chesterfield's letters, 1776.
La Colonie, Traité en Morale instructive, 1736.
Law, On the Fable of the Bees.
Lecky, Hist. of European Morals, 1869.
Le Prohon, Vol., Abortion, 1867.
Lieber, Manual of Political Ethics, 1838, 39.
Life's Evening, 1860.
M'Dowall's, J. R., Life, 1838.
Maltby, J., Sermon of Mor. Reform, 1845.
Mann, H., Thoughts for a young man, 1850.
Mason, J., Self-knowledge, 1814. B. C.
Mather, Essays to do good, 1815. B. C.
Meikle, The Traveller.
Mercier, Manuel de Morale, 1858.
Messinger, Sentiments on resignation.
Mitchell, J., Serm. on Mor. Reform.
Moral Almanac, 1847.
Moral Societies' Conv., Albany, 1819.
Moral Societies in N. Y., 1819. P. 65.
More, H., Christian Mor., 1831. B. C.
Newman, T., Progress of vice, 1755.
Œconomy of Human Life, 1752, 1790.
Opie, Illustrations of Lying, 1833. B. C.
Osborne, S. G., Beer shop evil.
Owen, Fashionable World, 1806. B. C.
Pamphlets relating to practical Morals, Vols. 1370, 1534, 1716, 1787.

Music, Historical, Elementary and Miscellaneous (continued).

Encyclopédie Méthodique, Framéry, 2 vols.

Estienne, Lettres sur la, 1854.

Fétis, A. Stradivari, Biog.

Graham, G. F., Essay on Mus. Comp.

Hastings, T., Elem. of Vocal M., 1839.

" The Musical Reader, 1819.

Higgins, The Philosophy of Sound, 1838.

Hood, G., Hist. of, in N. Engl., 1846.

Hullah, Wilhem's Method. P. 400.

" Selection of Pieces. P. 400.

Inquiry..Nature and Design of Music, 1831.

Johnson, A. N., Musical Class Book, 1845.

Jones, Thorough Bass.

Jones, Sir W., Musical Modes of the Hindus, 1812.

Kiesewetter, Verhandelingen, German and French.

" Hist. of Modern Music, 1848.

La Madeleine, Théories du Chant, 1854.

Lind, J., Concert. P. 266.

Liszt, F., Life of Chopin, 1863.

Liverpool Mus. Festivals, 1823, 27, 29, 30, 33, 36. P. 400.

Maatschappij: Tot bevorderung der Toonkunst, 1854–6.

Mason, L., Musical letters, 1854.

" Manual of vocal music, 1844.

Mendelssohn, Letters, 1865.

Moore, J. W., Encyclopædia of, 1854.

Musical Directory, Lond., 1853.

Musical Fund Soc., Phil'a, 1856.

N. Y. Musical Fund, 1830. P. 615.

North, E., Address, Uses of Music, 1858.

Novello, Voice and vocal art, 1856.

Ortigue, Dict. de Plain-Chant, 1854.

Pamphlets relating to, Vols. 400, 803, 1042, 1371–1373, 1717–1719.

Patriot's Cal., Marseilles Hymn, 1794. Alm. 54.

Quichérat, Principes de, 1846.

Richardson's Catalogue, 1855.

Rimbault, Bibliot. madrigaliana, 1847.

Romagnesi, Romances, Chansonnettes, Nocturnes.

Rossini, Memoirs of, Lond., 1824.

Rousseau, J. J., Dict. de musique, v. 12, 13.

Roussier, Sur différens points de l'harmonie, 1755.

Royal Mus. festival, 1834.

Royal Society of Musicians, 1856.

Scudo, Critique et Littérature musicales, 1850.

Music, Historical, Elementary and Miscellaneous (continued).

Spencer, C. C., Treatise on, 1850.

Sight Singing, 1842.

Sontag, H., Life of, 1852.

Van Tassel, Phonographic Harmonist, 1846.

Walker, J. C., Irish bards, 1818.

Wheatstone, Transmis. of Mus. Sounds. P. 400.

Wilhem's Method.

" Hullahism.

Willard, N. A., Mus. of Hindostan, 1834.

Winthrop, R. C., Addr. Mus. Festiv., Bost., 1857. P. 287.

See Bibliography; Fine Arts.

Music, Collections and Single Authors. Baker, B. F., School chimes, 1853.

Beethoven, Fidelio, Opera, 1840. P. 41. B. C.

Bellini, Sonnambula. P. 616.

Benjamin, L. A., Normal School song book, 1851.

Biblos Kaloumene Euterpe, Const'ple, 1830.

Bradbury, W. B., Flora's festival, 1847.

" The Jubilee, 1858.

" The Young choir, 1841.

Commuck, Indian melodies, 1845.

Dana, M. S. B., Northern Harp, 1841.

" Southern Harp, 1841.

Eastman, L., Masonic melodies, 1825.

Hastings, T., Crystal fount, 1847.

Hullah, Song book, 1866.

Kingsley, G., Juvenile choir, 1848.

Mason, L., Boston school song book, 1841.

" Madrigals and glees, 1843.

" Juvenile lyre, 1835.

" Bost. Juvenile Singing School, 1843.

Music, Misc. Coll., Lond., 1815–25.

Music Coll. for Piano, 1800–25.

Musical Olio, (Olmsted), 1805.

Nederlandsche Muzijk, A Collection of, by various authors, 1837–50.

Root, G. F., Acad. vocalist, N. Y.

Rossini, Cenerentola.

Sanders, C. W., Young Vocalist, 1847.

Scott, T., Harmonica lyrica, Lond.

Shaw, O., Mus. Olio, etc., 1807.

Vocal Companion, 1802.

Watson, H. C., Ladies' Glee Book, 1854.

Webster, W. C., School chorister, 1850.

Willard, J. D., The Arion, 1862.

Woodbury, I. B., Chorus Glee-book, 1850.

See Dramas; Operas.

Myrick, J. Life of, 1755.

Mysteries. Dendy, W. C., Philosophy of, 1845.
- Dissertation on the Pagan, 1766.
- Dupuis, Origine des cultes.
- Hitchcock, E. A., Christ the spirit, 1861.
- Hone, W., Ancient mysteries.
- Jamblichus, De Mysteriis.
- " On the Mysteries, 1821.
- Mysteries of Isis.
- Ouvaroff, Mys. of Eleusis, 1817.
- Sainte Croix, Mystères du Paganisme, 1784.
- Shakespeare Society, Coventry Mys.
- Taylor, T., Eleusin. and Bacc. Myst. Pamph'r 15, 16.
- Viollet le Duc, Ancien Théatre Français.
- *See* Mythology; Superstitions.

Mysticism. Behmen, J., Theosoph. philosophy, 1691.
- Brown, J. P., The Dervishes, 1868.
- Delafield, J., Myst. and Secret Societies, 1857.
- Madden, R. R., Phantasmata, 1857.
- Schmid, Myst. Allemand, XIV$_e$ siècle, (Ac. Mor., 1847).
- Taylor, I., Nat. Hist. of enthusiasm.
- Upham, T. C., M'me Adorna's life, 1847.
- " Madame Guyon's and Fénélon's lives, 1847.
- *See* Friends; Enthusiasm.

Mythology. Banier, A., Mythol. and Fables explained, 1740.
- Bell's New Pantheon, 1790.
- Betham, Etruria Celtica, 1842.
- Biog. Univ., Mythologique, 3 v.
- Brinton, D. G., Myths of the New World, 1868.
- Bryant, J., System of Mythology, 1776.
- Bulfinch, T., The age of fable, 1863.
- Colebrooke, Mythology of the Hindus, 1831.
- Collin De Plancy, Dictionnaire infernal, 1826.
- Court de Gébelin, Le monde primitif, 1777.
- Disser. on Prim. objects of idolatry, 1817. P. 1220.
- Dwight, M. A., Grecian and Roman Mythology, 1849.
- Encyc. Méthodique: Antiquités.
- Gale, T., Court of the Gentiles, 1671.
- Goropius, Hermathena; Hieroglyph., 1580.
- Gould, S. B., Origin of religious belief, 1869.
- " Myths of the Middle Ages, 1869.

Mythology (continued).
- Hamilton, A., Fairy Tales, 1849.
- Hodgson, Myth. for versification, 1866.
- Jones, Sir W., Works; Gods of Greece and India, 1807.
- Keightley, Fairy Mythology, 1850.
- Knight, R. P., Worship of Priapus, 1865.
- Montfaucon, Antiq. Explained, 1722–5.
- Muller, M., Essay, Comp. Mythol., 1867.
- Mysteries of Isis, 1858.
- Newton, J. F., Three Enigmas, 1821.
- Nimrod: A Discourse, (Apperley), 1826.
- Pococke, E., India in Greece, 1856.
- Ramsay, Travels of Cyrus, 1814.
- Rolle, Recherches sur le Culte de Bacchus, 1824.
- Ruskin, The Greek myths of cloud and storm, 1869.
- Shakespeare Soc., Fairy Mythology, (Halliwell).
- Smith, W., Dict. of Gr. and Rom. Mythology and Biog., 3 v.
- Taylor, T., Eleusin. and Bacchic Mys. Pamph'r 8.
- Thorpe, Yule-tide Stories, 1853.
- Tooke, A., Pantheon, 1845.
- Tyler, On primitive culture, 1871.
- Vestiges of Civilization, 1851.
- White, C. A., Student's Mythology, 1870.
- Wilson, H. H., Hindu Mythol., 1862.
- *See* Antiquities; Religions; Hindoos; Classical Lit.; Delusions; Mysteries; Pre-historic Times.

N.

Nadir Shah. Hanway, N., History of, 1753.
- Jones, W., Histoire de Nadir, (Works), v. 11, 12.
- Nadir, History of, 1742. P. 1250.

Names. Arthur, W., Dictionary of, 1857.
- Bowditch, Suffolk surnames, 1857, 58.
- Brady, Dissertation on, 1822.
- Buchanan, Ancient Scottish Names, Misc. Scot., v. 4.
- Court de Gébelin, Noms de famille, v. 8.
- Dixon, H. B., Surnames, 1857.
- Du Cange, Familles d'Outre Mer, France: Docts. inédits., 1869.
- Ferguson, English surnames, 1858.
- Förstemann, Altdeutsches Namenbuch, 1856.
- Lower, M. A., Dictionary of family names, 1860.
- Nichols, Christian names, 1857.
- Nicolas, Battle of Agincourt.

Names (continued).
Onderdonk, H., jr., Names of persons and places on Long Is., N. Y.
Pott, A. F., Die Personennamen, 1859.
Salverte, E., Essai sur les noms d'hommes, etc.
Sims, Scottish Surnames, 1862.
Taylor, I., Words and places, 1865.
Yonge, History of Christian names, 1863.
See Genealogies.

Nantucket, Ms. Crèvecœur, Letters of an Amer. Farmer.
Macy, O., History of, 1835.
Nantucket Papers, 1856.

Napier, Sir C. Buist, Errors in life of.

Napier, C. J. Indian misgovernment.
Rathborne, Gov't of Scinde, 1854.

Napier, John. Napier, M., Memoirs of, 1834.

Napier, Sir W. F. P. Bruce, H. A., Life of, 1854.
Napier, W. F. P., Tracts collected on his History, 2 v. 1831-41.

Naples. Blume, Iter Italicum, 1835-48.
Calabria, Lond., 1832.
Capecelatro, Istoria della Città e Regno, 1724.
Colletta, History of, 1734-1856.
Costanzo, Istoria del Regno di, 1735.
Craven, Travels in Abrucci, 1838.
Descrizione del Monast. di Mon. Casino, 1731.
Dolomieu, Earthquakes in Calabria, 1783.
Giannone, Histoire du Royaume, 1742.
" Anecdotes ecclésiastiques, 1753. B. C.
Gladstone, Letters on Persecutions of, 1851.
Gondon, La Terreur dans le Royaume, 1851.
Grant, J., Adventures of an Aide-de-Camp, 1851.
Joanna of Sicily, Life of, 1824.
Maceroni, Col., Memoirs, 1838.
Mazochius, Actorum S. Januarii vindiciæ, 1759.
Paulinus, Mus. Borgiani Velitris, 1793.
Spallanzani, L., Travels in the Sicilies, 1798.
Swinburne, Travels in, 1777-80.
Toppi, Biblioteca Napoletana, 1678.
See Sicily; Italy; Rome; Bibliography.

Napoleon Family. Bonaparte family, by the Berkeley men, 1852.
Gregorovius, Corsica and the B. family, 1855.

Napoleon I. Abbott, J. S. C., History of, 1855.
" N. at St. Helena, 1855.
Abell, E., Recollections of, at St. Helena, 1845.
Abrantès, Duchesse d', Memoirs of, 1836.
Answer to O'Meara's Napoleon, 1823.
Antommarchi, The Last Days of, 1825.
Bausset, Private Mem. of Court of, 1805-14. B. C.
Bonaparte, Lucien, Memoirs, 1836. B. C.
Bourrienne, Life of, 1832. B. C.
Carnot, Exposé, 1814.
Cathcart, Comm. on the War in Russia, 1812-13.
Caulincourt, Recollections, 1838.
Cevallos, Usurp. of Crown of Spain, 1808.
Chambray, Expédition de Russie.
Channing, W. E., Essay on, 1827.
Chateaubriand, Of Buonaparte, 1814.
Chênedollé, Napoleon le Grand, 1808.
David, Picture of Coronation.
Delalonde, Statue à Cherbourg.
Edwards, E., Napoleon Medals, 1837.
Forsyth, W., Captivity of, at St. Helena, 1853.
French Pretender unmasked, 1815. P. 392.
Goldsmith, Secret Hist. of Cabinet of, 1810.
Gourgaud, Memoirs of, 1824.
" Napoleon and the Army in Russia, 1825.
Haley, Abbott unmasked, 1855.
Hall, B., Voy. to Eastern Seas; and interview with, 1817.
Hazlitt, Life of, 1828.
Headley, J. T., Napoleon and his Marshals, 1846.
" Imperial guard of.
Holland, Lord, Foreign Reminis., 1850.
Humblet, Accomplissement de la Prophétie, 1808.
" Non plus ultra.
Jomini, Life of, 1864.
Labaume, Campaign in Russia.
Langon, Evenings with Cambacéres, 1837.
Las Casas, Mém. de Sainte Hélène, 1823, 24. B. C.
" Mem. of St. Helena, 1818.
Lee, H., Life of, 1835.
Maceroni, Col., Memoirs, 1838.
Maitland, Narr. of Surrender, 1826.
Manuscript brought from St. Helena, 1817.
Meadley, Two Pairs of Hist. Portraits, Pamph'r 18.

Napoleon I (continued).
Montholon, Captivity at St. Helena, 1846.
Müffling, Campaign of 1813, 14.
Napoleon I, Correspondance, 7 v.
" Confid. corresp. of, and Josephine, (Abbott).
" Œuvres choisies, (Pujol), 1843.
" Istoria di: Venezia, 1807, 15 v.
Napoleon and the Marshals, 1848.
Ney, Marshal, Memoirs of, 1834.
Noyes, T., Two sermons, 1809.
O'Meara, Napoleon in Exile, 1822.
Pélet, Napoleon in Council, 1837.
Peltier, Trial for a libel on, 1803. B. C.
Phillips, C., Dethronement of.
Pinch, W., Death of.
Plunder and partition, 1804.
Poore, Life and Campaigns of, 1851.
Porter, R. K., Campaign of 1812.
Rapp, Memoirs, 1823.
Récit Hist. de la Campagne en Italie, 1797.
Relation de la dernière campagne, 1815.
Reply to Irwin, 1798.
Sainsbury, J., Napoleon Museum, 1844.
Scott, Sir W., Life of, 1827.
" Paul's Letters, 1840.
Sneed, J., Rise and fall of, 1866. P. 1491.
Stutterheim, Battle of Austerlitz.
Tchuykevitch, On the war of 1812.
Thiers, Hist. of the consulate and empire.
Villemain, Souvenirs d'Histoire, 1855.
Walsh, Letters on the Fr. gov't, 1810.
Wilson, R., Journal, 1812-14.
See France, History of; Spain; Waterloo.

Napoleon III. Almanach de Napoleon, 1855.
Briffault, F. T., The Prisoner of Ham, 1846.
De Puy, L. Napoleon and his Times, 1852.
Henrichs, Aperçu de ses actes, 1857. P. 1773.
Napoleon III, Œuvres, 1856.
" Works, vol. 1-4, and memoir, 1852.
" Voyage en Algérie, 1860.
Napoleon et l'Italie, 1859.
O'Brien, P., Notes of interviews, 1852.
Pascal, A., Histoire de, 1853.
Persigny, Relation, 1837.
Rogeard, Sayings of Labiénus, 1865.
Rogers, B. B., An enquiry, 1855.
Roth, Life of, 1856.

Napoleon III (continued).
Schœlcher, Hist. du Deux Décembre, 1852.
Smucker, History of, 1858.
Ténot, Paris, Déc , 1851, 1870.
See France, Revolutions.

Narcissa. Pierquin, Tombeau de, 1851.

Narcotics. Anstie, Stim. and Narcotics, 1864.
Beard, G. M., Stim. and Narcotics, 1871.
Parrish, J., The Probe, No. I-IV, Phil'a, 1869.
See Opium; Stimulants; Temperance; Tea; Tobacco; Wine.

Narragansett, Rh. Is. Updike, Hist. of Ch., 1847.

Nash, R. Life of, 1762.

Nash, S. Journal, 1776.

Nashotah. Kip, A few days at Nashotah, 1849.
Nashotah Sem., Catalogues.
Seabury Miss. papers.

Nashua, New Hamp. Directory, 1864.
Fox, C. J., History of, 1846.

Nashville, Tenn. Directory, 1861.
Tennesee, Reports on the Capitol.

Nason, R. Genealogy, 1859.

Nassau, Bahamas. Decript. of, 1869.

Nassau, Ger. Belgium and Nassau.
Breval, Hist. of House of, 1734.
Head, Bubbles from the Brünnen.

Nassau, N. Y. Knox, J. P., Hist. disc., 1841.

Natal, South Africa. Arbousset, Tour in S. Africa, 1852.
Mann, Dr., Description of, 1860.
Methley, Information, 1850.
See Africa, South.

Natick, Mass. Bacon, O., History of, 1856.
Biglow, W., History of, 1560-1830.
Jacobs, S. S., Nonantum and N., 1853.

National Armory. *See* United States.

Nationality. *See* Naturalization; Aliens.

National Politics. *See* Political, American; Congressional Speeches; U. S., Political.

Native Americans. *See* American party.

Natural History: General and Miscellaneous. Acad. of Phil'a, Cat. of Crania, 1857.
Adams, A., Manual of, for travellers, 1854.
Ælianus, De natura animalium, 1784.

Natural History: General and Miscellaneous (continued).

Agassiz, L., Contributions, Nat. Hist. of U. S., 1857-62.

" Methods of study, 1863.

Albertus Magnus, Liber Secretorum, 1496.

Allen, R. L., Domestic Animals, 1848.

Baird, Cyc. of Nat. Sciences, 1858.

Barrington, D., Miscellanies, 1781.

Bell, A. N., Knowl. of living things, 1860.

Bingley, Useful Knowledge, 1818.

Brown, T., Taxidermist's Manual, 1859.

Buc'hoz, Manuel Econ. des Plantes, 1782.

Buckland, F. T., Curiosities of, 1858, 1860.

Buffon, Hist. Naturelle, 1750-83.

Cooper, Miss, Rural Hours, 1850.

Cuvier, Animal Kingdom, 1827-35.

" Prog. des Sciences Nat., 1789.

Darwin, C., Origin of Species, 1860.

" Variation of animals and plants, 1868.

Dawson, J. W., Misc. papers, 1860-63.

Dekay, Progress of the Nat. Sci. in the U. S., 1826.

Delafosse, Notions d', 1846.

Dict. des Sciences Naturelles, 1816-30.

Dumas, J., Balance of organic nature, 1844.

Duncan, P. M., Transformations of insects, 1871.

Ed. Cab. Lib., Lives of Zoölogists.

Edwards, M., Cahiers d'hist. nat., 1858.

Encyc. Méthodique, Hist. Nat.

Flint, T., Lectures on Nat. History, 1833.

Forskal, Descriptiones, 1775.

Geoffroy, Directions for preparations in, 1846.

Goldsmith, Hist. of Earth and Animated Nature, 1833.

Good, The Book of Nature, 1837.

Gosse, Life in...animals, 1857.

" The Wonders of the deep sea, 1854.

Hall, J., Addresses, Auburn and Cambridge, 1843, 48. P. 74.

Hartwig, The Sea and its Wonders, 1861.

Harvey, W. H., Sea-side Book, 1854.

Housset, Mémoires d'Hist. Nat., 1787.

Huxley, Origin of species, 1863.

Jesse, E., Gleanings in, 1854.

Kabinet der Natuurlijke Historien, 1719-21.

Kirby's Wonderful Museum, 1820.

Knapp, Jour. of a Naturalist, 1838.

Natural History: General and Miscellaneous (continued).

Leeuwenhoek, Send-brieven, aan de Kon. Soc. te Lond., 1718.

Linnæus, On the study of Nature, 1772.

Lyell, C., Antiquity of man, 1863.

Martyn, W. F., New Dictionary of, 1785.

Mass. Educ., Report on Museum, 1859. P. 551.

Mivart, Genesis of species, 1871.

Mudie, Obs. of Nature, 1833.

Naturalist's Library: Jardine, 1833-1844.

Neckam, De Naturis rerum, (Chron. G. B.).

Numan, Verhandeling, 1851.

Oken, L., Elem. of physio-philos., (Ray Soc.).

" Allgemeine Naturgeschichte, 1833-43.

Orr, Circle of the Sciences, 1855.

Pamphlets relating to, vols. 804, 1535, 1869. B. C. vol. 48.

Peck, On the Slug worm, 1790. P. 36.

Piso, W., De Indiæ re naturali, 1658.

Plinius, C. S., Natural History, (Bohn).

Plutarch, Morals, Goodwin's ed., 1870.

Quatrefages, Metamorphoses of man and animals, 1864.

Rafinesque, Hist. of Natural Science, 1840.

Redfield's Chart of An. Kingdom.

Reeve, Torpidity of Animals, 1809.

Richter, Vischkundige Onderwyser, 1790.

Rolleston, Forms of animal life, 1870.

Ruschenberger, Hist. Acad. Nat. Sci., Phil'a, 1852.

" First book of, 1846.

Scheuchzer, Bijbel der Natuur, 1784. P. 107.

Schouw, The Earth, Plants and Man, 1852.

Seba, A., Rerum Nat. Thes. Descriptio, 1738.

Selys-Longchamps, Phénom. périod. du Regne animal, 1841, 46.

Siamese Twins, 1831. P. 199.

Smellie, W., Philosophy of, 1827.

Smithsonian Contributions, 1856-70.

" Preserving specimens of, 1852.

Somerville, Mrs., Molec. and microscopic science, 1869.

Spectacle de la Nature, or Nature displayed, (Le Pluche), 1740-48.

Stark, J., Elements of, 1828.

Stieren....der Zibethmaus. P. 205.

Sulivan, View of nature, 1794.

Sullivan, J., Cat. of his Cabinet, 1838.

Natural History: General and Miscellaneous (continued).

Swainson, W., Discourse on, Lardner, 106.

Temminck, Misc. publications.

Thorp, C., Field-club of Tyneside, 1853. P. 395.

Townsend, P. S., Disc., Lyc. of Nat. Hist., N. Y., 1820. P. 85.

Turner, S., Sacred Hist. of the World, 1832. B. C.

Tyson, Homo Silvestris, (Pygmies), 1699.

U. S. Nav. Lyceum......preserving Articles, 1824. P. 551.

Valentini, Museum Museorum, 1700.

Vincentius, Speculum Naturale, 1494.

Wagner, A., Andeutungen...des Org. Leben, 1845.

Walker, A., Intermarriage.

Waterton, C., Essays on, 1851.

See Aquaria; Botany; Man; Mineralogy; Nature; Zoölogy, etc.

Natural History; Particular Countries. Adams, A., Notes on, Belcher's Voyage, 1843-46.

Azara, Quadrupèdes du Paraguay, 1801.

Bancroft, E., Nat. Hist. of Guiana, 1769.

Barton, Nat. Hist. of Penn'a, 1799.

Catesby, Nat. Hist. of Carolina, etc., 1754.

Darwin, C., Voy. of H. M. S. Beagle, 1845.

Descourtilz, Voy. d'un Naturaliste, 1809.

Gay, Hist. fisica de Chile, 1849.

Godman, American Nat. Hist., 1826-28.

" Rambles of a Naturalist, 1833.

Goeze, Europaische Fauna, 1797.

Gosse, The Canadian Naturalist, 1840.

Hernandez, Plantarum Anim. et Min. Mexi. Historia, 1651.

Hughes, Nat. Hist. of Barbadoes, 1750.

Josselyn, New England's Rareties discovered, 1672.

Kingsley, C., Glaucus, 1855.

Knapp, Journal of, Gr. Brit., 1838.

Massachusetts, Survey on Zoölogy, Botany and Geology, 1838-41.

Molina, Storia Nat. del Chili; *and in Eng.*, 1808, 09, 10.

Morgan, L. H., American beaver.

New York, Nat. Hist. of the State, 1842-70.

Nicolson, Hist. Nat. de Saint Domingue, 1776.

Piso, W., De Indiæ re naturali, 1658.

Pontopidon, Nat Hist. of Norway.

Quatrefages, Rambles in France, Spain, Sicily, 1857.

Natural History; Particular Countries (continued).

Ray Society, Publications to 1869.

Romans, Nat. Hist. of Florida, 1776.

Rousselot de Surgy, Hist. Nat. de Penn'ie, 1768.

Russell, A., Nat. Hist. of Aleppo, 1756.

Siebold, F., Schinesischer und Japanischer Naturgeschichten, 1837.

Sloane, Nat. Hist. of Jamaica, 1707-1725.

Suckley, Nat. Hist. of Washington and Oregon, 1860.

Tennent, J. E., Nat. Hist. of Ceylon, 1859.

U. S. Naval Exped., Chile, 1849-52.

U. S. Expl. Exped., Wilkes, 1844-54.

U. S., Pac. Railroad Rep., 1853-54.

Vermont Report, (Young), 1856.

Victoria, Aust., Productions, 1861, 66.

White, G., Nat. Hist. of Selborne, 1851.

Wied-Neuwied, M., Naturgesch. v. Brasilien, 1833.

See Botany; Mineralogy; Zoölogy, etc.

Natural History; Serials. Acad. of Nat. Sci., Phil'a, Jour., 1817-69.

" Proceedings, 1841-68.

Allgem. Schweiz. Gesellschaft, 1855-1867.

Annals of Natural History, Lond., 1858-70.

Boston Soc. of Nat. Hist., Memoirs, v. 1, 1869.

" Journal, 1834-63.

" Proceedings, 1841-68.

Elliott Soc., S. Carolina, 1853-58.

Essex Co. Nat. Hist. Soc., 1852.

Essex Institute, Communications, 1867.

Harvard University, Museum of Zoölogy. Bulletins to 1871.

Linnean Soc. Transactions, v. 1-20.

Lyceum of Nat. Hist. of N. Y., Annals, 1824-70.

Magazine of Nat. Hist., 1829-40, Lond.

Miscellanea curiosa, (Academ. Cæs. Leop.), 1670-97.

Nat. Hist. Soc. of Hartford, Trans., 1836.

Nat. Hist. Soc. of Montreal, 1857. P. 551.

Naturalists' Miscellany, (Shaw and Nodder), Lond., 1789-1813.

Naturforschende Gesellschaft in Bern, 1856-64.

Naturforsch. Gesellsch. in Emden, 1859-64.

N. Y.; Rep. of Cabinet of Natural History, 1848-70.

Ray Society, Publications, 1845-69.

Natural History; Serials (continued).
Soc. des Sci. Nat. de Neuchatel, 1835-1845.
Soc. des Sci. Nat. de Strasbourg, 1862.
Soc. Helvétique des Sci. Nat. *See* Allgemeine.
Zoölogical Soc., Lond., Trans., 1830-1868.
" Proceedings, 1830-70.
See Scient. Periodicals and Trans.

Naturalization. Atocha, Memorial, 1852.
Essay on, 1816.
Hanway, Nat. of the Jews, 1753.
Hay, G., Of Expatriation, 1814.
Hunt, W., Speech on the Laws of, 1845. P. 487.
Lowell, Review of Hay.
Martin, L., Charge, 1813.
Massachusetts, Report on Aliens, 1811.
Obser. on impressment, 1806.
Page, J., Address on aliens, 1779.
Palma, Principio di nazionalità, 1867.
Pamphlets, vol. 980.
Plowden, Rights of Brit. subjects, 1784.
Pumroy, J. N., Defence of our Laws, 1845.
Question whether a Jew, 1753. P. 1026.
Republic, The, periodical, 1841-54.
Rhodes, J. R., Speech, N. Y. Assem., 1855. P. 530.
Sanderson, Repub. Landmarks, 1856.
Sons of the Sires, 1855.
Two Tracts... Aliens in England, 1814.
Tucker, J., Letter concerning, 1753.
Willard, J., Nat. in the colonies, 1859. P. 1684.
See American Party; Emigrants; Suffrage.

Natural Philosophy. Adams, G., Lectures on, 1794.
Arnott, N., Elements of Physics, 1829.
Bacon, F., Works.
Bacon, R., Opera inedita, (Chron. G. B.).
Bailey, S., On Berkeley's Theory of vision, 1842.
Barker, G. F., Forces of nature, 1863. P. 1207.
Bartlett, W. H. C., Elements of: Mechanics, 1850.
Bird, G., Elem. of Nat. Phil., 1839.
Blair, D., Grammar of, 1821, 24.
Blake, J. L., Conversations on, 1831.
Boscovich, Opera pert. ad Opticam, 1785.
Boyle, R., Philos. works, 1725.
" Christian virtuoso.
Brard, Dictionnaire, 1855.
Brewer, Guide to Scientific Knowl., 1851.

Natural Philosophy (continued).
Bridgewater Treatises, 1832, 33, etc.
Brisson, Principes de Physique, 1799.
Codazza, Sci. papers, 1852-3.
Colden, First causes in matter, 1746.
Comstock, J. L., System of, 1847.
Conv. on Latent Heat, 1830. P. 402.
Cooper, C. C., Identities, 1848.
Correlation of Forces. (Youmans' ed.).
Dana, J. D., Laws of Cohesion, 1847. P. 272.
Darwin, E., Temple of Nature, Notes, 1803.
Démonville, Examen des Ouvrages de M. Azaïs, 1846.
Desaguliers, De Natuurkunde, 1736, 1746.
Dexter, Phil. Apparatus, 1842. P. 551.
Draper, J. W., Text-book of, 1848.
Dumas, J., Balance of organic nature, 1844.
Eaton, A., Philosophical Instructor, 1824.
Edwards, J., Tremors affecting Telescopes. P. 74.
Euler, L., Letters on Nat. Philosophy, 1833.
Faraday, M., Forces of matter, 1860.
Ferguson's Lectures, 1814.
Fresnel, A., Œuvres, 1868.
Frick, Phys. Technik, 1856.
Hamilton, Bishop, Works, 1809.
Herschel, Prelim. Disc. on Study of, Lardner, 46.
Horne, G., Sir I. Newton's case, 1753. P. 1207.
Horsford, E. N., Publications, 1846-1849.
Hunt, R., Elementary Physics, 1855.
" Poetry of Science, 1854.
" Researches on Light, 1844.
Imison, Elem. of Sci. and Art, 1808.
Joyce, Scientific Dialogues, 1846.
Johnston, J., Manual of Nat. Phil., 1846.
Knight, G., Attract. and repulsion, 1754.
Knight, R. & G., Catal. of Apparatus.
La Croix, Motions of Floating Bodies.
Lardner, Pop. Lectures on Science and Art, 1846.
" Treatise on Mechanics, 67.
Lavoisier, Mémoires, 1862.
Lawson, W. M., Introd. Lect., 1836.
Magnen, Democritus Reviviscens, 1648.
Marcet, Introduction to.
Martin, B., Philosophical Grammar, 1738.
Mather, C., Christian Philosopher, 1721.

Natural Philosophy (continued).

Maupertuis, P., Œuvres, 1756.

Melancthon, Initia Doctrinæ Physicæ, 1550.

Metcalfe, S. L., Caloric, Agency in Nature, 1843.

Miscellanea Curiosa, 1723-27.

Mitford, Pendulum experiment.

Motte, A., The Mechanical powers, 1733.

Muller, J., Prin. of Physics and Meteorology, 1847.

Musschenbroek, Beginsels d. Natuurkunde, 1739.

Newton, Sir I., Nat. Phil. Principia, 1713, 1848.

Nichol, Cyclopædia of Phys. Sci.

O'Gallagher, Investigation of Nature, 1785.

Olmsted, D., Introduction to, 1844.

" Compendium of....1847.

Palmer, E., Catal. of apparatus, 1840.

Pamphlets, vol. 1870.

Parker, R. G., Compendium of.

Parkinson, On Mechanics, 1863.

Passement, Déscr. des télescopes, 1737.

Peirce, B., Phys. and Celest. Mechanics, 1855.

Phelps, A. H. L., Nat. Phil. for Schools, 1848.

Phillips, R., Mech Causes of Phenom., 1818. P. 402.

" One hundred Aphorisms.

Pike, Catal. of Instruments.

Pike, S., Phil. Sacra, 1815. P. 303.

Piola, Meccanica analitica, 1825.

Plateau, Figures of equilibrium of a liquid mass withdrawn from the action of gravity; Smithson. Rep., 1863, 64, 65, 66.

Playfair, J., Outlines of, 1814.

" Prog. of Math. and Phys. Sci.

Poisson, Traité de Mécanique, 1833.

Porta, Magiæ Naturalis, 1607.

Pouillet, Physique expérimentale, 1836.

Powell, B., Hist. of Nat. Phil.

Pratt, J. H., Prin. of Mechan. Phil., 1836.

Priestley, J., Experiments, 1779.

" Exper. on air, 1781.

" Hist. of discov. on light and colours.

Principles of, 1748.

Pritchard, Optical Instruments.

Questions traitées, 1639, 41.

Riolan, J., Prælectiones, 1602.

Rose, H., Qual. Analysis of Inorgan. substances, 1844.

Silliman, B., First Principles of, 1859.

Smeaton, Misc. Papers, to Royal Soc., 1814.

Snowball, Cambridge course, 1864.

Somerville, M., Connection of the phys. sciences, 1842.

Sonnet, Notions de Physique, 1857.

Stallo, J. B., General Principles of, 1848.

Stamkart, Burgerlijke Tijdsbepaling, 1747.

Swift, M. A., First lessons in, 1851.

Taylor, Janet, Diurnal Register, 1844.

Taylor, R., Scientific Mem. of Learned Soc., 1837-52.

Tomlinson, Pneumatics, 1848.

" Cyclopædia of Sci., 1868.

Tyndall, J., On radiation, 1865.

" Heat as means of motion, 1863.

" On sound, 1867.

Troughton, Catal. of instr.

Wal, Prijsverhandeling, 1833.

Walferdin, Echelles Thermométriques.

Walker, A., Lectures on, 1780.

Wandelaincourt, Man. des Jeunes Physiciens, 1778. B. C.

Wilkins, J., Math. and Phil. Works, 1802.

Winkler, Beginselen d. Natuurkunde, 1768.

Wolf, C., Elem. Matheseos univ., 1741.

Young, T., Lectures on, 1807.

See Arts; Electricity; Engineering; Heat; Hydrostatics; Hydraulics; Magnetism; Meteorology; Microscope; Optics; Science; Tides, etc.

Natural Religion and Theology.

Babbage, Ninth Bridgewater Treatise, 1837.

Bate, J., Answer to Chubb and Collins, 1746. P. 333.

Bell, C., The Hand, 1837.

Bentham, J., Influence of.

Bentley, R., Works: Confut. of Atheism, 1836.

" Remarks on Collins, 1737.

Bergier, Esame del Materialismo, 1835.

Berkeley, Minute Philosopher, 1803.

Bible of Nature, 1842.

Black, The, Dwarf, 1821. P. 1536.

Boulanger, Principles of Chr. rel., 1795.

Bridgewater Treatises, 1835.

Brougham, Discourses on, 1827. B. C.

Buchanan, R., Author of evil, 1843.

" Modern priestcraft, 1840.

Buckland, Geol. and Min. in Reference to, 1837.

Bulkeley, B., Observations on, 1757.

" Bolingbroke's writings, 1765.

Bullock, T., Writings, 1724, 30.

Natural Religion and Theology (continued).

Chalmers, T., External Nature and Const. of Man, 1833.

Cicero, Nature of the Gods, 1853.

Common sense, 1751.

Concise Examinations, 1856.

Correspondent, The, Period., N. Y., 1827–29.

Cudworth, Intel. System of the Universe, 1837.

Culte des Théophilanthropes, 1798. P. 608.

Derham, Astro-theology, 1741.

" Physico-theology, 1716.

Dove, A Creed founded on Truth, 1750. P. 337.

Dunton, J., Religio Bibliopolæ, 1720.

Ellis, New Britain, 1820.

Emanuel, Janus on Zion, 1816. P. 337.

Everett, L. S., Of the Free Inquirers, 1831. P. 1260.

Farrar, Hist. of free thought, 1863.

Five Letters, 1737.

Free, The, Inquirer, Period., N. Y., 1729–30.

Free Thinking....stated, 1713.

Gale, T., The Court of the Gentiles, 1669.

Geometry....infidelity, 1734.

Green, J., Dispute with Carlile, 1837. P. 1536.

Hamilton, Bishop, Works, 1809.

Heinzen, K., Letters to a Pious Man, 1826. P. 528.

Herbert, E., Lord, Relig. of the Gentiles, 1705.

Herttell, T., Of Infidelity, 1845. P. 1720.

Howitt, Hist. of Supernatural, 1863.

Hurd, R., Remarks on Hume, 1777. P. 334.

Jackson, J., Remarks on Tindal, 1749.

Jones, C., Who am I? Lond.

Kate, L. Ten, Den Scheppen, etc., 1716.

Lewis, T., Discourse on, 1849. P. 528.

Magalotti, Lettere contro l'ateismo, 1837.

Martin, T., On Brougham's Paley, 1836. P. 337.

Messengers of truth, 1833.

Mirabaud, Sys. of nature, (Holbach).

Monthly Jubilee, Phil'a, 1855.

Moore, J., Propositions of, 1736.

Morgan, The Moral Philosopher, 1738.

" Defence of Moral Philosopher, 1737. P. 444.

Movement and Anti-Persecution Gazette, 1845.

Muir, Exam. of T. Paine, 1795.

Natural Religion and Theology (continued).

Munch, F., Treatise on Religion, 1847. P. 528.

Nairne, Atheism and Pantheism, 1848. P. 63.

Nieuwentyt, Gebruik der Werelt-Beschouwingen, etc., 1730.

Origine des principes, (Meister), 1768.

Paine, Theological Works, 1831. B. C.

Paley, Works, vol. 4, 1830.

Pamphlets relating to, vols. 336, 337, 528, 806, 1374, 1375, 1536, 1720.

Pascoa, G., The Cosmopolitan, 1855.

Patten, T , Religion of Nature, 1759. P. 371.

Payson, S., Of Illuminism, 1802.

Plato, Against the Atheists, 1845.

Priestley, J., Letters to a Phil. unbeliever.

Principles of a Rationalist, 1721.

Principles of Deism, 1711.

Prout, W., Chemistry, etc., with reference to, 1845.

Pye, S., Moses and Bolingbroke, 1765.

Queries to Collins, 1713.

Remarks upon a Late Discourse, 1737.

Revision, or the pruning knife, 1857.

Reynolds, G. W. M., Errors of Chr. rel., 1832.

Robinson, A., On Hall's Mod. Infidelity, 1800. P. 337.

Shaftesbury, Characteristicks, 1733.

Sharp, G., On the Law of Nature, 1809.

Smith, J. A., Sense of touch, 1837.

Smith, S. S., Princip. of Nat. and Revealed.

Stewart, J., Revel. of Nature, 1841.

Tindal, M., Christianity old as creation, 1730.

" Defence of Rights, 1708.

Toland, Tetradymus, 1720.

" Nazarenus, 1718.

True and faith. account of Veritas. P. 1720.

Truth ascertained, 1736. P. 444.

Vind of Divine Attributes, (Collins), 1710. P. 340.

Whewell, Indications of a Creator.

Whiston, Astron. princ. of religion, 1717.

Willatts, C., Serm., Rel. of Nature, 1756.

Williams, D., Letter to Collins, 1713.

Williams, T., Answer to Hollis, 1796.

Wollaston, W., Rel. of Nature, 1738.

Young, E., Centaur not fabulous, 1806.

See Atheism; Christianity, (Evidences of); Collins; Deism; Infidelity; Paine; Reason; Soul.

Nature. Aikin, J., Calendar of Nature, 1785. P. 605.
Bange, Boek der Natuur, 1839.
Boyne, Cursory remarks, 1815.
Bushnell, Nature and Supernatural, 1858.
Darwin, E., Zoönomia, 1803.
" La Zoönomie.
Emerson, R. W., Essays, 2d series.
Ewbank, T., The world a workshop, 1855.
Good, Book of Nature, 1837.
Howitt, Pictorial Calendar of the Seasons, 1854.
Humboldt, Aspects of Nature, 1849.
" Kosmos, 1845–62.
McCosh, The Supernatural and N., 1862.
Marsh, G. P., Man and Nature, 1864.
" Uomo e la natura, 1870.
Martinet, Catech. of Nature, 1818. P. 402.
Mudie, Obs. of Nature, 1833.
Neckam, De naturis rerum, (Chron. C. B.).
Œrsted, The Soul in Nature, 1852.
Polehampton's Gallery of, 6 v.
Polwhele, R., Pictures from: Sonnets, 1786.
Priest, J., Wonders of, 1825.
Rafinesque, Analyse de la, 1815.
Reiche, C. C., 15 discourses of wonders of, 1791.
St. Pierre, B. de, Etudes sur la nature.
" Studies of Nature, 1798.
" Harmonies de la nature.
Somerville, Molecular and micr. science, 1869.
Sulivan, View of N., 1794.
Tucker, A., Light of nature pursued, 1831.
Tyndall, Fragments of Science, 1871.
See Cosmogony; Earth; Man; Nat. History; Philosophy; Theology; Medicine.

Naunton, Sir R. Memoirs, 1814.
Fuller, T., Worthies of England.

Naval, Miscellaneous. Anderson, A., Speech, Steam Navy, 1852. P. 406.
Boynton, Navies of Europe, 1865.
Butler, J., American Bravery, 1812–15.
Carroll, Star of the West, 1857.
Cespedes, Regimiento de Nav., 1606.
Clavel, Brit. Dominion of the Seas.
Da-Olmi, D'Hygiène Navale, 1828.
Dickerson's Exposure, 1864.
Douglas, H., Warner's discoveries, 1864. P. 416.
Falconer, Univ. Marine Dict., 1830.

Naval, Miscellaneous (continued).
France, Naval, Mémoire, 1777.
" Ordinance, 1689.
Fulton, R., Torpedo war.
Jal, Archéologie navale, 1840.
La Serre, La Marine Française, 1661–1785.
McClellan, J. L., Guns burst on the Egmont.
Marine Soc., (Hanway), 1775.
Marine Societies, 1835.
Pamphlets, Naval, Vols. 521, 807, 993, 1376.
Pecquet, Plan de Comptabilité pour la Marine. P. 10.
Sargent, J. O., Improvements in N. Warfare, 1844. P. 274.
Totten, Naval Text Book, 1841.
U. S. Boat Armaments, 1852.
" Uniform of, 1852.
" Armored vessels, 1864.
Ward, J. H., Naval tactics, 1859.
Zusto, Estrazione della nave La Fenice, 1789.
See France; Great Britain, Navy; U. S., Navy.

Naval, Flogging. Essay on Flogging in, 1849.
Porter, Speech on Flogging in, 1850.
Stockton, Speech on Flogging in, 1852. P. 521.

Naval History and Battles. Allan, Battles of Brit. Navy.
Bonfils, Hist. de la Marine Française, 1845.
Bouvet de Cresse, Hist. de la Marine de tous les Peuples, 1824.
Brandt, G., Vie de Ruyter, 1698.
Cooper, J. T., Hist. U. S. Navy, 1840.
Cruise of the Somers.
Dawson, H. B., Battles of U. States, 1858.
De Peyster, Battle of the Baltic, 1658.
Duncan, Victory over the Dutch, 1797.
Field of Mars, to 1801.
Grasse, French fleet, 1781–2.
Hist. Gén. de la Marine, 1744.
Impartial account of fleet, 1702.
Kimball, H., Amer. Naval Battles, 1831.
Leech, S., 30 years from home, 1843.
Lipenius, Nav. Salomonis, 1660.
Morisot, Orbis Marit. Gen. Historia, 1643.
Narrative of the proceedings, Toulon, 1744.
Narrative, U. S. Brig Vixen, 1813.
Ralfe, Battle of Navarin, 1829. P. 392.
Russell, E., Against French fleet, 1692.
Steele's Naval chronologist.

Naval History and Battles (cont'd).
Thysius, Historia Navalis, 1657.
See France; Great Britain; United States.

Naval Architecture. Annesley, Syst. of Naval Archit., 1822
Barney, Collins's Steamers, 1855. P. 529.
Beaufoy, Naut. Experiments, 1834.
Collection of papers, 1791.
Estancelin, Destruction des bois de construction, 1845. P. 23.
Forbes, R. B., New Rig for Ships, 1849. P. 74.
Francis, Metallic Life-boats, 1854.
Genet, Upward Forces of Fluids, 1825.
Great Republic ship, 1853.
Green, W. P., Raising masts.
Griffiths, J. W., Treatise on Marine and Naval Archit., 1851.
Mickles, Snag Nullifier, 1843. P. 529.
Peake, Rudiments of Naval Archit., 1849.
Plates of masts, 1791.
Remarks on the Calumnies...on Shipbuilders, 1814.
Shreve, Removal of Snags, 1847. P. 205.
Sullivan, J. L., Naval Architecture, 1823.

Naval Schools. Amer. Jour. of Ed., 1864, 65.
Marine Soc., (Hanway), 1758, 75.
U. S. Nav. School, Annapolis.

Navigation. Abbink, Zee-regt, 1856.
Am. Assoc'n, Report on the Coast Survey, 1858.
Amer. Ephemeris, 1856-68.
Atkinson, J., Epitome of the art, 1759, 1778.
Bache, N. Y. Sailing Directions, 1856. P. 529.
Blackborrow, On Longitude, 1678.
Blundeville, His exercises, 1622.
Blunt, E. M., Guide du Navigateur, 1821.
Blunt, J., Shipmaster's Assist., 1822.
" West Coast of N. A., 1849. P. 274.
" Amer. Coast Pilot, 1812.
Bowditch, N., Amer. Pract. Navigator, 1802, 21.
Brady, Young Sailor's Assistant, 1848.
Brown, R., Speech, Nav. Laws, 1847.
Bureau des Longitudes, Annuaire, 1826-57.
Busby, Propulsion of Naviga. Bodies, 1818. P. 74.
Cassini, Montres marines, 1770.
Chabert, Horloges marines, 1785.
Cumings, Western pilot, 1810.

Navigation (continued).
Curtis, M., The Arte of, 1609.
Dana, R. H., Seaman's friend, 1841.
Davies, C., Elements of, 1846.
Diston, J., Lowerstoft to London. P. 1626.
Döllen's Transit Instrument, 1870.
Ericsson, Petition to Congress, 1848.
Fleurieu, Voy. pour éprouver les horloges marines, 1773.
Fournier, Hydrographie, 1679.
Gietermaker, 't Vergulde licht der Zeevaart, 1706.
Givry, Pilote Français, 1845.
Great Britain: Board of Trade; Sailing directions, 1859, 61.
Greenwood, Sailor's Sea-book, 1850.
Harlaem River improvement, 1857.
Heather, North American Pilot, 1801.
Hillary, Preservation from Shipwreck, 1823. P. 429.
Holden, Sermon on, 1680. P. 1005.
India and Australia Steam Co. P. 434.
Instruction Nautique....pour le Mississippi.
King, R., Speech, On Navig. laws, 1819.
Konink. Ak.: Over den Paalworm.
Leeuw, Op de koopvaardijschepen, 1857.
Lindsay, W. S., Letters on Eng. Nav. laws, 1849.
Lövenörn, Direct. for Cattegat.
Macgregor, Statistics of navig. laws.
Macpherson, Annals of Commerce and, 1805.
Martensen, Haandbog för Skippere.
Maury, Explan. Directions of Wind Charts, 1854.
" Abstract Log, 1848.
Mendoza, Tables for navig., 1805.
Mills, R., Am. Lighthouse Guide, 1845.
Nanninga, Pract. Zeeman, 1815.
" Van den Scheepsbouw, 1812.
Nautical Almanac, Lond., 1766-1872.
N. Y. Yacht club, 1848-62.
Norie, North Sea directions.
Palmer, J., Catholique Planisphaer, 1658.
Pamphlets relating to, vols. 426, 529, 807, 993, 1537.
Pilote, Le, de Terre Neuve, 1784.
Pilote de St. Domingue, 1781.
Ricardo, J. L., Anatomy of the Nav. Laws, 1847.
Schuylkill Nav. Company, Reports, 1822-62.
Seamanship: practice, 1795.
Seyxas, Theatro Naval Hidrographico, 1704.
Truxton, T., On Lat. and Long.; and the Compass, 1794.

Negro Races (continued).
Prince, Nancy, Life of, Bost., 1853.
Proceedings, Convention of Colored people, Albany, 1851. P. 560.
Prot. Ep. Ch, N. Y., St. Philip's Ch., 1851. P. 200.
Prot. Epis. Freed. Commiss., 1866.
Smith, T. P., Colored Schools, 1850.
Soc for the support of Colored Home, 1850–56. P. 627.
Sojourner Truth, Narrative.
Statis., People of Col., Phil'a, 1849.
Suffrage question, N. Y. P. 958.
Sweet, S. N., Address, Colored Bapt. Ch., 1834.
Un. St., Commerce, Charleston, S. C., 1823.
" Reports of Bureau of Refugees and Freedmen, 1866, 1867, 68.
" Report for Tenn. and Ark., 1864. P. 1681.
Van Evrie, J. H., Negroes and Slavery, 1853.
Vassa, G., (Equiano), Life, 1791, 1837.
Wheatley, P., Elegiac Poem, 1770.
" Memoir of, 1834.
White, G., Life of, 1810. P. 1701.
Whitfield, J. M., America and other poems, 1853.
Yates, Rights of colored men, 1838. P. 185.
See Slavery; Liberia; Colonization; Africa.

Negro River, S. America. Wallace, Travels on, 1853.

Neill, W. Autobiography, 1861.

Nelson, D. On Infidelity, and his life.

Nelson, H., Lord. Clarke, J. S., Life of.
Evans, T. A., Nelson Coat; Nelson Sword.
Manby, Nelson gallery.
Nelson, H., Lord, Dispatches and Letters.
" Letters to Lady Hamilton, 1814.
Pamphlets, Vol. 379, Serm., Trafalgar Vict.
Pearce, P. H., Victory and Bronte.
Pettigrew, Memoirs of, 1849.
Rotta, P. R., Ode on, 1805. P. 1388.
Southey, R., Life of, 1861.
Townsend, J., Serm., Death of, 1806.
White, J., Life of.

elson, J. Walsh, T., Journal of.

eology. *See* Rationalism; Theology.

Nesbitt, J. Hurrion, J., Serm. on, 1728.

Nesle, Marquise C. de Mailly de. L'imposture de, 1756.

Nesselrode. Gal. des Contem., Vie de, 1845.

Nestorians. Grant, The Nestorians or Lost Tribes, 1841.
" Les Nestoriens.
Laurie, Dr. Grant and the N., 1853.
Nestorians of Persia, Phil'a.
Perkins, J., Eighteen Years in Persia, 1843.
Smith, E., Researches, 1833.
Stoddard, D. T., Narrative of, 1857.
Tyler, W. S., Life of Lobdell, 1859.
See Kurdistan; Persia.

Netherlands. Aa, Van der, Leven van Willem den V, 1806–9. B. C.
Abbink, Proeve van Staat-kundige Fabeln, 1848.
" Leven van Willem II, 1849.
Abrégé de l'Histoire de, 1759.
Aitzema, Saken van Staat en Oorlogh, etc., 1621–97.
" Nederlantsche Vrede-handeling, 1650.
" Herstelde Leeuw, 1650, 51.
" Notable Revolutions, 1650, 1651.
Alkemade, Nederl. displegtigheden.
Barnwell, De Witt's Times.
Basnage, Ann. des Prov. Unies, 1719.
Batavia Sacra, 1714.
Beaumarchais, Le Hollandois, 1738. B. C.
Beeldsnijder, Smeekschriften der N. Edelen, 1567.
Beijerman, Geschiedenis der Nederlanden, 1830.
Belgium, Coll. de Docts. sur les Anc. Assemblées, 1600.
Beverningk, Verbael Gehouden, etc., 1725.
Bijsterbos, Provinciaale Wet, 1855.
Bonaparte, L., Hist. Documents, 1820.
Bor, Nederl. Oorlogen, 1555–1600.
Bosscha, Staats-Omwenteling, 1813.
Bowdler, T., Letters, 1787.
Brandt, Hist. of Reformation, 1720.
Breval, Hist. of the House of Nassau, 1734.
Britaine, Dutch Usurpation, 1672.
Brune, Campagne en Batavie, 1800–1.
Burnet's Travels, 1685.
Butler, C., Minutes of Civ. and Eccl. Hist. of, 1826.
C., H. J. Z., Nasporing van, 1567–1672.
Carleton, Sir D., Embassy to, 1615–20.
Carr, Sir J., Tour through, 1806.
Chronyke van Vlaenderen, 1725, 36.
Cluverius, Batavische Out-Heeden, 1719.

Netherlands (continued).

Costerus, Hist. Verhaal, 1572–1673.

Dagverhaal...Nat. Vergadering, 1796–1798.

Davies, C. M., History of, 1841–44.

De Peyster, Battle of the Baltic, 1658.

De Witt, C. and J., Vie de, 1709.

De Witt, J., Brieven, 1652–69.

" Secrete Resolutien, 1653–68.

" Polit. Maxims of the Republic, 1702.

Du Lignon, Hollande consolée, 1752.

Esquiros, Dutch at home, 1861.

Estrades, Lettres et Négociations, 1743.

Frederick Henry, Het Leven, 1737. B. C.

Friesland, Toestand, 1859.

Froger, Verdediging der Landgrenzen, 1849.

Giustiniano, Delle Guerre di Flandra, 1609.

Grattan, T., History of, Lardner, 41.

Grondwettige Herstelling van Nederlands Staatwezen, 1785.

Grimestone, Hist. of, to 1608.

Grotius, H., De antiq. reipub. Batavicæ, 1610.

" Apologeticus eorum qui Hollandiæ, etc., 1618.

" Holl. Rechtsgeleertheyt, 1649.

H. V., Historie de Gravelike Regeering in, 1662. B. C.

Hall, F. A. van, Publications, 1828–1840. B. C.

Hedendaagsche Historie, 1750–53.

" ....Friesland, 1785–88.

" ....Overyssel, 1781.

Hist. Abr. des Prov. Unies, 1701.

Holcroft, Travels, 1804.

Hooft, P. C., Nederl. Historien, 1656.

Jonge, J. C. de, Résolutions des Etats généraux, 1576.

Jurisprudentia Heroica, Christyn, 1668.

Kampen, Beschrijving van het k. der Nederl., 1827. B. C.

Kernoux, Abrégé de l'histoire de la, 1778.

Keverberg, Vom Königreiche der, 1836.

Koenen, Der Nijverheid in.... 1856.

Kok, Vaderl. Woordenboek, 1785-96.

Koning, Voorvaderlijke Levenswijze, 1810.

La Fayette, Mém. de Hollande, 1856.

Lange, Der Oude Batavieren, 1730.

La Sagra, Voy. en, et en Belgique, 1839. B. C.

Lauts, Ontdekkingen der Nederl., 1835. P. 30. B. C.

Le Clerc, Hist. des Provinces-Unies, 1723–28.

Leeuwen, Batavia illustrata, 1685.

Netherlands (continued).

Liefde, De, Founders of the Dutch Republic, 1869.

Ligtdal, Despotisme de la maison d'Orange, 1785.

Limburg, Betrekkingen van het hertogdom, 1848.

Luzac, La Richesse de la, 1778.

Maatschappij der Ned. Letterkunde, 1849.

Maerlant, Spiegel historiael, 1288.

Maestricht, Engravings of.

Martinet, Het Vaderland; beschryving, 1830–33.

Meerten, Reis door het k. van Nederl., 1223–33.

Meteren, Histoire van de Oorlogen der, 1315–1611.

Motley, J. L., Rise of the Dutch Republic, 1856.

" History of the United Neth., 1861-68.

Nederl. Historie, 1572–1611.

Nederl. Jaerboeken, 1766–87.

Netherland Historian, 1671–74.

Netherlands, Doc'ts, 1816–51.

" Manifesto, 1702.

Palm, V. d., Gedenkschrift van Nederl. Herstelling, 1816. B. C.

Pars, Catti Aborigines Batavorum, 1745.

Paulus, Unie van Utrecht, 1775–77. B. C.

Polanen, Brieven, 1816.

Prinsterer, Proeve over de zamenstelling, etc., 1826, 30.

Quetelet, Statist. des Pays Bas, 1829.

Recueil de pièces diplom., 1830–32.

Recueil des Représentations....1787.

Réglemens....des Eglises Wallones.

Reynolds, Sir J., Journey to, 1809.

Rhiyn, Hydrogr. Kaart van de Zuider zee, 1846.

Romans, B., Annals of, from Charles V, 1778.

Royaards, Bijdragen der Nederl., 1830.

St. Simon, Guerres des Bataves et Romains, 1770.

Schiller, Hist. of Revolt of Netherl., 1847.

Scriverius, Batavia Illustrata, 1609.

Sjoerds, Jaarboeken van Friesland, 1768–71.

Spranckhuysen, Triumphe, teghen de Silver-Vlote, 1628.

Staring, Aardkunde van, 1844.

Strada, De Bello Belgico, 1578–90.

Stuart, M., Vaderl. Historie, 1822.

Vaderlandsche Historie, 1758.

Valkenier, Verwerd Europa, 1675.

Wagenaar, Vaderl. Historie, 800–1751.

New England (continued).
Church, T., History of Philip's war, 1772, 1829, 46.
Clarke, J., Ill Newes from, 1652.
Coolidge, History of, 1860.
Cotton, J., Abstract of the laws of, 1655.
Dillingham, Orat., N. E. Soc., Phil'a, 1847. P. 63.
Dreuillette, Narré du Voy., 1650, 51.
Drake, S. G., Settlement of, 1856.
" Old Indian Chronicle, 1867.
" British Archives on, 1860.
Dummer, Defence of N. E. Charters, 1745.
Dwight, T., Travels in, 1821.
Edwards, J., Thoughts on the Revival of 1740.
Eliot, J., The Day Breaking, 1647.
" Brief Narrative, 1670.
Elliott, C. W., New England Hist. to 1776.
Everett, E., Oration, First settlement of, 1821.
Exam. of Commer. pretensions, 1814.
Farmer, Geneal. of First Settlers, 1829.
Felt, J. B., The Customs of, 1853.
Fleming's Register, 1772, 86.
Further accompt, 1659.
Further queries, 1690.
Gillies, Hist. Coll.: Revivals of 1740.
Good Newes from, 1648.
Gorges, Sir F., Planting of.
Hall, J. P., Discourse, N. E. Soc., N. Y., 1847.
Hayward, J., New England Gazetteer, 1839, 1857.
Hewett, Gazetteer of, 1829.
Higginson, New England's Plantation, 1630.
Hillard, G. S., Address, N. E. Soc., N. Y., 1851.
Hopkins, M,, Oration, 1854.
Hoyt, Hist. of Indian Wars on the Connecticut river, 1824.
Hubbard, W, Gen. Hist. of N. Eng., 1815, 48.
" Narr. of troubles, 1677, 1801.
" The same, Drake's ed., 1865.
Humble address of the Publicans, 1691.
Jenks, W., Address, N. E. H. G. Soc., 1852.
Jen(n)ison, W., Lash for a Lyar, 1658.
Johnson, E., History of, 1654.
Josselyn, N. E. Rarities, 1672.
" Two Voyages to, 1674.
Keith, G., Tr. from N. Hampshire to Caratuck, 1706.
" Reply to I. Mather, 1703.
Knight, Mme., Journal, 1704.

New England (continued).
Lechford, Plain dealing, 1642.
Levett, Voy. to New England, 1624.
Lucas, S., Essays, 1862.
Marsh, G. P., Address, N. E. Soc., N. Y., 1845.
" The Goths in N. E., Disc., 1843.
Mass. Hist. Soc., Collections.
Mather, C., Magnalia Christi Americana, 1702, 1820, 53.
Mather, I., Day of trouble near, two sermons, 1673.
" Early history of N. E., 1677, 1864.
" Philip's war, 1862.
" Elijah's Mantle, 1722.
" Revol. in N. E. Justified, 1690.
" Remarkable Providen., 1856.
Mauduit, Hist. of N. Eng. Col., 1776.
Modest Enquiry, Lond., 1707.
Morse, J., History of, 1809.
" Compend. History of, 1808.
Morton, N., N. England's Memorial, 1826, 55.
Morton, T., N. E. Canaan, 1632.
Mourt, G., Relation, 1622, 1865.
Neal, D., History of, 1720, 47.
New and Further Narr., 1676.
New England, Laws, 1641.
New E. and her institutions, 1835.
New England Business Directory, 1849, 1856, 1860.
New England's First Fruits, 1643; repr., 1865.
New England Historic-Genealogical Register, 1848–71.
New England Soc., N. Y., Celebrations, 1855, 59, 64, 68, 70.
News from New Eng., 1676.
N. Y. Hist. Soc. Coll., S. 2, V. 3, 1648–51.
Old England forever, 1740.
Oliver, P., Puritan Commonwealth, 1856.
Owen, R. D., Reconstruction without N. E., 1863.
Pages from Eccl. History of, 1740–1840.
Palfrey, History of, 1858–64.
Penhallow, Hist. of Wars of, 1703–1726.
Planters Plea, (White), 1630.
Phips, W., Action with the French, 1691.
Present State of N. E., 1675.
Prince, T., Chronolog. History of, 1736.
Relig. Intelligence, 1800.
Review of the Rise of, etc., 1774.
Robbins, T., Hist. View of Planters of, 1815.

New Hampshire Local History. *See* Amherst; Andover; Atkinson; Bedford; Candia; Campton; Charlemont; Chester; Concord; Coos Co.; Dublin; Dunbarton; Dunstable; Exeter; Hampton; Keene; Littleton; Londonderry; Manchester; Mason; Merrimac Valley; Nashua; N. Boston; N. Ipswich; Orford; Portsmouth; Rindge; Templeton; Warner; Warren; Wilton.

New Haven, Conn. Bacon, L., Thirteen Discourses, Centennial, 1839.

Barber, J. W., Views in 1825.

" Hist. and Antiq. of, 1831, 1870.

Beecher, C. E.. Truth stranger than Fiction, 1850.

Croswell, H., 40 years in Trinity parish, 1856.

Dutton, S. W. S., History of North Church, 1842.

Dwight, T., Statist. Acct. of, 1811.

Kingsley, Hist. Disc. 200th Anniv., 1838.

New Haven Colony Hist. Soc., Papers, 1865.

New Haven Col., Records, 1638–1665.

New Haven Directories, 1840-68.

Trumbull, B., Discourse, 1773.

See Yale College; North Haven.

New Ipswich, New Hamp. History of, 1786–1852, (Kidder).

Newington, Conn. Brace, J., Hist. discourse, 1855.

New Jersey. Armstrong, Hist. of Fort Nassau, 1853.

Barber, J. W., and H. Howe, Hist. Collections, 1844.

Brown, A. H., Hist. Presb. Church in.

Carpenter, W. H., History of, 1854.

Doane, G. W., Goodly heritage of, Disc., N. J. Hist. Soc., 1846.

Elizabethtown, Bill in Chancery, 1747.

Eumenes, Letters on the Constitution, (Griffith), 1799.

Field, R. S., Prov. Courts of; N. J. Hist. Soc. Coll.

Foster, J. Y., N. J. in the Rebellion, 1868.

Gordon, T. F., Gazetteer of; and History, 1834.

Green, A., Baccal. Addresses, College of, 1822.

Haven, C. C., Thirty days in, 1776–77.

Historical notes, 1842.

Lawrence, W. B., Colonization of, 1842. P. 11.

Letter from a gentleman, 1764.

Lloyd, N. J. Annual Register, 1846.

Morris, L., Letters, 1738–1846.

Mulford, Civ. and Polit. Hist. of, 1848.

New Jersey (continued).

New Jersey: Geol. Survey, 1831–68.

" Revolutionary Corresp., 1848.

N. J. Central R. Road Guide, 1864.

New Jersey Hist. Soc., Coll. and Proc., 1846–66.

N. J. Register, Potts, 1837.

New Jersey Congr. Elect., 1838.

Pyne, Hist. of First Reg't, 1871.

Scot, G., Model of Gov't of, 1685.

Scott, J. W., Of the Legis. Council, 1842. P. 197.

Smith, S., Hist. of Nova-Cæsaria, to 1721.

Tatham, N. J. Monopolies, 1852. P. 81.

Thompson, T., Missionary Voyage to, 1758.

Whitehead, W. A., East Jersey hist.

" Robbery of Treasury in 1768.

" Hist. of Perth Amboy and vicin., 1856.

New Jersey; Local History. *See* Bergen; Camden; Elizabethtown; Essex; Harlingen; Hudson Co.; Jersey City; Millstone; Newark; New Brunswick; Paterson; Perth Amboy; Princeton; Raritan; Salem; Trenton; Union Co.; Westfield.

New Jerusalem Church. *See* Swedenborg.

New London, Conn. Brainard, W. F., Address at Groton Heights, 1825.

Caulkins, History of, 1660–1845.

New London, Navy Yard, 1862, 66.

Newman, J. H. Achilli *vs.* Newman.

Froude, On the Grammar of Assent, 1871, (Studies).

Newman, Apologia pro vita sua, 1865.

Rowan, Review of, 1852.

Newman, T. Pickard, Serm., Death of, 1758. P. 381.

Newman, W. Pritchard, G., Memoir of, 1837.

New Mexico. Abert, Examination of.

" Report; with Cook's and Johnston's, 1846–47.

Bartlett, J. R., Explorations in, 1854.

Brackenridge, Early Discoveries in, 1857.

Clever, C. P., Her Resources, 1868.

Cremony, Life with the Apaches, 1868.

Davis, W. W. H., El Gringo, 1857.

" Span. Conquest of, 1869.

Edwards, Doniphan's campaign, 1848.

Emory, Mexican boundary survey, 1848.

New Mexico (continued).
Gregg, Commerce of the Prairies, 1844.
Pike, Z. M., Exped. to West of Louisiana, 1807.
" Voy. au Nouveau Mexique, 1812.
U. S. War Dept. Reports, 1850.
Weightman, Memorial, 1851.
See Arizona; Mexico; Rocky Mts.

New Orleans. Clapp, T., Sketches, 1857.
Cooke, J. H., Narrative of Attack, 1814.
Faithful picture, 1807.
Gleig, Campaign of Brit. army at.
Hall, A. O., Manhattaner in New Orleans, 1851.
Howard Assoc., 1853.
Mémoires sur, 1804.
New Orleans, San. Commiss. on Epidem. Fever, 1853.
New Orleans as it is, 1850.
New Orleans Directory, 1855.
Norman's, B. M., Descrip. of, 1845.
Tranchepain, Ursélines à, 1727–33.
U. S., N. O. riots, 1866.
See War of 1812–14; Jackson, A.; Louisiana.

Newport, Rh. Is. Cahoone's Sketches of, 1842.
" Visit to Grand-papa, 1840.
Controversy on the Old Stone Mill, (Hammett), 1851.
Mason, Reunion of sons of, 1859.
Newport Directory, 1858, 71–2.
Newport Long Wharf, 1863.
Redwood Library, Catalogue and hist.
Ross, A. A., Civil and rel. hist. of, 1838.
United Congr. Church, Hist., 1834.

New Rochelle, N. Y. Bolton, R., jun., Guide to, 1842.

New South Wales. *See* Australia.

Newspapers, History of, etc. Almanack of British, 1841.
Andrews, History of, 1859.
Buckingham, Specim. of newsp. press, 1850.
Chalmers, Life of Ruddiman. *Eng. Newsp.*, 1794.
Cobden, R., On the "Times," 1864.
Coggeshall, Newsp. Record, 1856.
Fifty Years Recollections, 1837.
Follett, Press of W. N. York, 1847.
Gt. Brit., Report on Newsp. stamps, 1851.
Hunt, F. K., Hist. of, 1850.
Mitchell, Newspaper directory, 1851.
Munsell, Typog. miscellany, 1850.
Nichols, Lit. anecdotes, v. 4, 1812.
Newspaper duties, 1836. P. 425.

Newspapers, History of, etc. (cont'd).
Periodical press, Inquiry, Lond., 1824.
Rowell, The men who advertise, 1870.
" Amer. Newsp. directory, 1869.
Streeter, G. L., Period. of Salem, Mass., 1768–1856. P. 233.
Timperley, Encyc. of typ. anecd., 1842.
Thomas, Printing in America, 1810.
Westmacott, C. M., Stamp duties, 1836. P. 1242.
Wilmer, Our press gang, 1859.
Wisconsin Editorial Assoc'n, 1859-70.
See Press, Liberty of; Periodicals.

Newspapers, American. Alta California, San Francisco, 1849–52.
American Weekly Messenger, Phil'a, 1814, 15.
American Star, Mexico, 1847.
Aurora, Philadelphia, 1796.
Boston Atlas, 1841–52.
Boston Commercial Gazette, 1818, 19.
Boston Chronicle, 1768.
Boston Evening Post, 1767–75.
Boston Gazette, 1758, 59, 62.
Boston News Letter, 1762, 1826.
Boston Recorder, 1825, 28, 31–32.
Boston Weekly Messenger, 1815–19.
Boston Weekly Transcript, 1856–61.
Buenos Ayres Newsp., 1849, 50.
Cabinet, The, Selections, 1815.
Chicago (Church,) Record, 1859–62.
Christian Register, Boston, 1836–60.
Church Register, Phil'a, 1826–29.
Columbian Centinel, Boston, 1793–1818, 22, 26, 28–32.
Columbian Star, Washington, 1823–26.
Connecticut Courant, 1774–1819, imp.
Connecticut Mirror, 1813–20.
Dakotah Friend, 1850–52.
Dunlap's Maryland Gazette, 1777.
Farmer's Chronicle, Conn., 1793.
Federal Galaxy, Vt., 1797.
Federal Gazette, Baltimore, 1808–13.
Gazette Française, Phil'a, 1845–46.
Independent Chronicle, Boston, 1776–1783, 94, 1800–1807.
Independent Gazetteer, Phil'a, 1791.
Kansas Herald of Freedom, 1855–56.
Liberator, The, Boston, 1831, 34.
Massachusetts Spy, 1795, 1800–17.
Missouri Republican, 1822–24.
Mor. and Pol. Telegraph, 1796.
National Intelligencer, 1813–69, imp.
National Gazette, Phil'a, 1823–41.
National Recorder, Phil'a, 1819–21.
New Engl. Palladium, Boston, 1801–27.
New England Republican, Danbury, 1805–6.

Newspapers, American (continued).
Newspapers, Miscellaneous, 160 vols.
Nieuwsbode, De, Sheboy an, 1849–57.
Niles's National Register, 1811–49.
North American, 1847–48, Mexico.
Ohio State Journal, 1845–46.
Pamphlets, vol. 1242.
Pennsylvania Chronicle, Phil'a, 1767–1771.
Pennsylvania Gazette, 1779–80.
Pennsylvania Packet, 1771–79.
Presbyterian, Phil'a, 1841–71.
Richmond Enquirer, 1861–63.
Richmond Examiner, 1863–65.
Richmond Sentinel, 1864–65.
Salem Gazette, 1790–1815.
Santa Fé Gazette, 1858, 9.
United States Gazette, 1804–17.
United States Telegraph, 1828.

Newspapers, New York. Albany Argus, 1813–71.
Albany Daily Advertiser, 1815–45.
Albany Daily Statesman, 1856–7.
Albany Dutchman, 1849, 50.
Albany Evening Atlas, 1850–56.
Albany Evening Journal, 1835–71.
Albany Freeholder, 1845–47.
Albany Gazette, 1784–1822.
Albany Herald, 1846.
Albany Microscope, 1832–38, imp.
Albany Morning Express, 1854–55, 68, 1870, 71.
Albany Register, 1793-1819, 21, 22.
Albany Spectator, 1844–47.
Albany State Register, 1854–6.
Albion, The, N. Y., 1849.
Amer. Daily Citizen, Albany, 1842–44.
Asmonean, N. Y., 1852–54.
Atlas and Argus, Albany, 1855–60. *See* Albany Argus.
Balance and Repos., Hudson and Alb., 1801-11.
Boys' Daily Journal, Ogdensburgh, 1855–57.
Chenango Free Democrat, 1850.
Christian Intelligencer, N.Y., 1830–71.
Christian Visitant, Albany, 1815–16.
Church Journal, New York, 1853–54.
Churchman, N. Y., 1854–55.
Columbian Gazette, Utica, 1813.
Columbian Mercury, Canaan, 1794.
Courrier des Etats Unis, 1840–59, 1862.
Daily Advertiser, N. Y., 1787, 1789–95.
Evening Mirror, New York, 1844–55.
Examiner or N. Y. Recorder, 1855, 56.
Family Newspaper, Albany, 1838–39.
Franco-Américain, Le, New York, 1841–47.

Newspapers, New York (continued).
Franklin Gazette, Malone, N. Y., 1855-1859.
Herald, New York, 1794–1797.
Herkimer American, 1812–15.
Home Journal, New York, 1850.
Hudson Weekly Gazette, 1785–1803.
Illustrated American News, N. Y., 1851.
Illustrated News, P. T. Barnum, 1853.
Illustrated N. Y. News, 1851.
Independent, N. Y., 1854–1871.
Journal and Telegraph, Albany, 1832–1834.
Jefferson and St. Lawrence Cos., Newspapers, 1812–52, imp.
Jeffersonian, The, (Greeley), Albany, 1838–39.
Log Cabin, (Greeley), 1840.
Nation, The, N. Y., 1866–68.
National Advocate, N. Y., 1819–22.
National Observer, Albany, 1826–31.
National Police Gazette, N. Y., 1850–1859, 1861–65.
New World, 1842.
N. Y. American, 1831–33.
New York Bapt. Register, 1826–55.
N. Y. Columbian, 1809–10, 1818–21.
N. Y. Commercial Advertiser, 1820–29, 1831–33, 35–44, 46–48.
N. Y. Daily Times, 1851–71.
N. Y. Daily Tribune, 1842–71.
New Yorker, The, 1838, 39.
N. Y. Evangelist, 1834–53, 57–64, 69, 1871.
N. Y. Evening Post, 1810–12, 19, 30, 60–63.
New York Gazette, 1805–20.
N. Y. Herald, 1802–1811.
N. Y. Herald, Weekly, July, 1838-July, 1856.
" Daily, July, 1861–June, 1863.
N. Y. Journal and Patron of Industry, 1821.
New York Leader, N. Y., 1862.
N. Y. Newspapers of 1851, specim.
N. Y. Newspapers of 1855, specim.
N. Y. Observer, 1855–70.
N. Y. Recorder, 1855.
N. Y. Reformer, Watertown, 1851.
N. Y. Spectator, 1820–21.
N. Y. Statesman, Alb., 1820–22, imp.
N. Y. Statesman, N. Y., 1824–28.
N. Y. Tablet, 1857.
North American, Watertown, N. Y., 1835–39.
Northern Budget, Troy, 1802, 03.
Northern New Yorker, Gouverneur, 1850.

Newspapers, New York (continued).
Northern N. Y. Journal, Watertown, 1859–62.
Northern State Journal, Watertown, 1848–50.
Northern Whig, Hudson, 1811–23.
Ogdensburgh Daily Journal, 1863–64.
Ogdensburgh Sentinel, 1854–58.
Old Settler, Keeseville, 1847–56.
Peoples' Democratic Guide, 1841–2.
Phare, Le, de New York, 1852, 53.
Plaindealer, Leggett, 1830–31.
Plebeian, Kingston, N. Y., 1805, 06.
Potsdam Courier, 1856–59.
Progrès, Le, N. Y., 1855.
Protestant Churchman, 1843–48, 54–6.
Repub. Advocate, Batavia, N. Y., 1820–23.
Rochester Observer, 1827.
St. Lawrence American, Ogdensburgh, 1855–59.
St. Lawrence Advertiser, 1850.
St. Lawrence Free Press, 1854.
Schoharie Observer, 1818–23.
Schoharie Republican, 1819–24.
Spectator, N. Webster, 1797–1802.
Spirit of the Times, N. Y., 1851–3.
Standard, Albany, 1829.
Voice of the People, Albany, 1858.
Watertown Register, 1830–50.
Weekly Journal, Ogdensburgh, 1857, 1858.
World, The, N. Y., 1868–71.
Yonkers Examiner, 1856–59.
Young America, N. Y., 1856.
See Periodicals.

Newspapers, British Colonies. Antigua Weekly Gazette, 1842, 44.
Canada Newspapers, 1848–51.
Canadien, Le, 1850.
Colonial Herald, Prince Edward, 1837–1840.
Examiner, The, Toronto, 1850.
Evening Courier, Montreal, 1850.
Globe, Toronto, 1850.
Minerve, La, Montreal, 1848–50.
Moniteur Canadien, 1850.
Pays, Le, Montreal, 1853, 54, 57.
Royal Gazette, Prince Edward Island, 1837–44.
See Periodicals.

Newspapers, European. Amsterdam Gazette, 1744–69.
Courier du Bas Rhin, 1789–94.
Courier van Europa, 1783, 84.
Dublin Courant, 1723–25.
Europische Staats Secretaris, 1763.
Examiner, The, London, 1810–20, 58–1860.

Newspapers, European (continued).
Flying Post, 1709.
Galignani's Messenger, Paris, 1851.
Illustrated London News, 1842–59.
Illustrated News of the World, 1858–1860.
Journal de Constantinople, 1846–56.
Journal Politique, Leyde, 1805–09.
Liverpool Chronicle, 1849–52.
London Chronicle, 1780–81.
London Gazette, Oct. 24, 31, 1851.
Mist's Weekly Journal, 1722.
Moniteur, Le, Paris, 1789–1836.
Moniteur de l'Exposition Universelle, 1865, 66.
Moniteur Ottoman, 1831-36.
Nouvelles Extraordinaires, 1784–98.
Nouvelles Politiques, 1799–1804.
Post, De, van den Neder Rhijn, 1781–1787.
Presse d'Orient, Smyrne, 1855.
Railway Chronicle, Lond., 1844–49.
Railway Times, Lond., 1855–58.
Rehearsal, The, 1704–8.
Saturday Review, Lond., 1860–62.
Spectator, London, 1831–33,
Times, Daily, London, 1832–37, 41–71.
" Index to, 1862, 63, 67–69.

Newstead Abbey. Irving, W., Description of.

Newton, Sir I. Brewster, Sir D., Life of.
Horne, G., Case of I. N. and Mr. Hutchinson, 1753. P. 1207.
Newton, I., Correspondence, 1851.
" Two Letters to Le Clerc, 1754.
Library Use. Knowl., Life of.
Rigaud, On the Principia, 1838.

Newton, I. Hague, W., Discourse, 1859.

Newton, Rev. J. Letters, 1819.
Evans, C., Sermon on.

Newton, R. Jackson, T., Life of.

Newton, T. Life of, (Pocock).

Newton, Mass. Jackson, W., History of, 1854.
Newton, Ms., Notice of, 1852.

Newtown, N. Y. Riker, Annals of, 1852.

New Utrecht, L. I. De Sille, Hist. of settlement of, 1660.

New York Central College, McGrawville. Reports, 1849-56.

New York City. Alvarez, Guia de, 1863.
Barnard, J. G., Defences of, 1859.
Barnes, D. M., Draft riots, 1863.
Bayley, J. R., Catholic Ch. in, 1870.
Bayley, R., Account of fever in, 1795.

New York City (continued).

Beekman, J. W., On the Founders of, 1870.

Booth, History of, 1859.

Bourne, W. O., Hist of Public School Society, 1870.

Boyd's Tax Book, 1857.

Brick Church Memorial, 1861.

Brief Treatise on the N. Y. Police, 1812.

Browne, J. H., The Great Metropolis, 1869.

Bulls and bears, 1854.

Commodities of Manati, 1650.

Cozzens, J., Geolog. Hist. of, 1843.

Davis, A., Hist. of New Amsterdam, 1854.

Dawson, H. B., Sons of Liberty, 1776.

De Forest, New York in olden time, 1833.

De Voe's Market History of, 1862.

Disosway, Earliest Churches of, 1865.

Disturnell, Description of, 1847.

Dix, J. A., Sketches of, 1827.

Duer, W. A., Hist. Address, 1848.

Dunshee, School of the Ref. Prot. Dutch Ch., 1633–1853.

Ely, Journal of Alms-house preacher, (1st, 2d series), 1812, 13.

Englishman's Sketch-book, 1828.

First Baptist Church, 1829. P. 466.

Francis, J. W., New York, 1800–57, a discourse.

" Old New York, 1858.

Free School Society, 1814. P. 552.

General Society of Mechanics, Reports, 1845–54.

Glentworth, Election frauds, 1838.

Gobright, N. Y. Sketch-book of.... trades, 1858.

Great Metropolis, Doggett, 1846, 53.

Greenleaf, Hist. of Churches of all denominations to 1846.

Hardie, J., Acc'ts of Epidemics, 1799, 1805, 22.

" Description of N. Y., 1827.

Harkness, J., Reformed Dutch Church burned, 1840.

High Life in N. Y., 1844. P. 496.

King, C., Progress of last fifty years, 1852.

Martyrs....at Wallabout Bay, 1855.

Mathews, J. M., Fifty Years in, 1858.

Michaëlius, J., Letter, 1628.

Moulton, View of New Orange, 1673.

New Jersey Rep. on N. Y. Encroachments, 1855.

N. Y. City; Documents, 1853–55.

" Census, 1865.

" Maps of Senate and Assembly Districts.

New York City (continued).

N. Y. City; Manual of the Corporation, (Valentine, etc.), 1841–70.

" Mortality, 1804–53.

N. Y. City, Growth of N. Y., 1865. P. 1806.

" Manual of the corporation, (Valentine), 1841–70.

" Quarantine, 1857–67. P. vol., 1807.

" Guia, 1855.

N. Y. City Mission and Tract Society, 1872.

New York State, Report on the harbor, 1857, 60.

New York as it is, 1837.

N. Y. Chamber of Commerce, History, 1867.

New York City in the Revolution; Papers, 1861.

New York Guides, 1817, 53.

New York in Slices, 1849.

New York Jour. of Commerce, Abuses, 1853.

New York, Sketch of, 1853.

New York, Walks about, 1865.

New York, Strangers' Guide, 1817.

Olden Time in, 1833.

Old Merchants of, (Scoville), 1863–1870, 5 v.

Pamphlets relating to, vol. 531, 1806.

Paulding, Affairs of New Amsterdam.

Picture of New York, 1807, 28, 48.

Plain Statement on real estate, 1818. P. 75, 1806.

Public School Soc., 1828, 32, 42.

Reminiscences of the City, 1855.

Remonstrance.......Pilot Law, 1857. P. 529.

Remonstrance..Ships and Piers, 1857.

St. Jude's Prot. E. Free Church, 1846. P. 543.

Skillman, Police reports, 1828, 9.

Skinner, T. H., Mercer St. Church, 1845.

Smith, M. H., Sunshine and shadow in, 1869.

Soc. for the Ref. of Juv. Delinquents, Rep., 1832, 35–55, 57, 64.

Spring, G., Hist. Discourses, 1858.

Stanton St. Bapt. Ch., 1860.

Stone, W. L., History of, 1868.

Stryker, Hist. Disc., Broome St. Ch., 1860.

Thompson, J. P., Hist. of the Tabernacle, 1857.

Thorburn, G., Reminiscences of, 1845.

Valentine, Hist. of the city, 1853.

" Plots below Wall St.

Van Nest, 21st Dutch Church.

New York City (continued).

Vertoogh van N. Nederland, 1649–50.

Watson, J. F., Historic tales of olden time, 1832.

Wealthy Citizens of, 1842.

Williams, E., New York in 1833, 1834.

Wilson's Copartnership Direct., 1856.

Witches of N. Y., (Thompson), 1859.

Wood, F., Communications, 1856–57.

See Yellow Fever.

New York City Directories. Boyd's Pict. Directory, 1859.

Doggett, Directory, 1842–52.

Elliot, 1812.

Franks, 1786. Repr.

Longworth, Alm. and Directory, 1797–1841. Wanting, 1799, 1801, 2, 3, 11, 12, 13, 14.

Low, 1796.

New York Business Direct., 1840, 41.

New York Merc. Un. Direct., 1850–51.

N. Y. Pictorial Directory, 1851.

Rode's, 1850–55.

Trow's, 1856–71.

Wilson's Bus. Direct., 1852, 56.

New York City University. *See* University.

New York State: Geography, Statistics, Travels, etc. Account of a Journey to Niagara, Quebec, 1765.

Asher and Adams, Atlas and Gazetteer of, 1870.

Beck, N. F., Road from Erie to the Hudson, 1827.

Brockett, L. P., Geography of, 1847.

Burr's County Atlas, 1829.

" Guide to Map.

Child, L. M., Letters from, 1845, 1848.

Clinton, D. W., Letters on the resources of, 1822.

Crèvecœur, Voyage dans l'état de, 1801.

Denton, D., Desc. of New York, 1670.

Dewey, Buffalo and N. York Railway Hand-book, 1849.

Disturnell, Gazetteer of, 1842.

" State Reg., 1858.

" State Guide, 1842.

" Western traveler, 1844.

Donck, A. v. d., Beschr. van Nieuw Nerderlant, 1656.

Dwight, T., Travels in, 1821.

Evening Journal Almanac, 1858–72.

Forest Arcadia of North N. Y., 1864.

Fowler, J., Tour in New York, 1820.

French, J. H., Gazetteer, 1860.

Gaine's N. Y. Almanac, 1766, 70.

" Univ. Register, 1776, 86, 1802.

Goodenow, Top. and statis. Manual of, 1811. P. 17.

New York State: Geography, Statistics, Travels, etc. (continued).

Gordon, T. F., Gazetteer of, 1836.

Hamilton, T., Men and Mann. in America, 1831, 33.

Hammond, S. H., Wild Northern Scenes.

Headley, J. T., The Adirondacks, 1849.

Holley, O. L., N. Y. State Reg., 1843–47.

Holt, N. Y. State Register, 1804–06.

Hough, N. Y. Civil List, 1855–69.

Jogues, New Netherland, 1642–44.

Lambrechsten, Disc. of N. Netherland, 1818.

Longworth, Pocket Alm., 1817.

Mather, J. H., Geography of, 1847.

Milbert, Itinéraire du Hudson, 1828.

Miller, J., Descr. of Province and city, 1695.

Munro, Descr. of the Genesee country, 1804.

N. Y. Almanac, (Meriam), 1857, 58.

N. Y. Manual for the Legislature, 1842–71.

N. Y. Pocket Alm., 1761, 70, 88, 95.

N. Y. State Register, Disturnell, 1847.

New York State Tourist, 1840.

N. Y. State Business Directory, 1850, 59, 67, 70.

N. Y. Statistics, Pamp. vol., 1247.

N. Y. Traveller, 1845.

O'Callaghan, Register, 1626–73.

O'Reilly, Sketches of Rochester and Western N. Y., 1838.

Pocket Guide, Hudson R. and Erie canal, 1824.

Post, Fevers of Genesee country, 1823.

Rivington's Alm., 1774.

Seymour, H., Lect. on Topog. and hist. of, 1856.

Smith, C., Gentleman's Alm., 1801.

Spafford, Pocket Guide on the Canals, 1824.

" Pocket Book of the towns, etc., 1825.

" Gazetteer of, 1813, 24.

Street, A. B., Saranac and Racket, 1860.

" The Indian Pass, 1869.

Tanner, Hand-book, 1844.

Timon, Bp. J., Missions in Western N. Y., 1862.

Vertoogh, Een, van de Colonie, 1676.

Vertoogh van Nieu Nederland, 1650.

West Indische Reize, 1705.

Williams, E., New York in 1833.

" Register, 1830–45.

Wooley, C., Two Years' Journal, 1679.

See Canals; Railroads; Education, etc.

New York State, History of, etc.

Account of settlement of, 1735.
Allen, E., On the Claims of N. York, 1774.
Asher, Dutch Books on, 1867.
Barber, J. W., Pict. History of, 1846.
Barton, J. L., Remin. of West. N. Y., 1848.
Belden, New York, Past and Future, 1849.
Brief and True Narrative, 1650.
Brodhead, J. R., History of, vol. I, 1609–64; vol. II, 1664–1691.
Buccaneers, The, Fict., 1826.
Butler, B. F., Const. Hist. of N. Y., 1847.
Campbell, W. W., Border Warfare of, 1831, 49.
Carpenter, W. H., History of, 1853.
Chassanis, Assoc'n pour Exploration.
Clinton, De W., Nat. Hist. and Resources of, 1822.
" Antiq. of West. N. Y., 1818.
" Disc., Indians of, 1811.
Cluny, A., Dutch colonies, 1769.
Colden, Completion of Canals, 1825.
" Vindica. of Steamboat right, 1818.
Congregational Churches of, 1848–67.
Connecticut, Rep. on Boundary, 1857.
Democratic Conventions, 1849, 56.
Donck, Van der, Remonstrance, 1649.
Dunlap, W., History of, 1837, 1844.
Eastman, History of, 1833.
Fontaine, Mem. of a Huguenot Fam.
Form of Prayer, 1762.
Gerard, London and New York, 1853.
Hammond, J. D., Hist. of Political parties in, to 1840.
Hasenclever, P., Case of, 1774.
Hastings, H. P., Constitut. Reform.
Herinneringen eener reize, 1832.
Hoffman, C. F., The Pioneers of, 1847.
Horsmanden, N. Y. Conspiracy, 1741.
Hotchkin, Hist. of Settlement of Western N. Y., 1848.
Hough, Results of N. Y. Census, 1855, 1865.
Hurlbut, Civil office and Polit. ethics, 1844.
Jenkins, J. S., Hist. of Political parties in, 1783–1844.
" Lives of the Governors of, 1851.
Jottrand, Comm. sur la Nouvelle Constitution de, 1847.
Kapp, F., Gesch. der Deutschen im Staate N. Y., 1869.
Kent, Disc., N. Y. Hist. Soc., 1829.
Keyen, Von Neu Niederland und Guajana, 1672.

New York State, History of, etc. (continued).

Lambrechsten, Ontdekking van Nieuw Nederland, 1818.
" The same: translation.
Lerow, Duties of Officers.
L. I. Hist. Soc., Danker's voy., 1679.
Macauley, J., History of, 1829.
Massachusetts Bay, The case of.... boundary, 1764.
Michaëlius's Letter, 1628.
Moulton, Hist. of State of N. Y., 1826.
Munsell's Hist. Series: Indian Treaties.
N. Y. Colony: Journal of Dutch Commis'rs, 1663, (Blue Laws).
" State of the Right, 1773.
" Colonial History, 11 v.
" Documentary Hist., 4 v.
" Provincial Congress. Journals, 1775–77, 2 v.
N. Y. State: Comm'rs treaties, 1784–91.
" Legislature, Speeches in, 1861–63. Pam. vols. 246, 1247, 1248.
" Mil. appointments, 1786–1802. MS.
" Public Documents; Series of reports of various departments collected, 1845–65.
N. Y. Colonial Tracts, 3 v., (O'Callaghan).
New York Historical Society, Collections, 1809–70.
" Proceedings, 1843–49, 57.
New York Marriages to 1784.
Niles, S., Serm., Mass. Miss. Soc., 1801, P. 1598.
O'Callaghan, Hist. of New Netherland. 1846, 48.
Photog. Senate Album, 1858.
Prot. Episc. Church, N. Y., Journals.
Rees, Nederl. Volkplantingen in N. A., 1855.
Republican Conventions, 1810, 1828. etc.
Russell, Harper's N. Y. Class-book, 1847.
Seymour, H., Lect. on the History of, 1856.
Smith, W., Hist. of, to 1732.
" Hist. of, to 1762.
Squier, Aborig. Monuments of, Smithson. Contr. 2.
State of Controversy with N. H., 1782.
Street, A. B., Hist. of Council of Revision, 1859.
Tibbets, Finances of the Canal fund, 1829.
Turner, O., Hist. of Phelps and Gorham's purchase, 1851.

New York State, History of, etc. (continued).

Uncle Philip's Conversations, 1844.

Vertoogh, etc, 1650.

" Representation of N. Neth., trans., (H. C. Murphy).

Yates, Hist. of, 1824.

Young, A. W., First lessons in gov't.

Whitehead, W. A., East. bound. of N. Jersey, 1866.

Zenger, Libel controversy, 1732.

See Canals; Education; New Hamp. Grants; Railroads, etc.

New York State, History: Local. *See* Albany; Auburn; Augusta; Batavia; Binghampton; Buffalo; Champlain Lake; Chautauqua; Chemung County; Chenango Co.; Claverack; Clinton; Columbia Co.; Cooperstown; Cortland Co.; Danville; Delaware Co.; East Hampton; Essex Co.; Fishkill; Flushing; Franklin Co.; Genesee; Glen Cove; Glenville; Gloversville; Greene; Hempstead; Herkimer; Holland Purchase; Hudson; Huntington; Lewis Co.; Little Britain; Long Island; Nassau; Newburgh; New Rochelle; Newtown; N. Utrecht; Oneida Co.; Onondaga Co.; Orange Co.; Oswego; Otsego; Owego; Oxford; Palmyra; Port Jervis; Poughkeepsie; Putnam; Queens Co.; Rochester; Rome; Rye; St. Lawrence Co.; Saratoga; Schenectady; Schoharie Co.; Seneca Co.; Sherburne; Southampton; Southold; Spencertown; Staten Is.; Steuben Co.; Suffolk Co.; Syracuse; Ticonderoga; Troy; Tryon Co.; Utica; Warsaw; Washington Co.; Watertown; Westchester Co.; West Point; Whitehall; White Plains; Yonkers.

New York in the Civil War. Albany Army Relief Bazaar, 1864, Collections.

" Photographs of (35).

Boudrye, L. N., Hist. 1st N. Y. Cavalry, 1865.

Brooklyn Fair, Hist., 1864.

Clark, J. H., Iron Hearted Regt., 115th N. Y.

Clark, O. S., 116th N. Y. Regt., 1868.

Clark, R. W., Heroes of Albany, 1866.

Corcoran, Gen. M., Captivity of, 1862.

Dewitt Guard. P. 1246.

Eddy, R., Hist. 60th N.Y. Regt., 1864.

Ellsworth (44th) N. Y. Vet. Assoc., Proc., 1871.

Judd, D. W., 33d N. Y. Vol., 1864.

Knipe, J. F., Testimony on Price, 1864. P. 1589.

Mil. Assoc'n of N. Y., Proc., 1860–69.

N. Y. Adj. Gens. Reports, 1861–69.

New York in the Civil War (cont'd).

N. Y. Adj. Gens. General Orders, 1861, 1864.

" Army list, 1862.

" Roll of the Volunteers, 8 v.

" Bureau of Mil. Statistics, 1–5th Reports, 1864–68.

" Soldiers' Home, Agent's Rept., 1864.

" Legislative speeches, 1861–63.

N. Y. City, Memory of A. Lincoln, 1865.

New York County: Reports of volunteering Commit., 1863–66.

" Enrolment lists.

N. Y. 2d Comp. of 7th Regt. Hist., 1864.

Old, The, Guard, 1863–66. N. Y., Period.

Oneida Volunteers, Reception, N. Y., 1861. P. 2504.

Pinckney, S. R., Nat. Guard Manual, 1864.

Rogers, W. H., Hist. of 189th Regt., 1865.

Spirit of The Fair, N. Y., 1864.

Stevens, G. T., Three Years in the Sixth Corps, 1867.

Swinton, W., Hist. of the 7th Regt., 1870.

U. S., Rolls of Honor of soldiers interred in the Nat. Cemeteries, 1865–1870.

Willson, A. M., Disaster—Triumph, 126th N. Y. Regt., 1870.

See Civil War.

New York State: Biographical. Berrian, Recollections, 1850.

Boone, Life Sketches of the Legislature, 1868, 69, 70.

Bungay, Off-hand takings, 1854.

Fisher, Physicians of Westchester Co.

Gorrie, Black River. Confer., Mem., 1852.

Harlow, Legislature of 1867.

Hunt's Amer. Biog. Panorama, 1849.

Jenkins, J. S., Lives of the governors, 1851.

Murphy, Biog. of Legislature, 1859, 1860, 61, 62–3.

Livingston, Biog. of Am. now living, 1851.

N. Y. Chamber of Commerce, (Stevens), 1867.

N. Y. Geneal. and Biog. Record, 1870-1871.

Old Merchants of N. Y., (Scoville), 1863–70.

Pamphlets, Biographical, N. Y., vol. 1858.

Q., O. P., Sketches of the N. Y. Press, 1844.

North America (continued).
Butel-Dumont, His. des Col. Anglaises, 1755.
Burnaby, Travels, 1759, 60.
Campbell, H., Travels in, 1791, 92.
Carver, Travels, 1766–68.
Chabert, Voyage dans, 1750.
Chastellux, Voyage, 1780–82.
Cooper, R., History of, 1805.
Davenport, Gazetteer and Geog. Dict. of, 1842.
Denys, Desc. géog. et hist. des costes de, 1672.
Description de l' Amérique, 1638.
Douglass, W., British settlements in, 1755.
Force, P., Tracts on the colonies of, 1836–46.
Gordon, J. B., Hist. and Geog. Mem. of, 1820.
Hall, B., Travels in, 1827, 28.
Harmon, Voy. and Tr. to the Pacific, 1820.
History of the Brit. Dominions in, 1773.
Hodgson, A., Remarks during a journey in, 1819, 21.
Humphreys, Hist. Soc. Prop. Gosp. to, 1728.
Johnston, J. F. W., Notes on, 1851.
Kingdom, Amer. and Brit. Colon., 1820.
Knox, J., Campaigns in N. A., 1757–1760.
La Hontan, Voyage to, 1735.
Laon, Voy. au Cap de Nord, 1654.
La Pothérie, Hist. de l'Amérique septentrionale, 1722.
Logan, J. K., Notes of a journey, 1838.
Lyell, Travels in, 1845.
McGee, History of Irish Settlers in, 1852.
Marquette, Récit de voyages, 1673. Repr. 1855.
" Voy. et Découverte, 1673; repr. 1845.
Moser, N. A. nach den Fried., 1783.
Murray, C. A., Travels in, 1834–36.
Murray, Hugh, Hist. of travels and discov. in, 1829.
Murray, H. A., The land of the slave and free, 1855.
North Amer. and West Indies Gazetteer, 1778.
Present State, Mitchell, 1767.
Present State of Brit. Empire, 1768.
Rafinesque, Travels, 1836.
Robin, Nouveau voyage, 1781.
Rogers, Robert, Account of, 1755.
Russell, R., Agric. and climate of, 1857.

North America (continued).
Saxe-Weimar, Travels through, 1825, 1826.
Shirreff, Tour through, 1835.
Stansbury, P., Pedestrian Tour in, 1822.
State of Brit. Col., 1755.
Stuart, J., Three years in, 1833.
Sutcliff, R., Travels in, 1804–6.
Talbot, J., History of North America, 1820.
Trollope, A., Travels, 1862.
Tudor, H., Travels in, 1834.
Welby, Visit to, 1821.
See America; Canada; Louisiana; Florida; S. Carolina; New England; United States; Mexico; British Colonies; North W. Coast.

North America, British. Bouchette, Brit. Dominions in, 1832.
Buckingham, J. S., Provinces of Brit. Am., 1843.
Canada, Northwest Territory, 1858.
Coke, Subaltern's Furlough, 1833.
Doyle, W., Brit. Dominions in.
Haliburton, Resources of, 1857.
Hooker, W. J., Bot. of the Northern parts, 1833.
Macgregor, British America, 1832.
Murray, Hist. and descr. acc't of, Edinburg Cab. Lib.
Richardson, Fauna Boreali-Americana, 1837.
Sleigh, Pine forests and hacmatack clearings, 1853.
Smith, M., British Possessions in, 1814.
See Canada; New Brunswick, etc.

Northampton Co., Eng. Baker, Hist. of, 1822–41.
Beauties of England and Wales.
Marcus, M., Letter, 1822. P. 389.
See Ecton.

Northampton, Mass. Allen, W., Hist. Discourse, 1854.
Bridgman, T., Inscript. in grave yards of, 1850.
Williams, S., Hist. of, 1815.
See Hampshire Co.

Northborough, Ms. Allen, J., Two Hist. Sermons, 1842, 67.
" Hist. sketch of.

Northbridgewater, Ms. Directory, 1869.
Kingman, B., History of, 1866.

North Brookfield, Ms. Snell, T., Sermon, 40th anniv., 1838.
" Sermon, 50th anniv., 1848.
" Hist. sketch of the town, 1854.
" Hist. sketch of the church, 1854.

Norway (continued).
La Martinière, Voyage, 1676.
Lamotte, Voy. principalement en Norwége, 1813.
Norway, Statistik, 1862.
Price, E., Norway and its Scenery, 1853.
Smithson. Rep., 1866, Statistics of Mountains and Lakes of.
Sturleson, Chronicle of Kings of, 1844.
Taylor, B., Northern travel, 1858.
Wyndham, F. M., Wild life in, 1861.
See Sweden.

Norway, Me. Noyes, D., History of, 1852.

Norwich, Conn. Bond, A., Hist. Discourse, 1860.
Caulkins, History of, 1660–1845.
Gilman, D. C., Hist. Discourse, 1859.
Morgan, Centenary Sermon, 1849.
Norwich Jubilee, 1859.

Norwich, Eng. Gould, G., Baptists of, 1860.
Norwich, History of, 1768.
Reed, A., Congregationalism in, 1842.

Nothing. Essay on, Arnot, 1795. P. 1777.

Nott, E. Backus, J. T., Fun. address, 1866. P. 1857.
Nott, E., 50th Anniversary, 1854.
Union College, Pamphlets, 6 vols.
Union Coll. Mag., Mar. 1862. P. 1857.

Nott, Sir W. Stocqueler, Memoirs of, 1854.

Nottinghamshire, Eng. Beauties of Engl. and Wales.

Nourse, J. Van Rensselaer, C., Disc. on.

Nouvelle France. *See* Canada; Jesuit Missions; North America.

Nova Scotia. Allan, J., Mil. opera. during Am. Revolution, 1867.
Belcher's Alman., 1846–59.
Bouchette, North America, 1832.
Chabert, Voyage, 1751.
Cunabell's Almanac, 1859.
Dawson, J. W., Agriculture in, 1856.
" Acadian Geol., 1855.
" Scien. papers, 1860–63.
De Peyster, J. W., Settlement of. P. 976.
Diéreville, Voyage de l'Acadie, 1710.
Gesner, Indust. Resources of, 1849.
Haliburton, Hist. and Statist. acct. of, 1829.
" The Old Judge, 1849.
Hamilton, P. S., N. S. for Emigration, 1858.
Hist. Géog. de la Nouvelle Ecosse, 1649.

Nova Scotia (continued).
Howe, J., Speeches, etc., 1858.
Little, O., Trade in Northern Colonies, and Descr. of, 1748.
Marrant's Journal, 1785–90.
Marsden, Mission to N. S., 1810.
Martin, M. R., Brit. Col. Lib. V. 6.
Mémoires des Comm. du roi. Eng. and Fr. 1755.
Monro, A., Account of, 1855.
Moorson, Letters from Nova Scotia, 1830.
Nova Scotia: Record commission, 1858, 1859.
" Census, 1861.
Nugent's Almanac, 1856.
Pichon, Mémoires du Cap. Bréton, 1718.
Present State of, 1787.
Provin. Wesleyan Alm., 1859.
Rameau, France aux Colonies, 1859.
Robertson, J., Hist of Miss. of Secession Church from 1765.
Whipple, J., Hist. of Acadia, 1816.
Williams, C. R., The neutral French, 1841.
See Canada; British Colonies; New Brunswick; Gold.

Novels. *See* Fiction.

Noyes, G. A. Withington, Fun. Sermon, 1852.

Noyes, G. F. Campaign Sketches, 1863.

Noyes, W. C. Fisher, S. W., Discourse on, 1866. P. 1858.

Nubia. Burckhardt, Travels in, 1819.
Russell, M., Hist. of Nubia.
See Abysinia; Egypt; Ethiopia; Nile river.

Nullification. *See* Secession; Civil War; South Carolina; State Rights.

Nullum Tempus Act. Portland, Duke of, Case, 1768.

Numbers. Aristoteles, Metaphysics, (T. Taylor).
Barlow, T., Theory of Numbers, 1811.
Byrne, O., Dual Arithmetic, 1864.
See Arithmetics; Mathematics.

Numismatics. Addison, Dialogue on Medals.
Akerman, Numismatic Manual, 1840.
" Introd. to Study of coins, 1848.
" Tradesmen's Tokens, 1648–1672.
" Forgeries of money.
Asiatic Soc. of Bengal, Hindoo coins.
Begerus, Regum Roman. numis. aurea, 1700.
" Numis. Pontif. Romanorum, 1704.

Numismatics (continued).

Birchall's Eng. Prov. coins, 1796.

Bizot, Hist. Métal. de Hollande, 1688, 1690.

Bonicelli, De Numis. "Lucillam Aug. fil.," 1828.

Bowring, J., Decimal System, 1854.

Burn, J. H., Lond. Trademen's Tokens, 1600–1700, 1853, 55.

Bushnell, C. I., Amer. Tokens, 1798–1858.

" Three Amer. Tokens, 1859.

Cardwell, Coinage of the Gr. and Rom., 1832.

Conder, British provin. coins, last 20 years, 1798.

Charles I, Medals of, 1851.

Chijs, Incrementa Mus. Lug. Bat., 1842–45.

Cuper, Observationes, 1670.

Coins of German Emperors, imp.

Dickeson, Amer. Numis. Manual, 1859.

DuBois, Coins at Mint of U. S., 1846.

DuCange, Glossarium, Art. Moneta.

Durand, Fabrication des Monnaies Françaises, 1853.

Eckfeldt, Coins within the last century, 1842.

" New varieties, etc., 1850.

Edwards, E., Napoleon Medals, 1837.

" French Medals, 1789–1830.

England, T. R., Hebrew Medal, 1819. P. 401.

Erizzo, Le medaglie degli antichi, 1571.

Evelyn, J., Disc. of Medals.

Fleetwood, Acc't of Eng. money, 1745.

" Sermon on Clipping, 1694.

Folkes, Engl. Gold Coins, 1736.

Goltz, Hist. Imp. Rom. ex Numism., 1563.

Guillemot, Monuments Mérovingiennes, 1845.

Hennin, Manuel de Numismatique ancienne, 1830.

Hickcox, J. H., American Coinage, 1858.

Hist. Abr. des Prov. Unies, 1701.

Homes, H. A., The Design of Medals, 1863.

Humphreys, Coin Collector's Manual, 1853.

" Coinage of G. B. to the present time, 1854.

Jonge, J. C. De, Notices des médailles à La Haye.

Julien, Les Césars; Trad. De Spanheim, 1728.

Labbé, Bibliot. nummaria, 1672.

La Motraye, Travels, 1723.

Langlois, Num. des Nomes d'Egypte, 1852.

Numismatics (continued).

Leake, History of English money, 1745.

LeClere, Médailles des Provinces Unies 1723–28.

Leipzig, Stadtbibliothek, Münzkabinet, 1853.

Loon, Van, Nederlandsche Historipenningen, 1723.

Madden, F. W., Hist. of Jewish coinage, 1864.

Manutius, De vet. Notarum Explanatione, 1566.

Marsden, W., Numis. Orientalia, 1825.

Mease, J., Descr. of Amer. medals, 1821; also, N. Y. Hist. Soc. Coll., v. 3.

Monfalcon, Hist. de Lyon, 1851.

" Archéologie Lyonnais, 1856.

Monumenta Historica Britannica, (Petrie), 1848.

Nicolas, Hist. of Knighthood, Hist. of Medals, 1842.

Odericus, G. A., Dissertationes, 1765.

Orsini, Familiæ Romanæ, 1597.

Pamphlets relating to, vol. 962.

Phil'a Board of Trade on U. S. Mint, 1861. P. 962.

Pietraszewski, Numi Mohammedani, 1843.

Prime, Coins, Medals, 1861.

Rouillio, Prontuario delle Medaglie, 1577.

Revue de la Numis. Belge, 1842–8.

Riddell, Monograph of the dollar, 1845.

Ruding, Annals of Coinage of Great Britain, 1840.

Satterlee, Medals of Presidents, 1862.

Schoenemann, Vaterlandischen Münzkünde, 1852.

Selden, De Nummis, 1675.

Simon, J., Irish coins, 1749.

Snelling, Coinage of England, 1762, 63, 66.

Snowden, Medals of Washington, 1861.

" Descr. of Foreign Coins, 1860.

Soc. of Antiquaries, Archæologia, Lond.

Souvenirs Numismatiques, 1848.

Spanhemius, Numismatum Antiquorum, 1706.

Svenska Mynt, 1845.

Taylor, Gold and Silver Coin Exam., 1847.

Thomason, Memoirs during half a century, 1845.

Thompson, J., 750 fac-similes of coins.

" Coin chart manual, 1853.

Till, Roman Denarius, 1846.

Tindal's England, Medals of William III, Anne and George I.

Numismatics (continued).
Tornberg, Numi Cufici, 1848.
Tristan, Commen. Hist. de l'Empire Romain, 1657.
U. S. Mint, Reports, 1859-68.
Wyatt, T., Nat. Medals of Amer., 1854.
Yale College, Catalogue of coins, 1863.
See Bibliography; Currency; Inscriptions.

Numismatics: Sale Catalogues.
Bangs, Brother & Co., June, 1855. Priced.
Bangs, Merwin & Co., 1858-63.
Bolland, Cat. of the Coll. of coins of, 1841. Priced.
Bunau, Cat. bibliothecæ, 1750, 53.
Chaffers, Cat. Anc. and Mod., Lond., 1855. Priced.
Chambers's Collection, 1866.
Cogan's Sales, 1859, 60, 62, 63.
Coin Catalogues, 2 vols., 1840-48.
Curtis, J. K., Sale, 1858.
Eves's Coll., Toronto.
Finotti Coll., N. Y., 1862.
Hearne, J. A., Cat. of Numism. books for sale, 1847-53.
Heberle, Vente à Cologne, 1862.
Kerrick, T., Cat. of Roman Coins, 1852.
Leavitt's Sale. P. 962.
Lincoln & Son, Cat., Lond., 1856, 57, 60, 61. Priced.
Lilliendahl, Sale, 1863.
Mason & Co., Phil'a, 1869.
New York State Lib., Cat. of Coins and Medals, 1856.
Northwick Coll., Lond., 1859.
Robinson, A. S., Sale, 1862.
Roper's Sale, 1851.
Sage's Sale, 1859.
Sotheby's Sale, June, 1856. Priced.
Syke's Collection, Sale, 1824. Priced.
Woodward's Sales; May, Oct., 1863; May, Oct., 1864; Mar., 1865, N. Y. Some priced.
Young, M., Sale Cat., Lond., 1839.

Nuneham-Courtenay. Descrip., 1806. P. 1755.

Nunez de Balboa. Quintana, Life of, 1832.

Nuns; Nunneries. Bunkley, Test. of a novice, 1855.
Goodman, Sisterhoods in Church of Eng., 1863.
Hampden, C., N. in France, 1845. P. 1441.
Monk, M., Disclosures of, 1836.
Montalembert, Anglo Saxon Nuns, Monks of the West, v. 2.
Nunnery Question, Report, Lond., 1854. P. 1434.

Nuns; Nunneries (continued).
Priests and victims.
Protest. Sisters of Charity, A letter, 1826.
Reed, Six months in a convent, 1835.
" Supp. to Six months, etc.
Reflections on communities of women, 1815.
Review of Reply, 1835. P. 871.
St. George, Mary E., Answer to Six months in a convent.
See Sisters of Mercy.

Nuremburg. Wagenseil, De civ. commentatio, 1697.
See Bibliography.

Nursing. Nightingale, F., Notes on, 1860.
Training Institution, 1857.

O.

Oastler, R. Letters, 1835-47.

Oates, Titus. Dangerfield, Narrative of the Plot, 1679.
Impartial account of Parl., 1679.
Instrument...of the true Protestants, 1679. P. 1116.
Oates, T., Narr. of plot, 1679.
" Trials of, 1685.
Observator, 1685.
Some observations on the tryals, 1679.
See Great Britain; Pamphlets.

Oaths. Briefe Treatise, 1650.
Brownlee, W. C., Diss. on a civil oath, 1825. P. 13.
Higden, W., View of the Constitution, 1709.
Junkin, The Oath, a divine ordinance.
Hudson, C., Incompet. of Witnesses, 1838.
Leigh, Speech on Oaths, 1855. P. 530.
L'Estrange, Three pamphlets, 1680-81.
Lewis, E., Dissertation on, 1838.
Mass., Witnesses' Belief, 1838.
Our Political Oaths, 1855.
Phipps, J., Oaths Prohibited, 1781.
Steele, T., Iniquity of, 1829.
Willard, S., On Laying the hand on the Bible, 1689.

Oaths of Allegiance. Friendly conference, 1689.
Hellier, Obligation of Oaths, 1688. P. 1005.
Hint, The, 1737.
Lawfulness of, 1689.
Letter to a Diss. Clergyman, 1690.
Penn, W., Treatise on, Works, 1736.
Reflexions upon, 1661.
Sherlock, T., Vind. of Test Acts, 1718.
Stillingfleet, On the Oaths, 1689.

Onderdonk, B. T. Trial of.
No Church, etc., 1845.
Onderdonk, Statement of facts, 1845.
Plebs, Reply to, 1843.
Prot. Epis. Ch., N. Y., Report, 1845.
Puseyism and Episcopacy, 1845. P. 543.
Richmond, J. C., Conspiracy against, 1845. P. 543.
" Laugh of a layman.
St. Peter's Ch., Albany, Report, 1845.
Seabury, S., Fun. Sermon on, 1861.
Smith, J. A., Remarks.
Trapier, Narrative of facts, 1845. P. 72.
Trial tried, 1845.

Onderdonk, H. U. Statement of the Facts, 1827. P. 543.

O'Neale, J. Weems, Life of, 1818.

Oneida Community. Circular, The, 1851–68.
Dixon, Spiritual wives.
Free Church circular, 1850–51.
Hand book, 1847.
Noyes, J. H., Hist. of Socialisms, 1870.
" The Berean, 1847.
Oneida Association, Bible communism, 1853.
Oneida Assoc'n, Reports, 1849, 51; Hand book, 1867; Miscellanies.
Perfectionist, The, 1843–45.
See Perfectionists; Noyes.

Oneida County, N. Y. Directory, 1862, 1863, 69.
Jones, P., Annals of, 1851.
Tracy, W., Notices of men and events in, 1838.

Oneida Indians. Hough, F. B., Notices of P. Penet, 1866.

Onondaga County, N. Y. Directory, 1868.
Clark, J. V. H., Reminiscenses of, 1849.
Exam. of the opinion of the Ononda. Comm'rs, 1800. P. 195.
Geddes, G., Report on Industry, Agr., Aborigines, N. Y. Agr. Soc., 1860.
N. Y. St. Agric. Trans., 1859.
Onondaga Comm'rs on Milit. lands, Minutes, 1798 to 1802, 18 vols. MS.
Pioneer Ass'n, Proc., 1869.
See Salt; Syracuse.

Ontario, Canada. Hand book, 1852.
See Canada; Toronto.

Ontario County, N. Y. Dickson, Speech, 1834.
Directory, 1869.

Operas, Musical. Librettos, Pamphlets, vol. 1373, 1717–1719, 2524.
See Dramatic; Music.

Opinions, Religious. Bailey, S., Essays on the formation of, 1831.
Foster, J., Letters on, to Stebbing, 1735.
Palmer, Formation of Rel. Opin, 1860.
Reflections on Faith, 1790. P. 337.
Simonde, Progress of, 1827.
Stebbing, H., Religious Sincerity, 1718.
Sykes, Innocency of Error, 1715.
Wilks, S. C., Influence of a Moral Life, 1822. P. 339.
See Creeds; Reason.

Opium. Allen, N., The Opium Trade, 1853.
Carlyle, Engl. opium eater.
Collins, Theriaki, 1871.
Fry, W. S., Facts on, 1840.
Pam. v. 1234, (China).
Statement of claims, 1840.
See China; Narcotics.

Optics. Berkeley, Bp., Theory of vision, Works, vol. 6, 1843.
Boscovich, R. J., Opera pertin. ad opticam, 1785.
Brewster, Sir D., Treatise on Optics, Lardner, 8.
Faraday, Glass for optical purposes, 1830.
Jackson, I. W., Treatise on Optics, 1848.
Lardner, Account of Newton's Optics, Lib. U. K.
Martin, B., Visual glasses.
Priestley, J., Discourses on vision, 1772.
Thomin, Traité d'Optique mécanique, 1749.
See Natural Philosophy; Eye; Light; Spectrum Analysis.

Optimism. Blood, B., O..the lesson of ages, 1860.
Tuckerman, H. T., The Optimist, 1850.
Voltaire, Candide, ou l'optimiste.
See Theology; Philosophy.

Orange, Prince d'. Montgomery, Gen., Entretiens de, 1776.

Orange, N. J. Hoyt, Hist. 1st Presb. Church.

Orange Co., N. Y. Denniston, E., Survey of, N. Y. Ag. Soc. Tr., 1862.
Eager, History of, 1845-47.
Stickney, C. C., Hist. of Minisink region, 1867.

Orations. Pamphlets containing, vols. 77, 83, 88, 100, 101. B. C. 55.
See Addresses; Speeches; Agr., Hist., Law, Liter'y and Med. Addresses.

Orations, July 4. Abbot, D., Nashua, N. H., 1803.
Adams, J. Q., Boston, 1793, 1831.

Orations, July 4 (continued).
Alger, W. R., Boston, 1857.
Allen, Thomas, 1803: Pittsfield, Mass.
Atherton, C. C., Amherst, 1798.
Austin, J. T., Lexington, 1815.
Austin, S., Worcester, 1798.
Bangs, E., Worcester, 1800.
Barnard, D. D., Albany, 1835.
Bates, I. C., Northampton, 1812.
Bidwell, B., Sheffield, Conn., 1805.
Bigelow, T., Boston, 1853.
Blake, F., Worcester, Mass., 1812.
Boies, P., Blandford, Mass., 1814.
Boston Celebration, 1858.
Bradford, Alden, Wiscasset, Me., 1804.
Callender, J. Boston, 1797.
Choate, Oration, Boston, 1858.
Cogswell, N., Newburyport, 1808.
Cushing, C., Newburyport, 1832.
Dana, S., Groton, Mass., 1807.
Danforth, T., Boston, 1804.
De Saussure, Columbia, S. C., 1826.
Doane, G. W., Address, 1848.
" Burlington, 1852.
Douglass, F., Rochester, N. Y., 1852.
Drayton, W., Charleston, 1831.
Dunlap, A., Salem, Mass..
Dutton, W., Boston, 1805.
Dwight, T., Hartford, 1798.
Everett, D., Amherst, N. H., 1804.
Everett, E., Cambridge, 1826.
" Boston, 1858.
Fondey, W. H., Albany, 1838.
Force, P., On the Declaration of Ind.
Foote, H. G., Ogdensburgh, 1856.
Forrest, E., New York, 1838.
French, E., Dem. Repub., Boston.
Furman, R., Sermon, Charleston, S.C.
Gleason, B., Hingham, Mass., 1807.
Grimké, T. S., Charleston, S. C., 1833. P. 71.
Grosvenor, T. P., Hudson, 1808.
Hammond, Wells S., Cherry-valley, 1839. P. 63.
Hall, J., Boston, 1800.
Holmes, J. S., Boston, 1858.
Hunter, W., Newport, R. I., 1801, 1826.
Ingersoll, C. J., Phil'a, 1832.
Johnson, J. B., Albany, 1798.
Ketchum, H., New Haven, 1851. P. 88.
Langdon, C., Castleton, Vt., 1812.
Law, S. A., Stamford, N. Y., 1858.
Learned, W. F., Newburgh, N. Y.
Linn, A. L., Schenectady, 1822.
Livermore, E. S., Boston, 1813.
Lord, J. C., Buffalo, 1858.
Lathrop, S. K., Boston, 1866.

Orations, July 4 (continued).
Lowell, J., Boston, 1799.
Lunt, G., Newburyport, 1836.
McClay, W. B., New York, 1839.
Maxcy, J., Columbia, S. C., 1819.
Maxcy, M., Schenectady, 1803. P. 58.
May, S. J., Jamestown, N. Y., 1856.
Miles, W. P., Charleston, S. C., 1849. P. 52.
Mitchell, N., Charleston, S. C., 1848. P. 52.
Moseley, E., Newburyport, 1808.
Nichols, I., Salem, 1805.
Otis, C., Scituate, Ms., 1800.
Otis, H. G., Boston, 1788.
Paine, C., Boston, 1801.
Pamphlets containing Orations, July 4, and Feb. 22, Vols. 532, 995, 1809, 1871.
Parker, E. G., Boston, 1856.
Pickering, J., Salem, Mass., 1804.
Potts, George, Phil'a, 1826.
Powers, H. P., Ypsilanti, Mich.
Putnam, J. O., Lockport, 1856.
Quincy, Josiah, Boston, 1798, 1826.
Ramsay, D., Charleston, S. C., 1794.
Rantoul, R., Gloucester, Mass., 1853.
Richardson, E. J., Utica, N. Y., 1850.
Richardson, Luther, Roxbury, 1800.
Ritchie, A., Boston, 1808.
Rush, R., 1812, Washington.
Savage, J., Boston, 1811.
Starr, G., Schenectady, 1831.
Story, J,, Salem, Mass., 1804.
Sheldon, J., Buffalo, 1852.
Smith, G.W., Fairfield, N.Y., 1856, 9.
Smith, H., Albany, 1858.
Smith, J. C., Sharon, Ct., 1798.
Smith, O., Johnson, Vt., 1826.
Sullivan, W., Boston, 1803.
Sumner, C., Boston, 1845.
Sumner, G., Boston, 1859.
Thacher, P., Boston, 1807.
Tower, C., Frankfort, 1843.
Tuft, J., Charlestown, 1814.
Van den Heuvel, J. A., Ogdensburgh.
Verplanck, G. C., New York, 1809.
Warner, G. J., New York, 1797.
Waterman, E., Hartford, 1794.
Wells, J., New York, 1798.
Whipple, E. P., Boston, 1850.
White, W. C., Rutland, 1802.
Whittlesey, F., Rochester, 1842.
Wilder, J. N., Ballston, 1855.
Winthrop, R. C., Washington, 1848.
Zabriskie, J. C., Princeton, 1843.

Oratory. *See* Elocution; Rhetoric; Speeches.

Ovidius. Heinsius, Commentarius, 1758.

Owego. Pioneer Festival, 1855.

Owen, J. Cawdrey, D., Answer to, 1857.

Owen, J. Hughes, J., Sermon on, 1822.

Owen, Rob. Journal, 1851.

Oxenstiern, J. Epistolæ.

Oxford, Earl of. Jesse, Mem. of the Court.

Oxford, N. Y. Academy, Jubilee, 1856.

Oxford, Eng. Blacow, Account of riot, 1747.
- Gr. Brit. Parl.; Riots at, 1717.
- Oxford, Poll, 1818. *See* Berks.
- Oxford Guide, 1790.
- Railway tr., walk through, 1851.

Oxford University. Ayscough's case.
- Black, Ashmole Mss., 1845.
- Chalmers, A., Hist. of the Colleges, 1810.
- Copleston, Education at, 1810.
- " Reply to Edinb. Rev., 1810.
- Cox, G. V., Recollections, 1868.
- Douce, Library bequeathed to, 1840.
- Few Observations..All Souls' Coll.
- Gibbs, Bibliotheca Radcliviana, 1747.
- Great Britain, Report on University of, 1852.
- Hawkins, E., Representation of, 1853. P. 1384.
- Hinton, J., Dissenters in, 1792.
- Huddesford, G., Exeter College, 1755.
- Hughes, T., Tom Brown at, 1870.
- Ingram, Memorials of Oxford, 1837.
- Laud, Archbp., Letter to the Univ., 1641.
- Newton, R., Hertford Coll., Statutes, 1747.
- Nicklin, P. H., Report concerning, 1834. P. 156.
- Nowell, Expul. of six students, 1768.
- Oxford, The, Commission; Letters to Gladstone, 1852.
- Oxford, Bodleian library, 1697.
- " On Univ. charters, 1680.
- " Calendar, 1868.
- " Catalogue of all graduates, 1659–1850.
- " Corpus Christi Coll., Proc., 1730. P. 1030.
- " " Regulations, 1856.
- " Exeter College, 1755.
- " " Regulations, 1856. P. 1318.
- " " Vindication of, 1755. P. 1039.
- " Parecbolæ, 1721, 1808.
- " Visit of King of Prussia and Russia, 1814. P. 1037.

Oxford University (continued).
- Sandford, D. K., Letter on, 1822.
- Seebohm, Oxf. reformers of, 1498.
- Skelton, J., Pietas Oxoniensis, Rec. of founders, 1828.
- Smith, G., Lecture on, N. Y., 1864.
- Terræ filius, (N. Amhurst), 1726.
- Waagen, Treasures of Art in G. B., v. 3, 1854.
- Wood, Athenæ Oxonienses, 1691, 92.
- *See* Universities; Bibliography.

Oxford Co., Canada. Shenston, Gazetteer of, 1852.

Oxfordshire, Eng. Beauties of Engl. and Wales.
- Cooke's Topog Lib.
- Old and New Interest, 1753.
- Oxfordshire contest, England, (1751), Pam., vol. 935.

Oxford Tracts. Dibdin, T. F., Three letters, 1843.
- Oakeley, F., Tract XC.
- Pamphlets relating to, vols. 331, 776, 1270, 1292.
- *See* Church of England; Tractarianism; Newman; Pusey.

Oysters. Virginia, Report, 1858.

P.

Pacific Ocean and Voyages. Alcala-Galiano, Viage, para el Estrecho de Frica, 1802.
- Beechey, Voy. to Pacific and Beering Straits, 1825–28.
- Bligh, Mutiny on board the Bounty, 1790.
- Brosses, Navig. aux terres australes, 1756.
- Broughton, Voyage to North Pacific, 1795.
- Brouwer, Journal .... naer de custen van Chili, 1643.
- Browne, J. R., Etchings of a Whaling Cruise, 1846.
- Cheever, The Island World of the Pacific, 1851.
- Cook, J., Voyages, 1776–80.
- Coulter, Adventures in the Pacific, 1845.
- Dalrymple, Hist. Coll. of voy. to South Pacific.
- Ellis, W., Voy. of Cook, 1776–80.
- Entrecasteaux, D', Recherche de La Pérouse, 1808.
- Fanning, Voyages, 1830–37.
- Franchère, Voy. to N. W. Coast, 1811–1814.
- Frézier, Voyage to the South Sea, 1712.
- Habersham, North Pacific Exped., 1857.

Paine, Thomas (continued).

Letters to, on Rights of man, 1791. P. 1332.

Muir, Exam. of Age of Reason, 1795.

Ogden, U., Antidote to Deism, 1795.

Oldys, F., Life of, (Chalmers), 1791, 92.

Osborne, J., Poem on Age of Reason, 1795.

Paine, T., Writings, etc., 1792, 1824.

" Life of, Pol. Censor, 1796.

" Life of, Hist. Mag., Lond., 1800.

Plain Truth, Ans. to Common Sense.

Priestley, J., Answer to A. of R.

Protest against "Rights of man," 1792.

Rickman, Life of, 1819.

Scott, T., Answer to, 1815.

Sherwin, W. T., Life of, 1819.

Simpson, D., Plea for religion, 1824.

Southwick, S., Pleasures of Poverty, 1823.

Vale, G., Life of, 1837, 41.

Watson, R., Letters to T. Paine, 1796. B. C.

Winchester, E., Answsr to, 1796.

Wood, W. H. R., Age of Reason, 1862.

Paine, L. W. Six Years in Georgia Prison, 1852.

Painting. Barnard, G., Painting in Water Colors, 1855.

Barry, Lectures on, 1848.

Blanc, C., Les Peintres des Fêtes galantes, 1854.

" Catalogue des peintures de Rembrandt, 1861.

Bryant, W. C., Oration, Death of Cole.

Buchanan, Memoirs on, 1824.

Campanari, Ritratto di Colonna.

Correggio, Œuvres complètes.

Dryden, Works, Obs. on Du Fresnoy's art of, 1808.

Du Fresnoy, De Arte graphica, 1808.

Dunlap, Progress of arts of design in the U. S., 1834.

Eastlake, History of Oil painting, 1847.

Entwürfe. . Niederlandischen meisters. . xv jahrhundert, 1830.

Field, G., Rudiments of the Painter's art, 1850.

Fielding, T. H., Theory and Practice of, 1852.

Fuseli, Lecture on, 1848.

Gibbes, Deveaux's Memoir, 1846.

Gilpin, Essays on Picturesque beauty, 1808.

Hand-book for young artists, 1845.

Harrison, H., Mixture of water colors.

Hay, D. R., A Nomenclature of colors, etc., 1845.

Painting (continued).

Historic Gallery of Portraits and Paintings, 1811.

James, J. T., Flemish, Dutch and German Schools, 1822.

Jarves, J. J., Art Studies: Italy, 1861.

Kugler, The Italian Schools, 1855.

Lanzi, Hist. of, in Italy, 1847.

Latilla, Fresco, encaustic and tempera, 1842.

Leslie, C. R., Autobiography, 1860.

Merrifield, Mrs., Original treatises on, 1849.

Michiels, Histoire de la peinture Flamande, 1847–49.

Murray, H., On Landscape painting, 1853.

" On Portrait Painting, 1853.

Montaiglon, Hist. de l'Académie de Peinture, 1648–1664.

New Society. . . . Water colors, 1849.

Pamphlets relating to Painting, v. 996.

Phillips, T., Lect. on hist. and principles of, 1833.

Rembrandt, Œuvre de, (Blanc).

Reynolds, Sir J., Literary Works, 1835.

Ruskin, Modern Painters, 1835–60.

Sainsbury, W. N., Rubens's life, 1859.

Society of Antiquaries: Historical Paintings, 1770, 78, 81.

Soc. of Pai. in Water colors, 1836, 58.

South Kensington Museum, 1860.

Spooner, Dict. of Painters, 1853.

Traité de la Peinture, 1708.

Tuckerman, H. T., Artist Life, 1847.

Vasari, Lives of the most eminent painters, 1850–52.

Waagen, Treas. of Art in G. Britain, 1857.

Walpole, H., Works, Anecdotes of, 1798.

Ware, W., Lectures on Allston, 1852.

Whittock, Decorative Painter's Guide, 1841.

Wornum, R. N., Epochs of, 1847.

See Drawing; Fine Arts.

Paintings, Catalogues and Descriptions of. Amer. Art Union, 1852.

Amer. Exhib. of British Art, 1857. P. 1015.

Apsley House, Lond. P. 489.

Auction Sales, Catalogues, N. Y., P. 499.

Bangs, Brother & Co., N. Y., 1850.

Banvard, Holy Land, 1852. P. 1015.

Bayne's Europe, Panorama, 1849. P. 489.

Belmont Exhibition, N. Y., 1857. P. 1015.

Brewer's Mammoth Cave, etc. P. 489.

Bryan Gallery, N. Y., 1832. P. 499.

Paleontology (continued).
Koninck, Monogr. des genres Productus et Chonetes, 1847.
Lea, I., Papers, 1855–65, on the genus Unio.
" Fossils from the Sandstone.
Mantell, Medals of creation, 1853.
" Petrifactions, 1851.
" Geol. and Foss. of Sussex, 1827.
Martin, W., Knowledge of Extraneous Fossils, 1809.
Megatherium Cuvieri, (Ward), 1864.
Mitchill, S. L., Organic Remains, Cat. of, 1826.
Owen, R., Fossil Reptilia, 1853–64.
" The extinct sloth.
" Palæontographical Soc. Pub.
" Fossil mammalia in Darwin's Zoöl. of the Beagle.
Page's Geology, advanced text book.
Palæontographical Soc., Publications, 1848–70.
Parkinson, Oryctology, 1822.
" Exam. of Mineral Remains, 1820.
Phillips, J., Life on the Earth, 1860.
Pritchard, A., History of Infusoria, 1841.
Ray, Discourses, 1721.
Richardson, J., Foss. mammals of voy. of the Herald, 1854.
Soc. d'Emul. de Montbéliard, Foss. Jurassiques, 1860.
Ward, Casts of fossils.
Warren, J. C, Mastodon giganteus, 1842.
" Mastodon Skeleton, 1855.
Woodward, S. P., Manual of the Mollusca, 1851.
See Geology; Mineralogy.

Paleontology, of Particular Countries. Barrande, Graptolites de Bohéme, 1850.
Bosquet, Fossiles de Limburg.
Brander, G., Hampshire Foss., 1829.
Braun, Verzeichniss der..zu Bayreuth befindlichen Petrefacten, 1840.
Bush, Fossils of the crag.
Conrad, T. A., Fossil shells from the Andes.
" Tert. Form. of N. America, 1832.
Crawfurd, Fossils in Ava, 1830.
Davidson, Fossil brachiopoda, 1863.
Dawson, J. W., Air breathers, coal format. of Nova Scotia, 1863.
" Devonian flora, N. E. Amer.
" Devonian rocks of N. Scotia.
" Precarb. flora of Maine and N. Scotia.

Paleontology, of Particular Countries (continued).
Deane, J., Ichnographs, Mass., 1861.
Edwards, F. E., Eocene Mollusca, Eng., 1849.
Edwards, H. M., Recherches sur les Polypiers, 1848, 49.
" British Fossil Corals, 1850–1853.
Forbes, E., Echinodermata of Brit. Tertiaries, 1852.
Goldfuss, Petrefacta Germaniæ, 1826–1833.
Great Britain, Geol. Survey: Memoirs, 1846–48, 49–66.
Hall, J., Castoroides Ohioensis, 1846. P. 4° 3.
Haughton, S., Fossil plants of Devonian rocks.
" Granites of Ireland, 1858.
" Cyclostigma, 1859.
" Fossils from Arctic regions, 1859.
Hisinger, Lethæa Suecica, 1837.
Hodgson, W. B., Megatherium of Georgia, 1846.
Humboldt, Pétrifications en Amérique.
Jones, T. R., Entomostraca of Cretac. formation, 1849.
" Fossil Estheriæ, 1862.
King, W., Permian Fossils of Eng., 1850.
Koch, Missourium Theristocaulodon, 1843. P. 273.
Lea, I., Fossil Footmarks, Pottsville, Pa., 1855.
" Mollusk from Red Sandstone, 1855.
Leidy, Ancient Fauna of Nebraska.
" Extinct mammalian fauna of Dakota and Nebraska, (Ac. of Nat. Sci.), 1869.
" Cretaceous reptiles, U. S., Smithson. Contr., xiv.
Lindley, Fossil Flora of G. B., 1831–33.
Lycett, Mollusca of the Oolite, 1863.
Mantell, Fossils of Sussex, 1827.
" Fossils of the South Downs, 1822.
Mass., Hitchcock's Ichnology, 1858.
Meek, New Genera, Nebraska, 1857. P. 551.
Meek and Hayden, Of the Upper Missouri, 1856, Smithson. Contr. xix.
Miller, H., Cruise of the Betsey, 1858.
Morris, J., Mollusca from the great Oölite, 1853.
New York Nat. Hist., Palæontology, 1854–69.
Owen, R., Brit. Foss. Reptiles and Mammalia, 1849–69.
Palæontographical Society, Publication, Lond., 1848–70.

Paleontology, of Particular Countries (continued).
Phillips, J., Fossils of Cornwall, Devon, 1841.
Sharpe, Mollusca, Engl., in the chalk, 1856.
Warren, J. C., Conn. Sandstones, 1854.
Wood, S. V., Crag Mollusca, Eng., 1849–55.
Wright, Oölitic echinodermata.
Wyman, Fos. Mammals, S. America, 1849–52.

Palermo, Sicily. Amari, Vespro Siciliano, 1843.
Hager, Picture of, 1800.
Mortillaro, Guida, 1836.
Mount-Edgcumbe, Revolution in 1848.
See Sicily.

Palestine. Bibliotheca Sacra, Papers on Geog. of, 1845–60.
Coleman, L., Geog. and Atlas of Holy Land, 1871.
Early Travels in Palestine, 1848.
Edwards, H., Colonization of, 1846.
Hahn-Hahn, Letters from the Holy Land, 1849.
Headley, J. T., Sacred mountains, 1852.
Henniker, Visit to Mt. Sinai and Jerusalem, 1823.
Ingraham, Index to map of.
La Brocquière, Travels in 1432–33.
Macgregor, Rob Roy on the Jordan, 1869.
Millard, Tr. in Petra and Holy Land, 1841, 2.
Montague, E. P., Exped. to the Dead Sea, 1849.
Newman, J. P., Dan to Bersheba, 1864.
Olin, Tr. in Egypt and Holy Land, 1843.
Osborn, H. S., Palestine, 1859.
Robinson, E., Bibl. Researches, 1838.
" Later Researches, 1852.
" Depression of the Jordan, Bibliot. Sacra, 1848.
" Geography of, 1865.
Saulcy, F. De., Journey in, 1854.
Schwarz, Rabbi, Geography and Hist. of, 1850.
Seaton's Map of.
Stanley, Sinai and Palestine, 1857.
Strauss, Helon's Pilgrimage, 1824.
Thomson, W. M., Land and the Book, 1857.
Upham, T. C., Letters from, 1855.
Wilson, W. R., Travels in, 1847.
See Dead Sea; Jerusalem; Syria; Turkey.

Paley, W. Meadley, G. W., Memoirs of, 1809, B. C.

Palfrey, W. Palfrey, J. G., Life of, (Sparks, 17).

Palissy, B. Morley, H., Life of, 1853.

Palliser, H. Hunt, R. M., Life of, 1844.

Palm, Van der. Hengel, Meritorum commemoratio, 1840. P. 33, B. C.

Palmer, Mrs. Cowper, W., Sermon on, 1845.

Palmer, W. Life and Career, 1856.

Palmer, W. B. L., Few Words on, 1856.

Palmerston, Lord. Bulwer-Lytton, Life of, 1871.
Palmerston, Two tours, 1815, 1818.

Palmyra. Porter, J. L., Researches, 1855.
Prescot, B., Sculptures at, 1830.
See Antiquities; Syria.

Palmyra, N. Y. Eaton, H., Early History of, 1857.

Pamphlets: Reprints. Collection of tracts on the Revolution of 1688, 3 v., f°.
Fugitive Pieces, 1765, 2 v.
Harleian Miscellany, 1808, 11. 12 v.
Masères, F., Select tracts......Wars, Charles I., 1815, 2 v.
" Occasional Essays collected, 1809.
Miscellanea Scotica, 1818, 3 v.
Morgan, J., Phœnix Britannicus, 1732, 2 v.
Oldys, Essay on Pamphlets. *See* Morgan.
Pamphleteer, The, 1813–28, 25 v.
Phenix, The, 1707, 8, 2 v.
Phenix, The, Gowans, 1835.
Remembrancer, The, Almon, 1775–84, 18 v.
Somers, Collection, (W. Scott), 1815, 13 v.
See Bibliography.

Pamphlets, New York State Library collection, 2,000 vols. Miscellaneous in their contents:
American authors, volumes, 2, 4, 6, 8, 9, 13, 18, 50, 52, 56, 76, 81, 91, 99, 103, 194, 198, 199, 220, 227, 230, 231, 260, 261, 266, 269, 454, 522, 576, 578, 580, 581, 587, 615–618, 636–638, 736, 741, 742, 744, 750, 751, 753, 861, 863, 1016, 1025, 1104, 1110, 1113, 1114, 1349, 1350, 1781. B. C. 5, 24, 43, etc.
British, vols. 706, 720, 721, 729, 762, 1041, 1110, 1626–1628. *See* Great Britain.
Dutch, vols. 623, 966, 1782. *See* Dutch.
French, vols. 523, 747, 748, 1783. *See* France.
German, vols. 609, 842, 991, 999, 1109, 1784.
Italian, vols. 661, 992, 1785.
See also, for others under the various subjects.

Perfumes. Farina, Eau de Cologne, 1830. P. 614.
Morfit, Manuf. of perfumery, 1847.
Rimmel, Book of, Lond., 1867.

Periodicals. *See* Scientific; Medical; Education; Temperance, etc.

Periodicals, History of. Camusat, Hist. des Journaux, 1734.
Eichhorn, Geschichte der litteratur, 1805–12.
Fifty Years' Recollections, 1837.
Follett, Press West. New York, 1847.
Namur, Bibliog. bibliologique, 1838.
Nichols, Lit. Anecd., v. 8, 1812.
Timperley, Encyc. of typ. anecd., 1842.
See Newspapers; Societies for Printing.

Periodicals, American, Literary and Miscellaneous. Albany Bouquet, 1835.
Albany Quarterly, 1832, 3.
Albion, N. Y., 1849–1861.
Alleghany Magazine, Meadville, 1816.
American Apollo, Boston, 1791.
American Eclectic, N. Y., 1841, 42.
American Farmer's Mag., 1858.
American Freemason's Magazine, 1859, 1860.
American Laborer, 1842.
Am. Literary Mag., (Sprague), 1847.
Am. Magazine, Bost., 1743–1746.
Am. Magazine, N. Y., 1787, 88.
Am. Mag. and Repos., (Wood), 1841, 1842.
Am. Mag. of Useful Knowl., Boston, 1834–37.
Am. Masonic Record, Albany, 1827-31.
Am. Monthly Mag., (Herbert, Benjamin), 1832–38.
Am. Monthly Mag., (Willis), 1829–31.
Am. Monthly Mag., (Holley), 1817–18.
Am. Mor. and Sent. Mag., N. Y., 1797.
Am. Museum, (Carey), 1787–92.
Am. Museum, Balt., 1838–9.
Am. Pioneer, Cinc., 1842–3.
Am. Pub. Circular, N. Y., 1855–59.
Am. Pub. Circular and Lit. Gaz., (Childs), 1863–71.
Am. Quar. Register, (Stryker), 1848–1851.
Am. Quar. Review, Phil'a, 1827–37.
Am. Register, (Brown), 1807–10.
Am. Register, Phil'a, 1817, 18.
Am. Review, (Brown), N. Y., 1801-2.
Am. Universal Mag., Phil'a, 1797–8.
Am. Whig Review, N. Y., 1845–52.
Analectic Mag., Phil'a, 1813–20.
Anglo-American Magazine, 1852–55, Toronto.

Periodicals, American, Literary and Miscellaneous (continued).
Antiquarian, Lansingburgh, 1845–47.
Anti-Slavery Record, N. Y., 1835–37.
Archivo Americano, Buénos-Aires, 1849, 50.
Arcturus, N. Y., 1846.
Atlantic Mag., N. Y, 1824, 25.
Atlantic Monthly, N. Y., 1857–70.
Atlantis, Buffalo, Germ., 1857. P. 523.
Ballou's Pictorial, Boston, 1855–59.
Baltimore Magazine, 1807.
Baltimore Phœnix, 1841–42.
Baltimore Repertory, 1811.
Banker's Magazine, N. Y., 1846–65.
Belding's North Western Review, 1857, 1858. P. 533.
Belles-Lettres Repos., N. Y., 1819–21.
Bibliot. Canadienne, 1823.
Book-buyer, (Scribner), 1867–71.
Boston Magazine, 1783–86.
Boston Monthly Magazine, 1825.
Boston Museum, 1850.
Branch's Daily Hand, N. Y., 1859.
Broadway Journal, (Poe), 1845.
Brownson's Quarterly Review, 1844–1864.
Bryant's Am. Merchant, 1859.
Carey's Library of Choice Lit., (covers), 1836.
Casket, The, Phil'a, 1832–6.
Cincinnati Miscellany, (Cist), 1844–46.
College Courant, N. Haven, 1868-71.
Colonizationist, Bost., 1834.
Columbian Magazine, Phil'a, 1786, 87, 1789.
Columbian Phenix, Bost., 1800.
Comet, The, Bost., 1811, 12.
Companion and Weekly Miscel., Balt., 1804–5.
Continental Monthly, 1862–64.
Corsair, The, 1839, 40.
Cozzen's Wine Press, 1854–61.
Crayon, The, N. Y., 1855–60.
Critic, The, Leggett, 1828, 29.
Criterion, The, N. Y., 1855-6.
Cronica politica, Lima, 1827.
De Bow's Review, N. Orleans, 1846-61.
Delaware Register, 1838-9.
Democratic Review, N. Y., 1838–52.
Eclectic Magazine, 1844–60.
Eclectic Museum, 1843.
Emblem: Odd Fellows' Mag., 1856–7.
Emerald, The, Boston, 1806, 7, 8.
Emerson's Magazine, N. Y., 1858.
Family Magazine, N. Y., 1834–40.
Fantasque, Le, Québec, 1848–9.
Farmer, J., Collections and Monthly Lit. Jour., 1822–24.

Periodicals, American, Literary and Miscellaneous (continued).

Farmer's, Mech., Manuf. and Sportsman's Mag., N. Y., 1847.
Farmer, The, and Mechanic, N. Y., 1847–50.
Fort Edward Institute Mag., 1857.
Friend, Albany, 1815.
Friend of Progress, 1864, 5.
Gazette Française, Phila., 1846.
Gen. Repository and Review, Camb., 1812, 13.
Genius of Univ. Emancipa., (Lundy), 1830.
Gentleman's Mag., Burton's, 1838.
Gleaner, 1801.
Gleason's Line of Battle Ship, 1858–9.
Gleason's Pictorial. *See* Ballou.
Green Mountain Repository, 1832.
Harper's New Monthly Mag., 1850–59.
Historical Magazine, N. Y., 1858–70.
Hive, Northampton, 1804.
Home Monthly, (Arey), Buffalo, 1859–1861.
Illustrated News, N. Y., 1851, 53.
Independent Reflector, N. Y., 1752.
International Magazine, New York, 1850–52.
Iron Platform, 1863–64.
Knickerbocker, The, New York, 1833–1855.
Knoxiana, Galesburg, Ill., 1851–53.
Laborer, The, Gouverneur, N. Y., 1853.
Lady's Book, 1834.
Ladies' Companion, 1838–44.
Lit. and Sci. Repository, N. Y., 1820–1822.
Literary Gazette, 1821, Phil'a.
Literary Magazine, 1803–08, Phil'a.
Literary Miscellany, Cambridge, 1805, 1806.
Literary Union, Syracuse, N. Y., 1849–1850.
Literary World, New York, 1847–53.
Literary and Phil. Repertory, Middlebury, Vt., 1812–14.
Littell's Living Age, Boston, 1844–63.
Long Island Journal of Phil., 1825.
Maryland Colonization Journal, 1841–1843.
Massachusetts Magazine, 1789–95.
Massachusetts Quarterly Review, 1847–1850.
Mechanic's Journal, Albany, 1846–7.
Metropolitan Magazine, N. Y., 1836–1841.
Merchants' Magazine, N. Y., (Hunt), 1839–71.
Military and Nav. Mag. of the U. S., 1833–36.

Periodicals, American, Literary and Miscellaneous (continued).

Military Gazette, N. Y., 1860.
Minerva, The, N. Y., 1822–25.
Mirror of Taste and Dram. Censor, Philadelphia, 1810–11.
Monthly Anthology and Boston Review, 1804–11.
Monthly Chronicle of Events, Boston, 1840–42.
Monthly Magazine, C. B. Brown, N. Y., 1799, 1800.
Monthly Magazine, E. Sargent, 1843.
Monthly Military Repository, N. Y., 1796, 7.
Monthly Recorder, New York, 1813.
Monthly Register, Mag. and Rev., Bristed, 1807, 8.
Monthly Repository, New York, 1831–1834.
Monthly Review, Charleston, 1806.
Montreal Museum, 1832.
Moonshine, Baltimore, 1807.
Museum of For. Lit. and Sci., Phil'a, 1836–46.
Nation, The, N. Y., 1866–68.
National Government Journal, 1823, 4.
National Magazine, Baltimore, 1830–1831.
National Magazine, A. Stevens, N.Y., 1852.
National Quar. Review, N. Y., 1860–1866.
National Magazine, Lyon, Richmond, 1799.
Naval Magazine, N. Y., 1836, 7.
New England Family Mag., 1845, 6.
New England Mag., Boston, 1831–35.
New Englander, New Haven, 1842–71.
New England Quarterly Mag., 1802.
New Hampshire Repository, 1846.
New Haven Gazette and Conn. Mag., 1786.
New Mirror of Literature, Morris and Willis, 1843, 44.
N. Y. Periodicals of 1851. Specim.
N. Y. Periodicals of 1855. Specim.
N. Y. Literary Gazette, J. G. Brooks, 1826.
N. Y. Literary Journal, 1819–21.
N. Y. Magazine, 1790, 92-95, 97.
N. Y. Magazine, No. 1, 1814, Hardie.
N. Y. Mirror, 1823-45; wanting vol. 4 and 6.
N. Y. Missionary Magazine, 1800–03.
N. Y. Quarterly, 1852–55.
N. Y. Review, 1825, 26, 1837–42.
N. Y. State Mechanic, Albany, 1842, 1843.
N. Y. Visitor, 1838–40.
N. Y. Weekly Magazine, 1795.

Periodicals, American, Literary and Miscellaneous (continued).

Nightingale, The, Boston, 1796.
Nineteenth Century, N. Y., 1848, 49.
North American Magazine, Fairfield, 1833–38.
North American Review, Boston, 1815–1871.
Norton's Literary and Educ. Register, 1854.
Northern Light, Albany, 1842–44.
Northwestern Journal of Ed., 1850.
Observer, 1807, Baltimore.
Observador Lusitano, 1815.
Odd Fellows' Literary Magazine, 1848–1849.
Olden Time, Pittsburgh, 1846.
Old, The, Guard, N. Y., 1863–66.
Onward, (M. Reid), 1869.
Opal, The, Utica Asylum, 1852–59.
Ordeal, Boston, 1809.
Orion, Richards, Georgia, 1842–44.
Orphan's Friend, Balt., 1804.
Parthenon, N. Y., 1827.
Parthenon, Union Coll., 1832–34.
Pastime, Schenectady, 1807.
Patriota Brasileiro, 1830.
Penn'a Jour. of Pris. Discipline, 1845–1857.
Periodicals, Miscellaneous, 1825–54.
Philadelphia Magazine, 1799.
Phil'a Monthly Magazine, 1798.
Phil'a Repertory, 1810, 11.
Phil'a Repository, 1802–05.
Phrenological Journal, N. Y., 1865–1867.
Pioneer, San Francisco, May, 1855.
Plough, Loom and Anvil, N. Y., 1848–1857.
Political Economist, (Carey), 1824.
Polyanthos, Boston, 1805–14.
Popular Educator, N. Y., 1853–4.
Portfolio : Dennie, 1801–27.
Portico, Baltimore, 1816–18.
Prisoner's Friend, Bost., 1848–57.
Provincial, 1852, 53, Halifax, N. S.
Putnam's Magazine, N. Y., 1868–69.
Putnam's Monthly Mag., N. Y., 1853–1857.
Rafinesque's Atlantic Journal, 1832–3.
Rambler's Magazine, N. Y., 1810.
Revue du nouveau monde, N. Y., 1849–1850.
Rhode Island Lit. Repos., 1814–15.
Round Table, N. Y., 1866–68.
Rural Magazine, Hartford, 1819.
Rural Repository, Hudson, N. Y., 1824–51.
Rural Visiter, Burlington, N. J., 1810.
Saturday Magazine, Phil'a, 1821–22.
Saturday Courier, 1838–48.
Silk Grower, Phil'a, 1839.
Southern Liter. Messenger, 1835–1848, 1850–2, 54, 55.
Southern Quarterly Review, 1842–56.
Spirit of the Fair, N. Y., 1864.
Stranger, The, Albany, 1814.
To-Day, Boston, 1852.
Truth's Advocate, Cincin., 1828.
Union Monthly, Albany, 1867.
U. S. Democratic Review, 1856–59.
U. S. Literary Gazette, Bost., 1824–26.
U. S. Magazine, Newark, 1794.
U. S. Magazine of Science, Arts, etc., 1854.
U. S. Review, Phil'a, 1834.
U. S. Review, N. Y., 1853–55.
U. S. Rev. and Gazette, Boston, 1826–1827.
U. S. Service Mag., N. Y., 1864–66.
Universal Asylum and Columb. Mag., Phil'a, 1790–92.
University Quarterly, N. Haven, 1860–1861.
Virginia Hist. Register, 1848–53.
Waldie's Select Lib., (covers), 1836–38.
Weal Reaf, Salem, Ms., 1860.
Weekly Register, Lynchburg, Va., 1864.
Western Gleaner, Pittsburgh, 1814.
Western Monthly Review, Cincinnati, 1827–29.
Western Messenger, Louisville, 1837.
Western Quarterly Review, Cincin., 1849.
Western Review, Lexington, Ky., 1819–1821.
Williams Quarterly, 1857–59.
Worcester Magazine, 1786–88.
Yale Literary Magazine, 1842, 45–58.
Yankee Doodle, 1846, 7.
Zodiac, The, Albany, 1836.
See Scientific Journals; Education; Agriculture; Arts, etc.; Registers; Almanacs.

Periodicals, American, Religious.

Adviser, The, v. 3, Vt., 1811.
Alleghany Magazine, Meadville, 1816.
Am. and For. Chr. Union Monthly, N. Y., 1850–68.
Amer. Baptist Magazine, Bost., 1817–1832.
Amer. Baptist Memorial, 1855, 56.
Amer. Christian Record, 1860.
Amer. Church Monthly, N. Y., 1857, 1858.
Amer. Educ. Soc., Am. Quar. Reg., Bost., 1829–43.

Periodicals, American, Religious (continued).

Amer. Home Miss. Soc.: Home Missionary, 1829–60.

Amer. Miss. Register, N. Y., 1822–25.

Amer. Quar. Church Review, N. Haven, 1848–71.

Amer. Quar. Observer, 1833–34.

Amer. Soc.: Jewish Chronicle, 1845–1847.

Amer. Sunday S. Magazine, 1823, 27.

Amer. Unit. Assoc'n, Quar. Journ., 1854–59.

" Monthly Journal, 1860–69.

Associate Presb. Mag., Albany, 1838–1842.

Baltimore Lit. and Relig. Mag., 1838–1841.

Baptist Memorial, 1848, 51. *See* Am. Baptist.

Baptist Missionary Magazine, 1845,6,7.

Baptist Preacher, 1847–8.

Biblical Repertory, Princeton, 1829–1871.

Biblical (American) Repository, Andover and N. Y., 1831–48.

Bibliotheca Sacra, Andover, 1844–60.

Brownson's Quar. Review, 1844–64.

Chicago Record, 1857–62.

Christian Advocate, (Presb.), 1823–34.

Christian Disciple, Bost., 1813–23.

Christian Examiner, Boston, 1827–69.

Christian Herald, N. Y., 1816.

Christian History, Prince, 1743-45.

Christian Journal, Swords, 1822–24.

Christian Magazine, N. Y., 1806–11.

Christian Magazine, Geneva, N. Y., 1833–34.

Christian Messenger, N. Y., 1832–35.

Christian Monitor, N. Y., 1812–13.

Christian Observatory, Bost., 1847–50.

Christian Palladium, Albany, 1847–49.

Christian Review, Bost., 1837.

Christian's, Scholar's and Farmer's Mag., N. J., 1789.

Churchman's Magazine, Hartford, 1821, 22.

Churchman's Monthly Magazine, N. Haven, 1804–11.

Churchman's Monthly Mag., N. Y., 1854–59.

Churchman's Repository, Mass., 1820.

Church Record, Hawks, 1840–2.

Church Review. *See* Amer. Quarterly.

Circular, The, Oneida Community, 1851–68.

Columbian Register, Washington, 1828.

Congregationalist Quarterly, Boston, 1859–69.

Connec. Evangel. Mag., 1800–8.

Correspondent, The, N. Y., 1827–29.

Periodicals, American, Religious (continued).

Cry from the North, Bost., 1827, 8.

Danville Quarterly Review, 1861, 62.

Enquirer for Truth, Canton, Ohio, 1827.

Episcopal Magazine, Phila., 1820, 1.

Evangelical Guardian, N. Y., 1817.

Evang. Record, Lexington, Ky., 1812, 13, imp.

Evangelical Review, 1855–60.

Evergreen, The, New Haven, 1844–53.

Five Points House of Industry, Record, 1858–9.

Foreign Miss. Chronicle, 1833–42.

Free Inquirer, N. Y., 1829–30.

Gospel Herald, 1821–26.

Guardian, The, N. Haven, 1819, 20.

Halcyon Luminary, N. Y., 1812–13.

Home, School and Church, Phila., 1850–59.

Hopkinsian Magazine, 1831–2.

Lit. and Evang. Mag., Richmond, 1826–28.

Lit. and Theological Review, N. Y., (Woods), 1834–39.

Magazine of the Ref. Dutch Church, N. Brunswick, 1826–30.

Meth. Conference, Miss'y Notices, 1816–25.

Methodist Magazine, N. Y., 1822–27.

Methodist Quar. Review, N. Y., 1841, 42, 45, 48–61, 63.

Missionary Herald, Boston, 1821–71.

Monthly Relig. Mag., Bost., 1844–54.

New Brunswick Review, 1855.

New Englander, N. Haven, 1842–71.

N. Y. Ecclesiologist, 1848–53.

Panoplist, Boston, 1806–20.

Perfectionist, The, J. H. Noyes, 1843–1845.

Pittsburgh, Pa., Recorder, 1822–24.

Plain Truth, Rochester, 1829.

Presbyterial Critic, Balt., 1855, 6.

Presbyterial Reporter, Milwaukee, 1852.

Presb. Church, Home and Foreign Record, 1851.

" Missionary Chronicle, 1833–49.

Presbyterian Mag., Janeway, Phila., 1821, 22.

Presbyterian Magazine, Van Rensselaer, Phila., 1855–58.

Presb. Quar. Review, Phil'a, 1853–62.

Presbytery Reporter, Alton, Ill., 1851–1865.

Prot. Episc. Church, Spirit of Missions, 1836–62.

Protestant Quarterly Review, Phil'a, 1850–53.

Periodicals, American, Religious (continued).
Quar. Christian Spectator, 1829–39.
Quarterly Theol. Magazine, Burlington, N. J., 1813–14.
Quarterly Theol. Review, Ely, Phil'a, 1818, 19.
Radical, The, Boston, 1866, 67.
Religious Intelligencer, New Haven, 1816–28.
Religious Magazine, Bost., 1828–29.
Religious Repository, Concord, N. H., 1808.
Shekinah, The, Brittan, 1831–33.
Sacred Circle, N. Y., 1855.
Southern Meth. Pulpit, 1846–50.
Spirit of the Pilgrims, Bost., 1828–33.
Theol. and Lit. Jour., (Lord), N. Y., 1848–60.
Theol. Magazine, N. Y., 1795–97.
Theol. Review, Balt., 1822.
Tiffany's Monthly, 1856–59.
Unitarian, The, Whitman, 1834.
United Breth. Miss'y Intelligencer, 1828, 48.
Universalist Quarterly, 1851.
Universalist Union, 1837.
Utica Christian Repository, 1822–26.
Vehicle, or Chr. Magazine, N. Y., 1814.
Virginia Evang. Mag., 1818–20.
Western Messenger, Louisville, 1837.
Western New York Bap. Mag., 1823.

Periodicals, British, Literary and Religious. Aldine Mag., 1839.
Anti-Jacobin Review, 1798–1804.
Archæologist, The, Lond., 1842.
Art Journal, Lond., 1847–69.
Athenæum Journal, Lond., 1828–63, 1870, 71.
Athenian Gazette, 1691.
Baptist Annual Register, 1795.
Bee, or Litt. Intell., Edinburgh, 1791–1793.
Belle (La) Assemblée, 1810–33.
Bentley's Miscellany, Lond., 1839–42.
Bentley's Quarterly Review, 1859.
Blackwood's Edinb. Magazine, 1817–71.
British Critic, 1793–1815.
British Mag. and Reg. of Eccl. Intel., 1832–40, 43–45, 48.
Campbell's For. Monthly Mag., 1842–4.
Chamber's Edin. Journal, 1832–60.
Chimney Sweeper's Friend, 1825.
Christian Moderator, 1826.
Christian Observer, Lond., 1802–40, 43.
Christian Physician, 1836.
Christian Remembrancer, 1819–27.
Christian Witness, 1845.
Church and State Review, 1862–64.

Periodicals, British, Literary and Religious (continued).
Church Miss'y Intelligencer, 1855–58.
Classical Journal, 1826–28.
Colonial Mag. and Commercial Mar. Journal, 1840–42.
Companion to the Newspaper, Lond., 1833–6.
Congreg. Magazine, Lond., 1818–44.
Constitutional Magazine, Lond., 1768.
Cook, (Eliza), Journal, 1849–53.
Critical Review, 1756–90.
Director, The, Dibdin, 1807.
Dolman's Magazine, 1847, 8.
Dublin Review, 1836–70.
Dublin Univ. Mag., 1833–69.
Eclectic Review, 1805–46.
Edinburgh Review, 1802–71.
Edinburgh Monthly Review, 1819–21.
European Magazine, 1784, 86, 97, 99.
Evangelical Magazine, London, 1793–1854.
Exchange, The, 1862.
Fine Arts Quarterly Review, 1863, 67.
Fisher's Colonial Magazine, 1842–45.
Foreign Quarterly Review, 1827–46.
Fortnightly Review, 1865–71.
Fraser's Magazine, 1850–61, 64–69.
Gentleman's Magazine, 1731–71.
Gentleman's and London Mag., 1759. 1765, 67–72.
Gospel Missionary, London, 1854.
History of the works of the learned, 1699–1710.
History of the works of the learned, 1737–38.
Home Miss'y Mag., Lond., 1820.
Household Words, London, 1850–56.
Hogg's Weekly Instructor, Lon., 1848, 1849.
Howitt's Journal of Lit., 1847, 8.
Illust. Lond. News, 1842–60.
Illust. News of the World, 1858–6
Imperial Mag., 1829.
Irish Presbyterian, 1854–8.
Knight's Penny Magazine, 1860.
Literary and Biog. Mag., Lond., 1788–1794.
Literary Chronicle, 1823.
Literary Gazette, 1818–51, 58–60.
London Magazine, 1732–85.
London Magazine, 1820–29.
London Review, 1777, 78.
London Review, 1835, 36.
Marlborough Magazine, 1848.
Mercurius Politicus, De Foe, 1716–20.
Microcosm, 1788.
Monthly Lit. and Sci. Lecturer, 1850
Monthly Magazine, 1799

Periodicals, British, Literary and Religious (continued).
Monthly Miscellany, Dec., 1708.
Monthly Review, London, 1749–1806.
Museum, The, London, 1746–7.
National Review, Lond., 1855–60.
New Miscellany, London, 1737, 38, 39.
New Monthly Magazine, 1822–25.
North British Review, 1844–71.
Notes and Queries, Lond., 1849–71.
Penny Magazine, 1832–45.
People's Journal, 1846–48.
People's and Howitt's Journal.
Philadelphian Magazine, (Stearns), 1788, 9.
Political Magazine, 1781–7.
Political Register and New books, 1767–1769.
Portfolio, The, 1835–7.
Poor Man's Guardian, 1847.
Punch and Lond. Charivari, 1841–58.
Quarterly Review, Lond., 1809–71.
Register of the Arts, Lond., 1824–32.
Rehearsals, The, 1704–08.
Repertory of Arts, 1794–1806.
Repertory of Inventions, 1830–48.
Retrospective Review, Lond., 1820-1828, 53, 54.
Theol. Repository, London, 1773–88.
United Service Journal, 1829–60.
Westminster Magazine, 1777.
Westminster Review, 1824–71.
Whisperer, The, 1770.
Willis, G., Current Notes, 1854–62.

Periodicals, European, etc. Algemeene Konst-en Letter-Bode, 1793.
Algemeene Vaderl. Letter-Oefeningen, 1783.
Alliance Evangélique, Genève, 1850.
Ami de l'Enfance, Paris, 1835–57.
Amsterdam, Gazette, 1744–69.
Annalen der Verbr. des Glaubens, 1857–1859.
Annales de la prop. de la foi, 1828–52.
Annales d'hygiène, Paris, 1829–71.
Annuaire de l'Instruction Publique, Paris, 1851–58.
Archives du Christianisme, 1840.
Archives du Magnétisme animal, 1820–1823.
Bernard, J. *See* Nouvelles.
Bibliothèque Américaine, Paris, 1807.
Bibliothèque Britannique, La Haye, 1733–1746.
Bibliothèque Italique, Genève, 1728–1734.
Chinese Repository, Macao, 1832–51.
Eco di Savonarola, Lon., 1847.
Friend, Honolulu, 1848.

Periodicals, European, etc. (cont'd).
Gazette Litt. de l'Europe, Amst., 1768–70.
Hawaiian Spectator, 1838.
Indo-Chinese Gleaner, 1818–9.
Italia del popolo, Losanna, 1849–50.
Janus Verrezen, Utrecht, 1787–95.
Journal Asiatique, Paris, 1822–67.
Letter-kundig Genootschap, Mengelingen, 1843–51.
Literarisch Verein, Nürnberg, Jahresbericht, 1841–65.
Maandelyke Uittreksels, Amst., 1716, 67, 70.
Mercure de France, 1756–67.
Merg der Akad. Verhandelingen, 1738.
Middelaer, De, 1840–43.
Minerve Française, 1818–20.
Mnemosyne, Leyden, 1852–61.
Museum Hist. Phil. Theol., Bremæ, 1728, 9.
Nouvelles de la Répub. des Lettres, Bernard, 1700–10.
Pastorale Brieven, 1686, 87.
Philosooph, De, 1766–69.
Polytechnische Centralhalle, 1851–56.
Post van den Neder-Rhijn, 1781–87.
Questions traitées, 1639–41.
Revue Anecdotique, 1851.
Revue Bibliog. des Pays Bas, 1822–30.
Revue Contemporaine, 1852–64, wants 1856 and 7, 62.
Revue de bibliog., Paris, 1840–45.
Revue de l'Instr. publique, 1842–58.
Revue des Deux Mondes, 1851–70.
Revue Encyclopédique, Paris, 1820–31.
Revue Independante, Leroux, Sand, 1841–4.
Tijdschrift toegewijd aan het Zeewezen, 1830–35.

Periodicals. Odd Numbers of, Pamphlets, vols. 264, 265, 533, 708, 712, 724, 1629, 1630.

Perkins, J. H. Channing, W. H., Memoir of, 1851.

Perkins, M. A. Duncan, A. G., Fun. Sermon on.

Perkins, T. H. Cary, Memoir of, 1856.

Perry, O. H. Calvert, G. H., Orat., Battle of L. Erie, 1854.
Irving, W., Spanish papers, v. 2.
Mackenzie, A. S., Life of, 1835.
Niles, J. M., Life of, 1821.
Perry, O. H., Documents, 1821.
Perry, Statue inaug., 1860.
See Erie, Lake, Battle of.

Perry, Lt. Stephens, W. W., C. Martial of, 1855.

Philips, R. Dean, A., Discourse, 1844. P. 1464.

Phillipopolis, Turkey. Constantinos, Encheiridion, 1814.

Hackett, H. B., Tour to, Bibliot. Sac., 1860.

Phillips, Miss E. Parsons, T., Sermon on.

Phillips, S. Tappan, D., Disc., Fun. of, 1802. P. 554.

Taylor, J. L., Memoir of, 1856.

Phillips, W. Speeches and Letters, 1870.

Stowe's Men of the Time, 1868.

Phillpott. *See* Philpot.

Phillpotts, Bp. Writings, (collection), 3 v.

Edinburgh Review, Rejoinder, 1852. P. 331.

Philology. *See* Bibliography; Classical; Ethnology; Languages; Orient. Lit.

Philomena, S. Memoria, 1835.

Philosophy. Abélard, Ouvrages inédits, 1836.

Albertus Magnus, Liber Secretorum, 1496.

Ahrens, Das Natur-recht, 1846.

Alletz, Harmonies de l'Intell. humaine, 1845-46.

Aristotle, Metaphysics, (T. Taylor).

Atkinson, H. G., Letters on Man's Nature, 1851.

Averroes, De Substantia Orbis.

Bacon, Lord, Works, 1824, 61.

Bacon, R., Opera inedita, (Chron. G. B.).

Bailey, S., Essays on the pursuit of Truth, 1831. B. C.

Barbay, In Aristot. Phil. Introductio, 1690. B. C.

Barruel, El Viennesi, 1801.

Bates, E., Rural Philosophy, 1803.

Baxter, A., Enquiry on Soul, 1745.

Beale, L. S., Protoplasm, 1870.

Beauvais, Manuel de, 1832.

Bentham, J., Works, 1843.

Berkeley, Bp., Works, 1843.

Bielfield, Elements of Universal Erudition, 1770.

Boerhave, Study of Physick, 1719.

Boëthius, Consolations of, 1811. B. C.

Bouttier, Essai de Phil. Franç., 1844.

Boyle, R., Philosophical Works, 1725.

Brenan, J., Old and new logic, 1838.

Cælius, L., Antiquæ lectiones, 1516.

Chalybäus, H. M., Phil. from Kant to Hegel, 1854.

Chardon, Mélanges, 1812.

Philosophy (continued).

Charma, A., Saint Anselme, 1853.

Cicero, Hist. ant. Philosophiæ, 1782.

Coleridge, S. T., Works, 1854.

Comte, Cours de Philosophie positive, 1830-42.

" Phil. of the Sciences, Lewes, 1853.

" The Positive Philosophy, Martineau, 1854.

Condillac, Traité des Systèmes, 1771.

Condorcet, Œuvres, 1847.

Cory, I. P., Inquiry into objects of, 1833.

Cousin, V., Cours de Philosophie, 1828.

" Introd. to Hist. of, Linberg, 1832.

" Course of Hist. of, Wight, 1852.

" Destiny of Modern Phil.

" Elements of Psychology, Henry, 1834.

Cros, Théorie de l'Homme, 1836.

Cudworth, Intell. System of the Universe, 1837.

Davy, Consolations in travel, 1830.

Defoe, D., World of Cartesius.

Degerando, Hist. comp. des systèmes.

Delavigne, Manuel....au Baccalauréat, 1836.

De Quincey, Writings, 17, 18, 1851-54.

Des Cartes, R., Epistolæ, 1683.

" Principles of, 1853.

" Conduct of the Reason, 1850, 53.

Dick, The Christ. Philosopher, 1831.

Drummond, Sir W., Acad. questions, 1805.

Durfee, J., The Panidea, (Works), 1849.

Enfield, History of Philosophy, 1837.

Essays on Truth, G. Hawley, 1856.

Faber, Thes. Eruditionis Scholast., 1696.

Fichte, Characteristics of the Present Age, 1847.

Field, G., Analogical Philosophy, 1836.

Fischer, P., Beobachtung in Natürlichen Dingen, 1782.

Fishbough, Macrocosm and Microcosm, 1856.

Fleming, W., The Vocabulary of, 1860.

Foxius, De Naturæ Philosophia, 1622.

Franck, A., La Kabbale, 1843.

Girard, Rénovation philosophique, 1838.

Giusti, Corso di Filosofia, 1836.

Green, J. H., Spiritual phil. of Coleridge, 1865.

Grote, G., Companions of Socrates, 1867.

Philosophy (continued).

Gruyer, Du Spiritualisme au xix siècle, 1835.

Hamilton, Bishop, Works, 1809.

Hamilton, Sir W., Discussions on Philosophy, 1852.

" Lectures on Metaphysics, 1859.

Harris, James, Philos. arrangements, 1779.

" Hermes or .. Universal Grammar, 1786.

Hartley, De l'Homme, ses facultés, 1802.

Hazlitt, Essays on the Principles of human action. B. C.

Helvetius, System of nature, 1810.

Hemisterhuis, F., Œuvres philosophiques, 1846.

Iamblichus, De mysteriis.

" On the mysteries, (Taylor).

Jamieson, G., Essentials of, 1859.

Jarves, J. J., Why and What am I? 1857.

Johnson, S., Introduction to, New Lond., 1743.

Jouffroy, T., Philosophical Miscell., 1838. B. C.

Kirwan, R., Metaphys. Essays, 1811.

La Chambre, Système de l'Ame, 1665.

Lewes, Biog. History of, 1857.

McCosh, Typical Forms, 1856.

Malebranche, Search after truth, 1694.

Mansel, H. L., Limits of relig. thought, 1859.

Masson, D., Recent Brit. Philos., 1866.

Marsh, J., Remains of, 1843.

Melancthon, Select. Declamationum tom. 5, 1670.

" Comm. de Anima, 1544.

Mendelssohn, Philosophische Schriften, 1790.

Métaphysique, La, 1753.

Mocenicus, Univ. Instit. ad hom. perfectionem, 1581.

Monestier, Vraie Philosophie, 1774.

More, H., Philos. writings, 1712.

Morell, Hist. of Spec. Phil. in the 19th Cent., 1847.

" Philos. Tendencies of the Age, 1848.

Müller, Chips from a German workshop, 1870.

Murdock, J., Sketches of German Philos., 1843.

Murray, Outlines of Hamilton's Phil., 1871.

Naigeon, Philosophie Anc. et moderne, (Encyc. Méth.).

Neckam, De naturis rerum.

Œrsted, The Soul in Nature, 1852.

Ogilvie, Philosophical Essays, 1816.

Philosophy (continued).

Paine, T., Age of Reason, 1794.

Pamphlets relating to Philosophy, vols. 1542, 1721, 1789.

Paracelsus, Three Books of, 1657.

Park, R., Pantology, 1841.

Pascal, B., Pensées, 1844.

" Thoughts, (Wight), 1859.

Plotinus, Opera, 1492.

" Select works, 1817.

Plutarch, Morals, Goodwin's ed., 1871.

Prantl, Die Gegenwartige Aufgabe der, 1852.

Priestley, J., Discussion of Materialism, 1778.

" Disq. on Matter and Spirit, 1775-82. B. C.

Psychological Speculations, 1827.

Purchot, Institutiones Philosophicæ, 1711.

Rauch, Psychology, 1840.

Riolan, Opuscula, 1602.

Ritter, Hist. of Ancient, 1838.

Schlegel, Weisheit der Indier, 1808.

Sorbière, Lettres, 1660.

Spencer, H., First principles, 1870.

" Principles of Biology, 1866.

" Principles of Psychol., 1855.

Stewart, D., Works, 1855.

Tenneman, Manual of Hist. of, 1852.

Tongiorgi, S., Instit. philosophicæ, N. Y., 1864.

Tyler, S., Progress of Phil., 1858.

Vanuxem, Essay on Ultim. Principles, 1827.

Vincentius, Speculum Morale, 1494.

" Speculum Doctrinale, 1494.

Volney, Les Ruines, 1792. B. C.

Voltaire, Œuvres.

Warden, R. B., View of man and law, 1860.

Westenrieder, V., Von den Nominalisten, 1786.

Whewell, W., Hist. of sci. ideas, 1858.

" Phil. of discovery, 1860.

Wieland, C. M., Socrates out of his senses, 1797.

See God; Logic; Man; Mental Phil.; Moral Phil.; Nature; Science; Soul; Theology.

Philpot, J. Examination of, 1555, (Parker Soc.).

Phipps, Sir W. Pond, E., Life of, 1847.

Sparks's Am. Biog., vol. 7: Life.

Phlegon. Chapman, J., Answer to Sykes, 1735. P. 1272.

Phlegon examined, 1734. P. 336.

Phlegon re-examined, 1735.

Sykes, Diss. on eclipse, 1732.

Whiston, Six dissertations, 1734.

Physiognomy. Brown, R., On truth of, 1807.

Chyromancie, 1619.

Evelyn, J., Digression on, 1697.

Franzius, J., Scriptores physiog. veteres, 1780.

Frœlichius, Bibliot. Physiognomiæ, 1644.

Lavater, J. C., Essays on Phys., 1860.

Redfield, J. W., 12 qual. of mind, 1850.

" Resem. of men and animals, 1852.

Walker, A., Physiognomy founded on physiol., 1834.

Physiology, Animal, Human. Abernethy, Physiol. lectures, 1821.

Adamucci, Syst. Mécan. des fonct. nerv., 1808.

Adélon, Physiol. de l'homme, 1823.

Adriani, De pulmon. structura.

Agassiz, Comparative Embryology, 1849.

Bacon, F., Life and Death.

Barry, M., Researches in Embryology, 1838–41.

Beaumont, Of Digestion, 1833.

Bell, A. N., Knowl. of living things, 1860.

Bell, C., Papers on Physiology, 1832, 1834, 35, 41.

Bichat, Phys. Researches on Life and Death, 1827. B. C.

Blatchford, On Equivocal Generation, 1844. Muns. P. 5.

Bleuland, Otium Acad., 1828.

Blumenbach, Anthropological treatises, 1865.

Bordenave, Essai sur, 1778.

Boucheron, Du Système pileux, 1837.

Broca, On hybridity, 1866, (Anthrop. Soc.).

Brodie, B., Mind and matter, 1857.

Bromm, Entwicklungs-gesetze der org. Welt, 1858.

Buchanan, J., Phil. of Human Nat., 1812.

Cælius, L., Antiquæ lectiones, 1516.

Carpenter, Animal Physiol., 1853, 59.

" Principles of human, 1853.

Clark, W., Report on Animal Phys., 1834.

Cole, De Secretione, 1674. P. 1711.

Combe, A., Physiology of Digestion, 1836. B. C.

" Management of infancy, 1850.

Coxe, Harvey's claims, on circulation of the blood.

Cutter, C., Anatomy and Physiol., 1847, 49.

Dalton, J., Treatise on, 1861.

Darby, J. T., Supra-renal capsules, 1859.

Physiology, Animal, Human (cont'd).

Darwin, E., Zoönomia, 1803.

Dean, J., Substance of the medulla oblongata, (Smithson. Contr. xvi).

Doellinger, Von den Fortschritten, 1824.

Douglas, L., Functions of Liver, spleen, etc., 1816. P. 86.

Draper, J. W., Human Physiol., 1856.

Du Bois, On Animal Electricity, 1852.

Dumas, J., Balance of Organic Nature, 1844.

Dunglison, Human Physiology, 1850.

Edwards, H. M., Outlines of Anat. and Phys., 1841.

Elliotson, Human Physiology, 1840.

Fearn, J., Color images, 1831.

Flint, A., jr., Physiol. of man, 1866, 7, 70.

Geoffroy, Des monstruosités humaines, 1822.

Hammond, W. A., Physiol. mem., 1863.

Hasselt, De Metamorph. Ranæ temporariæ, 1820.

Henry, W. C., Physiology of the Nervous system, 1833.

Hildrop, The brute creation, 1742.

Housset, Mémoires physiologiques, 1787.

Hunter, W., Med. commentaries, 1762.

Jackson, S., Organ. molecular action, 1856. P. 272.

Jarvis, E., Primary Physiology, 1850.

" Practical Physiology, 1848.

" Phys. and laws of health.

Johnson, A. B., Phys. of the Senses, 1856.

Joslin, B. F., Phys. Explan. of beauty of form, 1837. P. 64.

Kiernan, Anat and Phys. of the liver, Roy. Soc. Tr., 1833.

Kobelt, De l'Appareil génital, 1851.

Kolk, Sanguinis coag. historia.

Lambert, T. S., Pop. Anatomy and Physiol., 1852.

" Hygienic physiol., 1851.

Lawrence, W., Lectures, 1848.

Le Cat, Couleur de la peau humaine, 1765.

Lehmann, Chemical physiol., 1856.

Liebig, Motion of the juices, 1850. P. 551.

" Analyse organ. Körper.

" Organic analysis.

Lewes, G. H., Phys. of common life, 1857.

Macnish, The Philosophy of sleep, 1834. B. C.

Malpighi, Structure des Viscères, 1683.

Marchant, Système nerveux, 1846.

Matteuci, Physical Phenom. of living beings, 1847.

Pierpont, J. Bacon, E., Address, 1844.
Dix, J. R., Pulpit portraits, 1854.
Hollis Street Soc., Boston, Proc. 1838, 1839, 41.
Pierpont, J., Reply to Bost. Assoc'n, 1846.

Pietrowski, R. Escape from Siberia, 1863.

Pigeons. Bonaparte, C. L., Sur les ordres des, 1855.
New and comp. treatise, 1802.
Selby, Naturalist's Library.
See Birds; Ornithology; Poultry.

Piggott, J. Stennett, J., Serm., Death of, 1713. P. 365.

Pigmies. *See* Pygmies.

Pigot, Lord. Observations, Madras, 1776.

Pike, Z. M. Whiting, H., Life of, Sparks, 15.
Niles, J. M., Life of, 1821.

Pinckney, C. C. Garden, A., Eulogy on, 1825.

Pinkney, W. Pinkney, Rev. W., Life of, 1853.
Story, J., Sketch of, (Misc. Wri.).
Wheaton, W., Life of, 1826.

Pinto, F. M. Voyages advantureux, (16th Cent.).

Piozzi, Mrs. H. L. Autobiography and letters, 1861.
" Letters to Conway, 1843.
Delany, Mrs., Correspondence, 1862.
Wharton, Queens of Society, 1860.

Pirates. *See* Buccaneers.

Pisa. Nuova guida, 1833.

Pisciculture. *See* Fish Culture.

Pitcairn's Is. Belcher, Mutineers of the Bounty and their descendants, 1871.
Bligh, W., Voy. and mutiny in the Bounty, 1792.
Brodie, W., Pitcairn's Is., 1850.
Shillibeer, Nar. of Briton's Voy., 1817.

Pitman, J., Family. Descendants, (Thurston), 1868.

Pitt, William, Earl of Chatham.
Almon, J., Anecdotes of life of, 1810.
Elijah's Mantle, 1807. P. 397.
Enquiry into the Conduct of, 1766.
Examination of the Principles, 1766.
Letter from the anonymous....1761.
Macaulay, T. B., Essays, Misc.
Pitt, W., Correspondence.
" Letters to his nephew.
Right Honorable Annuitant, 1761.
Thackeray, F., Hist. of, 1827.
See Junius.

Pitt, Rt. Hon. W. Beddoes, T., Essay on, 1795. P. 573.
Commercial policy of......and Peel's, 1847.
Gifford, J., History of Political Life of, 1809.
Green, W., Portraits of, and Fox, 1808.
Meadley, G. W., Two pairs of Hist. portraits. Pamph'r 18.
Orme, J. B., Muse's tribute.
Reply to the charges....1821.
Rose, G., Brief Examination, 1799.
Smith, G., Three English Statesmen, 1868.
Stanhope, Life of, 1861.
Tomline, G., Life of, 1821.
Tooke, J. H., Two portraits, 1788. P. 411.
View of Relative Situations, 1804.
Waterhouse, B., Essay on, 1831.

Pittsburg, P'a. American, The, Pioneer, 1842, 43.
Beanjeu, Bataille du Malangueulé, 1755.
Craig, N. B., History of, 1851.
Jones, S., Pittsburgh in 1826.
Loomis, A. W., Oration on Fort Duquesne, 1859.
Lyford's Directory, 1837.
Olden, The, Time, Monthly, (Craig), 1846.
Pittsburg, Directory, 1859, 65.
Pittsburg, Its Resources, 1845.
Thurston, Pittsburg as it is, 1857.
See Du Quesne, Fort.

Pittsfield, Mass. Field, History of, 1844.
Pittsfield, Septuagenarian Celebration, 1870.
Smith, J. E. A., History of, 1869.
See Berkshire Co.

Pittston, Me. Hanson, History of, 1852.

Pius VI. Beccatini, Storia di Pio VI, 1841.
Merck, De, Mort de, 1814.

Pius VII. Gaschet, Lettres apologétiques, 1809.

Pius IX. Dowling, J., Life of, 1849. P. 1491.
Maguire, Pontificate of, 1871.
Montalembert, Pius IX and France, 1859.
Newspapers, vol. 12, 13, Italian, 1848, 1849.
Proceedings, New York City, 1847.
Twiss, T., The Letters of, considered, 1851.
See Rome.

Pizarro, F. Balboa, Life of Balboa and F. P.
Campe, J. H., Pizarro and the Conquest.
Quintana, Life of, 1832.

Plagiarism. Almelooveen, Opuscula, 1686.
Amer. Whig Review, vol. 10.
Douglas, J., Milton vindicated, 1751.
Jackson, W., The Four Ages, 1798.
Munro, J., Defence of Self, 1790. P. 1239.

Plague. Assalini, Observations on, 1806.
Bennett, W. J. E., Sermon on, 1849.
Donaldson, P., Review of Systems, 1821.
France: Algeria, Explor. Scient., 1847.
Harris, W., De peste, 1721.
Kingsley, C., Who Causes? 1854. P. 2500.
Lupton, Fast Sermon, 1720.
Payn, T., Sermon on, 1722.
Rowlandson, Two Sermons, 1623.
Russell, A., Nat. Hist. of Aleppo, 1756.
Russell, P., A treatise of the plague, 1791.
Tyndall, Dust and Disease, 1871.
See Contagion; Quarantine; Medicine; Yellow Fever.

Plagues. Fleming, G., Animal plagues, 1871.
See Cattle.

Plainfield, Ms. Porter, J., Hist. Sketch of, 1834.

Plantagenets. The Greatest of the, 1871.

Plata, La. *See* La Plata.

Plated Ware. Burton, Catalogue of.
Elkington, Catalogue of.
See Arts.

Plato. Gale, T., Court of the Gentiles, 1671.
Grote, G., Plato and companions of, 1867.
Plotinus, Opera: Comment. Mars. Ficini, 1492.
Proclus, Hist. of Restor. of Platonism.
" Commentaries on, (Taylor), 1816.
Woolsey, T. D., On Platonic philos., Bibliot. Sac., 1845.
See Philosophy; Classical Lit.

Plattsburgh, N. Y. Moore, A. C., On battle of, 1844.
See Champlain Lake.

Playfair, J. Life, in Works.

Playing Cards. *See* Cards; Engraving.

Plays. *See* Dramas.

Plinius, C. Masson, Vita, 1709.
Plinius, Epistolæ, Lipsiæ.
" Letters, Melmoth, 1805.

Plot of 1604–6. *See* Gunpowder plot.

Plot of 1679. *See* Oates, T.

Plumer, W. Plumer, W., jr., Life of, 1860.

Plummer Family. Descendants, Salem Athenæum.

Plurality of Worlds. Brewster, D., More worlds than one, 1870.
Chalmers, T., Astronom. discourses.
Fontenelle, Conversations on, 1767.
Whewell, W., Plurality of, with Introduction by Hitchcock, 1854.

Plymouth, Eng. Hand-book to. P. 1755.
Worth, History of, 1871.

Plymouth, Ms. Banvard, Plymouth and the Pilgrims, 1851.
Baylies, F., Hist. of New Plymouth, 1830, with S. G. Drake's Supp't.
Bradford, W., Hist. of Plymouth Col., Young's Ed.
" The same; Mass. Hist. Soc. Coll., 1856.
Cheever, G. B., Repr. of Journ. of the Pilgrims, 1848.
Clark, J. S., Hist. discourse, 1856.
Everett, E., Oration, Dec. 22, 1824.
" Pilgrim fathers, 1853, v. 3.
Hunter, J., Founders of New Plymouth, 1849.
Mass.; Records of the Col. of P., 1633-1692, 1855–59.
Morton, N., New England Memorial, 1669. Repr., 1826, 55.
Moore, J. B., Lives of the Gov'rs, 1620–1692.
Mourt, Relation, 1622.
" The same, repr., 1865.
Plymouth Co., Ms., Directory and roll of honor, 1867.
Pilgrim Soc., Celeb., 1853.
Russell, W. S., Guide to, 1855.
Scott, B., Pilgrim fathers not persecutors, 1866.
Steele, A., Brewster's Life, 1857.
Thacher, J., History of, 1835.
Webster, D., Hist. disc., 1843.
Winthrop, R. C., Hist. disc., 1870.
Young, A., Repr. of Chronicles of the Pilgrims.
See Puritans; New England; Mass.

Plymouth Christians. Babb, On Cottle. 1824.
Cottle, Strictures on, 1823.

Plymouth Ch., Brooklyn. Manual, 1848.
Shearman, Revival in, 1858.

Pneumatic Dispatch. Beach, A. E., N. Y., 1867, f°.

Pneumatics. Hero of Alexandria, Pneumatics of, 1851.

Lardner, Treatise on.

Tomlinson, P. for beginners, 1848.

See Natural Philosophy; Air; Meteorology.

Pocahontas. Neill, E. D., Virginia Comp., 1869.

" Coloniz. of America, 1871.

Pocahontas, a drama, 1837.

Pocahontas's memory vindicated, 1847. P. 976.

Webster, M. M., Pocahontas, a legend, 1840.

See Virginia.

Pocock, E. Life of, (Twells), 1816.

Poe, E. A. Works and Memoir, (Griswold).

Whitman, S. H., Poe and his critics, 1860.

Poetry, Treatises, etc., on. Aristotle, Treatise on Poetry, 1850.

Barrett, S., Grammatical Analysis of, 1831.

Blom, Friesche Dichtkunst, 1840.

Burman, Poetische Verrukking, 1762.

Campbell, H. Y., Ossiana. Pamph'r 15.

Campbell, T., Essay on Eng. Poetry. 1848.

Carey, J., Pract. Versification, 1809.

Cary, H. F., Lives of the poets, from Johnson to 1846.

Cazé, Systême de Versification, 1843.

Chevreau, Œuvres Mêlées, 1697.

Dwyer, Poetry of the Hebrews, 1830. P. 19. B. C.

Duyse, Nederlandsche Versbouw, 1854.

Edgeworth, R. L., Readings on, 1816.

Elzevier, Drie Dichtproeven, 1761.

Emerson, J., Poetic reader, 1832.

Essays on various subjects, 1780.

Fauriel, Hist. of Provençal Poetry, 1860.

Geysbeek, Over het Puntdicht, 1810. P. 230.

Hazlitt, Lectures on the Eng. Poets, 1845.

Holland, J., Psalmists of Britain, 1843.

Hood, Literature of Labor, 1852.

Hunt, L., Works, Criticisms, vol. 1, 2. 1854.

" Book of the Sonnet, 1867.

Hurd, Works, Notes on Horace, 1811.

Johnson, S., Lives of the poets.

Jones, Sir W., Works, Poésie Orientale, 1807.

Maerlant, Spiegel of Rijm-kronik, 1849.

Poetry, Treatises, etc., on (continued).

Manners, C. R., Review of poetry, 1779.

Marmontel, Poètique Française, 1763.

Montgomery, J., Lectures on General Literature, 1830, 31.

" Lectures on Poetry, etc., 1833. B. C.

Neale, H., Lectures on, 1829.

Pasquali, Istituzioni di Estetica, 1827.

Phrases Poeticæ, 1626.

Pinnock, Catechism of.

Poematum cantu, 1673.

Puttenham, Art of Eng. Poesie, 1589.

Reed, H., Lectures on the Brit. Poets, 1857.

" Lect. on Eng. Lit., 1855.

Richards, G., Differ. of Anc. and Mod. Poetry, 1789. P. 1013.

Schlegel, F. von, Romance poetry.

Sidney, Sir P., Apologie for.

Swift, J., Works; M. Scriblerus, 1812-1813.

Talfourd, T. N., Poetic Talent of the age. Pamph'r 5.

Taylor, H., Notes from Books, 1849.

Taylor, W., Hist. Survey of German Poetry, 1830.

Temple, Sir W., Works, 1720.

Walker, Rhyming Dict., 1852.

Warton, Hist. of English Poetry, 1824.

White, R. G., National Hymns, 1861.

See Rhetoric; Literary History; Drama, Treatises on.

Poetry: Collections, American and British.

Aikin, J., Select Works of British Poets, 1831. B. C.

Alexander, C. F., Sunday book of, 1865.

Anti-Jacobin, Poetry of the, 1801, 54.

Asylum for Fug. Pieces, 1785.

Barnwell, New Orleans book.

Boston Book, 1836-50, 4 v.

British Poets, Bohn's ed., 4 v.

Brydges, Brit. Bibliographer, 1810-14.

" Restituta, 1814-16.

Camden Society Publications, 1838-58.

Chalmers, A., English Poets, to Cowper, 1810.

Cheever, G. B., Amer. Common-place book of, 1843.

Coggeshall, Poets of the West, 1860.

Columbian Muse, N. Y., 1794.

Dana, C. A., Household Book of, 1858.

Dodsley, Coll. of diff. Authors, 1775.

Eastman, L., Masonic Melodies, 1825.

Ellis, G., Early Eng. Met. Romances, 1848.

" Early English Poets, 1811.

Poetry: Collections, American and British (continued).

Everest, Poets of Connecticut, 1847.

Fuller Worthies' Library, (Grosart), Miscellany, vol. I, II, 1870, 71.

Gallagher, W. D., Selections, Western, 1841.

Gem, The, 1848.

Griswold, R. W., The Female Poets of America, 1849.

" Poets of America, 1860.

Halliwell, Early Engl. Miscel., 1855.

Hart, J. S., Class Book of, 1845.

Hayward, T., The British Muse, 1738.

Hazlitt, Select British Poets, 1824. B. C.

Hemenway, Poets of Vermont.

Hill, G., Select. from Catholic Poets, 1867.

Hunt, J. H. L., Book of the Sonnet, 1867.

" Selections from Eng. Poets.

Hutchinson Family, Book of Words of, 1851.

Jacobite Minstrelsy, 1640–1734, 1829.

Kettell, Specimens of Am. Poetry, 1829.

Knickerbocker Gallery, 1855.

Knox, V., Elegant extracts, 6 v., 1818.

Moore, F., Songs of Am. Revolution, 1856.

" Lyrics of Loyalty, 1864.

" Songs of the Soldiers, 1864.

" Rebel Rhymes, 1864.

" Pers. and Polit. ballads, 1864.

Moore, J. S., Ballad Poetry of Gr. Br., 1853.

Morley, H., Cavalier and Puritan song, 1868.

Murphy, H. C., Anthol. of New Netherland, 1865.

Nation, The, Ballads and Songs of, 1846.

New Foundling Hospital for Wit, 1768–71, 1786.

New York Book of Poetry, 1837.

Nichols, J., Select Collection of poems, 1782.

Palgrave, The Golden Treasury, 1863.

Pamphlet volumes of American Poetry, vols. 620, 1391, 1392, 1722, 1845.

Pamphlet volumes of British Poetry, vols. 397, 398, 534, 642, 810, 1012, 1013, 1017, 1018, 1019, 1043–1046, 1115, 1385–1391, 1543, 1723–1728, 1790–1792, 1845, 2512.

Pauline, The, No. I, 1831.

Pearce, G., A Collection, etc., 1775.

Percy, Relics of Ancient English Poetry, 1839.

Percy Society, Publications, 1840–52.

Poet, The, Vol. 1, No. 1, 1849.

Poetry: Collections, American and British (continued).

Poetical Register, 1800–12.

Poetical Review, No. I, II, 1852.

Poet's Magazine, 1842.

Poet's Magazine, No. I, II, Albany.

Read, T. B., Female Poets of Amer., 1849.

Ritson, J., Caledonian muse, 1821.

Scott, Sir W., Minstrelsy of Scottish Border, 1839.

Southey, R., Brit. Poets, Chaucer to Johnson.

Taylor, E., Sabbath Recreations, (Pierpont), 1839.

Wilkins, Political ballads, 1600–1700.

Wreath, The, Hartford, 1824.

See Ballads; Satires; Songs; Quotations; Bibliography.

Poetry, American. Adams, G. Z., Musings, 1835.

Adams, J., Death of Mrs. Turell, 1735.

" Poems, 1745.

Adams, J. Q., Dermot M'Morrogh, 1832.

" Poems on Religion and Society, 1848.

Alasco, Phil'a, 1857.

Aldrich, T. B., Course of True Love, 1859.

" Poems, 1863.

Allen, Mrs. B., Pastorals, 1806.

Allen, W., Wunnissoo, 1856.

Allston, W., Lectures and Poems, 1850.

Alsop, R., Poem to George Washington. P. 47.

" Charms of Fancy, 1856.

" Enchanted Lake, Tr.

" *See* Echo, 1807.

Anarchiad, Repr., 1861.

Andrews, E. W., Wash. Benev. Soc., 1816.

Aquarelles, by S. Sombre, 1858.

Arey, H. E. G., Household Songs, 1855.

Aristocracy, Phil'a, 1795.

Arnold, J. L., Poems, 1797.

Astrop, Orig. Poems, 1835.

Atalantis, (W. G. Simms), 1832.

Atlee, Religion of the Sun, 1826.

Ayres, J. A., Legends of Montauk, 1849.

B., M. E., Poems and tales, 1851.

Bacon, E., Ægri Somnia, 1843.

" Vacant Hours, 1845.

Bacon, W. T., Poems, 1840.

Ball, B. W., Elfin land, 1851.

Ballou, H., Miscel. poems, 1852.

Barlow, Joel, Elegy on T. Hosmer.

" Hasty Pudding, 1773, 1847.

Poetry, American (continued).

Barlow, Joel, The Vision of Columbus, 1787.
" The Columbiad, 1807.
Barrett, S. A., Maintonomah, 1849.
Bartlett, J., Physiognomy, 1810.
Bartley, Lays of Virginia, 1855.
Batchelder, Border Adventures, etc., 1851.
Bates, D., Eolian, 1849.
Beach, E. T. P., Pelayo, 1864.
Benedict, E. C., Mediæval hymns, 1867.
Benedict, F. L., Shadow Worshipper, 1857.
Benjamin, P., Poetry, 1842.
" Infatuation, 1844.
Benjamin, S. G. W., Constantinople, etc., 1860.
Bethune, G. W., Lays of Love and Faith, 1848.
Bennett, E. T. B., Song of the rivers, 1855.
Bigelow, J., Poem, Phi Beta Kappa, 1811. P. 42.
Bleecker, A. E., Works in prose and verse, 1793.
Boker, G. H., Plays and poems, 1856.
" Konigsmark, 1869.
Boston city: by Phillipiad, 1849.
Bourne, W. O., Sale of a Distillery, 1845. P. 534.
Brackenridge, Divine Revelation, 1774.
Bradstreet, A., Poems, 1678.
Brainard, J. G. C., Poems of, 1847.
" Occasional, 1825.
Brannan, Vandyke Browne, 1865.
Bridal of Vaumond, 1817.
Brooks, C. E., Ballads, 1866.
Brooks, C. T., German Lyr. Poetry, 1853, 63.
Brooks, J. G., Rivals of Este, 1829.
" Poem, Phi Beta Kappa, 1826.
Brooks, M., Judith, 1820.
Brooks, N. C., History of the Church, 1841.
Brower, W. S., Y. M. C. Ass'n, Alb., 1859.
Brown, J. W., Michael Agonistes, 1843. P. 620.
Brown, W. A., Harp of Nature, 1846.
Bryan, The Mountain Muse, 1813.
Bryant, J. H., Poems, 1855.
Bryant, W. C., Poems, 1847.
Bucktail Bards, 1819.
Buckwheat, The, Cake, 1831.
Bulfinch, S. G., Poems, 1834.
Bulkley, O. H. A., Niagara, 1848.
Burges, T., Valley of Alvarado, 1847.
Burroughs, C., Poetry of Religion, 1851.

Poetry, American (continued).

Butler, C. M., Themes for the Poet, 1852.
Butler, F. A. K., Poems, 1844.
Butler, J. H., Wild Flowers, 1843.
Butler, W. A., Two Millions, 1858.
C., E. H., The Chaplet, 1846.
Calvert, F., Cœlestes et Inferi, 1771.
" Gaudia Poetica, 1769.
Camp, P., Poems, 1859.
Canning, J. D., The Harp and Plow, 1852.
" Poems, 1838.
Caprices, (E. S. Miller), 1849.
Case, W., Revolutionary Memorials, 1778, (Dodd), 1852.
Chandler, E. M., Works, 1835.
Channing, W. E., The Woodman, etc., 1849.
Chase, Elizabeth, Miscellaneous, 1821.
Chester, A. G., Delta Phi Society, 1855.
Chester, J. L., Greenwood Cemetery, 1843.
Cheves, Sketches, 1849.
Child, Mrs., The Coronal, 1832.
Chivers, T. H., Virginalia, 1853.
Chronicles of Yonkers, 1864.
Clark, W. G., Past and Present, 1834.
Clarke, G. W., Dreams of Pindus, 1829.
Clarke, McD., Poems, 1836.
" Afara II, 1843.
Coffin, R. S., Misc. poems, 1818.
" Oriental Harp, 1825.
Cole, F. W., Poems, 1845.
Colgan, W. J., Poems, 1844.
Colman, J. F., Island Bride, 1846.
Colton, G. H., Tecumseh, 1842.
Columbia's Naval Triumphs, 1813.
Condottier, 1821.
Cone, S. W., Proud Ladye, 1840.
Consolatory Odes: P. Quince, 1799.
Cottage garland, 1847.
Coxe, A. C., Advent, 1837.
" Christian ballads, 1840.
" Athanasion, 1840.
" Misc. Poems, 1835–45.
Craigenfelt, Fashionable Satires, Visit from the moon, 1832.
Cutler, E. J., War poems, 1867.
Dabney, R., Poems, 1812, 1815.
Dana, R. H., Poems, 1850.
Davidson, L. M., Amir Khan, 1829.
Davidson, M. M., Writings, 1843.
Davis, B. W., Poetry for the people, 1855.
Davis, R. B., Poems, 1807.
Dawes, R., Valley of Nashaway, 1830.
" Poems, 1839.

Poetry, American (continued).

Day, S. M., Pencillings, 1850.
Denison, C. W., The American Village, 1845.
Devereux, R., Poet pieces, 1803.
Discipline of earth and time, 1854.
Dix, S. A., Poem, Merc. Lib. Assoc'n, Bost., 1848.
Doane, G. W., Works, v. 1.
Don Paez, by a Virginian, 1847.
Drake, J. R., Culprit Fay, 1844. P. 260.
" The Croakers, Bradford Club, 1860.
Duganne, A. H., Mission of intellect, 1853.
Durfee, J., Whatcheer or Roger Williams, (Works).
Dwight, T., Conquest of Canaan, 1785.
" Greenfield Hill, 1794.
" Triumph of Infidelity, 1788.
Dyer, S., Songs and Ballads, 1857.
Eastburn, J. W., Yamoyden, 1820.
Eastman, C. G., Poems, 1848.
Echo, The, And other Poems, 1807. Ed. by Alsop.
Effigy, The, Burning, 1795.
Ellet, E. F., Poems, 1835.
Elliot, J., Poet. and Misc. Works, 1798.
Emigrant, The, Cincinn., 1833.
Emmons, R., Battle of Bunker Hill, 1841.
" The Fredoniad, 1827.
Epistle to Zenas. P. 45.
Evans, N., Poems, 1772.
Everest, C. W., Vision of death, 1837.
Everett, A. H., Poems, 1845.
Experience by a Green Mountain girl, 1821.
Extracts from Humbuggiana, 1847. P. 99.
Fairfield, S. L., Poems, 1823.
" Lays, 1824.
" Last Night of Pompeii, 1832. B. C.
" Abaddon, 1830.
" Poems and Prose Writings, 1841.
Family and guest, 1850.
Farmer, C. M., The Fairy, 1847.
Farmer, H. T., Imagination, 1819.
Fay, T. S., Ulric or the Voices, 1851.
Felton, J. B., The Horse-Shoe, 1849.
Fenner, Poems, 1846.
Fessenden, T. G., Terrible Tractoration, 1803, 1806.
" Democ. unveiled, 1805.
" Original Poems, 1806.
" Ladies' Monitor, 1818.

Poetry, American (continued).

Fields, J. T., Poems, 1849.
" Poem, Merc. Lib. Assoc'n.
Fitz Clarence, N. Y., 1838.
Flagg, W., Anat. of Female beauty, 1834.
Flint, M. P., The Hunter, 1826.
Follen, Mrs., Poems, 1839.
Fosdick, W. W., Ariel, etc., 1855.
Foster, W. C., Poetry, 1805.
Freneau, P., Miscell. Works, 1788.
" Poems, 1809, 61.
Fresh Hearts that Failed, 1860.
Frisbie, L., Misc. Writings, 1823.
Frothingham, N. L., Metrical Pieces, 1855.
Gallagher, W. D., Erato No. I, 1835.
" Erato II, III, 1837.
Genin, The Napolead, 1833.
Gibson, W., Vision of Fairy Land, 1853.
Giles, D. S., A Collection, Ann Arbor, 1845.
Gilman, C., Verses of a Life Time, 1849.
Goodrich, S. G., The Outcast, 1836.
Gordon, N. M., Alleghan, 1856.
Gotham, N. Y., 1823.
Gould, H. F., Poems, 1841, 1850.
Grate, C., Eugene, 1842.
Grattan, H. P., The Bottle, 1848.
Grayson, W. I., The Hireling and Slave, 1855.
Guest, M., Poems, 1824.
Hale, Sarah J., Three Hours, 1848.
Hall, Mrs. J., jr., Phantasia, 1849.
Halleck, F., Poetical Works, 1847.
" Fanny, 1821.
" Alnwick Castle, 1827, 1845.
" The Croakers, 1845, 60.
Hardy, D., Poems, 1858.
Harney, J. M., Crystalina, 1810.
Harris, T. L., Lyric of the Golden Age, 1856.
Harte, Bret, Poems, 1871.
Harwood, J. E., Poems, 1809.
Headsman, The, 1840.
Hemenway, Poetry of Vermont, 1858.
Hempstead, T., Poems, 1859.
Heroes of the Last Lustre, (Mines), 1858.
Hersey, A. C., Poet. Effusions, 1835.
Hewitt, J. H., Misc. Poems, 1838.
Hill, G., Ruins of Athens, 1839.
Hitchcock, D., Poet. Works, 1806.
Hoffman, C. F., Vigil of Faith, 1842.
" The Echo, 1844.
" Love's Calendar, etc., 1858.
Holland, J. G., Bitter-Sweet, 1859.

Poetry, American (continued).

Holland, J. G., Kathrine, 1867.

Holmes, O. W., Poems, 1849.

" Astræa, the Balance of Illusions, 1850.

Honeywood, St. John, Poems with Prose, 1801.

Horace in N. Y., (Clason), 1826. P. 1722.

Horsford, M. G., Indian Legends, 1855.

Hosmer, W. H. C., Pioneers of Western N. Y., 1838.

" Yonnondio or Warriors of the Genesee, 1844.

Hoyt, R., The Koh-i-noor, 1852. P. 88.

" Edward Bell.

Humboldt, G., Poems, 1857.

Humphreys, D., Miscellaneous Works, 1790.

" Discours en Vers, 1786.

" Happiness of Amer., 1790.

Hymns for the Sick Room, 1860.

James, Maria, Wales, 1839.

Judd, S., Philo, 1850.

Judson, E., An Olio, 1852.

Kennedy, T., Songs of Love and Liberty, 1817.

Key, F. S,, Poems of, 1857.

Knight, H. C., Poems, 1821.

Know-Nothing, 1854.

Krause, W. E. F., America, 1869.

Ladd, J. B., Remains, 1832.

Landis, J., Letter, 1854.

" Life of the Messiah, 1851.

Landscape sketched in N. H., 1821. P. 534.

Lane, G. C., Poems, 1860.

Lash, The, by Swammerdam, 1840.

Lawson, J., The Maniac, 1811.

Lays of the Kansas Emigrants, 1854. P. 103.

Leisure Hours, (Leggett), 1825.

Leland, C. J., Hans Breitmann, 1869.

Lesdernier, Voices of life, 1853.

Lewis, E. A., Myths of the Minstrel, 1853.

Lewis, H. C., Lyre of Love, 1818.

Lewis, Sarah A., Records of the heart, 1844.

Lincoln, E., The Village, 1816.

Linen, J., Songs of the Seasons, 1852.

Linn, J. B., Powers of Genius, 1802.

" Miscel. Works, 1795.

" Valerian, 1805.

Longfellow, H. W., Poems, 1844.

" Poetry of Europe, 1845.

" Waif and Spanish Student, 1845.

" Belfry of Bruges, 1846.

" The Estray, 1847.

Poetry, American (continued).

Longfellow, H. W., Evangeline, 1850.

" Golden Legend, 1852.

" Hiawatha, 1855.

" Miles Standish, 1858.

" Tales of a Wayside Inn, 1863.

" New England Tragedies, 1868.

Low, S., Winter Displayed, 1784.

" Poems, 1800.

Lowell, J. R., Fable for Critics, 1848.

" Biglow papers, 1848.

" Poet. Works, 1860.

" Under the Willows, 1869.

Lunt, G., Poems, 1839.

M'Jilton, J. N., Sovereignty of Mind, 1841.

Mack, R., Kyle Stuart, 1834.

Mackellar, T., Tam's Fortnight Ramble, 1847.

McLeod, C. D., Plasmion, 1841. P. 83.

McMasters, Silver Pictures, 1856.

MacMullen, J., Poem, Columbia Coll., Alum. Assoc'n, 1858.

March, D., Yankee Land, 1840.

Markoe, P., The Times, 1788. P. 66.

Marsden, Rev. J., Leisure hours, 1812.

Marsh, W., England, 1839.

Mellen, G., Martyr's triumph, etc., 1833.

Melville, H., Battle pieces, 1866.

Mengwe, A Poem, 1825.

Merrick, J. L., Pilgrim's Harp, 1847.

Merry, R. *See* Poetry, British.

Midnight, 1858.

Miller, J., Songs of the Sierras, 1871.

Mitchell, J. K., Indecision, 1839.

Mormoniad, 1858.

Morris, G. P., Poems, 1860.

Morris, R., The Past and Future.

Moses; or the Man who Supposes, 1866.

Munford, W., Poems, 1798.

Muzzy, H., Poems, 1821.

Myers, P. H., Poem, Euglossian Soc., 1841.

My Native Land, Va., 1827.

Mynehieur von Herrick, 1824.

Nack, J., Legend of the Rocks, 1827.

" Carl Rupert, 1839.

" The Immortal, 1850.

" Romance of the Ring, 1859.

Neal, J., Battle of Niagara, 1819.

Nicholls, A., Danvers, 1852.

Nichols, L. H., Poems, 1857.

" Songs of the Hearth, 1851.

Northmore, T., Washington, 1809.

No Slur, (Richmond), 1840.

Nothing to Eat, 1857.

Poetry, American (continued).
Ode: Atlantic Tel., (Fenn), 1858.
Odiorne, T., Prog. of Refinement, 1792.
Old things and new, 1835.
Olio, The, 1823.
Oliver, J. E., Class Poem, Harv., 1849.
Orig. Poems, Albany. P. 1722.
Orton, J. R., Arnold and Poems, 1854.
Osander, Misc. Poems, 1812.
Osborn, S., Poems, 1823.
Ostrea, 1857.
Ouabi, (Morton), Boston, 1790.
Our Chronicle of '26, 1827.
Paine, R. T., Works in Verse and Prose, 1812.
" The Ruling Passion, 1797. P. 88.
" Invention of letters, 1819.
Paine, T., Poems, (Rickman).
Paradise of Fools, 1831.
Parker, H. W., Poems, 1850.
Parmelee, H. L., Poems, 1865.
Parnassian shop, 1801.
Passaic, The, 1842.
Paulding, J. K., Lay of Scottish Fiddle, 1813.
" Backwoodsman, 1818.
Peck, J., A short Poem, 1817.
Peirson, L. J., Forest Minstrel, 1846.
Percival, J., Clio, No. III, 1827.
" Poem, Phi Beta Kappa Soc., 1825.
" Poet. works, 1861.
Pierce, W. L., The Year, 1813.
Pindar, Jonathan, Probationary odes, 1796.
Pierpont, J., Airs of Palestine, 1840.
Pinkney, E. C., Poems, Balt., 1838.
Pinkster Ode, Albany, 1803.
Pious remains, 1764.
Pise, Pleas of Religion, 1833.
Pleasures of Religion, 1820. B. C.
Poe, E. A., Works, v. 2, 1850.
Power, T., Secrecy, 1832.
Pratt, S. D., Inklings, 1852.
Pray, I. G., Prose and Verse, 1836.
Price, J. H., Miscellany, 1813.
Progress of Society, 1817.
Quincy, J. P., Charicles, 1856.
Rafinesque, The World, 1836.
Ray, W., Poems, 1821, 26.
Read, T. B., Wagoner of the Allegany, 1863.
" Summer Story, Sheridan's Ride, 1865.
Redden, Idyls of battle, 1864.
Reid, J., King Slavery's council.
Reporter, The, Prin. by S. Snowden, 1812.
Reveries by Nemo, 1846.

Poetry, American (continued).
Richards, W. C., Electron, 1858.
Ritchie, A. C. M., Pelayo, 1838.
" Reviewers reviewed, 1837.
Robinson, P., Immortality, 1846.
Rogers, D., Liberty and Equality, 1804.
Rogers, E. P., Missouri Compromise, 1856.
Rouquette, Wild Flowers, 1848.
" Fleurs d'Amérique, 1856.
Rowson, Susanna, Poems, 1804.
Rudder, The True Light, 1850.
Saint John, P., Death of Abel, 1793.
St. Jonathan, Lay of a Scald, 1838., (A. C. Coxe).
Sands, R. C., Yamoyden, etc., 1835.
Sangster, C., Hesperus, 1860.
Sargent, L. M., Hubert and Ellen, 1813.
Saxe, J. G., Poems, 1861.
Schoolcraft, H. R., The Rise of the West, 1841.
" Helderbergia, 1855.
Scott, J. M., Blue Lights, 1817.
" Sorceress, 1817.
Scott, M. Y., Deaf and Dumb, 1819.
" Fatal Jest, 1819.
Sewall, J. M., Misc. Poems, 1801.
Shaw, J., Poems, 1810.
Sigourney, Mrs., Moral Pieces, 1815.
" Traits of the Aborigines, 1822.
" Scenes in my native land, 1845.
" Pleasant memories, 1844.
Simms, W. G., Early Lays, 1827.
" Southern Passages, 1839.
" Atalantis, 1832.
" Vision of Cortes, 1829.
" Donna Florida, 1843.
" Egeria, 1853.
Shatzel, J., The Mexican, 1841.
Shippey, J., Specimens, 1841.
Smith, D. E., Destiny, Delta Phi, 1846.
Smith, J., Mirror of Merit, 1808.
Smith, Seba, Powhatan, 1841.
Smith, W., Poems, 1786.
Snowden, R., The Columbiad, 1800 ?
Snelling, W. J., Truth, 1831.
Some Lines....about Shakers, 1846.
Soldiers' Companion, 1862.
Song leaves, 1852.
Song of the Sexton. Muns. P. 9.
Songs in the night, 1802.
Southwick, Pleasures of Poverty, 1823. P. 99, 931.
Spear, T. G., Sylvan scenes, 1838.

Poetry, American (continued).
Sprague, C., Curiosity, 1820. P. 63.
" Centennial Ode, 1830. P. 20. B. C.
" Writings, 1843.
Sprague, H., Gloversville, N.Y., 1859.
Sprawn of Ixion, 1846.
Stagg, E., Poems, 1852.
Stansbury, J., Loyal Verses, 1775-83. Muns. Hist. Series, Repr.
Stoddard, R. H., The King's Bell, 1863.
Stone, H., Freedom, 1864.
Story, Joseph, Power of Solitude, 1804.
Story, W. W., Nature and Art, 1844. P. 37. B. C.
Street, A. B., Drawings and Tintings, 1844.
" Frontenac, 1849.
" Poems at Hamilton, Yale Coll. and Pittsfield, 1850, 51, 52.
" Poems, 1867.
Strother, J. H., The Golden Calf, 1854.
Stuart, C. D., Ianthe and other P. P. 1843.
Sukey, (Walter), 1821.
Swanwick, J., Poems, 1797.
Sweet, H. D. L., Twilight Hours, 1870.
Taggart, C., Poems, 1834.
Tappan, W. B., Poems and lyricks, 1842.
Tator, H. H., Hercules, 1856.
Taylor, B., Poems of Home, 1855.
" Poems of the Orient, 1855.
" Poet's Journal, 1863.
Thaxter, A. W., P. at Harvard, 1850.
Times, The, No. I, Standish, jr., 1809.
Triumph of Peace, N. Y., 1840.
Trumbull, J., Poetical Works, 1820.
" M'Fingal, 1776, 82, 91, 1806.
Twins, The,..by J. Verity, 1856.
Two Poems, Newburyport, 1829.
Tyler, R., jr., Ahasuerus, 1842.
Umphraville, Siege of Baltimore, 1817.
Vail, J., Noah's Flood, 1796.
Village, The, (Lincoln), 1816.
Vision of Rubeta, (Osborne), 1838.
Waddell, Texas, etc., 1844.
Walter, Wm. B., Sukey, 1821.
Wanderer, The, Trenton Falls, 1823.
Ware, H., Works, V. 1.
Warren, Mrs. M., Poems, 1790.
Warren, O. G., Dream of the Highlands, 1840.
Waterford Literary Society, 3 Poems.
Waterston, R. C., Merc. Lib. Ass'n, Boston, 1845.
Webber, S., War, 1823.
Webster, M. M., Pocahontas, 1840.

Poetry, American (continued).
Wheatley, P., Poems, 1773, 1802, 34.
" Elegiac Poem, 1770.
Whitfield, J. M., America, 1853.
Whitman, Leaves of Grass, 1855.
" Drum-taps, 1865, 6.
Whitney, T. R, The Ambuscade, 1845.
Whittier, J. G., Poems, 1838.
" Poems of Abolition, 1838.
" Lays of My Home, 1843.
" Poems, 1849.
" In War Time, 1864.
Whitwell, Experience, 1806. P. 44.
Wife of Leon, (Warfield), 1844.
Wigglesworth, E., Day of Doom, (1662), 1867.
Wilcox, C., Age of Benevolence, 1822.
" Remains, 1828.
Wilder, J. N., Rochester, 1857.
" Y. M. Ass'n, Albany, 1858.
Willis, N. P., Sketches, 1827.
" Fugitive Poetry, 1829.
" Poem with other Poems, 1831.
" Bianca Visconti, 1839.
" Tortesa, the Usurer, 1839.
" Sacred Poems, 1843.
Winter, W., Queen's Domain, 1859.
Withington, O. W., The Pilgrim, 1849.
Wolcott, R., Poet. Meditations, 1725.
" On J. Winthrop, 1750.
Wolf, Ethel, The Glad New Year, 1867.
Woodworth, Melodies, Songs, Ballads, 1830.
Wright, N. H., Boston, a poem, 1819.
Yellott, G., Maid of Peru, 1848.
See Ballads; Hymns; Songs.

Poetry, British. Academ. Contributions, Camb. Univ., 1795.
Adams, J., Charles Edward, 1847.
Akenside, M., Pleasures of Imagination, 1803. B. C.
" Poetical Works, 1857.
American War, 1781, (Cockings).
André, J., Cow Chace, 1781.
Andrew, J., Anatomie of Baseness, 1615. Fuller Misc., 1871.
Anketell, J., Poems, 1795.
Anstey, C., Poet. Works, 1808.
" New Bath guide, 1766.
Armstrong, J., Art of Health, 1744. P. 1012.
Arnold, C., Commerce, 1751.
Ashburnham, Elegiac sonnets, 1795.
Auction, The, a town eclogue, 1778.
Aurelia, 1783.
Aytoun, Lays of the Scottish Cavaliers 1851.

Poetry, British (continued).

Bacon, Sir F., Poems, (Grosart), 1870.
Bailey, P. J., Festus.
" The Age, 1858.
" The Mystic, 1856.
Baillie, J., Poetical Works, 1851.
Bakewell, T., Moorland Bard or poetry of a weaver, 1807.
Bale, Bp. R., The temptacion, 1548. Fuller Misc , 1871.
Ball, W., Night Watches, 1834. B. C.
Baptistery, The, 1852–54, (Williams).
Barbauld, A. L., Works, 1826. B. C.
Barham, R. W., Ingoldsby legends, 1856.
Barrard, B., Abol. of Death, 1827.
Barton, B., Mem. and Poems, 1850.
Bath, 1748.
Beach, W. W., Abradates, 1765.
Beattie, J., Poet. Works, 1854.
" The Minstrel and other Poems, 1811.
Beauty, or Art of charming, 1735.
Bidlake, J., Poems, 1794.
Bishop Bonner's Ghost, 1789.
Black Gowns and Red Coats, 1834.
Blair, R., The Grave, 1755, 1807, 47.
" Poet. Works, 1854, (Beattie).
Blake, W., Poems, (Gilchrist), 1863.
Bloomfield, R., (Brit. Poets).
Booker, L., The Hop garden, 1799.
Bounden, J., Fatal curiosity, 1805.
Bourne, V., Poetical Works, 1826.
Bowdler, H. M., Poems and Essays, 1803.
Bowles, W. L., Poet. Works, 1855.
Braithwait, R., Barnabæ Itinerarium, 1818.
Branagan, T., Avenia, 1840.
" Pleasures of contemplation, 1818.
Brandon, I., Instruction, 1811.
Brecknock, T., Prejudice detected, 1752.
Bridges, Divine wisdom and prov., 1737.
Bright, J. H., Palmyra, 1822.
Britannia, 1730.
British Blessings, 1844.
British, The, Patriot, 1794.
Brooke, Lord, Fulke Greville Works, 1870, (Grosart).
Brown, Dr., Cure of Saul, 1763.
Browne, M., Piscatory eclogues, 1750?
Browne, W., Works, 1772.
Browning, E., Aurora Leigh, 1857.
" Poems, 1858.
" Napoleon III.
Browning, R., Men and Women, 1856.

Poetry, British (continued).

Browning, R., Ring and the Book, 1869.
" Sordello, 1869.
" Poems, 1868, 69.
Brunswick, The, 1829.
Brydges, E., Sonnets, 1785.
Bucke, C., Fall of the leaf, etc., 1819.
Budget, The, 1795.
Building, On the, of a monastery, 1795.
Burges, J. B., Birth....of love, 1796.
Burgoyne, J., Poetical Works, 1808.
Burns, R., Poems, N. Y., 1788.
" Poems, 1845, 65, 68.
Butler, F. A. K., Poems, 1844.
Butler, S., Poetical Works. B. C.
" Hudibras, 1847.
Byron, Lord, Works, 1840.
Cambrian and Salopian Minstrel.
Campaign of one day, 1816.
Campbell, T., Poetical Works, 1846.
Canning, G., (Brit. Poets), 1851.
Carlisle, Earl of, Poems, 1773.
Carter, Mrs. E., Poems, Lond., 1816.
Catherall, S., Essay on the conflagration, 1720.
Cayley, G. J., Sir R. Mohun, 1849.
Chamberlain, T., Windsor, 1846.
Charms of liberty, 1709.
Charter House School, 1827.
Chatterton, Poetical Works, 1842.
Chaucer, G., Works, 1561, 1843.
Cheffins, S., Sighs of the poor, 1825.
Cheltenham poetical alphabet, 1832.
Childe Harold's monitor, 1818.
Christmas, H., Trans. from Camoens, 1835.
" The Voyage, 1833.
Churchill, Poet. Works, 1855.
Churchyard, T., Fun. of F. Knowles.
" Good will, 1815.
Clark, C., Doctor's doings.
Clark, J., The fortun. discovery, 1807.
Cleveland, J., Works, 1687.
Clifford, M. M., Poems, 1808.
Cobbold, E., The Galley, 1835.
Cockings, G., Poems.
" Benevolence, 1772.
" The American war, 1781.
Coleridge, S. T., Works, vol. 7, 1854.
Coll. of Poems on the Pretender, 1775.
Collins, W., Poetical Works, 1771.
Colman, G., Pieces in verse, 1787.
Colvil, The Whigs' Supplication, 1751.
" The Cyrnean hero, 1772.
Combe, W., Dr. Syntax's tours.
Common sense, 1819.
Compliments to Painters, 1797.
Conciliad, The, 1761.

Poetry, British (continued).

Congreve, W., Poet. works, 1784, 1840.
Conversation, (by E. Lloyd), 1767.
Cook, E., Sot-weed factor, 1708.
Cook, Eliza, Melaia, etc.
Coronation, 1821.
Corporation, The, 1775.
Cossack, The, 1815.
Cotton, C., Works of, 1734.
Cotton, N., Poet. works, 1806.
Courtier, P. L., Pleasures of solitude, 1802. P. 1723.
Cow, The, of Haslemere, 1754.
Cowley, A., Select Works, 1777.
Cowley, Mrs., Maid of Arragon, 1780.
Cowper, W., Works, 1847, 1853, 54.
Coxe, R. C., Wood notes, etc., 1848.
Crabbe, G., The Village, 1783. P. 1012.
" Poetical Works, 1847.
Crambe repetita, 1799.
Crashaw, R., Complete Works, 1858.
Creation, 1852.
Crichton, A., Festival of Flora, 1818.
Croly, G., Angel of the world, 1821.
Cromwell, T., The School boy, 1816.
Crowe, W., Lewesdon Hill, 1788.
Cumberland, R., Retrospection, 1812.
Cunningham, J., On a pile of ruins, 1761.
Curate, The, (by E. Lloyd), 1766.
Dale, T., Outlaw of Taurus, 1820. P. 397.
Dalton, J., Two Epistles, 1745. P. 1012.
" Descrip. poem, 1755.
Darwin, E., Temple of Nature, 1804.
" Botanic Garden, 1795.
Davis, J., The American Mariners.
Day, T., Devoted Legions, 1776.
" Dying Negro, 1787.
De Foe, D., True born Englishman, 1701.
" Jure Divino, 1706.
" Moderation displayed, 1709.
De La Mayne, Love and honour, 1742.
Denham, Sir J., Court of Cupid, 1770.
" Cooper's Hill, 1709. P. 397.
Description of Summer, 1786.
Deserter, The, 1836.
Diabo-lady, 1777.
Diaboliad, 1777.
Dibdin, C., Mons. Mong-tong-paw.
Dibdin, T. F., Bibliography, 1812.
Dick, R., Spiritual Dunciad, 1859. P. 1728.
Dissertator in Burlesque, 1701.
Dodd, W., African prince, 1755.
" Thoughts in prison, 1813.

Poetry, British (continued).

Don Juan in search, 1839.
Donne, J., Poet. Works, 1855.
Douglas, G., Descr. of May, 1752.
Drummond, W., Poetical Works, 1856.
Dryden, J., The Medall, 1682. P. 1012.
" Absalom and Achitophel, 1708. P. 810.
" Religio Laici, 1710. P. 910.
" Works, 1808, 1854.
Dutton, T., The Wise Man of the East, 1800.
Dyer, J., The Fleece, 1757.
Eagle's, The, Masque, 1808.
Ecclesia Dei, 1848.
Edwards, S., Copernican System, 1728.
Elijah's Mantle, (Pitt), 1807. P. 397.
Elliott, E., Corn Law Rhymes, 1831.
Ellis, W. R., Brief Narr. with Poems, 1832. P. 81.
Ellwood, T., Davideis, 1712, 92.
Eloisa en déshabille, (Matthews), 1801.
Emmett, Belshazzar's Feast, 1836.
England's Helicon, 1614.
Epistola ad Augustum, 1828.
Erskine, R., Gospel Sonnets, 1798.
Essay on Wind.
Evans, J., Poet. Garland, 1808.
Exton, R. B., A Discourse, 1832. P. 1824.
Fables for Grown Gentlemen, 1761.
Faction Displayed, 1709. P. 138.
Falconer, W., The Shipwreck, 1843.
" Poet. Works, 1854.
Fall of Man, (by G. M.), 1840.
False Honor, 1844.
Fellows, J., Grace Triumphant, 1820.
Fenton, E., Works, 1802.
Fergusson, R., Poems, 1815.
Fitz James, O., The Wandsworth Epistle, 1762.
Fleming, W., Destroying Angel, 1825.
Fosbroke, T. D., Monastic Life, 1795.
Foxton, T., Night Piece, 1719.
Francis, B., The Conflagration, 1786.
Fribbleriad, The, 1761.
Friendship, 1769.
Fry, J., Select Poems, 1805.
Fudge Family in England, 1823.
Gaggin, J., Poems, 1808.
Garth, Sir W., Works, 1769.
Gay, J., Trivia, 1795.
" Poet. Works, 1854.
Gaynam, J., Marlborough Conquers, 1708.
Gibbons, T., Juvenilia, 1750.
Gifford, H., A Poesie of Gilloflowers, 1580; Fuller Misc., 1871.

Poetry, British (continued).

Gifford, W., Baviad and Mæviad, 1811.
" Poems, (Brit. Poets), 1851.
Glover, R., Leonidas, 1770.
Godwin, C. G., Reproving Angel, 1835. P. 397.
Goldsmith, O., Poetical Works, 1856.
Gower, J., Confessio Amantis, 1857.
Graces, The, An Epistle, 1775.
Grahame, J., Poetical Works, 1856.
Grant, C., Restor. of Learning in the East, 1807.
Grattan, H. P., The Bottle, 1848. P. 534.
Gravener, T., Leviathan drawn out, 1832. P. 397.
Gray, D., Poems, 1864.
Gray, T., Poetical Works, 1855.
Gr. Br., Rolls: Chron.: Metr. Chron. of Scotland.
" " Political Poems and Songs.
Greeks, The, a Jeremiad, 1817.
Green, M., The Spleen, 1804.
Green, W. E., Dedic. of Solomon's Temple, 1854.
Gregg, St. G., Ambition, 1840.
Griffin, G., Poet. Works.
H., G., Unsuccessful suit, 1829.
Halcomb, J., Peace, 1814.
Hall, Jos., Satires, 1824.
Hall, T., Benevolence, 1788.
" Poems, 1804.
Hallam, A. H., Remains, 1863.
Halls, J. J., Clouds and Sunshine, 1849.
Hammond, J., (Brit. Poets), 1851.
" Love elegies, 1757.
Hankinson, T. E., The Druids, 1827.
Harbart, W., Proph. of Cadwallader, 1604. Fuller Misc., 1871.
Hardyknute, 1740.
Harte, W., Essay on Satire.
Hawkshaw, Dionysius, 1842.
Hay, W., Immortality, 1754.
Hayes, S., Duelling, 1775.
Hayley, W., Poems and Plays, 1785.
Hearne, Robert of Gloucester's and P. Langloft's Chronicles, 1724–5.
Heber, R., Palestine, 1828. B. C.
Hemans, F., The League of the Alps, etc., 1826. B. C.
" Poet. Works.
Herbert, G., Poems and Country Parson, 1824. B. C.
Herbert, W., Attila, (Works).
" The Guahiba, 1822. P. 1389.
Herrick, R., Poet. Works of, 1825.
Hewitt, Mrs., Meditations, 1830.
Hill, A., Works, 1753.

Poetry, British (continued).

Hobbes, T., Life by himself. Trans. from Latin, 1680.
Hobson, T., Christianity, Light of the World, 1745.
Hodgson, P., Gov't of the Passions, 1775.
Hogg, J., Poetical Works, 1826.
Holford, Miss, Margaret of Anjou, 1816. B. C.
Home: A Poem, 1806.
Homer's Battle of the Frogs.
Hood, T., Poetical Works, 1856.
" Prose and Verse, 1845.
" Whims and Oddities, 1854.
" Dream of Eugene Aram, 1831.
Hope, The, that is in us, 1843.
Howard, M., The Conquest of Quebec, 1768.
Howard, H., Earl of Surrey, Poetical Works, 1854.
Howie, J., Queen in Scotland, 1842.
Hoyland, F., P. and translations, 1763.
Hudibrastick Brewer, 1714.
Hughes, J., Court of Neptune, 1700.
" The House of Nassau, 1702.
Hughes, T. S., Belshazzar's Feast, 1818. P. 397.
Hull, T., Richard Plantagenet, 1774.
Humanity, the rights of nature, 1788.
Hunt, L., Juvenilia, 1802.
Hurdis, J., Village Curate, 1790.
" Tears of Affection, 1794.
" Adriano, 1790.
Influences of Sensibility, 1810.
Inglis, M. M., Misc. collection, 1838.
Injured, The, Islanders, T. C. D., 1779.
Ironside, Canto of Spenser, 1714.
Irwin, E., Eclogues, etc., 1774–98.
Jacob, H., Bedlam, 1723.
James I, Essayes of a prentise, 1584, repr., 1814.
Jemmat, C., Miscellanies, 1768.
Jeopardy and hope of Gt. Br., 1835.
Johnson, S., Vanity of human wishes, 1749.
" London, a poem, 1750.
" Poet. Works, 1855.
Katherine Hill, MS., 1730.
Keate, G., Epis. to Voltaire, 1768.
" Epist. to A. Kauffman, 1781.
" Poet. Works, 1781.
Keats, J. Works, 1854.
Keble, J., The Christian Year, 1848.
" Lyra innocentium, 1850.
Kent, J., Fall...of Zion, 1828.
King, W., Works, 1776.
Kingsley, C., Poems, 1856.
Kitchener, J., Trans. from Casimir, etc., 1821.

Poetry, British (continued).

Landon, L. E., Complete Works, 1856.
Langhorne, Fables of Flora, 1773.
Langtoft, P., Chronicle, 1724-5.
Layamon's Brut, 1847.
Lay of the Sea, 1853.
Lays of Poland, 1836.
Lays of Straiton House.
Lewis, M. G., Life and Poems, 1839.
Liberal, The, Hunt and Byron, 1822-1823.
Lilliput Levee, 1868.
Lloyd, R., Night, 1761.
Lockhart, Spanish Ballads, 1856.
Loe, W., Songs of Zion, 1620; Fuller Misc., 1871.
Logan, J., Poems, 1781.
" Poems, (British Poets), 1851.
Lok, H., Poems, Sonnets, 1597. Fuller Misc., 1871.
Longland, R., Vision of Pierce Plowman, 1550.
Lopez, F. De, The Piscopade, 1748.
Loves of the Saints, 1835.
Lyttelton, G., Works, 1801.
Lytton, Chronicles, 1868.
Macaulay, T. B., Pompeii, 1819. P. 398.
" Lays of Ancient Rome, 1852.
McCreery, The Press, 1803.
McGregor, M. *See* Mason, W.
Mackay, C., Songs and Poems, 1834.
Mac Neill, H., Works of, 1815.
Madge's addresses, 1777.
Makarony Fables, 1768. P. 1002.
Malcolm, D., Sorrows of love, 1814.
Mallet, D., Poet. works, 1805.
Marjoribanks, Slavery, 1792.
Markham, G., Teares of the beloved, 1600. Fuller Misc., 1871.
Markland, Art of shooting flying, 1735.
Marriott, W. S., Old and mod. times, 1855.
Marvell, A., Poet. works, 1726, 1857.
Mason, W., Isis, 1749.
" Odes, 1756.
" Epist. to Shebbeare, 1777.
" The Dean and the Squire, 1782.
" Elegies, 1763. P. 1012.
" Epist. to W. Chambers, etc., 1805.
Mathias, T. J., Pursuits of Literature, 1794, 1805.
" Epist. from Kien Long, 1794.
Maurice, T., Kien Long, 1795.
" Crisis of Britain, 1798, 1803.
" On Sir W. Jones, 1795.
" To Mem. of H. Hope, 1811.

Poetry, British (continued).

Mayne, W. E., Field and Factory, 1849.
Méle Ephémeria, 1783. P. 1013.
Melmoth, C., Ode to Garrick.
Memoirs of a Goldfinch, 1819.
Merivale, J. H., Orlando, 1814.
Merry, A., Dying Words of 18th Cent., 1800. P. 398.
Merry, R., Pains of memory.
" Paulina, 1787.
Mickle, W., Poet. works.
Middleton, S., Pompeii, 1835. P. 398.
Millikin, J. H., Poetical fragments, 1823.
Milnes, R. M., Poems of many years, 1846.
Milton, J., Paradise Lost, 1808, 39, 50.
" Poems, 1791, 1851.
Milward, T., Peleia, or the old woman, 1763.
Minot, L., Poems, 1352, (Ritson).
Moffet, W., Irish Hudibras, 1755.
Moncrieff, W. T., Poems. P. 1726.
Montague, M., Names, etc., 1853.
Montague, Lady, Works, vol. 3, 1837.
Montgomery, J., Harp with a Sabbath tone.
" On R. Reynolds, 1816.
" Poetical Works, 1845.
Montgomery, R., Hero's Funeral, 1853.
Moore, T., Corruption and Intolerance, 1808.
" Poetical Works, 1837, 56.
More, H., Slavery, 1788.
" Ode to Dragon, etc., 1777-88.
" Poems, (Brit. Poets), 1851.
Mundus dramaticus, the new Rosciad, 1852.
Murphy, A., Works, 1786.
My Dog Brace, by Cal. Currens, 1844.
New Popular Rhymes, 1843.
New, The, Jerusalem, Ancient Hymn.
Newton, C., Arnold, 1856.
Newton, John, Battle of the Beard, 1858.
Nicol, Wm., Scraps by the Printer, 1849.
Normanby, Temple of Death, 1709.
Norton, Hon. Mrs., Child of the Islands, 1846.
" Poems, 1833.
Noyes, R., Distress, 1806.
Nun's Path, by Huntingford, 1787.
Nuptial Dialogues, 1753.
Nut Brown Maid, (Arnold's Chronicles).
Ode, Odes, 1765-1814.
Ode....on leaving S. Carolina, 1783.

Poetry, British (continued).
Odes and Addresses, 1705–1829.
Ogilvie, J., Paradise, 1769.
Orme, J. B., Monody to Pitt, 1806.
Orphans, The, a Romance, 1814.
Osborne, J., Scripture and Reason, 1795.
Osro and Tylo, 1755. P. 1043.
Ossian, Poems, 1801, 16.
" Poems, (Macpherson) 1792,1805.
Overbury, Sir T., Misc. Works, 1856.
Oxford Sausage, 1822.
Paddock, R., Thoughts in Adversity, 1800.
Painter's Primer, 1810.
Palace, The, Martyr, 1840.
Paper Lantern for Puseyites, 1843.
Paradise of Coquettes, (Brown), 1816.
Paradise of Dainty Devices, 1576, (Brydges's Brit. Bibliog.).
Parnell, Poet. Works, 1855.
Parson-ography, 1857.
Parson's, The, Choice, 1821.
Parsons, W., Ode to a Boy, 1796.
Partridge, S. W., Idea of a Christian, 1858.
Pasquin, A., Poet. Epis. from Gabrielle D'Estrées, 1788.
Patent, The, 1776.
Patmore, Children's Garland, 1866.
Patriot, The, 1804.
Patriot, The, a Pind. address, 1767.
Patriot, The, Vision, 1778.
Patriotism, a Mock Heroic, 1763.
Paul, Sir J. D., Ruth, 1841.
Peace, W., Christian Conflict, 1853.
Peacock, T. L., Phil. of Melancholy, 1812.
Pearce, P. H., Victory and Bronte.
Peat, J., On a Plurality of Worlds, 1856.
Pelly, J. K., Christ's Pers. Reign, 1837.
Penrose, T., Flights of Fancy, 1775.
Percy, W., Cœlia, (1594), 1818.
Philips, J., Poems, 1744.
" Cyder, 1708.
Phillips, C., Emerald Isle, 1813.
" Lament of the Emerald Isle, 1818.
Physic and its phases, 1858.
Physiology-Hygiene, 1848.
Pickering, A., Sorrows of Werter, 1788.
Piers Ploughman's Vision, 1856.
Pindarics, to P. Pindar, 1800.
Plutus, Or Spirit of the age, 1857.
Poem, Poems, Poetic, 1676–1854.
Poems by a young lady, 1815.

Poetry, British (continued).
Poetical Essays, 1791.
Poetical Sketches.
Political Nomenclature, 1838.
Pollok, Course of Time, 1828.
Polwhele, R., Pictures from nature, 1786.
Pomfret, J., Poems, 1785, 91.
Pope, A., Poet. Works, 1797, 1808, 1858.
" Dunciad, 1729, 50.
" Epistles, 1734–7.
Pope, W., The Wish, 1710.
Popish, The, Divan, 1809.
Pordage, S., Azaria and Hushai, 1682.
Powers, The, of Britain, 1813.
Praed, W. M., Poetical Works, 1852.
" Lillian and other Poems, 1850.
Pratt, S. J., The Contrast, 1808.
" Triumph of Benevolence, 1786
" Humanity, 1788.
Prime, The, Minister, 1835.
Prior, J., Invit. to Malvern, 1851.
Prior, M., Poetical Works, 1784.
Probationary Odes, 1788.
Procter, A. A., Legends and Lyrics, 1858.
Procter, B. W., Dramatic Scenes, 1857.
Prophecy of Liberty, 1768.
Prospect of Liberty, 1767.
Pye, H. J., War elegies of Tyrtæus imitated, 1795.
" Carmen Seculare, 1800.
Quarles, F., Divine poems, 1717.
Queen's, The, Voyage, 1842.
Quizzical Quorum. P. 1013.
Radcliffe, A., Poems, 1816.
Radical Monday, 1821.
Raleigh, Sir W., Works, v. 8, 1829.
Ramsay, Allan, Works, Edinb.
Randolph, T., Poems, 1638.
Rawlins, E. A., Famine in Ireland, 1847.
Reed, E. J., Corona, etc.
Reed, T., Believer's hope, 1825.
" Ascension of Christ. P. 1013.
Reflections from Shakspeare's Cliff, 1851. P. 398.
Request, The, 1762.
Revolution, The, Canto 1, 1791. P. 1016.
Rhodes, S., Poetical Miscellanies.
Richards, G., Aboriginal Britons, 1791.
" Poem, 1791–5.
Richardson, C., Poems, 1806.
Richardson, G. F., Poetic hours, 1825.
Richardson, J., Poems, (Brit. Poets), 1851.
Richardson, R., Muse of Whitby, 1837.

Poetry, British (continued).

Rickman, T. C., Poetical scraps, 1803.
Rival, The, Demons, 1836.
Robinson, T. R., Juven. Poems, 1807.
Rodolph, a contin. of Don Juan, 1832.
Rogers, S., Pleasures of Memory, 1796.
" Jaqueline.
Room, C., Herculaneum, 1828.
Rosciad, The, of Covent Garden, 1762.
Rossetti, D. G., Poems, 1870.
Rota, P. R., Death of Nelson, 18C5.
Rout, The, by TB. CC., 1769.
Royal, The, Brood, Pindar, jr., 1813.
Rowden, F. A., Introd. to Botany, 1801.
Rowe, N., Works, 1703.
Russell, T., Sonnets, 1789.
Ryan, On Sacred Subjects, 1824.
Ryves, Eliz., Poems, 1777.
Sackville, T., Works, 1859.
Satyr against Brandy, 1683.
Saunders, J., Chaucer's Tales, 1845.
Scott, J., Four Elegies, 1760.
Scott, J., House of Mourning, 1817. P. 398.
Scott, Sir W., Poetical Works, 1840, 1857, 66.
Scribbleomania, 1815.
Search after Claret, 1691. P. 1013.
Senators, The, London, 1772.
September, London. P. 1002.
Seward, A., Ode, Gen. Eliott, 1787.
" Poet. Works, 1810.
Shadwell, Medal of J. Bayes, 1682.
Sharp, R., Letters....in verse, 1835. B. C.
Shakeshaft, J., Faith and Works, 1824.
Shakespeare, W., Poems, 1842.
Shelley, P. B., Poet. Works, 1855.
" Queen Mab, 1829.
Shenstone, W., Works, 1764, 9.
Shooting, 1784.
Sidney, Sir P., Misc. works, 1860.
Shelton, J., Poet. Works, 1856.
Skerries Light-house, 1842. P. 620.
Smart, C., Immensity of God, 1751. P. 1013.
Smith, A., City Poems, 1857.
" Life Drama, 1856.
" Edwin of Deira, 1862.
Smith, C., Poems, (Brit. Poets), 1851.
Smith, E., Fragments, 1810.
Smith, H., Poetical Works, 1851.
" Rejected Addresses, 1851.
Smith, Sir S., On Escape of, 1798.
Smollett, T., Poet. Works, 1855.
Solitude: by J. C., P. 1723.

Poetry, British (continued).

Somerville, W., Works, 1851.
" The Chace, 1796.
Songs....not by J. M. Neale, 1848.
Southey, C., Birth-day, 1855.
" Solitary Hours, 1846.
Southey, R., Roderick, 1815. B. C.
" Poet. Works, 1860.
Southwell, R., Poet. Works, 1856.
Spencer, J., Hermas, 1772.
Spencer, W. R., Year of Sorrow. P. 1013.
Spenser, E., Works, 1825. B. C.
Sprat, T., Plague of Athens, 1675.
State, The, Farce, a lyrick, 1756.
Stevenson, J. Hall, Works, 1795.
Stewart, W., Chron. of Scotland, 1858.
Stonehouse, J., Verses, occasional, 1794.
Suckling, J., Poems, 1646.
Surrey, Earl of. *See* Howard.
Swift, T., Temple of Folly, 1787.
Swinburne, A. C., Atalanta, 1866.
Sylvestre's Du Bartas, 1641.
Taylor, Jane, Writings.
Taylor, Jer., Poems, Fuller Misc., 1870.
Tecumseh....Of the West, 1828.
Tennyson, A., Poems, 1842, 1870.
" In Memoriam, 1851.
" The Princess, 1848.
" Ode to Wellington, 1852. P. 398.
" The Third Napoleon, 1854.
" Maud, 1855.
Thackeray, W. M., Ballads, 1856.
Thistlethwaite, J., Predic. of Liberty, 1776.
Thomson, James, Anc. and Med. Italy, 1735.
" Seasons, 1777, 1814.
Thornton, B., Battle of the Wigs, 1768.
Tighe, M., Psyche, 1852.
Timbuctoo. P. 398.
Timperley, Songs of the Press, 1845.
Tomlinson, J. W., Pentachord, 1843. P. 398.
" Eleventh Hour, 1843.
Tracts for the improvement, 1848.
Travellers, The, A Satire, 1778.
Tupper, M. F., Proverbial Philosophy, etc., 1846.
" Poems, 1851.
Vaughan, H., Works, (Grosart), 1871.
" Sacred Poems, 1856.
Vaughan, W., Golden Fleece, (in part), 1626.
Visions of the West. Railways, 1838.

Poetry, British (continued).

Walker, J., Three Original Poems, 1796.

Waller, E., Works, 1729.

Ward, T., England's Reformation, 1814.

Warreniana.

Warton, J., Poems, 1794.

Warton, T., Works, 1856.

Welsted, L., Works, 1787.

West, Mrs., The Mother, 1809.

West Indian eclogues, 1787.

Whalley, T. S., Edwy and Edilda, 1800.

" Mont Blanc, 1788.

Whiffin, R., Loves of the Roses, 1835. P. 398.

White, H. K., Works, 1856.

Whitehead, W. Elegies, 1757.

Whittle, T., Of the Elect, 1829.

Williams, Sir C. H., Works, 1822.

Wilson, A., Poet. Works, 1820.

Wolcott, Peter Pindar's Works, 1800.

Wordsworth, W., Poet. Works, 1854.

" Yarrow revisited, 1835.

Wreath, The, 1824.

Wyatt, T., Poet. Works, 1854.

Wyntown, A., Cronykill of Scotland.

Young, Edward, Works, 1802.

" Night Thoughts, 1851.

Young, J. W., Scraps, 1849.

See Bibliography; Hymns; Ballads; Songs.

Poetry, Danish. Feldborg, Selections from, 1816.

Poetry, Dutch. Alphen, H., Gedigten, 1778. B. C.

Apollo's Nieuwe-Jaers Gift, 1745.

" Kermis-Gift, 1763.

Bosch, M., Stichtelyke Gedichten, 1775.

Bowring's Batavian Anthology.

Broeckhoff, Dichtkundige Bespiegelingen, 1770.

Cats, J., Dichterlyke Werken, 1818.

Costa, I. Da, Aan Nederland, 1844. P. 33. B. C.

Does, 'S Gravenhage, 1688.

Eigenbaat, De. P. 110.

Elzevier, Drie Dichtproeven, 1761.

Hagen, J., Verzameling van Bruiloftsverzen, 1835.

Helmers, Nagelaten Gedichten, 1814. P. 110.

Hoogvliet, A., Zydebalen, 1740.

" Eerkroon, 1743.

" Abraham, de Aartsvader, 1744.

" Lof de Drukkunste door Coster, 1741.

Poetry, Dutch (continued).

Hoogvliet, A., Vervolg der Mengeldichten, 1753.

Hoogstratten, Republyk van Venetie, 1715.

Huygens, Koren-Bloemen, 1672.

Janssonius, R. B., Lentebladen, 1844.

Kiehl, Die Liebe u. d. Leben.

Kortebrant, Lof der Drukkunst.

Kraeyvanger, Dichtlievende lente en zomer, 1735.

Kumpel, Vaderl. Gedenkstukken.

Lodensteyn, Uytspanningen, 1727.

Mengelpoezij, Door T. H. M. F., 1778.

Moonen, A., Poëzy, 1700.

Murphy, H. C., Anthol. of N. Netherland, 1865.

Onveranderlyke Santhorstsche Geloofsbelydenis, 1786.

Opregte, De, Zandwoorder Speel-Wagen. B. C.

Overbeke, Rym-Werken, 1719.

Pamphlets of Dutch Poetry, vol. 110.

Parnassus Kunstkabinet, 1735.

Pluimer, Gedichten, 1692.

Pollius, M., Mengeldichten, 1745.

Poot, Gedichten, 1722.

" Vervolg, 1735.

Post, E. M., Gedichte, 1789.

Potgieter, E. J., Mount Vernon, 1861.

Scheltema, Dichtstukjes, 1848.

Slicher, Weegschaal....1786.

Smits, D., Gedichten, 1740.

" Izraels Baälfegorsdienst, 1737.

" De Rottestroom, 1750.

Sprong, H. van der, 1841. B. C.

Swaanenburg, W. van, Parnas, 1724.

Tafereel, De, 1720.

Thijm, Gedichten, XIIe–XVI Eeuw.

Vaderlandsche Zeeheld, 1781.

Van Zant, Een niew liedt, Albany, 1802.

Vink, N., De Redding-maatschappij, 1847.

Voet, Uitzicht van Nebo, 1753.

Volks-Liedjens, 1790–93.

Vondel, Hekeldigten, 1707.

" Poëzy of verscheide Gedichten, 1682.

" Trans. of Virgil and Ovid, 1659.

" Treuerspelen, 1660–62.

Wits, Stigtelyke bedenkinge, 1693.

Wolff, E. B., De Natuur, 1784.

" Econ. Liedjes, 1791.

Woordt, Gedichten, 1843.

Zeeus, Jakob, Gedichten, 1721–26.

See Dramas; Literature, Dutch.

Poetry, French. Aix, D', Annales poétiques....de la France, 1839.
Almanach Chantant, 1855.
Amérique Délivrée, 1783.
Art Iatrique, (Bourdelin), 1776. P. 612.
Audet, Syndics de Genève. P. 1104.
Avrigny, D', Le Départ de la Pérouse, 1807.
Baudoin, Rêveries, 1841.
Béranger, Poems, (Young), 1850.
Besnier, Le Mexique Conquis, 1752.
Boileau, Œuvres Poétiques, 1857.
Bonaparte, L., Charlemagne, 1814, and in Eng.
Boulay-Paty, Odes, 1844.
Bourgeois, Christophe Colomb, 1773.
Canonge, Poëmes Nouvelles, 1839.
Chénier, J., Œuvres diverses, 1816.
Chevreau, U., Œuvres meslées, 1697.
Colet, Le Monument de Molière, 1843.
Delille, J., Œuvres, 1808–22.
" Rural philosopher, 1804.
Deschamps, Etudes Françaises, 1829.
Dion, Tableau d'Hist. Universelle, 1807.
Duault, Poésies, 1823.
Du Boccage, La Colombiade, 1756.
Fénélon, Œuvres, vol. 3, 1837.
Fernand, Poésies, 1860.
Frederick II, Œuvres Poétiques, 1847–1850.
Gay, Dernier jour de Pompéii.
Hugo, V., Songs of Twilight, 1836. P. 398.
La Fontaine, Contes et Nouvelles, 1764.
" Fables, 1857.
" E. Wright's English trans., 1841.
La Motte, Odes, 1709.
Langtoft, P., Chronique, (Hearne).
Lemay, L. P., Essais poétiques, 1865.
Le Mercier, L'Atlantiade, 1812.
Le Suire, Le Nouveau Monde, 1781.
Malherbe, Œuvres, 1837.
Marmontel, Les Incas, 1817.
Martin-Maillefer, Les Fiancés de Caracas, 1829.
Masson, G., La Lyre Française, 1867.
Nivernois, Fables, Eng. and Fr., 1799.
Mätzner, Altfranzösische Lieder, 1853.
Petits Poétes Français, 1838, 39.
Poëmes sur l'Amérique, 1756.
Rapin, Christus patiens, 1720, Trans.
Raynouard, Poésies des troubadours.
Rouquette, Fleurs d'Amérique, 1856.
Roure, La Conquête du Mexique, 1811.
Rousseau, J. B., Œuvres Poétiques, 1837.

Poetry, French (continued).
Salm, La Princesse de, Œuvres, 1842.
Travers, Gerbes glanées, 1859.
Trésor, Le, du Parnasse, 1763. B. C.
Turgot, A. R. J., Œuvres, v. 9.
Villiers, L'Art de Prêcher à un abbé, 1642.
Voltaire, Œuvres, 1785–89.
" Henriade, 1797.
" The Henriade, Eng., 1797.
" La Pucelle.
Voyage d'Amérique, 1786.

Poetry, Gaelic. Fugitive Pieces, Macpherson's fragments, 1765.
Highland Soc. Report, by Mackenzie, On Ossian, 1805.
Ossian, Macpherson's ed.
Stewart, A. and D., Coll. of works of Highland bards, 1804.
See Language, Irish.

Poetry, German. Bethune, Specimens of, 1848.
Brooks, C. T., German lyrics, 1853.
" German....Songs and ballads, 1863.
Bürger, Leonora. Trans.
Follen, Works, vol. 1, 1841.
Goethe, Select Minor Poems, 1839.
" Dramatic works, (Swanwick).
" Faust, Hayward's, Taylor's tr.
Heine, H., Poems, Engl.
Körner, C. T., Lyre and Sword, 1834.
" *See* Uhland.
Klopstock, Der Messias, 1780.
Lonicer, J. A., Ständ und Orden der H. Rom. Kath. Kirchen, 1585.
Neuhofer, G. A., Gedichte, 1804.
Nibelungenlied, 1840.
Schiller, F. von. Sämmtliche Werke, 1836.
" Die Glocke, 1839. P. 620.
" Minor Poems, 1839.
" Maid of Orleans, 1843.
Uhland, German Songs, 1842.
Umbreit, F. W. S., David and Jonathan, 1844.
Voss, Gedichte, 1802.
Wagenseil, J. C., Von der Meister Singer....Anfang, etc., 1697.
Wieland, Oberon, 1791. B. C.

Poetry, Greek. *See* Greek Authors.

Poetry, Hungarian. Bowring, Poetry of the Magyars, 1830.

Poetry, Italian. Alfieri, L'America Libera, 1784.
Ariosto, Orlando Furioso, 1829.
" Hoole's trans., 1791.
" Satirici e burleschi sec. xvi, 1787.

Poetry, Italian (continued).
Bartolomei, L'America, 1650.
Berni, Enchanted Lake, 1806.
" Opere burlesche, 1760.
Botta, C., Il Camillo, 1853.
Callimacho, La Chioma di Berenice.
Cattuffio, Baiamonte Tiepolo, 1769.
Clericetti, Canto, 1851.
Collezione....in dialetto Veneziano.
Colpo d'occhio, 1848.
Contarini, Poesie, 1778.
Conti, G., Opere originali, 1819.
Cotta, G., Dio: Sonetti ed inni, 1820.
Dante, La Commedia, Tommaseo, 1837.
" Commedia, 1854.
" La Commedia, in Eng., (Cary), 1845.
" The new Life, (Norton), 1859.
" Œuvres, Rhéal, 1845, 52.
Fantoni, G., Poesie, 1823.
Forteguerri, N., Il ricciardetto, 1789.
Franceschinis, F., Morte di Socrate.
" L'Atenaide, 1837.
Giusti, G., Versi editi ed inediti, 1856.
Grazeosa canzone. P. 1785.
Graziani, Conquisto di Granata.
Guarini, B., Il pastor fido, 1590.
Hunt, L., Ital. poets, trans. into Eng. prose.
Marini, Suspicion of Herod, 1646. P. 398.
Marino, G. B., L'Adone, 1789.
" Murder of the Innocents, (Crashaw), 1834.
Mathias, C. J. Componimenti lirici scelti, 1802.
Metastasio, P. B., Dramas and Poems, Trans.
Monti, V., Opere inedite e rare, 1834.
Neri, Saggi di rime, 1700.
Ogone, Il vero lume, 1790.
Parini, Il mattino, 1818.
Petrarcha, F., Rime. P. 1785.
" Sonnets, 1859.
" Poems, Bohn's ed., 1859.
Pezzoli, L., Prose e poesie, 1853.
Pimbiolo Opere postume, 1824.
Poeti del primo secolo, 1816.
Polcastro, G., Opere, 1833.
Politiano, A., Stanze.
Ponte, L. Da, Composizione e traduzione, N. Y., 1807–30.
Pyrker, La Tunisiade, 1827.
Redi, F., Bacco in Toscana, 1821.
Romanze, 1838.
Scritti, Italiani vicende, Malta, 1848.
Tansillo, L., The Nurse, 1800.
Tasso, Gerusalemme liberata, 1745, 1844.

Poetry, Italian (continued).
Tasso, Trans. Wiffen, 1846, 54.
" Opere, 1724.
Teatro moderno, 1838–41.
Vannetti, C., Opere, 1826–31.
Varano, A., Opere scelte, 1818.
Villardi, F., Varie operette, 1832.
Vittorelli, J., Opere ed. e postume, 1841.

Poetry, Latin. Augurello, G. A., Iambicus, 1505.
Auratus. *See* Dorat.
Bardomachia, 1800.
Boethius, Metres in Cons. of Phil., 1811, (Lat. and Eng.).
Bottarelli, J. G., Ad J. Com. de Westmorland, 1759.
Bourne, V., Poet. Works, 1825.
Calvert, Gaudia Poetica, 1769.
Capella, M., Satyricon, 1600.
Catullus, Venet., 1502.
" Traj., 1680.
" Trans. Kelly, 1854.
Causton, P., Tunbrigialia, 170.
Claudianus, C., Cpera, 1650, 1760.
Cotton, J. D., Lachrymæ elegiacæ, 1765.
Dorat, J., Poematia, 1586.
Dufresnoy, De arte graphica, and trans., Dryden and Mason.
Ekker, A. H. A., Exeunte Octobri, 1868.
Este, C., Carmina quadragesimalia, 1741.
Estienne, H., Principum monitrix musa, 1590.
Excerpta e Test. Vet. Versibus, 1828.
Flaccus, C. V., Argonauticon, 1724.
Gr. Brit.: Rolls: Chronicles of Great Britain.
Grove, R., De Sanguinis circuitu, 1685.
Holdsworth, E., Muscipula, 1709.
Horatius, Q. F., Opera, 1779, 1815, 28, 1853.
" En Français, Sommer, 1855.
" English Trans., Buckley, Smart.
" Opere, Gargallo, 1830.
Iscanus, J., De bello Trojano.
Jortin, J., Lusus poetici, 1748. P. 1012.
Juvenalis, Satiræ, 1486, 1750, 1825.
" Satires, Trans. of Holyday, Gifford, Hodgson, Dryden, Evans, Madan.
" Trans. in Dutch, 1709.
Juvencus, Hist. Evangelica, 1490.
Leeuwen, Lycidas Ecloga, 1856.
" Octaviæ Querula, 1857.
" Carmen elegiacum, 1864.
Lennep, Van, Carmina, 1790.
Lucanus, M. A., Pharsalia, Trans., Riley.

Poetry, Latin (continued).
Lucretius, T. C., De rerum natura, Ed. Wakefield.
" Trans. of Good, Watson.
" Natura delle cose, Marchetti.
Lycophron, Cassandra, 1566.
Mantuanus, B., Adolescentia, 1634.
Martialis, M. V., Epigrammata, 1617, 1693.
" Trans., Lond., 1865.
Okes, Epigrammata, 1819.
Ovidius, P., Opera, 1591, 1629.
" Eng. Trans., Riley, Sandys.
" Dutch Transla., Hoogvliet, Vondel, Valentine.
" French Trans., Le Sage, 1850.
Ossian, Phingaleis, (M'Donald).
Pamphlets of Latin Poetry, vol. 1393.
Pedo Albin., Elegiæ, 1755.
Persius Flaccus, Satiræ. *See* Juvenalis.
" Eng. trans., Howes, etc.
Pervigilium Veneris, 1712.
Petronius Arbiter, Satyricon, 1629.
" Eng. trans. *See* Propertius.
Planta, Mauritiados, 1647.
Poetæ Latini minores, 1731, 1789.
Polignac, Anti-Lucretius, 1749.
Politianus, Opera, 1553.
Pope's Messiah, Phillips's Splendid Shilling, Lat., 1752.
Propertius, Elegiæ, 1780.
" 1680. *See* Catullus.
" Trans., Bohn's ed.
Prudentius, A., Opera, 1613.
Rombise, Itin...Galliæ, 1639.
St. John, T. P., Annus Mirabilis, 1848.
Schurman, Anna M., Opuscula, 1652. B: C.
Secundus, Trans. *See* Propertius.
Severus, P. C., Ætna, 1715.
Sidonius, C. S., Opera, 1609, 14.
Silius Italicus, Punicorum lib., 1798.
Statius, B. P., Silvæ, Thebäis, Achilleis, 1494.
Tibullus, Carmina, 1798.
" 1502, 1680. *See* Catullus.
" Trans. *See* Catullus.
Virgilius, P. M., Opera, 1717, 59, 1803, 1823.
" English Trans., Davidson, Martyn, Buckley.
" French Tr., Delille, Sommer.
" Dutch Trans., Vondel.
Vitrioli, Xiphias, 1745.
See Latin Authors.

Poetry, Oriental. *See* Oriental Literature; Arabic; Persian; Sanscrit.

Poetry, Portuguese. Camoens, Os Lusiadas, 1818.
" Lusiad, Mickle, 1798.
Duraò, Caramuru, Poëme Brésilien, 1829.
Ercilla, L'Araucana, 1776, 1824.

Poetry, Russian. Bowring, Russian poets.

Poetry, Spanish. Alvarez, F., Puren indomito, 1862.
Botello, F., El nuevo mundo, 1701.
Castellanos, Elegias, 1589.
Conti, G., Scelta da poesie Castigliane, sec. xvi, 1819.
Lima University, 1816.
Lockhart, Anc. Spanish ballads.
Manrique, J., Coplas, 1779.

Poetry, Swedish. Cavallius, Sveriges Hist. och Politiska Visor, 1853.
Klemming, Flores och Blanzeflor, 1844.
Tegner, E., Poems, 1848.
" Frithiof's Saga.

Pohlman, S. C. Sprague, W. B., Discourse on.

Poisons. Accum, Chemical re-agents, 1817.
" Culinary poisons, 1820.
Chevallier, A., Sur les empoisonnements, 1848.
Christison, R., Hemlock and Conia, 1836.
Ducachet, H. W., Action of Poisons, 1817. P. 86.
Fontana, Venom of the Viper, etc., 1787.
Hammond, W. A., Physiol. Memoirs, 1863.
Hasheesh Eater, (Ludlow).
Hendrickson, C., On Trial of J. Hendrickson, 1855. P. 516.
Koelliker, Upas Antiar, 1857. P. 551.
Orfila, Traité des Poisons, 1826.
" Treatise on, 1826.
" Traité de Toxocologie, 1852.
Otto, F., Detection of, 1857.
Swinburne, J., Papers, 1862.
Taylor, A. S., Pois. in Med. jurisprudence, 1859.
Wooler, J. S., Great Burdon case, 1855.
See Chemistry; Medicine.

Pola, Austria. Allason, Antiquities of, 1819.

Poland. Connor, Account of, (Coll. Voy., 4).
Dunham, History of, Lardner, 29.
Forman, C., Election of King, 1733.
Galecki, History of, 1843.
Hordynski, Hist. of Polish Revolution, 1833.

Poland (continued).
Johnston, R., Trav. through Russia and Poland, 1815.
Jones, S., History of, 1795.
Kraitsir, Hist. of Slavonians and Poland, 1837.
Krasinski, Russia and Europe, 1854.
Lays of Poland, 1836. P. 1792.
Mably, Gouvernement de, 1794, 95.
Mackintosh, Account of partition of, Works, 2.
Mém. Hist. de Pologne, 1795.
Montalembert, Insurrection of, 1863.
Pamphlets relating to, vol. 1443.
Poland, Const. charter, 1815. P. 1443.
Recueil de documents, 1853.
Regnard, Voyage, Œuvres, 1837.
Remembrances of a Polish Exile, 1835 B. C.
Russia, Droits des dissidents, 1766.
Saxton, L. C., Fall of, 1851.
Some remarks, 1726.
Tochman, G., Poland, Russia and the U. S., 1844. P. 17.
Turkey and Russia, 1766.
Williams, C. H., Account of, 1822.
See Russia.

Polari, C. Herinneringen eener reize naar Nieuw York, 1832.

Pole, R., Abp. Hook, W. F., Life of, 1869.
Ridley, Review of Phillips.

Police. Boston, Report, 1856.
Brereton, Writings, 1825–46.
Colquhoun, Police of the Thames, 1800.
" Police of London, 1800.
Considerations on seditious practices, 1795.
Deykes, Pavements of London, 1824. P. 139.
Duchatelet, De la Prostitution, 1837.
" Prostitution in Paris, 1846.
Ducpétiaux, Question des Mort-nés, 1848.
Fielding, H., Works, Increase of robbers, vol. 10, 1806.
Fielding, J., Plan for prevent. robberies, 1755. P. 403.
Frégier, Des Classes dangéreuses dans les grandes villes, 1840.
Gerard, London and New York, Police of, 1853.
Gr. Brit., London Police, 1816.
" Rep. on Constabulary force, 1839. B. C.
" Police: Bills, 1848.
Mather, J. C., On Metrop. Police Law.
N. Y. City, Reports, 1856–58.
N. Y. Metr. Pol. Regulations, 1858.
Noxon, Speech, Met. Police, 1858.

Police (continued).
San Francisco, Ordinance.
" Address of Comm. of Vigilance, 1856.
Sauveur, De la Police des Décès, 1843.
Skillman, N. Y. Police reports, 1830.
Vidocq, Memoirs, as Agent of.
Vivien, Le Préfet de Police, 1845.
Unlawful Meetings, Lond., 1848.
Waters, T., Recollections, 1853.
See Punishments; Convicts; Crime; Health; Prisons; Statistics.

Polignac, Diana de. Mémoires, 1796.
" Confession de, 1789.

Politeness. *See* Etiquette; Gentleman; Self Culture; Woman.

Political Economy. Baring, On the Commutation Act, 1786.
Bascom, J., Pol. Econ., a text-book, 1861.
Bastiat, Harmonies économiques, 1860.
" Popular fallacies.
Bell, A., Prohib. of grain for distilling, 1808. P. 1472.
Bowen, F., Am. pol. economy, 1870.
Brereton, Writings, 1825–46.
Cadet de Vaux, Des Disettes, 1812.
Carey, H. C., Principles of, 1837, 8.
" Harmony of interests, 1849, 50.
" Manual of Social Science, 1864.
" Miscellaneous writings, 1838–1868.
Carey, M., Twenty-one golden rules, 1824.
" Fifty-one reasons, 1824.
" Olive Branch, 1814, 32.
" Cursory views, 1826.
Casaux, Effets de l'impôt, 1787.
Chalmers, G., Consid. on commerce, 1811.
Chalmers, T., Connection with morals, 1832.
" Civic Econ. of towns, 1823.
Colton, C., Public Econ. of U. S., 1848.
Cotton, R., Disc., of Foreign war, 1690.
Comber, W. T., State of National subsistence, 1808.
Condorcet, Œuvres, 1847.
Conversations on, 1817.
Cooper, T., Lectures on, 1829.
Corbet, Causes of Wealth, 1841.
Davenant, Polit. and Comm. Works, 1771.
Demeunier, Economie politique, Encyc. Méth.
De Quincey, T., Logic of, 1844.
Dove, P. E., Elem. of pol. science, 1854.

Prisons (continued).

Parchappe, Plans des Prisons, 1853.

Paul, G. O., Defects of, 1784.

Peacock, J , In a French Prison, 1814.

Peirce, B. K., Half century with juv. delin., 1869.

Penn., Reports of the Peniten., 1831–1853.

" Rep. of Eastern Pen., 1834, 58–1866.

" Rep. of Committees, 1830, 34–1866.

Penn. Journ. of Prison Disc., 1845–57.

Penn. Penitentiary system. P. v. 164.

Penn. System in France, 1847. P. 162.

Pentonville, La Prison de, 1848.

Phelps, R. H., Hist. of Newgate and Wethersfield Prisons, 1860.

Phil'a County Prisons, Reports, 1848-51. P. 162.

" House of Refuge, Reports, 1845–53. P. 161, 162; 1860–67, and specials.

Phil'a Soc. for alleviating......1859. P. 539.

" Penn'a system defended, 1867.

Powers, G., Auburn State Prison, Report, 1828. P. 16. B. C.

Preston House of Correction, Eng., Calendar, 1819. P. 1016.

" Report, 1858.

Prison Assoc. of N. Y., Reports, 1844–1869.

" Special report of Wines and Dwight, 1867.

Prison Disc., Auburn System, 1839. P. 164.

Prison Disc., Lond., 1835.

Prison Disc. Soc., Boston: Reports, 1826–53.

Prisoner's friend, Boston, 1849–57.

Prisons, Des, de Philadelphie, 1796.

Providence, R. I., House of Reformation, Report, 1848. P. 159.

Public instruction in, 1846.

Rat-trap, The, 1857.

Roscoe, W., Penitentiaries in the U. S. A., 1827.

Smith, G. W., Defence of solitary confinement, 1833. P. 164.

Sneed, Hist. of Kentucky Penitentiary, 1860.

Soc. for the Improv. of P. Disc., Treadmill, 1823. P. 403.

" Reports, 1821, 22; Rules, 1818, 1822.

Soc. for Reform. of Juv. delinq., N. Y., Reports, 1828–67.

Soc. pour le patronage des jeunes détenus, 1833–52.

Prisons (continued).

Sumner, G., The Penn'a System of Prison Disc in France, 1847. P. 20.

Suringar, Bestaan, Nederl. Genoots.. tot..Gevangenen.

" My Visit to Mettray, 1845.

Tallack, Humanitarianism, 1870.

Tennessee, Peniten. Reports, 1857, 59.

Thoughts on prison labor, 1824.

Tracts on, 1861–62.

Vidal, Prisons de Sardaigne, 1857.

Vind. of the Separate system, 1839. P. 164.

Wisconsin, Ann. Report, 1856.

Whately, R., Thoughts on secondary punishments, 1832.

See Police; Punishments; Convicts; Reform Schools; Crimes.

Privateering. Appeal to the Government, 1819.

Coggeshall, Hist. of, 1812–1814.

Congrès de Paris, 1856.

General Armstrong privateer, Coll. of papers, 1833.

Practice of, Gallison, 1819.

Proposed Memorial, 1819.

Taylor, R. B., Memorial for losses, 1819.

See Buccaneers; Neutrals.

Probabilities. Condorcet, Discours sur. Œuvres, v. 1.

De Morgan, A., Essay on, (Lardner's Cyc.).

Galloway, T., Treatise on, 1839.

La Place, Essai sur les prob., 1814.

Quetelet, Théorie des Probabilités, 1846.

See Mathematics; Insurance.

Proclus. Fabricius, Vita à Marino, 1703.

Proclus, Works, Taylor's trans.

Proclus, Abp. Analecta, 1630.

Procter, W. Orde, Sermon on, 1839.

Proctor, E. G. Eichelberger, L., Discourse, 1851.

Prognostications. *See* Prophecy; Second Sight; Astrology.

Progress. Bunsen, C., God in history, 1870.

Everett, E., Remarks on progress, 1853.

Froude, Short Studies, 2d series, 1871.

Hamilton, R., Prog. of Society, 1830.

Hampden in the 19th century, 1834.

Mably, Du Développement, 1795.

Magoon, E. L., Westward Empire, 1856.

Nott, S., Improvement of the people, 1831.

Protestantism (continued).

Burnet, Hist. of Ref. of Ch. of Eng., 1781.

Campbell, J. N., The Reformation, 1844.

Carey, M., Views on Catholic Conspiracy in 1641.

Catholic Association reviewed, 1825.

/Challoner, Beginning of, 1832.

Chauncy, Doct. of Godliness, 1737.

Chillingworth, Works, 1836.

" Religion of, 1854.

Cobbett, Hist. of, in Engl., 1825.

Colton, C., Protestant Jesuitism, 1836.

Conder, J., Condition of Prot. dissenters, 1853.

Crespin, Galerie Chrétienne, 1837.

Crisp, J., Prot. compendium, 1840.

Dalhusius, Salvation of Protestants, 1689. P. 357.

De Beaulieu, Protestants safe, 1687.

De Coetlogon, Prot. Ref. considered, 1818.

Developments of, 1849.

Dialogue between two, 1686.

Dominis, Archiep., Suæ profec. consilium, 1616.

" My motives, 1827.

Du Moulin, A Replie, 1675.

Evans, C., Former Days, Lond., 1778.

Fox, J., Book of Martyrs, 1684, 1830.

Fratelli, C., Vereenigingh der twee Religien, 1725. P. 109.

Froude, Prospects of, (Short studies), 1871.

Gardiner, H. W., Emanc. of Protest. churches, 1825.

Gillett, E. H., Life of Huss, 1863.

Gilly, W. S., Our Prot. forefathers, 1836.

Haller, C., Conversion to Cath. Ch., 1822.

Hardwick, C., History of the Church, 1865.

Harmony of Protestant Confessions, 1832.

Hawkins, E., Sermon, 1850.

Heidelberg Catechism, 1654.

Heylin, Hist. of the Reformation of the Church of England, 1849.

Historical Collections, (Hickes), 1674.

Hist. of Prot. ch. in Hungary, 1854.

Hopkins, J. H., End of controversy.

Hopkins, S. M., Prot. of 19th Century.

Horne, T. H., Prot. Memorial, 1835.

Horton, R. W., Prot. securities, London, 1828.

Hurst, J. F., Hist. of rationalism, 1865.

Knibbe, Katechisatie, 1724. B. C.

Koefler, Reformbewegung in Deutschland, 1500.

Protestantism (continued).

Labadie, Des Geloofs de gereformeerde Kerke, 1682.

Leahey, Narr. of conversion.

Letter to a Member...on Union, 1689.

Luther, Bulla In cœna Domini, 1769. P. 109.

" Wittemberg Theses.

" Life of, illustrated, 1853.

McCrie, Hist. of Refor. in Italy, 1833.

" Hist. of Refor. in Spain, 1829.

M'Gavin, W., The Protestant, 1833.

M'Gee, T. D., Lect. on causes, 1853.

" Ref. in Ireland, 1853.

Massingberd's Hist. of, in England, 1844.

Merle d'Aubigné, Hist. de la Réformation.

" History of the Reformation, 1849.

" Hist. of the Ref., time of Calvin, 1863-9.

Millar, Prin. of Ref. churches, 1731.

Moehler, J. A., Symbolism, 1843.

Molesworth, Not a new Religion, 1835.

Mystery of iniquity, 1689.

National Club, Address, 1852-56.

Nolan, L. J., Of leaving church of Rome.

No Protestant Plot, 1675.

O'Donnoghue, H. C., Hist. of Ch. of Rome, 1830.

Palmer, S., Prot. Diss. Catechism.

Pamphlets on Protestantism, vols. 1048, 1425-1429, 1628, 1735, 1774.

Popery always the same, 1746.

Popery of Protestantism, 1850.

Protestant Almanac, 1693-98, 1841, 1851, 52, 55.

Protestant Association, Tracts, 1839.

Protestant Catechism, 1778, 80.

Protestant Dissenters' Committee, 1796, 1813.

Prot. Meeting, Liverpool, 1835.

Protestant Quar. Review, 1850-53.

Protestant's Resolution, 1766.

Protestants' Union, 1813.

Ranke's Hist. of Ref. in Germany, 1845.

Reflections on the Reformation, 1688.

Roussell, Cath. and Prot. Nations compared.

Sayous, Ecrivains de la Réformation, 1841.

Schaf, P., Principles of, 1845.

Sleidan, Hist. de la Réf. *Lat. and Fr.* 1767.

" De Stat. Rel. Car. V. Cæs., 1556.

Société Evang. de Genève, 1833-53.

Some considerations, 1680.

Protestantism (continued).
Some dialogues, 1687.
Spalding, M. J., Review of Aubigné, etc., 1860.
Strype, Reformation in Engl., 1736–38.
Tercentenary Anniv. of Heidelberg Catech., 1863.
Témoin de la Vérité, 1850.
Tillotson, Serm., Prot'm Vindicated, 1680.
Upham, C. W., Principles of: a Sermon, 1826. P. 106.
Weninger, F. X., Prot. and Infidelity, 1862.
Weiss, Hist. de la Réformation, 1854.
Young, M., Life of A. Paleario, 1860.
Zurich, The, Letters, 1537–1602.
See Church; Presbyterian; Puritans; Roman Catholic Church, etc.; Augsburgh Confession; Sisters of Mercy.

Protozoa. *See* Natural History; Zoölogy; Microscope; Zoöphytes.

Proudfit, A. Forsyth, J., Memoirs of, 1846.

Proverbs. Apostolius, M., Parœmiæ, 1619.
Ben-Sira, Proverbia, 1597.
Bohn, Polyglott of foreign Proverbs, 1857.
" Hand-book of, Ray's, etc., 1855.
Book of Crests, (Mottoes), 1854.
Draxe, Bibliot. Scholastica, 1654.
Erasmus, Adagiorum chiliades quatuor, 1574.
Grose, F., Glossary and Proverbs, 1811.
Hazlitt, W. C., Eng. Proverbs and phrases, 1869.
Herbert, G., Jacula prudentium, (Works).
Luther, M., Spruch-und-schatz Kastlein, 1824.
Lycosthenes, Apotheg. ex opt. Script., 1684.
Nopitsch, Handb. der Sprichwörter, 1833.
Reusnerius, Symbola heroica, 1650.
Trench, On the lessons in, 1856.
Tupper, Philos. of Proverbs, 1851.
See Emblems; Maxims; Quotations; Bible.

Providence. Berkeley, Theory of Vision, 1733. P. 236.
Birch, T., Serm., Const. of Man, 1749. P. 1006.
Bridges, Divine Wisdom, 1737.
Bridgewater Treatises, 9 vols.
Bunsen, C. De., God in history, 1868–1870.
Croly, G., Divine Providence, Lond., 1834.

Providence (continued).
Drummond, Sir W., Academ. questions, 1805.
Durham, Prize Essay, 1804.
Franck, A. H., Footsteps of Prov., 1788.
Gorman, J. B., Phil. of animated existence, 1845.
Gregory, T., Doctrine of, 1694.
Pilkington, Doctrine of, 1838.
Priest, J., Wonders of, 1825.
Proclus, Essay on Providence.
Rotheram, Sermon on, 1762.
Salvien, Opera, 1684.
" De la providence, 1701.
Sanford, M., Punitive Justice, 1855. P. 558.
Thurling, Things of Time, 1837. P. 339.
Young, E., Vindication of, Sermon, 1747. P. 370.
See Predestination; God; Theol.

Providence, Rh. Is. Hagar, W., Hist. First Bapt. Church.
Pitman, J., Centennial disc., 1836.
Providence, Marr. and Deaths, 1859–1866.
Providence Directory, 1832, 61, 62.
Rhode Island Hist. Coll., v. 5.
Snow, E. M., Statistics of, 1855–60.
Staples, W. R., Annals of, 1843.
Tucker, M., Centennial Serm., 1843.
See Brown University.

Provoost, Bp. Norton, J. N., Life of.
Perry, Fragment on.

Prudden, N. Robbins, T., Sermon, Death of.

Prussia. Atkinson, E. W., Mem. of Queenss of, 1856.
Campbell, J., Court of Frederick, 1842.
Cappe, N., Serm. on victory of, 1757.
Carlyle, T., Life of Frederick the Great.
Cernitius, Vies des Electeurs de Brandenbourg, 1707.
Denina, Vita di Federico II, 1789.
Dover, Lord, Life of Frederick II, 1839.
Franckel, Thanksgiving Serm. on victory of, 1757.
Frederica de Prusse, Mémoires, 1812.
Frederick II, Œuvres, 1846–53.
Germanic Empire, 1803. P. 1322.
Krug, Statistik, 1805.
Letters of Times Corresp't on the war, 1870–71.
McCabe, Hist. of the war, 1870–71.
Mémoires ....de la Maison de Brandebourg, 1787.

Pym, J. Forster, J., Life of.
Smith, Gold., Three Engl. Statesmen.

Pyramids. Belzoni, Discov. in Egypt, 1822.
France: Description de l'Egypte.
Gabb, T., Finis Pyramidis, 1806.
Greaves, J., Descrip. of; Churchill's Voy.
Lepsius, Denkmaeler aus Aegypten, 1842–45.
Smyth, C. P., The Great Pyramid; Quar. Jour. of Sci., 1871.
Ward, A., Around the Pyr., 1864.
See Egypt.

Pyrenees. Inglis, H. D., France and the Pyr., 1840.
See France; Spain.

Pyrenees, (Basses), Fr. Annuaire, 1845.

Pythagoras. Gale, T., Court of the Gentiles, 1671.
Hierocles, On the Golden verses of.
Pamphlets, vol. 1542.
Somers, Coll. of Tracts; Lloyd, Life of.
Taylor, T., Fragments of the Pythagoreans, 1822.

Q.

Quackery. Phil'a Med. Soc., Quack Med., 1828. P. 87.
Reese, Humbugs of N. Y., 1838.
Thomson, J., The steam quack. P. 713.
Ticknor, C., On Quackery, 1844.
See Medicine; Delusions.

Quadrupeds. *See* Mammalia; Zoölogy; Mastodon.

Quakers. *See* Friends, Society of.

Quarantine. Caldwell, Thoughts on, 1834.
Clark, H. G., Sanitary meas. preferable, 1852.
Harris, E., Pestilential diseases, 1858. P. 501.
Henry, W. C., Laws of contagion, 1834.
Maclean, C., Quarantine laws, 1824.
" Suggestions on the Plague. Pamph'r 16.
MacMichael, Opinions on Contagion. Pamph'r 25.
National Quarantine Conven., Proc., 1857, 59, 60.
New Jersey, Report on N. Y. Quar., 1858. P. 501.
New York, Removal of, 1858.
" Reps. on, 1856, 7. P. 1807.
" Letter of Sec. of State, 1863.
" Comm. from Governor, 1865, 1866.

Quarantine (continued).
New York, Leg. Rep. on Quar. laws, 1846.
Papon, I. P., De la Peste.
Russell, P., Of the Plague, 1790.
Swinburne, Report, N. Y., 1865.
Staten Island, Quarantine, 1858.
See Cholera; Contagion; Health; Plague; Yellow Fever.

Quebec. Adams, A., Sermon, Victory at, 1759.
Canada Directory, 1857, 1871.
Hawkins, Annals of the diocese, 1849.
Hawkins, Directory, 1844, 5.
Henry, Campaign against, 1775.
Lyttelton, Letter on bill, 1774.
Mayhew, J., Sermon on reduction of.
Melvin, J., Jour. of exped. to, 1776.
Quebec, Mémoire conc. les Grèves du Sault-au-matelot..du Seminaire, 1830.
Quebec Directories, 1852, 53.
Quebec Papers, 1775, 76.
Quebec, Pictures of, 1830, 51.
" Hand book, 1850.
Reminiscences of, 1862.
Séminaire de, 200e anniversaire, 1863.
Siége de Quebec, 1759, 1847.
Silliman, B., Tour in, 1819.
Winter, R., Sermon on, 1759.

Queen's Co., N. Y. Onderdonk, H., jr., Sketches of, 1851.
" Q. C. in olden times, 1865.
Queen's Co. Agric. Soc., Addresses before, 1858–62.

Queensland, Australia. Emigration to. P. 1683.

Queenstown. Van Rensselaer, Narr. of affair at, 1812.

Quiche Lang. *See* Languages, Indian.

Quincy family. Acct. of, 1857.

Quincy, J., jr. Quincy, J., Mem. of the Life of, 1825.

Quincy, Josiah. Addresses, etc., 1798–1856.
Everett, E., Remarks, 1864, v. 4.
Gannett, E. S., Discourse on, 1864.
Mass. Hist. Soc., Proc., 1864.
Quincy, E., Life of, 1867.
Walker, J., Memoir of, Mass. Hist. Soc.

Quincy, Ms. Cutler, Hist. discourse, 1828.
Dorchester and Q. Directory, 1869.
Lunt, W. P., Century discourses, 1839.
Whitney, G., History of, 1827.
" Centen. discourse, 1840.

Railroads, Construction, etc. (continued).
Lushington, Broad Gauge, 1846. P. 428.
Marivault, Des chemins de fer, 1839.
Martin, R. M., Railways, 1849.
Melville, H. S., Narrow Gauge, 1846. P. 428.
Navier, On Railways and Locomotive Engines, 1836.
Nicholson, P., Railway masonry, 1840.
Obser...en los E. U. Mejicanos, 1833. P. 284.
Obs. on Mr. Strutt's bill, 1847.
Observations on Gauge, Lond., 1846.
O'Rielly, H., Reform in railroad management, No. 3, 4, 5, 1867.
Palmer, H. R., A new principle, 1824.
Pamphlets relating to, vols. 1203, 4, 5.
Pim, J., Atmospheric R. R., 1841.
Rail Road Tolls, N. Y. P. v. 1248.
Railroad... Moral View, 1845. P. 339.
Railway eccentrics, on Guage, 1846.
Railway Chronicle, Lond., 1844-49.
Railway Magazine, Lond., 1836-39.
Railway Times, Lond., 1855-58.
Reply to "Obs." on Gauge, 1846.
Rightway, L., Railways, 1851.
Routes to the East, 1857.
Sidney, Speed on, 1847.
Slie, War of the Gauges, 1854.
Société d'Encouragement .... Freins automoteurs.
Stevens's plan in 1812, (Albany Inst. Coll.).
Strickland, W., Reports on, 1826.
Sullivan, J. L., Principles of, 1830.
Train, G. F., Observations on street R. R.
Tredgold, Treatise on, 1825.
Truth without fiction, (Private freight expresses), 1867.
Vose, G. L., Hand-book of Construction, 1857.
Weale, Ensamples of railways, 1843.
Whiting, W., 20 years war against the R. R., 1860.
Wishaw, Analysis of railways, 1838.
With, E., R. R. Accidents, 1856.
Woods, E., On Railway constants, 1841.
See Engineering.

Railroads, British. A. B. C. Railway Guide, 1854.
Adam, W., On the Great North Road, 1832. P. 1553.
Andrew, W. P., Railways in Bengal, 1853.
Atkinson, Caledonian R. R., 1842.
Barlow, On the Liv. and Manch. R. R., 1837.

Railroads, British (continued).
Bombay, Baroda Central, 1854.
Booth, H., Hist. of Liv. and Manch. R. R., 1831.
Bradshaw's Railway Guide, 1847, 51, 1852, 53, 57, 71.
Cape Town R. R., 1858. P. 1553.
Clarke, H. G., Excursion Guide, London. P. 1573.
Eastern Counties R. R., 1852-59.
Great Britain; India R. R., 1857.
Hudson, G., Report of evidence of, 1850.
Letter to the Rt. Hon, L'd J. Russell, on India R. R., 1848. P. 1553.
Liverpool and Manch. R. R., 1830.
London and Southwestern, 1846. P. 428.
Manchester R. R., Description of, 1835.
Pamphlets on British Railroads, vol. 428.
Railroads, London and Brighton, 1836.
Railway Chronicle, 1844-49.
Railway Magazine, 1836-39.
Railway Times, 1855-58.
Reasons for direct line to Manchester, 1846. P. 428.
Scrivenor, Railways of Great Britain, 1849.
Upper India R. R. Co., 1852.

Railroads, European. Amsterdam naar Rotterdam, Verslag, 1851.
Austria, Den Semmering.
" Eisenbahn Coursbuch, 1851.
Belgium: Comptes rendus, 1844-51.
Chatelain, Atlas des Chemins de fer, 1855.
Chemin de fer de Namur, 1845.
Compagnie.... de l'Espagne.
Dobson, E., Railways of Belgium, 1834-42.
Duplessy, Chemins de fer de l'Alsace 1842.
Est-il-vrai! Réponse...des interêts matériels, 1864.
France: Railroads; Sureté d'exploitation, 1858.
" Documents, 1823-1860.
" Bridges, Notices, 1859.
" Législation des chemins de fer.
" Situation générale, 1861.
Ghega, Chemin du Semmering.
" Uebersicht, Oesterreich, 1852.
Grande Société...Russe, Assem., 1861.
Mount, In the, Cenis Tunnel, 1866. P. 1553.
Prussia, Statis. Nachrichten, 1863.
Società Anon....Firenze à Livorno, 1841. P. 546.
Société Autrichienne, Assemblée, 1861.

Railroads, U. S.: PENNSYLVANIA (continued).
Catawissa, Williamsport & Erie, 1853, 1855.
" Case with Phil'a & Erie, 1866.
Huntingdon & Broadtop & Coal Co., 1853, 57.
Little Schuylkill & Susquehanna, 1835, 38, 39.
Mine Hill & Schuylkill, 1853, 4, 6.
North Pennsylvania, 1853-58.
Pamphlets on, vols. 285, 545, 1203, 1814.
Pennsylvania: Auditor's Rep., 1864-1870.
Penn'a R. R. Co. Reports, 3 vols. to 1867.
Pequa R. R. Co., 1849.
Phil'a and Columbia, 1854.
Phil'a & Reading, 1834-67.
Phil'a & Sunbury, 1852.
Phil'a, Easton & Water Gap, 1852, 1853.
Phil'a, Wilm., and Baltimore, 1835-57.
Pittsburgh & Alloghony, 1843.
Sunbury & Erie, 1854-60.
Susquehanna Co., 1852, 54.
Williamsport & Elmira, 1850, 56, 58, 1859.

SOUTHERN. Alabama Central, 1859.
Alabama & Florida, 1848, 58.
Brunswick & Florida, 1855.
Cairo & Fulton, Arkansas, 1856, 55.
Chesapeake & Ohio, 1868.
Georgia Railroads, 1859.
Macon & Western, 1848.
Memphis, Helena & St. Louis, 1869.
Mobile & Ohio, 1848, 49.
Nashville Cham. of Commerce, 1856.
Newcastle & Frenchtown, Del. 1849.
New Orleans, Mobile & Texas, 1871.
New Orleans, Opelousas & Great Western, 1868.
Pamphlets on Southern, vol. 1815.
Petersburgh (Va.) R. R., 1847.
Pope, South Western Tenn., 1846.
Raleigh & Gaston, N. C., 1840.
Richmond & York, 1849.
Southern R. R. Co., Miss., 1845.
Tennessee Com'rs Rep., 1857, 59.
Texas Western R. R., 1855.
Virginia & Tennessee, 1856.
Wilmington & Manchester, N. C., 1853.

VERMONT. Connecticut & Passumpsic Rivers, 1846, 49, 64.
Connecticut River R. R., 1863, 64.
Pamphlets, vol. 1817.
Quincy, J., Letter to Stockholders, 1852.

Railroads, U. S.: VERMONT (continued).
Rutland & Burlington, 1848-52, 54-58, 1860, 63.
Rutland & Whitehall, 1852, 54, 59.
Vermont Comm'rs Reports, 1856-66, 1868.
Vermont & Canada, 1859.
Vermont & Massachusetts, 1849, 64-66, 1868.
Vermont Central, 1850-52, 65.
Vermont Valley, 1851-55; mortgage, 1862, 63.
Western Vermont, 1851.

WESTERN. Ohio Falls Marine R. R., 1853.
Pamphlets on Western, vol. 1818.
Whittlesey C., R. R. with Lake Superior, 1853.

WISCONSIN. La Crosse & Milwaukee, 1855-1857, 63.
La Crosse & Milwaukee Bondholders' Deed, 1858.
Milwaukee & Beloit, 1857.
Milwaukee & Horicon, 1856.
Milwaukee & Mississippi, 1852-57.
Milwaukee & St. Paul's, 1866.
Mineral Point, R. R., 1857.
St. Croix & Lake Superior, 1850.
St. Croix & Lake Superior: Acts of Congr. and Wisconsin, 1866.
Watertown & Mississippi, 1857.
Wisconsin, Report of Board, 1853.
Wisconsin & Superior, 1856.

Raleigh, Sir W. Drake, S. G., Memoir of, 1862.
Edwards, E., Life and Letters of, 1868.
Harris, J. M., Life of, M'd. Hist. Soc.
Kingsley, C., Essays, 1859.
Napier, M., Lord Bacon and Sir W. R.
Raleigh, Works, Life of, by Birch.
" Collection of four tracts, 1618, 26, 48, 17.
Thomson, Mrs. A. T., Life of, 1841. B. C.
Tytler, P. F., Life of, Edin. Cab. Lib., 11.
Van Heuvel, El Dorado, 1844.

Ralston, R. Cuyler, C. C., Sermon on, 1836.
Green, A., Fun. Address, 1836.

Rambach, A. J. Petersen, In Memoriam, 1856.

Ramcke, J. H. Senior, Biography of.

Ramel, Gen. J. P. Journal, 1799.
Narrative of deportation, 1799.

Rammohun Roy. Fox, W. J., Disc. on, 1833.

Ramsay, M. L. Ramsay, D., Memoir 1845.

Reform, Moral, Political (continued). Dewey, A Lecture, 1852.

Greeley, H., Hints towards Reforms, 1850.

" Association discussed, 1847.

Ingestre, Viscount, Meliora, 1852, 53.

Mangles, R. D., Reasons for being a Reformer, 1840. P. 1384.

Michelet, The People, 1846.

Penitent Female's Refuge, Report, 1823. P. 509.

Reese, Humbugs of N. Y., 1838.

Smith, C. B., Philosophy of Reform, 1846.

Wells, E. M. P., Address, 1835.

See Morals; Political Economy; Civilization; Social Science; Society for the Reform. of Manners.

Reformation. *See* Protestantism.

Reformed Church, N. A. Graham, D., Proceedings, 1811.

Sabelis, B., Thoughts on declension, 1836.

Sprague, W. B., Annals of the American Pulpit, v. 9, 1869.

See Associate; Associate Reformed.

Reformed Presbyterian Church. Our Polit. Oaths, 1855.

Narr. of occurrences, 1834. P. 895.

Pamphlets relating to Reformed Presbyterians, vols. 895, 905, 915, 922.

Reform Presb. Ch., Proc. of Gen. Synod, 1848.

Reform Principles, 1862.

Sprague's Annals of the Amer. Pulpit, v. 9, 1869.

Reformed Presbyterian Ch., Scotland. History of, 1842.

Reformed (Protestant Dutch) Ch., U. S. Amerman, A., On the Classis of Montgomery, 1823.

Bergen, N. Jersey, Centennial of the Church, 1861.

Brief....van de Classis van Amsterdam aan N. Y., 1772.

Brownlee, W. C., Life of, 1860.

Buddingh, De Kerk in N. America, 1851, 53.

Corwin, Manual of, 1859.

" Manual of, 1869.

Demarest, D. D., History of, 1856.

Dewitt, T., Hist. Disc., N. Y., 1857.

Dortsma, Het Aanwesen, 1772.

Ferré, Van den Heidelberg. Catechismus, 17[illegible]3–86.

Ferris, I., Characteristics of, 1848.

Hudson First R. D. C., 1854. P. 547.

Knox, J., Memorial of, N. Y., 1858.

Leydt, J., Ware Vryheit tot vrede, 1760.

Magazine of R. D. Church, 1826–30.

Reformed (Protestant Dutch) Ch., U. S. (continued).

Michaëlius, Letter, N. Y., 1628.

New Brunswick Review, 1855.

Pamphlets relating to the Ref. Church, vol. 547.

Reddingius, Over den Heidelberg. Cat., 1806, 7.

Ref. Prot. Dutch Ch. of N. A., Proceedings, 1771–1812.

" Minutes, 1806–1868.

" Proceedings of Ministers of N. Y. and N. J., for union, 1771.

" Liturgy of, 1856, 57.

" Address to....the Secession, 1822.

" Message to Ministers, Tracts, 1856.

" Message to Ruling elders, Tracts, 1856.

" Synod of N. Y. city, Proc., 1840, 56.

" Synod of Albany, Proc.

Remarks on lib. of conscience, 1828.

Ritzema, J., Aan J. Leydt, N. Brunswick, Phil'a, 1763.

Taylor, B., Classis of Bergen, 1857.

Van Nest, A. R., Sermon, 1859.

" Life of G. W. Bethune, 1867.

Van Zandt, A. B., Rightful name of the church, 1867.

Reform Schools. Boston H. of Industry and Ref., Report, 1851. P. 162.

California Ref. School, Rep., 1860.

Chicago Reports, 1856–60, 63.

Clark, T. M., Discourse, Ref. Sch., Hartford, 1852.

Colonie de Mettray, 1853–9.

Connecticut, Reports on, 1853, 58. P. 507; 56, 57. P. 1820.

Houses of Refuge and Ref., 1857. P. 507.

Houses of Refuge: Conven. of Managers, 1860.

Howe, S. G., Letter on, for girls, 1854.

Lamarque, Colonies des jeunes détenus, 1850.

Maine: Ref. Sch. Reports, 1856–8.

Mass.; Ref. Sch., Docts., 1847–57. P. 159, 507.

Murray, P. J., Ref. Schools, 1854.

Orphans' Home, Pittsburgh, 1860.

Pamphlets regarding, vol. 1820.

Providence, 7th Report, 1858. P. 507; 1861, 63.

Rochester Juv. Asylum, 1854.

Soc. for the Ref. of Juv. Delin., N. Y., Repts., 1825, 47–64.

Relics. Toursel, Worship of Holy Relics, Cath. pulpit, 19.

See Ronge, John; Treves.

Relief Church, Scotland. Struther's, G., History of, 1858.

Thomson, A., Hist. of Secess. Church.

Religion, Religions. Adams, H., Compendium of Various Sects, 1784.

Brerewood, Inquiry, 1635.

Child, L. M., Prog. of rel. ideas, 1855.

Colloquies on, 1837.

Constant, De la Religion, 1824–5. B.C.

Dupuis, Origine des Cultes, 1821.

Essay in favour, etc., 1728.

Evelyn, John, History of, 1850.

Glade, Du Progrès Religieux, 1838.

Gould, S. B., Origin of Belief, 1869.

Hay, W., Religio Philosophi, 1753.

Hunt, J., Relig. Thought in England, 1871.

Hunt, Leigh, Rel. of the Heart, 1853.

Moore, G., Man and his Motives, 1848.

Morell, Philosophy of Religion, 1849.

Norton, A., Thoughts on True and False, 1820. P. 8. B. C.

Novissima tuba, 1632. P. 1795.

Occasional Paper, 1–10, 1697.

Orr, J., Theory of Religion, 1762.

Parker, T., Ten Sermons on, 1855.

Plain Truth, Rochester, N. Y., 1829.

Puffendorf, S., Nature and Qualification of, 1698.

Renan, Studies of Relig. Hist., 1864.

Robbins, T., All Religions, 1823.

Ross, A., View of all Religions.

" Les religions du Monde, 1666.

Rupp, Hist. of Relig. denominations, 1844.

Sismondi, Progress of Relig. Opinions, 1827. P. 65.

Steele, E., Five Discourses, Nature of, 1805.

See Bible; Christ; Theology; Mythology; Antiquities.

Religion in America. *See* U. States, Religion in.

Religion, Practical. Adam, T., Private Thoughts, 1825.

Advice to a Young Christian.

Alleine, Alarm to the Unconverted.

Baptistery, The, (J. Williams), 1844.

Bartoli, L'Eternità consigliera, 1832.

Baxter, R., Select Prac. Writings, 1831.

" Saint's Everlasting Rest.

" Call to the Unconverted.

" Principles of Love, 1671.

Beveridge, W., Private Thoughts.

Religion, Practical (continued).

Beecher, H. W., Life Thoughts, 1858.

Bernard, S., Opera, 1781.

Bogatzky, Golden Treasury. 1797.

Bogue, D., Sermon, 1800.

Breeden, Plain Things, 1846. P. 262.

Brodbelt, Orig. Essays, 1796.

Brown, J., Remains, 1792.

Buck, C., Religious Anecdotes.

Bunyan, Pilgrim's Progress.

" Holy War.

Burkitt, Poor Man's Help, 1804.

Cameron, J., The Messiah, 1770.

Carson, J., Revealer of Grievances, 1811.

Cecil, Friendly Visit, 1820. P. 339.

Charbonnel, J., Dèvotion à la sainte famille, 1850.

Cheap Repository Tracts, H. More, 1800.

Clarke, J., Why are you a Christian?

Cottage Dialogues, 1821.

Couling, The Saints Perfect, 1647.

Dickinson, J., Familiar Letters, 1745.

Devout Meditations, (J. Howe).

Divine Breathings, (Lucas), 1792.

Divine Maxims, 1755.

Doddridge, Rise and Progress, 1812.

Dolman, J., Contemplations, 1755.

Dream, The, Lond., 1747.

Drexelius, H., Prodromus æternitatis, 1628.

" Palæstra Christiana, 1648.

Dutton, A., Letters, 1823.

Edwards, T., Conversions in Northampton, 1636.

" Treatise on the affections, 1746.

Experimental Knowledge, 1849.

Felltham, Resolves, 1709.

Flower, T., Union with Christ, 1840.

Foster, J., Importance of, 1827.

Fuller, Thomas, The Holy State.

Gastrell, Necessity of, 1697.

Grosvenor, The Mourner, 1783. P. 615.

Guide to Heaven, 1815. P. 231.

Harrison, T., Topica sacra, 1658.

Hasted, F., Writings, 1861–3.

Herbert, G., Works, 1846.

Hervey, J., Meditations.

Hobson, Garden Enclosed, 1647.

Hooker, H., Uses of adversity, 1846.

Hopkins, E., Exposition of the Ten Commandments.

Huntington, W., Bank of faith, 1805.

Inmens, Pious Communicant, 1801.

Jackson, L., Letter to a Young Lady, 1756. P. 338.

James, J. A., The Anxious Enquirer.

Religion, Practical (continued).

Jay, W., Morn. and Eve. Exercises, 1841. B. C.

Jenks, B., Prayers for Families, 1813. B. C.

Johnson, A. B., Religion in the Present Life, 1841.

Kempis, Imitation of Christ, 1805, 12.

" Little Kempis, Boston, 1836.

" Nachfolge Christi, 1810.

Kenn, T., Crown of Glory, 1725.

Krummacher, The Parables, 1858.

Law, W., Address to the Clergy, 1796.

Letters to a Young Christian, 1858.

Macduff, J. R., Grapes of Eshcol, 1861.

McLeod, Power of True Godliness, 1816.

Malan, C., Theogenes, Am I a Child of God? 1828.

" Convent of Rolle, 1825.

Martineau, H., Devotional Exercises, 1833. B. C.

Martineau, J., Endeav. after Christ. life, 1844. B. C.

Meade, W., Companion to the Font, 1846.

Meikle, J., The Traveller, 1812.

" Solitude Sweetened, 1811.

Melmoth, Importance of Relig. Life, 1849.

More, H., Reflections on Prayer, 1820. B. C.

" Practical Piety, 1812. B. C.

Newton, R., Sermons to Children, 1860.

Ogden, U., Address.......Salvation, 1785.

" Theological Preceptor, 1772.

Osorio, De gloria: de Nobilitate christiana, 1671.

Palmer, R., Closet Hours, 1851.

Pamphlets relating to, American, vols. 90, 93, 219, 232, 495, 623, 2527, 2528.

Pamphlets relating to, British, vols. 338, 339, 623, 1433, 1736–1741, 1795, 1796.

Pastor's Daughter, (Payson), 1835.

Payson, E., Conversations, 1833.

Pearsall, R., Sacred dialogues, 1765.

Phelps, A., The Still Hour, 1860.

Phillips, R., On Watchfulness. P. 623.

Poole, M., Apology for, 1673.

Ridley, T., Strictures on party in religion, 1841. P. 1275.

Romaine, W., Works of, 1837.

Rowe, Mrs. E., Devout exercises, 1739. P. 1433.

Rowland, H. A., Way of peace, 1853.

Rundell, Relig. in the Soul, 1845.

Ryle, J. C., Writings, 1853.

Religion, Practical (continued).

Satchel, J., Thornton Abbey, 1806.

Scougal, H., Life of God in the soul of man, 1801, 27.

Sedgwick, J., Fragments, 1826.

Serle, A., Christ. Husbandry, 1825. P. 339.

Shepard, T., Sound Believer, 1649.

Sherlock, Discourse on Death, 1814. B. C.

Slie, The Closet, 1853. P. 78.

" Closet Cyclopædia, 1851. P. 495.

Society for Pro. Chr. Knowl, Tracts.

Spencer, I. S., Pastor's sketches, 1850, 1855.

Spring, G., Ess. on Christ. character, 1813.

Steel, R., Antidote, 1667.

Sturm, Morn. Communings, 1858.

Styles, T. L., Alarm in Zion, 1828.

Taylor, I., Saturday evening, 1833. B. C.

Taylor, J., Holy living and dying, 1810, 11. B. C.

Upham, T. C., Interior or hidden life, 1854.

Valsecchi, Fondamenti della rel., 1834, 1835.

Vives, L., Opera, 1782–90.

Wadsworth, B., Guide to the doubting, 1720.

Wilberforce, W., Practical View of the prevailing religions, 1840.

Williams, R., Exper. of spir. life, 1652.

Wilson, Bp. T., Sacra privata.

" Knowl. and practice of, 1742. B. C.

Worcester, N., Last Thoughts, 1829. B. C.

Young, View of Afflictions, 1667. P. 390.

See Theology; Christ; Morals; Biography; Religions.

Religious, Dutch Language. Alardin, De Geluksaligheyd, etc., 1738.

Alberthoma, Leere der Waarheid, 1757. B. C.

" Prin. of the Chr. Religion, (Westerlo), 1789.

Appelius, Aanmerkingen, 1762.

Arndt, Waare Christendom, 1747.

Augustinus, Alleenspraeck der siele.

Bijbelsch Dagschrift, 1840–42. B. C.

Binning, H., Ettelijcke gronden, 1678.

Bouman, De Werkzaamheden...1728.

Burgh, Gereformeerde Bloem-Hof, 1721. B. C.

Crucius, Gulde Regeln, 1656.

Dortsma, Der Naam-Remonstranten, 1772. P. 109.

Religious, Dutch Language (cont'd). Drelincourt, Vertroost. der Ziele, 1719. B. C.
Drelincourt, Gebruyk van des Avondmael, 1709. B. C.
Driessen, Evang. Zedekunde, 1717.
Du Moulin, Vrede de Ziele, 1680.
Elgersma, De Herder Israels, 1664.
Espagne, J. d', Alle de Werken van, 1678.
Guthrie, W., Des Christens groot interest, 1745. B. C.
Hagen, Husselyk Handboek voor Christenen, 1834. B. C.
" Verborgenheyt der Godsaligheyt, 1716. B. C.
Hellenbroek, De Kruis Triomph... 1764.
Heymenberg, Moses en Aaron, 1710.
Hier beghynt: Vertroestinghe, 1500.
Hillenius, Eenige Keurstoffen, 1755.
Huysinga, Nodinge Betragtinge, 1716. B. C.
Hulk, Troost-rijcke Leere, 1666. P. 634.
Kemp, Van der, Drie Brieven, 1719. B. C.
Lampe, Oeffeningen, 1720.
Lossius, Gumal en Lina, 1809, 10.
Meiners, Jesus, etc., 1725.
Mel, De Lust der heiligen..1728.
Mollerus, Handt-Boecken. B. C.
Neugerger, Dagelijck Gebede.
Niel, Balsem uyt den Boom des Levens, 1683. B. C.
Pamphlets relating to Religion, Dutch, vols. 109, 632, 634.
Renesse, De Voorsienigheyt, 1658. B. C.
Royaards, Van Jesus Koningrijk, 1799. P. 568.
Rulæus, Kerck-heyligingh, 1670
Saldenus, De Wegh des levens, 1666.
Schacht, De Noodzakelykheid, etc., 1762.
Schortinghuis, Het innige Christendom, 1750. B. C
Smytegelt, Pract. Leer-Reedenen.
Spranckhuysen, Balsem, 1731. B. C.
Swartte, Oude...Waarheid, 1727.
Themmen, Het Vervolg, 1764.
Udemans, Geestelyck roer, 1655.
Verloren, Den, Zondaar. B. C.
Vieroot, Wegwyzer, 1764.
Westerhout, Afbeedsel, 1745.
Wilkinson, Heyligen pilgrom, 1661.
Willemsem, Een Graaggetrouw Rentmeester, 1779.
Willet, Meditatien op den Ps. 122. B. C.
See Theological; Sermons.

Religious, French. Bonnet, Sermons, Prière du Seigneur, 1837.
" Famille de Béthanie, 1838.
Bourdaloue, L., Œuvres, 1837.
Fénélon, Œuvres, vol. 1, 1836.
Joli, Œuvres mêlées, 1702.
Jules Chrétien, on Dialogues, etc., 1805.
Loys, Œuvres spirituelles, 1613.
Saurin, J., Sermons, 1776.
Soc. Belg., Traités évangéliques, 1838. B. C.
Thurlot, Thrésor de la doct. chrétienne, 1653.
Vinet, Indifférentisme religieux, 559.

Religious, German. Christliche Handreichung, 1821.
Luther, Spruch-und Schatz-Kastlein.
Starke, J. Fr., Tägl. Handbuch, 1710.
Stilling, J. H. Jung., Siegsgeschichte der Chr. rel., 1814.
Theologia, Germanica, 1856.
See Theology.

Religious Biography. *See* Biography.

Religious Ceremonies. Vanity and Mischief of, 1690.
Picart, Cérémonies rel. de tous les Peuples, 1783.
See Roman; Mythology; Ritualism.

Religious Liberty. *See* Toleration; Inquisition.

Religious Opinions. *See* Opinions.

Religious Orders. De Lolme, Hist. of the Flagellants.
See Military Orders; Knights.

Religious Societies. *See* Benevolent; Missions.

Rembrandt, P. Blanc, C., L'Œuvre de, décrit, 1859.
See Painting.

Renfrew, Scot. Crawfurd, Hist. of, 1782.
Renfrew, Meeting on the distress, 1816.

Rennell, T. Life of, 1824. P. 1494.

Rensselaer Co., N. Y. Eaton's Geol. Surv., 1822.
Directory, 1870–71.

Rensselaer Polytechnic Institnte. Reports and Catalogues, 1825–66.

Rensselaerwyck, N. Y. Pepper, C., Account of.
Van Rensselaer, C., Manor of. From Burlington Gazette, 1844.
See Albany.

Reptiles. *See* Herpetology.

Revolutionary War, Partial Histories, etc. (continued).

Bartlett, J. R., Destruct. of the Gaspee, 1861.

Bernard, Gov., Letters on Government and trade of, 1763–68.

" Letters to the Ministry, 1767.

Black List of the Attainted, etc., 1802. P. 40.

Bleecker, Capt. L., Orderly Book, 1779. N. Y., 1865.

Bradford Club, No. 3, French fleet under De Grasse, 1781–2.

" No. 6, Northern Invasion of 1780, Hough, 1866.

" No. 7, Corresp. of Col. J. Laurens, 1777–8.

Bland Papers, 1840–43.

Bland, R., Inquiry into the rights of the Col., 1769.

Bloodgood, The Sexagenary, or Reminiscences of, 1833.

Boston Massacre, 1770.

Boston Orations: Massacre of 1770.

Brown, Capt. T., Memoirs, (Bushnell), 1862.

Burgoyne, Exp. from Canada, 1780.

Bushnell, C. I., L. Hanford's Life, 1863.

Case, W., Revolutionary memorials, 1852.

Chalmers, G., Polit. annals of, 1780.

" Introd. to Hist. of revolt, 1845.

Clark, G. R., Campaign in Illinois, 1778, 9.

Clark, H., Disc. at Hubbardstown, 1859.

Clark, T., Naval Hist. of U. S., 1814.

Clinton, G., Correspondence, 1842.

Clinton, Sir H., Let. on his conduct, 1784.

Coghlan, Mrs., Memoirs, with anecdotes of, 1795.

Collection of Letters, Newburgh, 1783.

Collection of Papers, 1764–75, by Almon.

Collection of Papers, N. Y., 1778.

Cooper, J. F., Naval History of, 1840.

Cowell, Spirit of '76 in Rhode Island, 1830.

Curwen, Journal, 1775–84; Loyalists.

Dawson, H. B., Battles of, 1858.

" Sons of Liberty in N.Y., 1859.

" Stony Point Attack, 1863.

" How's Diary, 1865.

" Corresp. on Gen. Putnam, 1860.

Detail of Services in 1776–79.

Deux-Ponts, Count W. De., My Campaigns, 1780–81. 1868.

Dickinson, John, Polit. writings, 1801.

Revolutionary War, Partial Histories, etc. (continued).

Drayton, Memoirs of, in South Carolina to 1776.

Dring, T., Jersey Prison Ship, 1831.

Eelking, Die Deutschen hülfstruppen im Nordamerikanischen Befreiungskriege, 1776–83.

Ellet, The Women of the Am. Rev., 1848–50.

Estaing, Extrait d'un Journal, 1782.

Exiles in Virginia, 1777.

Fanning's Narrative, 1775–83.

Force, P., Notes on History of Decl. of Independence, 1855.

Fox, E., Revolutionary Advent. of, 1838.

Freneau, Poems during the War, 1809.

Gage, T., Letters, 1769.

Garden, Anecdotes of the Revol. War, 1st, 2d series.

Gentz, Principles of, compared with French rev., 1800.

Gibbes, R. W., Doc. History of, 1764–1782.

Girod, Voyage d'un Suisse pendant, 1786.

Godefroy, Estampes des Evénemens de la guerre.

Graham, Gen. S., Memoir of, 1862.

Graves, W., Letters, 1781.

Gray, D., Narrative as spy, 1776–82.

Graydon, A., Rem. of men and events of, 1811, 22, 46.

Great Britain, Stamp Act, 1765.

Griffith, W., Hist. notes from 1754–75.

Grigsby, Virginia Conv. of 1776.

Haven, C. C., Thirty days in New Jersey, 1776–77.

Headley, J. T., Chaplains and clergy of the Rev., 1864.

Heath, W., Military events during, 1798.

Henry, J. J., Hardships in Campaign against Quebec, 1775.

Hewes, Traits of the Tea Party, Bost., 1835. *See* Thatcher.

Hildreth, Journal of Arnold's command, 1775.

Historical anecdotes, 1777.

Hist. Doc'ts from the Old Dominion, March, 1776—Aug. 1776.

Howe, Gen., Report on his conduct in 1779.

Hubbard, J. N., Border adventures of Van Campen, 1842.

Hull, W., Revolutionary services of, 1848.

Humphreys, D., Miscellaneous works, 1790.

Indians, The, or Massacres in Wawasink, 1846.

Izard, R., Correspondence, 1774–1804.

Revolutionary War, Partial Histories, etc. (continued).

Jacob, Cresap's life, 1866.

Jenkins, J. S., Lives of Patriots and Heroes of the Rev., 1849.

Johnson, Joseph, Traditions and Reminiscences of the Rev. in the South, 1851.

Jour. d'un officier de l'Armée Navale, 1781, 82.

Judson, L. C., The Sages and heroes of, 1852.

Kapp, F., Der Soldatenhandel Deutscher Fürsten, 1775–83, 1864.

Kidder, F., Hist. of Boston Massacre, 1770.

Lamb, R., Journal of occurrences to 1783.

Laurens, H., Correspondence, 1861.

Lee, H., Campaign of 1781 in the Carolinas, 1824.

" Mem. of Southern Dept. of the U. S., 1812.

Lewis, Gen. A., Orderly Book, 1776. *See* Hist. Docts.

McAlpine, Advent. from 1773 to 1779.

Mackenzie, R., On Tarleton's Hist. of 1780, 81.

Magoon, Orators of the Rev., 1848.

Marshall, C., Passages from his diary, 1774–77.

Martyrs of Wallabout Bay, 1855.

Massachusetts, Penobscot Expedition.

Massachusetts Prov. Cong. 1774.

Meigs, R. J., Jour. of Exped. against Quebec, 1775.

Melvin, J., Expedition to Quebec, 1775.

Military Journals of Lyon & Haws, 1758–75.

Minutes of the trial for Conspiracy, Lond., 1786. Repr. 1865.

Moody, J., Narrative of, (Bushnell), 1865.

Moore, F., Diary of the Revolution, 1860.

" Songs and Ballads of, 1856.

Morris, Margaret, Private Journal, 1836.

Moser, Nord. Am. nach den Fried, 1783.

Moultrie, Memoirs of N. and S. Caro., 1802.

Munsell's Hist. Series, No. 1–7, 1857–1860.

Narrative, Exchange of Prisoners, at the Cedars, 1777.

Nash, S., Journal, 1776–77, (Bushnell), 1861.

Neilson, C., Burgoyne's campaign, Bemis's Heights, 1844.

New England Convention, 1780.

New Jersey, Executive correspondence, 1776–86.

New York, Jour. of Prov. Cong., 1775–1777.

New York City in the Rev., 1861.

Niles, H., Principles and Acts of the Revolution, 1822.

Onderdonk, H., Incidents in Queen's Co., 1846.

" Incidents in Suffolk and King's Co., 1849.

Pennsylvania: Col. Rec., Min. of Exec. Coun., 1852, 53.

" Archives, 1664–1786.

Peterson, Heroes of the Revolution, 1848.

Political Register, Lond., 1767–9.

Potter, I. R., Life and Adventures of, 1824.

Pratt, G. W., Vaughan's Exped., 1777, Burning of Kingston.

Putnam, I., Mem. of the life of, 1839.

Ramsay, Hist. Rev., S. Carolina, 1785.

Remer, Amerikanisches Archiv, 1777, 1778.

Riedesel, Gen., Leben und Wirken, 1856.

" Memoirs and letters, 1868.

Riedesel, Mme., Berufs-reise, 1776–83.

" Journals and letters, 1827, 1867.

Rochambeau, Comte de, Memoirs, 1838.

Sabine, L., The American Loyalists, 1847, 64.

Saffell, Records of the war, 1858.

Sampson, Deborah, A Continental Soldier, 1797.

Scott, W., Rioting in America, 1775. P. 1455.

Seventy-Six Soc. Pub., S. Deane papers; Galloway's examination; Massachusetts papers; Maryland papers, 1855–7.

Simcoe, Military Journal, 1844.

Sketches of Bunker Hill, 1844.

Smith, J. J., Amer. Hist. Curiosities, 1847, 60.

Smith, S., Memoirs, (Bushnell), 1776–1786, 1860.

Smith, T. M, Legends of the war, Louisville, 1855.

Sparks, J., Corresp. of Am. Rev., 1853.

Sprengel, Die Geschichte der, 1784.

Stone, E. M., Invasion of Canada in 1775.

Stone, W. L., Border wars of, 1846.

Street, A. B., Battle of Saratoga, 1858.

Sullivan's campaign, 1842.

Sullivan, W., The Public men of, 1783–1815, 47.

Talbot, S., Hist. sketch of the Rev., and Life of, 1803.

Revolutionary War, Partial Histories, etc. (continued).
Tarleton, Campaigns of 1780, 81.
Thacher, J., Military Journal, 1823.
Thatcher, B. B., Tales of the Revol., 1846.
" Traits of the Tea party, Hewes's life, 1835.
Townsend, J., Army under Howe, 1846.
Trescot, The diplomacy of the revolution, 1852.
United States, Votes and proceedings of Congress, 1774.
" Declaration by Congress, 1775.
" Address to Ireland, 1775.
" Observations on, 1779. P. 47.
" American Archives, (P. Force), 1774–6.
Van Rensselaer, Hist. Disc. of Lake George, 1855.
Wallabout prison-ship series, N.-York, 1865.
Washington, G., Writings, (Sparks), 1833–37.
" Monuments of, 1800.
Washington's Head-Quarters, Newburgh; Cat. of relics in, 1858.
Watson, E., Men and Times of, 1856, 1861.
Watson, H. C., Camp-fires of the Rev., 1852.
Wells, W. V., Life of S. Adams, 1855.
West India Merchant, 1778.
Wilkinson, E., Letters, Charleston, S. C., 1838.
Wilmot, J. E., Losses of the loyalists, 1783.
Witherspoon, J., Misc. works, 1803.
See under the several States; United States; Orations, July 4, Washington, G.

Revolutionary War, Controversy regarding it, chiefly Pamphlets, etc. Abingdon, Thoughts on Burke's Letters, 1780.
Adams, J., Twenty-six letters on, 1780.
Additions to Plain Truth, 1776.
Address, (Dalrymple), 1775.
Address to Prot. Dissenters, Lond., 1774.
Address to the People of Gt. Br., from Congress, 1774.
Address to the Rulers, 1778.
America Vindicated, 1774.
America's Appeal, 1775.
American Querist, (Cooper), 1774.
Americans Roused, 1774.
Anderson, J., Interest of G. B., 1782.
Answer from Elect. of Bristol, 1777.

Revolutionary War, Controversy regarding it, chiefly Pamphlets, etc. (continued).
Anticipation, (of debate in Parl.), 1779.
Appeal to Reason, 1778.
Appeal to the World, 1769, Boston.
Appeal to the People of Great Britain, 1775. P. 117.
Articles of Confederation, 1777.
Auberteuil, Administration de Lord North, 1784.
" Essais....sur les Anglo-Américains, 1782.
Authentic Papers, 1774.
Baillie, H., Boston and Quebec Acts, 1775.
Bancroft, E., Remarks on the Review of the Controversy, 1769.
Boston Massacre, 1770, Orations on.
Brown, J., Sermon, 1763.
Burgoyne, J., Speeches, 1778.
Burke, E., Speech, Taxation, 1774.
Campbell, G., Fast Sermon on, 1778.
Cappe, N., Fast Sermon, York, 1776.
Cartwright, J., Letter to Abingdon, 1778.
Case of American Loyalists, 1783.
Causes of the Distractions, 1774.
Champion, Reflections on Parties, 1776.
Charters of the Provinces, 1760.
Claim of the colonies, 1765.
Complaint against a Speech, 1775.
Complete Debate, House of Commons, 1782.
Conciliatory Address, London, 1775.
Congress, The, Canvassed, by A. W. Farmer, 1774.
Considerations on certain polit. trans., S. Carolina, 1774.
Consid. on the Bill for Peace, 1782.
Considerations on the dependencies, 1769.
Consid. on the expediency of admitting, Lond., 1770.
Considerations on the propriety of imposing taxes, (Dulaney), 1765.
Consid. on the late Act, Edinburgh, 1776.
Considerations on the measures, Robinson, Lond., 1774, 76.
Consider. on the prov. treaty, Lond., 1783.
Consid. sur l'Admission, 1779.
Consider. upon the Amer. inquiry, Dallas, 1779.
Considerations upon the rights of the colonists, N. Y., 1766.
Consolatory thoughts....1782.
Constitutional answer to Wesley, 1775.
Constit. Right of G. B., 1768.
Conway, Speech, Parl., 1780.

Revolutionary War, Controversy regarding it, chiefly Pamphlets, etc. (continued).
Reed, J., Reprint of Reed & Cadwalader pamphlets, 1863.
Reflections on the Rise, 1780.
Remarks on the principal acts, (Lind), 1775.
Robinson, M., Peace the best policy, 1777.
Scott, W., Sermon, 1775.
Second Thoughts, London, 1777.
Sewall, Jona., Origin of Am. contest, 1775.
Shebbeare, Answer to Queries, 1775.
" Essay .... on Nat. Soc., 1776.
Short hist. of conduct of ministry, 1766.
Smith, H. W., Nuts for Future Historians, 1856.
Strictures, (Hutchinson), 1776.
Thoughts on government, 1776.
True merits of a late treatise, 1776.
True State of Proc of Parl., 1774.
Tucker, J., Four Tracts, 1774.
" Humble Address, 1775, 76.
" True interest of Great Britain, 1776.
" Cui Bono ?, 1781.
Tumultibus, De, Americanis, 1776.
View of the Controversy, N. Y., 1774; Lond., 1775.
Wesley, J., Some Observations, 1776.
" Calm Address, 1777.
Zubly, J. J., Sermon, Prov. Cong. of Georgia, 1775.

Reynard the Fox. Bost., 1865.
Percy Soc., Pub. v. 12.

Reyner. Family genealogy, (Whitmore).

Reynolds, Sir J. Jackson, W., The four ages, 1798.
" Northcote, Life of, 1817.
Reynolds, Works and memoir, E. Malone, 1809.
" Works and memoir, Beechey, 1852.

Rheims, France. *See* Reims.

Rhetoric. Adams, J. Q., Lectures on, and Orat., 1810.
Aristides, A., Opera, 1829.
Aristotle, Treatise on, 1850.
Baron, A., Rhétorique, (Encyc. Pop.).
Blair, H., Lectures on, 1817.
Boileau, Œuvres, 1745. B. C.
Bouhours, Art of Criticism, 1705.
" Art of Rhetoric, 1728.
Brookfield, 1st Book in Composition.

Rhetoric (continued).
Burrowes, Essay on Style, Roy. Irish Ac., 5.
Campbell, G., Philosophy of. B. C.
Cicero, De Oratore, 1822. B. C.
Copleston, Prælectiones Academicæ, 1828.
Comenius, Ars Oratoria, 1664.
Edwards, T., Canons of Criticism, 1765. B. C.
Eloquence du temps, enseignée, 1707.
Farnabius, Index Rhetoricus, 1689.
Fromondus, Labyrinthus, 1634.
Hobbes, T., Works, vol. 6, 1839–45.
Home, H., Elements of Criticism, 1768.
" The Art of Thinking, 1813. B. C.
Hurd, Works, Critical dissertations, 1811.
Jamieson, Questions to Rhetoric.
La Motte, Réflexions sur la critique, 1716.
Libanius, Præludia oratoria lxxii, 1606.
Melancthon, Elem. rhetories, 1572.
Mills, A., Outlines of rhetoric, 1854.
Morley, C., Guide to Composition, 1838.
Newman, S. H., System of, 1851.
Parker, R. G., Rhetorical readings, 1836.
Parsons, S. H., Grammatical Reader, 1836.
Pinnock, Catechism of Rhetoric.
Quackenboss, G. P., First lessons in.
" Course of, 1855.
Reed, H., Lect. on Eng. Lit., 1855.
Reid, A., English composition, 1839.
Riccius, De imitatione, 1845.
Rutilius, De fig. sententiarum, 1768.
Sheridan, T., Rhetorical Grammar, 1783.
Spengel, Rhet. bei den Alten, 1842.
Whately, R., Elements of, 1834.
See Classical Literature; Elocution; Language; Taste; Poetry, treatises on; Preaching; Criticism.

Rhett, R. B. Wallace, D., Life of. P. 1229.

Rheumatism. *See* Medicine.

Rhin, France. Annuaire, 1816, 1846.

Rhine River. Belgium and Nassau, tourist's guide.
Carr, Tour through Holland, 1807.
Champney's Panorama of, 1849.
Hoffman, Der Römerstadte.
Hooff, Navigation du Rhin, 1826.
Hugo, The Rhine, 1845.
Ritchie, Heath's Pictor. Annual, 1832, 1833.
See Belgium; Netherlands.

Roman Catholic Church, England (continued).

Soames, The Romish Reaction, 1843. P. 331.

Stewart, R., Sermon at Paris, 1687.

Vigo, Romish Bishops in G. B., 1850.

Warren, S., Queen or Pope, 1850.

Wiseman, Card., Appeal to Reason, 1850. P. 347.

Wix, Polit. power to Papists, 1822. P. 345.

Wordsworth, C., Bp. of Rome in England, 1850. P. 455.

See Church of England; Authority.

Roman Catholic Ch., Emancipation in Great Britain. Andrews, R. C., Letter to Peel, 1828.

Arguments for, 1813.

Baldwin, W. J., Appeal, 1823.

Brief warning, 1829.

Catholic Emancipation, 1825.

Catholic State Wagon, 1829.

Claims of Rom. Cath., 1812.

Claims of....1816.

Clarence, Speech, 1829.

Colchester, C., Speeches, 1828.

Dangers with which, 1817.

Devon Meeting, 1829.

Dillon, Catholic Claims, 1813.

England, H. C., Letter on, 1790.

Evans, W. D., Legal disabilities, 1813.

Firth, W., Letter to H. Bathurst, 1813.

Four Letters by a lay Catholic, Lond., 1825.

French, D., Letter to Lord Gifford, 1824. P. 345.

Furness, W. H., Sermon on, 1829.

Garratt, T., Appeal to Protestants, 1829.

Grenville, Lord, Letter on, 1810.

Hippisley, Sir J. C., Letters on Cath. claims, 1813.

Holland, Lord, Letter to Shuttleworth, 1827.

Horton, R. W., Letter on, 1826.

James, M., Letters on Cath. relief bill, 1829.

Lefroy, Speech, Const. Club of Ireland, 1827.

Letter to a Protestant Dissenter, 1812.

Letter to G. Silvertop, 1826.

Letter to Viscount Milton, 1827.

Letters to a Prot. Dissenter, 1813.

Look before you Leap, 1825.

Midland Cath. Ass'n, London, 1826. P. 346.

Miller, G., Policy of R. C. Ch., 1826.

Peel, R., Speech, 1817; Papers.

Short letter to Wellington, 1829.

Sparrow, Eccl. rm, 1833.

Roman Catholic Church, Emancipation in Great Britain (continued).

Stonard, J., Letter to Bp. of Chester, 1829. P. 347.

Substance of a Speech, 1810.

Sussex, Duke of, Speech, Cath. relief bill, 1829.

Van Mildert, Speech, H. of Lords, 1825.

Wardle to his Countrymen, 1828. P. 347.

Wrangham, Catholic Claims, 1829.

Roman Cath. Ch., Ireland. Address, Cath. of Ireland.

Brennan, Ans. to Finnegan, 1788.

Burke, E., Letter to Langrishe, 1792. P. 348.

Butler, C., Address to Prot., 1813.

" Memoirs of the Irish Catholics.

Carey, M., Vindiciæ Hibernicæ, 1837.

" Conspiracy of the Catholics in 1641.

Carlisle, Lord, Letter, 1795.

Croly, An Essay on, 1834.

" Address to lower orders, 1835. P. 342.

Dwyer, Popery Unmasked, 1852. P. 342.

Elrington, Remarks on J. H. L., 1827.

Foster, J. L., Speech, 1817.

Grattan, H., Speeches, Miscellanies.

Parnell, H., Penal laws, 1825.

Peter Plymley's letters, (S. Smith), 1809.

Stipendiary Priesthood, 1835.

Walsh, Hist. of the hierarchy and Irish Saints, 1854.

Wyse, Hist. of Cath. Assoc'n, 1829.

See Irish Churches; Ireland.

Roman Catholic Church, Liturgies and Private Devotions. Ange Conducteur, Paris.

Book of Cath. Prayers, Coll. S. J., Dublin, 1850.

Bona, Le Phénix, 1858.

Catholic Manual, Balt., 1831.

Choir Manual, Sisters of Mercy, N. Y., 1856.

Collet, M., Christian Student. P. 1742.

Daily Exercise, N. Y., 1846.

Daily Piety, N. Y., 1854.

Devout Manual, N. Y., 1860.

Diamante, El, N. Y., 1858.

Flowers of Piety, Selected, N. Y.

Furlong, J., Companac an Criosdaig.

Garden of the Soul, N. Y., 1861.

Golden Book, N. Y., 1854.

Golden Manual, N. Y., 1854.

Herbert, Lady L., Methods of hearing Mass, 1722.

Roman Catholic Church, Liturgies and Private Devotions (continued).
Horstius, Paradise of the soul, 1858.
Key of Heaven, N. Y., 1860.
Kyrie Eleison, Monasterii, 1854.
Libellus precum, Georgiopoli, D. C., 1831.
Liguori, A., Mission-book, 1858.
Little Flowers of Piety, N. Y., 1859.
Manuel de Piété, Paris, 1856.
Manual of Christ. Soldier, Soc. of St. Vincent de Paul, 1861.
Manual of Piety, Balt., 1856.
Manual of Prayers, Seminaries, N.Y., 1859.
Martin, H., Medulla Missæ, Germanica, 1750.
Nakatenus, Cœleste Palmetum, 1854.
Officium Beatæ Mariæ; MS. on vellum.
Paradise Gärtlein, N. Y., 1859.
Paradise of the Christian Soul, N. Y., 1858.
Paroissien des petits enfants, Montréal, 1861.
Path to Paradise, N. Y., 1862.
Rayment, B., The Divine Office, V. I, 1806.
R. C. Ch., Graduale Romanum, 1848.
" Missale Romanum, 1856.
" Breviarium Romanum, 1851.
" Ordo adm. sacr. in Missione Anglicana.
" Excerp. ex Rituali Romano, 1857.
" Ordinario de la Misa, Paris, 1826.
Rosa Mystica, Lyon.
Rosarist's Companion, Chicago, 1845.
St. John, A., The Raccolta, Indulgenced Prayers, N. Y., 1859.
St. John's Manual, N. Y., 1857.
St. Vincent's Manual, Balt., 1857.
Seraphic Manual, N. Y., 1859.
Star of Bethlehem, N. Y., 1859.
True Piety, Baltimore.
Ursuline Manual, N. Y., 1857.
Visitation Manual, (F. de Sales), 1858.
Way to Heaven, N. Y., 1860.
Xavier, F., Novena, Montreal, 1850.
See Prayers; Liturgies.

Rome, Ancient. Abbott, H., Antiquities of, 1820, f°.
Adam, A., Roman Antiquities, 1814.
Ammianus Marcellinus, Rerum gestarum lib. xviii, 1693.
Arnay, D', Private Life of the Romans, 1808.
Arnold, T., Hist. of the later Commonwealth, 1845.
" History of Rome, 1843.

Rome, Ancient (continued).
Arthur, W., Lect., Church in the catacombs, 1849.
Becker, W. A., Gallus, or Roman Scenes, 1844.
Blackwell, Mem. of the Court of Augustus, 1753.
Burges, D., Account of R. Senate, 1729. P. 1037.
Burgess, R., Circus on the Via Appia, 1828.
Burton, E. D., Antiquities of, 1821.
Cassiodorus, M A., Var. Epist. lib. xii, 1472.
Chapman, Roman Senate, 1750.
Cooper, Rev., History of, 1818.
Crévier, Hist. of the Rom. Emperors, 1755.
Diaz, Hist. del Senado, 1867.
Duruy, Histoire Romaine, 1855.
Dyer, Hist. of the City, 1865.
Echard, L., Roman History, 1726.
Eliot, S., The Liberty of, 1849.
Ferguson, Hist of prog. and termination of Republic, 1805.
Fosbroke, Encyc. of Antiquities, 1825.
Gell, Topography of, 1834.
Gibbon, Decline and Fall of Roman Empire, 1820, 39, 53.
Goldsmith, O., Roman history, 1793.
Grævius, Thesau. Antiq. Rom., 1735–1737.
Gruterus, Inscriptionum Rom. Corpus, 1616.
" Inscriptiones Antiquæ, 1707.
Hooke, N., Roman History, 1821.
Kennett, B., Antiquities of, 1820.
Kingsley, C., The Roman and Teuton, 1868.
Kip, Catacombs of Rome, 1854.
Koen. Baier. Ak., Theodosius, 1859.
Livius, Hist. of, 1849, 50.
Lumisden, Antiquities of, 1812.
Mably, Osservazioni sopra i Romani, 1766.
Malden, Prof., History of, Lib. U. K.
Manutius, De quæsitis, 1576.
" Ant. Rom.: de legibus, 1557.
Merivale, Hist. of Romans under the Empire, 1850–62.
" Conversion of the Empire, 1865.
Michelet, Hist. of the Republic, 1847. B. C.
Mommsen, History of, 1868.
Montfaucon, B. De, Antiq. Explained, 1721–5.
Montesquieu, Consid. sur la grandeur des Romains, 1748. B. C.
Newman, F. W., Regal Rome, 1852.
New Roman history, 1785.

Rome, Ancient (continued).
Niebuhr, Roman History, 1842.
Nieupoort, Rituum apud Rom: explicatio, 1767.
Pancirolus, Notitia utraque dignitatum, etc, 1608.
Pinnock's Goldsmith, with questions, 1845.
Pollio, (Egnatius de Prin. Romanorum), 1544.
Pomponius, Rom. Hist. Compend., 1544.
Polybius, Gen. history, (Hampton).
Rich, A., Of St. Peter's chair, 1851. P. 1220.
Rich, Dict. of Gr. and Rom. Antiq., 1860.
Rollin, Ch., Hist. Rom., Eng. and Fr., 1769–73.
Rombise, A. de, Itinerarii, et rerum Roman., 1639.
Rossi, Cav. de, Roma sotteranea, 1864, 1867.
Sallengre, Thes. Antiq. Roman.
Schlosser, Hist. of, 1837.
Schmitz, Hist. of, to A. D. 192.
Short Roman History, 1773.
Silius Ital., Lib. xvii Punicorum, 1798.
Sismondi, Fall of Roman Empire; Lardner's, 97, 98.
Sketches of domestic manners of, 1823.
Souligne, De, London and Old Rome, 1701. P. 1606.
Spanhemius, Numismatum Antiquorum, 1706.
Suetonius, Lives of Twelve Cæsars, 1796, 1855.
Tacitus, Opera, Works, 1801, 1794.
Tristan, J., Comment. Historiques, 1657.
Vertot, R. A. De, Hist. des rév. de la république, 1806. B. C.
" On the Roman Senate, 1721.
Wiseman, Remarks on St. Peter's Chair, 1833.
See Classical Literature; Italy; Latin Authors; Fine Arts; Antiquities.

Rome, Modern. About, The Roman Question.
" Rome contemporaine, 1861.
Barker, H. A., Painting of.
Bonaparte, J., Sac de Rome en 1527.
Bryce, J., Holy Roman Empire, 1866.
Cancellieri, La Semaine Sainte.
Chumacero, Excessos que se cometen en Roma, 1633.
Doria and the Revolution, 1849.
Dyer, T. H., Hist. of the City, 1865.
Eaton, C. A., Rome in the 19th cent., 1854.
Gell, Topog. of Rome, 1834.

Rome, Modern (continued).
Gillespie, Rome in 1843, 4.
Hall, N., Land of the Forum, 1855.
Head, G., Rome, a Tour of many days, 1849.
Humphreys, H. N., Rome illustrated, 1840.
Kingsley, C., Roman and Teuton, 1864.
Kip, W. I., Christmas Holidays in Rome, 1846.
" The Catacombs of Rome, 1854.
Maguire, J. F., Rome, its ruler and inst., 1858.
Miley, J., History of Papal states, 1850.
Mt. Edgcumbe, Revolution of 1848.
Neligan, R , its churches, schools, 1858.
Newspapers, vol. 12, 13, Italian, 1848, 1849.
Roma, Notizie pel anno, 1832.
" Pianta topografica, 1748, 1799, 1829.
Samber, Roma illustrata, 1721.
Seymour, M. H., Mornings..at Rome, 1849.
Story, W. W., Roba di Roma, 1864.
Tofanelli, Sculture e pitture nel Mus. Capitol., 1843.
Vasi, Itinerario di Roma, 1824.
Wiseman, Card., Ceremonies of Holy Week,
See Italy; Bibliography.

Rome, N. Y. Knox, W. E., Semi-centennial Sermon, 1850.
Oneida Co., Directory, 1862.

Romero, M. Dinner to, 1864.

Romeyn, J. B. Rowan, S. N., Sermon on, 1825. P. 62.

Romilly, Sir S. Life of, 1841.
Belsham, T., Sermon on, 1818.

Romney, G. Hayley, W., Life of, 1809.

Ronge, J. Andresen, Account of, 1845. P. 390.
Laing's Notes, 1846.
Ronge, J., Coat of Treves, 1845.
See Treves.

Roome, Mrs. R. Stanford, J., Sermon on, 1820.

Root Family. Genealog. records, 1870.

Roscoe, W. Bowles, W. L., Lessons in Criticism to, 1826.
Roscoe, H., Life of, 1833. B. C.

Roscommon, Ir. Weld, I., Survey of the county, 1832.

Rose. Amer. Rose culturist, 1852.
Buist, The Rose Manual, 1847.
Parsons, S. B., History of, and cultivation, 1847.
See Horticulture; Flowers.

Russell, J., Duke of Bedford. Correspondence, 1842–6.

Russell, J., Earl. Grey, Earl, Colonial Policy of, 1853.

Russell, Lady Rachel. Letters, 1792.
Berry, Memoirs of, 1844.

Russell, T. Morse, J., Serm., Death of, 1796. P. 554.
Warren, J., Eulogy on, 1796.

Russell, Lord Wm. Russell, Rachel, Trial of, 1792.
" Russell, Lord John, Life of, 1847.

Russia. Account of Livonia, 1701.
Ackersdijck, Verhaal eener Reize in, 1835.
Anthing, F., Campaigns of Gen. Suwarrow, 1799.
Beauplan, Description of the Ukraine.
Bell, R., History of, Lardner.
Bulgarin, Ivan Vejeeghen, or Life in, 1832. B. C.
Catherine II, Memoirs of, 1859.
" Mémoires par elle-même, 1859.
Cathcart, Commen. on War of, 1812.
Cobden, R., What Next? 1856.
Cochrane, J., Pedest. Journey, 1824.
Collins, P. M., Voyage on the Amoor, 1860.
Cottrell, Recollections of Siberia, 1840, 1841.
Custine, Russia, 1844.
Daschkaw, Princess, Memoirs, 1840.
Eckardt, J., Modern Russia, 1870.
Eustaphieve, A., Strictures, (Tchuykevitch).
" Resources of, 1812, 13.
Fletcher, R. in the 16th Cent., (Hakluyt Soc.).
Fowler, G., Lives of Sovereigns of, 1858.
Granville, Travels to St. Petersburg, 1829.
Grenville, Lord, Speech, On Treaties, 1802.
Guagnino, Della Sarmatia Europea, 1606.
Gurowski, Russia as it is, 1854.
Hagemeister, Commerce of New Russia, 1836.
Hamel, Early Voyages to Northern R., 1857.
Hanway, J., Trade with the Caspian, 1753.
" Account of, Coll. of Voy., 5.
Harper, R. G., Corresp. on the Russian victories, 1813.
Haxthausen, A. Von, The Russian Empire, 1856.

Russia (continued).
Herberstein, Notes upon Russia, 1851.
History of Eudoxia, 1816.
Hist. of R. under Peter, 1835.
Hommaire de Hell, Russie méridionale, 1843–5.
" Travels in Crimea, the Caucasus, etc., 1847.
Johnston, R., Travels through, and Poland, 1815.
Jourdier, Voyage agronomique, 1861.
Kelly, W. K., History of, 1854.
Kinglake, Invas. of Crimea, 1863, 68.
Labaume, Campaign of 1812.
Latham, R. G., Races of Russia, 1854.
Le Bruyn, C., Travels into Muscovy, 1737.
Le Perski, Verwisselinge van Russland, 1742.
Lingard, v. 5, p. 261; Russian Company.
Macarius, Travels, (Orient. Trans. Fund).
Marx, E., Serf and Cossack, 1854.
Maxwell, J. S., The Czar, his Court and People, 1848.
Milton, J., Works, History of Moscovia.
Muscovy, Churchill, Supp. vol. 1.
Niemcewicz, Captivity in, 1794–96.
Olearius, Travels, 1633–39.
Otto, Hist. Russ. literature, 1839.
Pallas, Voyages dans plusieurs provinces de, 1793.
Pamphlets relating to Russia, vols. 825, 1443, 1479.
Pinkerton, R., Misc. Obs. on the present state, 1833.
Political pict. of Europe, 1806.
Porter, R. K., Campaign of 1812.
Potocki, Voyage, Astrakhan, 1829.
Pradt, Comparison of, with England, Pamph'r 24.
Recueil de Doc'ts, 1853.
Reinbeck, G., Travels from St. Petersburgh, 1805, Phillips's Coll.
Revelations of Russia, 1844.
Ritchie, Pict. Annual, 1832, 3.
Russia: Droits des dissidents, 1766.
Russia under Nicholas I, 1841. B. C.
Sauer, Geog. exped. to North, 1785–1794.
Schnitzler, Aperçu Général de, 1844.
" Secret History of, 1847.
Schrenk, Reise nach dem Nord-osten, 1848.
Staat van't Russische Keizerryk, 1744.
Strangford, Lord, R. and Central Asia, 1869.
Taylor, B., Travels in, 1855.

Russia (continued).

Tchuykevitch, War of 1812.

Tegoborski, Productive Forces of, 1857.

Timkowski, Travels to China, 1827.

Tochman, G., Russian Policy to the U. S., 1844. P. 17.

Tooke, W., History of, 1800.

" View of, 1799.

U. S. Sen., Banks's Report on Treaty, 1868.

Urquhart, D., Mystery of the Danube, 1851.

Ustrialoff, Nicholas I, 1854. P. 1443.

Van Halen, Narr. of travels, 1828.

Walsh, R., Correspond. with R. G. Harper. P. 9.

Whitworth's Acc't, (Fugitive pieces), 1758.

Wilbraham, Tr. in Transcaucasian Provinces, 1837.

Willoughby, H., Travels in; Pinkerton, 1.

Wilson, R., Private Journal, 1812–14.

Ysenbeek, Der Doopsgezinden, 1848.

See Crimean War, 1854; Poland; St. Petersburgh; Siberia; Kamtschatka.

Rust. *See* Moulds; Smut.

Rutgers, H. McMurray, W., Sermon, Death of, 1830. P. 268.

Rutgers College, N. J. Centennial celebration, 1870.

Catalogues, 1856, 62–65.

Inaug. of W. H. Campbell, 1863.

Rutgers Female College. 25th anniversary, 1864.

Catalogues and commencements, 1843–1868.

Rutland, Vt. Town reports, 1861–67.

Centennial celebration, 1870.

Rutland Directory, 1867.

Rutland Herald, 1867–68.

Rutland Co., Vt. Agric. Soc. Reports, 1857–62.

Almanac, 1862.

Williams, C. L., Statistics of the bar of, 1847.

Rutlandshire. Beauties of Engl. and Wales.

Rutledge, J. Flanders, Lives of the Chief Justices.

Van Santvoord, Lives of the Chief Justices.

Ruyter, M. De. Brandt, G., La Vie de, 1698.

Ryder, J. C. Belden, Account of, 1834.

Rye, Eng. Durham, J. G., Address on Conflagration in, 1813. P. 1738.

Rye, N. Y. Baird, C. W., Hist. of, 1871.

S.

Sabbath. Am. and For. Sabbath Union, 1844, 46.

Blatchford, S., Sermon, 1826.

Bowdler, C., Abolition of, 1833. P. 490.

Brerewood, E., Treatise on Sabaoth, 1630.

Considerations on the Sabbath mails, 1829. P. 15. B. C.

Cox, R., Liter. of the Sabbath Question, 1865.

De Coetlogon, Sermon, Profanation of, 1776.

Edwards, J., Sabbath Manual, (A. Tract S.).

Exposition of unconstitutional law of N. Y., 1826. P. 14. B. C.

General Union for observance, 1828.

Hall, W., Plea for, 1845.

Hessey, J. A., Lectures on history of, 1860.

Higgins, G., Errors respecting. Pamphleteer 27.

Hooker, Horace, Temporal benefits of, 1835. P. 1753.

Horton, T. G., Holiday or Holy-day, 1856. P. 1563.

Hughes, T. S., Letter to Higgins respecting. Pamph'r 27.

Humphrey, H., On Sanctification of, 1829. B. C.

Jay, W., Prize Essay on, 1827.

Krauth, C. P., Lutherans and Sunday, 1856. P. 1444.

Logic of Col. Johnson's Report, 1829. P. 72.

Low life, 1764.

Maguire, R., Discussion on, 1858. P. 1444.

N. Y. Sabbath Committee, 1860.

" Doc'ts, 1858–62.

N. Y. State Sabbath Convention, 1844.

Orr, J., Sanctification of, 1808. P. 1444.

Pamphlets relating to the Sabbath Observance, 490, 1444.

Pearson, C, Letter on obser., 1855.

Permanent Sab. Documents, etc.

Quinton, J. A., Prize Essay, 1849.

Remarks on the existing..laws, Mass., 1816. P. 490.

Sabbath, The Ends of the, Albany. P. 490.

Sabbath Desecration, 1850. P. 490.

Seventh Day Baptist Conference, 1843, P. 490.

Simpson, Civil Mandates, 1793. P. 320.

Society for Promoting, etc., Lond., 1833. P. 490.

Sainte Croix (continued).
Knox, J. P., St. Thomas and St. Croix, 1852.
Tuckerman, J., Winter Residence in, 1837. P. 210.
West, Beschreibung von, 1794.

St. David's College. Williams, R., Working of, 1851. P. 386.

Saint Denis Abbey. History of, 1795.

Saint Domingo and Hayti. Atwood, T., Hist. of the Isle, 1791.
Bellin, Débouquemens au Nord de, 1768.
Briefe and Perfect Journal, 1655.
Brown, W. W., Revolutions of, 1855. P. 958.
Charlevoix, Histoire de, 1730, 31.
Charmilly, Answer to B. Edwards, 1797.
Chastenet, Nav. aux côtes de, 1787.
Clark, B. C., Plea for Haiti, 1853.
Courteney, W. S., Gold Fields of, 1860.
Cri, Le, d'un Colon de, 1795.
Dalmas, Hist. de la Révolution de, 1814.
Descourtilz, Voyage d'un naturaliste, 1809.
Desperrières, Fièvres de, 1780.
Ducœurjoly, Manuel des Habitans, 1802.
Edwards, B., Hist. of W. I., 1797.
Elliott, C. W., Revolution of, 1855.
Fabens, Resources of, 1862, 69.
France, Débats....dans l'Affaire des Colonies, 1795.
Gouy, Jour. Hist. de toutes les assemblées, 1788.
Grégoire, H., Liberté à Haïti, 1824.
Guillermin, Révolution de, 1808.
" Précis des Evénemens, 1811.
Hilliard d'Auberteuil, Etat présent de, 1776.
Journal de St. Domingue, 1765.
Laujon, Hist. de la dernière Expedition de, 1802.
Lee, Mem. of Touss. L'Ouverture, 1854.
L'Ouverture, History of, 1803.
Madiou, Histoire de Haiti, 1848.
Malenfant, Des Colonies et de, 1814.
Moreau de St. Méry, Descr. of Spanish part of, 1797–98.
Pons, Situation politique, 1790.
Pradt, Pièces relatives à, 1818.
Rainsford, M., Hist. Acct. of Hayti, 1805.
Recueil de Pièces, remises, 1788.
Redpath, J., Guide to Hayti, 1860.
Rural Code of Hayti.
Seul, Du, parti à prendre, 1819.
Smith, J. M., Lect. on Haytien Revolution, 1841. P. 958.

Saint Domingo and Hayti (continued).
Toledo, Objeciones, 1812.
Walton, W., Pres. State of Span. Col., 1810.
Willis, N. P., Trip to the Tropics, 1853.
Wimpffen, Voyage à, 1788.
Wright, E., Lesson of, 1861.
Wurtz, Mémoires: 1, 2, 1820, 22.
See West Indies; French and Spanish Col.

Saint Evremond, C. De. Œuvres, Vie, par Des Maizeaux.

St. Francis Xavier College, N. Y.
Catalogues, 1860–70.

St. George, Va. Slaughter, History of, 1847.

St. Helena Is. Beatson, Tracts on, 1816.
Selberg, Reise nach, 1846.
See Napoleon I.

St. Jago Is. Descourtilz, Voy. d'un naturaliste, 1809.

St. John, Lord Bolingbroke. *See* Bolingbroke.

St. John's Is. Egmont, Memorial, 1764. P. 1684.

St. Lawrence Co., N. Y. Directory, 1859, 62.
Hough, F. B., History of, 1853.
Jefferson and St. Lawrence Co. Newspapers, 1812–52.
Saint Lawrence American, 1855–59, (Newsp.).
St. Lawrence Co. Advertiser, 1850.
St. Lawrence Free Press, 1854.

St. Lawrence River. Journal de l'Expédition, 1759.
See Canada.

St. Leonard's, Eng. Ross's Hastings.

St. Louis, Mri. Chouteau, A., Settlement of, 1858. P. 971.
Edwards, The Great West, 1860.
Illinois Directory, 1855.
Lyford's Directory, 1837.
Pamphlets relating to, vol. 475.
Reavis, Future of, 1871.
St. Louis, Ann. Reviews of commerce, etc., 1851–5.
Saint Louis, Description of, 1858.
" Thoughts about, 1854.
St. Louis Cha. of Comm., Report on Navig., 1842.
St. Louis Directory, 1857, 59.
St. Louis Register, 1821, 22, Newsp., v. 4.

St. Louis Church, Buffalo. *See* Buffalo.

St. Louis University, Mri. Catalogues, 1842–64.

Saint Lucia Is. Breen, History of, 1844.
Uring, N., Hist. of his Voyages, 1722.

St. Malo, France. Robidou, B., Hist. d'un beau pays, 1861.

St. Mark's Church, N. Y. Anthon, Sermon, 1845.

St. Mary's Falls. Ship Canal Co. Lands, 1858, 62, 63.

St. Mary Overy Church, London. Taylor, W., Annals of, 1833.

St. Nicholas Society. Banquet to the Prince of Orange, 1852.
Beekman, J. W., Address, Dec. 4, 1869.
Betts, W, Anniv. Add., 1851.
Duer, W. A., Address, 1848. B. C. P. 50.
Hoffman, C. F., Discourse, 1847.

St. Pancras Parish. Cansick, Epitaphs in, 1869.
State of the Parish, 1845.

Saint Patrick's Cathedral, Dublin. Mason, W. M., History of, 1820.

St. Paul's. Minnesota, Rise of.

St. Paul's Cathedral. Hist. Sketch, 1837. P. 253, 616.
Guide to, 1850. P. 1710.
Plan for Worship in, 1839.

St. Paul's Coll., Mri. Giddings, Acc't of, 1855. P. 215.

St. Petersburg. Plan en relief de. P. 41. B. C.
See Russia.

St. Peter's Church, Albany. To the Members, J. Tayler *et al.*, 1816.
To the Congregation, No parishoner, 1816.
Report to the Vestrymen, 1816.
Answer of the members, 1816.
Finan. Reports, 1830, 32, 36.
Reports to the Vestry, 1845, 49, 70, 71.
To the parishioners, 1868.
Orphans' Home, Rep., 1866–70.
Review of a Pam., by Spencer, 1846.

St. Peter's Lake. Logan, W. E., Report of Survey of, 1850. P. 274.

St. Pierre, J. H. B. de. Œuvres: Vie de.

St. Saviour's Church, Lond. Taylor, W., Annals of, 1833.

St. Simon, Duc de. Mémoires, 1789.
" Memoirs, 1857.

St. Stephen's College, Annandale, N. Y. Reports and catal., 1863–1871.

St. Thomas' Church, Whitemarsh, Md. Millett, D. C., History of, 1864.

St. Thomas' Is. Belgium, Enquête sur, 1846.
Knox, J. P., Hist. acct. of, 1852.

St. Thomas' Rectory. Wilson, H. B., Letter, 1851.

St. Vincent, Earl of. Naval anecdotes, 1805.

St. Vincent Is. Shephard, C., History of, 1831,
Uring, Intended settlement of, 1725.

Sainte Beuve, C. A. Galerie des Contem., Vie de, 1845.

Saints. Ansart, Hist. de Reine d'Alise.
Butler, C., Lives of the Saints, 1838.
Discourse concerning invocation of, 1684.
Gennaro, *S.*, Novena, 1816.
Newman, Lives of English Saints, 1844.
Patrick, Sts., Bridget and Columba, Lives of.
Philomena, *S.*, Memorie, 1835.

Salem, Mass. Colman, Install. of J. Flint, 1821. P. 105.
Emerson, B., Jubilee discourse, South Church, 1855.
Essex South Conference.
Felt, J. B., Annals of, 1845–49.
" Did the first church, etc., 1856.
First Cong. Church, Corresp., 1832. P. 262.
Flint, J., Hist. Discourses, 1845, 46. P. 105.
Howard St. Church, Eccl. Counc., 1850.
Massachusetts Hist. Soc. Coll., I, 6, Hist. of.
Mills, R. C., Hist. 1st Bapt. Church.
Morison, First Church, Hist of, 1853.
Salem, City Documents, 1857–70.
Salem, Reports, etc., 1854–58.
Salem Directory, 1832, 42, 46, 50, 51, 1853, 55, 57, 59, 64.
Story, J., Hist. Discourse, 1828.
Tabernacle Church, 1821, 32, 63.
Upham, C. W., Hist. of First Church, 1867.
" Hist. of Witchcraft in, 1692.
White, D. A., Hist. of First Church, 1861.
Worcester, S. M., Centennial Disc., 1835.
" Mem. of the Tabernacle Church, 1855.

Salem, N. J. Johnson, R. G., Historical account of, 1839.

Salisbury, Conn. Reid, Hist. address, 1845.

Satire and Satires (continued).
Pope, A., The Dunciad, 1729.
Quevedo, T. De, Works, 1798.
Ritchie, A. C. M., Reviewers Reviewed, 1837.
Rogeard, A., Propos de Labiénus, 1865.
Satiræ duæ, (Scioppius), 1617.
Spain vindicated, 1825.
Strother, J. H., The Golden Calf, 1854.
Swift, J., Tale of a Tub.
Tafereel, Het groote, der dwaasheid, 1720.
Trollopiad, The, N. Y., 1837.
Trumbull, J., M'Fingal, 1782, 91, 1806.
Ward, N., Cobbler of Agawam, 1843.
Wolcott, J., Peter Pindar's Works, 1794.
See Humor; Latin Authors; Poetry.

Saumarez, Admiral de. Ross, Memoirs of, 1838.

Sauquoit, N. Y. McGiffert, Hist. discourse, 1860.

Savannah, Ga. Siege of, 1779, (Hough), 1866.

Savary, J. M. R. *See* Rovigo, Duke.

Savery, J. Bourne, Miniature of, 1830. P. 390.

Savings Banks. Bank for Savings, N. Y., Report, 1863, 68.
" Memorial to Congress, 1866.
Beaumont, Essay on, Pamphleteer, v. 7.
Becher, J. T., Friendly Societies, 1824.
Bowles, J., Reasons for, 1817.
Buffalo Savings Bank, Report, 1859.
Christian, E., Plan for, 1816.
Denio, H., Funds of Depositors, 1853. P. 464.
France: Caisses d'Epargne, 1851, 54, 1856.
Friendly Advice to Indust. Persons, 1816.
Girard, F., Des caisses de retraites, 1850.
Hawkins, J. B., Savings Banks: Suggestions, 1857.
Haygarth, Explanation of Bath Inst., 1816. P. 1821.
Manchester and Salford, Report on, 1845. P. 252.
Martou, Institutions de prévoyance, Encyc. Pop.
Massachusetts, Reports on, 1846–54.
Mass. Loan Fund Assoc'ns, 1862–65.
N. Y. Supt's Reports, 1858–66, 68–71.
" Unclaimed deposits, 1863.
" Special Report, Keyes, 1868.
Nicoll, Acct. of York Bank, 1817.
Observations on Benefit Clubs, 1827.

Savings Banks (continued).
Pamphlets relating to Savings Banks, vols. 535, 1821.
Paris: Bakers: Compte de la caisse de service, 1856.
Penn'a, Reports on, 1848, 52, 63, 66.
" Report on Phil'a Inst., 1836. P. 1821.
Pénot, Instit. de prévoyance, (Soc. de Mulhouse).
Provident Fund Soc. of N. Y., 1866.
Provident Inst., Bost., Laws, 1842.
Savings Inst., Newark, 1847.
Sixpenny Savings Bank, N. Y., 1853. P. 252.
Suffolk Savings Bank, Laws, 1855.
Syracuse Savings Inst., Laws, 1861.

Savory, W. Cox, J., Sermon on, Lond., 1854.

Savoy. *See* Sardinia; France.

Sawin, T. E. Descendants of, 1866.

Saxony. Philipps, History of Princes Ernest and Bernard, 1740.
Shoberl, House of, 1816.
Stanford, J. F., Rambles in, 1842.
See Germany.

Saybrook Platform. Congr. Churches of Connecticut.

Scammell, A. Coffin, C., Life of, 1855.

Scandal. Barret, Serm., Evil of, 1711. P. 365.
Durham, J., Treatise on, 1740.
Woodward, J., Baseness of Slander, 1787.

Scandinavia. Acerbi, Travels through, 1802.
Clarke, E. D., Travels, 1816.
Coxe, W., Travels, 1787.
Crichton, A., Scandinavia, a history. Ed. Cab. Lib.
Dunham, S. A., Hist. of; Lardner's Cyc.
Herbert, W., Horæ Scandicæ, 1842.
Howitt, W. & M., Lit. of Northern Europe, 1852.
Keyser, R., Religion of the Northmen, 1854.
Kong. Nord. Oldskrift-Selskab; Annaler, 1836–38.
Laing, The Krimskringla, 1844; Trans.
Mallet, Northern Antiquities, 1847.
Müller, Chips from German workshop, v. II.
Nilsson, Primitive inhabit. of 1868.
Nordiske Literatur Samfund, 1847–51.
Rietz, J. E., Skänska Skolväsendets Hist., 1848.
Sinding, History of, 1866.
Taylor, B., Northern travel, 1858.

Science (continued).

Comte, Philos. of the Sciences, 1853.

Cream of Scientific Knowledge, 1841. B. C.

Dick, T., The Chr. philosopher, 1830

Dict. des Sci. Philosophiques, 1844–52.

Dusseau, Verbeenigen in zachte deelen, 1850.

Epitome of science, 1811.

Ewbank, T., World a work-shop, 1855.

Excelsior, Lond., 1854.

Garnett, Annals of Philosophy, 1801.

Germain, S., Consid. sur l'état des, 1833. P. 10.

Haughton, Rev. S., Scientific Papers collected, 1851–63.

Hellingwerp, Wiskoustige Oeffening, 1718.

Herschel, Manual of Scientific Inquiry, 1849.

Historical Essay on origin, etc., 1749. P. 253.

Jamieson, G., Essentials of Philos., 1859.

Johnson, F. G., Philosoph. Charts, 1855.

Lardner, Museum of Science and Art, 1854, 55.

" Course of Lectures, N. Y., 1842.

Meiners, History des Sci. en Grèce, 1748.

Orr's Circle of the Sciences, 1854–5.

Pamphlets, Scientific, vols. 23, 74, 79, 92, 205, 222, 233, 255, 272–274, 402, 551, 662, 749, 781, 826, 827, 858, 907, 923, 1014, 1024, 1049, 1050, 1206, 1207, 1797, 1822, 1874.

Peirce, Phys. and Celest. Mechanics, 1855.

Potter, A., Sci. applied to the Arts, 1842.

Quetelet, A., Papers, 1863–5.

Quetelet, E., Papers, 1863–8.

Timbs, Year-book of facts in Science, 1839–60.

Tyndall, Fragments of Science for the unscientific, 1871.

Wechniakof, Economie des travaux scientifiques, 1870.

Whewell, W., Philos. of discovery, 1860.

" Hist. of inductive sciences, 1857.

" Hist. of Scien. ideas, 1858.

Vincentius, Speculum Doctrinale, 1494.

Wing, H. R., Effects of studying the Sciences, 1834. P. 237.

Youmans, E. L., The future demanded. Selected addresses, 1867.

See Knowledge; Philosophy; Physics; Arts; Natural Philosophy; Natural Hist.; Geology; Biography, Scientific.

Sciences, Classification of. Bacon, F., Novum Organon.

Charma, A., Une nouvelle classification, 1859. P. 1207.

Coleridge, S. T., Method, Encyc. Metropol.

Comte, Cours de Philosophie.

" Positive Philos., (Martineau).

Palermo, F., Classazione dei libri, 1854.

Park, R., Pantologia, 1841.

Spencer, H., Class. of the sciences, 1864. P. 1207.

See Bibliography.

Scientific Discourses. Bowdoin, J., Amer. Acad. of Arts and Science, 1780.

Brande, W. T., Lond. Inst., 1819.

Brougham, Disc. on the Objects of, etc., 1827. B. C.

Davy, Sir H., Six Lectures, 1827.

Forbes, J. D., Brit. Assoc'n, 1834.

Foulke, W. P., Ac. of Sci., Phil'a, 1854. P. 100.

Frick, W., Univ. of Maryland, 1831. P. 587.

Gregory, O., Oration, Phil. Soc., London. Pamph'r 13.

Luke, S., Lect., Chester Mech. Ass'n., 1838. P. 1822.

Lyman, C. S., Address on Sci. Ed., Sheffield School, 1867.

Northampton, Marq. of, Addr., Royal Soc., 1840.

Poinsett, J. R., Disc., Objects of the Nat. Inst., 1841.

Townsend, P. S., Disc., Lyceum of Nat. Hist., N. Y., 1820.

Watkins, T., Columbian Inst., Washington, 1826. P. 581.

Whewell, W., Lecture, 1854.

See Am. Assoc'n; British Assoc'n, etc., the Ann. Addresses.

Scientific Periodicals. Academician, (Picket), N. Y., 1818–20.

Amer. Journal of Photography, 1861.

Amer. Jour. of Science, (Silliman), 1819–72.

Amer. Mineral. Jour., (Bruce), 1814.

Amer. Repertory of Arts, Science and Man., (Mapes), N. Y., 1840–42.

Amer. Polytechnic Journal, 1853, 4.

Annales des mines, 1860, 61.

Annales d'Horticulture, (Leide), 1859–1862.

Annals and Mag. of Natural History, 1858–70.

Annals of Philosophy, (T. Thompson), 1813–20.

Annals of Science, Cleveland, O., 1853.

Annual of Scient. Discovery, Boston, 1850–71.

Anthropological Review, 1863–66.

Scientific Periodicals (continued).

Appleton's Mechanic's Mag., 1852–54.

Arcana of Science and Art, 1828–38.

Astron. Jour., Camb., Mass., (Gould), 1849–52.

Berg und Hüttenmänische Zeitung, Freiberg, 1860.

Boston Jour. of Phil., 1824–26.

Bulletin des Sciences, Hist., Antiq., Philol., 1824–31.

Bulletin des Sci. technologiques, 1824–1831.

Canadian Journal of Industry, Science and Art, 1852–65.

Canadian Naturalist and Geologist, 1863–69.

Civil Engineers Journal, Lond., 1838–1867.

Daguerrian Journal, 1850–53.

Echo du Monde Savant, 1841.

Edinburgh Philos. Jour., (Brewster), 1819–32.

Edinburgh New Phil. Jour., (Jameson), 1826–72.

Elliot, American Museum, 1822.

Emporium of Arts and Sciences, 1812–1814.

Ethnological Journal, 1848, 49.

Farmer and Mechanic, 1847–50.

Genees-Natuur en Huishoud-kundige Jaarboeken, 1780. P. 107.

Geologist, The, (Moxon), Lond., 1842, 1843.

Geologist, The, (Mackie), London, 1862–4.

Gill's Technological Repository, 1827–1830.

Göttingische Gelehrte Anzeigen, 1854–1863.

Humphrey's Jour. of Photog., 1853–1856.

Jahrbuch für Mineralogie, etc., (Leonhard), 1830–57.

Journal des Connaissances usuelles, 1833.

Journal of Design and Manuf., 1849–1852.

Journal of Organic and Med. Chem., 1852. P. 98.

Journal of Botany, (Hooker), 1834–42.

London, Edin. and Dublin Phil. Mag., 1832–72.

London Geolog. Journal, 1846, 47.

London Jour. of Arts, Sciences, etc., 1820–47.

Long Island Jour. of Phil., 1825.

Magazine of Nat. History, London, 1829–40.

Mechanics' Magazine, London, 1823–1872.

Monthly Lit. and Sci. Lecturer, London, 1850.

Mining Magazine, N. Y., 1853–60.

Scientific Periodicals (continued).

Nash, Ladies' Diary, N. Y., 1819–21.

N. Y. Med. and Philosoph. Journal, 1809–11.

Nicholson's Jour. of Nat. Phil., 1797–1813.

North Western Jour. of Edu., Sci., etc., 1850.

Paxton's Magazine of Botany, 1834, 1839–49.

Philosophical Magazine and Journal, 1793–1826.

Plough, Loom and Anvil, 1848–57.

Quarterly Journal of Science, (W. T. Brande), 1817–30.

Quarterly Journal of Science, London, 1864–71.

Quarterly Mining Review, 1830–35.

Répertoire de chimie, 1858–60.

Repertory of Patent Invent., 1830–48.

Repertory of Arts and Manuf., 1794–1817.

Scientific American, N. Y., 1846–72.

Scientific Journal, (Marratt), N. Y., 1818.

Scientific Tracts, Serial, Boston, 1832.

Timbs, Year-book of facts in Science, 1839–60.

United States Magazine of science, art, etc., 1854, 55.

Zeitschrift für das Berg-Hütten und Salinen....wesen in dem Preuss. Staate, 1859–60.

Zeitschrift für Mineralogie, (Leonhard), 1825-29.

See Arts, and the several Sciences.

Scientific and Learned Societies, Transactions and Journals.

Acad. Cæs. Leop. Car. Nat. Cur., 1818-20.

Academia Gandavensis: Annales, 1818-1820.

Academia Groningana, Annales Academici, 1815–37, 53–58.

Academia Leopoldina: Miscellanea curiosa, 1671–97.

Academia Lugduno-Batava: Annales Academici, Hagæ, 1837–1840, 53–54, 56–57.

" Museum Anatomicum, Sandifort, 1793–1827.

Académie de Belgique, Annuaire, 1846–1868.

" Mémoires, 1840–71.

" Bulletin, 1848–71.

Académie de Bordeaux, Recueil, 1839, 1842–53.

" Séances publiques, 1820–35.

Académie de Caen, Mémoires, 1855.

Académie...de Lyon, Classe des Sciences, 1851–56.

Académie de Metz, Mémoires, 1821–1848, 61–62.

Scientific and Learned Societies, Transactions and Journals (continued).

Acad. of Nat. Soc., Phila., Proc., 1841–69.

" Journal, 1817–68.

" History of, Ruschenberger, 1860.

Acad. of Sci. of St. Louis, Trans., 1857-69.

Albany Institute, Trans., 1850–70.

Allgemeine Schweizerische Gesellschaft für die Gesammten Naturwissenschaften, 1819–66.

" Denkschriften, 1860–62, 1865, 67.

Amer. Acad. of Arts and Sci., Memoirs, 1785–1850.

" Proceedings, 1846–8.

Am. Assoc. for Adv. of Science, Proc., 1848–69.

Am. Ethnological Soc., Trans., 1845, 1848.

Am. Inst. of the City of N. Y., Trans., 1842–68.

Am. Oriental Soc., Journal, 1849-66.

Am. Philos. Soc., Trans., 1789–1869.

" Trans. Hist. and Lit. Comm., 1819, 38.

" Proceedings, 1838–64.

Am. Statist. Assoc., Coll., 1847.

Anthropological Soc., Journal, 1863–1866.

" Transactions, 1863–66.

Asiatic Society of Bengal, Bibliot. Indica, 1848–60.

Bataafsch Genootschap te Rotterdam, 1784.

Bataviaasch Genoot. der Kunsten en Wetenschappen, 1780–1850.

Boston Society of Nat. Hist., Proc., 1841–68.

" Journal, 1834–63; Memoirs, 1866–69.

" Condition and doings, 1868. P. 1822.

Botanical Soc. of Edinburgh, 1838–41.

British Assoc. for Adv. of Sci., Proc., 1831–69.

Cagnola Fondazione Scien., 1856.

Columbian Chem. Soc., Phil'a., 1813.

Connect. Acad. Arts and Sci., 1810.

Elliott Soc. of Nat. Hist., S. C., 1853–58.

Essex Institute, Proc., 1848–67.

Essex Nat. Hist. Soc., Jour., 1852.

Ethnological Soc. of London, Proc. & Trans., 1848–68.

Franklin Institute, Journal, 1826–72.

Friesch Genootschap, 1840–57.

Geographical Soc. of Lond., Journal, 1834–70.

Scientific and Learned Societies, Transactions and Journals (continued).

Geolog. Soc. of Dublin, Jour., 1844–64.

Geolog. Soc. of London, Trans., Journal and Proc., 1811–68.

Geolog. Soc. of Penn'a, Trans., 1835.

Georg-Augusts-University, Göttingen, Nachrichten, 1859–63.

Georgetown Observatory: Annals, 1852.

Göttingische gelehrte Anzeigen, 1856–1858.

Hist. Soc. of Science. Publications of treatises of the middle ages.

Hollandsche Maatsch. der Weetenschappen, 1777-81.

Hollandsche Maatsch. van Fraijekunsten, 1840. B. C.

Hume, A., Lists of books of learned Soc., 1853.

Institut de France, Acad. des Sci. Mémoires, 1692–1862, imp.

" Comptes Rendus, 1838–62.

" Annuaire, 1840.

" Biog. Hist. of French Academy, (Edwards, E.), 1864.

Institution of Civil Engineers, Jour. Lond., 1836–40.

Institut National Genèvois, Mémoires, 1859–68.

Instituto Hist., Geog. e Ethnog., Rio de Janeiro, Revista trimensal, 1839–63.

Instituto Nacional de Geografia....de la Republica Mexicana, Boletin, 1839–51.

Istituto Lombardo, Milano, Memorie, 1812–63.

" Atti, 1860, 62.

Istituto Nazionale Italiano, Bologna, Memorie, 1806–13.

Internat. Congress of Pre-hist. Archæology, Norwich, 1868.

Italian Sci. Association, Atti, 1846.

Kaiserlich k. Ak. der Wissenchaften, Sitzungsberichte, Wien, 1857, 58, 63, 64.

" Almanach, 1858, 63–4.

Kaiserlich k. Geographische Gesellschaft, Mittheil., 1859–64.

Kaiserlich k. Geolog. Reichsanstalt, Jahrbuch, 1850–66.

Konink. Ak. der Wetenschappen, Verhandelingen, 1854–68.

Konink. Zool. Genoots., Jaarboekje, 1852–57.

Koeniglich Baier. Akad. der Wissenschaften, Monumenta Boica, 1763–1849.

" Abhandlungen, 1763–1866.

" Gelehrte Anzeigen, 1850–60.

" Sitzungsberichte, 1860–66.

Scientific and Learned Societies, Transactions and Journals (continued).

Koeniglich Gesellschaft der Wiss. zu Göttingen. *See* Götting. gelehrte Anzeigen.

Linnean Soc. of London, Trans., 1791–1846.

Lit. and Phil. Soc. of N. Y, Trans., 1815.

Lyceum of Nat. Hist. of N. Y., Jour., Annals, 1822–67.

Maatschappij der Neder. Letter-kunde, 1849.

McLurian Lyceum, Contr., 1827. P. 92.

Manchester Lit. and Phil. Soc, Mem., 1785–98.

Maryland Academy, 1837.

Med. & Phys. Soc. of Bombay, Trans., 1838.

Meding, Acad. Leopoldino-Carolina, 1854. P. 222.

Microscopical Society, Lond., Trans, 1862–68.

Mineralogical (Imperial) Society of St. Petersburgh, Trans., 1830.

National Ac. of Sciences, Wash., Annual, 1863–66.

National Institution, Washington, 1840–46.

Natur. Hist. Soc., Montreal, Reports, 1828–53, 63–65.

Naturforschende Gesellschaft, in Emden, 1859–66.

Naturforschende Gesellsc., Bern, 1855–1864.

Natuur en Geneeskundige Soc.: Verhandelingen, 1779–80.

Nederlandsche Entomol. vereeniging, 1858–9.

New Orleans Ac. of Sci., Report, 1858.

New York State Instit. of Civil Eng. Trans., 1849.

Overysselsche Vereeniging, 1841–57.

Palæontographical Soc. Publications, 1848–69.

Palma, Principio di nazionalità, 1867.

Peabody Ac. of Sci., Salem, Reports, 1–3, 1869–71.

Physikalisch Verein zu Frankfort, 1851–54.

Provinciaal Friesch Genootschap, Werken, 1835–7.

Provinciaal Utrechtsch Genoot. van Kunsten en Wetenschappen, 1845–1859.

Ray Society, Lond., Publications, 1845–69.

Royal Botan. Soc. of London, Proc., 1839, 57.

Royal Irish Acad., Trans., 1787–1849.

" Proceedings to 1864.

Royal Physical Society of Edinburgh, Proc., 1854–66.

Royal Soc. of Edinburgh, Trans., 1788–1867.

Royal Soc. of London, Trans., 1665–1869.

Russisch k. Gesellsch. f. d. Gesammte Mineralogie, 1842, 57, 58.

Smithsonian Institution, Wash'n, Reports, 1846-69.

" Contributions, 1848–71.

" Misc. Collections, 1862–69.

Soc. Acad. de Nantès, Annales, 1831-1846.

Soc. Asiatique, Journal, 1822–67.

Société Chimique de Paris, 1858-60.

Société de Géographie, Bulletin, 1844-1853.

Société des Sciences, Liége, Mémoires, 1843–60.

Société des Sciences de Lille, Mémoires, 1851, 52.

Soc. des Sci. Nat. de Neuchatel, 1835-1845.

Société des Sciences Naturelles de Strasbourg, Mémoires, 1862.

Soc. Géologique de France, Bulletin, 1844–54.

Soc. Helvétique des Sci. Nat., Mémoires, 1829–53..

Soc. Libre de l'Eure, Recueil, 1841–50.

Society of Arts, London, Journal, 1852-1869.

Soc. for Encour. of Arts, London, 1819.

Soc. for Prom. of useful Arts, N. Y., Trans., 1791–99, 1807. *See also* Albany Institute.

Society of Antiquaries, London, 1779–1867.

Society of Antiquaries of Scotland, Archæologia, 1792–1857.

" Proceedings, 1851-60.

Statistical Soc. of Lond., Journ., 1839–1868.

Svenska Akad., Hanlingar, 1832–37.

Taylor, R., Scientific Memoirs, 1837–1852.

Zoölogical Society of London, Trans., 1830–62.

" Proceedings, 1857–68.

See Arts; Agriculture; Horticulture; Medicine; Education; History; Literary; Bibliography; and Special Sciences.

Scilly Is. Heath, R., Acct. of, Pinkerton's Voy.

Scipio Africanus. Berwick, Life of, 1817.

Scituate, Mass. Deane, S., History of, to 1831.

Sclavonians. *See* Slavonians.

Scofield, A. Trial before Presb., 1845.

Scoresby, W. Scoresby, Life of, 1861.

Scotch Propag. Soc. Reports and Sermons, (12), 1763-1840.

Scotland. Abbott, J., A Summer in, 1848.

Abercrombie, Scots' Warriors, 1329-1514.

Anderson, J., Collections on Mary, Queen of, 1727.

Anderson, J., Western coasts of, 1786.

Baillie, Proceedings against, 1704.

Balcarres, Account of, 1833.

Bannatyne, R., Journal, 1570-73.

Bannatine Club, Publications, No. 1, 2, 3, 1836.

Beauties of, (Forsyth), 1805.

Bigelow, A., Rambles in, and Ireland, 1817.

Boece, Book of the Chronicles of, (Chr. of G. B.).

Boswell, J., Tour to the Hebrides, 1810.

Brand, J., Descr. of Orkney and Zetland, (Pinkerton, 3).

Brown, J., Hist. of Scotch Churches, 1823.

Browne, J., Highland Clans, 1843.

Buchanan, G., Rerum Scot. Historia, 1762.

" Hist. of Scotland, (Aikman).

" De jure regni, 1689. P. 1396.

Buchanan, J. L., Trav. in Western Hebrides, 1793.

Buchanan, R., Land of Lorne, 1871.

Buckle, H. T., Hist. of Civilization, v. 2, 1861.

Burt, Uncommon Customs of, 1754.

Calendars of the Ancient Charters, (Ayloffe), Lond., 1772.

Calendar of State papers, 1509-89.

Carrick, J. D., Life of Sir W. Wallace, 1840.

Carstares, State papers, 1688-1709.

Chalmers, G., Caledonia, Hist. and Topographical, 1807, 10, 24.

Charles I, Proclamation in 1638.

Crawfurd, G., Lives of State Officers, 1726.

De Foe, Hist. of Union with England, 1786.

Description of the Regalia of, 1843.

Douglas, Agr. of Roxburgh.

Edinburgh University Calendar, 1860, 1867.

Forbes, Jacobite Memoirs of 1745.

Fraser, R., Fisheries of, 1803.

Fraser, R. W., Kirk and Manse, Views, 1857.

Scotland (continued).

Garnett, T., Tour through the Highlands and Western Isles, 1800.

Gilpin, W., Obs. on the Highlands, 1808.

Glasgow University Calendar, 1868-70.

Gordon, R., Earldom of Sutherland, 1813.

Grant, A., Superstitions of Highlanders, 1811.

Grant, J., Mem. of W. Kirkaldy, 1849.

Great Britain, Report on Universities of, 1837.

Grose, F., Antiquities of, 1797.

Hamilton, W., Life of Sir. W. Wallace, 1816.

Heron, R., Hist. of, 1796.

Home, J, Works, Rebellion of 1745.

Hooke, Secret Negot. for the Pretender, 1760.

Innes, C., S. in the Middle Ages, 1860.

Irving, J., Hist. of Dumbartonshire, 1860.

Johnstone, Rebellion of 1745

Keith, History of, 1540 to 1568.

Kerr, R., Hist. of Reign of Robert I, 1306-71.

Knox, J., Works, Hist. of the Reformation in S.

Labanoff, Lettres de Marie Stuart, Reine, 1844.

Laing, History of, 1819.

Lawson, J. P., Hist. of Epis. Ch. in, 1844.

Lindsay, Lives of the Lindsays, 1849.

Lockhart, J. G., Peter's letters to his kinsfolk, 1819.

Logan, J., The Scottish Gael, 1833.

McCallum, Hist. of the Culdees, 1855.

M'Crie, Sketches of Scottish History, 1849.

" Lives of Veitch and Brysson.

McKenzie, G., Antiquity of the royal line, 1685.

M'Lellan, I., Residence in, 1834.

McNicol, On Johnson's Hebrides, 1779.

Macpherson, James, Hist. of rebel. in 1745.

Macpherson, John, Diss. on the Anc. Caledonians, 1768.

Maitland, W., History of, to 1603, 1757.

Martin, M., Descr. of Western Islands of, (Pinkerton, 3).

Miller, H., Scenes and Legends of North of, 1851.

" Cruise of the Betsey, 1858.

Miscellanea Scotica, 1818-20.

Moore, G., Anc. Pillar Stones of, 1865.

Naismith, Agr. of Clydesdale, 1806.

Napier, J., Montrose and the Covenanters, 1838.

Ossianic Society, Trans., 1857.

Ossian's Poems.

Scott, R. Adventures, 1850.

Scott, Tho. Force of truth, 1841.
Scott, J., Life of, 1823.

Scott, Sir W. Adolphus, On Authorship of Waverley, 1821.
Allan, G., Life of, 1835.
Ballantyne and Lockhart Controversy, 1838, 39.
Bonaparte, L., Reply to his history of Napoleon, 1829.
Chambers, R., Life of, 1832. P. 15. B. C.
Depping, Wayland Smith, 1847.
Hogg, J., Anecdotes of, 1834.
Hunnewell, Lands of Scott, 1871.
Irving, W., Crayon miscellany.
Lockhart, J. G., Life of, 1838.
Maginn, Fraserian papers, 1857.
Robberd's Mem. of W. Taylor, Letters of, 1843.
Scott, Sir W., Autobiography, 1831. B. C.

Scott, Gen. W. Galphin case, 1852.
Headley, Life of, 1861.
Mansfield, E. D., Life of, 1846.
New York City, Reception of, 1849.
Papers for the People, 1852.
Potter, W., War in Florida, 1836.
Scott, W., Life of, 1852.
" Memoirs, by himself, 1864.
See Mexico, War with the U. S.

Scranton Family. Descendants, 1855.

Scranton, Pa. History and Directory, 1867, 68.

Scrooby Church. Hunter, J., Collections, 1854

Sculpture. Barbédienne, Collec., Paris. P. 499.
Bottman, Cours d'Anatomie, 1788.
Canova, A., Engravings from, Portfolio 4.
Chiaramonti Museum, Engravings of the Hall, Portfolio 4.
Clarac, Musée du Louvre, 1847.
Disney, J., Museum of anc. marbles, 1849.
Elgin Marbles, selected from Revett, 1816, 4°.
Ellis, Elgin and Phigaleian Marbles. Lib. E. K.
" Townley Gallery of Sculpture.
Flaxman, Compositions from Dante, 1831.
" Illustrations of the Iliad and Odyssey.
" Illust. of Æschylus, 1831.
" Illust. of Hesiod, 1831.
" Lectures on Sculpture, 1838.
Fogelberg, B., L'Œuvre de, 1856.

Sculpture (continued).
Great Britain, Report on the Elgin Marbles, 1816. Pamph'r 8. *See also*, Elgin Marbles.
Hay, E. W. A., Roman Monument at Colchester, 1821. P. 401.
Hope, Costume of the Ancients, 1841.
Mêmes, Hist. of Sculpture, Painting and Architecture, 1831. B. C.
Mercey, Etudes sur les Beaux Arts, 1855.
Montfaucon, Antiquity Explained, 1721–25.
Montaiglon, Hist. Acad. de Sculp. à Paris, 1853.
Newton, C., Sculptures at Wilton House. 1849. P. 1220.
" Sculptures from Halicarnassus. P. 1220.
Pio-Clementine Museum, Engravings of the Halls. Portfolio 4.
Powers's Greek Slave, 1848. P. 499.
Quatremère, Canova et ses ouvrages, 1834.
Spooner, Dict. of Sculptors, 1853.
Thom's Tom O'Shanter, 1833. P. 499.
Visconti, Œuvres; Musée Pie Clémentin, 1818.
" Monumens du Musée Chiaramonti, 1822.
Worsley, Museum Worsleyanum, 1824.
See Fine Arts; Engraved Stones.

Sea. *See* Naval; Navigation; Ocean; Shipwrecks.

Seabury, S. Perry, W. S., Fragment on.
Jarvis, A., Discourse on, 1796.

Seal of the U. S. Columb. Mag., 1786.

Seals. Prime, W. C., Coins and Seals, 1861.
Wadhams, A., Use of, 1865.

Seamen. Amer. Bapt. Mariner's Society, 1857. P. 549.
Amer. Bethel Soc., Reports, 1838–53.
Amer. Seam. Friend Society, History, 1858. P. 549.
" Report, 1860.
Boston Port Society, Report, 1858. P. 549; 1836, 44.
Boston Seaman's Friend Society, Reports, 1832. P. 90; 1856, P. 1823.
Brazer, Addr., Seaman's Ass'n, 1836.
Canada, Return on desertions of, 1857. P. 567.
Churchman's Miss. Assoc'n for, 1848.
Colton, W., Sea and Sailor, 1851.
Cooke, J., Sermon, 1789.
Dana, R. H., jr., Seaman's Friend, 1841.
" Two years before the Mast, 1869.
Forbes, R B., An Appeal on, 1854.

Sermons, American, Volumes of.
Adams, J. W., 1851.
Alexander, J. W., Consolation, 1853.
Armstrong, W. J., 1853.
Baptist Preacher, 1847-8.
Barnard, J., Janua cœlestis, Bost., 1750.
Bedell, G. T., Phil'a, 1835. B. C.
Beecher, H. W., N. Y., 1868.
Beecher, Lyman, 1809-32.
Buckminster, J. S., 1815. B. C., 1839.
Castleman, T. T., S. for servants, 1851.
Chauncy, C., Five Sermons, Bost., 1816.
" Twelve Sermons, 1765.
Clark, D. A., Works, 1846.
Clark, R. W., Collected, 1848-63.
Clowes, T., Albany, 1816.
Colman, B., Discourses, Bost., 1747.
Colman, H., 1833. B. C.
Davies, S., 1845. B. C.
Dedham Pulpit, 1840.
Dewey, O., Works, 1847.
Doane, G. W., Works, 1861.
Duché, J., 1799.
Duffield, Princeton Pulpit, 1852.
Dwight, T., 1828. B. C.
Edwards, J., 1844.
Eliot, A., Twenty Sermons, Bost., 1774.
Emmons, N., 1812.
Flint, J., Salem, Mass., 1852.
Follen, C., Works, vol. 2, 1841.
Foxcroft, T., Bost., 1719.
Hemmenway, M., Bost. 1767, 92.
Hitchcock, E., Amherst, 1850.
Hooker, T., Saints Dignitie, 1651.
Hopkins, S., Salem, 1803.
Lathrop, J., Hartford, 1789.
" Northampton, 1803.
Lee, C., Conn., 1824.
Linn, William, New York, 1791, 94.
Mason, J. M., Works, N. Y., 1849.
Mather, C., Bost., 1717.
Mather, I., Bost., 1710.
Mather, S., Self-justiciary, 1706.
Mayhew, J., Seven Sermons, Bost., 1749.
" Practical Discourses, Bost., 1760.
Mayo, A. D., Albany, 1852, 1860.
National Preacher, N. Y., 1826-29.
Nott, Eliphalet, Schenectady, 1810.
Nott, Sam., jr., Bost., 1841.
Olds, Gam. S., Greenfield, 1815.
Olin, S., Works, N. Y., 1852.
Osgood, David, Boston, 1824.
Palfrey, J. G., Bost., 1834. B. C.

Sermons, American, Volumes of (continued).
Pamphlets containing sermons, American, vols. 25, 28, 29, 61, 62, 78, 80, 82, 94, 95, 104-106, 111, 189, 202, 238, 267, 288, 441, 453, 556-559, 574, 635, 641, 652, 755, 862, 864, 868, 870, 884, 894, 1596-1606, 2503, 2519, 1824.
Parker, T., Boston, Sermons, 1846-56; 1841-52.
Pemberton, E., Bost., 1727.
Proudfit, Alexander, Salem, N. Y., 1798, 1815.
Quincy, S., Charlestown, S. C. 1750.
Richards, James, Albany, 1849. B. C.
Romeyn, J. B., N. Y., 1816.
Rudder, W., Albany, 1858-61.
Sewall, J. Four Sermons, Bost. 1741.
Simmons, G. F., Six Sermons, Albany, 1856.
Smalley, J., Conn., 1803.
Smith, Gerrit, Peterboro, 1861-64.
Smith, S. S., Newark, 1709.
Smith, William, London, 1762.
Sprague, W. B., Albany, 1843-65.
Stillman, S., Bost., 1808.
Stoddard, S., Three Sermons, Bost., 1717.
" Safety, etc., Bost., 1742.
Strong, N., Sermons, Hartford, 1798.
Swett, W. G., Five Sermons, Bost., 1843. P. 106.
Swift, J., Discourses, Middlebury, 1805.
Tennent, G., Discourses, Bost., 1743.
Thacher, S. C., Bost., 1824.
Things new and old, Portland, 1845. B. C.
Thornton, Pulpit of the Revolution, Bost., 1860.
Wainright, Bp., 34 Sermons, N. Y., 1856.
Ware, H., Works, Bost., 1846.
Willard, S., Boston, 1684, 86.
Williston, S., Millenial Discourses, Utica, 1849.
" Serm. practical, Hudson, 1812.
Winslow, B. D., N. Y., 1841.
Witherspoon, Works, Phila., 1800-01.
Worcester, S, Six Sermons, 1800.
See Political Sermons; Slaves, Fugitive; Massachusetts; Connecticut.

Sermons, British, Volumes of. Alison, Archibald, 1815. B. C.
Allestree, R., Forty Sermons, 1684.
Balguy, Thomas, 1817. B. C.
Bates, G. F., 1816, 17.
Beard, J. R., 1831. B. C.
Blair, Hugh, 1802. B. C.

Sermons, British, Volumes of (cont'd).

Booth, A., 1770–1804.
Bowdler, Mrs. H., Bath, 1815.
Bridge, W., 1823. B. C.
Bright, G., Six Sermons, 1695.
Buchanan, C., 1812.
Burder, G., Village Sermons, 1808.
Butler, W. A., 1857.
Calamy, B , 1690, 1704.
Calamy, E., 1641–1663.
Cappe, N., 1818. B. C.
Catcott, A. S., 1753.
Catholic Pulpit, 1849. P. 380.
Chalmers, T., 1817, B. C. 1823.
Chevalier, T., Hulsean Lectures, 1826, 1827.
Church of England, Homilies, 1832.
Clarke, S., A Collection, 1705-25.
" Works, 1738.
Cole, T., Luxury, Infidelity, 1761.
Collier, J., Discourses, 1726.
Conybeare, J., Oxford, 1722–51.
Cooper, E., 1818.
Copleston, E., 1830–48.
Cotes, H., 1813–17.
Creighton, J., Lond., 1780–96.
Creyghton, R., 1720.
Croly, G., 1831–52.
Cummings, John, 1846–54.
Dawes, Sir W., 1704–13, 1696–1712.
Dealtry, W., 1812–49.
Dodwell, W., Oxford, 1743–60.
Dorman, W., Twelve Serm., 1744.
Doughty, J., Ten Discourses, 1761.
Evanson, E., Three Discourses, 1773. P. 373.
Fawcett, J., 1801. B. C.
Five Sermons, 1738.
Foster, James, 1774, 5. B. C.
Foster, John, 1853.
Fothergill, G., 1745–58.
Froude, R. H., Remains, 2d vol., 1838.
Garbett, J., 1843–51.
Gill, J., 1777.
Graver Thoughts, etc. (Boyd), 1862.
Griffith, T., 1756–70.
Hall, Robert, Works, 1832.
Hales, J., Remains of, 1688. B. C.
Hardy, N., 1848–1661.
Hare, Francis, 1700–30.
Hawkins, E., 1818–43.
Horsfall, S., 1808. P. 1560.
Horsley, S., 1811. B. C.
Hughes, O., Five Sermons, 1743–6.
Hull, W., The Mirrour of Majestie, 1615.
Irving, Edward, 1823.
Jay, William, 1805, 1807. B. C.

Sermons, British, Volumes of (cont'd).

Johnson, Samuel, 1812.
Jortin, J., Discourses, 1746.
Kennet, B., Twenty Sermons, 1727.
Kettlewell, J., 1696.
Kingsley, C., 1858.
Latimer, H., Fruitful Sermons, 1578.
" Parker Soc. Publications.
Leighton, R., Works, 1825.
Leland, J., 1769.
Lloyd, W., 1673–90.
Mangey, T., Lond., 1717–19.
Manning, H. E., 1838–52.
Mant, R., 1795–1836.
Marsh, G., 1737.
Maurice, F. D., What is revelation? 1859.
" The Patriarchs, 1867.
" Lectures on Luke, 1864.
Mitchell, M., Five Sermons, 1848.
Murray, J., Sermons to Asses, 1819.
Ogden, S., 1780.
Orton, Job, Discourses to the Aged.
Paley, W., Works, vols. 5, 6, 1830.
Palmer, Sam., 1771-1814.
Pamphlet vols. of Sermons, British, 359–380, 705, 717, 728, 737, 746, 758, 830–837, 911, 1005–1009, 1028-1032, 1459–1466, 1556–1565, 1618, 1619, 2500, 2517.
Parr, S., Works, vol. 2, 5, 6, 1828.
Patrick, S., 1670–1707.
Pearson, J., Twelve Sermons, 1803.
Pelling, E., 1679–1692.
Pope, J., 1792.
Porter, J. S., 1829–49.
Porteus, B., Works, 1811.
Practical Sermons, London, 1845.
Preston, J., 1630–38.
Price, Richard, 1794. B. C.
Pulpit, The, 1830–35.
Raikes, H., 1842–51.
Randolph, F., 1799.
Reeves, Wm., 14 Sermons, 1729.
Rennell, T., 1792–98.
Reynolds, E., 1634–8.
Reynolds, H. R., Christian Life, 1865.
Robinson, R , 1773–1781.
Rogers, John, 1719.
Rosewell, S., 1705–19.
Scott, Sir W., Works, vol. 8, 1840.
Secker, T., Works, 1792.
Sermons on duties of Children, 1813.
Sherlock, T., 1704–1729.
Sherlock, W., 1683–1704.
Smalridge, G., 1702–1716.
Smith, H., Twelve Sermons, 1769.
Sprat, T., 1676–1696.

Shakers (continued).

Dunlavy, J., The Manifesto, 1818.

" True Church of Christ, 1847. P. 540.

Dyer, J., Character of Mary Dyer, 1826.

" Review of the Portraiture, 1824.

Dyer, Mary, Portraiture of, 1824.

" Reply to Review of Portraiture, 1824.

Evans, F. W., Origin of, 1859.

" Tests of Divine Inspiration, 1853.

" Second appearing of Christ through the female, 1853.

Green, C., A View of the Millennial Church, 1848.

Investigator, The, or a Defence of the Order, 1846.

Leonard, W., On Divine Inspiration.

Mace, F., Dialogues on, 1838.

New Hampshire, Case of. Law Lib.

New York, Report on, 1849.

Rathbun, D., Letter to Whittaker.

Rathbun, V., Some Brief Hints, 1781.

Return of Departed Spirits, (Thomas), 1843.

Shakers, Testimonies concerning Ann Lee, 1827.

" Brief Exposition of the Regulations, etc., 1830, 46, 51, 1862.

" Society of Believers: A Declaration, 1815. P. 9. B.C.

" Memorial for Exemption, 1862. P. 1260.

Some lines....about Shakers, 1846.

Youngs, Testimony....2d Appearing, 1856.

Shakespeare, W. Ayscough, Index to passages and words, 1827. B. C.

Bacon, Delia, Philosophy of Plays of, 1857.

Bowdler, Family Shakespeare, 1831.

" Prospectus of, 1831. P. 1242.

Boydell, John, Cat. of the Pictures in the Shakespeare Gallery, 1810. P. 996.

" Prospectus for Am. edit. of, 1848. P. 1242.

" Plates to Shakespeare.

Bucknill, J. C., Mad folk of, 1867.

Burton, W. E., Bibliot. Dram., Cat. of Library of.

Campbell, J., His Legal acquirements, 1859.

Campbell, T., Life of, 1846.

Clarke, Mrs., Concordance to, 1845.

Clarke, C. C., Characters of, 1863.

Coleridge, S. T., Lectures on, (Works, v. 4).

Collier, J. P., Notes on text, 1853.

Shakespeare, W. (continued).

Craft, Z., Monument to Shakespeare. Pamph'r 22.

Dodd, W., Beauties of, selected, 1830. B. C.

Dolby, T., Shakespearian Dictionary, 1832. B. C.

Drake, N., Shakespeare and Times, 1817.

" Memorials of, 1828.

Dyce, A., A few notes on, 1853.

Edwards, T., Supp. to Warburton's edition of, 1765. B. C.

Evans, J., Shakespeare's Seven ages, 1831. B. C.

Fairholt, Home of, illustrated, 1848.

Farmer, R., Essay on the learning of, 1821. P. 710.

Guizot, F. De, S. and his times, 1852.

Hackett, J. H., Notes, Criticisms, 1863.

Halliwell, J. O., Curiosities of criticism, 1853. P. 1242.

" Obs. on emendation, 1853.

" Last days of, 1863.

" List of works on, 1867.

Hamilton, N. E., On Collier's edition, 1860.

Hazlitt, Characters of his plays, 1845.

Holmes, N., Authorship of, 1866.

Hows, J. W. S., Shakesp. Reader, 1855.

Hudson, H. N., Lectures on, 1848.

Hunter, J., New illustrations of, 1845.

Hurst, J. F., Why Americans love... 1856. P. 513.

Ireland, S., Misc. papers (forged), 1796.

Ireland's, W. H., Confessions, 1805.

Jackson, Z., His genius justified, 1819.

Jameson, A., Char. of women of, 1866.

Johnson, S., Obs. on the plays, v. 10.

Kellogg, His delineations of insanity, etc., 1866.

Kemble, J. P., Macbeth and Richard III, 1817.

Lamb, C., On the tragedies of.

Landor, W. S., Exam. of, before Sir T. Lucy, 1834.

Lenox, J., On the folio editions of, 1862.

Maginn, Shakespeare papers, 1856.

Malone, E., Letter to R. Farmer, 1792.

Montagu, E., Essay on, 1810.

Nares, R., Glossary, Wright's ed., 1867.

Pamphlets relating to Shakespeare, vol. 710.

Reflections from Shakespeare's Cliff, 1851. P. 398.

Richardson, W., On Richard III, Lear, Timon, Hamlet, 1784.

Shoemakers. Lives of, 1849.

Shoes. Meyer, H., Why the shoe pinches, 1861. P. 1223.

Plumer, J. C., Improved lasts, 1860.

Shooting. *See* Hunting.

Shore, James. Craig, E., Case of, 1849.

Eardley, Appeal for, 1849.

Shore, John. *See* Teignmouth, Lord.

Shoreham, Vt. Goodhue, J. F., History of, 1861.

Short Hand. Barton, M. H., Something new, 1830–33.

Fauvel-Gouraud, Cosmo-phonography, 1850.

Gould, M. T. C., Analytic Guide and Key to the Art, 1823.

Gurney, T., Brachygraphy, 1825.

Lewis, J. H., Hist. of Stenography, 1816.

N. Y. Constit. Conv., 1821, Gould's Stenog. report of the debates, MS.

Pitman, I., Man. of Phonog., 1845, 53.

" Phonog. instructor, 1853.

" Reporter's Companion, 1853.

Shelton, Tachygraphy, 1647.

Stenog. Nachrichten aus Lissa, 1856. P. 513.

Towndrow, Stenography, 1832.

Univ. Phonographer, 1852. P. 513.

See Alphabets; Cypher; Phonography; Writing.

Shrewsbury, C. Talbot, Duke of.

Coxe, W., Priv. Correspondence of, 1821.

Vernon, Letters to, 1696–1708.

Shrewsbury, Mass. Sumner, J., Hist. Sermon, 1812.

Ward, A. H., Hist. of, 1717–1829.

Shropshire. Beauties of England and Wales.

Shunk, F. R. Champneys, B., Address on, 1849. P. 1493.

Siam. Crawfurd, J., Jour. of Embassy to, 1830.

Malcom, H., Trav. in S. E. Asia, 1839.

Mouhot, H., Travels in, 1864.

Roberts, E., Embassy to Siam, 1832–1834.

Turpin, Hist. of, Pinkerton, 9.

Varen, B., Descriptio, 1673.

See Asia, Southern.

Siamese Twins. Hist. acct. of. P. 199.

Morehead, Lives of.

Siberia. Atkinson, T. W., Orient. and West. Siberia, Explor., 1858.

" Travels, Upper and Lower Amoor, 1860.

Siberia (continued).

Bell, J., Travels to divers parts of Asia, 1764.

Cochrane, J., Pedest. Journey through, 1824.

Collins, P. M., Voy. on the Amoor, 1860.

Cottrell, C. H., Recollections of, 1840, 1841.

Dobell, Travels in, 1830.

Erman, Travels in, 1848.

Fischer, Nations établies en Sibérie, 1798.

Palmer, A. H., Memoir on, 1848. P. 50. B. C.

Pietrowski, R., Escape from, 1863.

Pumpelly, R., Across America and Asia, 1870.

Sarytschew, G., Voy. N. E. of Siberia, 1807. Phillips' Coll.

See Russia; Kamtschatka; Tartary.

Sibthorp, R. W. Dodsworth, Remarks on, 1842. P. 722.

Sicily. Amari, M., Guerra del vespro Siciliano, 1843.

Bartlett, W. H., Pictures from, 1863.

Bigelow, A., Travels in, 1827.

Brydone, Tour through Sicily, 1813.

Byng. Adm., British Fleet at, 1739.

Cluverius, P., Sicilia antiqua, 1619.

Ferrara, F., Guida, 1822.

Forbin, Souvenirs de la Sicile, 1823.

Galt, Travels, 1812.

Gemmellaro, Progr. della Scienze in, 1833.

Græviuus, Thesaurus Antiquitatum, 1737.

Hoare, R. C., Classical Tour, 1819.

Hughes, T. S., Travels in, 1820.

James, J., Sketches of Travel in, 1820.

Oxford Essays, (Duff), 1857.

Petit, Politique des Normands dans, 1846.

Pietrasanta, Le antichità della Sicilia, 1834–42.

Quatrefages, Rambles, 1857.

Spallanzani, L., Tr. in the Two Sicilies, 1798.

Spalding, Italy and Italian Islands, Ed. Cab. Lib.

Swinburne, H., Travels in the Two S., 1777–80.

Thompson, W. H., Observatiens in, 1809.

Tuckerman, H. T., Sicily, 1856.

See Naples; Palermo.

Sickles, D. E. Tucker, G. J., Letter from, 1858. P. 488.

Siddons, S. Boaden, Memoir of, 1827.

Campbell, T., Life of, 1835. B. C.

Galindo, Mrs., Letter to, 1809.

Slavery in the United States (cont'd).

Brodnax, Speech, Va., 1832.

Brown, B. G., Address, St. Louis, 1862.

Brown, J., Am. Slavery, 1840. P. 663.

Buffalo Presbytery on A. B. C. F. M., 1845. P. 626.

Bushnell, H., A. Discourse on, 1839.

Butler, R. R., Speech, Harpers' Ferry inv., 1859.

Cairnes, The Slave power, 1862.

Carey, M., Slave Representation, 1814.

Caste and Sl. in the Am. Church, 1843.

Chambers, W., Amer. Slavery, 1857.

Chandler, E. M., Essays, 1836.

Chase, H., The North and the South, 1857.

Cheever, The Fire and Hammer, etc., 1858. P. 560.

" Guilt of Slavery, 1860.

Child, Appeal to Abolitionists, 1844. P. 560.

Coffin, J., Acc't of Insurrections, 1860. P. 1210.

Coles, Hist. of Ordinance of 1787.

Colonization and Abolition. P. 56.

Conkling, C., Slavery abolished.

Consid. on the Missouri Quest., 1820.

Constitution expounded, 1850.

Conway, M. D., The Golden hour, 1862.

Day, W., S. in America, 1841.

Desul. remarks: Sl. in Missouri, 1856.

Drew, North Side View of, 1856.

Duffield, G., Sermon on, 1840.

Dunning, H. N., Design of Agitation, 1861.

Effect of Secession, 1861.

Elder, Emancipation policy, 1856.

Ellison, Sl. and Secession, 1861.

England, Bp., Works, Letters on, 1849.

Essay in Vindication, etc., 1764.

Fisher, E., The North and South, 1849.

Foster, S. S., Brotherhood of Thieves, 1843. P. 663.

Free Soil Ass'n of D. of Columbia, Addr., 1849.

French Protestants: Lettre, 1857. P. 1104.

Friends, Soc. of, Address, 1822.

" Proceedings, 1840,62. P. 1213.

" Appeal, 1858. P. 958.

Garrison, W. L., Addresses, 1832, 54, 57.

Giddings, J. R., Exiles of Florida, 1858.

Goodell, W., Our National Charters, 1863.

" Am. Constitutional Law on, 1845. P. 626.

" Am. Slave Code, 1853.

Grahame, J., Who is to blame, 1842.

Greeley, H., History of the Struggle, 1856.

Slavery in the United States (cont'd).

Green, B., Things for Northern men, 1836.

" Church carried along, 1836.

Grimké, A., Appeal to Women. P. 560.

Grimké, S. M., An Epistle to the Clergy.

Grosvenor, C. P., Address, 1834.

Helper, Impending Crisis, 1857.

" No Joque, 1867.

Hildreth, Despotism in America, 1854.

Inquiry, Prospects of Africans in U.S., 1839.

James, H., Sermon, Our Duties, 1847.

Jay, W., Amer. Colon. and Anti-slavery Societies, 1835. B. C.

" Address, 1849.

Kemble, F. B., Journal, Georgia Plantation, 1858 to 59.

Kettell, Southern wealth, 1860.

Lanphear, O. T., Discourse, Lowell, 1856.

Learned, J. D., View of, Slaves west of the Missis., 1826.

Leggett, Political Writings, 1840.

Legion of Liberty, 1843.

Leisler, J., Letters on Free Soil, 1850.

Liberty, 1837.

Liberty Bell, 1842.

Livermore, Founders of the U. S. on Negroes, 1862.

Louisville, Ky., Workingmen's Addr., 1849.

M'Carter, Border Methodism and Slavery, 1858.

McDonough, J., Self-emancipation, 1862.

Marshall, T., Abolition of, in Virginia, 1832. P. 15. B. C.

Mass. Hist. Soc. Coll., Ser. 1, v. 4, Belknap on S. in Mass.

Mattison, Crisis of 1860.

May, S. J., Disc., Sl. in the U. S., 1832.

" Recollections, 1869.

Mayo, A. D., Herod, John and Jesus, 1860.

Med, Case of, 1836.

Memorial of Boston to Congress, 1819.

Meth. Epis. Ch., Debates, 1844.

Moore, G. H., Sl. in Massachusetts, 1866.

Murray, H. A., The Land of the Slave and Free, 1855.

New Democratic Doctrine, 1856.

Northup, S., Narrative of kidnapping of, 1841.

Nott, S., Jr., The Remedy, 1856, 1857.

Olmsted, F. L., Our Slave States, 1860, 3 v.

" The cotton kingdom, 1861.

Slavery, Anti-Slavery Periodicals and Societies (continued).
Maryland Soc., Colon. Journal, 1841-1843.
Massachusetts Abol. Soc., 1841.
" Hist. of the division, 1841.
Massachusetts Colon. Soc., Reports, 1852, 53, 63.
New Jersey Soc., 1793. P. 1208.
N. Y. Anti-Sl. Conv., 1835.
N. Y. Soc. for Manumission, 1808.
N. Y. Young Men's Anti-Slav. Soc., 1834. P. 462.
Pennsylvania Abolition Soc., 1788, 92, 1838, (P. 889), 1853.
Phil'a Anti-Sl. Soc., 1835.
Quart. Anti-Sl. Mag., N. Y., 1835-7.
Société des amis des noirs, 1789.
Society for the Abolition, Lond., 1833.
Soc. for the Mitigation, etc., Lond., 1828. P. 437; 1823, P. 828.
Vermont Anti-Slav. Soc., 1836.

Slavonians. Bulgarian Catechism.
Krasinski, Relig. history of, 1869.
" Montenegro and the S., 1853.
Storch, Antiq. Katal., 1858.
Talvi, Hist. and lit. of Slavic nations, 1850.
Valentinelli, Spec. Biblio. de Dalmatia, 1842.
Wilkinson, J. G., Dalmatia and Montenegro, 1848.
See Albania; Servia; Russia; Poland; Dalmatia.

Sleep. Fosgate, B., Sleep Psychol. Considered, 1850.
Hall, W. W., Hygiene of the night, 1870.
Macnish, R., Philosophy of sleep, 1834.
Wakeman, B., Essay on Somnolency, 1815. P. 578.
See Health; Man; Nature.

Slidell. *See* Mackenzie, A. S.

Slingsby, Sir H. Original memoirs, 1640-60.

Sloan, A. Boardman, H. A., Sermon on, 1851. P. 95.

Sluyter, R. Currie, R. O., Memoir of, 1846.

Small-pox. Ac. de Méd., Rapports sur les vaccinations, 1836-50.
Bateman, State of vaccination, 1812.
Boylston, Hist. of Small-pox in New Eng., 1726.
Byrde, H. M., Diss. de epidem., 1824.
Dimsdale, On Inoculation, 1776.
Dodd, W., Sermon on vaccin., 1767.
Dordrecht, Prov. Commissie, 1819.

Small-pox (continued).
Duvillard, Influence de, sur la mortalité, 1806.
Fisher, J., Description of, 1834.
Gardane, Le Secret des Suttons, 1774. P. 611.
Gibbs, J., Vaccination, 1857. P. 405.
Greenhow, Value of vaccin., 1825.
Hallifax, J., Hospital Sermon, 1768.
Jenner, E., Baron, J., Life of, 1838.
Long, P. W., Dublin Institution, 1860.
Maddox, I, Sermon on, 1752.
Marc, La Vaccine, 1836.
Milton, Mass., Proceedings on, 1810. P. 1800.
Moore, J., History of, 1815.
Nahuys, G. J., De Bedroefden, 1777.
Providence, Report on, 1859.
Pruen, S., Of Inoculation, 1807. P. 1354.
Royal Jennerian Soc., 1827, 30. P. 1522.
Snow, E. M., Protec. of vaccination, 1869.
" Statistics of, Prov., 1859.
Waterhouse, B., Hist. of Cow-pox, 1800.
Watson, W., Exper. in inoculation. P. 126.
Wildrik, Kinderpokjes, etc.
Woodville, Hist. of Inoculation, 1796.

Smeaton, J. Reports, and life, 1814.

Smellie, W. Kerr, R., Memoirs of, 1811.

Smelt, C. E. Waddel, M., Life of, 1819.

Smelting. *See* Metallurgy.

Smet, P. J. De. Cinquante lettres, 1858.

Smith, Adam. Life of, Lib. U. K.

Smith, Charlotte. Scott, W., Memoir of.

Smith, C. J. Buell, S., Serm., Death of, 1770. P. 554.

Smith, D. Baldwin, A. C., Sermon on, 1862.

Smith, Elias. Life of, by himself.

Smith, Ger. Speeches, Sermons, Essays, 1856-61.
Hawley, F., Review of his discourses, 1858. P. 1261.

Smith, Goldwin. Welcome to, by citizens of N. Y., 1864. P. 1872.

Smith, Col. J. Life, with the Indians, 1799.

Smith, J. A. Manley, J. R., Exposition of Character of, 1841.

Smith, Sir James E. Memoirs and Corresp., 1832.

Smith, Jeremiah. Morison, J. H., Life of, 1845.
North Am. Review, July, 1845.

Smith, Capt. John. Hillard, G. S., Life of, (Sparks 2).

Simms, W. G., Life of, 1846.

Smith, J., Life of, 1630.

" Advertisements, 1631.

Smith, J. Relations with Burr, 1808.

Smith, J. B. Blair, S., Discourse on, 1799. P. 82.

Smith, John C. Corresp. and letters, 1846.

Smith, John Pye. Testimonial to, 1851.

Belsham, Answer to, 1809.

Smith, M. W. Memorial of, 1864.

Smith, N. Smith, D., Family of, 1849.

Smith, O. D. Eells, J., Sermon on, 1854.

Smith, P. Duim, Zedige Aanmerkingen, 1738.

Smith, R. Addr. to the People, 1811.

" Answer to R. Smith, 1811. P. 1580.

Smith, S. Memoirs of a soldier, 1776.

Smith, Sir S. Poem, Escape of, 1798.

Smith, Sidney. Holland, Lady, Memoirs of, 1855.

Tuckerman, H. T., Biog. Essays.

Smith, S. L. H. Hooker, E. V., Memoir of.

Smith, Rev. T. Journals, Portland, Me., 1821, 49.

Smith, W. Phillips, J., Memoirs of, 1844.

Smith, W. Colden, Letters on his Hist. of N. Y., (N. Y. Hist. Soc. Coll., 1868, 9).

Smith, W. A. Deems, C. F., Speech on trial of, 1856.

Smith, Sir W. S. Barrow, Sir J., Life of, 1848.

Smithfield, Eng. Gaspey, History of. P. 1774.

Smithsonian Institution. Barlow, W., Address and outlines of a plan for, 1847.

Choate, Speech, U. S. Senate, 1845.

Rhees, Account of, 1857.

Six articles from Boston Post, 1855. P. 1874.

Smithson. Instit., Contributions, 17 v.

" Miscell. Coll., 7 v.

" Reports to 1868.

Southern Lit. Mess. V, VI, VII.

United States, Report, 1842.

Varnum, J. B., Notice of, 1848.

Smollett, T. Anderson, R., Life of, 1803.

Scott, W., Memoir of.

Smut. Butin, J., Treatise on Smoth, Cazenovia, 1803. P. 205.

See Moulds; Agriculture.

Smylie, J. A. Van Court, J. H., Review of Presb. proceedings, 1850. P. 1416.

Smyrna. Arundell, Discoveries, 1834.

Lane, G. M., Paper on, Bibliot. Sac., 1858.

Smyrna, Guide Smyrnéen, 1840.

See Asia, Western; Turkey.

Smyth, Mrs. C. Abduction of, 1823.

Smythe, Sir S. E. De Coetlogon, Sermon on, 1778.

Snape, A. De la Pillonière, Answer to, 1717.

Pamphlets, vol. 351.

Prat, D., Answer on Bp. Hoadly, 1717.

Whitby, Answer to, 1717.

See Hoadly, B.

Snowden, Mrs. H. Greaves, T., Sermon on, 1763. P. 1461.

Soane, Sir J. Donaldson, View of life of.

Soap. Morfit, Manuf. of, 1847.

Social Science, Reforms, etc. Amer. Assoc'n Advan. of, Journal, 1869–1871.

Andrews, S. P., Science of Society, 1852.

Audiganne, Les Populations ouvrières, 1854.

Bancal, Du nouvel Ordre Social, 1792.

Barhydt, Industrial Exchanges, 1849.

Brindley, J., Infidelity of, 1841. P. 1720.

Brisbane, A., Social Destiny of Man, 1840.

Brownson, O. A., Essays, 1852.

Brun, Triomphe du Nouveau Monde, 1785.

Buchanan, R., Hist. of modern priestcraft, 1840.

Buckingham, J. S., National Evils.

" Considerations, 1846.

Buret, E., Misère des classes laborieuses, 1846. B. C.

Burke, E., Vindication of Natural Society.

Carey, H. C., Prin. of Social Science, 1858, 59.

" Manual of, 1864.

Catlow, Æsthetic medicine, 1867.

Couling, S., Laboring classes, condition, 1851.

Cousin, V., Justice and charity, 1848.

Curél, T., Des Enfans trouvés, 1845.

Davenport, A., Orig. of Man, etc., 1846.

Davies, Late Hours of Business, 1843. P. 429.

Songs (continued).
British Musical Miscellany, 1805.
Brooks, C. T., German lyric poetry, 1863.
Chodzko, Pop. poetry of Persia, 1842.
Christy's Melodies, 1854.
Clay Minstrel.
Columbian Songster, 1797.
Croker, T. C., Songs of Ireland.
Dempster's Ballad Soirees, 1858.
Dibdin, C., Sea Songs, 1845.
Drew, Fremont Songs, 1856.
Dutton's, Dollie, Songs, 1859.
Dyer, Songs and Ballads, 1857.
Forecastle Songster.
Gem, The, 1846.
Glover's Magazine.
Graham, J., Flowers of Melody, 1825, 1834.
Hager's, J. M., Concerts, 1863.
Hastings, Songs of Temperance.
Hayes, Ballads of Ireland.
Heine, Poems, Book of Songs.
Hullah, The Song Book, 1866.
Johnson, J. H., Union Songs, (50).
Kennedy, Songs of Love and Liberty, 1817.
Log Cabin Song book, 1840.
London Songster, 1767.
Lovers' Magazine. P. 1543.
Malvina, etc., Modern Syren, 1807.
Moore, F., Songs of Am. Revol., 1856.
" Lyrics of loyalty, 1864.
" Songs of the Soldiers, 1864.
" Rebel rhymes, 1864.
Moore, T., Poet. works, v. 4, 5.
Nason, E., Our National Song, 1869.
Nation, The, Ballads and Songs of, Dublin, 1846.
Palgrave, Golden Treasury, 1863.
Pamphlets, v. 534, A. D., 1760.
Pantomimic Songster, N. Y.
Percy Society Publications, 1840–52.
Songs of the Soldiers, (Moore), 1864.
Songs of the War, P. 1, 1863.
Stansbury, Loyal Verses of the Revolution, 1860.
Star Spangled Banner Coll., 1817.
Timperley, Songs of the Press, 1845.
Uhland, Körner, etc., tr. by Brooks.
Union Songs.
Universal Songster, Lond., 3 v.
Warren's, G. W., Singing classes, 1857.
Watson, H. C., Ladies' Glee book, 1854.
Watts, I., Songs, Moral. P. 398.
Whig Banner Songster, 1844.
Whig Songs, 1844. P. 1392.
See Ballads; Poetry.

Sonora. Browne, J. N., Adventures, 1869.
Rudo ensayo, 1761.
Mowry, Resources of, 1859.
See Mexico.

Sons of the Clergy. *See* Society of the Sons, etc.

Sophia Dorothea Consort of George I. Memoirs, 1845.

Soren, J. Narrative, Case of, 1800, 1813.

Sorghum. Haraszthy, Grapes and Sorgho, 1862.
Hedges, North. Sugar plant, 1863.
Hyde, J., Chinese cane, 1857.
Madinier, Canne de sorgho, 1858.
See Sugar.

Soto, F. De. Bradford Club....No, 5, Career of, (B. Smith).
Irving, T., Conquest of Florida by, 1835, 51.
Wilmer, Life and travels of, 1858.

Soul. Abiezer, Letter on, 1845.
Æneas Gazæus, De immort. animarum, 1655.
Alger, W. R., Doctrine of future life, 1864.
Bakewell, F. C., Nat. Evi. of a future life, 1840.
Batey, J., Thoughts on Immortality, 1843. Muns. P. 3.
Baxter, A., Inquiry into nature of, 1745.
Berkeley, Works, Three dialogues, 1713.
Broughton, Psychology, 1703.
Bush, Scripture Psychology, 1845. B.C.
" Anastasis, 1845. B. C.
Cicero, Immortality of the Soul, 1833. B. C.
Clarke, S., Proofs of Immortality, (Works).
" Immateriality of, 1712.
Coward, Second thoughts, 1702.
Coxe, Recognition in Heaven: Soul in brutes, 1845.
Fine, Resurrection of the body, 1851.
Gaudenzio, P., De animarum transmigratione, 1641.
Grove, H., Immateriality of, 1718. P. 1251.
Guizot, F., Immortality of, 1864. P. 1542.
Haddock, J., Psychology, 1850.
Hickok, L. P., Empirical psychology, 1857.
Hildrop, J., The brute creation, 1742.
Immortality of, (Parsons), 1714.
Man more than a machine, 1752.
Melancthon, De anima, 1544.
Mendelssohn, Unsterblichkeit der Seele, 1789.

Spain, Pamphlets relating to (cont'd).
Observations on the present Convention, 1739.
Observations, The, upon the treaty examined, 1730.
Observ. upon the treaty of Seville, 1729.
Pamphlets relating to Spain, vols. 841, 842, 1467.
Pereda, V. M. De, La Situacion contra el deséo nacional, 1848.
Policy of England, 1837.
Profit and loss of Gr. Brit. in the war, 1741.
Proposals for humbling, 1740.
Propriety of retaining Gibraltar, 1783.
Reply to a pamphlet, Popular prejudices, 1739.
Rodil, Manifiesto, 1836.
Ross, O. C. D., Spain and the war with Morocco, 1860.
Secker, Fast Sermon, War, 1741.
Some farther remarks, 1729.
Some observations, 1728.
Some observations on the plan of peace, 1736.
Series of wisdom....in our foreign negotiations, 1736.
Spain vindicated, 1825. P. 1627.
Treaty of Seville considered, 1733.
View of depredations of, 1731.

Spanish Colonies. Account of Span. sett. in Amer. 1762.
America, or descr. of W. I., 1655.
Bonnycastle, Domin. of Spain in Am., 1819.
Burke, W., Emancipation of Col. in America, 1808. P. 128.
Campbell, J., Span. Emp. in Amer., 1747.
Campillo, Nuevo Sistema de Gobierno, 1789.
Castellanos, Elegias, 1589.
Consid. sur l'Amér. Espag., 1817.
Coréal, Voy. aux Indes d'Espagne, 1722.
Helps, Spanish Conquest in America, 1855, 57.
Herréra, Conquêtes des Castellans, 1660.
Las Casas, Destruycion de las Indias, 1552.
" First voyages of Spaniards, 1699.
Letters of Verus, 1797.
Old England Forever, 1740.
Pamphlets relating to the Spanish American Colonies, 14, 15.
Robertson, Hist. of South America.
Robinson, W. D., Cursory View of Span. Amer., 1815.
Ternaux, Recueil de Mémoires, 1840.

Spanish Colonies (continued).
Ulloa, Rétablissement du commerce de, 1753.
Uricoechea, Mapoteca Colombiana, 1860.
Veitia, Norte de la contratacion de, 1672.
Walton, W., State of the Spanish Colonies, 1810.
" Dissensions of Span. Amer., 1814.
See America; North America; South America; Cuba; Mexico; Philippine Is., etc.

Sparks, J. Ellis, G. E., Memoir of, Mass. Hist. Soc.
Mahon, Correspondence, 1852–3.
Mayer, B., Memoir of. P. 1659.

Spectacles. *See* Eye; Optics.

Spectrum Analysis. Airy, Wave lengths for Kirchoff's lines; Roy. Soc. Trans., 1869.
Anal. of the Sun-beam, Am. Ch. Rev. Jan. '72.
Barnard, F. A. P., Undulatory theory of light, Smithson. Rep., 1862.
Brewster, D., History of, Inst. de Fr., Comptes, lxii, 17.
" Obs. on Solar Spectrum, Roy. Soc. Trans., 1860.
Browning, J., Spec. of Met. of Nov., Lon. Ed. and D. Phil. Mag., 1867.
De La Rue, Resear. on Solar physics, 1865. P. 1052.
Gibbs, W., Descr. of Spectroscope, Am. Jour. of Sci., 1863.
" Map of the Spectrum, A. J. S., 1867.
" Wave lengths of lines, A. J. S., 1869.
Guillemin, A., The Heavens, 1871.
Huggins, W., Exam. of micros. objects, Quar. Jour. of Mic. Sci., 1865.
" Lect., Results of, applied to Astron., Brit. Assoc'n.
" Spectra of chem. elements, Roy. Soc. Trans., 1864.
" Spectra of the Stars, Roy. Soc., 1868, 69.
" Roy. Soc. Proc., 1865.
Janssen, Phil. Mag., XXX, 78; XXXII, 315; Comptes Rendus, lvi. 538; liv. 1280.
Kirchoff, Chemical analysis, London, Edin. and Dub. P. Mag., 1860, 65.
Miller, W. A., Obs. on the Spectrum, Lectures on Pharm. Jour., 2d Ser., iii. 399.
Norton, Corona in Eclipse of Sun, Am. Jour. of Sci., 1870, 71.
Pasteur, Phosp. light of animals, Inst. de Fr., C. R., lix. 509.

Spenser, E. Works and Life.
Jortin, J., On poems of, 1734. P. 1238.

Spice Is. *See* Moluccas.

Spicer, T. Autobiography, 1860.

Spinola, A. Barry, G., Siege of Breda, by, 1627.
Deza, Istoria della famiglia, 1694.

Spinola, C. Broeckart, Life of, 1869.

Spinoza, B. Damiron, Mémoire sur, Inst. de Fr., Ac. Mor. et pol., 1844.
Jaquelot, Leven van, 1698.
Spinoza, Tract. Theol. Polit., Introd. to.
Toland, Letter on, 1704.
Willis, Life and ethics, 1870.

Spira, F. Brownlee, W. C., Fearful state of, 1814. B. C.

Spirit. *See* Holy Spirit.

Spirits. *See* Chemistry; Alcohol; Temperance; Wine.

Spiritualism. Apocatastasis, 1854.
Arnold, L. M., Hist. of Man, 1852.
Ballou, A., Views respecting, 1853.
Beecher, C., Review of, 1853.
Brittan, S. B., Review of Beecher, 1853.
Brown, W., Individuality, 1863.
Bush, G., Davis's Revelations, 1847. P. 45. B. C.
Capron, E. W., Explan. and Hist. of, 1850.
Capron, Singular Revelations, 1850. P. 563.
Close, F., Table turning, Lond., 1853.
Cooke, P., Necromancy, 1857.
Davis, A. J., Principles of Nature, 1850.
" Approaching Crisis, 1852.
" Philosophy of....intercourse, 1851.
" The Present age, 1853.
" The Great Harmonia, 1859.
" The Magic Staff, autobiog., 1859.
Dendy, Philosophy of Mystery, 1845.
Dewey, Hist. of the Rappings, 1850. P. 563.
Dods, J. B., Spirit manifestations, refuted, 1854.
Edmonds, J. W., Reply to Bishop Hopkins, 1855. P. 563.
" Spiritual Intercourse, 1856. P. 563.
" Spiritualism, 1854.
Ferguson, J. B., Spirit Communion, 1855. P. 563.
" Divine Illumination, 1855. P. 563.
" Statement of belief, 1854.

Spiritualism (continued).
Fish, W. H., Orthodoxy against, 1857. P. 563.
Gasparin, Turning Tables. P. 563.
" Science *vs.* Spiritualism, v. i, 1857.
Hare, R., Investigation of, 1856.
Henry, G. W., Shoutings in the Church.
Home, D. D., Incidents in my life, 1863.
Incidents of Personal experience, 1852. P. 93.
Kardec, Qu'est le Spiritisme? 1859.
King, D., An address, 1857.
Linton, Healing of the Nations, 1858.
M'Ilvaine, J. H., Mod. Divination, 1855. P. 213.
Mahan, A., Spiritualism, a discussion, 1855.
" Review of Mahan, 1855.
Mallery, D. G., Necromancy, 1857.
Mattison, H., Spirit Rapping, 1853.
New Engl. Spirit. Assoc'n, Constitution, 1854. P. 563.
Newton, A. E., Charges of belief in, 1854. P. 97.
Obs. on the Theol. Mystery, 1851. P. 219.
Owen, R. D., The debatable land, 1872.
" Footfalls, of another world, 1860.
Page, C., Psychomancy, 1853.
Pamphlets on Spiritualism, vol. 563.
Prichard, J., Table talk, 1853.
Pugh, G., S. an old epidemic, 1857.
Putnam, A., Spirit works, 1853. P. 101.
Return of Dep. Spirits, (Thomas), 1843.
Sacred Circle, *Period.*, N. Y. 1855.
Shekinah, *Period.*, N. Y., 1853.
Snow, H., Incid. of experience, 1852.
Society for Diffu. of Sp. Knowl., 1854. P. 563.
Thoughts...Review of Mahan, 1855. P. 563.
Tiffany's Monthly, 1856–59.
Toohey, Review: Dwinell's Sermon, 1857. P. 563.
Tuttle, Year book of, for 1871.
" Scenes in the Spirit world, 1855.
Tyndall, J., Fragm. of Sci., 1871.
Wilson, R. P., Spiritual Science, 1854. P. 563.
See Magnetism, Animal.

Spitzbergen. Dufferin, (Blackwood), Voyage, 1856.
Fabvre, Rapport, sur voyage à, 1839.
Le Roy, Narr. of four Russ. Sailors, Pinkerton, 1.
Martens, Voyage to. Hakluyt Soc., No. 18, 1855.
See Arctic; Russia; Voyages, Arctic.

Steam Navigation (continued).
Gr. Brit.: Patents for Marine Propulsion to 1859.
" Plan for volunt. exam. in steam, 1852.
Great Eastern Steamship. Descr.
Lloyd's Steamboat Directory, 1856.
Maine: Plan for short passage to London, 1850.
Memorial...impolicy of law on steamboats, 1840.
Miller, W. O., Submerged propeller, 1856.
Montgomery, Steam on Canals, 1858.
N. Y. and Galway Co., 1851. P. 529.
N. Y. Leg. Rep., Steam on the canals, 1872.
Pamphlets on, vol. 993.
Rainey, Ocean St. Nav., 1858.
Redfield, Letters to Com. Perry, 1841.
" Explosion of the New England, 1833.
Rumsey's Treatise, 1788.
Russell, J. S., Treat. on St. Navig.
Smyth, T., Sermon on loss of the Home.
Statements of, for 1840.
Steamboat disasters, 1843.
Stuart, C. B., Naval and Mail Steamers of U. S., 1853.
Sullivan, J. L., Steam-boat rights, 1822.
Woodcroft, B., Progress of steam navigation, 1848.
U. S., Explosions of steam boilers, 1838.
" Princeton Steamship.
See Fitch; Fulton; Engineering; Naval; Railways.

Stearns, A. Sewall, S., Discourse on, 1859. P. 1227.

Stearns, F. A. Life, 1862.
Tyler, W. S., Memorials of, 1864. P. 1055.

Stearns, G. I. Willard, S. G., Funeral Sermon, 1862. P. 1614.

Stearns, H. C. Hedge, F. H., Funeral of, 1857.

Stearns, S. H. Life and discourses, 1846.

Stebbing, H. Pyle, Answer on Hoadly.
Warburton, Answer to, 1746.

Stebbins, S. W. Wright, E., Funeral Sermon, 1844. P. 1611.

Steel. Dessoye, J. B. J., Propriétés de l'acier, 1857.
Ede, G., Management of, 1864.
Fairbairn, Iron manufacture, Bessemer process, 1869.
" Mech. properties of, Brit. Assoc'n, 1867, 69.

Steel (continued).
Hassenfratz, Fonte de l'acier, 1812.
Kerl, Metallurgy of, 1870.
Landrin, Traité de l'acier, 1859.
Overman, Manufacture of, 1851, 54.
Pearson, G., Exper. on Bombay steel, 1795.
Steel Memorial to Congress, 1865.
Vismara, Fusione dell Acciajo, 1825.
See Iron; Metallurgy.

Steele, J. & G. Family genealogy, 1859, 1862.

Steele, Sir R. Brief Reflections on, 1715. P. 343.
Drake, N., Essays, 1809, 14.
Montgomery, H. R., Life of, 1865.

Steele, S. N. Niles, H. E., Disc. at Funeral, 1854. P. 555.

Steffens, H. Story of My Career, 1863.

Stennett, S. Jenkins, J., Sermon on, 1795. P. 1564.

Stenography. *See* Short-hand.

Stephanini, J. Personal narrative, 1829.

Stephens, H. Greswell, Early Greek Press, 1833.

Stephens, R. Crapelet, Rob't Estienne, 1839.
Greswell, Parisian Typography, 1818.

Stephenson, G. Smiles, S., Life of, 1858.

Stereotype. Camus, Histoire de, 1802.
Jansen, De l'orig. de la gravure, 1808.
Lavallée, J., Report on, 1804. P. 1041.
Westreenen, De l'impr. stéréotype, 1833.
See Typography.

Sterling, John. Carlyle, T., Life of, 1851.
Sterling, J., Essays, with life, by Hare.

Sterne, L. Ferriar, J., Illustrations of, 1812.
Fitzgerald, P., Life of, 1864.
Scott, W., Life of.

Sterzinger, F. Zech, Zum Andenken des. 1787.

Stetson family. Barry, J. S., Geneal. mem. of, 1634–1847.

Steuben, F. W. von. Bowen, F., Life of. Sparks, 9.
Kapp, F., Life of, 1859.

Steuben Co., N. Y. Directory, 1868–9.
Denniston, Survey of, 1862.
McMaster, G. H., History of, 1853.
Steuben Co., Enlistments, 1867.

Stevens, J. H. Whitcomb, Sermon on, 1852.

Superstitions (continued).
Collin De Plancy, Dictionnaire infernal, 1826.
Croker, T. C., Researches, South of Ireland.
False Religion, 1730.
Grant, Sup. of Highlanders, 1811.
Hammond, H., Concerning Sup., 1655.
Herklots, Customs of Muss. of India, 1832.
Horst, Zauber-Bibliothek, 1821–26.
Lea, H. C., Superst. and force, 1861.
Madden, R. R., Phantasmata, 1857.
Manningham, T., Sermon on, 1692.
Merryweather, F. S., Glimmerings in the dark, 1850.
Pettigrew, T. J., Sup. in medicine, 1844.
Plutarch, Morals, Goodwin's ed., 1871.
Soane, Curiosities of literature, 1849.
Stillingfleet, Nature of, 1682.
Wright, T., England in the middle ages, 1846.
Young, D., The Morristown ghost, 1825.
See Witchcraft; Mythology; Delusions; Fairies; Natural Religion.

Surinam. *See* Guiana.

Surgery. Adams, J. J., Oper. for amaurosis, 1841.
Andry, Difformités du Corps, 1743.
Arnold, Opium in Surg., 1863.
Ballingall, Military Surgery, 1844. P. 406.
Bancal, Lithotritie, 1829.
Bell, B., System of Surgery, 1804.
Bly's Artific. legs, 1862.
Boston city hospital, Report, 1870.
Brainard, D., Traitement des fractures, etc., 1854.
Brit. and For. Orthopedic Assoc.
Brodie, Diseases of Joints, 1834. P. 210.
Canniff, Manual of, 1866.
Cheselden, Anat. of Human body, 1795.
Civiale, Retrécissemens de l'urètre, 1842.
" Traité de la Lithontritie, 1848.
Clendinen, A., Disloc. shoulder, 1815. P. 579.
Cooke, J., Inflam. of cavities, 1804. P. 575.
Cox, W. S., Essay on Hernia. P. 1568.
Dejean, Des Hernies, 1762.
Delagenèvrière, Les Hernies, 1768.
Deleau, Du Cathéterisme, 1838.
Gibson, W., Introd. Lect., Penn'a, 1843. P. 8.
Greenhow, Fractures of the leg, 1833.
Guillon, Retrécissements de l'Urètre.

Surgery (continued).
Hamilton, J., On regulating the practice of. Pamph'r 12.
Hawkins, C., Congen. tumor of the neck, 1839.
" Stricture of the colon, 1852.
" Encysted tumors, 1833.
Heurteloup, Hist. de la Lithotripsie, 1846.
Hints....Dissections, 1795.
Hoogvliet, J., Konst om Wonden te Sehowen, 1749.
Hosack, D., Tumors from the nose, 1825. P. 86.
Howship, J., Hunterian Oration, 1833.
Hull, S. G., On the nature of hernia, 1826. P. 12. B. C.
Humbert, Les luxations, 1835.
Jackson, W., Luxations of ankle, 1787.
Jones, J., Of Wounds and Fractures, 1776.
Larrey, Military Surgery, 1814.
Lawrence, W., Hunterian Orations, 1834, 46.
Le Roy d'Etiolles, Hist. de la Lithontritie, 1849.
L'Espinasse, Tart. emet. in tumoribus, 1822. P. 593.
Lidell, Gunshot wounds, 1863.
Low, D., Chiropodologia, London.
Major, J., Blistering and cautery, 1853. P. 1521.
March, Alden, Writings collected.
Martin, F., Déplacements du tibia, 1852. P. 945.
Maynard, J. P., Liquid adhesive plaster, 1848. P. 1714.
Medico-Chirurg. Review, Lond., 1820-1844.
Otto, C., Wundärtze, 1843.
Pamphlets relating to Surgery, vols. 1568, 1714.
Paré, A., Œuvres, 1585.
Pharmacopœia chirurgica, 1794.
Ranby, J., Gunshot wounds, 1760.
Riggs, J. W., Hernia and treatment, 1859.
Sanson, L. J., Traité de la Cataracte, 1832.
Sayre, A., Morbus coxarius, 1863. P. 1712.
Shipman, Address, Indiana Med. Coll., 1848. P. 196.
Sims, J. M., Silver sutures, 1857.
Stevens, A. H., On Lithotomy, 1838.
Stevens, G. T., Review of Fero's case, 1870
Sweet, W., Natural Bone-setting, 1844.
Swinburne, J., Writings collected.
Syme, J., Prin. and Practice of, Newton, 1866.

Surgery (continued).
Taylor, C. F., Angular curvature, 1863. P. 1359.
Tripler, Handbook of Military Surgery, 1862.
Use of the Dead, 1828.
Velpeau, Elements of operative, 1847, 1851.
Vigo, Opera ....in chyrurgia, 1521.
Walker. W. J., Compound fractures, 1845.
Warren, J. C, Disloc. of hip joint, 1826.
Water, De polypis uteri, 1824.
Willemier, De Otorrhœa, 1835. P. 593.
Wood, J. R., Ligat. of Carot. Artery, 1857. P. 516.
See Anatomy; Medicine; Eyes; Physiology; Teeth.

Surrey, Eng. Allen, T., History of the County, 1831.
Beauties of Eng. and Wales.
Berry, Pedigrees of families of.
Brayley, E. W., Topog. Hist. of, 1850.

Surveying. Atwell, G., Faithful surveyor, 1662.
Davies, C., Elements of, 1846.
Flint, A., Treatise on, 1825.
Grumman, On Surveyor's chains, 1859. P. 1223.
La Croix, Der Meetkunst, 1838.
Lee, T. J., Tables and formula for, 1853.
Massachusetts, Trigonometric survey of.
Moore, S., System of, 1796.
Perkins, Trigonometry and, 1852.
Puissant, Arpentage et nivellement.
See Mathematics; Engineering; Coast Survey.

Susquehanna River. Johnson, C. B., Letters, 1819.
Meginness, J. F., Hist. of Settlement of, 1857.
Perkins, G. A., Early times on, 1870.
See Wyoming.

Sussex, Duke of. Dibdin, Sermon on, 1843.
Pettigrew, Bibliot. Sussexiana, 1827.

Sussex, Eng. Beauties of England and Wales.
Berry, Sussex pedigrees.
Cooke's Topog. Library.
East Bourn village, descr., 1799.
Lee, W., History of Lewes, etc., 1795.

Sussex Co., N. J. Centenary, 1853.

Sutherland. Gordon, R., Geneal. Hist. of the family, 1813.

Sutherland, E., Countess of. Case of.

Sutner, G. C. v. Mussinan, Denkrede auf, 1837.

Sutton, R., Lord. Lexington papers, 1851.

Sutton, S. Herne, S., Life of, 1677.

Suwarrow, Gen. Anthing, Campaigns and life of, 1799.

Swalm, L. B. Life of, 1852.

Swartz, C. F. Pearson, H., Memoirs of, 1839.

Sweden. Acerbi, Travels, 1798, 9.
Arkiv till upplysning om Svenska.... historia, 1854.
Arwidsson, Svenska Fornsänger, Coll. of national songs, 1834–1842.
" Anders Schönbergs historiska bref, etc., 18 9–51.
" Handlingar, Finlands Häfder, 1846–53.
Aslak Bolts Jordebog, 1852.
Boisgelin, Tr. through, and Denmark, 1810.
Bremer, F., The Home, Life in Sweden, Fict.
Brunius, Skänes Historia, 1850.
Buch, L. von, Travels through, 1806–1808.
Cavallius, Sveriges Hist. och Pol. visor, 1853.
Crichton, Hist. of, Ed. Cab. Lib., 23.
De Lolme, Parallel of gov't of.
Dunham, History of, Lardner, 19.
Falkman, Halländska Kyrkshemmanen, 1848.
Fortia, Travels in, Pinkerton, 6.
Fryxell, History of Sweden, 1844.
Gaimard, Voyage en Scandinavie, 1838. P. 18.
Geffroy, Histoire de la, 1851.
Geijer, History of the Swedes, 1845.
Gustavus Vasa, History of, 1852.
Handlingar rörande Sveriges inre förhällenden, 1841.
Hiortdahl, Geol. undersögelser i Bergens, 1852. P. 1052.
Howitt, W., Lit. of Northern Europe, 1852.
Laing, Tour in, 1839.
Lastborn, Geneal. of noblemen of Swea and Gotha, since 1720.
Letter to Sir J. Banks, 1711. P. 409.
Letters between Gyllenborg and others, 1717. P. 1335.
Ljungberg, Sou développement, 1867.
Meredith, Bernadotte's life.
Munch, Symb. ant-rerum Norvegicarum, 1850.
Nordberg, Hist. de Charles XII.
Obs. upon a Pamphlet, 1717.

Temperance Periodicals and Societies (continued).

Maryland Ineb. Asylum, Rep., 1860.

Maryland Temp. Soc., Rep., 1841, 42.

Mass. Soc. for Supp. Intemp., Report, 1827, 34. P. 291.

Mass. Temp. Soc., Tracts, 1834. P. 630.

Mass. Temp. Union, Address, 1846.

National Temp. Convention, 1851, 68.

National Temp. Soc., N. Y., 1850. P. 630.

New British and Foreign, 1838. P. 291.

New Orleans Temp. Soc., Addr., 1841.

N. Y. City T. Alliance, 1855, 56.

N. Y. City T. Society, 1848.

N. Y. State Temp. Soc., Reports, 1830–1833, 48, 52, 53, 67, 68.

" Quar. Temp. Mag., 1833, 1834.

" Temp. Recorder, 1832–43.

" Temp. Tracts, 1854.

Pamphlets relating to Societies, vols. 291, 630.

Penn'a Soc. for discoura. use of ardent spirits, 1828. P. 5.

Phil'a Med. Soc., Report on spirits, 1829.

Richmond Soc. for Temp., 1830, 31.

Prohibitionist, The, 1854–7.

Soc. for the Supp. of Vice, 1813.

Son of Temperance and Rechabite, No. 7, 1847.

Sons of Temperance, 1846–51. P. 630.

Sons of Temp. of Va., Minutes, 1850.

United Kingdom Alliance, Report, 1858. P. 1472.

" Lees, on the Maine Law, 1857.

" Politics of Temperance, 1859.

" Prohib. in Gr. Brit., 1864.

" Monthly Papers, 1859.

U. S. Inebriate Asylum, Addresses, 1855. P. 291.

Van Loon, Sons of Temp. defended, 1846.

Washingtonian Home, Bost., 1860.

World's Convention, N. Y., 1853. P. 234.

Templar Knights. Du Cange, Familles d'outre mer.

See Knights.

Temple Family. Whitmore, Account of, 1856.

Temple, Rev. D. Sermon by, 1825. P. 1615.

" Life of, 1855.

Goodell, W., Fun. Sermon, 1851. P. 1612.

Temple, H. J. *See* Palmerston, Lord.

Temple, R. G., Earl. Letter concerning libels, 1764–70.

Temple, Sir W. Works, with Life of, 17[illegible]0.

Courtenay, Memoirs of, 1836.

Macaulay, T. B., Essay on.

Temple, New Hamp. Blood, H. A., History of, 1860.

Templeton, Mass. Adams, E. G., Hist. Discourse, 1857.

Tenants. Bishop, J., Law of tenants.

Teneriffe Is. Mortimer, G., Voyage to, 1791.

See Canary Is.

Tennent, G. Alexander, A., Biograph. sketches, 1845.

Tennent, W. Life of, 1816. P. 925.

Tennessee. Bokum, H., Sketches of East T., 1864.

Carpenter, W. H., Hist. of, 1854.

Crockett, D., Life of, 1833.

Haywood, J., Civil History, 1823.

" Natural Hist., 1823.

Nashville and Tenn. Directory, 1853.

Pamphlets, vol. 1829.

Putnam, A. W., Hist. of Middle Tenn., 1859.

Ramsey, J. G. M., Annals of, 1853.

Smith, J. G., Descriptive Review of, 1842.

Tennessee, Geolog. Survey, 1837, 39, 1841, 55–7, 1869.

" Agric. Report, 1860.

Tennyson, A. Bayne, P., Essays in Biog., 1857.

Brimley, G., Essays, 1868.

Kingsley, C., Papers, 1859.

Tent Worship. *See* Tabernacle.

Teonge, H. Diary, 1675–79.

Terrill, Gen. W. R. Burial of, 1862. P. 1856.

Test Acts, Eng. Answer to the Bp. of Oxford, 1688.

Case of the.... test acts, 1736. P. 848.

Church of Englandman's answer, 1790. P. 322.

Consid. on the danger, 1828.

Croft, G., Test laws defended.

Defence of Chris. liberty, 1807.

Defence of Relig. liberty, 1825.

Dispute, The, Adjusted, 1732.

Equal liberty of conscience, 1780.

Enquiry into the reasons, 1688.

Essay on imposing articles of relig., 1719.

Fox, C. J., Speech, repeal of, 1790.

History of the Test act, 1790.

Hoadly, Refutation of Sherlock, 1718.

Horsley, Case of Prot. Dissenters, 1790. P. 319.

Theological Education and Seminaries (continued).
Wheatly, Serm., Schools of Prophets, 1721. P. 367.
Willard, S., Directions in Study, 1735. P. 603.
Wotton, W., Method of Study, 1734. P. 341.
See Clergy; Church of Engl., Clergy; Preaching.

Theology, in English. Abbadie, Change in the Eucharist.
Aids to Faith, 1862.
Alberthoma, Princ. of Chr. rel., 1789.
Allen, E., Reason the only Oracle, 1784.
Andover Fuss, 1853. P. 96.
Andros, Divine efficiency, 1820.
Apostolical Fathers, 1810. B. C.
Bad Effects of Speculative Theology. P. 50.
Baptismal bonds, (Heywood), 1687.
Beasley, Answer to Channing, 1830. P. 200.
Beecher, L., Works, 1853.
Bellamy, J., Works, 1850.
Bentham, Heads of Lectures, 1774. P. 399.
Boston, T., A View of the Covenant of Grace, 1770. B. C.
Bradford, E., Strictures on Langdon.
Brake, Serm., Election, Rom. ix. 11, 1839. P. 378.
Bretschneider, Theol. of Germany.
Brothers, Revealed Knowledge, 1795.
Buck, C., Theolog. Dictionary, 1833.
Bunyan, J., Works, 1830. B. C.
Burch, Free grace, 1757.
Burrough, Lect. on Church Catechism, 1793. P. 301.
Burnet, Exposition of xxxix Articles, 1842.
Bush, Anastasis, 1845. B. C.
Bushnell, God in Christ, 1852.
Butler, J., Works, 1827.
Butler, T., Gospel Liberty, 1819.
Calvin, J., Institutes, 1587.
Carmichael, Theol. and Metaphysics of SS., 1840. B. C.
Chalmers, T., Institutes of, 1849.
Chillingworth, Works, 1836.
Christmas, Hampden Controversy, 1832–1848.
Chubb, T., Tracts, 1730.
Clarke, S., Works, 1738.
Clarkson, D., Works, Wyckliffe Soc., 1846.
Cogswell, W., Theol. class book, 1838.
Copleston, On Necessity and Predestination, 1821.
Cotton, J., Of the Cov't of Grace, 1671.

Theology, in English (continued).
Cudworth, Intel. Sys. of the Universe, 1837.
Cumming, H., Christian's Vade mecum, 1819.
Davies, Principles of Chr. Religion, 1726. P. 338.
De Quincey, Writings, 15, 16, 1851.
De Ronde, Princ. of the Christ. Rel., 1763.
Dewey, O., Disc. on Controv. Theol., 1846. B. C.
Dissertation....fall of man, 1723.
Dissertations, Lond., 1740.
Divine Rectitude, 1730.
Doddridge, P., Misc. works, 1830.
Dunlap, S. F., Vestiges of Spirit History, 1858.
Dwight, T., Theology explained, 1846.
Eachard, J., Works, 1705.
Edwards, B. B., Writings, 1853.
Edwards, J., 1st., Works, 1844.
Edwards, J., 2d., Works, 1842.
Ely, Calvinism and Hopkinsianism, 1811.
England, Bp., Works, 1849.
Engles, On prevailing errors, 1837. P. 631.
Erskine, E., Works, 1798.
Essays and Reviews, 1860.
Exam. of Dr. Tyler's Strictures, 1830.
Faber, G. S., Calvinistic controversy, 1804.
Fellowes, The Anti-Calvinist, 1801.
Fénélon, Works, vol. 1, 1836.
Fisher, E., Marrow of divinity, 1743.
Fletcher's, J. W., Appeal, Man's lost estate, 1814.
Forbes, D., Works.
Frith's Works. *See* Tyndale.
Fuller, A., Works. 1852.
Gastrell, F., Christian Institutes, 1709.
Gill, Doctrine of Predestination. P. 125.
Gouge, T., Works.
Gray, J., Mediatorial Reign, 1821.
Gregorius, Pope, Dialogues, 1689.
Greenfield, E., Publications, 1825–49.
Hampden, R. D., The 39 Articles, 1842. P. 330.
Harris, J., Man primeval, 1854.
Hasted, Works, 1862.
Heylin, J., Theol. lectures, 1761.
Hoadly, B., Writings coll., 1705–37.
Hodgson, F., Exam. of New School, 1839.
Hollingsworth, Lectures, 1835.
Hooker, R., Works, vol. 2, 1825.
Hopkins, S., System of, 1793.
" Dialogues.

Theology, in English (continued).

Horsley, Controv. with Dr. Priestley, 1821. B. C.

Howe, John, Works.

Hunt, J., Relig. thought in Eng., 1871.

Hurd, Works, vol. 5, 8, 1811.

James, H., Lectures and Miscellanies, 1852.

Jebb, J., Theol. Lectures, 1770. P. 1004.

" Works, 1787.

Jenks, F., Reply to Beecher on infant damnation, 1825. B. C.

Knapp, G. C., Lectures on, (Woods), 1831.

Knox, John, Works, Wodrow Soc.

Lardner, N., Works, 1788.

Law, W., Reply to Hoadly, 1717.

Leighton, Bp. R., Works, 1825.

Letters, Agency of fallen spirits, (Shedd), 1828.

Lindsey, T., Conv. on Divine Government, 1802.

" Inquiry into the Doctrine of the SS., 1818.

Mackay, Tubingen school, 1863.

Maclellan, Exclusive Deity, 1843. P. 317.

Mainard, Law of God ratified, 1674.

Malcom, H., Theol. index, 1868.

Malebranche, The Search after Truth, 1694.

Marsh, H., Lectures, 1810, 11, 22.

Marshall, W., Sanctification, 1769.

Martin, J., Disc. on Rom. x. 3, 1771. P. 372.

Martineau, H., Faith of the Universal Church, 1838. B. C.

Maurice, F. D., Theol. Essays, 1853.

Millar, D., Of Justification, 1748.

Milton, Treatise on Christ. Doctrine, 1825. B. C.

Miss. Soc. of Conn., Summary of doctrine, 1804.

More, H., Theol. Works, 1708.

Morell, Philosophy of Religion, 1849.

Morgan, E., Decrees and Free Agency, 1859.

Neander, History of Christ. Dogmas, 1858.

Norton, J., The Orthodox Evangelist, 1657.

Occasional paper, 1-10, 1697.

Ott, A crack in the wall, 1846.

Pacific Discourse, (T. Smith), 1688.

Pamphlets, Theological, vols. 65, 262, 295, 296, 307, 308, 586, 631, 653-655, 680-685, 866, 867, 871, 1249-1262, 1830, 1875, 2502, 2513.

Pamphlets, Theological, British, vols. 299-306, 340, 341, 444, 455, 707, 711, 760, 761, 845-847, 1004, 1028, 1033, 1570-1572, 1619.

Theology, in English (continued).

Pamphlets of Theological Controversy, vols, 354-358, 488, 600.

Park, E. A., Address, Cong. Min. of Mass., 1850.

Pearson, On the Creed, 1833.

Pecock, R., The Repressor, (Chron. G. B.).

Penrose, J., Writings, Coll., 1821-49.

Philosophy of Salvation, (Walker), 1846.

Pococke, R., Diatribæ, 1710.

Polhill, Precious faith consid., 1675.

Price, R., Four dissertations, 1777. B. C.

Priestley, Letters to Dr. Horsley, 1783.

" Inst. of Nat. and rev. relig.

Renan, E., Studies of Relig. History, 1864.

Replies to Essays and Reviews, 1862.

Ridgley, Body of Divinity, 1731.

Rowles, On divine truth, 1797.

Sandeman, Theron and Aspasia.

Scott, T., Treatises on, 1815.

Sharpe, W., Course of Sermons, 1816.

Shepard, T., Parable of the Virgins.

Silver, F., Miscellanies.

Smith, M., Epitome of, 1837.

Sparks, J., Comp. Tend. of Unit. and Trin. Doct., 1823. B. C.

Spring, G., Diss. on Rule of faith, 1844.

Spring, S., Moral disquisitions, 1815.

Squier, Sin not of God, 1855.

" Writings.

Storr & Flatt, Biblical Theol., 1836.

Swift, E., Serm., West. Theol. Serm.

Synod of Dort, 1619.

Taylor, Jeremy, Catholic faith, 1765. P. 343.

" Works, 1836-37.

Tillotson, J., Works, 1820.

Tracts for Priests and People, 1861, 62.

Tucker, A., The Light of Nature, 1831. B. C.

Tyndale, W., and J. Frith, Works.

" Dissertations. P. 307.

Upham, Letters on the Logos, 1828. B. C.

Walker, J., Essays, 1838.

Watson, R., Theol. institutes, 1825. B. C.

Watts, I., Works, 1810.

Weller, J., Free Grace, 1846. P. 306.

Westminster Assemb., Catechism, 1813.

" Confes. of faith, 1658.

Whelpley, The Triangle, 1832.

White, J. B., Obs. on Heterodoxy etc., 1839. B. C.

Willard, S., Body of Divinity, 1726.

Theology, in English (continued).

Wilson, J., Concessions of Trinitarians, 1845. B. C.

Wilson, J. P., Probation of man, 184.

Wilson, T., Instruction for Indians, 1792.

Witherspoon, Works, 1800-01.

Witsius, H., Econ. of the Covenants, 1798.

Woods, L., Works, 1851.

Worcester, N., The atoning sacrifice, 1829. B. C.

See Nat. Theol.; Bible; Christ; Church; Faith; Soul; Religion, practical; and various Churches; Catechisms; Bibliography; Creeds; Hoadly; Unitarian; Predestination; Trinity; Periodicals, religious, etc.

Theology, in Dutch. Buurt... Godgeleerdheid, 1776.

Byler, Heilige mengelstoffen, 1730.

Comrie, Verhandeling, 1744.

Elgersma, Zeedige verhandelinge, 1684.

Francken, A., Stellige Godgeleertheyd, 1757.

Hakvoord, De.... Schole van Christus, 1722.

Heijningen, Onfeilbaarheid der Apostelen, 1845.

Honert, Van Christus koningryk, 1742.

Labadie, Geloof der Evan. Kerke, 1672.

Leydekker, De Verborgentheid, 1729.

Leydt, Ware vryheyt, 1760.

Meyer, Het geloof van Abraham, 1757.

Pamphlets, Theol., Dutch, vol. 109.

Pastorale Brieven, 1688.

Vitringa, Gelove der alg. Kercke, 1691. P. 569.

See Sermons; Religion.

Theology, in Latin. Abelardus, P., Opera, 1616.

Abelly, L., Medulla Theolog., 1673.

Alfonsus, Adversus omnes hæreses, 1565.

Altenstaig, Lexicon Theologicum, 1576.

Ames, Bellarminus enervatus, 1629.

Annato, Apparatus ad pos. theol., 1705.

Aquinas, T. d', Catena Aurea, 1470.

" Tabula Quæstionum, 1512.

Augustinus, Opera, 1700.

" De gratia Dei, etc.

Baronius, Phil. theologiæ ancillans, 1641.

" Peccati mortalis, 1658.

Bay, J. de, Instit. Rel. Christianæ, 1626.

Bellarminus, R., De controversiis Christ. fidei, 1601.

Bellovissius, Decl. term. theologiæ, etc., 1586.

Bernardus, (Sanctus), Opera, 1781.

Theology, in Latin (continued).

Beza, Conf. Christ. fidei, 1573.

" Epist. theologicæ, 1575.

Calvin, Opuscula, 1563.

Canisius, De fide, spe et charitate, 1671.

Chrysostom, De virginitate, 1562.

" Panegyrics, 1775.

Cocceius, Opera, 1689.

Crellius, J., Opera, 1656.

Cyprianus, Opera, 1726.

Cyril of Alex., Co-substan. filii, 1514.

Damascenus, Sanct. imag. oppugnatores, 1554.

Dens, P., Theol. mor. et dogm., 1832.

Dionysius, Celestis hierarchia, 1503.

Doorenbos, B., De amore Dei, 1838. P. 592.

Fulgentius, F. C. G., Opera, 1587.

Garsias, P., Determinationes magistrales, 1489.

Gerson, J., Opera, 1502.

Giraldus Cambrensis, Opera, (Chron. G. B.).

Gregorius, De Virginitate, 1562.

Groot, Compendium Theol., 1851.

Hospinianus, Historiæ sacramentariæ, 1681.

" Concordia discors, 1678.

Jansenius, Augustinus de Hum. nat. Sanitate, 1643.

Joannes, Summa de Exemplis, 1597.

Leemhuis, J., Libertas volendi, 1847. P. 592.

Lightfoot, J., Opera, 1686.

Lombardus, P., Sententiarum lib. iv, 1634.

Melancthon, Corpus Doctrinæ Christianæ, 1565.

" Loci Communes Theol., 1547.

Netter, Fasciculi Zizaniorum, (Chron. G. B.).

Pamphlets, Theol., Latin, vol. 592.

Pareau, Series Compend. theol., 1848.

Paulus, Scrutinium Scriptorum, 1478.

Peter of Blois, Opera, 1847.

Proclus, Archiep., Analecta, 1630.

Roman Cath. Church, Canons, Catechisms.

Socinus, F., Opera, 1618.

Sulpicius, Opera, 1693.

Sutcliffe, De recta stud. theol. ratione, 1602.

Theramo, Consol. peccatorum, 1484.

Trithemius, De Scriptoribus eccles., 1494.

Turretini, Compendium theol., 1703.

Velleus, De Gratia universali, 1619.

Vincentius, Speculum doctrinale, 1494.

Toleration (continued).
Conference....Papist and Jew, 1678.
Consid. moving to tol., 1685.
Consid. on the state of subscription, 1774.
Davis, G. L., Day-Star of Freedom, 1855.
Debate, H. of Com., repeal of Test acts, 1790. P. 310.
Defence of considerations, 1774.
Defence of the charge of persecution, 1730.
Defence of relig. liberty, 1825.
Exam. of some arguments, 1712.
Exclusion of Rothschild, 1850.
Expedient for peace, 1688.
Delays Dangerous, 1739.
Dispute Adjusted, 1732.
Duncan, J., Persecutions for relig. opinion, 1825.
Ellis, J., Narrative, Rehoboth, 1795.
Evans, J., A preservative against uncharitableness.
" Relig. liberty, 1811. P. 1560.
Exposition of the Orthodox System, 1749.
Findley, Obs. on "The two sons of oil," 1[illegible]2.
Fownes, J., Principles of, 1790.
Forney, J. W., Address on relig. intol., 1855.
Great Britain; Conformity, 1701.
Grégoire, Liberté de Conscience à Haiti, 1824.
Hammond, H., Disarmer's dexterities, 1656.
Harvest, G., Letter to S. Chandler, 1749.
Herttell, Relig. doctrines as qualif. of witnesses, 1828. P. 24. B. C.
Hickes, G., Sermon, 1681.
Hill, R., Parochial Assessments, 1811. P. 320.
" Freedom in danger.
Hull, Eng., Proceedings of Dissenters.
Humble Proposals, 1650.
Hypocrisy Unmasked, 1776.
Inconveniences of Toleration, 1667.
Indulgence not Justified, (Perrinchief), 1668. P. 354.
Jottrand, Les Eglises d'Etat, 1849.
Kent, W., Conviction of W. Rice, 1811.
Letter on Toleration, 1808.
Letters of Philopatris, 1819.
Liberty the Support of Truth, 1732.
Locke, J., Works, vol. 6, 1823.
M'Neile, State in Danger, 1846. P. 347.
Mallet, J., Penal Laws, 1680.
Marsh, H., Letter on, 1810.
Mill, James, Principles of, 1837.

Toleration (continued).
Observations....Rom. Cath. Subjects, 1817.
O'Leary, M., Essay on, 1785. P. 1476.
Pamphlets relating to, vols. 318-320, 848, 1298, 1475–1477. B. C., 15.
Paston, J., Penal Laws, 1688.
Tax redux..the reconciler, 1689.
Penal Laws, 1680. P. 1475.
Penington, I., Liberty of Conscience, 1681.
Penn, W., Treatise on Persecution, (Works), 1726.
Philosopher, The, 1771.
Porteous, W., The Doct. of Toleration, 1778.
Potter, J., Charge to Clergy, 1719.
Priestley, Letter to Pitt, 1787.
Principles and Facts, 1856.
Protestant Reconciler, 1683.
Question....admis. of Cath. to Parl., 1801.
Ramsay, W., Rel. Liberty, 1856.
Randerson, Refusal to bury, etc., 1847.
Remarks on Liberty of Conscience, 1828. P. 10. B. C.
Right of Prot. Dissenters, 1789.
Roaf, On Head's Proclamation, 1838. P. 495.
Robertson, J., Wolverhampton Case, 1818. P. 316.
Sharpe, J., Serm. on Conscience, 1687, 1688.
Some remarks, Exeter, N. H., 1823. P. 1477.
South, R., Sermon, 1716.
Short Answer to Buckingham, 1685.
Steele, T., Iniquity of Oaths, 1829.
Strong, Cyprian, Christian forbearance, 1789.
Sturges, On Subscription, 1772.
Tate, Sermon, Matt. vii. 12.
Taylor, J., Works, Lib. of prophesying, 1836.
Toleration Act Explained, 1812.
True liberty, 1677.
Tucker, J., Relig. Intolerance, 1774.
Turgot, Mémoire sur, Œuvres, 7.
Underhill, Liberty of conscience, 1614-1661.
Vindiciæ Britannicæ, Christophilus, 1821.
Werenfels, Three Discourses, 1718.
Whitman, B., Relig. liberty, 1830.
William III, Of Lib. of Conscience, 1689. P. 408.
Wordsworth, C., Relig. Liberty, 1850. P. 455.
See Conformity; Test Acts; Authority; Liberty; Persecution; Rom. Cath. Emancipation; Oaths.

Tractarianism (continued).
Palmer, W., Letter to W. P., on Auricular Confession, etc., by Verax, 1841.
" Narrative of Events, 1843.
Pamphlets, vol. 330, 331, 776, 999, 1270, 1292.
Paper Lantern, 1843.
Pepys, H., Charges, 1842, etc.
Perceval, A. P., Letter to T. Arnold, 1842. P. 306.
Plain Sermons, 1839.
Plain Words, 1842.
Remarks upon the "Papal Aggression," 1851. P. 548.
Sanderson, R. B., Stagnation of Trade, 1842.
Ward, R., Jer. Taylor's Testimony, 1838. P. 331.
Weaver, View of Puseyism.
Willatts, C., Monitory Address, 1848.
Williams, A., Five Sermons, 1842.
Worthington, J. W., Tr. Tendencies, 1850.
See Church of England; Baptismal regeneration; Hampden; Newman; Pusey; Ritualism; Tradition.

Tracts. *See* Pamphlets.

Tract Societies. Amer. Tract Society, Boston, Reports, 1827–52.
" History of, 1857.
Amer. Tract Society, N. Y., Reports, 1826–64.
Appeal to Chr. Public, 1849.
Canada Rel. Tr. Soc. Report, 1839.
Hartford Tract Soc. 1859.
Jay, W., Letters on, 1853, 59.
Meth. Episc. Church, Tract Soc. Reports, 1854–57.
New Eng. Tr. Soc., Rep., 1821.
N. Y. City Tract Soc., Rep's, 1849–56.
Pamphlets, relating to, Vol. 297.
Prot. Epis. Tr. Soc., N. Y., Reports, 1843, 44.
Religious Tract Soc., Lond., Proc., 1800–20, 1848, 54.
Soc. des Livres relig., Toulouse, 1853.

Tracy. Family pedigree, Lond., 1854.

Tracy, E. C. Byington, E. H., Funeral discourse, 1862. P. 1614.

Trade. *See* Commerce; Navigation; Free Trade; Polit. Economy.

Trades. Advertisements of, Pam. V. 618.
Colwell, S., Claims of labor, 1861.
Freedley, E. T., Leading pursuits of the U. S., 1856.
Hints on the abuses of trade, 1827.
Pamphlets relating to Trades, vol. 298.
See Arts; Labor; Social Science.

Trades' Unions. Albany Iron Moulders' Coöp. Assoc'n, 1865.
Builders' Assoc'n, London, 1834.
Capital Coöperative Foundery Co., 1868.
Carpenters' and Joiners' Union, Const., Albany, 1864. P. 2520.
Central Assoc'n of Employers of Engineers, Lond., 1852.
Character, etc. of, 1834.
Coachmakers' Internat. Union, 1866.
Co-operative League, 1852.
Gen. Soc. of Mech. and Tradesmen, N. Y., Reports, 1862–68.
Hotel Keepers' Prov. Inst., London.
Manual Labor vs. Machinery, London, 1834.
Marriott, C., The Coöperative Principle, 1855.
Maskell, C., The Coöperative Principle, 1855. P. 2501.
Moore, E., Addr. Gen. Trades' Union, N. Y., 1833.
Nat. Assoc. for Soc. Sci. Rep., Trades' Societies; Strikes, 1860.
National Indust. Congr., 8th Proc., 1853.
New York Typog. Soc., Const., 1848.
Plummer, J., Causes and evils of strikes.
Saddlemakers' Union, Albany, 1853, 1854.
Samuelson, German workmen, 1869.
Thurlow, Unions abroad, 1869.
Workingmen's Coöp. Ass'n, Portland. 1864.
See Labor; Mechanics' Institutes; Wages.

Tradition. Benson, C., Writings, Coll., 1832.
Brett, T., Trad. necessary, 1718.
Close, F., Writings, Coll., 1837–56.
Daillé, J., Right use of the Fathers.
Hawkins, E., Sermon, 1818.
Pamphlets relating to, vol. 897.
Pearson, G., Doct. of Ch. of England, 1837. P. 331.
Powell, B., Tradition unveiled, 1841.
Russell, A. T., On Keble's Sermon, 1837. P. 331.
Shuttleworth, P. N., Not Trad. but Scripture, 1841.
Stillingfleet, Sermon on, 1687.
Taylor, I., Transmission of Books, 1859.
See Church; Tractarianism.

Train, G. F. Speeches, 1862, 64.

Transactions. *See* Scientific Societies.

Transcendentalism. Coleridge, S. T., Aids to reflection, 1839, 47.
Green, J. H., Spiritual Philos'y, 1865.

Transcendentalism (continued).
Greene, W. B., Transcendentalism, 1849.
Kant, E., Critique of pure reason, 1855.
Wirgman, T., Principles of Transcen., Phil. Pamph'r 23.
See Nature; Philosophy; Supernatural.

Translations. Clarke, J., Usefulness of, 1734. P. 1764.
Cubi y Soler, On translations.
Tytler, Principles of, 1813.
See Language; Classical Literature.

Transportation. *See* Punishments; Convicts.

Transubstantiation. Aylmer, Serm., 2 Pet. ii. 1, 1713. P. 265.
Cahill, Rev. Dr., Lecture, The Holy Eucharist, 1860.
Clagett, On John 6th, 1686. P. 356.
Jenkins, R. C., Difficulties of, 1843. P. 1501.
Leon, The Miraculous Host, 1822. P. 1554.
Marsh, W. T., A Sermon, 1846.
Pamphlets regarding, vol. 1249.
Parker, S., Reasons for....Test, 1688.
Payne, W., Adoration of the Host, 1685. P. 356.
Piers, O., Not Doct. of Church of England, 1836. P. 348.
Tillotson, Disc. against, 1684.
Transubstantiation, (Goodman), 1688.
See Communion; Rom. Cath. Church.

Transylvania. Boner, Its people, 1865.
Paget, Hungary and Transyl., 1839.
Paton, The Goth and Hun, 1851.
See Hungary; Roumania.

Trapnell, J. Trial of, 1847.

Trapping. Newhouse, S., Trapper's Guide, 1867.

Travels, Miscellaneous. Adams, J., Flowers of, 1797.
Carletti, Ragionamenti, 1701.
Carver, J., New Univ. traveller, 1779.
Charton, Tour du Monde, 1861, 62.
Clarke, E., Travels in Europe, Asia and Africa, 1816–24.
Costello, Jacques Cœur, 1847.
Evliya, Narrative of Travels, 1834.
Foster's Cabinet Miscellany, 1836.
Hall, B., Patchwork, 1841.
Harriot, J., Travels and adventures of, 1807.
Hoffman, The Monitor, 1862.
Houstoun, Works, Mem. of his travels, 1690–1753.
Jenkinson, Reys, 1558.
Johnson, J., Philosophy of, 1831.

Travels, Miscellaneous (continued).
La Motraye, Tr. through Europe, Asia and Africa, 1723.
Langsdorff, Voy. and Trav., 1803–7.
Martineau, How to Observe, 1838. B. C.
Mavor, General Collection of, 1810.
Melton, Zee-en Land Reizen, 1660–77.
Minturn, N. Y. to Delhi, 1858.
Mocquet, Trav. in Afr., Asia and Am., 1696.
Over the Ocean: by a Lady, 1846.
Pages, Travels round the World, 1767–1779.
Pfeiffer, Last Travels, 1861.
Portfolio, 1812.
Pumpelly, Across America and Asia, 1870.
Rapelye, Excursions, 1834.
Sargent, E., American Adventure, 1847.
Simpson, Sir G., Overland Journey around the World, 1841–42.
Smith, Capt. J., Trav. in Eur., Asia, Afr. and Am., 1593–1629.
Smith, T. W., Narrative of Life, travels, etc., 1844.
Taylor, B., At Home and Abroad, 1860.
Thompson, E., Sailor's Letters, 1766.
Wheeler, D., Journals of, 1835. P. 1212.
See Voyages, Collections of, and travels; and the several countries; Geography.

Travers, S. S. Pedigrees of Family, 1864.

Treacher, B. Bulkley, C., Sermon on, 1766.

Treadmill. *See* Punishments.

Treadwell, J. Olmsted, D., Memoir of.
Porter, N., Fun. Sermon, 1823.

Treason. Earbery, Hist. of Clemency, 1715. P. 1518.
Holcroft, T., Defence on Prosecution for, 1795. P. 412.
Jenkins, D., The Armies Indemnity, 1647.
Joyce, J., His Arrest for, 1794. P. 1545.
Method of the Proceedings in Impeachments, 1715. P. 1520.
Plowden, F., Rights of Subjects, 1784, 1785.
Rocks and Shallows discovered...bills of attainder, 1716. P. 1399.
Wilkes, M., Athaliah, Trials for Treason, 1795, P. 320.
Wilson, W. D., Attainder of Treason, 1863.
See Rebellion.

Treat, Capt. J. Vindic. of, 1815.

Trials (continued).
Pamphlets, Vols. 577, 714, 873, 882. B. C. 7.
Pennsylvania, vs. John Smith, 1809.
Peltier, Libel on Napoleon I, 1803. B. C.
Phillips, Capt. I., U. S. Navy, 1825.
Pillow's, Gen., Defence, 1848.
Porter, D., Foxardo Expedition, 1825.
Sampson, W., Trial of Lieut. Renshaw, 1809. P. 4. B. C.
Tyng, S. H., jr., Trial, N. Y., 1868.
Warren, S., Miscellanies.
Wheeler, E., Trial, 1805. P. 36.
Williams, J., Murder, Boston, 1819.
See Capital Punishment; Law Library Catalogue.

Trinidad, W. Indies. Adam, T., Farewell Sermon.
Burnley, Observ. on, 1842.
Gr. Brit., Geol. Survey of T., Wall, 1860.
Kingsley, C., At Last, 1871.
Marryatt, J., Speech on, 1822.
Peck, N., Report on, 1840.
Picton, A Letter on, 1804.
Political Acc't of, 1807.
Stephens, Crisis of the Sugar Colonies, 1802.

Trinity. Burgess, T., Writings, 1820–35.
Burgh, W., Answer to Lindsey.
Burnet, G., Judgment on, 1732.
Calm and Sober Inquiry, 1694.
Christian Layman, 1842.
Christian Liberty asserted, 1734.
Clayton, R., Essay on Spirit, 1751.
Coningsby, G., Sermon, Rom. i. 22.
Consid. on the Explications of, 1694.
Cornelius, E., Sermon on, 1826.
Craig, R., Treatise on, 1828.
Doctrine of the blessed, 1719.
Doctrine of, (Evanson), 1772.
Doctrine of, 1768. P. 312.
Emlyn, On 1 John, 5, 7, 1719. P. 313.
Eveleigh, Sermon, Zech. ii. 8–11, 1796. P. 313.
Essay on Religion, 1734. P. 444.
Essay towards Demonstration of, 1738.
Evans, J., Letter to Mr. Cumming, 1722. P. 341.
Forrest, J., Acc't of origin of Trin. theology, 1836.
Greene, W. B., The Doctrine of, 1847. P. 295.
Hawkins, J., Address to Dr. Priestley, 1788. P. 315.
Haywood, W., Exam. of Dr. Clarke's Doct., 1719. P. 312.
Howell, W., Sermon on 1 John, 5. 7, 1711. P. 365.

Trinity (continued).
Huntingford, G. I., Thoughts on, 1804.
Jackson, J., Exam. of Nye, 1715.
Jones, W., The Doctrine proved, 1795.
Letter to the Rev. Dr. Waterland, 1722. P. 353.
Lindsey, T., Writings, Coll., 1774–88.
Martin, Exam. of Emlyn on John V, 1719.
Newton, W., Curiosity in Religion, 1725. P. 312.
Nolan, Vind. of Bampton Lect., 1817. P. 303.
Obs. on Dr. Waterland, (Clarke), 1724. P. 353.
Pamphlets relating to the Trinity, vols. 311, 312, 353, 1250, 1620.
Prim. Chri'ty vindicated, 1712.
Randolph, T., Vindication of, 1754.
Remarks on Dr. Waterland's Defense, 1723. P. 353.
Remarks upon a late Dissertation, 1726.
Reply to the 2d defence, 1795.
Resignation no Proof, 1776. P. 315.
Richardson, J., Athanasian Creed, 1822. P. 304.
Rowles, S., Remarks on Priestley, 1784.
Some Considerations, 1721. P. 312.
Toulmin, J., Doct. of Unity, 1802. P. 316.
Treatise of, 1748. P. 312.
Two Letters, 1688. P. 357.
Two Schemes of, 1793. P. 652.
Vaillant, J., Scripture compared with, 1819.
Waterland, D., Arian Subscription, 1721.
" Hist. of the Controversy, 1736.
Wells, E., Letter to Clarke, 1713.
Williams, J., Vindication, 1695.
Williams, J., Sermon, Conn., 1850.
Wilson, J., Doctrine considered, 1835.
Whiston, W., The Doxologies, 1719. P. 314.
" Historical preface, 1711.
" Collec. of anc. monuments on, 1713.
Whitaker, E. W., Four Dialogues, 1786.
Worcester, N., Bible News, 1812.
See Arians; Christ; Unitarians.

Trinity Church, N. Y. Apol. for vote on the Bishop, 1859.
Berrian, W., Hist. of, 1847.
" Semi-centenn. Sermon, 1860.
" Report on state of, 1856.
Boorman, J., Letter to, 1855.
Church of Holy Evan., Rep. on, 1860.
Hobart, The Charter of, defended, 1813.

Turkey (continued).

Blount, H., Voy. to the Levant. Pinkerton, 10.

British diplom. and Turk. independence, 1838.

Browne, J. R., Yusef, or the journey, 1853.

Buckingham, J. S., Travels in, 1827.

Carlisle, Earl of, Diary in Turkish waters, 1854.

Chalcondile, Hist. de l'établissement de, 1650.

Charrière, Négociations dans le Levant, 1848.

Chateaubriand, Travels in, 1806, 07.

Chesney, The Russo-Turk. Campaigns, 1828.

Chishull, E., Sermon, Levant Comp., 1698.

" Travels in, 1747.

Christian, J. H. L., Cry from empty lands of, 1854.

Cobden, R., Sultan Mahmoud; 3 letters, 1835.

Colton, W., Land and Lee, 1850.

Combi, Guerra a Venetia, 1645.

Costumes of Turkey, 1814.

Cox, S. S., A Buckeye abroad, 1852.

Crowe, The Greek and Turk, 1853.

Crusius, Turco-Graeciæ viii lib., 1584.

Damer, Mrs. H., Diary of a tour, 1842.

Dekay, J. E., Sketches of, 1831, 32.

Du Cros, Voyages de Ville, 1669.

Durbin, Observations in the East, 1845.

Eardley, Christianity in, 1855.

Egnatius, De origine Turcarum, 1633.

Finlay, G., Hist. of Greece and empire of Trebizond, 1204–1461, 1851.

" Hist. of Greece under Othman domination, 1856.

Fontanier, Voy. en Orient, 1821–33.

Formby, H., Visit to the East, 1845. Churchman's Library.

Forsyth, Few Months in the East, 1861.

Fowler, Hist. of War with Russia, 1855.

France, Discussion dans les chambres, 1840.

Fraser, Journal. from Constantinople to Tehran, 1838.

Galt's Travels, 1809–1811.

Gaudry, Recherches en Orient, 1853–1854.

Gilson, Czar and Sultan, 1852.

Goodell, W., The Old and New, 1853.

Grassi, Charte Turque, 1825.

Great Britain, Turkey; Eastern Papers, 1854.

Grey, Earl, Speech on, 1855.

Griffith, Jour. across the desert, 1845.

Hammer, Storia dell Impero Ottomano, 1828–31.

Turkey (continued).

Hawes, J., Religion of the East, 1845.

Hints on the East. question, 1853.

Hist. of War in Bosnia, 1737–39.

Hobhouse, J. C., Journey through Albania, etc., 1813.

Horton, T. G., People and gov't of, 1854. P. 1479.

Keppel, G., Across the Balcan, and to ruins in Asia Minor, 1829.

Kinglake, J. A., Eothen, 1845.

Kinnear, J. G., Cairo, Petra and Damascus, 1839.

Kinneir, J. M., Tour through Asia Minor, etc., 1818.

Knolles, R., Historie of the Turkes, 1603.

La Brocquière, B. de, Travels to Palestine, 1432–33.

La Croix, J. Fr. de, Abrégé de l'histoire de, 1768.

Lake, W. M., Geog. Tour in Asia Minor.

Lamartine, A. de, Hist. of Turkey, 1855.

Laurent, P. E., Classical Tour, 1819.

Lavenden, Travels to Syria and Asia Minor, 1605. Churchill, Supp.

Leunclavius, Ann. Sultanorum Othmanidarum, 1588.

Livingston, E., Speech on Mission to, 1831.

Lucas, P., Voyage dans, 1720.

Macarius, Patriarch, Travels, Orient. Trans. Fund, 1836.

MacFarlane, C., Turkey and its Destiny, 1847, 48.

Madden, R. R., The Turkish Empire, 1862.

Martineau, H., Eastern life, 1848.

Moltke, Russians in Roumelia, 1828.

Monro, V., Ramble in Syria and to Stamboul, 1835.

Montague, Lady, Letters during travels, 1743, 66, 1837.

Morris, E. J., The Turkish Empire, 1855.

" Tour through, and Egypt, 1842.

Mouriez, Des intérêts Européens, 1842.

Naima, Annals of, 1591–1659, Orient. Trans. fund, 1832.

Nicholay, Travels in Turkey, 1550.

Nicolay, Voyages en, 1577.

Noguès, L'indépendance de, 1852.

Oriental Museum, Lond., 1854. P. 1479.

Oscanyan, C., The Sultan.... 1857.

Pamphlets relating to, vols. 825, 1479.

Pococke, R., Travels in the East, (Pinkerton, 10).

Porter, Sir J., Obs. on the Turks, 1771.

Turkey (continued).
Porter, Sir J., Aanmerkingen, 1770.
Powers of Europe and the great quarrel, 1855.
Ranke, L., Ottoman Emp. in 16th and 17th Centuries, 1845.
Ray, J., Coll. of Voyages, 1693, (Rauwolff).
Reid, J., Turkey and the Turks, 1846.
Ricaut, Hist. of Turk. Emp., 1623–77.
Robertus, Christ. Prin. Bello contra Turcas, 1088.
Rolamb, Journey to Constantinople, (Churchill).
Russell, W. H., The War to the death of Raglan, 1855.
Sal namé, (Almanac), 1269, A. H.
Sandwith, H., Siege of Kars, 1856.
" Hékim Bashi, 1864.
Sandys, G., Rel. of a journey, 1621.
Schneider, Mrs., Letters from Broosa, 1846.
Slade, A., Sketches of trav., 1828–31.
Smith, J. V. C., Travels in, 1852.
Southgate, H., Visit to Syrian church, 1844.
Spon, J., Voy. du Levant, 1675.
Strangford, S. S., Lord, Writings, 1870.
Thévenot, M., Voyages, 1683.
Thomson, C., Asia, Holy Land and Egypt, 1810.
Tott, Baron de, State of, 1785.
Tournefort, Voyage du Levant, 1718.
Turkey, Charte. P. 227, 1104.
" , Manifesto, 1853.
Ubicini, Lettres sur, 1851.
United, The, States and Turkey, 1868.
Urquhart, D., Resources of, and free trade, 1833.
Van Lennep, H. J., Travels in Asia Minor, 1870.
Vassif, Guerre contre les Russes, 1769.
Walpole, F., The Ansayrii and Travels, 1851.
See Albania; Armenia; Asia, West.; Constantinople; Crimean War; Egypt; Mohammedanism; Palestine; Slavonians; Syria; Wallachia.

Turkish Literature. *See* Oriental Lit.; Language.

Turkish Newspapers. Courrier de Constantinople, 1847–55.
Impartial, L', Smyrne, 1855.
Jeridéi Havadis, Constantinople, 1848–1854.
Journal Asiat. de Constantinople, 1852. P. 1485.
Journal de Constantinople, 1846–56.
Levant Herald, Constantinople, 1863–1865, Odd Numbers.

Turkish Newspapers (continued).
Moniteur Ottoman, 1831–36.
Presse d'Orient, 1855.

Turnbull, J. Brewer, S. K., Letter to, 1827. P. 1379.

Turner, D. Evans, J., Sermon on, 1798.

Turner, H. Turner, J., Descendants of, 1852.

Turner, Mrs. J. Memoir, 1827.

Turner, S. H. Autobiography, 1863.

Turner, T. Chishull, E., Sermon, 1714.

Turner, W. Wood, W., Fun. Discourse, 1794.

Turnip. Commerell, Bericht....of Mangel-Wortel, 1789. P. 205.

Turrettin, J. A. Clarke, Jos., Reply, 1749. P. 299.

Tuscany. Almanacco Tos., 1846.
Burke, E., Peep into, 1853.
Cosmo III, Travels and Life, 1821.
Crawford, M. S., Life in, 1859.
France: Docts. inéd., 1859, Négociations avec.
Gray, Mrs., Sepulchres of Etruria, 1840.
Trollope, T. A., Hist. of Florence to 1531, 1865.
Tuscany, Rapporto dell' Esposizione indust., 1850, 54.
See Etruria; Florence.

Tweddell, J. Hunt, P., Literary Remains of.

Twickenham, Eng. Richmond Handbook.

Tyler, Pres. J. Life of, 1844.
Confed. Congr., Proc. Death of, 1862.
Who and what is ? 1843.

Tyng, D. A. Tyng, S. H., Memorial of, 1858.

Tyng, S. H., Jr. Trial of, 1868.

Typography. *See* Bibliography; Engraving; Lithography; Block Books.

American Typographical History, etc.
Buckingham, Personal Memoirs, 1850.
" Specimens of Newsp. literature, 1850.
Follett, History of the Press of West. N. Y., 1847.
Munsell, Typog. miscellany, 1850.
New Hampshire Celebration, 1856.
New York Typograph Soc., 1850.
Pamphlets containing early printing, vol. 603.
Thomas, History of printing in Amer., 1810.

Typography: American Typographical History, etc. (continued).

Troy Typog. Assoc'n. Celeb.

Wisconsin Editor. Ass'n, 1857–70.

Wallace, J. W., Address on W. Bradford.

Art of Typography. Adams, T. F., Typographia, 1845.

Auer, Raumverhältniss der Buchstaben, 1849.

" Das Unser Vater in 608 lang., 1847.

" Naturselbstdruck, 1854.

Bertrand, Traité de, 1798.

Bodoni, Manuale tipog., 1818.

Brun, Manuel de la typog. Française, 1826.

" Handbuch der Buchdruckerkunst, 1828.

Camus, Hist. du polytypage et de la stéréotype, 1802.

Crapelet, Etudes pratiques, 1837.

" De la prof. d'Imprimeur, 1840.

Donlevy, The Graphic Arts, 1854.

Fertel, La science pratique de, 1423.

Fournier, H., Traité de la typographie, 1758.

" Manuel typographique, 1764.

Grattan, Printer's companion, 1846.

Gr. Brit., Patents on printing to 1859.

Guignes, Principes de composition orientale, 1790.

Hansard, Treatise on Printing and Typefounding, 1841.

Hoe, Printing Machines.

Hoogvliet, Lof der Drukkunste, 1740.

Johnson, H., Introd. to Logography, 1783.

" Tangible typography.

Johnson, J., Typographia, 1824.

Kortebrant, Lof der Drukkunste, 1740.

Long, T., Printing Machines.

Luce, Essai d'une nouvelle typog., 1740–70.

Luckombe, Hist. and progress of, 1770.

Momoro, Traité élémentaire, 1793.

Moxon, Mechanick exercises, 1677–83.

Palmer, E., Glyphography. P. 1235.

Partington, Printer's guide, Lond. P. 1222.

Peignot, Dict. de bibliol., 1802, 04.

Saunders, F., Print. ass't, 1839.

Savage, W., Decorative printing, 1822.

" Dict. of Printing, 1841.

Smith, Printer's grammar, 1755.

Stower, Printer's grammar, 1808.

Timperley, Printer's manual, 1838.

Trumbull, Pocket typographia, 1846.

Type Machine Co., 1862.

Typography: Art of Typography (continued).

Vinçard, L'Art du typographe, 1823.

Westreenen, Imprimerie Steréotype, 1833.

Wolf, Monum. typog. v. 1, Elenchus, 1740.

See Lithography; Stereotype.

Augsburg. *See* Bibliography.

Bamberg. *See* Bibliography.

Belgium. *See* Bibliography, Belgium.

Bibliography of Typography. Delandine, Mém. Bibliog., 1817.

Dupont, Hist. de l'imprimerie, 1854.

Namur, Bibliog. paléog. bibliol., 1838.

Peignot, Repert. bibliog., 1812.

Renouard, Cat. de sa bibliot., 1854.

Schubarth, Répert. der techn. Literatur, 1823.

Biographies of Printers, Booksellers, etc. Amoretti, Lett. s. d'Aldo Manuzio.

Baillet, Jugemens des Savans, 1730.

Beloe, v. 3, Early Printers, 1807.

Blancken, Bildnisse, 1725.

Buckingham, Personal Memoirs, 1852.

Dolet, E., Vie de.

Dunton, Life and Errors, 1818.

Falkenstein, Gesch. der Buchdruckerkunst, 1840.

Fifty Years' Recollections, 1837.

Gent, The Life of, 1832.

Hansard, Biography of Luke Hansard, 1829.

Hartzheim, Bibliot. Coloniensis, 1747.

Hillard, Mem. of J. Brown, 1856.

Hutton, Life of, by himself, 1816.

Iseghem, Biog. de Martens, 1852.

Johnson, Typographia, 1824.

Kerr, Life of Smellie, 1811.

Kervin, Bibliophiles Flamands, 1853.

Lackington, Confessions of, 1804.

La Serna Santander, Dict., Imprimeurs, 1805–7.

Maittaire, Hist. Typog. Parisiensium, 1717.

Malaspina, Cat. di Stampe, 1824.

Nichols, Anecdotes of W. Bowyer, 1782.

Nodier, Vie de: Par Wey, 1844.

Oettinger, Bibliographie Biographique Univ., 1854.

Perthes, C. T., Memoirs of, 1789–1843.

Reume, Imprimeurs Belges, 1848.

Saxius, Hist. Lit. Typ. Mediolan., 1665.

Teissier, Catalogus Auctorum, 1688.

Timperley, Encyc. of Typ. Anecd., 1842.

Typography: Biographies of Printers, Booksellers, etc. (continued).
Zeltner, Von dem Leben J. Luffts, 1727.
See Caxton, W.; Coster, L. J.; Gutenberg, J.; Bibliography; Biography of Printers.

Block-books. Ottley, Inv. of Prin. and Block-books, 1863.
Russia, Cat. Xylographes, 1852.
Sotheby, Principia Typographica, 1858.
Varusoltis, Xylographie Troyenne.
See History; and Engraving.

Caxton, W. Dibdin, Bibl. Spencer., V. 4, 1815.
Dibdin, Typ. Antiq., V. 1, 1810.
Knight, C., The Old Printer, 1854.
Lewis, Life of, 1737.

Coster, L. J. Kortebrand, Lof der Drukkunst, 1740.
Loosjes, Gedenkschriften, 1824.
Vries, A. De, Notice sur le Speculum, 1841.
See Bibliography, and *Haarlem*.

English Typographical History. Ames, Typ. Antiquities, 1749.
Atkyns, Origin of Printing, 1664.
Baskett, Case of, vs. Parson, 1720.
Blackstone, W., Clarendon press.
Clarigny, Hist. de... en Angleterre, 1857.
Cranwell, Books before 1600 at Cambridge.
Dibdin, Bibliot. Spenceriana, V. 4, 1815.
" Typ. ant. of England, Scotland and Ireland, 1810–19.
Fifty Years' recollections, 1837.
Greswell, Annals of Parisian Typog., 1818.
Herbert, Typ. Ant. of Great Britain, 1471–1600.
Johnson, Typographia, 1824.
Knight, C., The Old Printer and Mod. Press, 1854.
Lemoine, Typog. antiquities, 1797.
Middleton, Disserta., 1776, (Bowyer).
Palmer, Hist. of Printing, 1733.
Singer, Book printed, Oxford, 1468.
Timperley, Encyc. of Typog. Anecdote, 1842.
See Caxton, W.; *History of Typog.*

Festivals (Centennial) of Printing. Clessen, J. J., Drittes Jubel-fest.
Falkenstein, Geschichte, 1840.
Lessern, Typog. Jubilans, 1740.
Loosjes, Gedenkschriften, 1823.
Schmidt, Danckpredigten, 1640.
Seiz, Annus tertius sæc. Inven. Typ., 1742.
See Origin; Haarlem; Strasbourg; Mayence.

Typography (continued).
French Typographical History. Crapelet, Des Brevets d'Imprimeur, 1704–1840.
" Imprimerie en France, 1836.
Delandine, Cat. de la bibl. de Lyon, 1818.
Dupont, Hist. de l'Imprimerie, 1854.
Frère, De l'imprim. à Rouen, 1843.
" Bibliog. Normand, 1858–60.
Greswell, Annals of Parisian typog., 1818.
" Early Greek Press at Paris, 1833.
Laborde, L'Impr. à Strasbourg, 1439.
Maittaire, Hist. Typog. Parisiensium, 1717.
Monfalcon, Hist. de Lyon, 1851.
Notice de l'Imprimerie Roy. à Paris, 1842.
See Paris; Strasbourg; Origin; Bibliography.

Gazetteers of Typography. Clarke, Bibl. Misc., V. 2, 1806.
Cotton, Typog. Gazetteer, 1st series, 1831: 2d series, 1866.
Falkenstein, Geschichte, 1840.
La Serna Santander, Dictionnaire, V. 1, 1805.
Namur, Man. du Bibliothécaire, 1834.
Peignot, Dict. de Bibliologie, 1802.

German Typographical History. Denis, Wiens' Buchdruckergeschichte, 1782.
" Geschichte der k. k. Druckerei in Wien.
Hüpfauer, Druckstücke aus dem xv Jahrhunderte, 1794.
Hassler, K., Buchdrucker-geschichte Ulm', 1840.
Jaeck, Beschreibung der bib. zu Bamberg, 1831–35.
Kirchhoff, Gesch. der Deutschen Buchhandels, 1857.
Mezger, Augsburg's Druckdenkmale.
Panzer, Annales Typographici.
Zapf, Augsburg's Buchdruckergesch., 1786.
Zeltner, Kurz historie, J. Lufft, 1727.
See Bibliography; *Augsburg; Bamberg; Beuerberg; Erlangen; Mayence.*

Greek. Bowyer, Hist. of Printing, 1776.
Greswell, Hist. of Greek Press, 1833.
See Bibliography.

Gutenberg, J., His Acts, 1860.
Koehler, Urkunden J. Guttenbergs... 1741.
Née de la Rochelle, Eloge de: 1811
Winaricky, Jean Gutenberg, 1847.
Zapf, Ælteste Buchdruckergeschichte, 1790.

Typography (continued).

HAARLEM. Bowyer, Hist. of Printing, 1776.

Holtrop, Mon. typ. des Pays Bas, 1858–1861.

Koenen, Voorlezigen, 1856.

Kortebrand, Lof der Drukkunst, 1740.

Lichtenberger, Initia Typog., 1811.

Loosjes, Gedenkschriften, 1824.

Meerman, Conspectus Orig. Typog., 1761.

" Origines Typographicæ, 1765.

Seiz, Annus tertius sæc. Inven. Typ., 1742.

Vries, A. De, Eclaircissement, 1823.

" Guichard's notice, 1841.

Westreenen van Tiellandt, Boekdrukkunst in Nederland, 1829. B. C.

HISTORY OF TYPOGRAPHY. Alnander, Artis Typ. in Sveciæ, 1725.

Ames, Typog. Antiq., 1471–1600.

Baillet, Jugemens, V. 1, 1722.

Bagford's Essay, 1707.

Brunet, Imprimeurs imaginaires, 1866.

Clarigny, Hist de....en Angleterre, 1857.

Corbelli, Einfluss auf die Wissenschaften, 1779.

Cotton, Typog. Gazetteer, 1831, 66.

Crapelet, Des Progrès de, au XVI Siècle, 1836.

" Des brevets d'imprimeur, 1704–40.

Denis, Wiens' Buckdruckergeschichte, 1782.

Dibdin, Bibliog. Decameron, 1817.

Delandine, Cat. de la Bibl. de Lyon, 1818.

Dupont, Hist. de l'imprimerie, 1854.

Falkenstein, Gesch. der Buchdruckerkunste, 1840.

Frère, De l'Imprim. à Rouen, 1843.

Greswell, Annals of Parisian Typog., 1818.

Hassler, K., Buchdrucker-geschichte Ulm's, 1840.

Herbert, Typog. ant. of Great Britain, 1471–1600.

Hoffman, De Typog. in Reg. Poloniæ, 1740.

Jaeck, Beschreibung der Bib. zu Bamberg, 1831–35.

Johnson, Typographia, 1824.

Kirchhoff, Gesch. der Deutschen Buchhandels, 1857.

La Serna Santander, Dictionnaire, 1805–07.

Lemoine, Typog. Antiquities, 1797.

Luckombe, History of, 1770.

Maittaire, Annales typographici, 1719–1741.

Mezger, Augsburg's Druckdenkmale, 1840.

Typography: HISTORY OF TYPOGRAPHY (continued).

Munsell, History of Printing, 1839.

Palmer, General History of Printing, 1733.

Panzer, Annales Typographici, 1793–1803.

Renouard, Annales des Aldes, 1825.

Rossi, De Hebraicæ Typ. Orig., 1778.

Saxius, Hist. Typog. Mediol., 1745, (Argelati).

Watson, History of Art of, 1713.

Westreenen, Verhandeling, 1809. B. C.

See Biographies of Printers; Gazetteers; English, French, German, Typog.; and, Bibliography.

INVENTION OF TYPOGRAPHY. Baillet, Jugemens, v. 1, 1722.

Bagford's Essay, 1707.

Bernard, De l'origine, 1853.

Besoldus, Dissert. de, 1740, (Wolf).

Bockenhoffer, Brevis relatio, 1691.

Boecler, Oratio, 1640.

Bosscha, Carmen de, 1817, (Lennep).

Bowyer, Origin of Printing, 1776.

Boxhorn, De typog. inventione, 1640.

Braun, Notitia hist. lit., 1788.

Brehmen, Expositio inventionis, 1740, (Wolf).

Chevillier, Dissertation sur, 1694.

Clarke, A., Bibliog. misc., 1806.

Cotton, Typog. gazetteer, 1831, 66.

Diosdado, De prima typ. ætate, 1793.

Ellis, C., Invention of printing, 1703.

Fischer, Beschreibung typ. Seltenheiten, 1800–04.

Fournier, Dissertation, 1758.

Heineken, Idée d'une coll. d'estampes, 1771.

Jansen, De l'orig. de la gravure, v. 2, 1808.

Koehler, Urkunden J. Guttenbergs... 1741.

Kortebrand, Lof der drukkunst, 1740.

Laborde, Débuts de l'impr. à Strasbourg, Mayence et Bamberg, 1840.

Lambinet, Origine de l'imprimerie, 1798.

La Serna Santander, Dict. bibliog., 1805–07.

Lessern, Typog. jubilans, 1740.

Lichtenberger, Initia typog., 1811.

" Hist. de l'invention, 1825.

Lille, Catal. de la Bibliot., Essai, 1859, (Paeile).

Loosjes, Gedenkschriften, 1823.

Mallincrot, De ortu et prog. typ., 1639

Marchand, Hist. de l'Origine, 1740.

Meerman, Conspectus Orig. Typog., 1761.

Typography: INVENTION OF TYPOGRAPHY (continued).

Meerman, Uitvinding, etc., Ed. Gockinga, 1767.

Mentel, De vera orig. paræenesis, 1650.

" Brevis excursus...ad G. Naudæum, 1844.

Mercier, Supplément à Marchand, 1775.

Middleton, Dissertation on, 1776, (Bowyer).

Munch, Primaria Documenta de orig., 1740.

Ottley, Invention of, 1863.

Paeile, L'Invention de....1859. *See* Lille.

Panciroli, Rerum Memorabilium, 1646.

Relatio de origine typ., 1619.

Roy. Soc. Phil. Trans., 1703, 1707, 1727.

Schoepflin, Vindic. typog., 1760.

Sotheby, Principia typog., 1858.

Toland, Conjectura de inventione, 1726.

Vries, A. De, Notice sur le Speculum, 1841.

" Eclaircissements sur l'hist. de, 1823.

" Arguments des Allemands, 1845.

" Uitvinding der Boekdrukkunst, 1841.

" Brief over Guichard's notice, 1841.

Westreenen, Uitvinding der boekdrukkunst, 1809. B. C.

" Voortgang der Boekdrukkunst, 1829. B. C.

Willett, Memoir on, 1820.

Würdtwein, Bibliot. Moguntina, 1787,

Wolff, Monumenta Typographica, 1740.

See Gutenberg; Haarlem; Coster; Strasbourg; Mayence.

ITALIAN TYPOGRAPHICAL HISTORY. Hoffman, F. L., Liste des ouvrages sur l'imprimerie en Italie, 1852.

Quirini, Liber de edit. Romæ, 1467–72.

Renouard, Annales des Aldes, 1825.

Saxius, Hist. typog. Mediol., 1465.

Tiraboschi, Storia della lett. Italiana, 1805–13.

See Bibliography.

KOSTER, L. J. *See Coster, L. J.*

LITHOGRAPHY. *See* Lithography.

LYON. *See* Bibliography.

MAYENCE. Fischer, Beschreibung typ. Seltenheiten, 1800–04.

Heineken, Idée, etc., 1771.

Laborde, Débuts de l'impr. à Mayence, 1454.

Lambinet, Recherches sur l'Origine, 1798.

Marchand, Hist. de l'Orig. de l'Impr., 1740.

Typography: MAYENCE (continued).

Willett, Orig. of Printing, 1820.

Würdtwein, Bibliot. Moguntina, 1787.

Zapf, Buckdruckergesch. von Mainz, 1790.

See Gutenberg, J.; Invention.

NUREMBERG. *See* Bibliography.

PARIS TYPOGRAPHY. Crapelet, Etudes pratiques, 1837.

Crapelet, Robert Estienne, 1839.

Dupont, Imprimerie nationale, 1854.

Greswell, Annals of Parisian Typog., 1818.

Maittaire, Historia Typ. Parisiensinm, 1717.

Petit-Radel, Bibliot. Mazarine, 1819.

See French Typog. History.

PRINTERS. National Typ. Union.

See Biographies.

SPECIMENS OF PRINTERS. Austria, Geschichte der Druckerei....1850.

Bodoni, Manuale tipog., 1818.

Bruce, G., Son & Co., N. Y., 1869.

Caslon's Specimen, 1808, (Stower).

Chicago Press, Illinois, 1859. P. 298.

Falkenstein, Typenschau von Orient., 1840.

Figgins, V. & G., Lond., 1838.

Fournier, Manuel, v. 2, 1764.

Fry, Specimen, 1787.

Luce, Essai d'une Typog., 1771.

Mappa, A. G., Epreuves, 1780.

Miller, W., & Co., Edinb., 1834.

Munsell, J., Albany, 1858.

Ploos van Amstel, Amster., 1767.

Rand & Avery, Specimen Book, Bost., 1865.

Silberman, Album Typog., 1840.

Specimen of Dutch Typog., 1760–80.

Specimen Typog. de l'imprimerie roy.

Stower, Fry and Caslon, 1808.

Tauchnitz, Proben, Leipzig, 1831.

Trow, J. F., Specimens, N. Y., 1856.

Watson, Hist. of Art of Printing, 1713.

White, Foundry, N. Y., 1819.

Wood & Sharwood, Lond. P. 470.

See Alphabets.

STEREOTYPE. Auer, A., Naturselbstdruck, 1854.

Camus, Histoire de, 1802.

Jansen, De l'Orig. de la Gravure, 1808.

Westreenen, De l'impr. stéréotype, 1833.

STRASBOURG. Laborde, Débuts de l'impri. à Strasbourg, 1840.

La Serna Santander, Dict. bibliog., 1805–07.

Lichtenberger, Initia typographica, 1811.

United States, Constitution, Government and Politics (continued).

Political Mirror, 1835.

Political text-book for 1860.

Politics for Am. Christians.

Porter, W. D., State Sovereignty, 1860.

President's Messages, 1819–50.

Puglia, The Federal Politician, 1795.

Rawlins, Amer. dis-union, 1862.

Reed, H., Lectures on the Hist. of the Union, 1856.

Réponse aux princ. questions, 1795.

Republic of North America, 1863.

Robertson, G., Lecture, K'y, 1854.

Russell, R. W., America comp. with England, 1848.

Shurtleff, Gov't Instructor, 1849.

Smith, W. L., Court of U. S. and the several States, 1832.

Spofford's Polit. Register, 1849.

Stansbury, Constit. Catechism.

Story, Joseph, Const. Class-book, 1834.

Strictures by Massachusettensis, 1792. P. 96.

Strictures upon Const. powers of Congress, 1825.

Sullivan, J., Observations on, 1791. P. 94.

Tallmadge, Speech, U. S. Sen., Enlargement of Exec. power, 1838.

Taylor, J., Inquiry into principles of, 1814.

" Tyranny unmasked, 1822.

" New Views of Constitution, 1823.

Throop, M. H., The future, 1864.

Tocqueville, Democracy in America, 1836.

Towle, Hist. and Anal. of the Constitution, 1871.

Tremenheere, H. S., The Const. comp. with that of G. B., 1854.

Trescot, Foreign Policy of, 1849.

U. States, Constitution of, 1787.

" In Dutch, Albany, 1788.

" In German, Albany, 1788.

Van Buren, M., Course of pol. parties, 1867.

Voice from America, 1839.

Wheeler, Hist. of Congress, 1848.

Whiting, War powers of the President, 1862.

Williams, E., The Statesman's manual, 1789–1858.

Winchester, E., Political Catechism, 1796.

Witherspoon, J., Miscell. Works, 1803.

Woodward, A. B., Considerations on Exec. Power, 1809.

Wylie, S. B., Sentiments in 1803 and 1832. P. 894.

United States, Constitution, Government and Politics (continued).

Yates, Proc. and Debates of Convention of 1787, 1821.

Young, A. W., Gov't Class Book, 1842.

See Suffrage; Democracy; Elections; Government; Republic; State Rights; U. S. Polit. Pamphlets.

United States, Financial and Commercial. Am. Geog. Soc., Fin. credit of, 1862.

Atkinson, E., Lect. on cotton, 1865.

" Sen. Sherman's fallacies, 1868.

Atkinson, R. J., A view of the situation, 1867.

Bannan, B., Plan for currency, 1867.

Barnes, D., Speech on finan. cond., 1868.

Benton, T. H., Speech, 1840.

Blair, A., Speech, Nat. finances, 1868.

Bollman, E., Plan of new system, 1816.

Bond, W. K., Speech, 1838.

" Speech, Treasury Notes, 1840. P. 193.

Brissot, Commerce of, 1795.

Butler, B. F., The currency question, 1867.

Carey, H. C., The finance minister, 1868.

Champion, Considerations on comm., 1784.

Clarke, R. W., Speech, H. of R., On the Currency, 1868.

Clarke, S., Speech, H. of R., On finance, 1868.

Commercial conduct of, 1786.

Considerations on the nature of a funded debt, N. Y., 1790.

Cooper, P., Letter to H. J. Redfield, 1868.

Correspondence on Loan, 1822.

Cromelien, R., Specie payments, 1867.

Dean, G., Speech, Expenditures, 1852.

Derby, E. H., Prospects of the U. S., 1868.

Elder, W., Debt and resources of, 1863.

" How our debt can be paid, 1865.

Examination.... effect of the National banks, 1863. P. 1835.

Ferris, J. A., Financial Economy of, 1867.

Financial, The, Problem, 1868. P. 1833.

Gallatin, J., Two Letters to S. P. Chase, 1861.

" Government Finances, 1862.

Garfield, J. A., Speech, on the Currency, 1868.

Gould, C., Financial Scheme for, 1862.

Henderson, J. B., Speech, U. S. Sen., 1868.

High prices, causes and remedy, 1864.

United States, Financial and Commercial (continued).

Johnson, A. B., Our Monetary Condition, 1863.

" The Advanced value of Gold, 1862.

Kelley, W. D., Speech, on contraction of the currency, 1868.

Lanier, J. F. D., Remarks at Frankfort on, 1865.

Lord, E., Theories of currency, 1864.

McCulloch, H., Our National future, 1865.

McDuffie, G., Speech, on Deposits, 1834.

Mann, A., Jr., Corresp. on Paying Bonds in Paper, 1868.

Morrell, D. J., Speech, H. of R., 1868.

Morris, R., Organ. of the Debt, 1863.

National Commer. Conv., Bost., 1868.

National, The, Finances, Six Letters, 1868.

National Loan, Appeal, 1861.

Newcomb, S., Fin. Pol. in the Rebellion, 1865.

New Views of the Currency, 1866.

Our National Finances, No. 10, 11, 13, 15, S. P. Townsend, 1865–8.

Pamphlets relating to Currency, vol., 1833.

Pamphlets relating to Finance, vols. 1834, 1835.

Pamphlets relating to Internal Revenue, vol. 1836.

Pendleton, C. H., Payment of Debt in legal tender, 1867.

Reflections on the Policy, New York, 1786.

Remarks on the Currency, 1840.

Richardson, D. M., Resuming Specie Payments, 1866.

Rockwell, J. A., Speech, 1848.

Sherman, J., Speech, Funding Bill, 1868.

Stilwell, S. M., Gold and Paper, 1866.

Stokes, C., Notes on the Stocks of, 1839.

Talleyrand, Relat. Commer. avec l'Angleterre.

Three Financial Problems, 1868.

U. S., Kennedy's Report, 1842.

Walker, R. J., Review of our Finances, 1862, 63.

Wells, D. A., Our Burden and our Strength, 1864.

" Our Finan. Credit Abroad, 1866.

Williams, C. P., Review of the Finan. Situation, 1868.

Williams, J., Letter on the U. S. Banking System, 1868.

See Banks; Currency; Financial; Retrenchment.

United States, Geography, and Gazetteers. Appleton's American Travel., 1857.

Appleton's Railway Guide, 1852–71, imp.

Bache, Tide Tables.

Bradford, T. G., Illustrated Atlas, 1842.

Brown, S. R., Western Gazetteer, 1820.

Chapin, Reference Gazetteer of, 1839.

Cobb, Am. Railway Guides, 1850, 1.

Collins, S. H., Guide to.

Colton, J. H., Western Tourist, 1845.

Cooper, T., Information respecting, 1794.

Curtiss, D. S., Western Portraiture, 1852.

Darby, West. and Southwest. Guide, 1818.

" New Gazetteer of the U. S., 1833.

Disturnell, Guide, Eastern and Middle States, 1848.

" Railway and Steamship Guide, 1849–53.

" Springs: Bathing Resorts, 1855.

" The Great Lakes, 1863.

Doggett, U. S. R. R. and Steam Nav. Guide, 1848.

Ellet, Physical Geography of, Smithson. Contr., 2, 3.

Emigrant's Guide, 1818.

Evans, L., Analysis of Map of Brit. Col., 1755.

Fisher, R. S., Complete Gaz. of the U. S., 1853.

Forry, Climatic features of U. S., Am. Jour. of Sci., 47.

Foster, J. W., Mississippi Valley, 1869.

Guide between Washington, etc.

Harper's Gazetteer of the World, 1855.

Haskel, Gazetteer of the U. S., 1843.

Hayward, J., Gazetteer of the U. S., 1853.

Hewett, Am. Traveller, or Nat. Directory, 1825.

Hinckley, Traveller's Pocket-guide, 1848–49.

Lippincott, Gazetteer of the World, 1855.

Lloyd's Steamboat Guide, 1856.

Löher, Aussichten für Deutsche in N. A., 1853.

Lorain, Hints to Emigrants, 1819.

Marcy, The Prairie Traveler, 1847.

Melish, J., Trav. Directory, 1815.

" Geog. description of, 1816.

Miller, A., New Territories, 1818.

Mitchell, S. A., Princ. Routes, 1834.

Moore, S. S., Traveller's Directory, 1802.

United States, Geography, and Gazetteers (continued).
Morse, J., American Geography, 1792.
" American Gazetteer, 1797, 1810.
New American Cyclopedia, Appleton, 1863.
Northern Traveller, 1825.
Phelps, One Hundred Cities, 1853. P. 565.
Scott, J., U. S. Gaz., 1795.
" Geog. Dict. of U. S., 1805.
Southern Business Directory, 1854.
Smith, J. C., Guide for Travellers.
Steele's Western Guide Book, 1849.
Stevens, I. N., Address, Geog. Soc., 1858.
Tanner, Am. Traveller, 1844.
" Recent Surveys, 1830.
" The Central Traveller or guide, 1844.
Thompson, Z., Guide to Lake George, Montreal, etc., 1842.
Trip through the Lakes, 1857.
Tunis, Guide, 1859.
U. S., Pacific R. R. Reports, 1854.
Vade mecum for America, 1731.
Volney, Tab. du Climat et du Sol, 1803.
" View of the Soil and Climate of, 1804.
Webster, N., Elem. of Use. Knowl., 1808, 12.
Williams, Traveller's Guide, 1851.
" Tourist's Guide, 1856.
See United States, Travels in North America; Northwest Terr.; Geography; Climate; U. S., Lands.

United States, History of. American Annual Cyclopedia, Appleton, 1861–70.
American Archives, 1774–76.
American Historical Mag., 1836, New Haven.
American Pioneer, 1842–43.
American Remembrancer, 1795.
Anderson, J. J., School History, 1869.
Bancroft, G., Hist. of the United States, from discovery to 1777. 1838–66.
Barbaroux, Résumé de l'histoire de, 1824.
Barber, J. W., History of, 1832.
" Incidents in Am. Hist., 1847.
" Hist. Poet. Amer. Scenes, 1852.
Blunt, J., Hist. of formation of, 1825.
Bradford, A., Hist. of the Fed. Gov't, 1789–1839.
Butler, F., Complete History of, to 1820.
Callender, Hist. for 1796.
Chapin's Hist. Picture Gallery, 1856.

United States, History of (continued).
Cox, S. S., Eight years in Congress, 1857–65.
Davis, E., The Half Century, 1851.
Dawson, H. B., Battles of, by Sea and Land, 1858.
Eliot, S., Manual of, 1856.
Emerson, J., Questions to Goodrich's.
Farmer, J., Collections, Historical, etc., 1822–24.
Fergus, Hist. of the United States, Lardner, 53.
Frost, J., Book of the Colonies, 1846.
Gilij, Saggio di Storia Americana, 1780–1784.
Goodrich, C., History of, 1824.
Goodrich, S. G., Pictorial Hist., 1845.
Gordon, W., Hist. of Rise and Independence of, 1788.
Grahame, Hist. of, to Independence, 1827–36.
Great Britain: America, Correspondence, 1810, 46.
Grimshaw, W., Hist. of the U. S., 1820.
Guernsey, E., Hist. of, for Schools, 1848.
Hale, S., History of, to 1837.
Hamilton, J. C., History of, 1860.
Hazard, E., Hist. Coll. of State Papers of, 1792.
Hildreth, Hist. of the U. S. A., 1840–1852.
Hinton, J. H., Hist. of the U. S., 1834.
Histor. Catechism, 1834.
Historical Magazine, N. Y., 1858–68.
History of, Keene, N. H., 1821.
History of, N. Y., 1838.
History, New and Universal, of, 1827.
Holmes, A., American Annals, 1805.
Journal...Guerre du Micissippi, 1739.
Knapp, S. L., Lib. of Amer. Hist., 1835.
Latrobe, J. H. B., Hist. of Mason and Dixon's line, 1855.
Lossing, Pict. Hist. of, for Schools, 1854.
Ludlow, J. M., History of, 1862.
McCartney, Origin and Progress of, 1847.
McCulloch, Concise Hist. of, 1797, 1807.
Macpherson, Pol. Hist. of, 1860–67.
Madison, J., Papers of, 1840.
March, Reminiscences of Congress, 1850.
Martineau, H., Hist. of Am. compromises.
Mazzei, Recherches Hist. sur, 1788.
Modern view of, Lond., 1783.
Monroe, J., On Mission to France, 1794–6.

United States, History of (continued).
Munsell's Historical Series, 1857–60.
Murray, H., Pictorial Hist. of, 1851.
" Hist. of the U. S., Edin., Cab. Lib., 35.
Neff, Army and Navy Hist., 1845.
Patton, J. H., History of, 1860.
Peabody, E. P., Chronol. Hist. of, 1856.
Pélet, Précis de l'histoire de, 1845.
Perkins, S., Hist. from 1815 to 1830.
Philippi, Geschichte der V. F., 1827.
Pitkin, T., Polit. and Civ. Hist. of, 1763–97.
Political Mirror of Jacksonism, 1835.
Pritts, J., Mirror of Olden Time, 1849.
Ramsay, Hist. to 1808.
Saffell, Records of Rev. War, 1858.
Sanford, E., History of, 1819.
Scheffer, Hist. des Etats Unis, 1825.
Sena, Hist. de los Estados, 1807.
Sherman, Government Hist., 1860.
Smith, J. J., Am. Hist. Curiosities, 1847, 60.
Trescot, Dipl. Hist., Washington and Adams, 1789–1801.
Trumbull, B., Hist. of, 1810.
Tucker, G., History of, to 1841.
U. S., France, Négociations, 1793–1800.
Victor, Hist. of Am. Conspiracies, 1863.
View of the U. S. of America. P. 752.
Walsh, R., Appeal from Great Britain, 1819.
Washington, G., Diary, 1789–91.
Webster, N., History of, 1835.
Wells, National Hand-book, 1857.
White, H., Early Hist. of New England, 1845.
Willard, E., Late Amer. Hist., 1856.
Willson, M., Hist. for Schools, 1846.
Winterbotham, Hist. View of U. S., 1795.
Winthrop, J., Hist. of New England, 1630–49.
Wood, J., Adams's Administration, 1797–1801.
Woodbury, L., Disc., Am. Hist. Soc., Wash., 1837.
Wraxall, Records of Indian Aff., 1678–1751, MS.
See Historical Societies; America; North America; Civil War, 1861–1865; French War; Mexican War; Revolut. War; War of 1812; Bibliography.

United States, Lands. Bennet, H., Speech, 1852.
Jenkins, T., Speech, 1852, Giving away.

United States, Lands (continued).
Martin, T. S., Speech, 1852.
Schoonmaker, Speech, 1852.
Snow, W. W., Speech, 1852.
Strictures on the Land....Interest, 1781.
U. S. Land-Office Reports, 1847, 56, 1865–67.

United States, Military. *See* U. S. Army.

U. S., Military Academy. *See* West Point.

United States, Mint. Annual Reports, 1859, 60, 62–68.
" Instructions on business at, 1867.
" Rules of Assay, 1868.
" Denver Mint Reports, 1863, 64.
King, J. G., Speech, Branch Mints, 1851. P. 487.
Phil'a Board of Trade, Report on.
See Numismatics.

United States, Naval Academy. Rules and Regulations, 1850, 62.
Register, 1862, 63, 67, 68.
Marshall, History of Nav. Acad., 1862.
U. S., Report on Loyalty of Officers of, 1862.

United States, Navy. Boynton, Hist. of in the Rebellion.
Brief History of....Assimilated Rank, by W. S. W. R., 1850.
Cairo, Memorial for Naval Depot.
Clark, T., Naval History of, 1814.
Cooper, J. F., History of, 1840.
Dawson, H. B., Battles by Sea and Land, 1858.
Examination of the legality....1848.
Forbes, P. S., Petition to Congress.
Goldsborough, Naval Chronicle, 1824.
Goldsborough, Reply to Attack on the Navy, 1845.
Hamersly, Biog. of Living Offi., 1870.
Houston, S., Speech, U. S. Sen., Naval Retiring Board, 1856.
Isherwood, Remarks on his Defence of Wampanoag, 1868.
Hull, I., Court of Inquiry on, 1822.
Kimball, H., Amer. Naval Battles, 1831.
Lawrence, J., Chesapeake and Shannon, 1813.
Levy, U. P., Memorial, 1855.
Lyon, C., Increase of, 1854.
Memorial of U. S. Engineers, 1864. P. 1837.
Memorial of officers for increased pay, 1866.

United States, Political Pamphlets (continued).

Thoughts upon the Pol. Situation, 1788.

Treaty Discussed, 1795.

Tullius Americus, Strictures on L. J. Brutus, 1801.

Varnum, J. B., Address, Concord, 1800.

View of the N. E. Illuminati, 1799.

Wortman, T., Address to N. Y. on Jefferson, 1800.

See Adams; Aliens; Jefferson; Washington.

1802–1816.

Adams, J., Correspondence, 1809.

Address of State Comm., Penn'a, 1808.

Address to the peo. of N. E., A. Sidney, 1809.

American Dialogues of the Dead, 1814.

American Arguments, Neutral Trade, 1806.

Answer to War in Disguise, (Morris), 1806.

Appeal to the People, (Coleman), 1810.

Atcheson, American Encroachments, 1808.

Banks, H., Truth without Guile, 1808.

Barlow, J., Two letters, 1806.

Bayard, J. A., Speech, Embargo, 1809.

Bishop, A., Proofs of a conspiracy, 1802.

Bliss, H., An Oration, 1815.

Clopton, J., Speech, Non-importation, 1806.

Colvin, J. B., Republican economy, 1802.

Conduct of Washington compared, 1813.

Corrector, No. 1, 1815; No. 2, 1816, N. Y.

Cursory sketch of the motives, 1809.

Custis, G. W., Orat. on Lingan, 1812.

Exam. of Brit. doctrine, 1800.

Examin. of the Pres'ts Message, 1802.

Fessenden, T. G., Some thoughts, 1807.

Freyheit die treue Liebe, 1809.

Foreign Relations, 1810.

Gen. Rep. Comm. of N. Y. City, Addr., 1809.

Hartford Convention, 1815.

Inquiry into Relations with France, 1811.

Jefferson, T., Inaug. Speech and Reply to N. Haven remon., 1802.

Johnson, R. M., Speech, Ky., 1815.

Lewis, R. W., Oration, 1812.

Lynn, J., Address to citizens, 1804.

M'Henry, Letter to Speaker of H. of R., 1803.

Moseley, J. O., Speech, Embargo, 1809.

Niles, H., Things as they are, 1809.

United States, Political Pamphlets (continued).

Peace without Dishonor, (Lowell), 1807.

Pickering, T., Letter, Danger of war, 1808.

Politics for farmers, 1807.

Republican crisis, 1812.

Reviewers reviewed, 1816.

Sedgwick, Oration, 1811.

Sixth of August Fest., Litchfield, Conn., 1806.

Stanley, G. W., Oration, "Corruption," 1805.

Strachan, Disc. of George III, 1810.

Things as they are, 1809.

Touchstone to the People, 1812.

Tyrant, The, Caught, 1809. P. 75.

View of the Policy of, 1810. P. 1, B. C.

Vindication of the Measures, 1803.

Webster, N., Misc. Papers, 1802.

White, W. C., Avowals of a Republican, 1813.

Worcester, S., Serm., War, 1812.

See Neutrals; War of 1812; Washington Societies.

1817–1837.

Address of tate Conv., N. Y., 1828.

Address to the People of Maryland, 1832.

American Recorder, No. I, 1832.

Binney, H., Speech, Phil'a, 1832.

Brackenridge, H. M., To the Public, 1832.

Cabinet Literature, 1830.

Crisis, The, by Brutus, 1827.

Dorsey, J. L., Address, Maryland, 1831.

Essays of Camillus, Norfolk, 1841.

Essays on the Origin of the Fed. Gov't, 1830.

Falkland, On Foote's Resolutions, 1830.

Few Hints on Monar. and Repub., 1825.

Grimshaw, W., Exposition of the... Republic, 1822.

Hallett, B. F., Oration, Palmer, MS. 1836.

History of Extra Session of Congress, 1837.

Important facts for the People, 1832.

Jarvis, W. C., The Republican, 1820.

Letter to the Hon. D. Webster, by Marcellus, 1837.

Letters from Phil'a Comm. of Corresp., 1828.

Letters on the Richmond Party, 1823.

Letters of Wyoming, 1824.

McDuffie, State Rights, 1821

United States, Political Pamphlets (continued).

Nat. Rep. Conv. of Young Men, Wash., 1832.

Nat. Rep. Conv., Worcester, 1832.

Political Balance, 1832.

Romaine, State Sovereignty, 1832.

Republican Conventions, 1825.

Scriptural View of Pol., 1826.

Storrs, H. R., Pres. Election, 1828.

Two, The, Americas, 1824.

Van Rensselaer, J. S., Address, Schenectady, 1839.

Voice from the Interior, Who President ? 1828.

Wilde, R. H., Speech, "Deposits," 1834.

Woodbee Family, Sketch of, 1823.

1837-1853.

Andover Husking, Bost., 1842.

Bacon, D. F., The Mystery of Iniquity, 1845.

" Progressive Democracy, 1844.

Bancroft, G., Address, 1840.

Botts, J. M., Speech, Newark, 1853.

Brown, A. V., Speeches, 1854.

Buel, A. W., Speech on the Union, 1851.

Campbell, L. D., Speech, U. S. H. of R., 1850.

Cass, L., Speech, Wilmot Proviso, 1847.

Constit. meeting, Boston, 1850.

Defence of the Whigs, 1844.

Democratic Conventions, 1848, 52.

Democ. Rep. Meet., N. Y. City, 1838.

Democ. Republicans opposed, 1838.

Dem. Whig Ass'n, Addr., 1839.

Facts for the Laboring Man, 1840.

Graham, S., Letter to Webster on Compromises, 1850.

Green, W., Addr., Clay Club, Alexandria, 1845.

Harrison, W. H., Why Elect ?

Identity of Federalists with Whigs, 1840.

Jackson, W., Essay on rights of gov't, 1846.

Junius Tracts, (Colton), 1844.

Kurtze Geschichte der politische Parteien, 1850.

Leisler, J., Letters to Penn'a, 1850.

Loco-focoism Displayed, 1844.

Lowndes, Letters to Calhoun, 1843.

National Free Soil Conv., Buffalo, 1848.

Native American State Conv., Proc., 1845.

Northern States, Their Peril, 1850.

Peck, J. M., Prin. of Democracy, 1839.

United States, Political Pamphlets (continued).

Pictures of the Times, 1840.

Platforms, The, 1852.

Pumroy, J. N., Defence of our Naturalization Laws, 1845.

Religious Lib. in Danger, 1844.

Riell, H. E., Appeal to Voluntary Citizens, 1840.

Secret History of....Tyler Dynasty, 1845.

Smith, J., Mr. Van Buren's Letter, 1841.

Spencer, J. C., Corresp. with, 1842.

Stephens, Speech, Rights of Members, 1844.

Union Meet., N. Haven, Proc., 1850.

Utica Convention, Proc., 1848.

Venable, Speech, Internal Improvements, 1848.

Washington, Meet. of Opponents, 1840.

Whig Charge of Intolerance, 1852.

Whig Congr. Committee, 1844.

Whig Text-book, 1844.

Whig Nat. Convention, 1848.

Whig State Conventions, 1846, 48.

White, J. L., Speech, 1843.

Wilson, J. P., Serm., Perpetuity of the Union, 1851.

Winthrop, R. C., Vote on the War Bill, 1846.

Words of Counsel, 1850.

Yeadon, R., Speech, Charleston, S. C., 1844.

See Compromise; California; Missouri; American Party.

1854-1868.

Address, Democratic, 1854.

American Destiny, 1864.

Appleton, N., Letter on Slavery and Union, 1860.

Austin, R. F., Buchananism, 1858.

Barstow, B., Letter to Buchanan, 1857.

Bell, J., Relations with G. Brit., 1856.

Benton, T. H., Dred Scott Case.

Blair, M., Speech, Balt., 1860.

Bradford, S. D., Works.

Brooks, E., Speech, 1856.

Brown, A. V., Addr. on the Parties, 1856.

Browne, C., The U. S. Power and Constitution, Lond., 1856.

Buck, E., The Drift of the War.

Cairnes, J. E., The Revol. in America, 1862.

Cameron, S., Address, Phil'a, 1859.

Campaign of 1860.

Carey, H. C., Letters to the President, 1858.

Coggeshall, W. T., Address, Ohio, 1860.

United States, Political Pamphlets (continued).

Common Sense, Nashville, 1860.

Cosmopolitan Ideas on the Union, 1859.

Cowdin, E. C., The Presidential Issue, 1868.

Crosby, A., Pres. Posit. of the Seceded States, 1865.

Curtis, G. T., Suprem. of Congr. over the Territ., 1859.

Democratic Conventions, 1854, 56.

Democ. Conv., Montgomery, 1860.

Democ. State Cent. Comm., N. Y., Addr., 1859.

Disunion Convention, 1857.

Dix, W. G., The Presidency, 1856.

Dorr, J. A., Justice to the South, 1856.

Dougherty, D., The Peril of the Republic, 1863.

Eighteen Hundred and Sixty Assocn., Tracts.

Eighteenth Ward, N. Y., Repub. Fest., Speeches, 1860.

End of the Irrepr. Conflict, 1860.

Exhibition of Wolves, 1856.

Facts for the People, 1855.

Fast Day Sermons, 1861.

Goodloe, D. R., Federalism unmasked, 1860.

Gordon, G. W., On Bates for Pres't, 1860.

Halstead, Caucuses of 1860.

Hambleton, Review of the Parties, 1856.

Henry, C. S., Reasons for the Repub. Move., 1856.

Howe, J., Speech, Recruiting, 1856.

Hunt, E. B., Amer. Nationality.

Hunt, W., Speech, N. Y., 1859.

Impending crisis, No. 1, 2, 1862.

Infidelity and Abolitionism, 1856.

Kroeger, A. E., Our form of government, 1860.

Laboulaye, E., The U. S. and France, 1862.

Lee, F. A., Speech, Cooperstown, N. Y., 1856.

Letter to Americans, 1859.

Lewis, Tayler, Heroic periods of a Nation's Hist., 1866.

Lincoln, A., Debate with Douglas, 1858.

" Speech, 1858, 1860.

Loyal National League, Proc., 1863.

Maclay, W. B., Selection of letters, 1859.

Macon, N., Letters to O'Connor, 1862.

Mason, J. Y., Addr. Univ. of N. Carolina.

Moody, L., The destruction of Republicanism, 1863.

" Plain statement to Democrats, 1868.

United States, Political Pamphlets (continued).

Nott, B., Constitutional ethics, 1857.

" Remedy for the irrepr. conflict, 1860.

Pamphlets, Presid. elect., 1856, vol. 537.

Pamphlets, Politics, 1860–68, vol. 1838.

Parsons, T., The Constitution, 1861.

Pelletan, E., Address to King Cotton, 1863.

Plain facts.. in favor of J. Buchanan, 1856.

Plumb, D., Citizenship and suffrage, 1868.

Popular Sovereignty: reviewed, 1859.

Porter, W. D., State Sovereignty, 1860.

Presid. Platforms, 1856.

Pruyn, J. V. L., Remarks, H. of R. Gov't of the South. States, 1868.

Radical reconstruction, Sacram., 1867.

Recruiting in 1856.

Reed, W. B., Speech, Somerset, 1856.

Reeder, A. H., Speech, 1856.

Remarks on Popular Sovereignty, 1859.

Reminiscences.... 1856.

Reply to Prof. Hodge on the state of country, 1861.

Repub. Documents, 1859.

Repub. Nat. Conv., Proc., 1856.

Rise and progr. of outbreak, Harper's Ferry, 1859.

Scroggs, G. A., *et al.*, Speeches, 1860.

Seward, W. H., Speeches, 1860.

Shaffer, Letter, 1856.

Squatter Sovereignty, 1858.

South, The, a letter, 1856.

South alone should govern the South, 1860.

States against Territories, 1860.

Stephens, A. H., Speech against Secession.

Stringham, Address, 1856.

Union, The, Helper condemned, 1859.

Union as it was, Const. as it is, 1862.

Union Meet., Phil'a, Proc., 1859.

Walker, R. J., Appel, Lettre, 1856.

Yancey, W. L., Speech, Syracuse, 1860.

Washington Despotism Dissected, 1863.

Weller, *et al.*, Speeches, 1856.

Wilson, H., Speech, Repub. Party, 1856.

See Homestead Bills; Fremont; Slavery; Kansas; Civil War of 1861–1865; U. S. Constitution; Government.

United States, Railroads. *See* Railroads.

United States, Reconstruction. Pamphlets, vol., 1839: Speeches, etc., 1865–68.

United States, Travels South (continued).
Berquin-Duvallon, Tr. in Louisiana and the Floridas, 1806.
Buckingham, J. S., Slave States, 1842.
Coxe, Descr. of Carolana and Louisiana.
Day, Down South, 1862.
Featherstonhaugh, Excur. through Slave States, 1844.
Gilman, C., Recollections, 1838.
Ingraham, J. W., The Southwest, 1835.
Kirke, Among the Pines, 1862.
" My Southern friends.
Knight, Letters from South and West, 1824.
Lanman, Letters from the Alleganys, 1849.
Lilly, Early Hist. of Southern States, 1852.
Mackie, J. M., To Dixie and the tropics, 1864.
Milburn, Pioneers of Mississippi, 1860.
Olmsted, Our Slave States, 1856, 60.
" Seaboard Slave States, 1856.
" The Cotton Kingdom, 1861.
Paulding, J. K., Letters from the South, 1816.
Royall, Anne, Travels, 1826–30.
Tasistro, Random Shots, 1847.
Willis, N. P., Health trip, 1853.
See Slavery.

United States, Travels West. Ashe, Travels in America, 1806.
Atwater, C., Tour to Prairie du Chien, 1829.
Baxley, What I saw on the West coast, 1865.
Beste, The Wabash, 1855.
Birkbeck, M., Notes, 1818, 22.
Bowles, S., Across the Continent, 1865.
" Our new West, 1869.
Brackenridge, Voy. on the Missouri, 1816.
" Recoll. of persons and places, 1834.
Bradbury, J., Travels in the interior, 1809–11.
Bradford, W. J. A., Notes on the Northwest, 1846.
Brown, S. R., Western Gazetteer, 1820.
Burnet, J., Settlement of N. W. Territory, 1847.
Burton, Rocky Mountains and California, 1862.
Caird, Prairie Farming, 1859.
Carleton, R., The New Purchase, 1843.
Carver, J., Travels, 1766–68.
Coffin, C. C., Seat of Empire, 1870.
Colton, Western Guide, 1850,
Colton, C., Tour of the Lakes, 1830.
Conclin's River Guide, 1852.

United States, Travels West (cont'd).
Cuming, Tour in Ohio, Ky., etc., 1810.
Cumings, Western Pilot, 1825.
Dana, E., Geog. Sketches; Western States, 1819.
Darby, W., Emigrant's Guide, 1818.
Decalves, New Travels, 1796.
Domenech, Seven Years in Deserts, 1860.
Duden, Reise nach den Westlichen Staaten, 1824–27.
Ellet, Mrs., Summer Rambles.
Ellis, New Britain, Plain of the Missouri, 1820.
Evans, E., Pedestrian Tour, 1818.
Farnham, Life in Prairie Land, 1846.
Ferris, States of the Great West, 1856.
Finley, J. B., Autobiography: Pioneer Life, 1853.
Flagg, The Far West, 1838.
Flint, J., Letters from America, 1822.
Flint, T., Ten Years in Mississ. Valley, 1826.
" Geog. of the Western States, 1828.
Greeley, H., Overland Journey, 1859.
Hall, B. F., Hist. of the North Western Terr., 1849.
Hall, B. R., The New Purchase, 1855.
Hall, J., Letters from the West, 1828.
" The West, its Comm. and Product, 1848.
" Notes on the Western States, 1838.
" Sketches of the West, 1836.
Harris, T. M., Tour to the Northwest Territory, 1805.
Haswell, Phelps, Voyage to the Mississippi, 1773.
Hart, A. M., Hist. of Valley of the Mississippi, 1853.
Hawley, Tour from Mass. to Ohio, 1822.
Heart, The Western Country, 1792.
Hildreth, S. P., Pioneer History, 1848.
" Biog. of Early Settlers, 1852.
" Early History of, 1864.
Hoffman, C. F., A Winter in the West, 1835.
Houstoun, M. C. H., Hesperos, or Travels in the West, 1850.
Imlay, Topog. Descr. of West. Terr., 1792.
Keating, Expedition under Long, 1823.
Ker, H., Travels in the West, 1808–1816.
Kinzie, Early Days in the North West, 1856.
Kip, L., Army Life on the Pacific, 1858
Kirkland, Mrs., A New Home, Who'll follow? 1840. B. C.

United States, Travels West (cont'd).
Lanman, C., Summer in the Wilderness, 1847.
" Haw-ho-noo, 1850.
Lederer, Marches to the West of Carolina, 1669.
Lyford, Western Address Directory, 1837.
M'Call, Letters from the Frontiers, 1868.
McClung, Western Adventure, 1755–94.
Marcy, R. B., Army Life on the Border, 1866.
" Border Reminiscences, 1872.
Michaux, Voy. à l'ouest des Alleghanys, 1804.
Milburn, Rifle, Axe, etc., 1857.
Mills, S. J., Miss. Tour West of the Alleghanys, 1815.
Möllhausen, Diary to the Pacific, 1858.
Mullan, Capt. J., Mil. Road from Walhalla, 1863.
Nicollet, Report, Basin of Upper Mississippi, 1843.
Ogden, Letters from West, 1823.
Olmsted, F. L., Our Slave States, 1856, 1860.
Pagès, Travels, 1767–71.
Pamphlets relating to the West, Vol., 1840.
Parkman, F., Discov. of Great West, 1869.
Parkman, F., Jr., Prairie Life, 1852.
Peck, J. M., Guide for Emigrants, 1831, 37.
Perkins, J. H., Writings, 1851.
" Annals of the West, 1850.
Perrin-du-Lac, Travels, 1807.
Peyton, Over the Alleghanies, 1869
Pike, Z. M., Exp. to Sources of the Mississippi, 1805–07.
Pritts, J., Mirror of olden time, 1849.
Raynolds, Yellow-Stone River, 1868.
Richardson, A. D., Beyond the Mississippi, 1867.
Ruxton, Life in the Far West, 1849.
Sargent, G. B., Lecture on, 1858.
Schoolcraft, Trav. in the Mississippi Valley, 1825.
Smet, Voy. aux Montagnes Rocheuses, 1858.
" Western Missions, 1863.
" New Indian sketches, 1863.
Smith, T. M., Early settlement, 1855.
Steele, Mrs., Journey in the West, 1841.
Steele's Western Guide-book, 1836.
Strickland, W. P., Pioneers of the West, 1856.
Thomas, D., Travels in the West, 1816.
Thorpe, T. B., Mysteries of the Backwoods, 1846.
Topog. Descr. of Ohio, etc., (Cutler), 1812.
U. S., Pacific R. R. Reports, 1853–4.
Western Travellers'.....Guide, 1836.
Winthrop, T., Canoe and Saddle, 1863.
See Canada; North America; Mississippi River; Rocky Mts.; Oregon; United States Guides; North West Terr.

United States, Wars. Thomson, J. L., Hist. of the Wars of, 1854.
" Thrilling incidents in, 1848.
See Civil War, 1861–5; French War; Mexican War; Revolutionary War; War of 1812.

Universalism. Balfour, Doctrine on Satan, 1827. B. C.
Balfour's opinion of the devil.
Ballou, H., Dedica. Sermon, 1817.
" The Universalist pulpit, 1851.
" On the Atonement, 1805.
" Hist. of anct. Univ.
Ballou, H., 2d, Phraseology of the Jews on future state, 1844.
Bernard, D., Universalism weighed, 1853.
Blain, J., Death not Life, 1854. P. 630.
Boston Assoc'n Home Missionary Soc., Report, 1850. P. 524.
Braman, M. P., Discuss. with T. Whittemore, 1833.
Browne, J., Essay on Univ. Redemp., 1798.
Chapin, E. H., Serm., Install. of H. Bacon, 1842.
" What it is. P. 558.
Christian Messenger, N. Y., 1832–35.
Devol, Anti-Universalism, 1843. P. 267.
Emmons, On gen. judgment, 1791.
Empie, A., On Universalism, 1825. P. 65.
Foster, John, Letters on Future Punishment, 1849. P. 96.
Fuller, A., Letters on, 1802.
Gospel Herald, N. Y., 1821–26.
Hopkins, S., Future State of Sinners, 1783.
Hudson, C. F., Is evil eternal? 1859.
Huntingdon, Advoc. for devils, 1794.
Johnson, Rev. S., Everlasting punishment, 1786.
Kneeland, A., Lectures, 1824.
Layman's Letter, 1752.
Lee, L., Universalism examined, 1836.
Loveland, S. C., Corresp. with J. Laberee, 1818.
McClure, A. W., Lectures on.
Maurice, F. D., Theological Essays, 1853.

University Education (continued).
Hoyt. Add., Univ. Progress, 1870.
Hughes, T., Tom Brown at Oxford.
Inglis, R. H., Speeches, 1850, 53.
Inquiry into the Right of Appeal at Cambridge, 1751. P. 1574.
Jebb, J., Ed. Univ. of Cambr., 1774.
King's College, London. P. 156.
Knox, V., Liberal Education, 1789.
Krauth, Address, Penn'a College, 1834. P. 286.
Le Roy, Univ. de Liège, 1869.
Letter to the Rt. Hon. Sir R. Peel, 1828. P. 386.
Lindsley, P., Speech, Univ. Nashville.
London Univ. Calendar, 1868.
Louvain, Université de, Annuaire, 1863, 1864.
Malden, H., Study of Greek and Latin, 1831.
Marriott, C., Letter to Gladstone, Oxford, 1854.
Memorial on National University, 1852.
Miller, Present state of Camb., 1710.
Monk, Vindic. of Cambridge, 1818.
Newland, H., Thoughts on Lond. University, 1828.
Newman, J. H., Office of Univ., 1856.
" Discourse, 1852.
Oxford Commission, 1852.
Oxford Univ. Calendar, 1868.
Pamphlets relating to University Education, vols. 386, 1023, 1318, 1574.
Paris, Guide, 1867, Morin.
Pearson, G., Of abrogating religious tests, 1834.
Philograntus, Exam. at Cambridge.
Pillan, J., Three lectures on method, 1836.
Powell, Dissenters at Oxford, 1834. P. 1104.
Pratt, D. J., Statist. of Colleg. ed., Univ. Conv., Proc., 1866.
Pruyn, J. V. L., Volun. endowments for Colleges, Univ. Conv., 1867.
Pycroft, Guide for University honors, 1842.
Queen's College, Birmingham, 1851-52. P. 156.
Raumer, German Univ., 1859.
Remarks on the actual state of Camb., 1830.
Remarks on the prop. reform at Cambridge, 1855.
Remarks on the Rev. Dr. P.'s Sermon, 1758.
Rendu, Code Universitaire, 1846.
Reply to the....Edinb. Rev., 1810. P. 386.
Row, C. A., Letter on Univ. reform, 1850.

University Education (continued).
Sedgwick, A., Studies of the Univ.
Shoveller, Scholastic Educ., 1824.
Some account of Durham Coll., 1840. P. 386.
Tappan, H. P., University Education, 1851.
" Address, Mich. Univ., 1855.
Terræ filius, 1726.
Universitas Regia Fred., 1849, 52.
Univ. of Albany, Circular, 1852. P. 73.
" Speeches, 1852. P. 70.
" Memorial on National Univ., 1852. P. 173.
Univ. of London, Regul. for Degrees, 1839. P. 1574.
Univ. of Maryland, Memorial, 1830.
University of Sydney, N. S. W., 1851.
Venable, Address, 1859.
Yale College, Sci. School, Appeal for, 1856. P. 251.
Wagenseil, Priv. Univ. Altdorf., 1623.
Waterland, Advice to a Student, 1760. P. 387.
Wayland, Present Collegiate System, 1842.
Whewell, Of a Liberal Education, 1845.
" Eng. Univ. Education, 1838.
Wiseman, Card., Sermon on, 1852.
Wordsworth, C., Eccles. Commission, 1837.
Wratislaw, On the Cambridge System, 1850. P. 386.
See Education; Theological Education; Examinations; Cambridge; Oxford; Edinburgh.

University of Michigan. Catalogues, 1843-49, 1856-66.
Haven, E. O., Inaugural Address, 1863.
Tappan, H. P., Report, 1853.

University of N. Y. City. Anthon, Greek Professorship, 1851.
Hist. of Controversy in, 1838. P. 73.
Inaug. of H. Crosby, 1870.
Univ. of N. Y., Catalogues, etc., 1839-1871.
Vethake, Resignations, 1833.

University of Penn'a. Catalogues, 1845, 49, 51, 53, 54, 55, 57, 58, 1864, 66.
General Cat., 1849.
Bell's Memorial on Med. Ed., 1850.
Nicklin's Report on Oxford and Camb., 1834.
Philo. Math. Soc., Rep. on Rosetta Stone, 1856.
Wood, G. B., Hist. of, 1834.

University of Rochester, N. Y. Catalogues, etc., 1850-70.

V.

Vaudois. *See* Albigenses; Waldenses; Piedmont.

Vaughan, R. A. Memoir of, 1864.

Vaughan, W. Memoir of, 1839.

Vaux, Richard. Sketch of, Democ. Rev., 1847.

Vaux, Roberts. Pettit, Memoir of. Hist. Soc., Penn'a.

Vega, L. T. De. Holland, Lord, Account of, 1806.

Vegetarianism. Gleizès, Thalysie, 1840, 1842.
- Graham, S., Lectures.
- Graham Journal of health, 1837, 8.
- Health Almanac, 1842.
- Horsford, E. N., Value of. P. 210.
- Moncrieff, On the stomach, 1856.
- Plutarch, On eating of flesh. Morals, 1871.
- *See* Food; Health.

Vegetation. *See* Botany; Physiology, vegetable.

Veitch, W. Memoir of; autobiog., 1825.

Vellum. *See* Parchment.

Vendee, La, France. La Rochejaquelein, Memoirs.

Venezuela. Biggs, Miranda's revolution.
- Chesterton, Narrative, 1819, 20.
- Depons, Voy. to Terra Ferma, 1801–4.
- Giliij, F. S., Saggio di storia Americana, 1784.
- Hackett, Expéd., 1817, pour joindre les patriotes de.
- Hawkshaw, Residence in, 1838.
- Hippisley, Exped. to the Orinoco, 1817
- Lavaysse, Voyage de, 1813.
- Michelana, Exploracion....del Amazones, 1859.
- Paez, R., Wild scenes in, 1862.
- Recollections of a Service, 1828.
- Robinson, J. H., Expedition up the Orinoco, 1822.
- Venezuela, Constitution, 1817.
- " Official Docts., 1812.
- *See* New Granada; Guiana; Orinoco.

Venice. Bembo, Storia Vinitiana, 1522.
- Collezzione di carte pubb., 1806, 7.
- Combi, Guerra de Selim a', 1645.
- Contarini, Della repubblica, 1591.
- Daru, Hist. de la république, 1821.
- France: Docts. inéd., Relations des ambass. Vénitiens, 1500–1600.
- Flagg, E., History of, 1797–1849.
- Gratarol, P. A., Narr. apologetica, 1797.
- Gr. Brit., Calend. of State Pap. of MSS. at Venice, 1202–1509.

Venice (continued).
- Hazlitt, History of, 1860.
- Hist. de la Rév. de la république de, 1807.
- Howell, J., Survey of the signorie of, 1651.
- Howells, Venetian life, 1867.
- Hull, Select letters, 1764.
- Mauroceni, Hist. Veneta, 1521–1615.
- Memoria della Repubblica di, 1798.
- Raccolta cron., 1799.
- Raccolta di carte, 1797, 98.
- Raccolta (Nuova) di leggi, 1799.
- Ruskin, Stones of Venice.
- Saint Réal, Espagnols contre, 1781.
- Sanuto, M., Itinerario per Terra Firma, 1483, 1847.
- Sketches from Venetian Hist., 1832. B. C.
- Soravia, Le Chiese de Venezia, 1822.
- Vacani, Laguna di Venezia, e dei Fiumi, 1867.
- *See* Italy; Austria.

Ventilation. Am. Acad. of Arts, Report, 1848. P. 501.
- Amer. Calorifere Comp. Patent Stoves, 1854. P. 1805.
- Beck, Van, Beschrijving, etc., 1833.
- Bell, L. V., Method of ventilating buildings, 1848.
- Bernan, Hist. and Art of warming and, 1845.
- Boston, Report on school-houses, 1855-1857.
- Culver's Ventilators, 1856. P. 298.
- Gouge, H., A new system of, 1866.
- Griscom, Uses and abuses of air, 1850.
- Hadfield, T. J., Construction of fire-places, 1833.
- Heat and ventilation, 1851. P. 990.
- How to subdue smoke.
- Inman, Ventilation, warming, etc., 1836.
- Kelland, Laws of Conduction of heat, 1841.
- Kirkbride, Heating and Ventilating hospitals, 1850. P. 64.
- Jebb, Ventilation of prisons, 1844.
- La Cambre, Le Système à Paris, 1845.
- " Divers Systèmes de.
- Leeds, Lectures on, 1867.
- Pamphlets relating to, vol. 1865.
- Péclet, Traité de la Chaleur, etc., 1843.
- " Nouveaux Docts. rel. à la, 1853.
- " The same, 3e éd., 1860, 61.
- " Assainissement des Ecoles, 1846. P. 278.
- Reid, D. B., Illustrations of the Theory, 1844.
- " Vent. in Amer. Dwellings, 1858.

Virginia (continued).

Davis, J., First Settlers of, 1806.

Declaration of State of, 1620.

De Hass, Settlement and Wars of Western Va, 1851.

De La Warre, Relation, 1611.

Doddridge, Notes on, (Kercheval).

Exiles in Virginia, 1777, Gilpin, 1848.

Fisher, Alcinda Gold mine, 1839. P. 92.

Foote, W. H., Sketches of, 1850, 55.

Force's Tracts, Bacon's rebellion.

Grigsby, Convention of 1776.

Hakluyt, Virginia richly valued, 1609.

Hamor, R., True Discourse of, 1615.

" Reprint, 1861.

Harriot, De commodis incolarum, 1590.

Harrison, J. B., Letters in, 1828.

Hartlib, Va. Silk worm, 1695.

Hartwell, Present state of, 1727.

Hawks, Contrib. to Eccl. Hist. of, 1836.

Hist. Docts. of Old Dominion, 1776. Lewis's Orderly book.

Hopkins, S., Youth of the Old Dominion, 1856. Fict.

Howe, H., Historical Coll. of, 1845.

Howison, R. R., History of, 1846–48.

Hunter, R. M. T., Obs. on the Hist. of, 1855.

Hutchins, T., Topog. Descr. of Va., Penn., Md, etc., 1788.

Jefferson, T., Notes on, 1782, 87, 94, 1801.

" Observations sur la, 1786.

Jones, H., Present state of, 1724.

Joynes, T. R., Speech, Basis of represensation, 1829.

Keith, Sir W., Hist. of Brit. Plantations, 1738

Kercheval, Hist. of Valley of, 1833, 50.

Le Page du Pratz, Louisiana, or Western Va., 1763.

Letters descr. Virginia Springs, 1837.

Martin, J., Gazetteer of, 1835.

Mass., Message on Resolutions, 1844.

Meade, W., Old Churches.... Families of, 1857.

Mordecai, Virginia in by-gone days, 1860.

Neill, E. D., Hist. of Va. company, 1869.

" Engl. Coloniz. of America, 1871.

New Life of Virginea, 1612.

Norwood, Voyage to, 1649.

Nova Britannia, 1609. Force, 1.

Old Dominion Soc., Celeb., 1860.

Pamphlets relating to, vols. 1215, 1841.

Peirpoint, Gov., Letter, abuse of mil. power in, 1864.

Perfect Descr. of, 1649.

Plain facts: Rights of Indians, 1781.

Virginia (continued).

Pritts, Mirror of Olden Time, 1849.

Reformed V'a Silk Worm, 1655.

Reply, Case of Tobacco planters, 1733.

Riparian rights on the Potomac, 1859.

Robertson's Hist. of America.

Rosier, Voy. of Waymouth, 1605.

Rouelle, Treatise on Va. Min. waters, 1792.

Secret, The, out, or the reason why, 1857.

Semple, Hist. of Baptists in, 1810.

Short acco nt of, 1735.

Shrigley, True relation, 1699.

Smith, J., Travels, 1627.

" True relation of, Repr., 1866.

Stith, Discovery and Settlement of, 1747.

Strachey, Hist. of Travaile into, 1849.

" Laws Divine, 1612.

Summers, G. W., Anniv. of Settlement of Jamestown, 1860.

Taylor, J. B., Lives of Va. Bap. Min., 1838.

Thornton, J. W., First records, 1859.

Upshur, Speech, On Representation, 1829.

View of the Conduct of the Executive, 1825. P. 1841.

Views of the Constitution of, 1850.

Virginia, Proc. First Assem., 1619. N. Y. Hist. Soc. Coll., 1857.

" Case of the Planters of Tobacco, 1733.

" Vindic. of the Representation, 1733.

" Resolutions, 1799.

" Address of the Majority, 1799.

" Address of the Minority, 1799.

" Geological Survey, 1836–41.

" Population, 1840–46.

" Governor's Message, 1866.

Virginia, True Declaration, 1610. Force's tracts, 3.

Virginia and Maryland, 1655. Force's tracts, 2.

Virginia's Cure, 1662. Force's tracts, 3.

Virginia Almanack, 1802, 3, 1811–56, imp.

Virginia Directory, 1853, 1871–2.

Virginia Historical Register, (Maxwell), 1848–53.

Virginia Repository, 1802.

Virginia Richly Valued, 1609.

Whitmore, W. H., Cavalier dismounted, 1864.

Williams, E., Va. truly valued, 1650.

Wingfield, E. M., A Discourse of, Repr., 1860.

Voyages, Antarctic. Cook, J., 2d voyage, 1772–75.
Fanning's Voyages, 1792–32.
Ross, J. C., Voyage, 1839–43.
Weddell, Voy. to South Pole, 1822.
Wilkes, C., U. S. Explor. Exp., 1851.
Wilkins, P., Life of.

Voyages, Arctic. Arctic Regions, Grinnell search. P. vol. 500.
Arctic Rewards, 1856.
Back, Arctic Land Expedition, 1833–35.
Barrington, Possib. of approaching the Pole, 1843.
Barrow, Sir J., Chron. Hist. of, 1818.
" Voy. to, to present time, 1846.
Beechey, Voy. towards the North Pole, 1843.
Belcher, E., Last Voyage, 1852–54.
Bellot, Journal, 1855.
Burney, N. E. Voy. of Russians, 1819.
Button, T., Of a N. W. Passage, 1612. Bibliog. Misc.
Coxe, Russ. Discov. between Asia and Amer., 1780.
Davis, J., Voyages, 1585–87, (Hakluyt).
De Peyster, Dutch at the North Pole.
Digges, Sir D., Of the N. E. Passage, 1611. Bibliog. Misc.
Dufferin, Voy. to Iceland, Jan Mayen, Spitzbergen, 1859.
Edmond, C., Voyage, 1857.
Ellis, H., Voyage, for N W. Passage, 1747.
Fisher, A., Voy. of Disc. to, 1818.
Force, P., Remarks on English maps of, 1850, 51.
" Supp. to Grinnell Land, 1853.
Forster, J. R., Hist. of Voy. to the North, 1786.
Foxe, L., Nort-hwest Passage, 1635.
Franklin, Sir J., Exped. to the Polar Sea, 1822 and 1827.
Frobisher, Voy., Disc. of N. W. Passage, Pinkerton, 12.
" The same, Latin and French, 1577–78, 1675.
" True report, 1577.
Gatonbe, Voy. for N. W. Passage, Churchill, 2.
Goodsir, Voy. in Search of Sir J. Franklin, 1850.
Gr. Brit., Parl. Papers, Arctic Exped., 1834–52.
Hall, C. F., Arctic researches, 1860–62.
Hamel, J., Early Engl. Voy. to N. Russia, 1857.
Hayes, I. I., Arctic boat journey, 1854.
" Open Polar Sea, 1867.
Inglefield, Search for Sir J. F., 1853.

Voyages, Arctic (continued).
James, T., Strange and Dangerous voyage of, 1633.
Kane, E. K., The U. S Grinnell Expedition, 1853.
" Arctic Explorations, 1856.
Kennedy, W., Voy. of the Prince Albert, 1853.
King, R., Journey under Capt. Back, 1836.
Kotzebue, Voy. to Beering's Straits, 1815–18.
La Martinière, Voyage, 1676.
Lamont, Seasons with the Sea-horses, 1861.
La Poix de Fréminville, Voyage, 1819.
Leslie, Prof., Discov. in Polar Seas, 1831. B. C.
Letter to J. Barrow, on Polar Exped., 1819.
Letter from a Russian Officer, 1754.
Lyon, Capt., Journal of Disc. under Parry, 1824.
" Voy. in the Griper, 1825.
McClintock, Voyage of the Fox. 1860.
M'Clure, R., Voyage of Investigator, 1853–4.
M'Cormick, Wellington Channel, 1852.
M'Dougall, Voy. of Resolute, 1852–54.
Mackenzie, A., Voyage to the Frozen Ocean, 1789, 93.
Maupertuis, Journey to Polar Circle, Pinkerton, 1.
Middleton, C., Answer to Dobbs, 1743.
Müller, G. P., Découvertes des Russes, 1766.
Müller, S., Summary of Russ. N. E. Voy., 1761.
Murray, Disc. in Polar regions, (Edin. Cab. Lib.).
Noble, L. L, After icebergs, 1861.
O'Reilly, Greenland illust., 1818.
Osborn, S., An Arctic Journal, 1852.
" McClure's Discovery, 1856.
" Fate of Franklin, 1860.
Pagès, Voyages, 1767–76.
Parry, Voyages, 1st, 2d, 3d, 4th, 1819–1827.
Petermann, Search for Franklin, 1852.
Phipps, C. J., Voy. towards the North Pole, 1773.
Rae, J., Narrative of exped., 1846–47.
Richardson, Sir J., Arctic Searching Exp., 1851.
Ross, Sir J., Voyages, 1825–33.
" Explan. of Sabine's remarks, 1819.
Rundall, T., Narr. of Voyages to N. W., 1496–1831.
Sabine, J., Remarks on Ross's Voy. to Baffin's Bay, 1819.

Voyages, Arctic (continued).
Sargent, E., Arctic Adventure, 1857.
Sauer, Geog. and Astron. Exp. of Billings to Russia, 1785–94.
Seemann, B., Voy., Herald, 1845–51.
Scoresby, The Franklin Expedition, 1850.
Simpson, T., Narr. of Disc. by Hudson's Bay Co., 1836–39.
Snow, W. P., Voy. of the Prince Albert, 1853.
Sonntag, Grinnell Exped. of Kane.
Sutherland, Voy. in Baffin's Bay and Davis's Str., 1852–54.
Veer, G., Descr. of Three Voyages, 1594–96.
Weld, R., Arctic expeditions, a lect., 1850.
White, W., Prob. fate of Franklin, 1852.
Wrangell, F. Von, Voy. to Polar Sea, 1820–23, with Sabine's additions.
See Arctic Travels; Hudson's Bay; Greenland; Russia; Spitzbergen.

Voyages Around the World. Adventure and Beagle, Voy., 1826–36.
Anson, G., Voyage, 1740–44.
Arago, J., Voy. under Freycinet, 1817–1820.
Banks, Sir J., Voyage autour, etc., 1768–71.
Belcher, E., Voy. in Ship Sulphur, 1840–41.
Bennett, F. D., Whaling Voyage, 1833–6.
Betagh, Voy., 1719.
Bougainville, Baron, Jour. de la frégate Thétis, 1824.
Bougainville, L. de, Voy., 1766–69.
Byron, J., Voyage, 1769.
Campbell, A., Voy., 1806–1812.
Careri, Voyage du tour du monde, 1719.
Carteret, Philip, Kerr, vol. 12.
Cavendish, Sir T., Voy., 1599, in Lat., in Bry; Eng., in Harris, Kerr.
Circumnavigation and Prog. of discov., Edin. Cab. Lib., 21.
Clipperton, J., Kerr, vol. 10.
Cook, J., Voy., 1772–75.
Cooke, E., Voy., 1708–11.
Dampier, New Voyage around, 1699.
Dixon, Voy., 1785–88.
Drake, Sir F., The World Encompassed, 1653, 1854.
" Descrip. trium itinerum, Bry, 8.
" His Voyage, 1595. Hakluyt Soc.
" Revived, 1652.
Fanning, E., Voyages around, 1792–1832.

Voyages Around the World (cont'd).
Forster, J. R., Obs. in a Voy. around with Cook, 1778.
" Observ. faites pendant.
Forster, G., Voy. with Capt. Cook, 1777.
Funnell, W., Voy. round the World, 1703.
Hacke, Cowley's Voyage, 1699.
Heremite, Journael van de Nassausche Vloot, 1623–26.
Kotzebue, Voyage, 1823–26.
Krusenstern, Voyage, 1804–6.
La Barbinais, Voy. autour du Monde, 1728, 29.
La Pérouse, Voy. autour, 1785–88.
" Voy. around, Lond.
La Place, Circumnav. de l'Artémise, 1837–40.
Le Gentil, Voyage autour du Monde, 1725.
Lisiansky, Voy., 1803–6.
Marchand, E., Voyage en 1790–92.
Noort, O. van, Beschryvinghe van de voyagie, etc., 1598–1601.
" Descr. peric. navigationis, Bry.
Pagès, Voyages, 1767–76.
Pfeiffer, A Lady's Voy. around, 1852.
Philips, J., Voy. of Anson, 1744.
Pigafetta, Premier Voyage, 1519–22.
Portlock, Voyage, 1785–88.
Read, G. C., Narrative, 1840.
Reynolds, J. N., Voyage of Potomac, 1831–34.
Rogers, W., Voy., 1708–11, in French, Dutch and Eng.
Roquefeuil, Voyage, 1816–19.
Ruschenberger, Voyage, 1835–37.
Sack, Voyage to Surinam, etc., 1810.
Seemann, Voy. of the Herald, 1845–51.
Shelvocke, Voy., 1719–22.
Spilbergen, G., Voy., 1614.
Taylor, F. W., Voy. U. S. Ship Columbia, 1840.
Turnbull, Voy., 1800–4.
United States Expl. Expedition, 1838–1842.
Vancouver, Voy. to N. Pacific, 1790.
Vassar, Twenty Years around the World, 1861.
Voyages around the World. Edin. Cab. Lib., 34.
Vries, D. P. De, Korte Historiael, 1655.
" Translation, Murphy.
Wallis, Kerr, vol. 12.
Warriner, F., Cruise of the Potomec, 1835.
Weert, Nav., Fretum Magellanicum, 1598, Bry.
Wilkes, C., Un. St. Explor. Exped., 1851.

Voyages, Atlantic. Battel, A., Na Brasilien, 1589.

Chappell, Voyage to New Foundland, 1818.

Chastenet, Navigation aux côtes de St. Domingue, 1787.

Columbus, C., Letters, and Personal Narrative, 1827, 47.

Lee, Cruise of the Dolphin, 1852.

Relation d'une traversée d'Angleterre, 1812.

Uring's Voyages, 1728.

Wafer, Voy. to Isthmus of Darien, 1699.

Webster, W. H. B., Voy. to South Atlantic, 1828–38.

See the several Countries adjacent.

Voyages, Indian Ocean. Belcher, Voy. East Indian Archipel., 1843–46.

Broecke, Reysen....Oost Indien, 1634.

Forrest, T., Voy. aux Moluques, et N. Guinée, 1774–76.

Gilbert, T., From N. S. Wales to Canton, 1789.

Hall, B., Voy. to the Eastern Seas, 1816.

Jukes, J. B., Voy. of Fly, New Guinea, etc., 1842–46.

Kolff, Voy. through Moluccan Archip. 1825–26.

Léguat, Reyzen....Oost Indische eylander, 1690.

Linschoten, Voy. to East and West Indies, 1598.

" Navigatio, 1599.

" Hist. de la navig., 1619, 1638.

Pinto, F. M., Voyages de, 1830.

Prior, James, Voy. in the Indian Seas, 1810, 11.

Purmerent, Oost Indische Reys, 1651.

Reinaud, Voy. des Arabes, 9e Siècle.

Spilbergen, Oost en West Indische Voyagie, 1648.

Steele, R., Tour, 1810.

Wilson, H., Account of the Pelew Is., 1789.

Wood, W. M., Voy. in East Indies, 1859.

See Indian Ocean; Moluccas; Philippine; Sumatra.

Voyages, Pacific Ocean. Alcala-Galiano, Viage, para el Estrecho de Fuca, 1792.

Beechey, Voy. to Pacific, and Beering's Straits, 1825–28.

Bligh, W., Voyage, 1792.

" Mutiny on board the Bounty, 1790.

Broughton, Voyage to North Pacific, 1795.

Brouwer, Journael....naer de custen van Chili, 1643.

Voyages, Pacific Ocean (continued).

Browne, J. R., Etchings of a Whaling Cruise, 1846.

" Crusoe's Island.

Bulkeley, Voy., 1740, 41.

Burney, Hist. of Disc. in, 1819.

Callander, Voyages to the Southern hemis., 1766.

Campbell, A., Sequel to Bulkeley's Voy., 1747.

Cano, Juan S. del, Magellan's Voy., Byron.

Cheever, The Island World of the Pacific, 1851.

Cockburn, J., Journ. from Honduras, 1735.

Colnett, Voy. to South Atlantic, 1797.

Colton, W., Deck and Port, 1850.

Cook, J., Voy., 1772–75.

" Voy., 1776–80.

Coulter, Adventures in the Pacific, 1845.

Crozet, Voy. à la Mer du Sud, 1783.

Dalrymple, Hist. Coll. of voyages in, 1770.

" Voyages dans, par les Espagn. et Holland., 1774.

Dillon, Voy. aux iles de la mer du Sud, 1827, 28.

Ellis, W., Voy. of Cook, 1776–80.

Entrecasteaux, D', Recherche de La Pérouse, 1808.

Fanning, Voyages, 1830–37.

Fleurieu, Découvertes, S. E. de la Nouvelle Guinée, 1768, 9.

" Discov. of the French, 1768–1769.

Franchère, Voy. to N. W. Coast, 1811–1814.

Frézier, Voy. to the South Sea, 1712.

" Voy., Mer du Sud, 1712–14.

Gambóa, Viage al Estrecho de Magellanes, 1679, 80.

Habersham, North Pacific Exped.

Hawkesworth, Voyages of Cook, Wallis and Byron, 1773.

Hawkins, R., Obs. in his voy., 1593.

Holmesby, J., Voyages, 1745.

Jacobs, T. J., Scenes in the Pacific Ocean, 1844.

Jefferys, T., Voy. from Asia to America, 1761.

Jewett, J. R., Adventures on N. W. Coast.

Kerguelin, Voy. dans les Mers Australes, 1771–74.

Kotzebue, Voyage to, 1815–18.

Labillardiére, Voy. in search of La Pérouse, 1791–94.

La Borde, Hist. de la Mer du Sud, 1791.

Ledyard, Journ. of Capt. Cook's voy., 1776–79.

Voyages, Pacific Ocean (continued).
M'Konochie, Statist. and Comm. of Shores of, 1818.
Maurelle, Voy. North of California, 1775.
Meares, J., Voy. to N. W. Coast of Am., 1788.
Melville, Omoo, Adventures in, 1847.
Morrell, B., Four voy. to, and to Pacific Ocean, 1822–31.
Moulton, W., Voy. to Staten Island, 1799.
Müller, S., Voy. N. E. Coast of Am., 1761.
Oliver, J., Wreck of the Glide: The Fijiis, 1848.
Parkinson, S., Journal of a voyage, 1773.
" Voy. autour, 1794.
Paulding, H., Dolphin's Cruise, 1831.
Pernéty, Voy. to the Falkland Is., 1763, 1764.
" Voy. aux iles Malouines, 1763.
Péron, Voy. aux terres australes, 1800–4.
Porter, D., Cruise of the Essex, 1812–1814.
Raveneau, Jour. du Voy., 1684, 1705.
Relacion .... viage .. . S. M. de la Cabeza, 1785–86.
Reynolds, J. N., South Sea Exped., 1835, 36, 41.
" Corresp. with Dickerson, 1837–8.
Ross, J. C., Voy., 1839–43.
Smith, W., Voyage of Ship Duff, 1796–1802.
Stewart, C. S., Voy. of Vincennes, 1829, 30.
Tasman, Voy. of Disc., Pinkerton, 11.
Thomas, P., Anson's voyage.
Tyerman, S. Sea Islands, Asia, 1821.
Vancouver, Voy. of Disc., 1791–95.
Voy. du Wager, 1756.
Walpole, F., Four Years in Pacific, 1844–48.
Webster, W. H. B., Voy. under H. Foster, 1828.
Wilkins, P., Adventures.
See Polynesia; Hawaii; Tahiti; Fiji; Pacific Ocean.

Voyages, Miscellaneous. Albertinus, Hist. relation, 1609.
Atkins, J., To Guinea, Brazil and West Indies, 1735.
Boyle, R., Viaggi, 1734.
" Voyages, 1794.
Chase, Shipwreck of the Essex, 1821.
Cleveland, R. J., Narr. of N. England voyages, 1843, 58.
Coggeshall, G., Various Voy., 1799–1844.

Voyages, Miscellaneous (continued).
Colton, W., Cruise of U. S. Fr. Congress, 1850.
Coréal, Voy. aux Indes d'Espagne, 1722.
Cubero, Peregrinacion, 1688.
Dampier, Voy. to New Holland, 1699.
Dana, R. H., jr., Two years before the mast, 1869.
Delano, A., Voy. in N. and S. Hemispheres, 1817.
Dunham, J , Jour. of Voyages, 1850.
Durrett, De Marseille à Lima, 1720.
Fanning, Voyages, 1830–37.
Frederick, C., Reys na en door Indien, 1563.
Froger, Voy., Africa, Brazil, etc., 1695.
Gama, Voyage, Hakluyt Soc., Pub.
Ghillany, Geschichte der M. Behaim, 1853.
Gottfried, Zee en Landreizen, 1727.
Hakluyt Soc., Publications.
Holmesby, J., Voyages, 1745.
Lade, R., Voy. en Afrique, Asie et l'Amérique, 1744.
Le Blanc, V., Les Voyages, 1658.
Le Maire, Speculum Orien. et Occid. Nav., 1614–18. Spilbergen.
Lynch, Naval Life, 1851.
Major, R. H., Early Voy. to Australia, 1857.
" Life of Henry the Navigator, 1868.
Melville, Redburn, his first Voy., 1849.
Miroir Oost et West Indical, 1614–18. Spilbergen.
Morrell, Narr. of Four voyages, 1822–1831.
Noordt, O. van, Journael, 1602.
Patterson, S , Narrative of voy., 1825.
Pfeiffer, Second Voyage, 1855.
Pinto, F. M., Voyages avantureux.
Philoponus, H., Nova Navigatio, 1621.
Pyrard de Laval, Voy. aux Indes orient. et au Brésil, 1615.
Sandwich, Around the Mediterranean, 1738, 9.
Torrey, F. P., Cruise of the Ohio, 1840.
Uring, M., Hist. of his voyages, 1826.
Viaud, Strane Avventure, 1784.
See Buccaneers; Shipwrecks; Travels.

W.

Wabash Valley. Beste, The Wabash, 1855.
Cox, S. C., Early settlement of, 1860.
Ellsworth, The upper Wabash, 1838.

Wadsworth, J. S. Allen, L. F., Memorial of, N. Y. Agr. Trans., 1864.
Century Assoc'n, in honor of, 1865.

War of 1812, History, etc. (cont'd).
Van Rensselaer, Affair of Queenstown, 1815.
Vermont Official Papers, 1808.
War, The, Periodical, 1812-14.
Williams, S., Two Campaigns, 1870.
See United States, History.

War of 1812, Pamphlets and Sermons on. Address of Leg. of N. Y., 1811, 1813.
Address of Members of Congress, 1812. P. 57.
Address to N. Y. Republicans, 1813.
Address to Norfolk Co. P. 259.
Address to the Clergy of New England, 1814. P. 57.
Address to the Fair Daughters, 1811. P. 199.
Analysis of Corresp., U. S. and G. Brit., 1811.
Appeal to the People, Bost., 1811.
Austin, J. T., Oration, Peace of 1815.
Blake, F., Oration, July 4, 1812.
Blatchford, S., Sermon, Lansingburgh, 1815.
Bliss, H., Oration, Colebrook, Conn., 1815.
Cary, S., Fast Sermon, Bost., 1813.
Catlin, J., Sermon, New Marlborough, 1812.
Channing, W. E., Fast Sermons, July 23, Aug. 20, 1812.
Dow, M., Fast Sermons, Beverly, 1812, 1813.
Dwight, T., Fast Sermon, N. Haven, 1812.
Emerson, B., Sermon, Salem, 1812.
Emmons, N., Thanksgiving Sermon, 1813.
Essex Junto, 1812.
Exposition of the Causes, (Dallas), 1815.
Free Trade and no Impressment, 1813, Poem.
Gardiner, J. S. J., Fast Serm., Boston, 1812. P. 411.
Gillet, E., Sermon, Hallowell, 1812.
Griswold, Gov., Message to Conn. Legis., 1812.
Hampshire Co., etc., Conv. Proc., 1812.
Harper, R. G., Speech, Annapolis, Jan. 20, 1814.
Holcomb, R., Sermon, Sterling, Ms., 1812.
Jackson, R., and E. R. Potter, To their Constituents, 1813.
Lathrop, J., Sermon, Springfield, 1814.
Letter to a Mem. of Congress, 1812.
Lowell, J., Dispass. Inquiry, 1812; Perpetual War, 1812; Road to Peace, 1813; Peace without Dishonor, 1807; etc.

War of 1812, Pamphlets and Sermons on (continued).
M'Donald, J., Sermon, Albany, 1812.
McLeod, Scriptural view of, 1815.
Madison's, Mr., War, Dispass. Inquiry, Lowell, 1812.
Morse, Jed., Fast Sermon, Charlestown, 1812.
New, The, States: A Comparison, Bost., 1813.
New York, Conv. Rept., Proc., 1812.
Norfolk, Mess., Conv., Proc. on, 1812.
Osgood, D., Sermon, Protest, 1812.
Pamphlets relating to, vols. 752. B. C. vol. 3, 6, 7, 9, 54.
Parish, E., Fast Sermon, Byfield, Ms., 1811.
Perpetual War Policy, 1812.
Pickering, T., Unnecessary War, 1808. P. 1698.
" Danger of War, 1808.
Smith, J., Sermon, Salem, N. H., 1813.
Stanford, R., Speech, H. of R., U. S., 1812.
Stewart, C., Sermon, Montreal, 1815.
Ward, A., Speech, H. of R., U. S., 1814.
Webster, D., Addr., Wash. Benev. Soc., 1812.
Worcester, Mass., Proc. of Conv., 1812. P. 37.
See United States, Pamphlets, 1801-17.

War. Civil War of 1861-65; French War in America, 1745-60; Mexican War; Revolutionary War.

Warburton, W. Brown, J., Letter to Lowth, 1766. P. 352.
Letter to the Rev. Mr. W., 1742.
Letter to the Rt. Rev. Dr. Warburton, 1760.
Letter to Rev. Dr. Parr, 1789.
Lowth, R., Letter to, 1766. P. 352.
Pamphlets on the Warburton controversies, vol. 352.
Parr, Warburtonian Tracts, Works, 3.
Parry, Defence of Sherlock, 1760. P. 352.
Review of the Div. Legation.
Warburton, Letters, 1809.
" Literary remains, 1841.
" Corresp., Nichols's Lit. Illust., v. 2.
See Communion.

Ward Family. Descendants, 1851.

Ward, Rev. N. Dean, J. W., Memoir of, 1865.

Ward, R. P. Phipps, E., Memoirs of, 1850.

Ward, S. Gammell, Life of, Sparks, 19.

Wardlaw, R. Lynch, T. T., Glasgow Case, 1850. P. 809.
Wardlaw, Discourses on death of, 1854. P. 652.

Wardle, Col. Clarke, M. A., The Rival Princes, 1810.
Wardle, Col. To his Countrymen, 1828.

Ware, H., Jr. Robbins, C., Discourse on, 1843.
Ware, J., Memoir of, 1846.

Ware, M. L. Hall, E. B., Memoir of, 1853.

Ware, W. Bellows, Memorial of, 1852. P. 555.

Ware, Mass. Coburn, D. M., Hist discourse, 1851.
Hyde, W., Hist. Address, 1847.

Wareham, Mass. Nott, S., jr., Sixteen years preaching at, 1845.

Warming. Bull, M., Compar. value of fuel, 1827.
Derby, Anthracite fires, 1868.
Parker, T. N., Suggestions, 1836.
Peclet, Traité de la chaleur, 1861.
Prideaux, F. S., On Economy of, 1853.
Reid, On Ventilation and Warming.
Williams, On combustion of coal and smoke.
See Coal; Heat; Stoves; Ventilation.

Warner, Col. S. Chipman, D., Life of, 1858.
Houghton, G. F., Address on, 1849.

Warner, New Hamp. Long, M., History of, 1832.

Warren Family. Genealogy, 1854.

Warren, F. S. Pollock, The National Society, 1853.

Warren, John C. Warren, J. C., Life of, 1860.

Warren, Gen. Jos. Biog. of, 1857.
Bunker Hill Monument Association, Statue of.
Everett, A. H., Life of, Sparks, 10.
Everett, E., Inaugural of Statue of, v. 3.
Frothingham, R., Life of, 1865.
Loring, J. S., Lives of 100 Boston Orators, 1852.
See Bunker Hill.

Warren, Bp. J. Hughes, R., Defence of, 1796.

Warren, J. P. Plymouth Congr. Church, 1856. P. 484.

Warren, Me. Eaton, C., Annals of, 1851.

Warren, New Hamp. Little, W., History of, 1870.

Warren, Rhode Is. Fessenden, G. M., History of, 1845.
Spalding, A. F., Centen Disc., First Bapt. Church, 1864.
Tustin, Hist. Baptist Church, 1845.

Warsaw, N. Y. Warsaw Presb. Ch., Hist., 1841. P. 1416.

Warwickshire, Eng. Beauties of Engl. and Wales, 1815.
Universal Magazine, Descr., 1760. P. 1629.
West, W., Hist., Topog. and Directory of, 1830.

Washington, B. Story, J., Sketch of, (Misc. wri.).

Washington, George. Circular Letter, June 18, 1783.
Corresp. with J. Anderson, 1800.
Diary from 1789-91, 1858.
Epistles, Domestic, etc., Forged, 1796.
Fac-similes of his public acct's, 1844, f°.
Fac-similes of letters to Sinclair, 1844.
Farewell Address, 1796, 1810, 46, Eng. and Germ.
Journal, 1754: Repr. 1865.
Letters to A. Young, 1803.
Monuments of Patriotism, Phil'a, 1800.
Official Letters, 1775-83.
Political Legacies, Bost., 1800.
Revolutionary Orders, (Whiting), 1778-1782, 1844.
Will of, N. Y., 1800.
Writings, (Sparks's ed.), 1837.

Washington, George, Biographies, etc. Bancroft, A., Life of, 1833.
Clark, J., Life of, 1813.
Corry, Life of, 1807.
Craig, N. B., His first campaign, 1848.
Custis, G. W. P., Recollections of, 1860.
DeWitt, C., Histoire de, 1855.
Edmonds, C. R., Life of, 1839.
Everett, E., Life of, 1860.
Frost, J., Pictorial Life of, 1847.
Glass, F., Life of, in Latin, 1836.
Guizot, Etude hist. sur, 1855.
Headley, J. T., Life of, 1856.
Irving, W., Life of, 1855-59.
Kingston, J., Life of, 1813.
Kirkland, C. M., Memoirs of, 1857.
Marshall, J., Life of, 1823-35.
Paulding, J. K., Life of, 1848.
Pickell, J., New chapter of life, 1856.
Ramsay, D., Life of, 1807.
Rush, R., Domestic life of, 1857.
Simpson, S., Lives of W. and Jefferson, with a parallel, 1833.
Sparks, J., Life of, 1833.

Washington, G., Orations on Feb. 22, etc. (continued).

Pickman, B., Oration, Feb. 22, 1797, Salem.

Putnam, J. O., Orat., Paris, Fr.,1866.

Reed, W. B., Orat. Feb. 22, 1849.

Schenck, N. H., Orat., Balt., 1861.

Smith, C. A., Discourse, 1852.

Spaulding, J., Addr., Initiation of W. as Freemason, 1854.

Sprague, W. B., Albany, Feb. 22, 1847.

Stewart, K. J., Orat., Centenn., Freemasons, Newport, 1852.

Tator, H. H., Orat., Feb. 22, 1851.

Tyng, S. H., Centen. Celeb., Freemasons, N. Y., 1852. P. 1697.

Ullman, D., Orat., O. U. Amer., Feb. 22, 1856.

Warner, H. W., Oration on, N. Y., 1814. P. 58.

Washington's Birth-day, A Poem, J. Lovett, Albany, 1812.

Whipple, E. P., Oration on, 1850.

Whitney, T. R., Orat., O. U. Amer., Feb. 22, 1855.

Winthrop, R. C., Orat., Washington Monument, 1848.

" Address, Boston, Ball's Statue, 1859.

Wood, F., Scranton, Feb. 22, 1862.

Washington, G., Volumes and Pamphlets relating to. Appeal for the Fut. Preser. of the Home of, 1855.

Biddle, C. J., W. and André, 1857.

Binney, Formation of Farewell Add., 1859.

Collection of Letters of Half-Pay Officers, 1793.

Conduct, The, of, Compared, 1813.

Cooper, Miss S., Mount Vernon, 1859.

Dwight, Jasper, Letter to W., 1796, (Duane).

Gaspé, P. A. De, Canadians of Old, (Appendix), 1864.

Germanicus, Letter to the People, 1793.

Gibbs, G., Memoirs of Administration of, 1846.

Guizot, Etude Hist. sur, (De Witt), 1855.

" Monk and W., 1851.

Hayden, W. and his Masonic Compeers, 1866.

Headley, J. T., Washington and his Generals, 1847.

Hough, F. B., Washingtoniana, Proc. on Death of, List of Eulogies, 1865.

Jackson, James, Memoir on Death of, 1861.

Kennedy, P., Answer to Mr. Paine's letter to W., 1797.

Washington, G., Volumes and Pamphlets relating to (continued).

Ladies' Mount Vernon Assoc., Appeal, 1857. P. 502.

Lossing, Mt. Vernon, 1859.

" The home of, 1866.

Lowell, J., New-England Patriot, 1810.

M'Guire, Religious Opinions of, 1836.

Mahon, Lord, Letter to J. Sparks, 1852.

Minutes of a Conspiracy, repr., 1865.

Mt. Vernon Assoc'n Record, Phil'a, 1858–59.

Paine, T., Letter to, 1797.

Penn'a, Legis. Proc., Feb. 22, 1861.

Reed, W. B., Reprint of letters of, 1852.

Remarks occasioned by the late conduct of, 1796, 97.

Ritner, Vindication of, on secret soc., 1841. P. 184.

Schroeder, J. F., Maxims of, 1859.

Simpkinson, The Washingtons, a tale, with hist. appendix, 1860.

Sinclair, Sir J., Correspondence, 1831.

Sparks, J., Corresp. of the Am. Revolution, 1853.

" Letter to Lord Mahon, 1853.

" Strictures on Lord Mahon, 1852.

" Remarks on Reed's reprint, 1853.

Stanhope, Earl. *See* Mahon.

U. S., H. of Rep., Proc. on Sword of, Feb., 1843.

Washington, G., Fac similes of memorial Stones of the family in England, 1862.

" Centenn. Anniv. Washington, 1832. P. 504.

" Washington's Birth-day, Cong. banquet, 1852.

" Eere Penning, etc., Poems in Dutch of Erkelens and Brandis.

Washingtoniana, Balt., 1800.

Washington Exhibition Pictures, N. Y., 1853,

Washington's Head-Quarters, Newburgh, Cat. of MSS., etc., 1858.

Washington Monument Assoc'n, Penn., 1st Report, 1860.

Washington National Monument Soc. Report, 1855.

Wineberger, The Tomb of, 1858.

Word to Federalists. P. 44.

See Revolutionary War; U. S. Government.

Washington, Martha. Conkling, Memoir of, 1850.

Lossing, B. J., Life of, 1863.

Water-cure (continued).
Coffin, J. G., Discourses on cold and warm bathing, 1818.
Elmer, Gynecian Sanatorium.
Forbes, J., The Water-cure, 1847.
Graefenberg Manual.
Harsha, The Principles of, 1852. P. 515.
Humpage, E., Address, Brit. Assoc'n for Pro. Sci., 1847.
Lee, E., Hydro- and Homœopathy, 1848. P. 515.
New Graefenberg Water-cure, 1849. P. 210.
N. Y. Hydrop. School, 1855.
Nichols, M. S. G., Experience in, 1850.
Nichols, T. L., Introduction to, 1850.
Priessnitz Monthly, No. 1, 5, N. Y., 1861.
Rausse, Miscellanies, 1848.
Rausse, Graeffenberg.
Shew, J., Hand-book of, 1847.
Water-cure in America, 1849.
Water-cure Journal, 1846.
Wilson, J., Water-cure, 1847.

Waterford, Ir. Ryland, Hist. of, 1824.

Waterford, N. Y. Powell, M. C., Case of, 1858.

Waterland, D. Answer to the letter, 1731.
Letter to....1731.
Middleton, C., Letter to, 1731.
Pamphlets on the Waterland controversies, vol. 353.
Wetmore, J., Reply to Dickinson, N. Y., 1744.
See Arians; Trinity.

Waterloo. Campaign of; a poem, 1816.
Charras, Hist. de la Campagne, 1858.
Cotes, H., Sermon, 1815.
Gleig, Story of the battle of, 1847.
Grouchy, Observations sur, 1818.
Jomini, Life of Napoleon, 1864.
" Mil. Hist. of, 1864.
Kennedy, J. S., Battle of Waterloo, 1865.
Lenting, Leerredenen, Batavia, 1823.
Mudford, W., Campaign of 1815, 1817.
Scott, Sir W., Paul's Letters to his Kinsfolk.
Siborne, Hist. of War of 1815.
Southey, R., Life of Wellington, 1816.
Waterloo, Descr. of Panorama, 1816.
" Report on Siborne's Model of. P. 1022.
See Napoleon; Wellesley.

Waters, Mrs. A. Memoirs, Bost., 1817.

Waters, Mrs. S. Payson, S., Sermon on, 1802.

Waterton, C. Essays and Autobiog., 1851.

Watertown, Mass. Bond, Genealogies of.
Francis, C., Three Discourses, Hist., 1836.
" Hist. Sketch of, 1830.
Harris, W. T., Epitaphs in, 1869.

Watertown, N. Y. Common Almanac, 1823–55.
Right's...Hydraulic Works, 1855.
Watertown Directory, 1840, 50, 55, 59.
Watertown Register, (Newsp.), and continuations, 1830–50, imp.

Watertown, Wis. Description, 1856.

Water-Wheels, Water-Works. *See* Hydro-dynamics.

Watmough, J. G. Services of, 1814–1815. P. 1493.

Watson, E. Memoirs and Corresp., 1777–1842, 1856, 61.
Troup, R., Vindication of his claims, 1821.

Watson, J. F. Dorr, B., Memoirs of, 1861.

Watt, J. Arago, Eulogy on, 1839.
Smiles, Life of.
Watt, Correspondence of, on composition of water, 1846.

Wattles, N. Bacon, J., Fun. Sermon, 1798.

Watts, I. Chandler, S., Oration on. *See* Jennings.
Jennings, D., Sermon on, 1748.
Milner, J., Sermon on, 1748.
Moore, S. W., Memoir of, 1831. P. 1492.
Watts, I., Works, and Life by Burder, 1810.
" Choice Works and Life, Harsha, 1857.
Willson, J. R., Dr. W., anti-trinitarian, 1821.

Watts, M. Calamy, E., Sermon on, 1708.

Waves. *See* Hydro-dynamics.

Wax Work. Tussaud's Exhibition of, 1849. P. 489.

Waymouth, G. McKeen, Remarks on his voyage, Maine Hist. Coll., v. 5.
Rosier, Relation of the voyage of, (Mass. Hist. Coll., S. 3, v. 5).

Wayne, Gen. A. Armstrong, J., Life of, Sparks, 4.
Boyer, W.'s campaign, 1794.
Brice, W. A., Life of, 1868.
Moore, H. N., Life of, 1845.

Wayne Co., N. Y. Directory, 1867-8.

West Indies (continued).
Hamilton, A., Sixteen Months in the Danish Isles, 1852.
Herrera, Descr. Indiæ occidentalis, 1619.
" Descr. des Indes Occid., 1619.
" Hist. gen. de los Castellanos en, 1730.
" Hist. gén. des conquêtes, 1660.
" Gen. Hist. of the W. I., 1725.
Hist. et Comm. des Antilles Angloises, 1758.
Jefferys, T., Descr. of Span. Islands, 1762.
" West India Atlas, 1780.
Knox, J. P., St. Thomas, St. Croix, St. Johns, 1852.
Koromantyn Slaves, 1823.
Labat, Voy. aux isles de l'Amérique, 1722.
La Borde, Origine des Caraïbes, 1674.
Laet, De, Beschrijvinghe van West Indien, 1630.
" Hist. du Nouveau monde, 1640.
" Novus Orbis, 1633.
" Geoctroyeerde W. I. Compagnie, 1644.
Las Casas, Distruttione delle Indie Occidentali, 1630.
" The same in Germ. and Lat., 1578, 97.
" Découverte des Indes Occid., 1697.
Lavaysse, Voy. de Trinidad, Tobago, etc., 1813.
Linschoten, Voy. to East and West Indies, 1598.
" Nav. in Orien. Indiam, 1599.
" Hist. de la navig., 1638.
Maffei, Historiarum Indicarum lib. 16, 1614.
Marryatt, J., State of, 1818.
Martin, R. M., Brit. Col. Lib., v. 4, 1836.
Pamphlets on the West Indies, Vols., 435–438, 839, 840, 1483.
Pinckard, G., Notes on the West Indies, 1806, 1816.
Porteus, Lett. to Proprietors, 1808. P. 435.
Protection to W. I. Sugar, 1823.
Raynal, Hist. of trade in, 1777.
Real Bearings of W. I. Question, 1849, 1850.
Recueil d'arrests, 1720.
Ribaut, Voyage, 1569.
Rochefort, Hist. nat. et mor. des Antilles, 1667.
Society for Conv. of Negroes, Report, 1828.

West Indies (continued).
Schmidel, Verissima .... Descriptio, 1599.
Solorzano, Politica Indiana, 1703.
Some considerations.... Sugar, 1823.
Southey, T., Chronolog. Hist. of, 1827.
Statement of Claims, 1823.
Taylor, L. W., On negotiations with Gr. Brit., 1829.
Trollope, A., Travels in, 1860.
Weed, T., Letters from, 1843–62.
West India Ass'n of Glasgow, 1852. P. 438.
West India (Dutch) Company, three Treatises, 1630.
West India Manual, 1842.
West India Merchant, Lond., 1778.
West India Reporter, No. 39, 40, 42, 1831.
West India Planters, Comm. Reports, 1849, 50, 55.
West India Question, Lond., 1826.
West Indische Compagnie, 1651.
West Indische Zee en Land Reizen, 1705.
Willis, N. P., Health Trip to, 1853.
Willyams, Campaign in, 1794.
Wood, C., Speech, 1848.
Wsellinx, Vertoogh van te hand. op. West-Indien, 1608.
Wytfliet, Hist. Universelle, 1611.
Young, West-India Common-place book, 1807.
See Voyages; Columbus; America; Florida; France, Colonies; Slavery; Sugar; Barbadoes; Cuba; Dominica; Jamaica; Martinique; Porto Rico; Ste. Croix; St. Domingo; Tobago; Trinidad.

Westminster. Brayley, History of, 1836. P. 401.
Hawkins, J. S., On Antiquities of, 1807, 8.
Hopper, T., Letter on architects of the new palace, 1837. P. 1036.
Nicoll, D., Munic. institutions, 1853.
Saint James Church, Proc., 1846. P. 328.
Short narrative of.... bridge, 1738.
Westminster palace, Descr. of, 1850. P. 1515.

Westminster Abbey. Buckland, W., Sermon, 1848.
Neale, Hist. and Antiq. of, 1856.
Westminster Abbey.... guide, 1814
" Description of, 1827. P. 1710.

Westminster Assembly. Fletcher, J., Hist. of Independency, 1849.
Hetherington, History of, 1843.
Reid, J., Lives of members of, 1815.

Wisconsin (continued).
Ritchie, Wisconsin, 1858.
Rock County, History of, 1856.
Sketches of the West, 1847.
Smith, W. R., History of, 1854.
Watertown, Statistics, 1856.
Wisconsin, Geol. Survey, 1854, 57, 61, 1862.
" Geol. Sur. of Lead Regions, 1871.
" Report of Charities and Reform, 1871.
" Description of, 1853.
" Statistics, 1870.
" Bescrivelse over..1870.
" Ysladegau....1870.
" Same in Dutch, German.
" Advantages of Brown, Door & Oconto Co.'s, 1870.
Wisconsin Almanac, 1856, 7.
Wisconsin Editorial Assoc'n, Proc., 1857-69.
Wisconsin State Agr. Soc., Trans., 1851-69.
Wisconsin State Hist. Soc. Collections, 1855-68, 5 v.
See U. S., Travels West; Mississippi River.

Wisconsin Local History. *See* La Crosse; Madison; Milwaukee; Winnebago.

Wise, H. A. Hambleton, Biog. Sketch of, 1855.

Wiselius, S. J. Brouwer, Leven van, 1846.

Wiseman, Card. N. Bowyer, G., The Cardinal, 1850. P. 348.
Cumming, J., Lectures on, 1850.
Important Questions, 1854.
Palmer, W., Letter to, 1841.
Wiseman, Card., Speeches and Tour in Ireland, 1859.

Wisner, B. B. Fay, W., Sermon on, 1835. P. 1610.

Wistar, C. Caldwell, C., Eulogium on, 1818. P. 1230.
Tilghman, W., Eulogium on, 1818.

Wit. *See* Humor; Satire.

Witchcraft. Boulton's Vindication, 1722.
Calef, More Wonders of the Invisible World, 1700, 1823, 66.
Christmas, Cradle of the Twin Giants, 1819.
Chyromancie, 1619.
Cotta, Trial of, 1616.
Douce, Cat. of Books on, 1840.
Drake, S. G., Annals of, in New Eng., 1869.
Filmer, To the jurymen of Eng., respecting, 1680.

Witchcraft (continued).
Fowler, Salem witchcraft, 1861.
Giffard, Dialogue concerning, 1593. Percy Soc. Pub., v. 8.
Glanvil, Evidence concerning, 1681.
Halliwell, The Poetry of witchcraft, 1853.
Hutchinson, F., Hist. Essay on, 1718.
Mackinnon, W. A., Hist. of civilization, 1849.
Madden, R. R., Phantasmata, 1857.
Mather, C., Wonders of Invis. World, 1693; Repr., 1861, 66.
Poole, W. F., Mather and Salem witchcraft, 1869.
Random sketches, 1817. Muns. P. 8.
Scott, Sir W., Demonology and Witchcraft, 1830. B. C.
Some miscellany observations, S. Willard, 1692; Repr., 1869.
Spurious reprints, Deane, 1865.
Thacher, J., Essay, 1831.
Upham, C. W., Lectures on, 1832.
" Salem witchcraft, 1867.
Witches of N. Y., 1859.
Woodward, W., Delusion in N. England, Drake, 1866.
" Records of Salem W., 1864.
Wright, T., Sorcery and Magic, 1852.
See Delusions; Magnetism, Animal.

Witsius, Herman. The Covenants and Life of, 1798.

Witherspoon, J. Rodgers, J., Fun. Sermon, 1795.

Woburn, Mass. Bennett, Sermon, 1846.
Sewall, S., History of, 1868.

Wodrow, J. Wodrow, R., Life of, 1828.

Wodrow, R. Correspondence, 1709-31.

Wolcott, E. McClure, D., Serm., Death of, 1794. P. 80.

Wolcott, J. Pindarics, 1800.
Works and Life of.

Wolcott, Roger. Poems and Preface, 1725.
Perry, J., Disc. on Death of, 1767.

Wolfe, Gen. J. Sabine, Hist. Address, 1860.
Wolfe, Instruc. to Officers, 1768.
Wright, R., Life of, 1864.

Wolfe-Tone, T. *See* Tone.

Wolff, C. and A. Memorial of, Geneal., 1863.

Wolff, Jos. Researches, 1831-34.
" Narr. of Mission, 1845.

Wollaston, W. Burnet, T., Judgment on, 1732.

Wollstonecraft. *See* Godwin.

Wolsey, Card. Cavendish, G., Life of, 1827.
Fiddes, Life of, 1724.
Galt, J., Life of, 1846.
Library of Use. Knowl., Life of.

Wolverhampton, Eng. Staffordshire Directory, 1834.

Woman. Alexander, W., History of, 1796.
Alger, W. R., Friendships of, 1868.
Amer. Fem. Guard. Soc., Reports, 1849–55, 61.
Almanach des dames, 1855.
Amer. Woman's Ed. Ass'n, 1853–56. P. 226, 277.
Banister, Mrs., Hints on Education, 1856.
Beecher, C. E., Evils suffered by Am. Women, 1847.
Beecher, H. W., Addr. on Ment. Culture for, 1859.
Blackwell, E., Addr. on Med. Educ. for, 1856.
Brady, J. T., Addr. on Ment. Culture for, 1859.
Brother Jonathan's Wife, 1842. P. 1216.
Brown, D. M., Young-ladyism, Lond. P. 1793.
Brown, J., Sermon, Fem. Orphans, 1765.
Carlier, A., Marriage in the U. S.. 1867.
Challenge...or The Female War, 1697.
Chapone, Mrs., Works, 1818.
Child, L. M., Condition of, in all ages, 1845. B. C.
Clarke, M. C., World noted women, 1868.
Cleveland, Mrs. E. H., Lect., Female Med. Coll., Phil'a, 1858.
Craig, J., Use of church service on a late occasion, Lond., 1840.
Cushman, R. W., Amer. female ed., 1855.
Davies, E., Higher education of, 1866.
Défenses du Beau Sexe, 1753.
De Foe, D., Religious courtship.
Doctrine of Divorce, Agonistes, Albany,
Du Montier, Lettres à sa Fille, 1756.
Edwards, J., Disc., Pen. Fem. Refuge Soc., 1826.
Ellet, Mrs. E. F., Women artists, 1859.
Ellis, Mrs. S. S., Women of England, 1843.
" Mothers of England, 1844.
" Wives of England, 1843.
" Daughters of England, 1842.
Eminent women of the age, Parton, 1869.
Facts and important information, 1842.
Female Med. Educ. Soc., Bost., Reports, 1851, 52. P. 64; 1853–56, 64.

Woman (continued).
Fem. Med. Coll. of Penn'a, Announce., 1853–57.
Feyjoo, Defence of the women.
Fullom, History of, 1855.
Gisborne, T., Duties of the sex, 1801.
Green, Mrs., Letters of royal and illustrious, 1200–1500.
Gregory, J., Father's Legacy, 1779. P. 266.
Guardian Soc., Lond., Report, 1840. P. 472.
Gynæcological Society, Bost., Const., 1869.
Hale, S. J., Distinguished Women, 1850.
Hanway, Jonas, Journal in Eng., 1756.
Hayley, Essay on old maids, 1786.
Hays, Mary, Female biography, 1803.
Histoire litt. des femmes Françoises, 1769.
Holland, J. G., Titcomb's letters, 1867.
Houssaye, Men and women of the 18th century, 1852.
Jameson, Mrs. A., Characteristics of Shakespeare's W.
" Mem., Woman's mission, 1846.
" Biog. sketches of women celeb. in poetry, 1844.
Jones, Mrs. M. M., Woman's dress, 1865.
Kavanagh, J., English women of letters, 1863.
Knox, V., Liberal education of, 1789.
Kurtz, B., Choice of a wife, 1863.
Lambert, Marq. De, Réflexions sur, 1750.
Legouvé, Moral history of, 1860.
Lewis, Dio, Our girls, 1871.
Longshore, J. S., Addr. Fem. Med. Coll., 1850.
Loving words, 1860.
M'Elheran, Condition of, in Celtic nations.
Magdalen Soc., Phil'a, Report, 1859.
Mann, Horace, Lectures, 1859.
Mental improvement for a young lady, 1793. P. 606.
Michelet, La Femme, 1860.
Milburn, Rifle, Axe, etc., 1857.
Modern women, Linton, 1868.
Moreau, Hist. naturelle de la femme, 1803.
Mulock, D. M., A woman's thoughts about.
Necker, Mme., Study of Life of, 1844.
New, The, Bond of Love, N. Y., 1853.
New Engl., Female Med. Coll., Report, 1857, 58.
N. Eng. Female Moral Reform Soc., Bost., Report, 1857, 68.

Zoology, Comparative. Agassiz, Compar. Embryology, 1849.
" Principles of, 1848, 59.
Blainville, De, Ostéographie comparée ...d' animaux vertébrés, 1839-56, 4 v.
Browne, P. A., Trichographia Mamm., 1848. P. 1050.
Cuvier, Recherches sur les ossemens fossiles, 1812, 1825.
Dana, J. D., Classif. on Princ. of Cephalization, Edinb. New Jour., 1864.
Darwin, C., Origin of Species.
" Variation of Animals, 1868.
Harvard Coll., Mus. of Comp. Zoölogy, Bulletin, 1863-71.
Home, E., Lectures on, 1814-28, 6 v.
Huxley, Origin of Species, 1863.
Kidd, J., Lect., Comp. Anatomy, 1824.
Maclise, Comp. Osteology, 1847.
Mivart, Genesis of Species, 1871.
Owen, R., Comp. Anat. and Phys. of Invertebrates, 1855.
" Comp. Anat. of Vertebrates, 1866-68.
" Comp. Anat. of the Teeth, 1840-1845.
" Structure of the Skeleton, Orr's Circle, 1.
Quatrefages, Metamorphoses of Man and Animals, 1864.
Rolleston, Forms of Animal Life, 1870.
Siebold, C. T., Comparative Anatomy, 1854.

Zoophytes. Agassiz, Contrib. to Nat. Hist. U. S., 3, 4, Acalephs.
Baird, The Entomostraca, Ray Soc.
Bailey, Infus. of fam. Bacillaria.
Bowerbank, Brit. Spongiadæ, Ray Soc., 1864, 66.
Catlow, Drops of Water, 1851.
Dana, J. D., On Zoöphytes, Am. J. of Sci., 1846, 47, etc.
" Corals and Coral Islands, 1872.
Darwin, C., Researches, Voy. of the Beagle, 1845.
Dict. des Sci. Nat., 1816-30.

Zoophytes (continued).
Edwards, H. M., Recherches sur les polypes, 1838, 49.
Ehrenberg, Infusionsthierchen, 1830.
" Mikrogeologie, 1854.
Encyc. Méthod., Les Vers, 1791-1832.
Gosse, Life in its lower forms, 1857.
Landsborough, British Zoöphytes, 1852.
Mantell, Thoughts on Animalcules, 1846.
Owen, Anat. of the Invertebrates, 1855.
Pritchard, Hist. of Infusoria, 1841.
Siebold, Anat. of the Invertebrata, 1854.
U. S. Expl. Exped., 1838-42; Dana, J. D., Zoöphytes.
See Crustacea; Entomology; Mollusks; Microscope.

Zoroaster. Bleeck, A. H., Avesta; Religious books of the Parsees, 1864.
Bunsen, C. J., God in History, 1868-1870.
Bunsen, Ernest, Hidden Wisdom of Christ, 1865.
Hyde, Hist. relig. vet. Persarum, 1700.
Lord, H., Relig. of Persees, 1630. P. 1626.
Müller, Max., Essays on the Zendavesta, Chips, v. 1.
Trübner's Am. and Orient Record, Bibliography, 1867.
Zend-avesta, Texte Zend, Polonaise, Française, Pietraszewski, 1858-62.
See Parsees; Persia.

Zschokke, H. Autobiography, 1845.

Zuccarini. J. G. Martius, Denkrede auf, 1848.

Zuinglius, U. Croly, Hist. Sketches, 1842.
Robbins, R. D. C., Life of, Bibliot. Sac., 1851, 2.

Zurich. The Zurich Letters, 1537-1602, Parker Soc.

Zwaag-westeinde. Zwaag, Leerredenen, 1830.

FINIS.

www.ingramcontent.com/pod-product-compliance
Lightning Source LLC
LaVergne TN
LVHW021050110826
845150LV00001B/36

* 9 7 8 1 4 2 5 5 6 8 1 0 8 *